Recreation
Central Utah Veterans Home

AVIATION LAW

Fundamental Cases with Legal Checklist for Aviation Activities

Fourth Edition

AF722930

Gerard Pucci, B.S.M.E., J.D.
Member of Florida Bar
Registered Florida Professional Engineer

Book Donated from the
Personal Library of:
Roland Mower

KENDALL/HUNT PUBLISHING COMPANY
2460 Kerper Boulevard P.O. Box 539 Dubuque, Iowa 52004-0539

Copyright © 1970, 1974, 1977, 1981 by Gerard Pucci

Library of Congress Catalog Card No. 74—75405

ISBN 0—8403—2535—5

All rights reserved. No part of this publication may be reproduced, stored in a retrieval system, or transmitted, in any form or by any means, electronic, mechanical, photocopying, recording, or otherwise, without the prior written permission of the copyright owner.

Printed in the United States of America
10 9 8 7

Contents

SECTION TWO
Legal Checklist for Aviation Activities
Index for Section Two

Preface

This book was prepared and compiled by the author, for academic study by the undergraduate student.

The book is divided into two sections:

SECTION ONE contains the Cases, the Moot Court Practices, and the supplementary material such as Glossary and Extracts of Laws.

It presents, in readily available form, and in one brief volume, the landmark cases, as well as selected current cases in the area of aviation law.

The cases are arranged by subject, and they are presented in the form that they appear in the legal reports.

At the beginning of each case are headnotes which are a condensation of the main points of law covered by the cases and give a brief resume of the case to aid the student. The student may then proceed into the body of the case to see the reasoning of the court that led to the conclusions recited in the headnote.

The law cases contain a background and history of the development of aviation law. Many of the aviation cases refer to, and rely on, other and older branches of law; on these is based the comparatively new area of aviation law.

SECTION TWO contains a checklist for the student or pilot or other persons engaged in aviation activities. This Section can be used either by the student in conjunction with Section One, or independently by the pilot, repairman, fixed base operator, or other persons in aviation.

I am grateful for the repeated wise counsel of my good friend, Professor Robert Kane, for his encouragement and assistance in the preparation of this volume.

I owe a deep debt of gratitude to Roger F. Noreen, Vice President and Manager of West Publishing Company, for permitting the reproduction of these law cases from their National Reporter System, without which permission, this work would not have been possible.

Gerard Pucci
Miami, Florida

SECTION ONE

Aviation Law Fundamental Cases

Index to Cases in Section One

CHAPTER 1

Introduction to Section One

Relationship of Air Law to Other Branches of Law

The comparatively young field of aviation law has developed its own distinctive body of statutes, treaties, regulations, and case law. Nevertheless the cases in the field of aviation have borrowed from, and are related to, those other branches of the law that deal with transportation, railroads, admiralty, automobile, civil, military, international, and federal.

An analysis of the relation between aviation and the other specialized branches can be made, as the reader studies the selected cases.

The principles and conclusions of law, as they relate to aviation, are set forth in the headnotes of each case. Immediately following these headnotes, is the court's statement of the facts of the case; a history of how the facts developed; and a history of, and the reasons for, the conclusions recited in the headnotes.

The cases will point out the specialized rules, and laws, that have developed because of the distinctive nature of the airplane as a mode of transportation.

Who May Study This Book

This textbook is directed to the student who is interested in learning about the fundamental aspects of aviation law.

The student who can benefit from this book can be classified in the following manner:

1. Persons who are presently working in the aviation industry and who want to expand their knowledge of aviation law.
2. Undergraduate college students who want to become familiar with aviation law and who will go to work in the aviation industry before completing college.
3. Undergraduate students who will go on to complete college in a non-law field; these students may specialize in aviation or they may desire only an introduction to aviation.
4. Undergraduate pre-law students who may want an introduction to the case method of studying law, before entering law school.

It should also be noted that wherever students go to work as non-lawyers, the phase of law with which they will be most affected in their relations with the public is the area of liability to the public. In fact, product liability to the consumer has become one of the most important fields of law for the consumer as well as for the non-lawyer business man who deals with the consumer.

Although one of the primary subjects covered in this book is liability to the consumer in the aviation industry, many of the principles of liability presented here can be applied to other consumer fields.

How to Study This Book

One of the purposes of this book is to present complicated legal problems in simple, direct terms, for the non-law aviation student.

In the teaching of law, there are two methods. One of the methods is the "text method"—by which the principles and maxims of law are set forth in abstract statements. The other method is the "case method"—by which the student is given an actual case and is thereby shown how the law is applied to a particular set of facts.

In this book the author attempts to combine both of these methods.

It is analogous to the teaching of engineering science, in which the theory of the textbook is discussed in the lecture room, the application of the theory is demonstrated in the laboratory.

In law, the text provides the abstract theory, and the actual case provides the "laboratory" by which is demonstrated the application of the theory.

In this book the author hopes to present the "lecture room" and the "laboratory" in one volume. The method of presentation is threefold:

1. First, at the beginning of each Chapter of Section One is discussed the problems to look for, the solutions to those problems, and why the solutions are important to aviation.
2. Second, actual cases are reproduced exactly as they appear in the legal, National Reporter System. These cases relate to the subject matter of the Section under discussion.

   At the beginning of each case are headnotes which point out the principle or principles of law covered by that particular case. These headnotes are condensations of the case and are written by the publisher's legal staff, in order to simplify one or more aspects of the case.
3. Third, following the headnotes is the body of the case in which the court recites the facts of that particular case. The court then goes on to explain how it arrived at its decision, and the reasoning used to arrive at a conclusion.

From the above, it can be seen that the method used here is to alert the student to the problem, present to him the principle of law, and then show him the reasoning that produced the principle.

By this method, it is felt that the student learns how to read, write, and think analytically, and critically. After learning to analyze the law cases here, it is hoped that the student can then use his analytical ability in other areas of study.

CHAPTER 2

National Supremacy in Airspace

The United States is a Federation of States, and the authority of the Federal government is derived from the authority that is delegated by the several States to the Federal government. The specific authority that is delegated to the Federal government is set forth in the United States Constitution.

With the advent of air travel it soon became apparent that, in the matter of air travel and air regulation, there would be a conflict between the authority delegated to the Federal government, and the authority of the several States.

Some of the legal questions that arise in this area are:

1. Who has sovereignty over the airspace—the States or the Federal government?
2. It is acknowledged that the United States has sovereignty over the three nautical mile belt beyond the low water mark. How does this precedent in land and water rights affect the newer law of air rights?
3. Is there a difference between "Sovereignty" of air rights and "ownership" of air rights?
4. What are the spheres of authority to tax aircraft which are constantly moving from one state to another? Can all states tax the property equally? Are the states preempted of their taxing authority, by the Federal government?
5. Which branch of government has the jurisdiction over crimes on board aircraft? Are the State criminal laws violated? Are Federal criminal laws violated? Where is the crime committed when a plane is traveling at 600 miles per hour? Is the crime committed in one state, in a second state, or in both states?

This section sets forth the steps taken to delineate the responsibility and authority of these two branches of government.

Before reading the cases in this section, read and become familiar with the provisions of Extracts from the United States Constitution in Extract A, and with provisions of the Extracts from the Civil Aeronautics Act in Extract B.

Relationship of Federal and State Governments

The National responsibility for regulating air commerce has been acknowledged by the Congress of the United States and by the United States Supreme Court. Precedence for recognizing the Federal supremacy was developed from such cases as the Tidelands Oil Cases (U.S. v. Texas).

In addition, one of the first important cases that resolved the conflict in this area is the Causby Case. Both of these cases follow.

The relationship of Federal and State governments regarding their respective sovereign rights in the airspace is identified in the three cases of U.S. v. Causby, 328 U.S. 256 (1946), U.S. v. California, 332 U.S. 19 (1947), and U.S. v. Texas, 339 U.S. 707 (1950). The California and Texas cases are often referred to as the Tidelands Cases.

U.S. v. Texas is presented here because it is a later case and because it includes the principles of, and refers to, the U.S. v. California case.

In a scholarly and practical article entitled "*State Sovereignty v. Federal Sovereignty of Navigable Airspace*" in JOURNAL OF AIR LAW AND COMMERCE, Vol. 15, page 27 (1948), John C. Cooper analyzes the effect of the U.S. v. Causby and U.S. v. California (Tidelands Case) on the respective sovereignty rights of the state governments and the federal government in the airspace of the United States:

"By its decision in *United States v. Causby,* construing the Air Commerce Act of 1926 and the Civil Aeronautics Act of 1938, the Court has divided the airspace over the United States into two zones. In the lower zone next to the earth's surface, private property in the airspace is permitted and we must assume that in that zone normal relationships exist between State and Federal sovereignty as elsewhere in State territory. But in the upper zone (the navigable airspace) the rights of the Federal Government seem to have been considered so paramount that Congress was able to place the navigable airspace, as stated in the Court's opinion, "within the public domain." The opinion does not indicate what rights, if any, the subjacent State has in that part of the navigable airspace public domain lying over its surface territory.

"By its later decision in *United States v. State of California,* the Court found that the State of California is not the owner of the three-mile marginal ocean belt along its coasts or the lands underlying that belt. The opinion in that case indicates that the Court felt that paramount rights in and power over this ocean belt had been acquired directly by the Federal Government since the adoption of the United States Constitution. It must be noted that the *Causby* case is there cited, apparently to sustain the need for the Federal Government having a paramount position as against State sovereignty when national rights are involved.

"If these two cases are read together, surprising conclusions result. Either the several States may be held under these rulings to be entirely without sovereignty of right of control in the navigable airspace over their surface territories, or the power and rights of the Federal Government may be found so paramount in the navigable airspace as to produce the same legal result."

Please note that U.S. v. Causby is also pertinent to the section on "AIRPORTS AND LIABILITY." U.S. v. Causby is referred to, and cited in, all the cases in that Section. Therefore, when you read "AIRPORTS AND LIABILITY" in your class assignments, it would be helpful to read U.S. v. Causby again.

Refer to Extract A
U.S. Constitution, Article III, Section 2

339 U.S. 707

UNITED STATES v. STATE OF TEXAS.

(Cite as 70 S. Ct. 918)

No. 13, Original.

Argued on Motion for Judgment

March 28, 1950.

Decided June 5, 1950.

As Amended on Denial of Rehearing

Oct. 16, 1950.

The United States of America brought action against the State of Texas, for a decree declaring rights to an area under coastal waters, for injunction against trespass and for accounting, and the United States filed motion for judgment. The Supreme Court, Mr. Justice Douglas, held that the United States had dominion over the area, including oil thereunder, notwithstanding the acts of Texas extending boundary to a line 24 miles beyond the three-mile limit, and to the edge of the continental shelf.*

Judgment for plaintiff.

Mr. Justice Reed, Mr. Justice Minton and Mr. Justice Frankfurter dissented.

1. Courts

The United States Supreme Court in original actions, passing on controversies between sovereigns which involve issues of high public importance, is liberal in allowing full development of facts. U.S.C.A. Const. art. 3, § 2, cl. 2.

2. Courts

Where "equal footing" clause of resolution admitting Texas to the Union disposed of controversy between Texas and United States as to dominion over

*The decree proposed by the United States read in part:
"1. The United States of America is now, and has been at all times pertinent hereto, possessed of paramount rights *of proprietorship* in, and full dominion and power over, the lands, minerals and other things underlying the Pacific Ocean . . ."
The italicized words were omitted in the Court's decree. 332 U.S. 804, 805, 68 S.Ct. 20, 21, 92 L.Ed. 382.

minerals under coastal waters, evidence to establish meaning of "equal footing" was unnecessary and hearing to develop facts would not be allowed in action against Texas in Supreme Court. U.S.C.A. Const. art. 3, § 2, cl. 2; Joint Resolution March 1, 1845, 5 Stat. 797.

3. States

In resolution admitting state to the Union, clause providing that state shall be on "equal footing" with other states refers to political right and sovereignty, not economic stature or standing, but may have direct effect upon property rights. Joint Resolution March 1, 1845, 5 Stat. 797.

4. Mines and minerals
Navigable waters

In resolution admitting Texas to the Union, provision that Texas shall be on "equal footing" with other states negatived any implied, special limitation of any of the paramount powers of the United States, and Texas relinquished all claim to the marginal sea, including oil thereunder, to the United States. Joint Resolution March 1, 1845, 5 Stat. 797.

5. Navigable waters

Where low-water mark is passed, international domain is reached and property rights must be so subordinated to political rights as in substance to coalesce and unite in the national sovereign.

6. States

In resolution admitting state to the Union, provision that state shall be on "equal footing" with other states prevents extension of state's sovereignty into a domain of political and sovereign power of United States from which other states have been excluded, just as it prevents a contraction of sovereignty. Joint Resolution March 1, 1845, 5 Stat. 797.

7. States

Equality of states means that they are not less or greater, or different in dignity or power.

8. Mines and minerals
Navigable waters

Statutes of Texas extending boundary to a line 24 miles beyond three mile limit, and thereafter to outer edge of continental shelf, did not affect dominion of United States over such area, including oil thereunder. Vernon's Ann.Civ.St. Tex. art. 5415a.

708

Sol. Gen. Philip B. Perlman, Washington, D.C., for plaintiff.

Messrs. Price Daniel, J. Chrys Dougherty, Austin, Tex., for defendant.

709

Mr. Justice DOUGLAS delivered the opinion of the Court.

This suit, like its companion United States v. State of Louisiana, 339 U.S. 699, 70 S.Ct. 914, invokes our original jurisdiction under Art. III, § 2, Cl. 2 of the Constitution and puts into issue the conflicting claims of the parties to oil and other products under the bed of the ocean below low-water mark off the shores of Texas.

The complaint alleges that the United States was and is "the owner in fee simple of, or possessed of paramount rights in, and full dominion and power over, the lands, minerals and other things underlying the Gulf of Mexico, lying seaward of the ordinary low-water mark on the coast of Texas and outside of the inland waters, extending seaward to the outer edge of the continental shelf and bounded on the east and southwest, respectively, by the eastern boundary of the State of Texas and the boundary between the United States and Mexico."

The complaint is in other material respects identical with that filed against Louisiana. The prayer is for a decree adjudging and declaring the rights of the United States as against Texas in the above-described area, enjoining Texas and all persons claiming under it from continuing to trespass upon the area in violation of the rights of the United States, and requiring Texas to account to the United States for all money derived by it from the area subsequent to June 23, 1947.

Texas opposed the motion for leave to file the complaint on the grounds that the Attorney General was not authorized to bring the suit and that the suit, if brought, should be instituted in a District Court. And Texas, like Louisiana, moved to dismiss on the ground that since Texas had not consented to be sued, the Court

710

had no original jurisdiction of the suit. After argument we granted the motion for leave to file the complaint. 337 U.S. 902, 69 S.Ct. 1040, 93 L.Ed. 1716. Texas then moved to dismiss the complaint on the ground that the suit did not come within the original jurisdiction of the Court. She also moved for a more definite statement or for a bill of particulars and for an extension of time to answer. The United States then moved for judgment. These various motions were denied and Texas was granted thirty days to file an answer. 338 U.S. 806, 70 S.Ct. 36.

Texas in her answer, as later amended, renews her objection that this case is not one of which the Court has original jurisdiction; denies that the United States is or ever has been the owner of the lands, minerals, etc., underlying the Gulf of Mexico within the disputed area; denies that the United States is or ever has been possessed of paramount rights in or full dominion over the lands, minerals, etc., underlying the Gulf of Mexico within said area except the paramount power to control, improve, and regulate navigation which under the Commerce Clause the United States has over lands beneath all navigable waters and except the same dominion and paramount power which the United States has over uplands within the United States, whether privately or state owned; denies that these or any other paramount powers or rights of the United States include ownership or the right to take or develop or authorize the taking or developing of oil or other minerals in the area in dispute without compensation to Texas; denies that any paramount powers or rights of the United States include the right to control or to prevent the taking or developing of these minerals by Texas or her lessees except when necessary in the exercise of the paramount federal powers, as recognized by Texas, and when duly authorized by appropriate action of the Congress; admits that she claims rights, title, and interests in said lands, minerals, etc., and says that her rights include ownership and the right

711

to take, use, lease, and develop these properties; admits that she has leased some of the lands in the area and received royalties from the lessees but denies that the United States is entitled to any of them; and denies that she has no title to or interest in any of the lands in the disputed area.

As an affirmative defense Texas asserts that as an independent nation, the Republic of Texas had open, adverse, and exclusive possession and exercise jurisdiction and control over the land, minerals, etc., underlying that part of the Gulf of Mexico within her boundaries established at three marine leagues from shore by her First Congress and acquiesced in by the United States and other major nations; that when Texas was annexed to the United States the claim and rights of Texas to this land, minerals, etc., were recognized and preserved in Texas; that Texas continued as a State, to hold open, adverse and exclusive possession, jurisdiction and control of these lands, minerals, etc., without dispute, challenge or objection by the United States; that the United States has recognized and acquiesced in this claim and these rights; that Texas under the doctrine of prescription has established such title, ownership and sovereign rights in the area as preclude the granting of the relief prayed.

As a second affirmative defense Texas alleges that there was an agreement between the United States and the Republic of Texas that upon annexation Texas would not cede to the United States but would retain all of the lands, minerals, etc., underlying that part of the Gulf of Mexico within the original boundaries of the Republic.

As a third affirmative defense Texas asserts that the United States acknowledged and confirmed the three-league boundary of Texas in the Gulf of Mexico as declared, established, and maintained by the Republic of Texas and as retained by Texas under the annexation agreement.

712

Texas then moved for an order to take depositions of specified aged persons respecting the existence and extent of knowledge and use of subsoil minerals within the disputed area prior to and since the annexation of Texas, and the uses to which Texas has devoted parts of the area as bearing on her alleged prescriptive rights. Texas also moved for the appointment of a special master to take evidence and report to the Court.

The United States opposed these motions and in turn moved for judgment asserting that the defenses tendered by Texas were insufficient in law and that no issue of fact had been raised which could not be resolved by judicial notice. We set the case down for argument on that motion.

We are told that the considerations which give the Federal Government paramount rights in, and full dominion and power over, the marginal sea off the shores of California and Louisiana (see United States v. State of California, 332 U.S. 19, 67 S.Ct. 1658, 91 L.Ed. 1889; United States v. State of Louisiana, supra) should be equally controlling when we come to the marginal sea off the shores of Texas. It is argued that the national interests, national responsibilities, and national concerns which are the basis of the paramount rights of the National Government in one case would seem to be equally applicable in the other.

But there is a difference in this case which, Texas says, requires a different result. That difference is largely in the preadmission history of Texas.

The sum of the argument is that prior to annexation Texas had both *dominium* (ownership or proprietary rights) and *imperium* (governmental powers of regulation and control) as respects the lands, minerals and other products underlying the marginal sea. In the case of California we found that she, like the original thirteen colonies, never had *dominium* over that area. The first claim to the marginal sea was asserted by the National Government. We held that protection and control of it

713

were indeed a function of national external sovereignty. 332 U.S. 31-34, 67 S.Ct. 1664-1666. The status of Texas, it is said, is different: Texas, when she came into the Union, retained the *dominium* over the marginal sea which she had previously acquired and transferred to the National Government only her powers of sovereignty—her *imperium*—over the marginal sea.

This argument leads into several chapters of Texas history.

The Republic of Texas was proclaimed by a convention on March 2, 1836.[1] The United States[2] and other nations[3] formally recognized it. The Congress of Texas on December 19, 1836, passed an act defining the boundaries of the Republic.[4] The southern boundary was described as follows: "beginning at the mouth of the Sabine river, and running west along the Gulf of Mexico three leagues from land, to the mouth of the Rio Grande."[5] Texas was admitted to the Union in 1845 "on an equal footing with the original States in all respects whatever."[6] Texas claims that during the period from 1836 to 1845 she had

1. 1 Laws, Rep. of Texas, p. 6.

2. See the Resolution passed by the Senate March 1, 1837 (Cong.Globe, 24th Cong., 2d Sess., p. 270), the appropriation of a salary for a diplomatic agent to Texas (5 Stat. 170), and the confirmation of a charge d'affaires to the Republic in 1837. 5 Exec. Journ. 17.

3. See 2 Gammel's Laws of Texas 655, 880, 886, 889, 905 for recognition by France, Great Britain, and The Netherlands.

4. 1 Laws, Rep. of Texas, p. 133.

5. The traditional three-mile maritime belt is one marine league or three marine miles in width. One marine league is 3.45 English statute miles.

6. See Joint Resolution approved December 29, 1845, 9 Stat. 108.

brought this marginal belt into her territory and subjected it to her domestic law which recognized ownership in minerals under coastal waters. This the United States contests. Texas also claims that under international law, as it had evolved by the 1840's, the Republic of Texas as a sovereign nation became th owner of the bed and

714

sub-soil of the marginal sea *vis-a-vis* other nations. Texas claims that the Republic of Texas acquired during that period the same interest in its marginal sea as the United States acquired in the marginal sea off California when it purchased from Mexico in 1848 the territory from which California was later formed. This the United States contests.

The Joint Resolution annexing Texas[7] provided in part: "Said State, when admitted into the Union, after ceding to the United States, *all public edifices, fortifications, barracks, ports and harbors, navy and navy-yards, docks, magazines, arms, armaments, and all other property and means pertaining to the public defence* belonging to said Republic of Texas, shall retain all the public funds, debts, taxes, and dues of every kind, which may belong to or be due and owing said republic; and shall also retain *all the vacant and unappropriated lands lying within its limits,* to be applied to the payment of the debts and liabilities of said Republic of Texas, and the residue of said lands, after discharging said debts and liabilities, to be disposed of as said State may direct; but in no event are said debts and liabilities to become a charge upon the Government of the United States." (Italics added.)

The United States contends that the inclusion of fortifications, barracks, ports and harbors, navy and navy-yards, and docks in the cession clause of the Resolution demonstrates an intent to convey all interests of the Republic in the marginal sea, since most of these properties lie side by side, with, and shade into, the marginal sea. It stresses the phrase in the Resolution "other property and means pertaining to the public defence." It

715

argues that possession by the United States in the lands underlying the marginal sea is a defense necessity. Texas maintains that the construction of the Resolution both by the United States and Texas has been restricted to properties which the Republic actually used at the time in the public defense.

The United States contends that the "vacant and unappropriated lands" which by the Resolution were retained by Texas do not include the marginal belt. It argues that the purpose of the clause, the circumstances of its inclusion, and the meaning of the words in Texas and federal usage give them a more restricted meaning. Texas replies that since the United States refused to assume the liabilities of the Republic, it was to have no claim to the assets of the Republic except the defense properties expressly ceded.

7. Joint Resolution approved March 1, 1845, 5 Stat. 797.

In the California case, neither party suggested the necessity for the introduction of evidence. 332 U.S. 24, 67 S.Ct. 1661, 91 L.Ed. 1889. But Texas makes an earnest plea to be heard on the facts as they bear on the circumstances of her history which, she says, sets her apart from the other States on this issue.

[1] The Court in original actions, passing as it does on controversies between sovereigns which involve issues of high public importance, has always been liberal in allowing full development of the facts. United States v. State of Texas, 162 U.S. 1, 16 S.Ct. 725, 40 L.Ed. 867; State of Kansas v. State of Colorado, 185 U.S. 125, 144, 145, 147, 22 S.Ct. 552, 558, 559, 560, 46 L.Ed. 838; State of Oklahoma v. State of Texas, 253 U.S. 465, 471, 40 S.Ct. 580, 582, 64 L.Ed. 1015. If there were a dispute as to the meaning of documents and the answer was to be found in diplomatic correspondence, contemporary construction, usage, international law and the like, introduction of evidence and a full hearing would be essential.

[2] We conclude, however, that no such hearing is required in this case. We are of the view that the "equal footing" clause of the Joint Resolution admitting Texas to the Union disposes of the present phase of the controversy.

716

[3] The "equal footing" clause has long been held to refer to political rights and to sovereignty. See Stearns v. State, of Minnesota, 179 U.S. 223, 245, 21 S.Ct. 73, 81, 45 L.Ed. 162. It does not, of course, include economic stature or standing. There has never been equality among the States in that sense. Some States when they entered the Union had within their boundaries tracts of land belonging to the Federal Government; others were sovereigns of their soil. Some had special agreements with the Federal Government governing property within their borders. See Stearns v. State of Minnesota, supra, 179 U.S. pages 243-245, 21 S.Ct. pages 80-81. Area, location, geology, and latitude have created great diversity in the economic aspects of the several States. The requirement of equal footing was designed not to wipe out those diversities but to create parity as respects political standing and sovereignty.

Yet the "equal footing" clause has long been held to have a direct effect on certain property rights. Thus the question early arose in controversies between the Federal Government and the States as to the ownership of the shores of navigable waters and the soils under them. It was consistently held that to deny to the States, admitted subsequent to the formation of the Union, ownership of this property would deny them admission on an equal footing with the original States, since the original States did not grant these properties to the United States but reserved them to themselves. See Pollard's Lessee v. Hagan, 3 How. 212, 228-229, 11 L.Ed. 565; Mumford v. Wardwell, 6 Wall. 423, 436, 18 L.Ed. 756; Weber v. Board of Harbor Com'rs, 18 Wall. 57, 65-66, 21 L.Ed. 798; Knight v. United Land Ass'n, 142 U.S. 161, 183, 12 S.Ct. 258, 264, 35 L.Ed. 974; Shively v. Bowlby, 152 U.S. 1, 26, 14 S.Ct. 548, 557, 38 L.Ed. 331; United States v. Mission Rock Co., 189 U.S. 391, 404, 23 S.Ct. 606, 608, 47 L.Ed. 865. The theory of these decisions was aptly summarized by Mr. Justice Stone speaking for the Court in United States v. State of Oregon, 295 U.S. 1, 14, 55 S.Ct. 610, 615, 79 L.Ed. 1267 as follows:[8]

717

"Dominion over navigable waters and property in the soil under them are so identified with the sovereign power of government that a presumption against their separation from sovereignty must be indulged, in construing either grants by the sovereign of the lands to be held in private ownership or transfer of sovereignty itself. See Commonwealth of Massachusetts v. State of New York, 271 U.S. 65, 89, 46 S.Ct. 357, 361, 70 L.Ed. 838. For that reason, upon the admission of a state to the Union, the title of the United States to lands underlying navigable waters within the state passes to it, as incident to the transfer to the state of local sovereignty, and is subject only to the paramount power of the United States to control such waters for purposes of navigation in interstate and foreign commerce."

[4] The "equal footing" clause, we hold, works the same way in the converse situation presented by this case. It negatives any implied, special limitation of any of the paramount powers of the United States in favor of a State. Texas prior to her admission was a Republic. We assume that as a Republic she had not only full sovereignty over the marginal sea but ownership of it, of the land underlying it, and of all the riches which it held. In other words, we assume that it then had the *dominium* and *imperium* in and over this belt which the United States now claims. When Texas came into the Union, she ceased

718

to be an independent nation. She then became a sister State on an "equal footing" with all the other States. That act concededly entailed a relinquishment of some of her sovereignty. The United States then took her place as respects foreign commerce, the waging of war, the making of treaties, defense of the shores, and the like. In external affairs the United States became the sole and exclusive spokesman for the Nation. We hold that as an incident to the transfer of that sovereignty any claim that Texas may have had to the marginal sea was relinquished to the United States.

We stated the reasons for this in United States v. State of California, supra, 332 U.S. page 35, 67 S.Ct. pages 1658, 1666, 91 L.Ed. 1889, as follows: "The

8. The same idea was expressed somewhat differently by Mr. Justice Field in Weber v. Board of Harbor Com'rs, supra, 18 Wall. pages 65-66, 21 L.Ed. 798 as follows: "Although the title to the soil under the tidewaters of the bay was acquired by the United States by cession from Mexico, equally with the title to the upland, they held it only in trust for the future State. Upon the admission of California into the Union upon equal footing with the original States, absolute property in, and dominion and sovereignty over, all soils under the tidewaters within her limits passed to the State, with the consequent right to dispose of the title to any part of said soils in such manner as she might deem proper, subject only to the paramount right of navigation over the waters, so far as such navigation might be required by the necessities of commerce with foreign nations or among the several States, the regulation of which was vested in the General government."

three-mile rule is but a recognition of the necessity that a government next to the sea must be able to protect itself from dangers incident to its location. It must have powers of dominion and regulation in the interest of its revenues, its health, and the security of its people from wars waged on or too near its coasts. And in so far as the nation asserts its rights under international law, whatever of value may be discovered in the seas next to its shores and within its protective belt, will most naturally be appropriated for its use. But whatever any nation does in the open sea, which detracts from its common usefulness to nations, or which another nation may charge detracts from it, is a question for consideration among nations as such, and not their separate governmental units. What this Government does, or even what the states do, anywhere in the ocean, is a subject upon which the nation may enter into and assume treaty or similar international obligations. See United States v. Belmont, 301 U.S. 324, 331-332, 57 S.Ct. 758, 761, 762, 81 L.Ed. 1134. The very oil about which the state and nation here contend might well become the subject of international dispute and settlement."

719

And so although *domimium* and *imperium* are normally separable and separate,[9] this is an instance where property interests are so subordinated to the right of sovereignty as to follow sovereignty.

[5-7] It is said that there is no necessity for it—that the sovereignty of the sea can be complete and unimpaired no matter if Texas owns the oil underlying it. Yet as pointed out in United States v. State of California, once low-water mark is passed the international domain is reached. Property rights must then be so subordinated to political rights as in substance to coalesce and unite in the national sovereign. Today the controversy is over oil. Tomorrow it may be over some other substance or mineral or perhaps the bed of the ocean itself. If the property, whatever it may be, lies seaward of low-water mark, its use, disposition, management, and control involve national interests and national responsibilities. That is the source of national rights in it. Such is the rationale of the *California* decision, which we have applied to Louisiana's case. The same result must be reached here if "equal footing" with the various States is to be achieved. Unless any claim or title which the Republic of Texas had to the marginal sea is subordinated to this full paramount power of the United States on admission, there is or may be in practical effect a subtraction in favor of Texas from the national sovereignty of the United States. Yet neither the original thirteen States (United States v. State of California, supra, 332 U.S. pages 31-32, 67 S.Ct. pages 1664-1665, 91 L.Ed. 1889) nor California nor Louisiana enjoys such an advantage. The "equal footing" clause prevents extension of the sovereignty of a State into a domain of political and sovereign power of the United States from which the other States

720

have been excluded, just as it prevents a contraction of sovereignty (Pollard's Lessee v. Hagan, supra) which would produce inequality among

9. See the statement of Mr. Justice Field (then Chief Justice of the Supreme Court of California) in Moore v. Smaw, 17 Cal. 199, 218-219, 79 Am.Dec. 123.

the States. For equality of States means that they are not "less or greater, or different in dignity or power." See Coyle v. Smith, 221 U.S. 559, 566, 31 S.Ct. 688, 690, 55 L.Ed. 853. There is no need to take evidence to establish that meaning of "equal footing."

[8] Texas in 1941 sought to extend its boundary to a line in the Gulf of Mexico twenty-four marine miles beyond the three-mile limit and asserted ownership of the bed within that area.[10] And in 1947 she put the extended boundary to the outer edge of the continental shelf.[11] The irrelevancy of these acts to the issue before us has been adequately demonstrated in United States v. State of Louisiana. The other contentions of Texas need not be detailed. They have been foreclosed by United States v. State of California and United States v. State of Louisiana.

The motions of Texas for an order to take depositions and for the appointment of a Special Master are denied. The motion of the United States for judgment is granted. The parties, or either of them, may before September 15, 1950, submit the form of decree to carry this opinion into effect. So ordered.

Judgment for plaintiff.

Mr. Justice JACKSON and Mr. Justice CLARK took no part in the consideration or decision of this case.

Mr. Justice REED, with whom Mr. Justice MINTON joins, dissenting.

This case brings before us the application of United States v. State of California, 332 U.S. 19, 67 S.Ct. 1658, 91 L.Ed. 1889, to Texas. Insofar as Louisina is concerned, I see no difference between its situation and that passed upon in the California case.

721

Texas, however, presents a variation which requires a different result.

The California case determines, 332 U.S. page 36, 67 S.Ct. page 1667, that since "paramount rights run to the states in inland waters to the shoreward of the low-water mark, the same rationale leads to the conclusion that national interests responsibilities, and therefore national rights are paramount in waters lying to the seaward in the three-mile belt." Thus the Court held, 332 U.S. page 39, 67 S.Ct. page 1668, that the Federal Government has power over that belt, an incident of which is "full dominion over the resources of the soil under that water area, including oil." But that decision was based on the premise, 332 U.S. pages 32-34, 67 S.Ct. pages 1665-1666, that the three-mile belt had never belonged to California. The California case points out that it was the United States which had acquired this seacoast area for the Nation. Sovereignty over that area passed from Mexico to this country. The Court commented that similar belts along their shores were not owned by the original seacoast states. Since something akin to ownership of the similar area along the coasts of the original states was thought by the Court to have been obtained through an assertion of full dominion by the United States to this hitherto unclaimed portion of the earth's

10. Act of May 16, 1941, L. Texas, 47th Leg., p. 454, Vernon's Ann.Civ.St. art. 5415a.

11. Act of May 23, 1947, L. Texas, 50th Leg., p. 451, Vernon's Ann.Civ.St. art. 5415a.

surface, it was decided that a similar right in the California area was obtained by the United States. The contrary is true in the case of Texas. The Court concedes that prior to the Resolution of Annexation, the United States recognized Texas ownership of the three-league area claimed by Texas.[12]

The Court holds immaterial the fact of Texas' original ownership of this marginal sea area, because Texas was admitted on an "equal footing" with the other states by the Resolution of Annexation. 5 Stat. 797. The scope of

722

the

"equal footing" doctrine, however, has been thought to embrace only political rights or those rights considered necessary attributes of state sovereignty. Thus this Court has held in a consistent line of decisions that since the original states, as an incident of sovereignty, had ownership and dominion over lands under navigable waters within their jurisdiction, states subsequently admitted must be accorded equivalent ownership. E.g., Pollard's Lessee v. Hagan, 3 How. 212, 11 L.Ed. 565; Martin v. Waddell's Lessee, 16 Pet. 367, 10 L.Ed. 997. But it was an articulated premise of the California decision that the thirteen original states neither had asserted ownership nor had held dominion over the three-mile zone as an incident of sovereignty.

"Equal footing" has heretofore brought to a state the ownership of river beds, but never before has that phrase been interpreted to take away from a newly admitted state property that it had theretofore owned. I see no constitutional requirement that this should be done and I think the Resolution of Annexation left the marginal sea area in Texas. The Resolution expressly consented that Texas should retain all "the vacant and unappropriated lands lying within its limits." An agreement of this kind is in accord with the holding of this Court that ordinarily lands may be the subject of compact between a state and the Nation. Stearns v. State of Minnesota, 179 U.S. 223, 245, 21 S.Ct. 73, 81, 45 L.Ed. 162. The Court, however, does not decide whether or not "the vacant and unappropriated lands lying within its limits" (at the time of annexation) includes the land under the marginal sea. I think that it does include those lands. Cf. Hynes v. Grimes Packing Co., 337 U.S. 86, 110, 69 S.Ct. 968, 982, 93 L.Ed. 1231. At least we should permit evidence of its meaning.

Instead of deciding this question of cession, the Court relies upon the need for the United States to control the area seaward of low water because of its international responsibilities. It reasons that full dominion over the

723

resources

follows this paramount responsibility, and it refers to the California discussion of the point. 332 U.S. at page 35, 67 S.Ct. at page 1666, 91 L.Ed. 1889. But the argument based on international responsibilities prevailed in the California case because the marginal sea area was staked out by the United States. The argument

12. See the statement in the Court's opinion as to the chapters of Texas history.

cannot reasonably be extended to Texas without a holding that Texas ceded that area to the United States.

The necessity for the United States to defend the land and to handle international affairs is not enough to transfer property rights in the marginal sea from Texas to the United States. Federal sovereignty is paramount within national boundaries, but federal ownership depends on taking possession, as the California case holds; on consent, as in the case of places for federal use; or on purchase, as in the case of Alaska or the Territory of Louisiana. The needs of defense and foreign affairs alone cannot transfer ownership of an ocean bed from a state to the Federal Government any more than they could transfer iron ore under uplands from state to federal ownership. National responsibility is no greater in respect to the marginal sea than it is toward every other particle of American territory. In my view, Texas owned the marginal area by virtue of its original proprietorship; it has not been shown to my satisfaction that it lost it by the terms of the Resolution of Annexation.

I would deny the United States motion for judgment.

Mr. Justice FRANKFURTER.

Time has not made the reasoning of United States v. State of California, 332 U.S. 19, 67 S.Ct. 1658, 91 L.Ed. 1889, more persuasive but the issue there decided is no longer open for me. It is relevant, however, to note that in rejecting California's claim of

724

ownership in the off-shore oil the Court carefully abstained from recognizing such claim of ownership by the United States. This was emphasized when the Court struck out the proprietary claim of the United States from the terms of the decree proposed by the United States in the California case.*

I must leave it to those who deem the reasoning of that decision right to define its scope and apply it, particularly to the historically very different situation of Texas. As is made clear in the opinion of Mr. Justice REED, the submerged lands now in controversy were part of the domain of Texas when she was on her own. The Court now decides that when Texas entered the Union she lost what she had and the United States acquired it. How that shift came to pass remains for me a puzzle.

On Rehearing

Oct. 16, 1950. The petition for rehearing is denied. Mr. Justice JACKSON and Mr. Justice CLARK took no part in the consideration or decision of this application.

*The decree proposed by the United States read in part:
"1. The United States of America is now, and has been at all times pertinent hereto, possessed of paramount rights *of proprietorship* in, and full dominion and power over, the lands, minerals and other things underlying the Pacific Ocean . . ."
The italicized words were omitted in the Court's decree. 332 U.S. 804, 805, 68 S.Ct. 20, 21, 92 L.Ed. 382.

Refer to Extract A, U.S. Constitution, 5th Amendment; also Extract D, Tucker Act

328 U.S. 256

UNITED STATES v. CAUSBY et ux.

(Cite as 66 S. Ct. 1062)

No. 630.

Argued May 1, 1946.

Decided May 27, 1946.

1. Army and navy

Military airplanes are subject to rules of Civil Aeronautics Board where there are no army or navy regulations to the contrary.

2. Eminent domain

The owner's loss, and not the taker's gain, is the measure of value of condemned property. U.S.C.A.Const. Amend. 5.

3. Eminent domain

Market value fairly determined is the normal measure of recovery in condemnation proceeding, and that value may reflect the use to which the property could readily be converted as well as the existing use. U.S.C.A.Const. Amend. 5.

4. Eminent domain

Where federal Government permitted its airplanes to fly so low over plaintiffs land which adjoined municipal airport in North Carolina leased by federal Government as to deprive plaintiffs of use and enjoyment of their land for purpose of raising chickens, there was a "taking," so as to entitle plaintiffs to recover just compensation. Air Commerce Act of 1926, §§ 1 et seq., 6(a), 10, as amended, 49 U.S.C.A. §§ 171 et seq., 176(a), 180; Civil Aeronautics Act of 1938, §§ 1 et seq., 1(3), 3, 49 U.S.C.A. §§ 401 et seq., 401(3), 403; U.S.C.A. Const. Amend. 5; G.S.N.C. §§ 63-11 to 63-13.

5. Eminent domain

The fact that path of glide taken by airplanes in taking off and landing over plaintiffs' land, which adjoined municipal airport leased by federal Government, was approved by Civil Aeronautics Authority, did not prevent the flights over plaintiffs' land from constituting a "taking" entitling plaintiffs to just compensation, since the path of glide is not the "minimum safe altitude of flight" prescribed by Civil Air Regulations as the downward reach of navigable air space placed within public domain by Congress. Air Commerce Act of 1926, § 10, 49 U.S.C.A. § 180; U.S.C.A.Const. Amend. 5

6. Property

Landowner owns at least as much of the air space above the ground as he can occupy or use in connection with the land, and fact that he does not occupy it in a physical sense by erection of buildings and the like is not material.

7. Eminent domain

The meaning of "property," as used in Fifth Amendment prohibiting the taking of private property for public use without just compensation, is a "federal question," but it will normally obtain its content by reference to local law. U.S.C.A.Const. Amend. 5.

8. Eminent domain

A holding that flights by airplanes at low levels over plaintiffs' land, which adjoined municipal airport in North Carolina leased by federal Government, deprived plaintiffs of use and enjoyment of their land and constituted a "taking," so as to entitle them to just compensation, was not inconsistent with local law of North Carolina governing landowner's claim to immediate reaches of the superadjacent airspace. G.S.N.C. §§ 63-11 to 63-13; U.S.C.A.Const. Amend. 5.

9. Eminent domain

Flights by airplanes of federal Government over private lands are not a "taking," so as to entitle owner to just compensation, unless they are so low and so frequent as to be a direct and immediate interference with the enjoyment and use of the land. Air Commerce Act of 1926, §§ 1 et seq., 6(a), 10, as amended, 49 U.S.C.A. §§ 171 et seq., 176(a), 180; Civil Aeronautics Act of 1938, §§ 1 et seq., 1(3), 3, 49 U.S.C.A. §§ 401 et seq., 401(3), 403; U.S.C.A.Const. Amend. 5.

10. Courts

A claim for taking of private land by federal Government is a "claim founded upon the Constitution" and within jurisdiction of the Court of Claims to determine. Jud.Code, § 145(1), 28 U.S.C.A. § 250(1); U.S.C.A.Const. Amend. 5.

11. Courts

On certiorari from United States Supreme Court to Court of Claims, deficiency in findings of fact by Court of Claims cannot be rectified by statements in its opinion. 28 U.S.C.A. § 288.

12. Courts

On certiorari from United States Supreme Court to Court of Claims, Supreme Court would not examine evidence to determine whether it would support a finding of fact, if such finding had been made by Court of Claims. 28 U.S.C.A. §- 288.

13. Courts

In action against federal Government for alleged taking of plaintiffs' chicken farm, which was adjacent to municipal airport leased by federal Government as result of Government permitting its airplanes to fly so low over land as to destroy plaintiffs' use and enjoyment thereof, where Court of Claims held that an easement was taken, but its findings of fact contained no description as to whether the easement taken was permanent or temporary, it would be premature for Supreme Court to consider whether amount of award made by Court of Claims was proper. 28 U.S.C.A. § 288; U.S.C.A.Const. Amend. 5.

Mr. Justice BLACK and Mr. Justice BURTON dissenting.

On Writ of Certiorari to the Court of Claims.

Action by Thomas Lee Causby and wife, Tinie Causby, against the United States, to recover for the alleged taking by defendant of plaintiffs' home and chicken farm which was adjacent to a municipal airport leased by the defendant. To review a judgment of the Court of Claims in favor of the plaintiffs, 60 F.Supp. 751, the United States brings certiorari.

Reversed and remanded.

257

Mr. Walter J. Cummings, Jr., of Washington, D.C., for petitioner.

Mr. William E. Comer, of Greensboro, N.C., for respondent.

258

Mr. Justice DOUGLAS delivered the opinion of the Court.

This is a case of first impression. The problem presented is whether respondents' property was taken within the meaning of the Fifth Amendment by frequent and regular flights of army and navy aircraft over respondents' land at low altitudes. The Court of Claims held that there was a taking and entered judgment for respondent, one judge dissenting. 60 F.Supp. 751. The case is here on a petition for a writ of certiorari which we granted because of the importance of the question presented.

[1] Respondents own 2.8 acres near an airport outside of Greensboro, North Carolina. It has on it a dwelling house, and also various outbuildings which were mainly used for raising chickens. The end of the airport's northwest-southeast runway is 2,220 feet from respondents' barn and 2,275 feet from their house. The path of glide to this runway passes directly over the property—which is 100 feet wide and 1,200 feet long. The 30 to 1 safe glide angle[1] approved by the Civil Aeronautics Authority[2] passes over this property at 83 feet, which is 67 feet above the house, 63 feet above the barn and 18 feet above the highest tree.[3] The use by the United States of this airport is pursuant to a lease executed in May, 1942, for a term commencing June 1, 1942 and ending June 30, 1942, with a provision for renewals until June 30, 1967, or six

259

months after the end of the national emergency, whichever is the earlier.

1. A 30 to 1 glide angle means one foot of elevation or descent for every 30 feet of horizontal distance.

2. Military planes are subject to the rules of the Civil Aeronautics Board where, as in the present case, there are no Army or Navy regulations to the contrary. Cameron v. Civil Aeronautics Board, 7 Cir., 140 F.2d 482.

3. The house is approximately 16 feet high, the barn 20 feet, and the tallest tree 65 feet.

Various aircraft of the United States use this airport–bombers, transports and fighters. The direction of the prevailing wind determines when a particular runway is used. The north-west-southeast runway in question is used about four per cent of the time in taking off and about seven per cent of the time in landing. Since the United States began operations in May, 1942, its four-motored heavy bombers, other planes of the heavier type, and its fighter planes have frequently passed over respondents' land and buildings in considerable numbers and rather close together. They come close enough at times to appear barely to miss the tops of the trees and at times so close to the tops of the trees as to blow the old leaves off. The noise is startling. And at night the glare from the planes brightly lights up the place. As a result of the noise, respondents had to give up their chicken business. As many as six to ten of their chickens were killed in one day by flying into the walls from fright. The total chickens lost in that manner was about 150. Production also fell off. The result was the destruction of the use of the property as a commercial chicken farm. Respondents are frequently deprived of their sleep and the family has become nervous and frightened. Although there have been no airplane accidents on respondents' property, there have been several accidents near the airport and close to respondents' place. These are the essential facts found by the Court of Claims. On the basis of these facts, it found that respondents' property had depreciated in value. It held that the United States had taken an easement over the property on June 1, 1942, and that the value of the property destroyed and the easement taken was $2,000.

260

I. The United States relies on the Air Commerce Act of 1926, 44 Stat. 568, 49 U.S.C. § 171 et seq., 49 U.S.C.A. § 171 et seq., as amended by the Civil Aeronautics Act of 1938, 52 Stat. 973, 49 U.S.C. § 401 et seq., 49 U.S.C.A. § 401 et seq. Under those statutes the United States has "complete and exclusive national sovereignty in the air space" over this country. 49 U.S.C. § 176(a), 49 U.S.C.A. § 176(a). They grant any citizen of the United States "a public right of freedom of transit in air commerce[4] through the navigable air space of the United States." 49 U.S.C. § 403, 49 U.S.C.A. § 403. And "navigable air space" is defined as "airspace above the minimum safe altitudes of flight prescribed by the Civil Aeronautics Authority." 49 U.S.C. § 180, 49 U.S.C.A. § 180. And it is provided that "such navigable airspace shall be subject to a public right of freedom of interstate and foreign air navigation." Id. It is, therefore, argued that since these flights were within the minimum safe altitudes of flight which had been prescribed, they were an exercise of the declared right of travel through the airspace. The United States concludes that when flights are made within the navigable airspace without any physical invasion of the property of the landowners, there has been no taking of property. It says that at most there was merely incidental damage occurring as a consequence of authorized air navigation. It

4. "Air commerce" is defined as including "any operation or navigation of aircraft which directly affects, or which may endanger safety in, interstate, overseas, or foreign air commerce." 49 U.S.C. § 401(3), 49 U.S.C.A. § 401(3).

also argues that the landowner does not own superadjacent airspace which he has not subjected to possession by the erection of structures or other occupancy. Moreover, it is argued that even if the United States took airspace owned by respondents, no compensable damage was shown. Any damages are said to be merely consequential for which no compensation may be obtained under the Fifth Amendment.

It is ancient doctrine that at common law ownership of the land extended to the periphery of the universe—*Cujus*

261

est solum ejus est usque ad coelum.[5] But that doctrine has no place in the modern world. The air is a public highway, as Congress has declared. Were that not true, every transcontinental flight would subject the operator to countless trespass suits. Common sense revolts at the idea. To recognize such private claims to the airspace would clog these highways, seriously interfere with their control and development in the public interest, and transfer into private ownership that to which only the public has a just claim.

[2,3] But that general principle does not control the present case. For the United States conceded on oral argument that if the flights over respondents' property rendered it uninhabitable, there would be a taking compensable under the Fifth Amendment. It is the owner's loss, not the taker's gain, which is the measure of the value of the property taken. United States v. Miller, 317 U.S. 369, 63 S.Ct. 276, 87 L.Ed. 336, 147 A.L.R. 55. Market value fairly determined is the normal measure of the recovery. Id. And that value may reflect the use to which the land could readily be converted, as well as the exising use. United States v. Powelson, 319 U.S. 266, 275, 63 S.Ct. 1047, 1053, 87 L.Ed. 1390, and cases cited. If, by reason of the frequency and altitude of the flights, respondents could not use this land for any purpose, their loss would be complete.[6] It would be as complete as if the United States had entered upon the surface of the land and taken exclusive possession of it.

[4] We agree that in those circumstances there would be a taking. Though it would be only an easement of flight

262

which was taken, that easement, if permanent and not merely temporary, normally would be the equivalent of a fee interest. It would be a definite exercise of complete dominion and control over the surface of the land. The fact that the planes never touched the surface would be as irrelevant as the absence in this day of the feudal livery of seisin on the transfer of real estate. The owner's right to possess and exploit the land—that is to say, his beneficial ownership of it—would be destroyed. It would not be a case

5. 1 Coke, Institutes, 19th Ed. 1832, ch. 1, § 1(4a); 2 Blackstone, Commentaries, Lewis Ed. 1902, p. 18; 3 Kent, Commentaries, Gould Ed. 1896, p. 621.

6. The destruction of all uses of the property by flooding has been held to constitute a taking. Pumpelly v. Green Bay Co., 13 Wall. 166, 20 L.Ed. 557; United States v. Lynah, 188 U.S. 445, 23 S.Ct. 349, 47 L.Ed. 539; United States v. Welch, 217 U.S. 333, 30 S.Ct. 527, 54 L.Ed. 787, 28 L.R.A.,N.S., 385, 19 Ann.Cas. 680.

of incidental damages arising from a legalized nuisance such as was involved in Richards v. Washington Terminal Co., 233 U.S. 546, 34 S.Ct. 654, 58 L.Ed. 1088, L.R.A.1915A, 887. In that case property owners whose lands adjoined a railroad line were denied recovery for damages resulting from the noise, vibrations, smoke and the like, incidental to the operations of the trains. In the supposed case the line of flight is over the land. And the land is appropriated as directly and completely as if it were used for the runways themselves.

There is no material difference between the supposed case and the present one, except that here enjoyment and use of the land are not completely destroyed. But that does not seem to us to be controlling. The path of glide for airplanes might reduce a valuable factory site to grazing land, an orchard to a vegetable patch, a residential section to a wheat field. Some value would remain. But the use of the airspace immediately above the land would limit the utility of the land and cause a diminution in its value.[7] That was the philosophy of Portsmouth Harbor Land & Hotel Co. v.

263

United States, 260 U.S. 327, 43 S.Ct. 135, 67 L.Ed. 287. In that case the petition alleged that the United States erected a fort on nearby land, established a battery and a fire control station there, and fired guns over petitioner's land. The Court, speaking through Mr. Justice Holmes, reversed the Court of Claims which dismissed the petition on a demurrer, holding that "the specific facts set forth would warrant a finding that a servitude has been imposed."[8] 260 U.S. at page 330, 43 S.Ct. at page 137, 67 L.Ed. 287. And see Delta Air Corp. v. Kersey, 193 Ga. 862, 20 S.E.2d 245, 140 A.L.R. 1352. Cf. United States v. 357.-25 Acres of Land, D.C., 55 F.Supp. 461.

[5] The fact that the path of glide taken by the planes was that approved by the Civil Aeronautics Authority does not change the result. The navigable airspace which Congress has placed in the public domain is "airspace above the minimum safe altitudes of flight prescribed by the Civil Aeronautics Authority." 49 U.S.C. § 180, 49 U.S.C.A. § 180. If that agency prescribed 83 feet as the minimum safe altitude, then we would have presented the question of the validity of the regulation. But nothing of the sort has been done. The path of glide governs the method of operating—of landing or taking off. The altitude required

7. It was stated in United States v. General Motors Corp., 323 U.S. 373, 378, 65 S.Ct. 357, 359, 89 L.Ed. 311, 156 A.L.R. 390, "The courts have held that the deprivation of the former owner rather than the accretion of a right or interest to the sovereign constitutes the taking. Governmental action short of acquisition of title or occupancy has been held, if its effects are so complete as to deprive the owner of all or most of his interest in the subject matter, to amount to a taking." The present case falls short of the General Motors case. This is not a case where the United States has merely destroyed property. It is using a part of it for the flight of its planes.

Cf. Warren Township School Dist. v. Detroit, 308 Mich. 460, 14 N.W.2d 134; Smith v. New England Aircraft Co., 270 Mass. 511, 170 N.E. 385, 69 A.L.R. 300; Burnham v. Beverly Airways, Inc., 311 Mass. 628, 42 N.E.2d 575.

8. On remand the allegations in the petition were found not to be supported by the facts. 64 Ct.Cl. 572.

for that operation is not the minimum safe altitude of flight which is the downward reach of the navigable airspace. The minimum prescribed by the authority is 500 feet during the day and 1000 feet at night for air carriers (Civil Air Regulations, Pt. 61, §§ 61.7400, 61.7401, Code Fed. Reg. Cum.Supp., Tit. 14, ch. 1) and from 300 to 1000 feet for

264

other aircraft depending on the type of plane and the character of the terrain. Id., Pt. 60, §§ 60.350-60.3505, Fed.Reg. Cum.Supp., supra. Hence, the flights in question were not within the navigable airspace which Congress placed within the public domain. If any airspace needed for landing or taking off were included, flights which were so close to the land as to render it uninhabitable would be immune. But the United States concedes, as we have said, that in that event there would be a taking. Thus, it is apparent that the path of glide is not the minimum safe altitude of flight within the meaning of the statute. The Civil Aeronautics Authority has, of course, the power to prescribe air traffic rules. But Congress has defined navigable airspace only in terms of one of them—the minimum safe altitudes of flight.

[6] We have said that the airspace is a public highway. Yet it is obvious that if the landowner is to have full enjoyment of the land, he must have exclusive control of the immediate reaches of the enveloping atmosphere. Otherwise buildings could not be erected, trees could not be planted, and even fences could not be run. The principle is recognized when the law gives a remedy in case overhanging structures are erected on adjoining land.[9] The landowner owns at least as much of the space above the ground as he can occupy or use in connection with the land. See Hinman v. Pacific Air Transport, 9 Cir., 84 F.2d 755. The fact that he does not occupy it in a physical sense—by the erection of buildings and the like—is not material. As we have said, the flight of airplanes, which skim the surface but do not touch it, is as much an appropriation of the use of the land as a more conventional entry upon it. We would not doubt that if the United States erected

265

an elevated railway over respondents' land at the precise altitude where its planes now fly, there would be a partial taking, even though none of the support of the structure rested on the land.[10] The reason is that there would be

9. Baten's Case, 9 Coke R. 53b; Meyer v. Metzler, 51 Cal. 142; Codman v. Evans, 7 Allen 431, 89 Mass. 431; Harrington v. McCarthy, 169 Mass. 492, 48 N.E. 278, 61 Am.St.Rep. 208. See Ball, The Vertical Extent of Ownership in Land, 76 U.Pa.L.Rev. 631, 658-671.

10. It was held in Butler v. Frontier Telephone Co., 186 N.Y. 486, 79 N.E. 716, 11 L.R.A.,N.S., 920, 116 Am.St.Rep. 563, 9 Ann.Cas. 858, that ejectment would lie where a telephone wire was strung across the plaintiff's property, even though it did not touch the soil. The court stated pages 491, 492 of 186 N.Y., page 718 of 79 N.E.: ". . . an owner is entitled to the absolute and undisturbed possession of every part of his premises, including the space above, as much as a mine beneath. If the wire had been a huge cable, several inches thick and but a foot above the ground, there would have been a difference in degree, but not in principle. Expand the wire into a beam supported by posts standing upon abutting lots without touching the surface of plaintiff's land, and the difference would still be one of degree only. Enlarge the beam into a bridge, and yet space only would be occupied. Erect a house upon the bridge, and the air above the surface of the land would alone be disturbed."

an intrusion so immediate and direct as to subtract from the owner's full enjoyment of the property and to limit his exploitation of it. While the owner does not in any physical manner occupy that stratum of airspace or make use of it in the conventional sense, he does use it in somewhat the same sense that space left between buildings for the purpose of light and air is used. The superadjacent airspace at this low altitude is so close to the land that continuous invasions of it affect the use of the surface of the land itself. We think that the landowner, as an incident to his ownership, has a claim to it and that invasions of it are in the same category as invasions of the surface.[11]

In this case, as in Portsmouth Harbor Land & Hotel Co. v. United States, supra, the damages were not merely consequential. They were the product of a direct invasion of respondents' domain.

266

As stated in United States v. Cress, 243 U.S. 316, 328, 37 S.Ct. 380, 385, 61 L.Ed. 746, "* * * it is the character of the invasion, not the amount of damage resulting from it, so long as the damage is substantial, that determines the question whether it is a taking."

[7,8] We said in United States v. Powelson, supra, 319 U.S. at page 279, 63 S.Ct. at page 1054, 87 L.Ed. 1390, that while the meaning of "property" as used in the Fifth Amendment was a federal question, "it will normally obtain its content by reference to local law." If we look to North Carolina law, we reach the same result. Sovereignty in the airspace rests in the State "except where granted to and assumed by the United States." Gen.Stats. 1943, § 63-11. The flight of aircraft is lawful "unless at such a low altitude as to interfere with the then existing use to which the land or water, or the space over the land or water, is put by the owner, or unless so conducted as to be imminently dangerous to persons or property lawfully on the land or water beneath." Id., § 63-13. Subject to that right of flight, "ownership of the space above the lands and waters of this State is declared to be vested in the several owners of the surface beneath." Id. § 63-12. Our holding that there was in invasion of respondents' property is thus not inconsistent with the local law governing a landowner's claim to the immediate reaches of the superadjacent airspace.

[9] The airplane is part of the modern environment of life, and the inconveniences which it causes are normally not compensable under the Fifth Amendment. The airspace, apart from the immediate reaches above the land, is part of the public domain. We need not determine at this time what those precise limits are. Flights over private land are not a taking, unless they are so low and so frequent as to be a direct and immediate interference with the enjoyment and use of the land. We need not speculate on that phase of the present case. For the findings of the Court

11. See Bouve, Private Ownership of Navigable Airspace Under the Commerce Clause, 21 Amer.Bar Assoc.Journ. 416, 421-422; Hise, Ownership and Sovereignty of the Air, 16 Ia.L.Rev. 169; Eubank, The Doctrine of the Airspace Zone of Effective Possession, 12 Boston Univ. L.Rev. 414.

267

of Claims plainly establish that there was a diminution in value of the property and that the frequent, low-level flights were the direct and immediate cause. We agree with the Court of Claims that a servitude has been imposed upon the land.

[10] II. By § 145(1) of the Judicial Code, 28 U.S.C. § 250(1), 28 U.S.C.A. § 250(1), the Court of Claims has jurisdiction to hear and determine "All claims (except for pensions) founded upon the Constitution of the United States or * * * upon any contract, express or implied, with the Government of the United States."

We need not decide whether repeated trespasses might give rise to an implied contract. Cf. Portsmouth Harbor Land & Hotel Co. v. United States, supra. If there is a taking, the claim is "founded upon the Constitution" and within the jurisdiction of the Court of Claims to hear and determine. See Hollister v. Benedict & Burnham Mfg. Co., 113 U.S. 59, 67, 5 S.Ct. 717, 721, 28 L.Ed. 901; Hurley v. Kincaid, 285 U.S. 95, 104, 52 S.Ct. 267, 269, 76 L.Ed. 637; Yearsley v. W.A. Ross Construction Co., 309 U.S. 18, 21, 60 S.Ct. 413, 415, 84 L.Ed. 554. Thus, the jurisdiction of the Court of Claims in this case is clear.

[11,12] III. The Court of Claims held, as we have noted, that an easement was taken. But the findings of fact contain no precise description as to its nature. It is not described in terms of frequency of flight, permissible altitude, or type of airplane. Nor is there a finding as to whether the easement taken was temporary or permanent. Yet an accurate description of the property taken is essential, since that interest vests in the United States. United States v. Cress, supra, 243 U.S. 328, 329, 37 S.Ct. 385, 386, 61 L.Ed. 746, and cases cited. It is true that the Court of Claims stated in its opinion that the easement taken was permanent. But the deficiency in findings cannot be rectified by statements in the opinion. United States v. Esnault-Pelterie, 299 U.S. 201, 205, 206, 57 S.Ct. 159, 161, 162, 81 L.Ed. 123; United States v. Seminole Nation, 299 U.S. 417, 422, 57 S.Ct. 283, 287, 81 L.Ed. 316. Findings of fact on every "material issue" are a statutory

268

requirement. 53 Stat. 752, 28 U.S.C. § 288, 28 U.S.C.A. § 288. The importance of findings of fact based on evidence is emphasized here by the Court of Claims' treatment of the nature of the easement. It stated in its opinion that the easement was permanent because the United States "no doubt intended to make some sort of arrangement whereby it could use the airport for its military planes whenever it had occasion to do so." [60 F.Supp. 758.] That sounds more like conjecture rather than a conclusion from evidence; and if so, it would not be a proper foundation for liability of the United States. We do not stop to examine the evidence to determine whether it would support such a finding, if made. For that is not our function. United States v. Esnault-Pelterie, supra, 299 U.S. at page 206, 57 S.Ct. at page 162, 81 L.Ed. 123.

[13] Since on this record it is not clear whether the easement taken is a permanent or a temporary one, it would be premature for us to consider whether the amount of the award made by the Court of Claims was proper.

The judgment is reversed and the cause is remanded to the Court of Claims so that it may make the necessary findings in conformity with this opinion.

Reversed.

Mr. Justice JACKSON took no part in the consideration or decision of this case.

Mr. Justice BLACK, dissenting.

The Fifth Amendment provides that "private property" shall not "be taken for public use, without just compensation." The Court holds today that the Government has "taken" respondents' property by repeatedly flying Army bombers directly above respondents' land at a height of eighty-three feet where the light and noise from these planes caused repondents to lose sleep and their chickens to be killed. Since the effect of the Court's decision is

269

to limit, by the imposition of relatively absolute Constitutional barriers, possible future adjustments through legislation and regulation which might become necessary with the growth of air transportation, and since in my view the Constitution does not contain such barriers, I dissent.

The following is a brief statement of the background and of the events that the Court's opinion terms a "taking" within the meaning of the Fifth Amendment: Since 1928 there has been an airfield some eight miles form Greensboro, North Carolina. In April, 1942, this airport was taken over by the Greensboro-High Point Municipal Airport Authority and it has since then operated as a municipal airport. In 1942 the Government, by contract, obtained the right to use the field "concurrently, jointly, and in common" with other users. Years before, in 1934, respondents had bought their property, located more than one-third of a mile from the airport. Private planes from the airport flew over their land and farm buildings from 1934 to 1942 and are still doing so. But though these planes disturbed respondents to some extent, Army bombers, which started to fly over the land in 1942 at a height of eighty-three feet, disturbed them more because they were larger, came over more frequently, made a louder noise, and at night a greater glare was caused by their lights. This noise and glare disturbed respondents' sleep, frightened them, and made them nervous. The noise and light also frightened respondents' chickens so much that many of them flew against buildings and were killed.

The Court's opinion seems to indicate that the mere flying of planes through the column of air directly above respondents' land does not constitute a "taking." Consequently, it appears to be noise and glare, to the extent and under the circumstances shown here, which make the government a seizer of private property. But the allegation

270

of noise and glare resulting in damages, constitutes at best an action in tort where there might be recovery if the noise and light constituted a nuisance, a violation of a statute,[12] or were the result of negligence.[13] But the Government has not consented to be sued in the Court of Claims except in actions based on express or implied contract. And there is no implied contract here, unless by reason of the noise and glare caused by the bombers the Government can be said to have "taken" respondents' property in a Constitutional sense. The concept of taking property as used in the Constitution has heretofore never been given so sweeping a meaning. The Court's opinion presents no case where a man who makes noise or shines light onto his neighbor's property has been ejected from that property for wrongfully taking possession of it. Nor would anyone take seriously a claim that noisy automobiles passing on a highway are taking wrongful possession of the homes located thereon, or that a city elevated train which greatly interferes with the sleep of those who live next to it wrongfully takes their property. Even the one case in this Court which in considering the sufficiency of a complaint gave the most elastic meaning to the phrase "private property be taken" as used in the Fifth Amendment, did not go so far. Portsmouth Harbor Land & Hotel Co. v. United States, 260 U.S.

271

327, 43 S.Ct. 135, 67 L.Ed. 287. I am not willing, nor do I think the Constitution and the decisions authorize me, to extend that phrase so as to guarantee an absolute Constitutional right to relief not subject to legislative change, which is based on averments that at best show mere torts committed by Government agents while flying over land. The future adjustment of the rights and remedies of property owners, which might be found necessary because of the flight of planes at safe altitudes, should, especially in view of the imminent expansion of air navigation, be left where I think the Constitution left it, with Congress.

Nor do I reach a different conclusion because of the fact that the particular circumstance which under the Court's opinion makes the tort here absolutely actionable, is the passing of planes through a column of air at an elevation of eighty-three feet directly over respondents' property. It is inconceivable to me that the Constitution guarantees that the airspace of this Nation needed for air

12. Neiswonger v. Goodyear Tire & Rubber Co., D.C., 35 F.2d 761.

13. As to the damage to chickens, Judge Madden, dissenting from this judgment against the Government said, "When railroads were new, cattle in fields in sight and hearing of the trains were alarmed, thinking that the great moving objects would turn aside and harm them. Horses ran away at the sight and sound of a train or a threshing machine engine. The farmer's chickens have to get over being alarmed at the incredible racket of the tractor starting up suddenly in the shed adjoining the chicken house. These sights and noises are a part of our world, and airplanes are now and will be to a greater degree, likewise a part of it. These disturbances should not be treated as torts, in the case of the airplane, any more than they are so treated in the case of the railroad or public highway."

navigation, is owned by the particular persons who happen to own the land beneath to the same degree as they own the surface below.[14] No rigid Constitutional rule, in my judgment, commands that the air must be considered as marked off into separate compartments by imaginary metes and bounds in order to synchronize air ownership with land ownership. I think that the Constitution entrusts Congress with full power to control all navigable airspace. Congress has already acted under that power. It has by statute, 44 Stat. 568, 52 Stat. 973, provided that "the United States of America is * * * to possess and exercise complete and exclusive national sovereignty in the

272

air space [over] the United States." This was done under the assumption that the Commerce Clause of the Constitution gave Congress the same plenary power to control navigable airspace as its plenary power over navigable waters. H. Rep. No. 572, 69th Cong., 1st Sess., p. 10; H. Rep. No. 1162, 69th Cong., 1st Sess., p. 14; United States v. Commodore Park, Inc., 324 U.S. 386, 65 S.Ct. 803, 89 L.Ed. 1017. To make sure that the airspace used for air navigation would remain free, Congress further declared that "navigable airspace shall be subject to a public right of freedom of interstate and foreign air navigation," and finally stated emphatically that there exists "a public right of freedom of transit * * * through the navigable airspace of the United States." Congress thus declared that the air is free, not subject to private ownership, and not subject to delimitation by the courts. Congress and those acting under its authority were the only ones who had power to control and regulate the flight of planes. "Navigable air-space" was defined as "airspace above the minimum safe altitudes of flight prescribed by the Civil Aeronautics Authority." 49 U.S.C. § 180, 49 U.S.C.A. § 180. Thus, Congress has given the Civil Aeronautics Authority exclusive power to determine what is navigable airspace subject to its exclusive control. This power derives specifically from the Section which authorizes the Authority to prescribe "air traffic rules governing the flight of, and for the navigation, protection, and identification of, aircraft, including rules as to safe altitudes of flight and rules for the prevention of collisions between aircraft, and between aircaft and land or water vehicles." 49 U.S.C.A. § 551. Here there was no showing that the bombers flying over respondents' land violated any rule or regulation of the Civil Aeronautics Authority. Yet, unless we hold the Act unconstitutional, at least such a showing would be necessary before the courts could act without interfering with the exclusive authority which Congress gave to the administrative agency. Not even a

14. The House in its report on the Air Commerce Act of 1926 stated: "The public right of flight in the navigable air space owes its source to the same constitutional basis which, under decisions of the Supreme Court, has given rise to a public easement of navigation in the navigable waters of the United States, regardless of the ownership of adjacent or subjacent soil." House Report No. 572, 69th Congress, First Session, page 10.

273

showing that the Authority has not acted at all would be sufficient. For in that event, were the courts to have any authority to act in this case at all, they should stay their hand till the Authority has acted.

The broad provisions of the Congressional statute cannot properly be circumscribed by making a distinction as the Court's opinion does between rules of safe altitude of flight while on the level of cross-country flight and rules of safe altitude during landing and taking off. First, such a distinction can not be maintained from the practical standpoint. It is unlikely that Congress intended that the Authority prescribe safe altitudes for planes making cross-country flights, while at the same time it left the more hazardous landing and take-off operations unregulated. The legislative history, moreover, clearly shows that the Authority's power to prescribe air traffic rules includes the power to make rules governing landing and take-off. Nor is the Court justified in ignoring that history by labeling rules of safe altitude while on the level of cross-country flight as rules prescribing the safe altitude proper and rules governing take-off and landing as rules of operation. For the Conference Report explicitly states that such distinctions were purposely eliminated from the original House Bill in order that the Section on air traffic rules "might be given the broadest construction by the * * * [Civil Aeronautics Authority] * * * and the courts."[15] In construing the statute narrowly the Court

274

thwarts the intent of Congress. A proper broad construction, such as Congress commanded, would not permit the Court to decide what it has today without declaring the Act of Congress unconstitutional. I think the Act given the broad construction intended is constitutional.

15. The full statement read: "The substitute provides that the Secretary shall by regulation establish air traffic rules for the navigation, protection, and identification of all aircraft, including rules as to safe altitudes of flight and rules for the prevention of collisions between vessels and aircraft. The provision as to rules for taking off and alighting, for instance, was eliminated as unnecessary specification, for the reason that such rules are but one class of air traffic rules for the navigation and protection of aircraft. Rules as to marking were eliminated for the reason that such rules were fairly included within the scope of air rules for the identification of aircraft. No attempt is made by either the Senate bill or the House amendment to fully define the various classes of rules that would fall within the scope of air traffic traffic rules, as, for instance, lights and signals along airways and at air-ports and upon emergency landing fields. In general, these rules would relate to the same subjects as those covered by navigation laws and regulations and by the various State motor vehicle traffic codes. As noted above, surplusage was eliminated in specifying particular air traffic rules in order that the term might be given the broadest possible construction by the Department of Commerce and the courts." House Report No. 1162, 69th Congress, 1st Session, p. 12.
That the rules for landing and take-off are rules prescribing "minimum safe altitudes of flight" is shown by the following further statement in the House Report: ". . . the minimum safe altitudes of flight . . . would vary with the terrain and location of cities and would coincide with the surface of the land or water at airports." Id. at p. 14.

No greater confusion could be brought about in the coming age of air transportation than that which would result were courts by Constitutional interpretation to hamper Congress in its efforts to keep the air free. Old concepts of private ownership of land should not be introduced into the field of air regulation. I have no doubt that Congress will, if not handicapped by judicial interpretations of the Constitution, preserve the freedom of the air, and at the same time, satisfy the just claims of aggrieved persons. The noise of newer, larger, and more powerful planes may grow louder and louder and disturb people more and more. But the solution of the problems precipitated by these technological advances and new ways of living cannot come about through the application of rigid Constitutional restraints formulated and enforced by the courts. What adjustments may have to be made, only the future can reveal. It seems certain, however, that courts do not possess the techniques or the personnel

275

to consider and act upon the complex combinations of factors entering into the problems. The contribution of courts must be made through the awarding of damages for injuries suffered from the flying of planes, or by the granting of injunctions to prohibit their flying. When these two simple remedial devices are elevated to a Constitutional level under the Fifth Amendment, as the Court today seems to have done, they can stand as obstacles to better adapted techniques that might be offered by experienced experts and accepted by Congress. Today's opinion is, I fear, an opening wedge for an unwarranted judicial interference with the power of Congress to develop solutions for new and vital and national problems. In my opinion this case should be reversed on the ground that there has been no "taking" in the Constitutional sense.

Mr. Justice BURTON joins in this dissent.

Taxation

Taxation of aircraft, that were continually flying, landing, and being repaired in many different states, was an important question that had to be resolved. The authority of States in preference to the Federal government was decided. Then the question of which State could tax these aircraft arose—was it the State in which the airline was domiciled or was it every State into which the aircraft flew? This question was resolved by many cases, two of which are presented here: Northwest Airlines v. Minnesota, and Braniff Airways v. Nebraska. The States then further clarified the matter by agreeing to a Council of States Allocation Formula which is also reported in the cases which follow.

Refer to Extract A, U.S. Constitution, Article I, Section 8, Clause 3; also 14th Amendment

322 U.S. 292

NORTHWEST AIRLINES, Inc., v. STATE OF MINNESOTA.

No. 33.

Argued Oct. 19, 20, 1943.

Decided May 15, 1944.

Rehearing Denied Oct. 9, 1944.

See 65 S.Ct. 26.

1. Taxation

The state of domicile has jurisdiction to tax personal property of its corporations unless the property has acquired a permanent location, that is, a taxing situs elsewhere.

2. Commerce

The power of a state to tax personalty which is permanently attributable to the state is not less because the tax may be reflected in the cost of interstate transportation. U.S.C.A.Const. art. 1, § 8, cl. 3.

3. Commerce
Constitutional law
Taxation

Where Minnesota corporation operating fleet of airplanes in interstate commerce had principal place of business in Minnesota, home port of all airplanes was in Minnesota, all airplanes were in Minnesota from time to time during tax year, and none of airplanes had acquired permanent location elsewhere, Minnesota personal property tax imposed on entire fleet of airplanes did not violate the commerce clause or deny "due process of law." Minn.St.1941, §§ 272.01 and 273.01; U.S.C.A.Const. art. 1, § 8, cl. 3, and Amend. 14.

4. Commerce
Constitutional law
Taxation

Where Minnesota corporation operating fleet of airplanes in interstate commerce had principal place of business in Minnesota, home port of all airplanes was in Minnesota, all airplanes were in Minnesota from time to time during tax year, and none of airplanes had acquired permanent location elsewhere, the fact that the corporation paid personal property taxes for the year involved on some proportion of full value of its airplane fleet in some other states did not abridge the power of taxation of Minnesota as the home state of the fleet. Minn.St.1941, §§ 272.01 and 273.01; U.S.C.A.Const. art. 1, § 8, cl. 3, and Amend. 14.

5. Taxation

Where Minnesota corporation operating fleet of airplanes in interstate commerce had principal place of business in Minnesota, home port of all airplanes was in Minnesota, all airplanes were in Minnesota from time to time during tax year, and none of airplanes had acquired permanent location elsewhere, and, on date fixed for assessing personalty subject to tax, the corporation's scheduled route mileage in Minnesota was 14 per cent of its total scheduled route mileage, and scheduled plane mileage was 16 per cent of that scheduled, the doctrine of tax apportionment for instrumentalities engaged in interstate commerce was inapplicable. Minn.St.1941, §§ 272.01 and 273.01.

6. Taxation

"Permanently," as used in rule that state of domicile has jurisdiction to tax personal property of its corporations unless such property is permanently situated in another state, means continuously throughout the year, not a fraction thereof, whether days or weeks.

7. Taxation

The power of a state of origin to tax its own corporations for all their property within the state during the tax year cannot constitutionally be affected whether property takes fixed or indeterminate trips, so long as the property is not continuously without the state during the whole tax year, even though a percentage of the property was used outside of such state during the tax year but in no one visited state permanently. U.S.C.A.Const. art. 1, § 8, cl. 3.

Mr. Chief Justice STONE, Mr. Justice ROBERTS, Mr. Justice REED, and Mr. Justice RUTLEDGE, dissenting.

On Writ of Certiorari to the Supreme Court of the State of Minnesota.

Proceedings by the State of Minnesota against Northwest Airlines, Inc., to enforce payment of delinquent personal property taxes for 1939, imposed against the defendant. A judgment for the State of Minnesota was affirmed by the Minnesota Supreme Court, 213 Minn. 395, 7 N.W.2d 691, and the Northwest Airlines, Inc., brings certiorari.

Affirmed.

Mr. Michael J. Doherty, of St. Paul, Minn., for petitioner.

Messrs. Andrew R. Bratter and George B. Sjoselius, both of St. Paul, Minn., for respondent.

Mr. Justice FRANKFURTER announced the conclusion and judgment of the Court.

The question before us is whether the Commerce Clause or the Due Process Clause of the Fourteenth Amendment bars the State of Minnesota from enforcing the personal property tax it has laid on the entire fleet of airplanes owned by the petitioner and operated by it in interstate transportation. The answer involves the application of

293

settled legal principles to the precise circumstances of this case. To these, about which there is no dispute, we turn.

Northwest Airlines is a Minnesota corporation and its principal place of business is St. Paul. It is a commercial airline carrying persons, property and mail on regular fixed routes, with due allowance for weather, predominantly within the territory comprising Illinois, Minnesota, North Dakota, Montana, Oregon, Wisconsin and Washington. For all the planes St. Paul is the home port registered with the Civil Aeronautics Authority, under whose certificate of convenience and necessity Northwest operates. At six of its scheduled cities, Northwest operates maintenance bases, but the work of rebuilding and overhauling the planes is done in St. Paul. Details as to stopovers, other runs, the location of flying crew bases and of the usual facilities for aircraft, have no bearing on our problem.

The tax in controversy is for the year 1939. All of Northwest's planes were in Minnesota from time to time during that year. All were, however, continuously engaged in flying from State to State, except when laid up for repairs and overhauling for unidentified periods. On May 1, 1939, the time fixed by Minnesota for assessing personal property subject to its tax (Minn. Stat.1941, § 273.01), Northwest's scheduled route mileage in Minnesota was 14% of its total scheduled route mileage, and the scheduled plane mileage was 16% of that scheduled. It based its personal property tax return for 1939 on the number of planes in Minnesota on May 1, 1939. Thereupon the appropriate taxing authority of Minnesota assessed a tax against Northwest on the basis of the entire fleet coming into Minnesota. For that additional assessment this suit was brought. The Supreme Court of Minnesota with three judges dissenting, affirmed the judgment of a lower court in favor of the State. 213 Minn.

294

395, 7 N.W.2d 691.

A new phase of an old problem led us to bring the case here. 319 U.S. 734, 63 S.Ct. 1157, 87 L.Ed. 1695.

The tax here assessed by Minnesota is a tax assessed upon "all personal property of persons residing therein, including the property of corporations * * *." Minn. Stat. 1941, § 272.01. It is not a charge laid for engaging in interstate commerce or upon airlines specifically; it is not aimed by indirection against interstate commerce or measure by such commerce. Nor is the tax assessed against planes which were "continuously without the state during the whole tax year," New York Central & H.R.R. Co. v. Miller, 202 U.S. 584, 594, 26 S.Ct. 714, 716, 50 L.Ed. 1155, and had thereby acquired "a permanent location elsewhere," Southern Pacific Co. v. Kentucky, 222 U.S. 63, 68, 32 S.Ct. 13, 15, 56 L.Ed. 96; and see Cream of Wheat Co. v. Grand Forks County, 253 U.S. 325, 328-330, 40 S.Ct. 558, 559, 560, 64 L.Ed. 931.

[1,2] Minnesota is here taxing a corporation for all its property within the State during the tax year no part of which receives permanent protection from any other State. The benefits given to Northwest by Minnesota and for which Minnesota taxes—its corporate facilities and the governmental resources which Northwest enjoys in the conduct of its business in Minnesota—are concretely symbolized by the fact that Northwest's principal place of business is in St. Paul and that St. Paul is the "home port" of all its planes. The relation between Northwest and Minnesota—a relation existing between no other State and Northwest—and the benefits which this relation affords are the constitutional foundation for the taxing power which Minnesota has asserted. See State Tax Com. v. Aldrich, 316 U.S. 174, 180, 62 S.Ct. 1008, 1011, 86 L.Ed. 1358, 139 A.L.R. 1436. No other State can claim to tax as the State of the legal domicile as well as the home State of the fleet, as a business fact. No other State is the State which gave Northwest the power to be as well as the power to function as Northwest functions in Minnesota; no other state could impose a tax that derives from the significant legal relation of creator and creature

295

and the practical consequences of that relation in this case. On the basis of rights which Minnesota alone originated and Minnesota continues to safeguard, she alone can tax the personalty which is permanently attributable to Minnesota and to no other State. It is too late to suggest that this taxing power of a State is less because the tax may be reflected in the cost of transportation. See In re Delaware Railroad Tax, 18 Wall. 206, 232, 21 L.Ed. 888.

[3,4] Such being the case, it is clearly ruled by New York Central & H.R.R. Co. v. Miller, supra. Here, as in that case, a corporation is taxed for all its property within the State during the tax year none of which was "continuously without the state during the whole tax year." Therefore the doctrine of Union Refrigerator Transit Co. v. Kentucky, 199 U.S. 194, 26 S.Ct. 36, 50 L.Ed. 150, 4 Ann.Cas. 493, does not come into play. The fact that Northwest paid personal property taxes for the year 1939 upon "some proportion of its full value" of its airplane fleet in some other States does not abridge the power of taxation of Minnesota as the home State of the fleet in the circumstances of the present case. The taxability of any part of this fleet by any other State than Minnesota,

in view of the taxability of the entire fleet by that State, is not now before us. It was not shown in the Miller case and it is not shown here that a defined part of the domiciliary corpus has acquired a permanent location, i.e., a taxing situs, elsewhere.[1] That

296

was the decisive feature of the Miller case, and it was deemed decisive as late as 1933 in Johnson Refining Oil Co. v. Oklahoma, 290 U.S. 158, 54 S.Ct. 152, 78 L.Ed. 238, which was strongly pressed upon us by Northwest. In that case it was not the home State, Illinois, but a foreign State, Oklahoma, which was seeking to tax a whole fleet of tank cars used by the oil company. That case fell outside of the decision of the Miller case and ours falls precisely within it. "Appellant had its domicile in Illinois," as Mr. Chief Justice Hughes pointed out, "and that state had jurisdiction to tax appellant's personal property which had not acquired an actual situs elsewhere." 290 U.S. at page 161, 54 S.Ct. at page 153, 78 L.Ed. 238.[2] This constitutional basis for what Minnesota did, reflects practicalities in the relations between the States and air transportation. "It has been customary to tax operating airplanes at their overhaul

1. In the Miller case, the New York Central Railroad introduced evidence that during the taxable years in question, a proportion of its cars, ranging from about 12% to 64%, was used outside of New York. This figure was arrived at by using the ratio between Central's mileage outside of New York and its total mileage. The comptroller nevertheless ruled that all of Central's cars were taxable in New York, the State of domicile. On review of this ruling as applied in the first tax year involved, the New York Court of Appeals remitted the proceedings to the comptroller to determine whether any of the rolling stock was used exclusively out of the State. People ex rel. New York Cent. & H.R.R. Co. v. Knight, 173 N.Y. 255, 65 N.E. 1102. No such evidence was introduced for any tax year, although there was evidence to show "that a certain proportion of cars, although not the same cars, was continuously without the state during the whole tax year." 202 U.S. 584, 594, 26 S.Ct. 714, 716, 50 L.Ed. 1155. The comptroller made no reduction in the tax, and this action was affirmed by the Appellate Division (89 App.div. 127, 84 N.Y.S. 1088), the Court of Appeals (177 N.Y. 584, 69 N.E. 1129) and on review here.

2. In the Johnson Oil Refining Co. case, supra, this Court reaffirmed not less than three times that the State of domicile has jurisdiction to tax the personal property of its corporation unless such property has acquired an "actual situs" in another State. And by "actual situs" it meant, as its references to Union Refrigerator Transit Co. v. Kentucky, supra, and the Miller case indicate, what those cases required for "actual situs" before the constitutional power of the domiciliary State to tax could be curtailed, namely continuous presence in another State which thereby supplants the home State and acquires the taxing power over personalty that has become a permanent part of the foreign State. Surely the situs which personal property may acquire for tax purposes in a State other than that of the owner's domicile cannot be made to depend on some undefined concept of "permanence" short of a tax year, leaving the adequate size of the fraction of the tax year for judicial determination in each year. Such a doctrine would play havoc with the tax laws of the forty-eight states. It would multiply manifold the recognized difficulties of ascertaining the domicile of individuals. See State of Texas v. Florida, 306 U.S. 398, 59 S.Ct. 563, 830, 83 L.Ed. 817, 121 A.L.R. 1179; District of Columbia v. Murphy, 314 U.S. 441, 62 S.Ct. 303, 86 L.Ed. 329.

297

base."
Thompson, State and Local Taxation Affecting Air Transportation (1933) 4 J.Air L. 479, 483.

[5] The doctrine of tax apportionment for instrumentalities engaged in interstate commerce introduced by Pullman's Palace-Car Co. v. Pennsylvania, 141 U.S. 18, 11 S.Ct. 876, 35 L.Ed. 613, is here inapplicable. The principle of that case is that a nondomiciliary State may tax an interstate carrier "engaged in running railroad cars into, through, and out of the state, and having at all times a large number of cars within the state * * * by taking as the basis of assessment such proportion of its capital stock as the number of miles of railroad over which its cars are run within the state bears to the whole number of miles in all the states over which its cars are run." Union Refrigerator Transit Co. v. Kentucky, supra, 199 U.S. at page 206, 26 S.Ct. at page 38, 50 L.Ed. 150, 4 Ann.Cas. 493. This principle was successively extended to the old means of transportation and communication, such as express companies and telegraph systems. But the doctrine of apportionment has neither in theory nor in practice been applied to tax units of interstate commerce visiting for fractional periods of the taxing year. (Thus, for instance, "The coaches of the company * * * are daily passing from one end of the state to the other," in Pullman's Palace-Car Co. v. Pennsylvania, supra, 141 U.S. at page 20, 11 S.Ct. at page 877, 35 L.Ed. 613, citing the opinion of the court below in 107 Pa. 156, 160.) The continuous protection by a State other than the domiciliary State—that is, protection throughout the tax year—has furnished the constitutional basis for tax apportionment in these interstate commerce situations, and it is on that basis that the tax laws have been framed and administered.

[6] The taxing power of the domiciliary State has a very different basis. It has power to tax because it is the State of domicile and no other State is. For reasons within its own sphere of choice Congress at one time chartered interstate carriers and at other times has left the chartering and all that goes with it to the States. That is a practical fact of legislative choice and a practical fact

298

from
which legal significance has always followed. That far-reaching fact was recognized, as a matter of course, by Mr. Justice Bradley in his dissent in the Pullman's Palace-Car Co. case, supra, 141 U.S. at page 32, 11 S.Ct. at page 881, 35 L.Ed. 613. Congress of course could exert its controlling authority over commerce by appropriate regulation and exclude a domiciliary State from authority which it otherwise would have because it is the domiciliary State. But no judicial restriction has been applied against the domiciliary State except when property (or a portion of fungible units) is permanently situated in a State other than the

domiciliary State.[3] And permanently means continuously throughout the year, not a fraction thereof, whether days or weeks.

[7] Such was the unanimous decision in the Miller case or the Miller case decided nothing. The present case is precisely the case which Mr. Justice Holmes assumed the Miller case to be. By substituting Minnesota for New York we have inescapably the facts of the present case: "Suppose, then, that the state of Minnesota had taxed the property directly, there was nothing to hinder its taxing the whole of it. It is true that it has been decided that property, even of a domestic corporation, cannot be taxed

299

if it is permanently out of the State. * * * But it has not been decided, and it could not be decided, that a state may not tax its own corporations for all their property within the state during the tax year, even if every item of that property should be taken successively into another state for a day, a week, or six months, and then brought back. Using the language of domicil, which now so frequently is applied to inanimate things, the state of origin remains the permanent situs of the property, notwithstanding its occasional excursions to foreign parts." New York Central & H.R.R. Co. v. Miller, supra, 202 U.S. at pages 596, 597, 26 S.Ct. at pages 716, 717, 50 L.Ed. 1155.[4] Surely, the power of the State of origin to "tax its own corporations for all their property within the state during the tax year" cannot constitutionally be affected whether the property takes fixed trips or indeterminate trips so long as the property is not "continuously without the state during the whole tax year," New York Central & H.R.R. Co. v. Miller, supra, 202 U.S. at page 594, 26 S.Ct. at page 716, 50 L.Ed. 1155, even when, as in the Miller case, from 12% to 64% of the property was shown to have been used outside of New York during the tax year, but in no one visited State permanently, that is, for the whole year. And that is the decisive constitutional fact about the Miller case—that although from 12% to 64% of the rolling stock of the railroad was outside of New York

4. In speaking of "occasional excursions to foreign parts" and "random excursions" (202 U.S. at page 579, 26 S.Ct. at page 717, 50 L.Ed. 1155), Mr. Justice Holmes merely put colloquially the legally significant fact that neither any specific cars nor any average of cars was so continuously in any other State as to have been withdrawn from the home State and to have established for tax purposes an adopted home State.

3. In the most recent apportionment case to come before this Court, Nashville, C. & St. L. Ry. v. Browning, 310 U.S. 362, 60 S.Ct. 968, 970, 84 L.Ed. 1254, we merely sustained the application by the Tennessee Railroad Commission and the Tennessee Supreme Court (176 Tenn. 245, 140 S.W.2d 781) of a "familiar and frequently sanctioned formula" for apportionment on a mileage basis against the claim of the inapplicability of this formula in the circumstances of that case because of the disparity in the revenue-producing capacity between the lines in and out of Tennessee. Mathematical exactitude in making the apportionment has never been a constitutional requirement. That is the essence of the Browning holding. No suggestion can be found at any stage of that litigation in any wise touching the present problem, namely, whether the domiciliary State is constitutionally limited in taxing all the movables that come within it except by the Union Transit doctrine, that a proportion which had during the entire tax year been within another State cannot be taxed in the domiciliary State.

throughout the tax year, New York was nevertheless allowed to tax it all because no part was in any other State throughout the year.

To introduce a new doctrine of tax apportionment as a limitation upon the hitherto established taxing power of the home State is not merely to indulge in constitutional

300

innovation. It is to introduce practical dislocation into the established taxing systems of the States. The doctrine of tax apportionment has been painfully evolved in working out the financial relations between the States and interstate transportation and communication conducted on land and thereby forming a part of the organic life of these States. Although a part of the taxing systems of this country, the rule of apportionment is beset with friction, waste and difficulties, but at all events it grew out of, and has established itself in regard to land commerce.[5] To what extent it should be carried over to the totally new problems presented by the very different modes of transportation and communication that the airplane and the radio have already introduced, let alone the still more subtle and complicated technological facilities that are on the horizon, raises questions that we ought not to anticipate; certainly we ought not to embarrass the future by judicial answers which at best can deal only in a truncated way with problems sufficiently difficult even for legislative statesmanship.

The doctrine in the Miller case, which we here apply, does not subject property permanently located outside of the domiciliary State to double taxation. But not to subject property that has no locality other than the State of its owner's domicile to taxation there would free such floating property from taxation everywhere. And what the Miller case decided is that neither the Commerce Clause nor the Fourteenth Amendment affords such constitutional immunity.

Each new means of interstate transportation and communciation has engendered controversy regarding the

301

taxing powers of the States inter se and as between the States and the Federal Government. Such controversies and some conflict and confusion are inevitable under a federal system. They have long been the source of difficulty and dissatisfaction for us, see J.B. Moore, Taxation of Movables and the Fourteenth Amendment (1907) 7 Col. L.Rev. 309; Groves, Intergovernmental Fiscal Relations, Proceedings Thirty-fifth Annual Conference, National Tax Association, p. 105, and have equally plagued the British federal systems, see Report of the [Australian] Royal Commission on the Constitution (1929) c. XII (p. 127), c. XIX (p. 187), c. XXIII (at p. 259); Report of the [Canadian] Royal Commission on Dominion-Provincial Relations (1940) Bk. I,

5. And that the constitutional power of the domiciliary State to tax vessels is precisely the same as its power to tax rolling stock is conclusively shown by the Court's reliance in the Miller case on a case decided a week before, namely Ayer & Lord Tie Co. v. Kentucky, 202 U.S. 409, 26 S.Ct. 679, 50 L.Ed. 1082, 6 Ann.Cas. 205.

c. VIII, Bk. II, § B, c. III. In response to arguments addressed also to us about the dangers of harassing state taxation affecting national transportation, the concurring judge below adverts to the power of Congress to incorporate airlines and to control their taxation. But insofar as these are matters that go beyond the constitutional issues which dispose of this case, they are not our concern.

Affirmed.

Mr. Justice BLACK, concurring.

I concur in the judgment of the Court and in substantially all that is said in the opinion, but I would not in this case foreclose consideration of the taxing rights of States other than Minnesota.

I believe there is small support in reason or in the Constitution for the doctrine that the Commerce Clause in and of itself prohibits a state from applying its general tax laws to transactions and properties in interstate commerce unless it is able to make two correct prophecies as to what this Court ultimately may hold, namely [1] The permissible total of taxes which might be imposed by an aggregate of states on the taxed properties or transactions; and [2] The proportion of this total which the state itself

302

fairly may claim. See dissenting opinions in Adams Manufacturing Co. v. Storen, 304 U.S. 307, 316, 58 S.Ct. 913, 918, 82 L.Ed. 1365, 117 A.L.R. 429; Gwin, etc., Inc., v. Henneford, 305 U.S. 434, 442, 59 S.Ct. 325, 329, 83 L.Ed. 272. Extension of this dubious doctrine to the new problems of air transport gives promise of little but tax confusion.

The differing views of members of the Court in this and related cases illustrate the difficulties inherent in the judicial formulation of general rules to meet the national problems arising from state taxation which bears in incidence upon interstate commerce. These problems, it seems to me, call for Congressional investigation, consideration, and action. The Constitution gives that branch of government the power to regulate commerce among the states, and until it acts I think we should enter the field with extreme caution. See dissenting opinion, McCarroll v. Dixie Greyhound Lines, 309 U.S. 176, 183, 60 S.Ct. 504, 507, 84 L.Ed. 683.

Mr. Justice JACKSON, concurring.

This case considers for the first time constitutional limitations upon state power to tax airplanes. Several principles of limitation have been judicially evolved in reference to ships and to railroad rolling stock. The question is which, if any of these should be transferred to air transport.

We are at a stage in development of air commerce roughly comparable to that of steamship navigation in 1824 when Gibbons v. Ogden, 9 Wheat. 1, 6 L.Ed. 23, came before this Court. Any authorization of local burdens on our national air commerce will lead to their multiplication in this country. Moreover, such an example is not likely to be neglected by other revenue-needy nations as international air transport expands.

Aviation has added a new dimension to travel and to our ideas. The ancient idea that landlordism and sovereignty extend from the center of the world to the periphery

303

of the universe has been modified. Today the landowner no more possesses a vertical control of all the air above him than a shore owner possesses horizontal control of all the sea before him. The air is too precious as an open highway to permit it to be "owned" to the exclusion of embarrassment of air navigation by surface landlords who could put it to little real use.

Students of our legal evolution know how this Court interpreted the commerce clause of the Constitution to lift navigable waters of the United States out of local controls and into the domain of federal control. Gibbons v. Ogden, 9 Wheat. 1, 6 L.Ed. 23, to United States v. Appalachian Electric Power Co., 311 U.S. 377, 61 S.Ct. 291, 85 L.Ed. 243. Air as an element in which to navigate is even more inevitably federalized by the commerce clause than is navigable water. Local exactions and barriers to free transit in the air would neutralize its indifference to space and its conquest of time.

Congress has recognized the national responsibility for regulating air commerce. Federal control is intensive and exclusive. Planes do not wander about in the sky like vagrant clouds. They move only by federal permission, subject to federal inspection, in the hands of federally certified personnel and under an intricate system of federal commands. The moment a ship taxis onto a runway it is caught up in an elaborate and detailed system of controls. It takes off only by instruction from the control tower, it travels on prescribed beams, it may be diverted from its intended landing, and it obeys signals and orders. Its privileges, rights, and protection, so far as transit is concerned, it owes to the Federal Government alone and not to any state government.

Congress has not extended its protection and control to the field of taxation, although I take it no one denies that constitutionally it may do so. It may exact a single uniform federal tax on the property or the business to

304

the exclusion of taxation by the states. It may subject the vehicles or other incidents to any type of state and local taxation, or it may declare them tax-free altogether. Our function is to determine what rule governs in the absence of such legislative enactment.

Certainly today flight over a state either casually or on regular routes and schedules confers no jurisdiction to tax. Earlier ideas of a state's sovereignty over the air above it might argue for such a right to tax, but it is one of those cases where legal philosophy has to take account of the fact that the world does move.

Does the act of landing within a state, even regularly and on schedule, confer jurisdiction to tax? Undoubtedly a plane, like any other article of personal property, could land or remain within a state in such a way as to become a part of the property within the state. But when a plane lands to receive and discharge passengers, to undergo servicing or repairs, or to await a convenient departing schedule, it does not in my opinion lose its character as a plane in transit. Long ago this Court held that the landing of a ship within the ports of a state for similar purposes did not confer jurisdiction to tax. Hays v. Pacific Mail S.S. Co., 17 How. 596, 15 L.Ed. 254; City of St. Louis v. Wiggins Ferry Co., 11 Wall. 423, 20 L.Ed. 192; Morgan v. Parham, 16 Wall. 471, 21 L.Ed. 302; cf. Ayer & Lord Tie Co. v. Kentucky, 202 U.S. 409, 26 S.Ct. 679, 50 L.Ed. 1082, 6 Ann.Cas. 205. I cannot consider that to alight out of the skies onto a landing field and take off again into the air confers any greater taxing jurisdiction on a state than for a ship for the same purposes to come alongside a wharf on the water and get under way again.

What, then, remains as a basis for Minnesota's claim to tax this entire fleet of planes at their full value as property of the State of Minnesota? They have been within the state only transiently and in the same manner in which they have been in many states: to serve the public and to be serviced. The planes have received no "protection"

305

or "benefit" from Minnesota that they have not received from many others. It might be difficult, in view of the complete control of this type of activity by the Federal Government, to find what benefits or protection any state extends. But no distinction whatever can be pointed out between those extended by Minnesota and those extended by any state where there is a terminal or a stopping place.

But it is said that Minnesota incorporated the company. Of course it is her right to tax the company she has created and the franchise she has granted. I suppose there are many ways that she might constitutionally measure the value of this privilege. If she chartered a corporation on condition that all property it might acquire, tangible or intangible, should be taxable under her laws, I do not think a company which accepted such a charter could appeal to the Constitution to give back what it voluntarily contracted away. But no such stipulation has been made in the charter in this case. The tax imposed here is a general ad valorem property tax on the full value of every plane of the fleet operated by this company. Domicile of an owner is a usual test of power to tax intangibles, but has not generally been a conclusive test of taxability of tangible property situated elsewhere. If we should suppose that this corporation had a Delaware charter instead of a Minnesota one, and had nothing in Delaware except its agent, but operated otherwise in Minnesota exactly as it has done, would we say that the entire right to tax the fleet moved to Delaware because it was the corporation's state of domicile? I do not think that domicile, in the facts of this case, is decisive of Minnesota's claim to tax the tangible property of the company wherever situate.

It is strongly and plausibly advocated that the theory of apportionment of the total value among the several states of operation, heretofore applied to state taxation

306

of railroad rolling stock, be transferred to air transportation. This would mean that each state of operation (no one ventures to say whether flight alone or both flight and landing would be required) could tax a proportion of the total value.

The apportionment theory is a mongrel one, a cross between desire not to interfere with state taxation and desire at the same time not utterly to crush out interstate commerce. It is a practical, but rather illogical, device to prevent duplication of tax burdens on vehicles in transit. It is established in our decisions and has been found more or less workable with more or less arbitrary formulae of apportionment. Nothing either in theory or in practice commends it for transfer to air commerce. A state has a different relation to rolling stock of railroads than it has to airplanes. Rolling stock is useless without surface rights and continuous structures on every inch of land over which it operates. Surface rights the railroad has acquired from the state or under its law. There is a physical basis within the state for the taxation of rolling stock which is lacking in the case of airplanes.

It seems more than likely that no solution of the competition among states to tax this transportation agency can be devised by the judicial process without legislative help. The best analogy that I find in existing decisions is the "home port" theory applied to ships. See Hays v. Pacific Mail S.S. Co., City of St. Louis v. Wiggins Ferry Co., Morgan v. Parham, supra. There is difficulty in the application of this doctrine to air commerce, I grant. There is no statutory machinery for fixing the home port. If federal registration established statehood as it establishes nationality, the home port doctrine would be easy to apply. However, on the record before us it seems unquestioned that Minnesota is in an operational as well as in a domiciliary sense the home port of this fleet. On that doctrine Minnesota can tax the fleet, but its right to do so is exclusive,

307

for no other state can acquire jurisdiction to tax merely because it provides a port of call. I therefore concur in the conclusion reached by the opinion of Mr. Justice FRANKFURTER. I do not accept the opinion because it falls short of commitment that Minnesota's right is exclusive of any similar right elsewhere. It is, I know, difficult to judge and dangerous to foreclose claims of other states that are not before us. That is the weakness of the judicial process in these tax questions where the total problem that faces an industry reaches us only in installments. If the reasoning should hereafter be extended to support full taxation everywhere, it would offend the commerce clause, as I see it, even more seriously than apportioned taxation everywhere.

The evils of local taxation of goods or vehicles in transit are not measured by the exaction of one locality alone, but by the aggregation of them. I certainly do not favor exemption of interstate commerce from its "just share of taxation." But history shows that fair judgment as to what exactions are just to the passerby cannot be left to local opinion. When local authority is taxing its own, the taxed ones may be assumed to be able to protect themselves at the polls. No such sanction enforces fair dealing to the transient. In all ages and climes those who are settled in strategic localities have made the moving world pay dearly. This the commerce clause was designed to end in the United States.

The rule I suggest seems most consonant with the purposes of the commerce clause among those found in our precedents. But the whole problem we deal with is unprecedented. I do not think we can derive from decisional law a satisfactory adjustment of the conflicting needs of the nation for free air commerce and the natural desire of localities to have revenue from the business that goes on about them.

308

I concur in the affirmance of the judgment below, but only because the record seems to me to establish Minnesota as a "home port" within the meaning of the old and somewhat neglected but to me wise authorities cited.

Mr. Chief Justice STONE, dissenting.

In my opinion the Minnesota levy imposed an unconstitutional tax on petitioner's vehicles of interstate transportation in violation of the commerce clause, and for that reason the judgment below should be reversed.

Petitioner, a Minnesota corporation, is owner of a large number of airplanes which it uses exclusively in interstate transportation moving on regular schedules and over fixed routes extending through eight states between Chicago, Illinois and the Pacific coast, with the usual landing fields and maintenance bases at intermediate points, including Minneapolis and St. Paul, Minnesota. It is stipulated that on May 1, 1939, 14% of the total mileage of the prescribed interstate routes was in Minnesota and that 16% of the daily plane mileage of all petitioner's interstate planes was in that state.

Although the Minnesota statute taxing personal property directs that it shall be listed for taxation on May 1st of each year and assessed for taxation at its value on that date, Minn.Stat.1941 § 273.01, the state taxing authorities have levied on petitioner, and the Minnesota Supreme Court and this Court have sustained an annual tax on the full value of all its planes used in interstate commerce which have come into the state at any time during the year. It is evident that if, with the Minnesota tax now sustained, other states are left free to impose a further or comparable tax on the same property for the same tax period, a serious question is raised whether the tax is not a prohibited burden on interstate commerce.

It is no longer doubted that interstate business "must pay its way" by sustaining its fair share of the property

309

tax burden which the states in which the interstate business is done may lawfully impose generally on property located within them. See Western Live Stock v. Bureau, 303 U.S. 250, 254, 255, 58 S.Ct. 546, 548, 549, 82 L.Ed. 823, 115 A.L.R. 944, and cases cited. Obviously interstate business bears no undue part of that burden if the personal property tax imposed on it by a given state is—like a tax on real estate located there—exclusive of all other property taxes imposed by other states, as is the case with the taxation of vessels, Old Dominion S.S. Co. v. Virginia, 198 U.S. 299, 25 S.Ct. 686, 49 L.Ed. 1059, 3 Ann.Cas. 1100; Southern Pacific Co. v. Kentucky, 222 U.S. 63, 32 S.Ct. 13, 56 L.Ed. 96, and cases cited; cf. New York Central & H.R.R. Co. v. Miller, 202 U.S. 584, 26 S.Ct. 714, 50 L.Ed. 1155, or if the tax on its personal property regularly used over fixed routes in interstate commerce, both within and without the taxing state, is fairly apportioned to its use within the state, as has until now been the rule as to railroad cars. Marye v. Baltimore & Ohio R. Co., 127 U.S. 117, 123, 124, 8 S.Ct. 1037, 1039, 1040, 32 L.Ed. 94; Pullman's Palace-Car Co. v. Pennsylvania, 141 U.S. 18, 11 S.Ct. 876, 35 L.Ed. 613; American Refrigerator Transit Co. v. Hall, 174 U.S. 70, 19 S.Ct. 599, 43 L.Ed. 899; Union Refrigerator Transit Co. v. Lynch, 177 U.S. 149, 20 S.Ct. 631, 44 L.Ed. 708; Union Refrigerator Transit Co. v. Kentucky, 199 U.S. 194, 26 S.Ct. 36, 50 L.Ed. 150, 4 Ann.Cas. 493; Germania Refining Co. v. Fuller, 245 U.S. 632, 38 S.Ct. 63, 62 L.Ed. 521; Union Tank Line v. Wright, 249 U.S. 275, 39 S.Ct. 276, 63 L.Ed. 602; Johnson Oil Refining Co. v. Oklahoma, 290 U.S. 158, 54 S.Ct. 152, 78 L.Ed. 238.

If the tax levied here were held to be exclusive of all property taxes imposed on petitioner's airplanes by other states there could be no serious question of an undue burden on interstate commerce. That question arises now only because the rationale found necessary to support the present tax leaves other states free to impose comparable taxes on the same property used in interstate commerce which Minnesota has already taxed for the entire taxable year and at its full value.

Such, I think, is the necessary consequence of the Court's decision and judgment now given. They do not sustain the tax on the ground that Minnesota, as the state of petitioner's domicile, has exclusive power to tax respondent's

310

planes which pass in and out of Minnesota in performance of their interstate functions. They do not deny that the planes are constitutionally subject, to some extent, to personal property taxes by the states through which they pass. Our decisions, as will presently appear, establish that they are, and that vehicles of interstate transportation moving from the state of the owner's domicile over regular routes within the jurisdiction of other states also acquire a tax situs there, so that, to an extent presently to be considered, they may be taxed by each of the states through which they pass. In fact the record discloses that petitioner's interstate planes, already taxed by Minnesota for their full value, are in addition subjected to personal property taxes in six of the seven other states through which they fly.

But if petitioner's airplanes, which are taxable for some portion of their value in each of the states in which they carry on interstate transportation over fixed routes and regular schedules, are also taxed for their full value by Minnesota, the state of the domicile, it is evident that merely because they are engaged in interstate commerce they may be subjected to multiple state taxation far in excess of their value, and far beyond any tax which any one of the states concerned could under its established system of taxation impose on vehicles whose movements are confined within its territorial limits. It is a scheme of property taxation on which, so far as the decision now rendered gives us any hint, the commerce clause sets no restriction, but which is so burdensome in its operation as compared with the taxes imposed on intrastate vehicles that few interstate carriers could support it and survive economically.

The case thus sharply presents in a new form the old question whether the commerce clause affords any protection against multiple state taxation of the physical

311

facilities used in interstate transportation which, because they move from state to state, are exposed to full taxation in each, save only as the due process and commerce clauses may prevent. Although the question is new in form it is old in substance and this Court has considered it so often in other but similar relationships that the answer here seems plain.

Of controlling significance in this case are certain elementary propositions, so long accepted and applied by this Court that they cannot be said to be debatable here, although they seem not to have been taken into account in deciding this case either here or in the Minnesota Supreme Court. The first is that the constitutional basis for the state taxation of the airplanes, which are chattels, is their physical presence within the taxing state, and not the domicile of the owner. Union Refrigerator Transit Co. v. Kentucky, supra; Johnson Oil Refining Co. v. Oklahoma, supra, 290 U.S. 161, 162, 54 S.Ct. 153, 154, 78 L.Ed. 238, and cases cited. In this respect, as this Court has often pointed out, the taxation of chattels rests on a different basis than does the taxation of intangibles, which have no physical situs and may be reached by the tax gatherer only through exertion of the power of the state over the person of those who have some legal interest in the intangibles. Union Refrigerator Transit Co. v. Kentucky, supra, 199 U.S. 205, 206, 26 S.Ct. 38, 39, 50 L.Ed. 150, 4 Ann.Cas. 493; Schwab v. Richardson, 263 U.S. 88, 92, 44 S.Ct. 60, 62, 68 L.Ed. 183; Frick v. Pennsylvania, 268 U.S. 473, 494, 45 S.Ct. 603, 606, 69 L.Ed. 1058, 42 A.L.R. 316; Blodgett v. Silberman, 277 U.S. 1, 16-18, 48 S.Ct. 410, 416, 72 L.Ed. 749; Wheeling Steel Corp. v. Fox, 298 U.S. 193, 209, 210, 56 S.Ct. 773, 776, 777, 80 L.Ed. 1143; Curry v. McCanless, 307 U.S. 357, 363-366, 59 S.Ct. 900, 903-906, 83 L.Ed. 1339, 123 A.L.R. 162; Graves v. Elliott, 307 U.S. 383, 59 S.Ct. 913, 83 L.Ed. 1356; Graves v. Schmidlapp, 315 U.S. 657, 62 S.Ct. 870, 86 L.Ed. 1097, 141 A.L.R. 948; State Tax Com. v. Aldrich, 316 U.S. 174, 62 S.Ct. 1008, 86 L.Ed. 1358, 139 A.L.R. 1436.

A state may, within the Fourteenth Amendment, tax a chattel located within its limits, although its owner is domiciled elsewhere, Brown v. Houston, 114 U.S. 622, 5 S.Ct. 1091, 29 L.Ed. 257; Coe v. Errol, 116 U.S. 517 6 S.Ct. 475, 29 L.Ed. 715; Pullman's Palace-Car Co. v. Pennsylvania, supra; Old Dominion S.S. Co. v. Virginia, supra.

312

But due process precludes the state of the domicile from taxing it unless it is brought within that state's boundaries. Delaware, L. & W.R. Co. v. Pennsylvania, 198 U.S. 341, 25 S.Ct. 669, 49 L.Ed. 1077; Union Refrigerator Transit Co. v. Kentucky, supra; Frick v. Pennsylvania, supra, 268 U.S. 489 et seq., 45 S.Ct. 604 et seq., 69 L.Ed. 1058, 42 A.L.R. 316. It is plain then that for present purposes, and so far as the Fourteenth Amendment is concerned, respondent's airplanes, which are chattels regularly moving over fixed interstate routes, are subject in some measure to the taxing power of every state in which they regularly stop on their interstate mission.[6]

In some instances it may be that vehicles of transportation moving interstate are so sporadically and irregularly present in other states that they acquire no tax situs there, Hays v. Pacific Mail S.S. Co., 17 How. 596, 15 L.Ed. 254; City St. Louis v. Wiggins Ferry Co., 11 Wall. 423, 20 L.Ed. 192; Morgan v. Parham, 16 Wall. 471, 21 L.Ed. 302; Ayer & Lord Tie Co. v. Kentucky, 202 U.S. 409, 26 S.Ct. 679, 50 L.Ed. 1082, 6 Ann.Cas. 205, and hence remain taxable to their full value by the state of the domicile because they are not taxable elsewhere, New York Central & H.R.R. Co. v. Miller, supra; Southern Pacific Co. v. Kentucky, supra. But that is not the case as to any of the planes here involved. And our decisions establish that, except in the case of tangibles which have nowhere acquired a tax situs based on physical presence, and for that reason remain taxable at the domicile even if never present there, the state's power to tax chattels depends

313

on their physical presence and is neither added to nor subtracted from because the taxing state may or may not happen to be the state of the owner's domicile.

We need not consider to what extent the due process clause limits the taxing power of each state through which airplanes or other vehicles of interstate transportation pass, to the taxation of part only of their value, fairly related to their use within the state, or precluded the Minnesota Supreme Court from extending to tangible property moving in more than one state the rule of Curry v. McCanless, supra, and subsequent cases, permitting full taxation of intangibles by each state having a substantial relationship to the interest taxed. For we are dealing here with tangible instrumentalities of interstate commerce, entitled as such to the protection afforded by the commerce clause from unduly burdensome state taxation, even though the tax might otherwise be within the constitu-

6. We need not consider here whether the jurisdiction of a state over air above it—as distinguished from the control of a private landowner over air above his land—affords a basis for taxation of planes which regularly fly over the state but do not regularly land within its borders. For in six of the seven states, other than Minnesota, over which petitioner's airplanes regularly fly, they also make regular scheduled landings. Plainly those states have jurisdiction to tax a proportionate part of their value and to that extent the judgment of the Minnesota Supreme Court, permitting taxation in full by the domicile, is erroneous, and the cause should be remanded for further proceedings.

tional power of the state. And it is plain as this Court has often held, that if one state may impose a personal property tax at full value on an interstate carrier's vehicles of transportation, and other states through which they pass may also tax them for the same tax period, the resulting tax would be destructive of the commerce by imposing on it a multiple tax burden to which intrastate carriers are not subjected.

This Court has never denied the power of the several states to impose a property tax on vehicles used in interstate transportation in the taxing state. It has recognized, as we have seen, that such instruments of interstate transportation, at least if moving over fixed routes on regular schedules, may thus acquire a tax situs in every state through which they pass. And it has met the problem of burdensome multiple taxation by the several states through which such vehicles pass by recognizing that the due process clause or the commerce clause or both preclude

314

each state from imposing on the interstate commerce involved an undue or inequitable share of the tax burden. In Nashville, C. & St. L. Ry. v. Browning, 310 U.S. 362, 365, 60 S.Ct. 968, 970, 84 L.Ed. 1254, we recently considered "the guiding principles for adjustment of the state's right to secure its revenues and the nation's duty to protect interstate transportation." We declared that "The problem to be solved is what portion of an interstate organism may appropriately be attributed to each of the various states in which it functions." And, in sustaining the tax, apportioned according to mileage, upon the entire property, including rolling stock, of an interstate railroad, imposed by Tennessee, the state of the owner's domicile, in which its principal business office and over 70% of its trackage was located, we said that the state could not "use a fiscal formula * * * to project the taxing power of the state plainly beyond its borders."

This Court has accordingly held invalid state taxation of vehicles of interstate transportation unless the tax is equitably apportioned to the use of the vehicles within the state compared to their use without, whether the tax is laid by the state of the domicile or another.[7] Such an

7. The rule, generally applied, that vessels are taxable only by the domicile, Hays v. Pacific Mail S.S. Co., 17 How. 596, 597, 15 L.Ed. 254; St. Louis v. Wiggins Ferry Co., 11 Wall. 423, 430, 431, 432, 20 L.Ed. 192; Morgan v. Parham, 16 Wall. 471, 475, 21 L.Ed. 302; Transportation Co. v. Wheeling, 99 U.S. 273; 279, 280, 25 L.Ed. 412; Ayer & Lord Tie Co. v. Kentucky, 202 U.S. 409, 421, 26 S.Ct. 679, 682, 50 L.Ed. 1082, 6 Ann.Cas. 205; Southern Pacific Co. v. Kentucky, 222 U.S. 63, 68, 69, 77, 32 S.Ct. 13, 14, 15, 18, 56 L.Ed. 96, is no exception to these rules. For vessels ordinarily move on the high seas, outside the jurisdiction of any state, and merely touch briefly at ports within a state. Hence they acquire no tax situs in any of the states at which they touch port, and are taxable by the domicile or not at all. See Pullman's Palace-Car Co. v. Pennsylvania, 141 U.S. 18, 23, 11 S.Ct. 876, 878, 35 L.Ed. 613; Southern Pacific Co. v. Kentucky, supra, 222 U.S. 75, 32 S.Ct. 17, 56 L.Ed. 96. The suggestion in the earlier cases, see Hays v. Pacific Mail S.S. Co., supra, 17 How. 600, 15 L.Ed. 254; City of St. Louis v. Wiggins Ferry Co., supra; Morgan v. Parham, supra, that vessels were to be taxed exclusively at the home port, whether or not it was the domicile,

315

apportionment has been sustained when made according to the mileage traveled within and without the state, Pullman's Palace-Car Co. v. Pennsylvania, supra, 141 U.S. 26, 11 S.Ct. 879, 35 L.Ed. 613, or the average number of vehicles within the taxing state during the tax period. Marye v. Baltimore & Ohio R. Co., supra; American Refrigerator Transit Co. v. Hall, supra, 174 U.S. 82, 19 S.Ct. 604, 43 L.Ed. 899; Union Refrigerator Transit Co. v. Lynch, supra.[8]

But if the tax is laid without apportionment or if the apportionment, when made, is plainly inequitable so as to bear unfairly on the commerce by compelling the carrier to pay to the taxing state more than its fair share of the tax measured by the full value of the property, this Court has set aside the tax as an unconstitutional burden on interstate commerce, whether it be in form on the rolling

316

stock, Union Refrigerator Transit Co. v. Kentucky, supra; Union Tank Line v. Wright, supra; Johnson Oil Refining Co. v. Oklahoma, supra, or on the carrier's entire property, Fargo v. Hart, 193 U.S. 490, 24 S.Ct. 498, 48 L.Ed. 761; or on a franchise or right to do business, Allen v. Pullman's Palace-Car Co.,

was rejected in Ayer & Lord Tie Co. v. Kentucky, supra, and Southern Pacific Co. v. Kentucky, supra, and has never been revived. But where the vessels operate wholly on waters within one state, they have been held to be taxable there, Old Dominion Steamship Co. v. Virginia, 198 U.S. 299, 25 S.Ct. 686, 49 L.Ed. 1059, 3 Ann.Cas. 1100, and not at the domicile, Southern Pacific Co. v. Kentucky, supra, 222 U.S. 67, 72, 32 S.Ct. 14, 16, 56 L.Ed. 96, a result which, like the rule of apportionment in taxing railroad cars, avoids the burden of multiple taxation.

8. Similarly taxes by the state of domicile or other states on the carrier's entire property including rolling stock have been sustained if apportioned according to mileage, Pittsburgh, etc. R. Co. v. Backus, 154 U.S. 421, 14 S.Ct. 1114, 38 L.Ed. 1031; Adams Express Co. v. Ohio State Auditor, 165 U.S. 194, 17 S.Ct. 305, 41 L.Ed. 683; Id., 166 U.S. 185, 17 S.Ct. 604, 41 L.Ed. 965; American Express Co. v. Indiana, 165 U.S. 255, 17 S.Ct. 991, 41 L.Ed. 707; Adams Express Co. v. Kentucky, 166 U.S. 171, 17 S.Ct. 527, 41 L.Ed. 960; Wells, Fargo & Co. v. Nevada, 248 U.S. 165, 39 S.Ct. 62, 63 L.Ed. 190; St. Louis, etc., R. Co. v. State of Missouri ex rel. and to Use of Hagerman, 256 U.S. 314, 41 S.Ct. 488, 65 L.Ed. 946; Southern R. Co. v. Watts, 260 U.S. 519, 43 S.Ct. 192, 67 L.Ed. 375; Nashville, C. & St. L. Ry. v. Browning, 310 U.S. 362, 60 S.Ct. 968, 84 L.Ed. 1254, or a combination of relevant factors, Rowley v. Chicago & N.W.R. Co., 293 U.S. 102, 55 S.Ct. 55, 79 L.Ed. 222; Great Northern R. Co. v. Weeks, 297 U.S. 135, 56 S.Ct. 426, 80 L.Ed. 532. Likewise gross receipts taxes, if properly apportioned or otherwise limited to receipts from business done within the state, have been upheld, Erie R. Co. v. Pennsylvania, 21 Wall. 492, 22 L.Ed. 595; State of Maine v. Grand Trunk R. Co., 142 U.S. 217, 12 S.Ct. 121, 163, 35 L.Ed. 994, as explained in Galveston, etc., R. Co. v. Texas, 210 U.S. 217, 226, 28 S.Ct. 638, 640, 52 L.Ed. 1031; United States Express Co. v. Minnesota, 223 U.S. 335, 32 S.Ct. 211, 56 L.Ed. 459; Cudahy Packing Co. v. Minnesota, 246 U.S. 450, 38 S.Ct. 373, 62 L.Ed. 827; Pullman Co. v. Richardson, 261 U.S. 330, 43 S.Ct. 366, 67 L.Ed. 682; cf. New York, Lake Erie & W.R. Co. v. Pennsylvania, 158 U.S. 431, 15 S.Ct. 896, 39 L.Ed. 1043.

191 U.S. 171, 24 S.Ct. 39, 48 L.Ed. 134; Wallace v. Hines, 253 U.S. 66, 40 S.Ct. 435, 64 L.Ed. 782; Southern R. Co. v. Kentucky, 274 U.S. 76, 47 S.Ct. 542, 71 L.Ed. 934; cf. Norfolk, etc., R. Co. v. Pennsylvania, 136 U.S. 114, 10 S.Ct. 958, 34 L.Ed. 394.

Upon like principles this Court has consistently held that a tax laid by a state on gross receipts from interstate commerce, which is comparable to a property tax at full value on vehicles of interstate transportation, violates the commerce clause unless equitably apportioned. Galveston, H., etc., R. Co. v. Texas, 210 U.S. 217, 28 S.Ct. 638, 52 L.Ed. 1031; Meyer, Auditor of Oklahoma v. Wells, Fargo & Co., 223 U.S. 298, 32 S.Ct. 218, 56 L.Ed. 445; see Cudahy Packing Co. v. Minnesota, 246 U.S. 450, 453-455, 38 S.Ct. 373, 374, 375, 62 L.Ed. 827; Pullman Company v. Richardson, 261 U.S. 330, 338, 339, 43 S.Ct. 366, 368, 369, 67 L.Ed. 682. To the same effect as to capital stock taxes, see Atchison, etc., R. Co. v. O'Connor, 223 U.S. 280, 285, 32 S.Ct. 216, 217, 56 L.Ed. 436, Ann.Cas. 1913C, 1050, and cases cited.

In many the tax was held invalid although imposed by the state of the domicile of the taxpayer. Philadelphia & S.M. Steamship Co. v. Pennsylvania, 122 U.S. 326, 342, 7 S.Ct. 1118, 1123, 30 L.Ed. 1200, overruling State Tax on Railway Gross Receipts, 15 Wall. 284, 21 L.Ed. 164; Crew Levick Co. v. Pennsylvania, 245 U.S. 292, 38 S.Ct. 126, 62 L.Ed. 295; New Jersey Bell Telephone Co. v. Tax Board, 280 U.S. 338, 50 S.Ct. 111, 74 L.Ed. 463; Fisher's Blend Station v. Tax Commission, 297 U.S. 650, 56 S.Ct. 608, 80 L.Ed. 956; Puget Sound Stevedoring Co. v. Tax Commission, 302 U.S. 90, 58 S.Ct. 72, 82 L.Ed. 68; Adams Mfg. Co. v. Storen, 304 U.S. 307, 58 S.Ct. 913, 82 L.Ed. 1365, 117 A.L.R. 429; Gwin, White & Prince v. Henneford, 305 U.S. 434, 59 S.Ct. 325, 83 L.Ed. 272; see Western Live Stock v. Bureau, supra. The same rule is applied to the taxation by the domicile of goods carried interstate, Case of the State Freight Tax, 15 Wall. 232, 21 L.Ed. 146; Eureka Pipe Line Co. v. Hallanan, 257 U.S. 265, 42 S.Ct. 101, 66 L.Ed. 227; and the taxation of goods in transit generally, Hughes Bros. Timber Co. v. Minnesota, 272 U.S. 469, 47 S.Ct. 170, 71 L.Ed. 359.

317

In Galveston, H., etc., R. Co. v. Texas, supra, 210 U.S. 228, 28 S.Ct. 640, 52 L.Ed. 1031, in which a tax on gross receipts of a railway engaged in interstate commerce was condemned because not apportioned, the Court declared, "Of course, it does not matter that plaintiffs in error are domestic corporations." The like rule, applied to the taxation by the state of the owner's domicile of railroad property, including rolling stock, was approved in Nashville, C. & St. L. Ry. v. Browning, supra. And in Bacon v. Illinois, 227 U.S. 504, 511, 512, 33 S.Ct. 299, 301, 57 L.Ed. 615, the Court was at pains to point out that the power of a state to tax goods in transit is not affected by the fact that it is or is not the domicile of the owner. These cases clearly establish that, whatever relevance domicile may at times have to the power of a state under the due process clause to tax tangibles, it has none to the question whether the exercise of that power so burdens interstate commerce as to violate the commerce clause.

It cannot be said either in point of practicality or of legal theory that anything is added to Minnesota's power to tax by reason of the fact that all of petitioner's aircraft are registered with the Civil Aeronautics Authority with St. Paul, Minnesota, designated as their "home port." Section 501 of the Civil Aeronautics Act, 52 Stat. 1005, 49 U.S.C. § 521, 49 U.S.C.A. § 521, requiring the registration with the Authority of aircraft, merely provides that a certificate of registration "shall be conclusive evidence of nationality for international purposes." Neither the statute nor the regulations adopted under it attach any other consequences to the registration of airplanes at a particular "home port." The much more detailed provisions of R.S. §§ 4141, 4178 as amended, 46 U.S.C.A. §§ 17, 46, requiring registration of vessels at a particular home port and the painting of the name of that port on the stern of the vessel, have been held irrelevant to state power to tax, even though the port of enrollment is also one at which the vessel regularly calls, City of St.

318

Louis v. Wiggins Ferry Co., supra; Ayer & Lord Tie Co. v. Kentucky, supra; see Southern Pacific Co. v. Kentucky, supra, 222 U.S. 68, 73, 32 S.Ct. 14, 17, 56 L.Ed. 96.

Nor is it of any significance for tax purposes whether Minnesota is "as a business fact the home state of the fleet." While the existence of a business domicile has been thought to afford a basis for the state taxation of intangibles, on the theory that they have become localized there, Wheeling Steel Corp. v. Fox, supra, 298 U.S. 211 et seq., 56 S.Ct. 777, et seq., 80 L.Ed. 1143, the constitutional bases for the taxation of tangibles and of intangibles are, as we have seen, quite different, and under our decisions, to which we have referred, the only basis for the taxation of tangibles is their physical presence in the taxing jurisdiction. And even the taxation of intangibles of interstate carriers is subject to the rule of apportionment wherever the tax without it would subject the commerce to the burden of multiple state taxation. The "unit rule" for the taxation of interstate carriers applies to tangibles and intangibles alike and requires an equitable apportionment of the tax on both. Adams Express Co. v. Ohio State Auditor, 165 U.S. 194, 222, 226, 17 S.Ct. 305, 309, 311, 41 L.Ed. 683; Id., 166 U.S. 185, 223, 224, 225, 17 S.Ct. 604, 607, 608, 41 L.Ed. 965; Fargo v. Hart, supra, 193 U.S. 499, 24 S.Ct. 500, 48 L.Ed. 761; Meyer, Auditor of Oklahoma v. Wells Fargo & Co., supra, 223 U.S. 300, 32 S.Ct. 219, 56 L.Ed. 445; Wallace v. Hines, supra, 253 U.S. 69, 70, 40 S.Ct. 436, 437, 64 L.Ed. 782; Southern R. Co. v. Kentucky, supra, 274 U.S. 81, 47 S.Ct. 544, 71 L.Ed. 934.

Moreover, the difficulties of applying to aircraft a rule of taxation at a "home port" are essentially those which have led, long since, to the abandonment of the idea by this Court as applied to vessels. Compare City of St. Louis v. Wiggins Ferry Co., supra; Ayer & Lord Tie Co. v. Kentucky, supra. While it appears from the present record that petitioner maintains at St. Paul, Minnesota, its airplane and engine overhauling base, at which the principal repairs to planes and engines are made, it also operates maintenance bases at Chicago, Illinois, Minneapolis, Minnesota, Fargo, North Dakota, Billings, Montana, and Spokane and Seattle,

319

Washington, at which points it maintains crews of mechanics and maintenance equipment. It owns and leases hangars and office space at all of its stopping points, each of which are manned by its employees. On the tax day, May 1, 1939, petitioner's planes made no scheduled stop in St. Paul. Thus a number of states have a physical relationship to petitioner's business—by reason of the movement of planes, over the fixed routes, the landing of planes, the maintenance and operation of repair and service equipment, landing fields, hangars, and office buildings, with their attendant employees—which, for practical purposes, is as substantial in nature as that claimed for Minnesota.

Even if we could say on this record that Minnesota and it alone can be regarded as the "home state," we have no assurance that in taxing planes operated by other and more complex business organizations, one state will have any greater claim to that designation than several others, and the court's opinion furnishes no test to guide in the choice among them, if choice has any relevance. Nor does it say that the power to tax vehicles of interstate transportation at the domicile or the "home port" is exclusive. Obviously, unless it is deemed to be thus exclusive it does not foreclose any state within which the planes move on fixed routes from imposing a like tax burden. And if it is deemed to be exclusive the other states must be denied their just claims to collect an equitable tax on property regularly used within them in carrying on an interstate business. North Dakota, for instance, in taxing the planes regularly landing within its borders, is not taxing rights originating in and safeguarded by Minnesota, or exercising any rights attributable to Minnesota. No reason appears why North Dakota should be denied the right to tax the planes to the extent that they are within its borders, or why, to that extent, Minnesota

320

has any relationship to them sufficent either to enable it to tax them or to preclude North Dakota from taxing them.

The taxation of vehicles of interstate transportation in a business organized and conducted as is petitioner's is as capable of apportionment, and the insupportable multiple tax burden on interstate commerce is as readily avoided by apportionment of the tax, as in the case of the taxation of tangible and intangible property of railroads, railroad car supply companies, express companies, and the like which we have repeatedly held to be subject to the rule of apportionment. To refuse now to apply the rule of apportionment to petitioner's airplanes, after a half century of its application by this Court as the means of avoiding prohibited multiple state tax burdens on vehicles of interstate transportation; to extend to airplanes moving interstate over fixed routes on regular schedules, the rule that intangibles may be taxed at the business domicile whether or not taxed elsewhere; and to revive the abandoned doctrine that vessels may be taxed in full at their home port, while rejecting the correlative rule that they are exempt from taxation elsewhere, is to disregard the teachings of experience and of precedent. It subjects a new and important industry to state tax burdens, essentially discriminatory in their effect on interstate commerce, to which other interstate carriers are not subject and which it was the very purpose of the commerce clause to avoid.

Respondent places its reliance on New York Central & H.R.R. v. Miller, supra. There the Court sustained a franchise tax by the state of domicile including in its measure the full value of freight cars moving in and out of the state, often out of the taxpayer's possession for an indefinite time, and moving in the service of other roads on their independent business. The decision proceeded on the assumption, not tenable here but which the facts of that case were thought to support, that the cars were not

321

shown to have moved so regularly or continuously in any state or group of states outside the domicile as to gain a tax situs there. The Court in distinguishing the case from Pullman's Palace-Car Co. v. Pennsylvania, supra, which sustained a state tax on a foreign railroad corporation, measured by the intrastate mileage of cars passing in and out of the taxing state, said (202 U.S. at pages 597, 598, 26 S.Ct. at page 717, 50 L.Ed. 1155):

"But, in that case, it was found that the 'cars used in this state have, during all the time for which tax is charged, been running into, through, and out of the State.' The same cars were continuously receiving the protection of the state, and, therefore, it was just that the state should tax a proportion of them. Whether, if the same amount of protection had been received in respect of constantly changing cars, the same principle would have applied, was not decided, and it is not necessary to decide now. In the present case, however, it does not appear that any specific cars or any average of cars was so continuously in any other state as to be taxable there. The absences relied on were not in the course of travel upon fixed routes, but random excursions of casually chosen cars, determined by the varying orders of particular shippers and the arbitrary convenience of other roads. Therefore we need not consider either whether there is any necessary parallelism between liability elsewhere and immunity at home."

The present case raises the question which the Miller case found it unnecessary to decide but which this Court has consistently answered by requiring the apportionment of a tax on vehicles of interstate transportation according to their regular use within and without the taxing state. In the Miller case it appeared that the cars moved not only over the carrier's own tracks, but also were interchanged with other railroads, and thus, as the Court pointed out, moved about almost at random throughout the United States. No evidence was offered tending to show in what states the cars moved, or with what degree

322

of regularity they were present in any particular state or group of states other than New York. The Court was thus not called upon to consider whether New York could tax the cars if they moved between New York and other named states with such regularity that an "average of cars" could be said to be continuously so moving in those other states. Here, on the other hand, it is stipulated and found that all of petitioner's planes are "continuously engaged in flying from state to state in the course of [petitioner's] operations" and that those operations are on regular schedules along fixed routes through eight states. The total mileage of regular routes and the total daily mileage on those routes both in Minnesota and outside are definitely stipulated and found. Hence there is no warrant for saying that their presence in each of the states through which they pass is not as regular and continuous in nature as it is in Minnesota. These findings establish that, while no particular plane is permanently within any state, its planes are continuously flying in, and an average number or a percentage of the total is regularly, i.e., "permanently" within, each of the states through which they pass. Here, as was the case in Pullman's Palace-Car Co. v. Pennsylvania, supra [141 U.S. 18, 11 S.Ct. 877, 35 L.Ed. 613], the same planes are "running into, through, and out of" each of the states along petitioner's routes and an "average" of planes is continuously within each of those states.[9]

323

We are not now concerned with the proper apportionment of taxable values among the states outside the state of Minnesota. Since the movement of the planes, wherever they go, is over fixed routes and on regular schedules, they acquire a tax situs outside Minnesota to the extent that they do not move within it. Hence the extent to which they move in and are taxable by one state outside Minnesota rather than another is irrelevant. It is enough that the Minnesota tax is for full value and that Minnesota's fiscal formula imposes a prohibited burden

9. It is true that here there is no evidence of the average number of planes present within Minnesota or any other state during the tax year. But where the movement through the state is regular and continuous, as it is here and was not in the Miller case, apportionment may be made by showing the plane mileage or route mileage within and without the state. Pullman's Palace-Car Co. v. Pennsylvania, 141 U.S. 18, 11 S.Ct. 876, 35 L.Ed. 613; Nashville C. & St. L. Ry. v. Browning, 310 U.S. 362, 60 S.Ct. 968, 84 L.Ed. 1254, and cases cited. The Minnesota court here did not rest its decision on the ground that petitioner had sought to apportion by mileage instead of by average number of cars, and had introduced no evidence to support the latter type of apportionment. If it had it might well have remanded the cause to permit any deficiences of proof to be remedied. It held rather that regardless of the nature of proof of apportionment Minnesota, as the state of the domicile, could tax the cars for their entire value.

In this respect also the case is unlike the Miller case. There, as the record reveals, the carrier's evidence showed only the car mileage within and without the state, and its owned track mileage within and without the state. But since the cars moved over irregular routes without fixed schedules, car mileage afforded no basis of apportionment, without proof also that the cars were present in particular states with sufficient regularity to acquire a tax situs there. Owned track mileage likewise failed to afford a basis of apportionment, in the absence of some proof that the tracks were regularly used by the cars in question. Nor did the carrier lack opportunity to make fuller proof. The cause as it came here involved five successive tax years, as to each of which the carrier was afforded a hearing with opportunity to introduce evidence. The carrier having failed despite this repeated opportunity to introduce evidence which would, on any theory of apportionment, support a conclusion that any particular proportion of cars had acquired a tax situs elsewhere, this Court, as it pointed out, was not called upon to apply the rule of Pullman's Palace-Car Co. v. Pennsylvania, supra, or to consider whether, consistently with the commerce clause, property used as an instrumentality of commerce may be subjected to the risk of double taxation.

on interstate commerce because it is used "to project the tax power of the state plainly beyond its borders," to reach instruments of interstate commerce which are taxable elsewhere, and that the extent of that projection may be measured by comparing either the plane or the

324

route mileage over fixed routes in Minnesota with like mileage over fixed routes in the states outside Minnesota.

Both before and since the Miller case this Court has ruled that vehicles of interstate transportation regularly moving to and from the state of domicile from and to other states acquire a tax situs in the latter, and that the state of domicile cannot constitutionally levy on them on unapportioned property tax. Union Refrigerator Transit Co. v. Kentucky, supra; Johnson Oil Refining Co. v. Oklahoma, supra; Nashville, C. & St. L. Ry. v. Browning, supra. In Johnson Oil Refining Co. v. Oklahoma, supra, 290 U.S. 161, 162, 54 S.Ct. 153, 154, 78 L.Ed. 238, where the cars moved from and to Oklahoma to and from various states including Illinois, the state of domicile, we declared that the cars had acquired a tax situs outside Illinois and were to that extent not taxable by Illinois. The court rested its decision on the rule, stated without qualification, that "When a fleet of cars is habitually employed in several states–the individual cars constantly running in and out of each state–it cannot be said that any one of the states is entitled to tax the entire number of cars regardless of their use in the other states."[10] Those cases should control

10. In Union Refrigerator Transit Company v. Kentucky, 199 U.S. 194, 26 S.Ct. 36, 50 L.Ed. 150, 4 Ann.Cas. 493, it appeared that the cars of the Transit Company, the taxpayer, moved in and out of Kentucky, the state of domicile. The Transit Company disclaimed on the record any effort to prove that it had any cars which never came within the state, and sought to establish the number "permanently located" outside it only by proof of gross earnings within and without the state. In holding that the state of domicile could not tax tangible personal property "permanently located in other states" (199 U.S. at page 201, 26 S.Ct. at page 36, 50 L.Ed. 150, 4 Ann.Cas. 493), it is clear that the Court was limiting the taxing power of the state of domicile to the extent that the cars moving between Kentucky and other states had, under the rule of apportionment, gained a tax situs outside the state because they were "located and employed" there (199 U.S. at page 211, 26 S.Ct. at page 41, 50 L.Ed. 150, 4 Ann.Cas. 493). This is evident from its citation (199 U.S. at page 206, 26 S.Ct. at page 38, 50 L.Ed. 150, 4 Ann.Cas. 493) of Pullman's Palace-Car Company v. Pennsylvania, 141 U.S. 18, 11 S.Ct. 876, 35 L.Ed. 613, and American Refrigerator Transit Company v. Hall, 174 U.S. 70, 19 S.Ct. 599, 43 L.Ed. 899, as cases involving property "permanently located" in the taxing states. Both cases involved rolling stock continuously moving into and out of the taxing state and sustained taxes upon a proportion of the carrier's total rolling stock based respectively upon the track mileage or upon the average number of cars used within the taxing state. Had the Court intended to exempt, from the domicile's power to tax, only property which never came into the domicile it would have been necessary for it to discuss also the contention that the Union Transit Company had been denied the equal protection of the laws because railroads were taxed only upon the value of their rolling stock used within the state determined by the proportionate mileage within the state. 199 U.S. at pages 202, 211, 26 S.Ct. at pages 36, 41, 50 L.Ed. 150, 4 Ann.Cas. 493.

325

now. For here we are confronted with a scheme of taxation imposed on vehicles of interstate transportation located within the taxing state for only a limited and specified part of their active life. For the rest, they are in other states, moving over fixed routes of travel where, under our decisions, they plainly have a tax situs, and where they are in fact taxed in six of the seven states other than Minnesota through which they pass.

The tax now sustained is so obviously disproportionate to the protection afforded to the taxed property by the taxing state as to place a constitutionally intolerable burden on interstate commerce. But it is a burden which is capable of equitable adjustment which would satisfy constitutional requirements by the application of the principles of apportionment which this court has repeatedly sanctioned, and which it is the constitutional duty of the State of Minnesota to apply. The application of these principles does not call for mathematical exactness nor for the rigid application of a particular formula; only if the resulting valuation is palpably excessive will it be set aside. But a reasonable attempt must be made to tax only so much of the value as is fairly related to use within the taxing state. Union Tank Line v. Wright, supra 249 U.S. 282, 39 S.Ct. 278, 63 L.Ed. 602; Great Northern R. Co. v. Weeks, supra, 297 U.S. 144, 56 S.Ct. 431, 80 L.Ed. 532; Nashville Co. & St. L. Ry. v. Browning, supra, 310 U.S. 365, 60 S.Ct. 970, 84 L.Ed. 1254.

326

It is no answer to suggest that the states other than Minnesota have not asserted their constitutional power to tax or that we do not know how or to what extent they have exercised it. The extent to which one state may constitutionally tax the instruments of interstate transportation does not depend on what other states may happen to do, but on what the taxing state has constitutional power to do. The jurisdiction of Minnesota to tax "must be determined on a basis which is consistent with the like jurisdiction of other states." Johnson Oil Refining Co. v. Oklahoma, supra, 290 U.S. 162, 54 S.Ct. 154, 78 L.Ed. 238. Minnesota cannot justify its imposition of an undue proportion of the total tax burden which can be imposed on an interstate carrier by saying that other states have taken or may take less than their share of the tax. It is enough that the tax exposes petitioner to "the risk of a multiple burden to which local commerce is not exposed. Adams Mfg. Co. v. Storen, supra [304 U.S. 311, 58 S.Ct. 916, 82 L.Ed. 1365, 117 A.L.R. 429]." Gwin, White & Prince, Inc., v. Henneford, supra, 305 U.S. 439, 59 S.Ct. 328, 83 L.Ed. 272, and cases cited. To hold otherwise would be to measure Minnesota's power to tax, not by constitutional standards, but by the action of other states over which neither Minnesota nor petitioner has any control and to leave petitioner's tax to be measured from year to year, not according to any legal standard, but by the unpredictable uncontrolled action of other states.

The judgment should be reversed and the case remanded for further proceedings in the course of which the state court would be free, if so advised, to inquire to what extent, if at all, the tax may, in harmony with state law, be apportioned in conformity to principles heretofore announced by this Court, and to that extent sustained.

Mr. Justice ROBERTS, Mr. Justice REED, and Mr. Justice RUTLEDGE join in this dissent.

Refer to Extract B, Federal Aviation Act Section 1108, 49 U.S. Code 1508; also Extract A, U.S. Constitution, Article I, Section 8

347 U.S. 590

BRANIFF AIRWAYS, Inc.

v.

NEBRASKA STATE BOARD OF EQUALIZATION AND ASSESSMENT et al.

(Cite as 74 S. Ct. 757)

No. 476.

Argued March 12, 1954.

Decided June 1, 1954.

Action by airline for declaratory judgment of invalidity of Nebraska statutes authorizing assessment, levy and collection of ad valorem personal property tax on flight equipment of airline, an interstate air carrier, and for injunction against collection of such taxes assessed for previous years. The Supreme Court of the State of Nebraska, 157 Neb. 425, 59 N.W.2d 746, dismissed the petition, and the airline appealed. The Supreme Court, Mr. Justice Reed, held that where airline's aircraft made 18 stops per day in Nebraska, in which state airline rented ground facilities, purchased and paid for fuel, and picked up and discharged Nebraska freight and passengers, deriving therefrom approximately 1/10 of its revenue, airline received protection from state during such stops and derived benefit from such regular landings, and such regular contact with Nebraska was sufficient to establish Nebraska's power to levy the tax, even though the same aircraft did not land every day and none of the aircraft was continuously within state.

Affirmed.

Mr. Justice Frankfurter and Mr. Justice Jackson dissented.

1. Statutes

Fact that a uniform act is no longer recommended for enactment does not work a repeal, and, where adopted, such act continues in effect.

2. Carriers

Commerce

The federal acts regulating air commerce are bottomed on the commerce power of Congress, not on national ownership of navigable air space, as distinguished from sovereignty. Air Commerce Act of 1926, § 6(a), as amended by Civil Aeronautics Act of 1938, § 1107(i) (3), 49 U.S.C.A. § 176(a); Civil Aeronautics Act of 1938, §§ 1–1205 as amended 49 U.S.C.A. §§ 401–705.

3. Commerce

Existent federal air-carrier regulation does not preclude state of Nebraska from assessing, levying and collecting an ad valorem personal property tax on airline's flight equipment used in interstate commerce. R.R.S.Neb.1943, §§ 77–1244 et seq.; Civil Aeronautics Act of 1938, §§ 1–1205 as amended 49 U.S.C.A. §§ 401–705.

4. Commerce

State statutes authorizing assessment, levy and collection of an ad valorem personal property tax on airline's flight equipment used in interstate commerce were not violative of Commerce Clause of Federal Constitution. R.R.S.Neb. 1943, §§ 77–1244 et seq.; U.S.C.A.Const. art. 1, § 8, cl. 3.

5. Courts

On appeal from judgment of state Supreme Court, United States Supreme Court would not consider contentions not preserved by appellant in its statement as to jurisdiction.

6. Commerce

The Commerce Clause of the Federal Constitution does not immunize interstate instrumentalities from all state taxation, but such commerce may be required to pay a nondiscriminatory share of the tax burden. U.S.C.A.Const. art. 1, § 8, cl. 3.

7. Constitutional Law

The question of whether a commodity en route to market is sufficiently settled in a state for purpose of subjection to a property tax may be a commerce clause question, but bare question whether an instrumentality of commerce has a tax situs in a state for purpose of subjection to property tax is one of due process. U.S.C.A.Const. art. 1, § 8, cl. 3; Amend. 14.

8. Courts

Where airline timely raised and preserved its contention that its property was not taxable in Nebraska because such property had attained no taxable situs in that state, United States Supreme Court would consider such contention, even though airline erroneously relied upon commerce clause to support its position, and failed to specifically claim protection under due process clause of Fourteenth Amendment to Federal Constitution. U.S.C.A.Const. art. 1, § 8, cl. 3; Amend. 14.

9. Commerce
Constitutional Law

Constitutional power of state to impose tax on aircraft flying in interstate commerce cannot be logically distinguished from its power to impose taxes on boats plying the inland waters, and, so far as due process is concerned, the only question is whether the tax in practicable operation has relation to opportunities, benefits or protection conferred or afforded by the taxing state. U.S.C.A. Const. Amend. 14.

10. Commerce

Where airline's aircraft made 18 stops per day in Nebraska, in which state airline rented ground facilities, purchased and paid for fuel, and picked up and discharged Nebraska freight and passengers, deriving therefrom approximately 1/10 of its revenue, airline received protection from state during such stops and derived benefit from such regular landings, and such regular contact with Nebraska was sufficient to establish Nebraska's power to levy an apportioned ad valorem tax on such aircraft, even though the same aircraft did not land every day and none of the aircraft was continuously within the state. R.R.S.Neb.1943, §§ 77–1244 et seq.

11. Commerce

States other than those of corporate domicile may tax aircraft in interstate commerce on an apportionment basis in accordance with their use in the taxing state, and taxation by two or more states on an apportionment basis precludes taxation of all of the property by the state of domicile.

591

Mr. William J. Hotz, Sr., Omaha, Neb., for appellant.

Mr. C.C. Sheldon, Lincoln, Neb., for appellees.

Mr. Justice REED delivered the opinion of the Court.

The question presented by this appeal from the Supreme Court of Nebraska is whether the Constitution bars the State of Nebraska from levying an apportioned ad valorem tax on the flight equipment of appellant, and interstate air carrier. Appellant is not incorporated in Nebraska and does not have its principal place of business or home port registered under the Civil Aeronautics Act, 52 Stat. 977, 49 U.S.C. §§ 401–705, 49 U.S.C.A. §§ 401–705, in that state. Such flight equipment is employed as a part of a system of interstate air commerce operating over fixed routes and landing on and departing from airports within Nebraska on regular schedules. Appellant does not challenge the reasonableness of the apportionment prescribed by the taxing statute or the application of such apportionment to its property. It contends only that its flight equipment used in interstate commerce is immune from taxation by Nebraska because without situs in that state and because regulation of air navigation by the Federal Government precludes such state taxation.

This petition for a declaratory judgment of the invalidity of §§ 77–1244 to 77–1250 of the state tax statute[1]

592

and an injunction against the collection of taxes assessed under such provisions for previous years was filed as an original action in the court below by Mid-Continent Airlines, Inc., and tried upon stipulated facts. Subsequent to filing, but before the decision, Mid-Continent and appellant were merged on August 1, 1952, and appellant was substituted as the party plaintiff. Mid-Continent had been incorporated in Delaware with its corporate place of business in Wilmington in that state, and Braniff is incorporated in Oklahoma and has its corporate place of business in Oklahoma City. Pursuant to

1. Neb.Rev.Stat.1943, § 77–1244 et seq.

the merger Mid-Continent's main executive offices were moved from Kansas City, Missouri, and merged with appellant's in Dallas, Texas. The number of regularly scheduled stops in Nebraska, fourteen per day at Omaha and four at Lincoln, was not affected by the merger.

The home port registered with the Civil Aeronautics Authority and the overhaul base for the aircraft in question is the Minneapolis-St. Paul Airport, Minnesota. All of the aircraft not undergoing overhaul fly regular schedules upon a circuit ranging from Minot, North Dakota, to New Orleans, Louisiana, with stops in fourteen states including Minnesota, Nebraska and Oklahoma. No stops were made in Delaware. The Nebraska stops are of short duration since utilized only for the discharge and loading of passengers, mail, express, and freight, and sometimes for refueling. Appellant neither owns nor maintains facilities for repairing, reconditioning, or storing its flight equipment in Nebraska, but rents depot space and hires other services as required. The Supreme Court of Nebraska made no distinction as to taxability between those years when no flights were made into the state of domicile (Delaware) and those when flights did enter the state of new domicile (Oklahoma).

It is stipulated that the tax in question is assessed only against regularly scheduled air carriers and is not applied

593

to carriers who operate only intermittently in the state. The statute defines "flight equipment" as "aircraft fully equipped for flight,"[2] and provides that "Any tax upon or measured by the value of flight equipment of air carriers incorporated or doing business in this state shall be assessed and collected by the Tax Commissioner."[3] A formula is prescribed for arriving at the proportion of a carrier's flight equipment to be allocated to the state.[4]

The statute uses the allocation formula of the "proposed uniform statute to provide for an equitable method of state taxation of air carriers" adopted by the Council of State Governments upon the recommendation of the National Association of Tax Administrators in 1947.[5] Use of a uniform allocation

2. Id., § 77–1244(3).

3. Id., § 77–1245.

4. Ibid. This section provides that "The proportion of flight equipment allocated to this state for purposes of taxation shall be the arithmetical average of the following three ratios: (1) The ratio which the aircraft arrivals and departures within this state scheduled by such air carrier during the preceding calendar year bears to the total aircraft arrivals and departures within and without this state scheduled by such carrier during the same period; Provided, that in the case of nonscheduled operations all arrivals and departures shall be substituted for scheduled arrivals and departures; (2) the ratio which the revenue tons handled by such air carrier at airports within this state during the preceding calendar year bears to the total revenue tons handled by such carrier at airports within and without this state during the same period; and (3) the ratio which such air carrier's originating revenue within this state for the preceding calendar year bears to the total originating revenue of such carrier within and without this state for the same period."

5. Resolutions, The Eighth General Assembly of the States, 20 State Government 95.

formula to apportion air-carrier taxes among the states follows the recommendation of the Civil Aeronautics Board in its report to Congress.[6]

594

The Nebraska statute provides for reports, levy, and rate of tax by state average.[7]

Required reports filed by Mid-Continent for 1950 show that about 9% of its revenue and 11 1/2% of the total system tonnage originated in Nebraska and about 9% of its total stops were made in that state. From these figures, using the statutory formula, the Tax Commissioner arrived at a valuation of $118,901 allocable to Nebraska, resulting in a tax of $4,280.44. Since Mid-Continent filed no return for 1951 the same valuation was used and an increased rate resulted in assessment of $4,518.29. The Supreme Court of Nebraska held the statute not violative of the Commerce Clause and dismissed appellant's petition.[8]

Appellant argues that federal statutes governing air commerce enacted under the commerce power preempt the field of regulation of such air commerce and preclude this tax. Congress, by the Civil Aeronautics Act of 1938, 52 Stat. 977, 1028, § 1107 (i) (3), 49 U.S.C. § 176(a), 49 U.S.C.A. § 176(a), enacted:

> "The United States of America is declared to possess and exercise complete and exclusive national sovereignty in the air space above the United States, including the air space above all inland waters and the air space above those portions of the adjacent
>
> 595
>
> marginal high seas, bays, and lakes, over which by international law or treaty or convention the United States exercises national jurisdiction."

This provision originated in the Air Commerce Act of 1926, 44 Stat. 568, 572, § 6. The 1938 Act also declares "a public right of freedom of transit" for air commerce in the navigable air space to exist for any citizen of the United States. 52 Stat. 980, § 3, 49 U.S.C. § 403, 49 U.S.C.A. § 403.[9]

6. Multiple Taxation of Air Carriers, H.R.Doc.No.141, 79th Cong., 1st Sess. Recommendations by various interested groups as to the proper method of apportionment are included in that report and its appendices. See also Arditto, State and Local Taxation of Scheduled Local Airlines, 16 J. Air L. & Com. 162; Kassell, Interstate Cooperation and Airlines, 25 Taxes 302. Mr. Bulwinkle introduced bills in accordance with the recommendation of the C.A.B. report that the National Government should prescribe the method of state taxation of air carriers. The bills adopted the Council formula utilized by Nebraska. Neither was enacted. H.R. 3446, 79th Cong., 1st Sess.; H.R. 1241, 80th Cong., 1st Sess.

7. Neb.Rev.Stat.1943, §§ 77–1247, 77–1249.

8. Mid-Continent Airlines, Inc. v. Nebraska State Board of Equalization and Assessment, 157 Neb. 425, 59 N.W.2d 746.

9. That space was defined in § 10 of the Air Commerce Act and freedom for its navigation declared. This was continued by the Civil Aeronautics Act, 49 U.S.C. § 180, 49 U.S.C.A. § 180, in "airspace above the minimum safe altitudes of flight prescribed by the Civil Aeronautics Authority".

[1] The provision pertinent to sovereignty over the navigable air space in the Air Commerce Act of 1926 was an assertion of exclusive national sovereignty. The convention between the United States and other nations respecting international civil aviation ratified August 6, 1946, 61 Stat. 1180, accords. The Act, however, did not expressly exclude the sovereign powers of the states. H.R. Rep.No. 572, 69th Cong., 1st Sess., p. 10. The Civil Aeronautics Act of 1938 gives no support to a different view.[10] After the enactment of the Air Commerce Act, more than twenty states adopted the Uniform Aeronautics Act. It had three provisions indicating that the states did not consider their sovereignty affected by the National Act except to the extent that the states had ceded that sovereignty by constitutional grant.[11] The

596

recommendation of the National Conference of Commissioners on Uniform State Laws to the states to enact this Act was withdrawn in 1943.[12] Where adopted, however, it continues in effect. See United States v. Praylou, 4 Cir., 208 F.2d 291. Recognizing this "exclusive national sovereignty" and right of freedom in air transit, this Court in United States v. Causby, 328 U.S. 256, 261, 66 S.Ct. 1062, 1065, 90 L.Ed. 1206, nevertheless held that the owner of land might recover for a taking by national use of navigable air space, resulting in destruction in whole or in part of the usefulness of the land property.

[2,3] These Federal Acts regulating air commerce are bottomed on the commerce power of Congress, not on national ownership of the navigable air space, as distinguished from sovereignty. In reporting the bill which became the Air Commerce Act, it was said:

> "The declaration of what constitutes navigable air space is an exercise of the same source of power, the interstate commerce clause, as that

10. S.Rep.No.1661, 75th Cong., 3d Sess.; H.R.Rep.No.2254, 75th Cong., 3d Sess.; H.R. Conf.Rep.No.2635, 75th Cong., 3d Sess.

11. 11 Uniform Laws Annotated 159:

"§ 2. Sovereignty in Space.—Sovereignty in the space above the lands and waters of this State is declared to rest in the State, except where granted to and assumed by the United States pursuant to a constitutional grant from the people of this State.

"§ 3. Ownership of Space.—The ownership of the space above the lands and waters of this State is declared to be vested in the several owners of the surface beneath, subject to the right of flight described in Section 4.

"§ 4. Lawfulness of Flight.—Flight in aircraft over the lands and waters of this State is lawful, unless at such a low altitude as to interfere with the then existing use to which the land or water, or the space over the land or water, is put by the owner, or unless so conducted as to be imminently dangerous to persons or property lawfully on the land or water beneath. The landing of an aircraft on the lands or waters of another, without his consent, is unlawful, except in the case of a forced landing. For damages caused by a forced landing, however, the owner or lessee of the aircraft or the aeronaut shall be liable, as provided in Section 5."

12. See Conference Handbook, 1943, pp. 66-67. Efforts continue to draft an acceptable State Uniform Aeronautical Code. See Conference Handbook, 1948, p. 147.

under which Congress has long declared in many acts what constitutes navigable or non-navigable waters. The public right of flight in the navigable air space owes

597

its source to the same constitutional basis which, under decisions of the Supreme Court, has given rise to a public easement of navigation in the navigable waters of the United States, regardless of the ownership of the adjacent or subjacent soil." H.R.Rep.No. 572, 69th Cong., 1st Sess., p. 10.

The commerce power, since Gibbons v. Ogden, 9 Wheat. 1, 193, 6 L.Ed. 23, has comprehended navigation of streams. Its breadth covers all commercial intercourse. But the federal commerce power over navigable streams does not prevent state action consistent with that power. Gilman v. City of Philadelphia, 3 Wall. 713, 729, 18 L.Ed. 96. Since, over streams, Congress acts by virtue of the commerce power, the sovereignty of the state is not impaired. State of Oklahoma ex rel. Phillips v. Guy F. Atkinson Co., 313 U.S. 508, 534, 61 S.Ct. 1050, 1063, 85 L.Ed. 1487. The title to the beds and the banks are in the states and the riparian owners, subject to the federal power over navigation.[13] Federal regulation of interstate land and water carriers under the commerce power has not been deemed to deny all state power to tax the property of such carriers. We conclude that existent federal air-carrier regulation does not preclude the Nebraska tax challenged here.

[4–6] Nor has appellant demonstrated that the Commerce Clause otherwise bars this tax as a burden on interstate commerce.[14] We have frequently reiterated that the

598

Commerce Clause does not immunize interstate instrumentalities from all state taxation, but that such commerce may be required to pay a nondiscriminatory share of the tax burden.[15] And appellant does not allege that this Nebraska statute discriminates against it nor, as noted above, does it challenge the reasonableness of the apportionment prescribed by the statute.[16]

13. United States v. Chandler Dunbar Water Power Co., 229 U.S. 53, 60, 33 S.Ct. 667, 671, 57 L.Ed. 1063; United States v. Kansas City Life Ins. Co., 339 U.S. 799, 808, 70 S.Ct. 885, 890, 94 L.Ed. 1277; Federal Power Commission v. Niagara Mohawk Power Corp., 347 U.S. 239, 246 et seq., 74 S.Ct. 487, 491.

14. In its original petition appellant also alleged that the Nebraska statute is invalid under § 8, cl. 3, § 9, cl. 6, and § 10, cl. 3 of Art. I of the Constitution. While noting that such contentions were apparently "abandoned in brief and oral argument," the court below held such provisions of the Constitution not violated. Since appellant did not preserve such contentions in its Statement as to Jurisdiction, we do not consider such issues.

15. Western Live Stock v. Bureau of Revenue, 303 U.S. 250, 254, 58 S.Ct. 546, 548, 82 L.Ed. 823; Michigan-Wisconsin Pipe Line Co. v. Calvert, 347 U.S. 157, 165, 74 S.Ct. 396, 400.

16. See Pullman's Palace-Car Co. v. Commonwealth of Pennsylvania, 141 U.S. 18, 11 S.Ct. 876, 35 L.Ed. 613; Ford Motor Co. v. Beauchamp, 308 U.S. 331, 60 S.Ct. 273, 84 L.Ed. 304; Nashville, C. & St. L. Ry. Co. v. Browning, 310 U.S. 362, 60 S.Ct. 968, 84 L.Ed. 1254; Central Greyhound Lines of New York v. Mealey, 334 U.S. 653, 654, 662, 663, 68 S.Ct.

[7,8] The argument upon which appellant depends ultimately, however, is that its aircraft never "attained a taxable situs within Nebraska" from which it argues that the Nebraska tax imposes a burden on interstate commerce. In relying upon the Commerce Clause on this issue and in not specifically claiming protection under the Due Process Clause of the Fourteenth Amendment, appellant names the wrong constitutional clause to support its position. While the question of whether a commodity en route to market is sufficiently settled in a state for purpose of subjection to a property tax has been determined by this Court as a Commerce Clause question,[17]

599

the bare question whether an instrumentality of commerce has tax situs in a state for the purpose of subjection to a property tax is one of due process.[18] However, appellant timely raised and preserved its contention that its property was not taxable because such property had attained no taxable situs in Nebraska. Though inexplicit, we consider the

1260, 1261, 1265, 1266, 92 L.Ed. 1633; Ott v. Mississippi Valley Barge Line Co., 336 U.S. 169, 174, 69 S.Ct. 432, 434, 93 L.Ed. 585; Canton R. Co. v. Rogan, 340 U.S. 511, 514-516, 71 S.Ct. 447, 448-449, 95 L.Ed. 488. Multiple Taxation of Air Commerce, H.R.Doc.No. 141, 79th Cong., 1st Sess.; Arditto, State and Local Taxation of Scheduled Local Airlines, 16 Jour. of Air Law & Com. 162; Howard, State Taxation of Airplanes in Interstate Commerce, 10 Mo.L.Rev. 195; Welch, The Taxation of Air Carriers, 11 Law & Contemp. Prob. 584; Green, The War Against the States in Aviation, 31 Va.L.Rev. 835; Sutherland and Vinciguerra, The Octroi and the Airplane, 32 Cornell L.Q. 161; Saxe, Federal Control of State Taxation of Airlines, 31 Cornell L.Q. 228; Ternes, Aviation Taxation, 25 Mich. S.B.J. 23; Note, 57 Harv.L.Rev. 1097.

17. See e.g., Independent Warehouses v. Scheele, 331 U.S. 70, 72, 67 S.Ct. 1062, 1064, 91 L.Ed. 1346; Carson Petroleum Co. v. Vial, 279 U.S. 95, 49 S.Ct. 292, 73 L.Ed. 626; Champlain Realty Co. v. City of Brattleboro, 260 U.S. 366, 43 S.Ct. 146, 67 L.Ed. 309; General Oil Co. v. Crain, 209 U.S. 211, 28 S.Ct. 475, 52 L.Ed. 754; Coe v. Town of Errol, 116 U.S. 517, 6 S.Ct. 475, 29 L.Ed. 715; Brown v. Houston, 114 U.S. 622, 5 S.Ct. 1091, 29 L.Ed. 257; Powell, Taxation of Things in Transit, 7 Va.L.Rev. 167, 245, 429, 497.

18. See e.g., Johnson Oil Refining Co. v. State of Oklahoma, 290 U.S. 158, 54 S.Ct. 152, 78 L.Ed. 238; Frick v. Commonwealth of Pennsylvania, 268 U.S. 473, 45 S.Ct. 603, 69 L.Ed. 1058; Union Refrigerator Transit Co. v. Commonwealth of Kentucky, 199 U.S. 194, 26 S.Ct. 36, 50 L.Ed. 150; Delaware, L. & W.R. Co. v. Commonwealth of Pennsylvania, 198 U.S. 341, 25 S.Ct. 669, 49 L.Ed. 1077; Beale, Conflict of Laws, 533 et seq.; Moore, Taxation of Movables and the Fourteenth Amendment, 7 Col.L.Rev. 309; Page, Jurisdiction to Tax Tangible Movables, 1945 Wis.L.Rev. 125.

While the common-law concept of situs was recognized by this Court as a limitation on state power to tax tangible personalty prior to invocation of the Fourteenth Amendment as a defense to such taxation, the bases for such decisions varied and no consistent constitutional principle was applied. Compare the following cases: Hays v. Pacific Mail S.S. Co., 17 How. 596, 15 L.Ed. 254; Morgan v. Parham, 16 Wall. 471, 21 L.Ed. 302; City of St. Louis v. Wiggins Ferry Co., 11 Wall. 423, 20 L.Ed. 192; Marye v. Baltimore & O.R. Co., 127 U.S. 117, 8 S.Ct. 1037, 32 L.Ed. 94; Pullman's Palace-Car Co. v. Commonwealth of Pennsylvania, 141 U.S. 18, 11 S.Ct. 876, 35 L.Ed. 613; Adams Express Co. v. Ohio State Auditor, 165 U.S. 194, 17 S.Ct. 305, 41 L.Ed. 683. See also Hartman, State Taxation of Interstate Commerce, 13, 73 et seq.

A collection of this Court's decisions dealing with power to tax may be found in an Appendix to Miller Bros. Co. v. State of Maryland, 347 U.S. 340, notes 8-20, 74 S.Ct. 535, 540-546.

due process issue within the clear intendment of such contention and hold such issue sufficiently presented. See People of State of New York ex rel. Bryant v. Zimmerman, 278 U.S. 63, 67, 49 S.Ct. 61, 63, 73 L.Ed. 184, and cases cited; Wolfson and Kurland, Jurisdiction of the Supreme Court of the United States, 149 et seq.

[9] Appellant relies upon cases involving ocean-going vessels to support its contention that its aircraft attained no tax situs in Nebraska. See, e.g., Hays v. Pacific

600

Mail S.S. Co., 17 How. 596, 15 L.Ed. 254; Morgan v. Parham, 16 Wall. 471, 21 L.Ed. 302; Southern Pacific Co. v. Commonwealth of Kentucky, 222 U.S. 63, 32 S.Ct. 13, 56 L.Ed. 96. The first two cases were efforts to tax the entire value of the ships as other local property, without apportionment, when they were used to plow the open seas. The last case holds the state of corporate domicile has power to tax vessels that are not taxable elsewhere. A closer analogy exists between planes flying interstate and boats that ply the inland waters. We perceive no logical basis for distinguishing the constitutional power to impose a tax on such aircraft from the power to impose taxes on river boats. Ott v. Mississippi Valley Barge Line Co., 336 U.S. 169, 69 S.Ct. 432, 93 L.Ed. 585; Standard Oil Co. v. Peck, 342 U.S. 382, 72 S.Ct. 309, 96 L.Ed. 427. The limitation imposed by the Due Process Clause upon state power to impose taxes upon such instrumentalities was succinctly stated in the Ott case: "So far as due process is concerned the only question is whether the tax in practical operation has relation to opportunities, benefits, or protection conferred or afforded by the taxing State." 336 U.S. at page 174, 69 S.Ct. at page 434. In Curry v. McCanless, 307 U.S. 357, 59 S.Ct. 900, 83 L.Ed. 1339, the evolution of such restriction on state power was reviewed and the rule stated thusly:

> "When we speak of the jurisdiction to tax land or chattels as being exclusively in the state where they are physically located, we mean no more than that the benefit and protection of laws enabling the owner to enjoy the fruits of his ownership and the power to reach effectively the interests protected, for the purpose of subjecting them to payment of a tax, are so narrowly restricted to the state in whose territory the physical property is located as to set practical limits to taxation by others." Id., 307 U.S. at page 364, 59 S.Ct. at page 904.

[10] Thus the situs issue devolves into the question of whether eighteen stops per day by appellant's aircraft is sufficent contact with Nebraska to sustain that state's

601

power to levy an apportioned ad valorem tax on such aircraft. We think such regular contact is sufficient to establish Nebraska's power to tax even though the same aircraft do not land every day and even though none of the aircraft is continuously within the state. "The basis of the jurisdiction is the habitual employment of the property within the state."[19] Appellant rents its ground facilities and pays for fuel it purchases in Nebraska. This leaves it in the position of other carriers such as rails, boats and motors that pay for the use of local facilities so as to have the opportunity to exploit the commerce, traffic, and trade that originates in or reaches Nebraska. Approximately one-tenth of appellant's revenue is produced by the pickup and discharge of Nebraska freight and passengers. Nebraska certainly affords protection during such stops and these regular landings are clearly a benefit to appellant.

[11] Nor do we think that Nebraska's power to levy this tax was affected by the merger of Mid-Continent with Braniff. Since "The rule which permits taxation by two or more states on an apportionment basis precludes taxation of all of the property by the state of domicile," Standard Oil Co. v. Peck, supra, 342 U.S. at page 384, 72 S.Ct. at page 310, we deem it immaterial that before the merger Mid-Continent was domiciled in Delaware, a state through which its planes did not fly, and after the merger Braniff is domiciled in Oklahoma, a state through which these aircraft make regular flights.

Appellant urges that Northwest Airlines v. State of Minnesota, 322 U.S. 292, 64 S.Ct. 950, 88 L.Ed. 1283, precludes this tax unless that case is to be overruled. In that case Minnesota, as the domicile of the air carrier and its "home port," was permitted to tax the entire value of the fleet ad valorem although it ranged

602

by fixed routes through eight states.[20] While no one view mustered a majority of this Court, it seems fair to say that without the position stated in the Conclusion and Judgment which announced the decision of this Court, the result would have been the reverse. That position was that it was not shown "that a defined part of the domiciliary corpus has acquired a permanent location, i.e., at taxing situs, elsewhere." 322 U.S. at page 295, 64 S.Ct. at page 952. That opinion recognized the "doctrine of tax apportionment for instrumentalities engaged in interstate commerce," 322 U.S. at page 297, 64 S.Ct. at page 953, but held it inapplicable because no "property (or a portion of fungible units) is permanently situated in a State other than the domiciliary State." 322 U.S. at page 298, 64 S.Ct. at page 953. When Standard Oil Co. v. Peck, 342 U.S. 382, 384, 72 S.Ct. 309, 310, 96 L.Ed. 427, was here, the Court interpreted the Northwest Airlines case to permit states other than those of the corporate

19. Johnson Oil Refining Co. v. State of Oklahoma, supra, 290 U.S. at page 162, 54 S.Ct. at page 154, 78 L.Ed. 238. See also Pullman's Palace-Car Co. v. Commonwealth of Pennsylvania, supra; Ott v. Mississippi Valley Barge Line Co., supra.

20. Subsequent to the Northwest Airlines case, Minnesota enacted a tax statute incorporating an apportionment formula for allocation of the valuation of property of air carriers to Minnesota. Minn.Stat.1945, §§ 270.071-270.079, as amended, Minn.Laws 1953, c. 672, §§ 2-3, M.S.A. §§ 270.071-270.079.

domicile to tax boats in interstate commerce on the apportionment basis in accordance with their use in the taxing state. We adhere to that interpretation.

Affirmed.

Mr. Justice BLACK concurs in the result.

Mr. Justice JACKSON dissents for the reasons stated in his concurring opinion in Northwest Airlines v. State of Minnesota, 322 U.S. 292, 64 S.Ct. 950, 88 L.Ed. 1283.

Mr. Justice DOUGLAS, concurring.

Braniff Airways, in challenging the power of Nebraska to lay this ad valorem tax, claims only that its planes have no taxable situs in the State. It does not claim that no fraction of the aircraft, on an apportioned basis,

603

is permanently in the State. Nor does it attack this apportionment formula.

My understanding of our decisions is that the power to lay an ad valorem tax turns on the permanency of the property in the State. All the property may be there or only a fraction of it. Property in transit, whether a plane discharging passengers or an automobile refueling, is not subject to an ad valorem tax. Property in transit may move so regularly and so continuously that part of it is always in the State. Then the fraction, but no more, may be taxed ad valorem.

I mention these elemental points to reserve explicitly the validity of the apportionment formula that serves as the basis of this ad valorem tax. The formula used presents substantial questions. What might be an adequate formula for a gross receipts tax might be inadequate for an ad valorem tax. Moreover, when we are faced with a due process question, we have a problem we may not delegate to Congress.

I do not think the Court takes a position contrary to what I have said. But there are passages in the opinion which blur the constitutional issues as they are blurred and confused in the interesting report of the Civil Aeronautics Board, H.R.Doc.No. 141, 79th Cong., 1st Sess., entitled Multiple Taxation of Air Commerce. Hence I have joined in the judgment of the Court but not in the opinion.

Mr. Justice FRANKFURTER, dissenting.

One of the most treacherous tendencies in legal reasoning is the transfer of generalizations developed for one set of situations to seemingly analogous, yet essentially very different, situations. The doctrines evolved in adjusting rights as between the States to tax property bearing some relation to a number of States, and the taxing power of the States as against the freedom from

604

State interferences secured by the Commerce Clause, bear, of course, a practical relation to what it is that is taxed. It took a considerable time to make this adjustment in regard to taxation of railroad property and railroad income—to decide when the States are wholly excluded from levying certain taxes, when an ad valorem tax may levied on railroad property reasonably deemed to be permanently in a given State, and on what basis income from interstate railroad business may fairly be apportioned among different States. Even as to railroads, nice distinctions had to be made and the making of them has not been concluded.

It stands to reason that the drastic differences between slow-moving trains and the bird-like flight of airplanes would be reflected in the law's response to the claims of the different States and the limitations of the Commerce Clause upon those claims. The differences in result and the conflict even among those who agreed in result in Northwest Airlines v. State of Minnesota, 322 U.S. 292, 64 S.Ct. 950, 88 L.Ed. 1283, demonstrate not the contrariness or caprice of different minds but the inherent perplexities of the law's adjustment to such novel problems as the exercise of the taxing power over commerical aviation in a federal system. The problems canvassed in that case were unprecedented, and perhaps the most important thing that was there decided was the refusal of the Court to apply to air transportation the doctrines that had been enunciated with regard to land and water transportation.

The plain intimation of the case—that these novel problems, affecting the taxing power of the States and the Nation, call for the comprehensive powers of legislation possessed by Congress—found response in a resolution of Congress directing the Civil Aeronautics Board to develop the "means for eliminating and avoiding, as far as practicable, multiple taxation of persons engaged in air commerce * * * which has the effect of unduly

605

burdening or unduly impeding the development of air commerce." 58 Stat. 723, 49 U.S.C.A. § 425 note. The inquiry thus set afoot produced an illuminating report. See H.R.Doc.No.141, 79th Cong., 1st Sess., which analyzed the difficulties and also made concrete proposals.[21] The gist of these proposals was that Congress make an apportionment of taxes among the States over which air carriers fly, based upon relevant factors and in appropriate ratios. The basis of taxation by Nebraska, here under review, substantially reflects the factors which the Civil Aeronautics Board recommended to the Congress. It is one thing, however, for the individual States to determine what factors should be taken into account and how they should be weighted. It is quite another for Congress to devise, as the Civil Aeronautics Board recommended it should, a scheme of apportionment binding on all the States. Until that time, Nebraska may rely on one scheme of apportionment; other States on other schemes. And each State may, from time to time, modify the relevant factors.[22]

21. The proposal of this Report—that there be a uniform allocation formula to apportion taxes among the States—was adopted by the Council of State Governments. See 20 State Government 95. However no federal legislation has yet resulted.

22. In addition to the problem of conflict between apportionment schemes of various States, it must be borne in mind that these schemes cannot be regarded as abstract mathematical formulas, and hence they must be closely scrutinized to ensure their fairness as applied to a given situation. See Wallace v. Hines, 253 U.S. 66, 40 S.Ct. 435, 64 L.Ed. 782.

The exercise of the taxing power by one of the States by means of a formula, based on such criteria as tonnage, revenue, and arrivals and departures, may, in isolation, impose no unfair burden on commerce. And the adoption by all the States of such a basis for taxation, which only congressional action could ensure, would not offend the Commerce Clause. It is the diverse and fluctuating

606

exercise of power by the various States, even where based on concededly relevant factors, which imposes an undue burden on interstate commerce.[23]

The complexity of the proposals of the Board's Report—the items to be taken into account, the balance to be struck among them, the problem of giving the States their due without unfairly burdening an industry of vital national import—indicates how ill-adapted the judicial process is, as against the choices open to Congress, for dealing with these problems and how warily this Court should move within the limits of its own inescapable duty to act. The protection of interstate commerce against the burden of multiple taxation ought not to be left to litigation growing out of changes in the methods of taxation.

> "The immunities implicit in the Commerce Clause and the potential taxing power of a State can hardly be made to depend, in the world of practical affairs, on the shifting incidence of the varying tax laws of the various States at a particular moment. Courts are not possessed of instruments of determination so delicate as to enable them to weigh the various factors in a complicated economic setting which, as to an isolated application of a State tax, might mitigate the obvious burden generally created by a direct tax on commerce." Freeman v. Hewit, 329 U.S. 249, 256, 67 S.Ct. 274, 278, 91 L.Ed. 265.

607

This would not be the only instance in which a constructive adjustment of competing considerations requires congressional legislation and is beyond the scope of the judicial process. See Davis v. Department of Labor, 317 U.S. 249, 259, 63 S.Ct. 225, 230, 87 L.Ed. 246; Halcyon Lines v. Haenn Ship Ceiling & Refitting Corp., 342 U.S. 282, 72 S.Ct. 277, 96 L.Ed. 318; United States v. Standard Oil Co., 332 U.S. 301, 67 S.Ct. 1604, 91 L.Ed. 2067; United States v. Gilman, 347 U.S. 507, 74 S.Ct. 695.

It was not too difficult in Northwest Airlines to allow Minnesota to levy a personal property tax on the entire fleet of airplanes owned by a corporation of its creation, the principal place of business of which was also Minnesota. The State of Minnesota, as we said, was the only State that had such a hold on the planes. In the case before us, Nebraska has no such relation with the airplanes on which it seeks to impose an ad valorem tax.

23. Lest it be thought one formula of apportionment is clearly the appropriate one, it should be noted that the Board's Report sets forth three formulas proposed by responsible groups, in addition to that recommended by the Board. And while Nebraska adopted the factors recommended by the Board, it did not give them the same weight which the Board's proposed formula did. See H.R.Doc.No.141, 79th Cong., 1st Sess. 58.

This Court has held that a State may levy an ad valorem tax on the basis of a showing that the total time spent in a State by different units of a carrier's property is such that a certain proportion of that property may be said to have a permanent location in that State. Such a doctrine of apportionment, as the basis of property taxation, was adopted by this Court in Pullman's Palace-Car Co. v. Commonwealth of Pennsylvania, 141 U.S. 18, 11 S.Ct. 876, 35 L.Ed. 613, with relation to railroad cars; and in Ott v. Mississippi Valley Barge Line Co., 336 U.S. 169, 69 S.Ct. 432, 93 L.Ed. 585, with relation to barges. But boats and railroad cars which spend hours and days at a time in a State have a closeness and duration of relationship to that State obviously not true of planes which make brief stopovers for a few minutes.

The appealing phrase that "interstate business must pay its way" can be invoked only when we know what the "way" is for which business commerce must pay. Of course, the appellant must pay for the use of airports and other services it enjoys in Nebraska. It

608

must pay a tax on all its property permanently located in Nebraska. Like everyone else it must pay a gasoline tax. In fact it pays approximately $22,000 a year for the use of the airport, $14,000 a year in gasoline taxes, and appropriate property taxes on office equipment, trucks and other items permanently in Nebraska.

But only those who have a sufficiently substantial relation to Nebraska that they may fairly be said to partake of the benefits, though impalpable and unspecific, it gives as an ordered society, may be taxed because they partake of those benefits. And even then, of course, an undue burden must not be cast on commerce. Not unless Nebraska can show that appellant has airplanes that have a substantially permanent presence in Nebraska can Nebraska exert its taxing power on their presence. I do not believe that planes which pause for a few moments can be made the basis for the exercise of such power.[24] If Nebraska can tax without such a tie, every other State through which the planes fly or in which they alight for a few minutes can tax. Surely this is an obvious inroad upon the Commerce Clause and as such barred by the Constitution.

It cannot be said that for airplanes, flying regularly scheduled flights, to alight, stop over for a short time and then take off is so tenuously related to Nebraska that it would deny due process for that State to seize on these short stopovers as the basis of an ad valorem tax. But the incidence of a tax may offend the Commerce Clause, even though it may satisfy the Due Process Clause.

24. With the exception of one plane which remains in Nebraska overnight, all of the Company's planes remain in Nebraska for periods of between five and twenty minutes each day. Considering this brief time spent on the ground by planes which stop in transit, more than a bare assertion that flight equipment is "permanently" in Nebraska is called for to establish the requisite permanence for taxing purposes.

609

I am not unaware that there is an air of imprecision about what I have written. Such is the intention. Until Congress acts, the vital thing for the Court in this new and subtle field is to focus on the process of interstate commerce and protect it from inroads of taxation by a State beyond "opportunities which it has given, * * * protection which it has afforded, * * * benefits which it has conferred by the fact of being an orderly, civilized society." Wisconsin v. J.C. Penney Co., 311 U.S. 435, 444, 61 S.Ct. 246, 250, 85 L.Ed. 267.

Crimes on Aircraft

Another area in which there was a conflict of responsibility between the two Branches of Government, was the commission of a crime on board an aircraft. There was little precedence for this area of aviation law. It was difficult to determine over exactly what location of land, the crime was committed in a moving aircraft. There were few parallels in the common law jurisprudence of criminal law.

The Federal government had to enact a body of laws that would cover these new crimes against society.

These problems are illustrated in the two cases, U.S. v. Cordova, and U.S. v. Healy, which follow.

---

89 F. Supp. 298

UNITED STATES v. CORDOVA et al.

No. Cr. 42082.

United States District Court

E.D. New York.

March 17, 1950.

Information by the United States of America against Diego Cordova and Benito Santano charging the commission of certain offenses while on an airplane operating over the high seas. The District Court, Kennedy, J., held that an airplane was not a "vessel" within the admiralty and maritime jurisdiction of the United States and that the offenses were not punishable under the statute denouncing certain crimes committed on the "high seas."

Judgment in accordance with opinion.

1. Criminal law

The venue requirements of the statute relating to offenses on the high seas are satisfied if the crime within the jurisdiction of the United States Courts is committed. 18 U.S.C.A. § 3238.

2. Criminal law

Under the statute penalizing offenses committed on board an American "vessel" on the high seas, etc., the statute when speaking of a "vessel" within the admiralty and maritime jurisdiction of the United States evokes in the common mind a picture of a ship, and not of a plane. 18 U.S.C.A. § 7.

3. Criminal law

Where plane was in flight over the high seas when defendant assaulted the pilot and others thereon, acts of defendant could not be prosecuted under the statute dealing with crimes committed on a "vessel." 18 U.S.C.A. § 7.

4. Criminal law

Under the statute denouncing certain crimes committed "on" the "high seas" or other waters within the admiralty jurisdiction of the United States and out of the jurisdiction of any particular state, acts of defendant in assaulting certain persons on a plane flying "over" the high seas were not punishable under the statute. 18 U.S.C.A. § 7.

J. Vincent Keogh, United States Attorney, Brooklyn, N.Y. (M. Jay Meckler, Assistant United States Attorney, New York City, of counsel), for plaintiff.

Dominic M. Mello, Brooklyn, N.Y., for defendant Cordova.

KENNEDY, District Judge.

On March 30, 1949, an information was filed against the defendant Cordova, along with one Santano, the charge consisting of four counts: 1) that on August 2, 1948 Cordova assaulted one Machada, pilot of an airplane owned by Flying Tigers, Inc., an American corporation, while the plane was flying over the high seas from San Juan, Puerto Rico, to New York; 2) that at the same time and place Cordova assaulted one Santiago, stewardess of the air carrier; 3) that at the same time and place Cordova assaulted the codefendant Santano; and 4) that at the same time and place Santano assaulted Cordova.

The statutory bases for jurisdiction alleged in the information are respectively (a) the act forbidding striking, wounding and beating and simple assault within the admiralty and maritime jurisdiction of the United States, 18 U.S.C.A. § 455, now 18 U.S.C.A. § 113(d) and (e), (b) the act defining the admiralty and maritime jurisdiction, 18 U.S.C.A. § 451, now 18 U.S.C.A. § 7, and (c) the venue statute for the prosecution of crimes within the admiralty and maritime jurisdiction, 28 U.S.C.A. § 102, now 18 U.S.C.A. § 3238. The pertinent portions of these statutes, as they existed on August 2, 1948, the date of the alleged offenses, are given in the margin:[1]

1. Title 18 U.S.C.A. § 451, reads in part: "Places and waters applicable; on board American vessel on high seas or Great Lakes; on land under exclusive control of United States; guano islands. The crimes and offenses defined in this chapter shall be punished as herein prescribed:

"First. When committed upon the high seas, or on any other waters within the admiralty and maritime jurisdiction of the United States and out of the jurisdiction of any particular State, or when committed within the admiralty and maritime jurisdiction of the United States and out of the jurisdiction of any particular State on board any vessel belonging in whole or in part to the United States or any citizen thereof, or to any corporation created by or under the laws of the United States, or of any State, Territory, or District thereof."

Title 18 U.S.C.A. § 455 (part of the same chapter) is entitled "Felonious assaults; to murder or rape; other felony; with weapons; beating; simple assault." and reads in part: "Whoever shall unlawfully strike, beat, or wound another, shall be fined not more than $500, or imprisoned not more than six months or both. Whoever shall unlawfully assault another, shall be fined not more than $300, or imprisoned not more than three months, or both."

Title 28 U.S.C.A. § 102 is entitled "Offenses on the high seas." and reads: "The trial of all offenses committed upon the high seas, or elsewhere out of the jurisdiction of any particular State or district, shall be in the district where the offender is found, or into which he is first brought."

As will appear shortly, after the facts have been outlined, the revision of the criminal code has no bearing on the case: the relevant statutes are substantially the same now as they were at the time of the offenses set forth in the information.

When the trial commenced, the government moved to dismiss the fourth count of the information (which charges the codefendant Santano with assault upon the defendant Cordova), a jury was waived, and the cause was tried to the court. Motions appropriate to challenge the jurisdiction of the court over the offenses charged were made at every stage of the case. These included a motion addressed to the information, a motion for the direction of an acquittal at the end of the government's case, and the same motion at the end of the whole case, coupled with a motion in arrest of judgment.

The facts are simple and clear. At 6:42 P.M., New York time, the carrier plane DC-4 No. NC-90911 took off from San Juan Airfield in Puerto Rico, bound for New York. The plane is the property of Flying Tigers, Inc., an American corporation, and at the time of the flight was under charter to Air America, Inc., another American corporation, organized under the laws of California. On board when the flight began were 60 passengers and 6 crew members. Of the passengers 43 were adults, 11 were children under 2 years of age, and 6 were children over that age.

At 8:15 P.M. on August 2, 1948 the plane, travelling at an air speed of 180 m.p.h., was over the Atlantic Ocean on a course 324 degrees true bound for Charleston, S.C., having been on her course for 1 1/2 hours. This means that the plane was to the northward of the Bahama Islands at a point approximately 270 miles northwest of San Juan, Puerto Rico. The plane's altitude was 8,500 feet. At that time (8:15 P.M., August 2, 1948) the plane became tail heavy, and her indicated air speed fell from 180 miles per hour to 150 miles per hour. The nose was rising so fast that the automatic pilot could not make corrections which would keep the ship on an even keel, and it became necessary to adjust the instrument. At this juncture the steward notified the pilot Machada that there was a fight going on in the passenger compartment. Machada turned the controls over to his First Officer and went aft. What he found was a brawl in progress between the passengers Cordova and Santano, which the steward and the stewardess (one Santiago) had been attempting to stop in vain. The passengers had crowded aft to watch the fight; it was because of this fact that the plane had become tail heavy.

Machada intervened, with the result that the defendant Cordova bit him on the shoulder, and during this portion of the fracas Cordova struck not only his adversary Santano, but also the stewardess Santiago.

The story of the origin of the fight is an old one. Apparently when these planes leave from San Juan, the relatives and friends of the passengers participate in a bon voyage celebration, the principal attraction being Puerto Rican rum in large quantities. And to fortify themselves for the flight, on this particular occasion many of the passengers, including Cordova and Santano, had boarded the plane with bottles of rum in paper shopping bags, which they took to their seats. Cordova and Santano had been toasting each other effusively for the first part of the flight, but soon a dispute arose over a missing bottle. Cordova seems literally to have gone beserk: while the main object of his viciousness was Santano, anyone else who crossed his path, including the captain of the plane, was in danger. The efforts of Machada (the captain) to subdue Cordova were reasonable. He began by attempting to hold Cordova's arms. At that time the weather being warm, Machada was wearing no flight jacket, and Cordova, attempting to free himself, bit Machada in the shoulder, drawing blood and necessitating first aid treatment. Eventually Cordova was locked up in a compartment.

[1] The plane landed at La Guardia Field at 4:45 A.M. on August 3, 1948. Cordova and Santano were immediately apprehended in this District and charged with assault. It thus appears that the venue requirements of the statute, 28 U.S.C.A. § 102, heretofore quoted in the margin, are satisfied if a crime within the jurisdiction of the United States Courts was committed. It is also plain that Cordova did, in fact, and without just cause or excuse strike and bite Machada (count 1), Santiago (count 2), and Santano (count 3). The case under the third count is weaker than the others, because Santano was at least in the beginning himself an active participant in the fight. Later, however, he attempted to retreat when the pilot of the plane and the stewardess intervened and the striking or biting which were then committed by Cordova on all three victims clearly violated the terms of the specific substantive statute, 18 U.S.C.A. § 455, heretofore quoted in the margin.

But the statute condemning striking, wounding and beating, and simple assault, within the admiralty and maritime jurisdiction of the United States does not become operative unless the acts complained of meet one of two tests, 18 U.S.C.A. § 451: (1) Were those acts committed on the high seas, or on any other waters within the admiralty and maritime jurisdiction of the United States and out of the jurisdiction of any particular State? or (2) Were those acts committed within the admiralty and maritime jurisdiction of the United States and out of the jurisdiction of any particular State on board any vessel belonging in whole or in part to the United States or any citizen thereof or any corporation created by or under the laws of the United States, or of any State, Territory or District thereof?

The second question gives less difficulty than the other, and perhaps should be dealt with first. The answer that ought to be made turns on the question whether an airplane is a vessel, within the meaning of the statute, and obviously the answer should be in the negative.

In the famous Reinhardt case, Reinhardt v. Newport Flying Service Corp., 1921, 232 N.Y. 115, 133 N.E. 371, 18 A.L.R. 1324, Judge Cardozo, speaking for the unanimous Court of Appeals, held that a hydroplane, which had been moored in navigable waters and had begun to drag her anchor was within the admiralty jurisdiction. This holding was necessary for the decision of the case, because the problem before the court was whether the New York State Workman's Compensation Commission had jurisdiction to make an award to an employee engaged in attempting to save the plane when she was in danger of being wrecked. The lower courts had upheld the Commission's jurisdiction, but the Court of Appeals reversed. Once the conclusion was reached that while afloat in navigable waters a hydroplane is a "vessel" within the admiralty jurisdiction, it became clear that the jurisdiction of the Compensation Commission was excluded. Knickerbocker Ice Co. v. Stewart, 1919, 253 U.S. 149, 40 S.Ct. 438, 64 L.Ed. 834, 11 A.L.R. 1145.

Judge Cardozo was careful to point out in dictum that even a hydroplane, while in the air, is not subject to the admiralty, citing Crawford Bros, No. 2, D.C.Wash. 1914, 215 F. 269, 271, a case which held that the admiralty has no jurisdiction to enforce a lien for repairs against an airplane on the theory that it is a vessel. The rationale of the Crawford case was that planes "are neither of the land nor sea, and, not being of the sea or restricted in their activities to navigable waters, they are not maritime." A similar conclusion was reached, after the Reinhardt decision, in United States v. Northwest Air Service, Inc., 9 Cir., 1935, 80 F.2d 804. There an unsuccessful attempt was made to assert a maritime lien against an airplane libeled by the United States because of violations of the Air Commerce Act of 1926, 49 U.S.C.A. §§ 177(b), 181(b), the Tariff Act of 1930, 19 U.S.C.A. §§ 1454, 1459, and the Customs Regulations of 1931. The basis for the rejected maritime lien was the performance of work on the plane's engine while she was in a hangar on the shore of Lake Washington.

[2] Objection may be made that the cases so far mentioned are civil cases, and for that reason have no important bearing on questions of federal criminal jurisdiction. However, in McBoyle v. U.S., 1931, 283 U.S. 25, 51 S.Ct. 340, 341, 75 L.Ed. 816, Mr. Justice Holmes, construing the National Motor Vehicle Theft Act, held that it did not apply to a case where an airplane was stolen. The language of the criminal statute, 18 U.S.C.A. § 408 [now § 2311], was very broad: "The term 'motor vehicle' when used in this section shall include an automobile, automobile truck, automobile wagon, motor cycle, or any other self-propelled vehicle not designed for running on rails." Of course, literally an airplane is a self-propelled vehicle not designed for running on rails. But Mr. Justice Holmes reasons that Congress was using the word "vehicle" in the popular sense, and that even though airplanes were well-known in 1919 when the statute was passed, Congress had laid down a rule of conduct "in words that evoke in the common mind only the picture of vehicles moving on land." By parity of reasoning, when, 18 U.S.C.A. § 451, Congress speaks of a "vessel" within the admiralty and maritime jurisdiction of the United States, it evokes in the common mind a picture of a ship, not of a plane.

Similarly, in another criminal case, a statute, 18 U.S.C.A. § 469, making it a misdemeanor for any person to stow away on a vessel, was held inapplicable to a case where the defendant had stowed away on an airplane. U.S. v. Peoples, D.C.Cal.1943, 50 F.Supp. 462. The Reinhardt and McBoyle cases are discussed in the opinion, as well as Noakes v. Imperial Airways, D.C.S.D.N.Y.1939, 29 F.Supp. 412, where an airplane was denied the right to limit liability in the admiralty, a right which Congress has accorded to "vessels." After the decision in the Peoples case, Congress adopted the suggestion of the judge who wrote the opinion and modified the law specifically to include aircraft within its coverage, 18 U.S.C.A. § 2199, see 58 Stat. 111, Mar. 4, 1944.

Finally, and on the negative side, the Reinhardt case, even to the extent that it holds a drifting plane to be a vessel, has been legislated out of existence. The Air Commerce Act of 1926, 49 U.S.C.A. § 171 et seq., now contains a section, 49 U.S.C.A. § 177(a), providing that: "The navigation and shipping laws of the United States, including any definition of 'vessel' or 'vehicle' found therein and including the rules for the prevention of collisions, shall not be construed to apply to seaplanes or other aircraft or to the navigation of vessels in relation to seaplanes or other aircraft."

[3] It seems, therefore, clear on precedent and on principle that even after airplanes become well-known, both Congress and the courts, saving the Reinhardt case, refused, and still refuse, to consider them as vessels even when they were afloat. In the instant case the plane was in flight, and it seems beyond argument that Cordova's acts cannot be prosecuted under a statute dealing with crimes committed on a "vessel."

It now becomes necessary to return to the first branch of the statute, which denounces certain crimes committed on the high seas or other waters within the admiralty and maritime jurisdiction of the United States and out of the jurisdiction of any particular state, 18 U.S.C.A. § 451. Beyond any doubt, Cordova's misconduct took place over the high seas. Is it proper, then, in a criminal case, to extend federal criminal jurisdiction to a plane in flight *over* the high seas under the statute which speaks of crimes committed *upon* the high seas or *on* any other waters within the admiralty and maritime jurisdiction of the United States? It is, of course, ridiculous to suppose, as Mr. Justice Holmes says in the McBoyle case, that any criminal considers the text of the law before he murders or steals. At the same time it is important that a rule of conduct must be considered in the light of the "picture" it evokes in the common mind.

It is perhaps irrelevant, but I have little doubt that had it wished to do so Congress could, under its police power, have extended federal criminal jurisdiction to acts committed on board an airplane owned by an American national, even though such acts had no effect upon national security.[2] In U.S. v. Flores, 1933, 289 U.S. 137, 53 S.Ct. 580, 77 L.Ed. 1086, the Supreme Court of the United States went the extreme length of holding that the criminal jurisdiction of the United States, under this very statute, 18 U.S.C.A. § 451, was broad enough to include acts committed on an American flag vessel, even though she was within the territorial waters of another sovereign. The Court has even

2. The reason I mention "national security" is this. It seems clear that Congress can denounce as crimes acts affecting the well-being of the government, and committed by American nationals, even when those acts take place on land within the jurisdiction of a foreign sovereign. U.S. v. Bowman, 1922, 260 U.S. 94, 43 S.Ct. 39, 67 L.Ed. 149; United States v. Chandler, D.C.Mass.1947, 72 F.Supp. 230, affirmed 1 Cir., 1949, 171 F.2d 921, certiorari denied 1949, 336 U.S. 918, 69 S.Ct. 640, rehearing denied 1949, 336 U.S. 947, 69 S.Ct. 809. But Congressional power over vessels on the high seas, or in admiralty waters outside the jurisdiction of any state, is even wider. It can be exercised to punish acts (such as assault) which have no relationship to national security. A different theory of jurisdiction comes into play, namely, that the American flag vessel is itself territory of the United States. There are no international complications, as there might be for land crimes against a person.

suggested that a State of the union may make a regulation valid and effective to rule conduct on the high seas, so long as the federal government has not occupied the field Skiriotes v. Florida, 1941, 313 U.S. 69, 61 S.Ct. 924, 85 L.Ed. 1193. And on occasion the Supreme Court has not been over technical to ascertain whether the crime was committed on the ship itself or in adjacent waters. United States v. Holmes, 1820, 5 Wheat. 412, 5 L.Ed. 122. For such a case the expression "high seas" was held to have a general meaning, and a similar result was reached when the Court was dealing with the question whether the term "high seas" was applicable to the Great Lakes. United States v. Rodgers, 1893, 150 U.S. 249, 14 S.Ct. 109, 37 L.Ed. 1071.

But none of these cases, nor the principles on which they rest, would justify the extension of the words "high seas" to the air space over them. It is at this point that the case at bar, I think, becomes one of first impression. The proper approach is, nevertheless, to be gathered, for example, from United States v. Wiltberger, 1820, 5 Wheat. 76, 5 L.Ed. 37. In that case the master of an American ship lying in the river Tigris off Wampoa in China was charged with manslaughter committed on board the vessel. The prosecution was laid under the Act of April 30, 1790, 1 Stat. 112. One section of that statute dealt with murder committed on the high seas, or any river, haven, basin or bay out of the jurisdiction of any particular state. Another section of the *same statute* dealt with manslaughter committed upon the high seas, but the other places were not mentioned. The Court was asked by the government to transfer the broader jurisdictional scope over murder to the crime of manslaughter, and to make the offense punishable when committed on a river, which did not come within the place-coverage of the words "high seas." Chief Justice Marshall refused to make any such judicial extension of the legislative definition, even though he agreed with the government that it was extremely improbable that Congress actually intended to make a fine jurisdictional definition as between murder and manslaughter. In other words, Congress, having limited jurisdiction over manslaughter to the "high seas," the Supreme Court held that the denounced acts, committed elsewhere, could not be punished on any theory of a probable Congressional intent to include those places.

[4] The acts for which Cordova stands charged were vicious in the extreme. He jeopardized the lives of others on the plane, including a considerable number of infants. But it seems to be clear that those acts have not been denounced by a statute which forbids them when committed on board an American "vessel," or when committed on the "high seas."

The situation may call for correction. There has been for some years discussion by experts in the field of aeronautic law of how the problem can be solved. For example, the so-called de Wisscher Draft Convention of 1937 suggests that crimes of this character ought to be punishable under the laws of the state of which the victim is a national, or of which the accused is a national, or of the state where the airplane arrives, if, in the latter case, what was done affects its security interests. The British Air Navigation Act of 1920 provides that any offense committed on a British aircraft shall be deemed committed in any place where the offender may for the time be. It is my understanding that

French criminal law applies to French aircraft in flight any place in the world. Air Nav.Law 1924, Title V, Art. 20. Italian law, I have been told, also applies to Italian planes in flight anywhere, although this may be merely a civil code.[3]

What I gather is that there is little likelihood, if any, of an international agreement involving, as it necessarily would, difficult and delicate questions of sovereignty. However that may be, as the law now stands, acts like those committed by Cordova will go unpunished, unless the law of the domicile of the corporation can be considered to cover them.

I, therefore, find Cordova guilty of the acts charged. But I must arrest judgment of conviction since there is no federal jurisdiction to punish those acts.

I feel very strongly that the government should have the opportunity to review this decision. And I draw the attention of the United States Attorney to the procedure followed in U.S. v. Flores, supra, and also to the criminal appeals statute in its present form, 18 U.S.C.A. § 3731, which seems to give ample protection against appeal to the wrong court. For what it may be worth, I certify that my decision turns on no issue of fact, but merely the determination of a question of law, namely, the construction of 18 U.S.C.A. § 451 and § 455.[4]

3. For a resume of the efforts of the experts to cope with this problem and for otherwise unavailable books and documents discussing these efforts I am indebted to Mr. Arnold W. Knauth, a member of the New York Bar.

4. It is true that I have found the facts against Cordova, including intent, wilfullness, and lack of excuse. But I have construed the Statute on the basis of what the information says concerning the place of the offenses and this is a fact not in dispute nor capable of debate. It may seem odd that fact-finding and a verdict of guilty are combined with an order in arrest of judgment because of want of jurisdiction. But I thought this procedure wise because, in the event my decision is wrong, I can proceed to sentence under the mandate, and save another trial.

376 U.S. 75
UNITED STATES, Appellant,
v.
David Thomas HEALY et al.
(Cite as 84 S. Ct. 553)

No. 64.
Argued Jan. 6, 1964.
Decided Feb. 17, 1964.

The defendants were indicted for aircraft piracy and violation of Federal Kidnapping Act. The United States District Court for the Southern District of Florida dismissed the indictment before trial. The United States appealed. The Supreme Court, Mr. Justice Harlan, held that the Federal Kidnapping Act is not limited to kidnapping for pecuniary gain or for an otherwise illegal purpose, and that a private airplane is "aircraft in flight in commerce" within statute defining aircraft piracy as seizure or exercise of control, by force or violence or threat of force or violence and with wrongful intent, of an aircraft in flight in commerce.

Reversed and remanded with instructions.

1. Courts

The Supreme Court noted probable jurisdiction of government's direct appeal from dismissal of indictment charging aircraft piracy and violation of Federal Kidnapping Act. 18 U.S.C.A. §§ 1201(a), 3731; Federal Aviation Act of 1958, § 902(i) as amended 49 U.S.C.A. § 1472(i).

2. Criminal Law

Where in a criminal case a timely petition for rehearing is filed by the government within the permissible time for appeal, the 30-day appeal period begins to run from denial of petition for rehearing and not from date of entry of judgment. Rules of Supreme Court, rule 11, subd. 2, 28 U.S.C.A.; Fed.Rules Crim.Proc. rule 37(a) (2), 18 U.S.C.A.

3. Criminal Law

Petitions for rehearing by United States in criminal cases are appropriate; the practice of the Supreme Court is to treat such petitions as having the same effect on the permissible time for seeking review as do similar petitions in civil cases and in criminal cases in which the government has won below. Rules of Supreme Court, rule 11, subd. 2, 28 U.S.C.A.

4. Criminal Law

As respects the effect of rehearing petition on time for seeking review in criminal case, the inference is compelling that no difference in treatment is intended by the rules between appealable judgments and those reviewable by certiorari, or between criminal defendants and the United States. Rules of Supreme Court, rule 11, subd. 2, and rule 22, subd. 2, 28 U.S.C.A.

5. Criminal Law

The principle of strict construction of statutes permitting governmental appeals in criminal cases cannot be utilized to undermine a well-established procedural rule for criminal, as well as civil, litigation.

6. Criminal Law

Speedy disposition of criminal cases is desirable.

7. Criminal Law

The Supreme Court will not countenance the United States using petition for rehearing simply as a delaying tactic in criminal litigation.

8. Kidnapping

The Federal Kidnapping Act is not limited to kidnappings for pecuniary gain or for an otherwise illegal purpose. 18 U.S.C.A. § 1201.

9. Statutes

The maxim of strict construction of penal statutes is not a directive to invent distinctions neither reflective of policy behind congressional enactments nor intimated by the words used to implement the legislative goal.

10. Citizens

A trip to Cuba would have been lawful on April 13, 1962 only if travelers had had passports specifically endorsed for travel to Cuba. Presidential Proclamation No. 2914, Dec. 16, 1950, 50 U.S.C.A.App. note preceding section 1; No. 3004, Jan. 17, 1953, 67 Stat. c. 31; Immigration and Nationality Act, § 215, 8 U.S.C.A. § 1185.

11. Aviation

A private airplane is "aircraft in flight in commerce" within statute defining aircraft piracy as seizure or exercise of control, by force or violence or threat of force or violence and with wrongful intent, of an aircraft in flight in commerce; the quoted phrase is not limited to commercial airlines. Federal Aviation Act of 1958, § 902(i) as amended 49 U.S.C.A. § 1472(i).

12. Aviation

One of the purposes of the aircraft piracy amendment to statute was to provide a solution to the jurisdictional problems involved in fixing a locus for a crime committed in transit and in arresting a deplaning passenger who may have engaged in criminal activity over the territory of a different state. Federal Aviation Act of 1958, § 902(i) as amended 49 U.S.C.A. § 1472(i).

76

Stephen J. Pollak, Washington, D.C., for appellant.

Robert L. Shevin, Miami, Fla., for appellees.

Mr. Justice HARLAN delivered the opinion of the Court.

A federal grand jury alleged in an indictment, returned in the United States District Court for the Southern District of Florida, that on April 13,

1962, the appellees that kidnapped at gunpoint the pilot of a private Cessna 172 airplane and compelled him to transport them from Florida to Cuba. Count 1 of the indictment charged appellees with having violated 18 U.S.C. § 1201,[1] the Federal Kidnapping Act. Under Count 2, appellees were charged with the commission of "aircraft piracy" in contravention of a 1961 amendment to § 902 of the Federal Aviation Act of 1958, 75 Stat. 466, 49 U.S.C. (Supp. IV) § 1472(i).[2]

[1] The District Court dismissed the indictment on September 17, 1962 before trial. It held that a kidnapping is not "for ransom or reward or otherwise," as required by § 1201(a), unless committed for the pecuniary benefit of

77

the defendant and that a private airplane is not "an aircraft in flight in air commerce" within the meaning of the aircraft piracy provision, which it read as limited to commercial airliners. The Government's petition for rehearing, filed October 17, was denied on November 8. On December 5, the Government filed a notice of appeal to this Court under 18 U.S.C. § 3731, permitting direct appeal when the dismissal of an indictment is based on construction of the statute upon which the indictment is founded. We noted probable jurisdiction, 372 U.S. 963, 83 S.Ct. 1089, 10 L.Ed.2d 127. We conclude that the judgment of dismissal must be reversed.

I.

[2] Appellees contend that this Court is without jurisdiction and is thereby precluded from considering the case on its merits. They argue that, absent authorization by statute or rule, the filing of a petition for rehearing by the Government in a criminal case cannot extend the time for appeal. Rule 11(2) of this Court provides:

> "An appeal permitted by law from a district court to this court in a criminal case shall be in time when the notice of appeal prescribed by Rule 10 is filed with the clerk of the district court within thirty days after entry of the judgment or order appealed from."

It is undisputed that the notice of appeal was filed by the United States within 30 days from the denial of the petition for rehearing, although not within 30 days of the original entry of judgment. Since the petition for rehearing was filed within 30 days of the judgment, we are not faced with an attempt to rejuvenate an extinguished right to appeal. Cf. Allegrucci v. United States, 372 U.S. 954, 83

1. "(a) Whoever knowingly transports in interstate or foreign commerce, any person who has been unlawfully seized, confined, inveigled, decoyed, kidnapped, abducted, or carried away and held for ransom or reward or otherwise, except, in the case of a minor, by a parent thereof, shall be punished . . ."

2. "(1) Whoever commits or attempts to commit aircraft piracy, as herein defined, shall be punished–

"(2) As used in this subsection, the term 'aircraft piracy' means any seizure or exercise of control, by force or violence or threat of force or violence and with wrongful intent, of an aircraft in flight in air commerce."

S.Ct. 950, 9 L.Ed.2d 978. The question, therefore, is simply whether in a criminal case a timely petition for rehearing by the Government filed within the permissible time for appeal

78

renders the judgment not final for purposes of appeal until the court disposes of the petition—in other words whether in such circumstances the 30-day period prescribed by Rule 11(2) begins to run from the date of entry of judgment or the denial of the petition for rehearing.

The latter is the well-established rule in civil cases, whether brought here by appeal or certiorari, *e.g.,* United States v. Ellicott, 223 U.S. 524, 539, 32 S.Ct. 334, 337, 56 L.Ed. 535; Morse v. United States, 270 U.S. 151, 153-154, 46 S.Ct. 241, 242, 70 L.Ed. 518; Bowman v. Loperena, 311 U.S. 262, 264-266, 61 S.Ct. 201, 85 L.Ed. 177. That a rehearing petition, at least when filed within the original period for review, may also extend the time for filing a petition for certiorari by a criminal defendant is the unarticulated premise on which the Court has consistently proceeded. See, *e.g.,* Panico v. United States, 375 U.S. 29, 84 S.Ct. 19, 11 L.Ed.2d 1 (order extending time for filing entered 19 days after denial of petition for rehearing *en banc,* 45 days after original judgment of Court of Appeals); Corey v. United States, 375 U.S. 169, 84 S.Ct. 298, 11 L.Ed.2d 229 (petition for certiorari filed 30 days after denial of rehearing, 45 days after original judgment of Court of Appeals); Genovese v. United States, decided with Evola v. United States, 375 U.S. 32, 84 S.Ct. 24, 11 L.Ed.2d 106 (order extending time for filing entered 16 days after denial of rehearing and rehearing *en banc,* 49 days after entry of original judgment). In Craig v. United States, 298 U.S. 637, 56 S.Ct. 670, 80 L.Ed. 1371, this Court dismissed an application for a writ of certiorari as premature, "without prejudice to a renewal of the application within thirty days after action by the Circuit Court of Appeals on the petition for rehearing." This summary disposition plainly reflects an advertent decision that criminal judgments are nonfinal for purposes of appeal so long as timely rehearing petitions are pending.

[3] We have recently recognized the appropriateness of petitions for rehearing by the United States in criminal cases, Forman v. United States, 361 U.S. 416, 425-426, 80 S.Ct. 481, 486, 4 L.Ed.2d 412.

79

The practice of the Court has been to treat such petitions as having the same effect on the permissible time for seeking review as do similar petitions in civil cases and in criminal cases in which the Government has won below. United States v. Williams, 341 U.S. 58, 71 S.Ct. 595, 95 L.Ed. 747 (appeal from dismissal of indictment by District Court; notice of appeal filed 29 days after denial of motion for rehearing, 44 days after entry of original order); United States v. Smith, 342 U.S. 225, 72 S.Ct. 260, 96 L.Ed. 252 (appeal from dismissal of indictment by District Court; notice of appeal filed 28 days after denial of petition for rehearing, 109 days after entry of original order); United States v. Calderon, 348 U.S. 160, 75 S.Ct.

186, 99 L.Ed. 202 (petition for certiorari from Court of Appeals; order extending time for filing entered 28 days after denial of rehearing, 88 days after entry of original judgment).

[4] Appellees place great reliance on the absence of any statute or rule governing the effect of rehearing petitions of the Government, but both the civil and criminal procedural doctrines lack such a foundation. The wording of Rule 11(2) of this Court, as unilluminating on this issue as it may be standing alone, is virtually identical to that of Rule 22(2), which encompasses petitions for certiorari both by criminal defendants and the Government. The inference is compelling that no difference in treatment is intended between appealable judgments and those reviewable by certiorari, or between criminal defendants and the United States. We are constrained to read these rules as consistent with a traditional and virtually unquestioned practice.

[5] Rule 37(a) (2) of the Federal Rules of Criminal Procedure[3] does not alter this conclusion, since it sheds no

80

light on the relevance of a petition for rehearing. Nor can the principle of strict construction of statutes permitting governmental appeals in criminal cases, Carroll v. United States, 354 U.S. 394, 77 S.Ct. 1332, 1 L.Ed.2d 1442, be utilized to undermine a well-established procedural rule for criminal, as well as civil, litigation. No persuasive considerations of policy dictate a deviant standard for government appeals.

[6,7] Of course speedy disposition of criminal cases is desirable, but to deprive the Government of the opportunity to petition a lower court for the correction of errors might, in some circumstances, actually prolong the process of litigation—since plenary consideration of a question of law here ordinarily consumes more time than disposition of a petition for rehearing—and could, in some cases, impose an added and unnecessary burden of adjudication upon this Court.[4] It would be senseless for this Court to pass on an issue while a motion for rehearing is pending below, and no significant saving of time would be achieved by altering the ordinary rule to the extent of compelling a notice of appeal to be filed while the petition for rehearing is under consideration.

3. "Time for Taking Appeal. An appeal by a defendant may be taken within 10 days after entry of the judgment or order appealed from, but if a motion for a new trial or in arrest of judgment has been made within the 10-day period an appeal from a judgment of conviction may be taken within 10 days after entry of the order denying the motion. When a court after trial imposes sentence upon a defendant not represented by counsel, the defendant shall be advised of his right to appeal and if he so requests, the clerk shall prepare and file forthwith a notice of appeal on behalf of the defendant. An appeal by the government when authorized by statute may be taken within 30 days after entry of the judgment or order appealed from."

4. In this case, the record and legal issues plainly indicate the good faith of the Government in petitioning for rehearing. We would, of course, not countenance the United States' using such petitions simply as a delaying tactic in criminal litigation; there is, however, not the slightest basis for believing that it would try to do so.

We conclude that this appeal was timely filed and that the Court has jurisdiction to determine the case on its merits.

81

II.

[8] By interpreting 18 U.S.C. § 1201 to require a motive of pecuniary profit, the District Court disregarded the plain holding of Gooch v. United States, 297 U.S. 124, 56 S.Ct. 395, 80 L.Ed. 522, in which the defendant, who had seized and carried away a state peace officer attempting to effectuate his arrest, was held subject to prosecution under the statute. Prior to a 1934 amendment, the Federal Kidnapping Act had been applicable only if the person transported was held for ransom or reward. The wording was then changed to encompass persons held "for ransom or reward *or otherwise,* except, in the case of a minor, by a parent thereof," 48 Stat. 781. (Emphasis added.) The Court in Gooch, noting the ambiguity of the word "reward," found convincing evidence in the amendment's legislative history that the addition of "otherwise" was intended to make clear that a nonpecuniary motive did not preclude prosecution under the statute. The Senate Judiciary Committee, which quoted from a memorandum of the Justice Department and the House Judiciary Committee both had reported that the bill was designed to extend federal jurisdiction under the Act to cases of persons kidnapped and held "not only for reward, but for any other reason."[5] The Court's conclusion that the amended statute covered the facts before it was clearly in accord with the congressional purpose.

[9,10] The Courts of Appeals have consistently followed Gooch, *e.g.,* United States v. Parker, 3 Cir., 103 F.2d 857; Brooks v. United States, 4 Cir., 199 F.2d 336; Hayes v. United States, 8 Cir., 296 F.2d 657, and appellees do not challenge the authority of that case. While recognizing that the

82

statute is not limited to kidnappings for pecuniary gain, they assert that it is restricted to kidnappings for an otherwise *illegal* purpose. This contention is without support in the language of the provision, its legislative history, judicial decisions, or reason. The wording certainly suggests no distinction based on the ultimate purpose of a kidnapping; were one intended, the exclusion of parent-child kidnappings would have been largely superfluous, since such conduct is rarely the result of an intrinsically illegal purpose. Nothing in the reports or debates supports appellees' position. In two cases, Wheatley v. United States, 4 Cir., 159 F.2d 599, 600; Bearden v. United States, 5 Cir., 304 F.2d 532 (judgment vacated on another ground, 372 U.S. 252, 83 S.Ct. 875, 9 L.Ed.2d 732), Courts of Appeals have assumed that the applicability of the statute does not turn on the illegality of the ultimate purpose of the kidnapper. No policy considerations support appellees' strained reading of 18 U.S.C. § 1201. A murder committed to

5. S.Rep.No.534, 73d Cong., 2d Sess., Mar. 20, 1934; H.R.Rep.No.1457, 73d Cong., 2d Sess., May 3, 1934, p. 2.

accelerate the accrual of one's rightful inheritance is hardly less heinous than one committed to facilitate a theft; by the same token, we find no compelling correlation between the propriety of the ultimate purpose sought to be furthered by a kidnapping and the undesirability of the act of kidnapping itself. Appellees rely on the principle of strict construction of penal statutes,[6] but that maxim is hardly a directive to this Court to invent distinctions neither reflective of the policy behind congressional enactments nor intimated by the words used to implement the legislative goal.[7]

83

We hold that the District Court improperly dismissed the first count of the indictment.

III.

[11] The 1961 "aircraft piracy" amendment to the Federal Aviation Act makes it a federal crime, *inter alia,* to exercise control, by threat of force with wrongful intent, of "an aircraft in flight in air commerce," § 902(i), 75 Stat. 466, 49 U.S.C. (Supp. IV) § 1472(i). Examination of the provision itself and its relation to the rest of the statute, apart from reference to the legislative history, stands against the conclusion of the court below. The Cessna 172 was "an aircraft"; it was "in flight"; it was in flight "in air commerce." Appellees assert that had Congress intended to include private airplanes it could have referred to "any aircraft," but, standing alone, the phrase "an aircraft" is on its face an all-inclusive term. Appellees' contention that the statutory language refers only to commercial airlines is contradicted by the definition of air commerce in the original act, § 101 of the Federal

84

Aviation Act of 1958, 72 Stat. 737, 49 U.S.C. (Supp. IV) § 1301:

6. Chatwin v. United States, 326 U.S. 455, 66 S.Ct. 233, 90 L.Ed. 198, which involved the transporting of a girl to maintain a "celestial" marriage, is inapposite. There the element of coercion or deception, central to the crime of kidnapping, was absent.

7. Our disposition of this issue relieves us from considering whether appellees' ultimate purpose was unlawful and, if so, whether illegality of purpose, if not obvious, is a necessary element in the indictment. However, it may be observed that a trip to Cuba would have been lawful only if appellees had had passports specifically endorsed for travel to Cuba. See Presidential Proclamations No. 2914, Dec. 16, 1950 (64 Stat. A454); and No. 3004, Jan. 17, 1953 (67 Stat. C31); § 215 of the Immigration and Nationality Act of 1952, 66 Stat. 163, 190, 8 U.S.C. § 1185; Department of State Public Notice 179, 26 Fed.Reg. 492, Jan. 16, 1961. Appellees, without claiming lawfulness of purpose, argue that the burden of showing that they had not complied with the regulations governing travel to Cuba rests with the United States and that noncompliance has to be specifically alleged in an indictment.

The discussion concerning the legality of travel to Cuba points up how untenable is appellees' basic position. It would surely be anomalous were application of the Kidnapping Act made to turn on whether existing regulations permit travel to the point of destination without a passport, with an ordinary passport, or only with a passport specially endorsed.

"(4) 'Air commerce' means interstate, overseas, or foreign air commerce or the transportation of mail by aircraft or any operation or navigation of aircraft within the limits of any Federal airway or any operation or navigation of aircraft which directly affects, or which may endanger safety in, interstate, overseas, or foreign air commerce."

Without question, this definition covers the facts alleged in the indictment in this case. That the relation between the language of the "aircraft piracy" amendment and the above definition was not overlooked by the drafters is indicated by the different phraseology used in a contemporaneous amendment concerning concealed weapons. Section 902(*l*) of the amended act, 75 Stat. 466, 49 U.S.C. (Supp. IV) § 1472(*l*), makes it a crime to carry such a weapon "while aboard an aircraft being operated by an air carrier in air transportation." Thus Congress knew how to choose words to refer solely to commercial airliners when it wished to do so.

The conclusions drawn from the statute itself are confirmed by the legislative history. The House Committee on Interstate and Foreign Commerce reported, H.R.Rep. No. 958, 87th Cong., 1st Sess., U.S.Code Cong. and Adm. News 1961, p. 2563, that the term "air commerce" was used by design because of its broad scope as defined in existing law, p. 8. It specifically cited "the urgent need for stronger Federal laws applicable to criminal acts committed aboard commercial and private aircraft," p. 3, and noted that the subsection regarding weapons "would be limited to aircraft being used in air carrier commercial operations, whereas these other subsections [including that relating to aircraft piracy] would apply also in the case of private aircraft," p. 15.

85

[12] Comments during House debate accord with the Committee's understanding, see remarks of Congressman Harris (107 Cong.Rec. 16545) and Congressman Williams (107 Cong.Rec. 16547-16548). The remarks of Senator Engle, the sponsor of the aircraft piracy provisions in the Senate, during debate are explicit: "Yes; it applies to all airplanes in air commerce, which includes, of course, not only commercial aircraft, but private airplanes as well." (107 Cong. Rec. 15243.) The statements of members of Congress evincing a concern for the protection of passengers aboard commercial airlines, see, *e.g.*, remarks of Congressman Rostenkowski (107 Cong.Rec. 16552), do not reflect any intent to put private aircraft beyond the scope of the provision. Indeed, since one of the often-expressed purposes of the aircraft piracy amendment was to provide a solution to the jurisdictional problems involved in fixing a locus for a crime committed in transit and in arresting a deplaning passenger who may have engaged in criminal activity over the territory of a different State, see, *e.g.*, H.R.Rep. No. 958, 87th Cong., 1st Sess., pp. 3-5, one would suppose, absent any other evidence, a design to include private aircraft; these problems are as pertinent to acts committed aboard them as to those done on commercial airliners. Finding that the plainly expressed intent of Congress, as manifested both in the

statutory language and legislative history, was to include private aircraft within the scope of § 902(i), we conclude that dismissal of the second count of the indictment was also incorrect.

The judgment below is reversed and the case is remanded to the District Court with instructions to reinstate both counts of the indictment.

It is so ordered.

Reversed and remanded with instructions.

CHAPTER 3

Airports and Liability

The question of liability of airports due to the noise which results by their use is considered in the cases in this section.

The question raised is whether the noise created is a "taking" of the property of adjacent landowners, or whether the airport and airplane noise constitute a "tort" against the neighboring landowners.

A sovereign government can be sued only if it consents to be sued. The United States, by enactment of the Tucker Act in 1887, consented to be sued only in five situations, and expressly forbade lawsuits against the United States based on torts.

In 1946 the Federal Tort Claims Act was passed which, in general, permitted a citizen to sue the United States Government for torts committed by a Federal employee while acting within the scope of his employment.

Similarly, a sovereign State of the United States, cannot be sued unless it consents to be sued. In this section, the cases cover the provisions in state constitutions which permit the state to be sued.

A state constitution may contain a provision for compensation for "taking," in which case if a court declares the state's airport noise as a commission of a tort, then the adjacent landowner could not recover. If, however, the state constitution mentioned "damages" then the landowner could recover on the grounds that lawsuits against the state were permitted for "torts" in which "damages" are the result. In cases involving a "taking," the landowner is considered entitled to compensation for the taking of an easement over his property, by operation of the airport. In this situation the "taking" by the airport constitutes depriving the landowner of one or more useful functions of the land, due to the noise resulting from the airport operation.

We see that the U.S. Supreme Court's decision in British Airways v. Port Authority of N.Y. makes it possible to arrive at a novel conclusion regarding the question as to who is liable for damages caused by noise and vibration at a local government owned airport (either owned by a port authority or by a county) such as in British Airways and Griggs v. Allegheny cases respectively.

A logical and chronological analysis of this problem is as follows:

In Griggs v. Allegheny (1962) the county was held liable (not the Federal government) because the U.S. Supreme Court said the regulatory power of the Federal government did not preempt the regulatory and proprietary rights of local government (county) owned airports.

In 1973 in City of Burbank v. Lockheed (411 U.S. 624) the U.S. Supreme Court said that a local government (city) could not by city ordinance control noise at a private airport. The Federal government regulatory powers preempted the local government regulatory powers. At the same time the U.S. Supreme Court, in the same case, stated that a local government owned and operated airport may be permitted to control noise.

The Court, in the above two cases made a distinction between the local government regulatory (police) control over a private airport, and proprietary (ownership) control by local government over its own local airport.

In 1977 the Federal Courts have, in British Airways (see case in this chapter), preempted the regulatory and proprietary rights of the local government (port authority) over its own local airport.

The question then becomes,—since the Federal Government compelled the local government owned airport to accept conditions of noise and vibration—would the Federal government be liable for damages or would the local government be liable for damages caused by the noise and vibration?

The cases in this section analyze these opposing views. The following cases are reported in their entirety—Batten v. U.S., Griggs v. Allegheny, Thornburg v. Portland, Martin v. Seattle, and British Airways v. Port Authority of N.Y.

Refer to Extract A, U.S. Constitution, 5th Amendment; also Extract D, Tucker Act.

306 F. 2d 580

William J. BATTEN and Katie M. Batten, his wife; Donald G. Becker and Opal M. Becker, his wife; Don T. Campbell and Leta Mae Campbell, his wife; Ernest S. Horton and Margaret U.A. Horton, his wife; Ivan F. Huhs and Bernadine M. Huhs, his wife; Thomas N. Lee and Gladys M. Lee, his wife; Clyde A. Lewis and Dorothy L. Lewis, his wife; Edward Dale Moore and Fay L. Moore, his wife; John W. Stephens and Vada Stephens, his wife; and Ralph C. Weed and Mary T. Weed, his wife, Appellants,

v.

UNITED STATES of America, Appellee.

No. 6906.

United States Court of Appeals Tenth Circuit.

July 10, 1962.

Rehearing Denied Aug. 9, 1962.

Action by property owners presenting questions of whether there was a taking of property when there was no physical invasion of the affected property by operation and maintenance of military jet aircraft which produced noise, vibration and smoke. From an adverse judgment of the United States District Court for the District of Kansas, Walter A. Huxman, J., the property owners appealed. The Court of Appeals, Breitenstein, Circuit Judge, held that jet airplane operations from military base, which caused windows and dishes to rattle, smoke to blow into homes during summer months and noise which interrupted ordinary home activities and interfered with use and enjoyment of private homes but which did not render them uninhabitable, did not constitute a taking of an interest in the property for which compensation had to be paid by government, which did not operate any of the jets over the property.

Affirmed.

Murrah, Chief Judge, dissented.

See also 292 F.2d 144.

Eminent Domain

Jet airplane operations from military base, which caused windows and dishes to rattle, smoke to blow into homes during summer months and noise which interrupted ordinary home activities and interfered with use and enjoyment of private homes but which did not render them uninhabitable, did not constitute a taking of an interest in the property for which compensation had to be paid by government, which did not operate any of jets over property. U.S.C.A.Const. Amend. 5; 28 U.S.C.A. § 1346(a) (2).

Roger P. Marquis, Attorney, Department of Justice (Ramsey Clark, Asst. Atty. Gen., Newell A. George, U.S. Atty., and R. Stanley Ditus, Asst. U.S. Atty., on the brief), for appellee.

Harvey D. Ashworth and Raymond L. Spring, Topeka, Kan. (A. Harry Crane, Ward D. Martin, Arthur L. Claussen and Jack C. McCarter, Topeka, Kan., on the brief), for appellants.

Before MURRAH, Chief Judge, and LEWIS and BREITENSTEIN, Circuit Judges.

BREITENSTEIN, Circuit Judge.

This case presents the novel question whether a taking of property, compensable under the Fifth Amendment, occurs when there is no physical invasion of the affected property but the operation and maintenance of military jet aircraft on an Air Force Base of the United States produce noise, vibration, and smoke which interfere with the use and enjoyment of the property. The appellants-plaintiffs, owners of 10 homes at Pauline, Kansas, sued the United States under the Tucker Act[1] and base their claims on the use of jet aircraft at Forbes Air Force Base which adjoins the subdivision in which they live. They acquired their homes prior to the enlargement of the Base to accommodate jets. Recovery was denied on the ground that there was no taking of property in violation of the Fifth Amendment for which the United States was liable under the Tucker Act.[2]

The facts are not disputed. Forbes Air Force Base, originally known as Topeka Army Air Field, was a temporary World War II base used for training in the operation of propeller-driven aircraft. It was deactivated at an undisclosed date prior to 1948. In that year a tract, the southeastern corner of which adjoined the northwestern corner of the Base, was platted as a residential subdivision. The homes of the plaintiffs were built and acquired in the period 1949-1955. After the Korean War started the United States obtained land adjacent to the subdivision on the east to enlarge the Base for the accommodation of jet aircraft. Use of a lengthened runway, known as 13-31, began in September, 1955, and a ramp, parking area, and warm-up pad for jet planes were put into operation in the spring of 1956.

Since the enlargement of the Base, about 100 RB–47 and B–47 six-engine jet aircraft and about 40 KC–97 six-engine propeller-driven aircraft have been

1. 28 U.S.C. § 1346(a) (2). The United States District Court had jurisdiction because each claim was for less than $10,000.

2. The Tucker Act provides, 28 U.S.C. § 1346(a) (2) that an action may be maintained against the United States for a claim "founded . . . upon the Constitution, . . . or upon any express or implied contract with the United States." The last clause of the Fifth Amendment reads: "nor shall private property be taken for public use, without just compensation."

located there. Aircraft movements average about 4,000 monthly or about 130 daily and of these 70% are attributable to jets. This activity occurs usually between dawn and dusk, Monday through Friday, but occasionally on the week ends and at night.

The plaintiffs do not rely on flights over their properties to sustain their claims. The trial court found:

> "The Pauline Subdivision is outside the flying pattern of all aircraft operating from Forbes Air Force Base, and the Government does not claim or exercise any right to fly any planes over plaintiffs' property. However, on a few occasions, RB–47 and B–47 jet aircraft did fly directly over the plaintiffs' homes in Pauline, Kansas, Subdivision at low altitudes."

The jets use the 13-31 runway almost exclusively. The operating procedure is for the engines to be started on the parking ramp about 30 minutes before take-off. The ramp is 900 feet wide and at its nearest point is 650 feet from any property of the plaintiffs. After about 10 minutes the plane is taxied to the warm-up pad, located 2,000 feet from the nearest property of the plaintiffs, where final pre-flight checks are performed. During this period all 6 engines are running at idling speed. The plane is then moved to the take-off point. About one-half of the flights begin at the end of the 13-31 runway near Pauline and at a point 2,280 feet from the nearest property of the plaintiffs. About 30 seconds before take-off the engine power is advanced to maximum output. The planes are airborne some 50 seconds after start.

From April through October a water-alcohol injection system is used to increase the maximum power by 23%. The RB–47 and B–47 jets leave a characteristic trail of black smoke which is increased by the use of the water-alcohol injection system and which is quite heavy for about 70 seconds after the brakes have been released for take-off but which is exhausted within a mile from the end of the runway.

Maintenance work on the planes was done on the ramp 3,420 feet from the nearest property of the plaintiffs until May, 1960, when it was moved to a location about 1 1/2 miles therefrom. In the maintenance operations jet engines are run at power settings of from 50% to 100%. During a typical month the engines were operated for 84 hours in the 100% RPM range and for 211 hours in less than that range for maintenance purposes.

Ground power generators are used on the parking ramp to provide auxiliary power to start the jet engines and to recharge the batteries of the planes. From 4 to 10 of these generators may operate at the same time and on occasion they run from 8 to 10 hours at any time during the day and sometimes at night.

The mentioned activities produce sound and shock waves which cross the plaintiffs' properties and limit the use and enjoyment thereof. Strong vibrations cause windows and dishes to rattle. Loud noises frequently make conversation and the use of the telephone, radio, and television facilities impossible and also interrupt sleep. During engine operation in the 100% range the sound pressure level measured in decibels varies from 90 to 117 decibels on the plaintiffs' properties. Ear plugs are recommended for Air Force personnel when the sound pressure level reaches 85 decibels and are required at or above 95 decibels.

In the summer months when there is an easterly wind, the black smoke developed during jet take-offs occasionally blows across the plaintiffs' properties leaving an oily black deposit on the houses and laundry of the plaintiffs.

The court found that:

> "* * * plaintiffs have suffered a substantial interference of the use and enjoyment of their properties, which interference did not exist prior to the construction and activation of the new runway in September, 1955, and the new ramp in March or April, 1956."

The court further found that such interference "is of the same character as that noticed in varying degrees in the general area surrounding the Base" with greater adverse effect on the plaintiffs because of the proximity of their property to the Base.

Diminution in value of the 10 homes was found in amounts which varied from $4,700 to $8,800.[3] The trial court deemed United States v. Causby, 328 U.S. 256, 66 S.Ct. 1062, 90 L.Ed. 1206, to be a controlling precedent and held that there was no taking of an interest in the plaintiffs' properties for which compensation had to be paid.

The case at bar is one of first impression in the federal appellate courts and presents an issue of widespread current interest. The jet airplane is a great boon to the traveler but a veritable plague to the homeowners near an airfield. The noise, vibration, and smoke incidental to the operation and maintenance of jet planes disturb the peace and quiet in every residential area located near an airport used by the jets. This disturbance is felt not only by those whose property is crossed by the planes on take-offs or landings but also by those who live outside of the established flight patterns. The Supreme Court has allowed recovery under the Tucker Act to a landowner whose property was crossed by low-elevation flights of military planes on take-offs and landings.[4] The novelty in the instant case is that liability is asserted not because of disturbance in conjunction with any over-flights but because of the noise, vibration, and smoke alone which harass the occupants of nearby properties. The amount of harassment varies with the proximity of the property to the scene of jet operations.

No amount of sympathy for the vexed landowners can change the legal principles applicable to their claims. We do not have either a tort or a nuisance case. The plaintiffs sue under the Tucker Act and whether the applicability of that Act depends on a taking without compensation in violation of the Fifth Amendment or on an implied promise to pay for property taken, the claims are founded on the prohibition of the Fifth Amendment, "nor shall private property be taken for public use, without just compensation."[5]

In construing and applying this constitutional provision the federal courts have long and consistently recognized the distinction between a taking and consequential damages. In Transportation Company v. Chicago, 99 U.S. 635,

3. Stated in terms of percentages the diminution in value ranged from 55.3% to 40.8%.

4. United States v. Causby, supra. See also Griggs v. Allegheny County, 369 U.S. 84 82 S.Ct. 531, 7 L.Ed.2d 585.

5. United States v. Dickinson, 331 U.S. 745, 748, 67 S.Ct. 1382, 91 L.Ed. 1789.

642, 25 L.Ed. 336, the Supreme Court held that governmental activities which do not directly encroach on private property are not a taking within the meaning of the Fifth Amendment even though the consequences of such acts may impair the use of the property. The principle was repeated in United States v. Willow River Power Co., 324 U.S. 499, 510, 65 S.Ct. 761, 89 L.Ed. 1101, the Court saying that "damage alone gives courts no power to require compensation." We have recognized the rule in this circuit by our holding in Harris v. United States, 10 Cir., 205 F.2d 765, 767, that under the federal constitution "damages to property not taken are compensable only as a consequence of or incidental to an actual taking."

Because of this rule which denies the recovery of consequential damages in the absence of any taking, many state constitutions provide in substance that private property shall not be taken or damaged for public use without compensation.[6] However, the federal obligation has not been so enlarged either by statute or by constitutional amendment.

In Causby the Supreme Court held that the continuous invasions of the airspace superadjacent to the property of the landowner by military planes taking off and landing at a nearby base was "in the same category as invasions of the surface" and that the damages were not "merely consequential" but "the product of a direct invasion of respondent's domain."[7] The plaintiffs argue that the actual damage in Causby resulted from noise and vibrations and that if recovery is permitted for sound and shock waves traveling vertically, it should also be allowed for such waves traveling laterally. The unacceptability of this theory was demonstrated in Nunnally v. United States, 4 Cir., 239 F.2d 521, where recovery was denied because of diminution in value of a recreational cottage by practice bombing on an adjoining federal proving ground. The Fourth Circuit pointed out that there was no physical invasion of the plaintiff's property and that there was at the most a "sharing in the common burden of incidental damages" because the annoyance was the same as that to which everyone living in the vicinity was subject to varying degrees. The court said that to permit recovery would be to obliterate the carefully preserved distinction between "damage" and "taking."

We are cited to no decisions holding that the United States is liable for noise, vibration, or smoke without a physical invasion. In Causby, Griggs, and a number of lower court decisions such as Highland Park, Inc. v. United States, 161 F.Supp. 597, 142 Ct.Cl. 269; Herring v. United States, 162 F.Supp. 769, 142 Ct.Cl. 695, and Matson v. United States, 171 F.Supp. 283, 145 Ct.Cl. 225,

6. Richards v. Washington Terminal Company, 233 U.S. 546, 554, 34 S.Ct. 654, 58 L.Ed. 1088. In 2 Nichols on Eminent Domain (3d ed. 1950) § 6.44, pp. 324-325, there is a list of 25 states whose constitutions so provide. Interestingly every state within the Tenth Circuit, except Kansas, has so provided.

7. 328 U.S. 265, 66 S.Ct. 1068.

there were regular flights over the property. Absent such physical invasion recovery has been uniformly denied.[8]

Plaintiffs cite no cases with either facts or issues analogous to those with which we are concerned. Richards v. Washington Terminal Company, supra, allowed recovery because smoke and fumes were driven out of a tunnel by an exhaust fan in such manner that they were directed across plaintiff's property, but in so doing expressly recognized the invasion principle. United States v. Cress, 243 U.S. 316, 37 S.Ct. 380, 61 L.Ed. 746, and United States v. Kansas City Life Insurance Co., 339 U.S. 799, 70 S.Ct. 885, 94 L.Ed. 1277, cases of flooding and underflooding respectively, applied the same principle. Swetland v. Curtiss Airports Corporation, 6 Cir., 55 F.2d 201, 83 A.L.R. 319, was an action to enjoin a private nuisance and the decision rests on the theory of balance of conveniences.

In Armstrong v. United States, 364 U.S. 40, 48, 80 S.Ct. 1563, 4 L.Ed.2d 1554, the Court held that the total destruction of a lien was a compensable taking. Baltimore & Potomac Railroad Company v. Fifth Baptist Church, 108 U.S. 317, 332, 2 S.Ct. 719, 27 L.Ed. 739, sustained a recovery by a church for a nuisance created by a railroad operating in the District of Columbia under congressional authorization and the Court expressed doubt that such authorization would justify total deprivation of use without compensation. In discussing the meaning of the word "taken," the Court said in United States v. General Motors Corp., 323 U.S. 373, 378, 65 S.Ct. 357, 89 L.Ed. 311, that governmental action short of occupancy was a taking "if its effects are so complete as to deprive the owner of all or most of his interest in the subject matter."[9]

In the instant case there is no total destruction and no deprivation of "all or most" of the plaintiffs' interests. The plaintiffs do not suggest that any home has been made uninhabitable or that any plaintiff has moved because of the activities at the Base. The record shows nothing more than an interference with use and enjoyment.

Congress has placed the navigable airspace in the public domain and has authorized administrative regulation of minimum altitudes of flight.[10] The regulations so far as pertinent fix the minimum altitudes at 1,000 feet over congested areas and 500 over sparsely populated areas.[11] The airspace below such mini-

8. See Freeman v. United States, D.C.W.D.Okl., 167 F.Supp. 541, wherein the flights were alongside the plaintiff's land. In Pope v. United States, D.C.N.D.Tex., 173 F.Supp. 36, the complaint was based on the operation of an engine test cell by the Air Force and it was held that there was no taking because the test cell did not encroach on the plaintiff's land. Nuclear detonations by the Atomic Energy Commission at a site removed from the plaintiff's property was held not to be a taking in Bartholomae Corporation v. United States, 9 Cir., 253 F.2d 716, 718, 73 A.L.R.2d 1293, note 2.

9. Cf. United States v. Dickinson, supra, where the Court said: "Property is taken in the constitutional sense when inroads are made upon an owner's use of it to an extent that, as between private parties, a servitude has been acquired either by agreement or in course of time."

10. 49 U.S.C. §§ 1301(24) and 1348(a).

11. 14 C.F.R. § 60.17.

mums is within the dominion of the landowner. The over-flights considered in Causby invaded that dominion. In the situation confronting us the warm-ups occur 2,000 feet, the take-offs 2,280 feet, and the maintenance 1 1/2 miles from the nearest property of the plaintiffs. Causby contains nothing indicating that recovery could be had for noise, vibration, or smoke coming from the same vertical distances.

Each of these disturbing conditions is brought to the plaintiffs' properties through the air and they do not effect an actual displacement of a landowner from space within which he is entitled to exercise dominion consistent with recognized concepts of real property rights. Such displacement is a fact when occasioned by repeated airplane flights. Sound waves, shock waves, and smoke pervade property neighboring that on which they have their source but the disturbance caused thereby is only a neighborhood inconvenience unless they are intentionally directed to some particular property as was the case in Richards v. Washington Terminal Co., supra, or unless they force the abdication of the use of space within the landowner's dominion. The activities of which the plaintiffs complain are not directed against them or their property and do not arrogate to the government any of the plaintiffs' dominion over their properties. The situation is common to that found on all the private property surrounding the Base.

The vibrations which cause the windows and dishes to rattle, the smoke which blows into the homes during the summer months when the wind is from the east, and the noise which interrupts ordinary home activities do interfere with the use and enjoyment by the plaintiffs of their properties. Such interference is not a taking. The damages are no more than a consequence of the operations of the Base and as said in United States v. Willow River Power Co., supra, they "may be compensated by legislative authority, not by force of the Constitution alone." As we see the case at bar, the distinctions which the Supreme Court has consistently made between "damages" and "taking" control and compel denial of recovery.

Affirmed.

MURRAH, Chief Judge (dissenting).

It is agreed that subsequent to the establishment of the homes of these plaintiffs, the Government constructed these runways and warm-up pads nearby, for Jet Engine operation, and that, as a direct result of this operation, the "plaintiffs have suffered a substantial interference of the use and enjoyment of their properties * * *," with consequent substantial diminution of the values of such properties. It seems also agreed that the right asserted, i.e., the peaceful enjoyment of their homes, is a constitutionally protected property right, and that the admitted injury to such right is peculiar to these plaintiffs, who are similarly situated. In any event, "the constitutional provision is addressed to every sort of interest the citizen may possess," (see United States v. General Motors, 323 U.S. 373, 65 S.Ct. 357, 89 L.Ed. 311) and certainly includes the right to the peaceful possession of residential property. The economic interest asserted here, is no different from that "taken" in Causby and Griggs.

Both the trial Court and this Court have denied compensation, upon the premise that an actual physical invasion of the property damaged is a sine qua non to a constitutional taking, and the injury is, therefore, merely consequential; hence, not constitutionally compensable. It is my thesis that a constitutional taking does not necessarily depend on whether the Government physically invaded the property damaged.

It is true that, in the very nature of things, most constitutional takings are accompanied by actual physical invasion. See Transportation Company v. Chicago, 99 U.S. 635, 25 L.Ed. 336; Pennsylvania Coal Co. v. Mahon, 260 U.S. 393, 43 S.Ct. 158, 67 L.Ed. 322; Portsmouth Harbor Land & Hotel Company et al. v. United States, 260 U.S. 327, 43 S.Ct. 135, 67 L.Ed. 287; United States v. General Motors, supra; United States v. Causby, 328 U.S. 256, 66 S.Ct. 1062, 90 L.Ed. 1206; United States v. Dickinson, 331 U.S. 745, 67 S.Ct. 1382, 91 L.Ed. 1789; United States v. Kansas City Life Insurance Co., 339 U.S. 799, 70 S.Ct. 885, 94 L.Ed. 1277; Griggs v. Allegheny County, 369 U.S. 84, 82 S.Ct. 531, 7 L.Ed.2d 585; and, Nunnally v. United States, 4 Cir., 239 F.2d 521. But, the Government may surely accomplish by indirect interference, the equivalent of an outright physical invasion. "If regulation goes too far it will be recognized as a taking." Pennsylvania Coal Co. v. Mahon, supra, 260 U.S. p. 415, 43 S.Ct. p. 160. Thus, a "taking" was effected in Armstrong v. United States, 364 U.S. 40, 80 S.Ct. 1563, 4 L.Ed.2d 1554, by the destruction of the liens on property through governmental acquisition of title. The closing of a gold mine, by force of a wartime governmental regulation, without physical invasion was held not to be a constitutional taking in United States v. Central Eureka Mining Co., 357 U.S. 155, 78 S.Ct. 1097, 2 L.Ed.2d 1228, but not without recognizing that "action in the form of regulation can so diminish the value of property as to constitute a taking." There was forceful argument in dissent to the effect that to make the property owner's right to compensation turn on the physical act of taking, was to "permit technicalities of form to dictate consequences of substance." (See Mr. Justice Harlan's dissent, p. 181, 78 S.Ct. p. 1110.) It is admitted that the compensable damage in Richards v. Washington Terminal, 233 U.S. 546, 34 S.Ct. 654, 58 L.Ed. 1088, was not accompanied by an actual invasion, though the case is said to have been decided on the invasion theory. The facts and reasoning there are analogous to our situation, and serve to prove the recognition of a constitutional taking by indirect interference. The principal is analogous to trespass and nuisance. See cases collected in Harvard Law Review, June 1961 p. 1581.

As I view the precedents, especially in the context of their contrariety, the decisional process involves an analysis and evaluation of competing interests, i.e., the public versus private, within the framework of our social order—a jurisprudence of interest, if you please, in which the State imposes its will, subject only to the constitutional covenant that it will pay "just compensation" for "private property" which is "taken." The critical and definitive words are, to be sure, constitutional language which, as we know, are subject to formulations, depending upon a point of view. We start with the agreed proposition that not every governmental interference, which adversely affects a private economic interest, amounts to a constitutional taking. See United States v. Willow River Power Co., 324 U.S. 499, 65 S.Ct. 761, 89 L.Ed. 1101; Armstrong v. United States, supra; and, Nunnally v. United States, supra. "Frustration and appropriation are essentially different things." Omnia Company v. United States, 261 U.S. 502, 43 S.Ct. 437, 67 L.Ed. 773. As I reason, the constitutional test in each case is first, whether the asserted interest is one which the law will protect; if so, whether the interference is sufficiently direct, sufficiently peculiar, and of sufficient magnitude to cause us to conclude that fairness and justice, as between the State and the citizen, requires the burden imposed to be borne by the public and not by the individual alone.

Indeed, my brothers impliedly embrace this theory when they indicate that if the governmental interference in this case had rendered the plaintiffs' homes totally uninhabitable, the damages would have been compensable, as for a constitutional taking. But, they then say, that since there is "nothing more than an interference with use and enjoyment" of the property, the admitted damages are merely "consequential." This leaves me in doubt as to whether compensation is denied because the interest asserted is not one which the law will protect, as in United States v. Willow River Power Co., supra, or whether the interference with a protectable property right was not sufficiently direct, peculiar and grave to justify a conclusion of "taking." If the decision is based on the latter premise, I must inquire at what point the interference rises to the dignity of a "taking." Is it when the window glass rattles, or when it falls out; when the smoke suffocates the inhabitants, or merely makes them cough; when the noise makes family conversation difficult, or when it stifles it entirely? In other words, does the "taking" occur when the property interest is totally destroyed, or when it is substantially diminished?

My point of view leads me to conclude, contrary to my brothers, that the interference shown here was sufficiently substantial, direct and peculiar to impose a servitude on the plaintiffs' homes, quite as effectively as the overflights in Causby and Griggs, and the smoke and gases in Richards. I would, therefore, hold the damages constitutionally compensable.

Refer to Extract A, U.S. Constitution, 5th Amendment, and 14th Amendment.

369 U.S. 84
Thomas N. GRIGGS, Petitioner,
v.
COUNTY OF ALLEGHENY,
PENNSYLVANIA.
(Cite as 82 S. Ct. 531)
No. 81
Argued Jan. 16, 1962.
Decided March 5, 1962.
Rehearing Denied April 16, 1962.
See 369 U.S. 857, 82 S.Ct. 931.

Action by property owner against county for an alleged appropriation of his property resulting from take-off and landing of aircraft at county airport. The Court of Common Pleas, Allegheny County, dismissed exceptions taken by both parties and both parties appealed. The Pennsylvania Supreme Court, 402 Pa. 411, 168 A.2d 123, reversed the order dismissing county's exceptions and dismissed the property owner's appeal, and the United States Supreme Court granted the property owner's petition for writ of certiorari. The Supreme Court, Mr. Justice Douglas, held that where noise from aircraft landing and taking off made a home located off the end of the runway unbearable for residential use, there was a "taking" of an air easement over the property, and county, which had designed airport for public use in conformity with rules and regulations of Civil Aeronautics Administration, and not the Civil Aeronautics Board or airlines using the airport, was liable to property owner.

Reversed.

Mr. Justice Black and Mr. Justice Frankfurter dissented.

Eminent Domain

Where noise from airplanes landing and taking off made a home located off end of runway unbearable for residential use, there was a "taking" of an air easement over the property, and county, which had designed airport for public use in conformity with rules and regulations of Civil Aeronautics Administration, and not the Civil Aeronautics Board or airlines using airport, was liable to property owner. Federal Airport Act, §§ 1 et seq., 3(a), 4(a), 5, 6, 9 and (d) (1), 10, 13(a) (2), 49 U.S.C.A. §§ 1101 et seq., 1102(a), 1103, 1104, 1105, 1108 and (d), 1109, 1112(a) (2); Federal Aviation Act of 1958, § 101(24), 49 U.S.C.A. § 1301(24); U.S.C.A.Const. Amend. 14.

William A. Blair, Pittsburgh, Pa., for petitioner.

Maurice Louik, Pittsburgh, Pa., for respondent.

Mr. Justice DOUGLAS delivered the opinion of the Court.

This case is here on a petition for a writ of certiorari to the Supreme Court of Pennsylvania which we granted (366 U.S. 943, 81 S.Ct. 1672, 6 L.Ed.2d 854) because its decision (402 Pa. 411, 168 A.2d 123) seemed to be in conflict with United States v. Causby, 328 U.S. 256, 66 S.Ct. 1062, 90 L.Ed. 1206. The question is whether respondent

85

has taken an air easement over petitioner's property for which it must pay just compensation as required by the Fourteenth Amendment. Chicago, B. & Q.R. Co. v. Chicago, 166 U.S. 226, 241, 17 S.Ct. 581, 41 L.Ed. 979. The Court of Common Pleas, pursuant to customary Pennsylvania procedure, appointed a Board of Viewers to determine whether there had been a "taking" and, if so, the amount of compensation due. The Board of Viewers met upon the property; it held a hearing, and in its report found that there had been a "taking" by respondent of an air easement over petitioner's property and that the compensation payable (damages suffered) was $12,690. The Court of Common Pleas dismissed the exceptions of each party to the Board's report. On appeal, the Supreme Court of Pennsylvania decided, by a divided vote, that if there were a "taking" in the constitutional sense, the respondent was not liable.

Respondent owns and maintains the Greater Pittsburgh Airport on land which it purchased to provide airport and air-transport facilities. The airport was designed for public use in conformity with the rules and regulations of the Civil Aeronautics Administration within the scope of the National Airport Plan provided for in 49 U.S.C. § 1101 et seq., 49 U.S.C.A. § 1101 et seq. By this Act the federal Administrator is authorized and directed to prepare and continually revise a "national plan for the development of public airports." § 1102(a). For this purpose he is authorized to make grants to "sponsors" for airport development. §§ 1103, 1104. Provision is made for apportionment of grants for this purpose among the States. § 1105. The applications for projects must follow the standards prescribed by the Administrator. § 1108.

It is provided in § 1108(d) that: "No project shall be approved by the Administrator with respect to any airport unless a public agency holds good title, satisfactory to the Administrator, to the landing area of such airport or the site therefor, or gives assurance satisfactory

86

to the Administrator that such title be acquired." The United States agrees to share from 50% to 75% of the "allowable project costs," depending, so far as material here, on the class and location of the airport. § 1109.

Allowable costs payable by the Federal Government include "costs of acquiring land or interests therein or easements through or other interests in air space * * *." § 1112(a) (2).

Respondent executed three agreements with the Administrator of Civil Aeronautics in which it agreed, among other things, to abide by and adhere to the Rules and Regulations of C.A.A. and to "maintain a master plan of the airport," including "approach areas." It was provided that the "airport approach standards to be followed in this connection shall be those established by the Administrator"; and it was also agreed that respondent "will acquire such easements or other interests in lands and air space as may be necessary to perform the covenants of this paragraph." The "master plan" laid out and submitted by respondent included and required "approach areas"; and that "master plan" was approved. One "approach area" was to the northeast runway. As designed and approved, it passed over petitioner's home which is 3,250 feet from the end of that runway. The elevation at the end of that runway is 1,150.50 feet above sea level; the door sill at petitioner's residence, 1,183.64 feet; the top of petitioner's chimney, 1,219.64 feet. The slope gradient of the approach area is as 40 is to 3,250 feet or 81 feet, which leaves a clearance of 11.36 feet between the bottom of the glide angle and petitioner's chimney.

The airlines that use the airport are lessees of respondent; and the leases give them, among other things, the right "to land" and "take off." No flights were in violation of the regulations of C.A.A.; nor were any flights

87

lower than necessary for a safe landing or take-off. The planes taking off from the northeast runway observed regular flight patterns ranging from 30 feet to 300 feet over petitioner's residence; and on let-down they were within 53 feet to 153 feet.

On take-off the noise of the planes is comparable "to the noise of a riveting machine or steam hammer." On the let-down the planes make a noise comparable "to that of a noisy factory." The Board of Viewers found that "The low altitude flights over plaintiff's property caused the plaintiff and occupants of his property to become nervous and distraught, eventually causing their removal therefrom as undesirable and unbearable for their residential use." Judge Bell, dissenting below, accurately summarized the uncontroverted facts as follows:

> "Regular and almost continuous daily flights, often several minutes apart, have been made by a number of airlines directly over and very, very close to plaintiff's residence. During these flights it was often impossible for people in the house to converse or to talk on the telephone. The plaintiff and the members of his household (depending on the flight which in turn sometimes depended on the wind) were frequently unable to sleep even with ear plugs and sleeping pills; they would frequently be awakened by the flight and the noise of the planes; the windows of their home would frequently rattle and at times plaster fell down from the walls and ceilings; their health was affected and impaired, and they sometimes were compelled to sleep elsewhere. Moreover, their house was so close to the runways or path of glide that as the spokesman for the members of the Airlines Pilot Association admitted 'If we had engine failure we would have no course but to plow into your house'." 402 Pa. 411, 422, 168 A.2d 123, 128-129.

88

We start with United States v. Causby, supra, which held that the United States by low flights of its military planes over a chicken farm made the property unusable for that purpose and that therefore there had been a "taking," in the constitutional sense, of an air easement for which compensation must be made. At the time of the Causby case, Congress had placed the navigable airspace in the public domain, defining it as "airspace above the minimum safe altitudes of flight prescribed" by the C.A.A. 44 Stat. 574. We held that the path of the glide or flight for landing or taking off was not the downward reach of the "navigable airspace." 328 U.S. at 264, 66 S.Ct. 1062. Following the decision in the Causby case, Congress redefined "navigable airspace" to mean "airspace above the minimum altitudes of flight prescribed by regulations issued under this chapter, and shall include airspace needed to insure safety in take-off and landing of aircraft." 72 Stat. 739, 49 U.S.C. § 1301(24), 49 U.S.C.A. § 1301(24). By the present regulations[1] the "minimum safe altitudes" within the meaning of the statute are defined, so far as relevant here, as heights of 500 feet or 1,000 feet, "[e]xcept where necessary for takeoff or landing." But as we said in the Causby

89

case, the use of land presupposes the use of some of the airspace above it. 328 U.S. at 264, 66 S.Ct. 1062. Otherwise no home could be built, no tree planted, no fence constructed, no chimney erected. An invasion of the "superadjacent airspace" will often "affect the use of the surface of the land itself." 328 U.S. at 265, 66 S.Ct. at 1068.

It is argued that though there was a "taking," someone other than respondent was the taker—the airlines or the C.A.A. acting as an authorized representative of the United States. We think, however, that respondent, which was the promoter, owner, and lessor[2] of the airport, was in these circumstances the one who took the air easement in the constitutional sense. Respondent decided, subject to the approval of the C.A.A., where the airport would be built, what runways it would need, their direction and length, and what land and navigation easements would be needed. The Federal Government takes nothing; it is the

1. Regulation 60.17, entitled "Minimum safe altitudes, provides:

"*Except when necessary for take-off or landing,* no person shall operate an aircraft below the following altitudes:

"(a) *Anywhere.* An altitude which will permit, in the event of the failure of a power unit, an emergency landing without undue hazard to persons or property on the surface;

"(b) *Over congested areas.* Over the congested areas of cities, towns or settlements, or over an open-air assembly of persons, an altitude of *1,000 feet* above the highest obstacle within a horizontal radius of 2,000 feet from the aircraft. . . .

"(c) *Over other than congested areas.* An altitude of 500 feet above the surface, except over open water or sparsely populated areas. In such event, the aircraft shall not be operated closer than 500 feet to any person, vessel, vehicle, or structure. . . ." (Emphasis supplied except in catch lines.) 14 C.F.R. § 60.17.

2. In circumstances more opaque than this we have held lessors to their constitutional obligations. See Burton v. Wilmington Parking Auth., 365 U.S. 715, 81 S.Ct. 856, 6 L.Ed.2d 45.

local authority which decides to build an airport *vel non,* and where it is to be located. We see no difference between its responsibility for the air easements necessary for operation of the airport and its responsibility for the land on which the runways were built. Nor did the Congress when it designed the legislation for a National Airport Plan. For, as we have already noted, Congress provided in 49 U.S.C. § 1109, 49 U.S.C.A. § 1109, for the payment to the owners of airports, whose plans were approved by the Administrator, of a share of "the allowable project costs" including the "costs of acquiring land or interests therein or easements through or other interests in air space." § 1112(a) (2). A county that designed and constructed a bridge would not have a usable facility unless it had at least an easement over the land necessary for the

90

approaches to the bridge. Why should one who designs, constructs, and uses an airport be in a more favorable position so far as the Fourteenth Amendment is concerned? That the instant "taking" was "for public use" is not debatable. For respondent agreed with the C.A.A. that it would operate the airport "for the use and benefit of the public," that it would operate it "on fair and reasonable terms and without unjust discrimination," and that it would not allow any carrier to acquire "any exclusive right" to its use.

The glide path for the northeast runway is as necessary for the operation of the airport as is a surface right of way for operation of a bridge, or as is the land for the operation of a dam. See United States v. Virginia Electric Co., 365 U.S. 624, 630, 81 S.Ct. 784, 5 L.Ed.2d 838. As stated by the Supreme Court of Washington in Ackerman v. Port of Seattle, 55 Wash.2d 400, 401, 413, 348 P.2d 664, 671, 77 A.L.R.2d 1344, "* * * an adequate approach way is as necessary a part of an airport as is the ground on which the airstrip, itself, is constructed * * *." Without the "approach areas," an airport is indeed not operable. Respondent in designing it had to acquire some private property. Our conclusion is that by constitutional standards it did not acquire enough.

Reversed.

Mr. Justice BLACK, with whom Mr. Justice FRANKFURTER concurs, dissenting.

In United States v. Causby,[3] the Court held that by flying its military aircraft frequently on low landing and takeoff flights over Causby's chicken farm the United States had so disturbed the peace of the occupants and so frightened the chickens that it had "taken" a flight easement from Causby for which it was required to pay "just compensation" under the Fifth Amendment. Today the

91

Court holds that similar low landing and take-off flights, making petitioner Griggs' property "undesirable and unbearable for * * * residential use," constitute a "taking" of airspace over Griggs' property—not, however, by the owner

3. 328 U.S. 256, 66 S.Ct. 1062, 90 L.Ed. 1206.

and operator of the planes as in Causby, but by Allegheny County, the owner and operator of the Greater Pittsburgh Airport to and from which the planes fly. Although I dissented in Causby because I did not believe that the individual aircraft flights "took" property in the constitutional sense merely by going over it and because I believed that the complexities of adjusting atmospheric property rights to the air age could best be handled by Congress, I agree with the Court that the noise, vibrations and fear caused by constant and extremely low overflights in this case have so interfered with the use and enjoyment of petitioner's property as to amount to a "taking" of it under the Causby holding. I cannot agree, however, that it was the County of Allegheny that did the "taking." I think that the United States, not the Greater Pittsburgh Airport, has "taken" the airspace over Griggs' property necessary for flight.[4] While the County did design the plan for the airport, including the arrangement of its takeoff and approach areas, in order to comply with federal requirements it did so under the supervision of and subject to the approval of the Civil Aeronautics Administrator of the United States.[5]

Congress has over the years adopted a comprehensive plan for national and international air commerce, regulating in minute detail virtually every aspect of air transit—from construction and planning of ground facilities to

92

safety and methods of flight operations.[6] As part of this overall scheme of development, Congress in 1938 declared that the United States has "complete and exclusive national sovereignty in the air space above the United States"[7] and that every citizen has "a public right of freedom of transit in air commerce through the navigable air space of the United States."[8] Although in Causby the Court held that under the then existing laws and regulations the airspace used in landing and take-off was not part of the "navigable airspace" as to which all have a right of free transit, Congress has since, in 1958, enacted a new law, as part of a regulatory scheme even more comprehensive than those before it, making it clear that the "airspace needed to insure safety in take-off and landing of aircraft" is

4. We are not called on to pass on any question of "taking" under the Pennsylvania Constitution or laws.

5. 60 Stat. 174-176, as amended, 49 U.S.C. §§ 1108, 1110, 49 U.S.C.A. §§ 1108, 1110. The duties of the Civil Aeronautics Administrator have since been transferred to the Federal Aviation Agency Administrator. 72 Stat. 806-807.

6. The Federal Aviation Agency Administrator is directed to prepare and maintain a "national plan for the development of public airports in the United States" taking "into account the needs of both air commerce and private flying, the probable technological developments in the science of aeronautics [and] the probable growth and requirements of civil aeronautics." 49 U.S.C. § 1102, 49 U.S.C.A. § 1102. The detailed features of the federal regulatory and development scheme are found in 49 U.S.C. cc. 14 (Federal-Aid for Public Airport Development), 15 (International Aviation Facilities) and 20 (Federal Aviation Program).

7. 52 Stat. 1028, 49 U.S.C. § 1508, 49 U.S.C.A. § 1508.

8. 52 Stat. 980, 49 U.S.C. § 1304, 49 U.S.C.A. § 1304.

"navigable airspace."[9] Thus Congress has not only appropriated the airspace necessary for planes to fly at high altitudes throughout the country but has also provided the low altitude airspace essential for those same planes to approach and take off from airports. These airspaces are so much under the control of the Federal Government that every take-off from the every landing at

93

airports such as the Greater Pittsburgh Airport is made under the direct signal and supervisory control of some federal agent.[10]

In reaching its conclusion, however, the Court emphasizes the fact that highway bridges require approaches. Of course they do. But if the United States Highway Department purchases the approaches to a bridge, the bridge owner need not. The same is true where Congress has, as here, appropriated the airspace necessary to approach the Pittsburgh airport as well as all the other airports in the country. Despite this, however, the Court somehow finds a congressional intent to shift the burden of acquiring flight airspace to the local communities in 49 U.S.C. § 1112, 49 U.S.C.A. § 1112, which authorizes reimbursement to local communities for "necessary" acquisitions of "easements through or other interests in air space." But this is no different from the bridge-approach argument. Merely because local communities might eventually be reimbursed for the acquisition of necessary easements does not mean that local communities must acquire easements that the United States has already acquired. And where Congress has already declared airspace *free* to all—a fact not denied by the Court—pretty clearly it need not again be acquired by an airport. The "necessary" easements for which Congress authorized reimbursement in § 1112 were those "easements through or other interests in air space" necessary for the clearing and protecting of "aerial approaches" from physical "airport hazards"[11] —a duty explicitly placed on the local communities by the statute (§ 1110) and by their contract with the Government.

94

There is no such duty on the local community to acquire flight airspace. Having taken the airspace over Griggs' private property for a public use, it is the United States which owes just compensation.

9. Section 101(24) of the Federal Aviation Act of 1958 provides: " 'Navigable airspace' means airspace above the minimum altitudes of flight prescribed by regulations issued under this Act, and shall include airspace needed to insure safety in take-off and landing of aircraft." 72 Stat. 739, 49 U.S.C. § 1301(24), 49 U.S.C.A. § 1301(24).

10. 14 CFR § 60.18. The Administrator of the Federal Aviation Agency is directed to control "the use of the navigable airspace of the United States." 49 U.S.C. § 1303(c), 49 U.S.C.A. § 1303(c).

11. The term "airport hazard" means "any structure or object of natural growth . . . or any use of land . . . which obstructs the air space . . . or is otherwise hazardous to . . . landing or taking off of aircraft." 49 U.S.C. § 1101(a) (4), 49 U.S.C.A. § 1101(a) (4).

The construction of the Greater Pittsburgh Airport was financed in large part by funds supplied by the United States as part of its plan to induce localities like Allegheny County to assist in setting up a national and international air-transportation system. The Court's imposition of liability on Allegheny County, however, goes a long way toward defeating that plan because of the greatly increased financial burdens (how great one can only guess) which will hereafter fall on all the cities and counties which til now have given or may hereafter give support to the national program. I do not believe the Congress ever intended any such frustration of its own purpose.

Nor do I believe that Congress intended the wholly inequitable and unjust saddling of the entire financial burden of this part of the national program on the people of local communities like Allegheny County. The planes that take off and land at the Greater Pittsburgh Airport wind their rapid way through space not for the peculiar benefit of the citizens of Allegheny County but as part of a great, reliable transportation system of immense advantage to the whole Nation in time of peace and war. Just as it would be unfair to require petitioner and others who suffer serious and peculiar injuries by reason of these transportation flights to bear an unfair proportion of the burdens of air commerce, so it would be unfair to make Allegheny County bear expenses wholly out of proportion to the advantages it can receive from the national transportation system. I can see no justification at all for throwing this monkey wrench into Congress' finely tuned national transit mechanism. I would affirm the state court's judgment holding that the County of Allegheny has not "taken" petitioner's property.

376 P. 2d 100

Margaret K. THORNBURG, and Margaret K. Thornburg, Executrix of the Estate of Bernhart Mesch Thornburg, also known as Bernard M. Thornburg, deceased, Appellants,

v.

The PORT OF PORTLAND, a Municipal Corporation, Respondent.

Supreme Court of Oregon,

En Banc.

Argued and Submitted July 2, 1962.

Decided Nov. 7, 1962.

Action for inverse condemnation brought by property owners against owner and operator of airport. From an adverse judgment of the Circuit Court, Multnomah County, Paul R. Harris, J., the property owners appealed. The Supreme Court, Goodwin, J., held that property owner's proffered testimony concerning jet flights near his land was admissible in an action for an "inverse condemnation" based on alleged noise nuisance from planes.

Reversed and remanded.

Perry and Rossman, JJ., and McAllister, C.J., dissented.

1. Eminent Domain

A property owner claiming a taking under the eminent domain section of the Constitution must show more than merely the suffering of some damage. Const. art. 1, § 18.

2. Eminent Domain

A "taking" within meaning of the eminent domain section of the Constitution means any destruction, restriction, or interruption of common and necessary use and enjoyment of property of a person for a public purpose. Const. art. 1, § 18.

3. Eminent Domain

Easements can be taken by repeated low-level flights over private land, and when such easements have arisen, compensation must be paid to the owners of the land thus burdened. Const. art. 1, § 18.

4. Eminent Domain

If the government substantially deprives landowner of use of his land, such deprivation is a "taking" for which the government must pay, but if government merely commits some tort which does not deprive owner of use of his land, then there is no taking. Const. art. 1, § 18.

5. Eminent Domain

A nuisance can be such an invasion of rights of possessor of land as to amount to a taking, in theory at least, any time possessor is in fact ousted from the enjoyment of his land.

6. Eminent Domain

A taking occurs whenever government acts in such a way as substantially to deprive owner of useful possession of that which he owns, either by repeated trespasses or by repeated nontrespassory invasions called "nuisances."

7. Torts

A landowner has a right to be free from unreasonable interference caused by noise.

8. Eminent Domain

A nuisance can give rise to an easement, and a noise coming straight down from above one's land can ripen into a "taking" if it is persistent enough and aggravated enough, and the same kind and degree of interference with use and enjoyment of one's land can also be a taking even though the noise vector may come from some direction other than the perpendicular. Const. art. 1, § 18.

9. Eminent Domain

When government conducts an activity upon its own land which, after balancing question of reasonableness, is sufficiently disturbing to use and enjoyment of neighboring lands to amount to a taking thereof, the public and not the subservient landowner should bear the cost of such public benefit. Const. art. 1, § 18.

10. Eminent Domain

Property owner's proffered testimony concerning jet flights near his land was admissible in an action for "inverse condemnation" based on alleged noise nuisance from planes. Const. art. 1, § 18.

11. Eminent Domain

Ordinarily, in a case of continuing interference, whether it is substantial enough to constitute a taking is for the jury.

12. Eminent Domain

There can be a taking of private property by flights over land even though such flights are within the navigable airspace as defined by the law. Civil Aeronautics Act of 1938, § 601(a) (7), 49 U.S.C.A. § 551(a) (7); Const. art. 1, § 18.

13. Eminent Domain

Whether a noise nuisance caused by airplanes constitutes a taking for public use is a question for the jury. Const. art. 1, § 18.

James H. Clarke, Portland, for appellants. Wayne Hilliard, Cecil H. Greene, and Koerner, Young, McColloch & Dezendorf, Portland, on the briefs.

Lofton L. Tatum, Portland, for respondent. John G. Holden and Wood, Wood, Tatum, Mosser & Brooke, Portland, on the brief.

Before McALLISTER, C.J., and ROSSMAN, WARNER, PERRY, SLOAN, O'CONNELL, and GOODWIN, JJ.

GOODWIN, Justice.

A trial jury denied plaintiffs the compensation which they sought in an action for "inverse condemnation."[1] In so doing, the jury necessarily found that the Port of Portland had not taken the plaintiffs' property. The plaintiffs appeal.

The issues in their broadest sense concern the rights of landowners adjacent to airports and the rights of the public in the airspace near the ground. Specifically, we must decide whether a noise-nuisance can amount to a taking.

The Port of Portland owns and operates the Portland International Airport. It has the power of eminent domain. It has used this power to surround itself with a substantial curtilage, but its formal acquistition stopped short of the land of the plaintiffs. For the purposes of this case, the parties have assumed that the Port is immune from ordinary tort liability. Further, it is conceded that injuctive relief would not be in the public interest. Aircraft are not ordinarily operated by the Port itself, but by third parties which use its facilities. Air navigation and other related operations are, for all practical purposes, regulated by a federal agency. The Port merely holds the airport open to the flying public.

The plaintiffs own and reside in a dwelling house located about 6,000 feet beyond the end of one runway and directly under the glide path of aircraft using it. Their land lies about 1,500 feet beyond the end of a second runway, but about 1,000 feet to one side of the glide path of aircraft using that runway.

The plaintiffs contend that flights from both runways have resulted in a taking of their property. Their principal complaint is that the noise from jet aircraft makes their land unusable. The jets use a runway the center line of which, if extended, would pass about 1,000 feet to one side of the plaintiffs' land. Some planes pass directly over the plaintiffs' land, but these are not, for the most part, the civilian and military jets which cause the most noise.

The plaintiffs' case proceeded on two theories: (1) Systematic flights directly over their land cause a substantial interference with their use and enjoyment of that land. This interference constitutes a nuisance. Such a nuisance, if persisted in by a private party, could ripen into a prescription. Such a continuing nuisance, when maintained by government, amounts to the taking of an easement, or, more precisely, presents a jury question whether there is a taking. (2) Systematic flights which pass close to their land, even though not directly overhead, likewise constitute the taking of an easement, for the same reasons, and upon the same authority.

The Port of Portland contends that its activities do not constitute the taking of easements in the plaintiffs' land. The Port argues: (1) The plaintiffs have no right to exclude or protest flights directly over their land, if such flights are so high as to be in the public domain, i.e., within navigable airspace as

1. Inverse condemnation is the popular description of a cause of action against a governmental defendant to recover the value of property which has been taken in fact by the governmental defendant, even though no formal exercise of the power of eminent domain has been attempted by the taking agency. See, e.g., State by and through State Highway Comm. v. Stumbo et al., 222 Or. 62, 66, 352 P.2d 478, 480 (1960); Tomasek v. State Highway Comm., 196 Or. 120, 248 P.2d 703 (1952).

defined by federal law.[2] (2) The plaintiffs have no right to protest flights which do not cross the airspace above their land, since these could commit no trespass in any event. Accordingly, the Port contends, there is no interference with any legally protected interest of the plaintiffs and thus no taking of any property for which the plaintiffs are entitled to compensation. In short, the Port's theory is that the plaintiffs must endure the noise of the nearby airport with the same forbearance that is required of those who live near highways and railroads. The Port's arguments, supported as they are by substantial authority, prevailed in the lower court, even though they were not entirely responsive to the plaintiffs' case. (The plaintiffs founded their case upon a nuisance theory; the defendant answered that there was no trespass.)

The trial court proceeded as if the rights of the plaintiffs were limited by the imaginary lines that would describe a cube of airspace exactly 500 feet high and bounded on four sides by perpendicular extensions of the surface boundaries of their land. The trial court thus in effect adapted the law of trespass to the issues presented in this case, and held that unless there was a continuing trespass within the described cube of space there could be no recovery. The trial court accordingly adopted the view that even if there was a nuisance, a nuisance could not give rise to a taking.

This appeal requires us to decide whether, under the circumstances of this case, the landowner has a right to have the jury pass upon his claim. If we so hold, then we have necessarily decided that the owner's interest in the use of his land free from the inconvenience of noise coming in upon him from outside his boundaries is an interest for the taking of which the government must pay. It would, of course, remain for the jury, under proper instructions, to decide when such a taking has occurred.

There is no doubt that noise can be a nuisance. See cases collected in Annotation, 44 A.L.R.2d 1381, 1394 (1953) (dance halls); Lloyd, Noise As a Nuisance, 82 Pa. L.Rev. 567 (1934); de Funiak, Equitable Relief Against Nuisances, 38 Ky.L.J. 223 (1949); and Notes, 15 Or.L.Rev. 268 (1936). At common law, one could obtain a prescriptive right to impose an unreasonable noise upon one's neighbor, and hence an easement for a nuisance. Sturges v. Bridgman, L.R. 11 Ch.D. 852 (1879); Restatement, Property, § 451, Comment a. (The

2. The Air Commerce Act of 1926, as amended by the Civil Aeronautics Act of 1938, provided that the Civil Aeronautics Authority could prescribe air traffic rules. See 49 U.S.C. (1952) § 551(a) (7). One of these rules fixed 500 feet as the minimum safe altitude over persons, vehicles, and structures. 14 CFR 60.107 (1947 Supp.). There can be no doubt that Congress has, during all material times, denominated the airspace 500 feet above any person, vessel, vehicle or structure in other than congested areas as navigable airspace which is subject to a public right of transit. The authority of Congress to pass such legislation is bottomed on the commerce power, and the validity of the legislation is not in question. See Braniff Airways v. Nebraska State Board, 347 U.S. 590, 596, 74 S.Ct. 757, 98 L.Ed. 967 (1954); Smith v. New England Aircraft Co., Inc., 270 Mass. 511, 525, 526, 170 N.E. 385, 69 A.L.R. 300 (1930).

authorities do not all agree about when the prescriptive period begins to run,[3] but that problem is not before us now.) It is clear the freedom from unreasonable noise is a right which, in a proper case, the law will protect. On similar principles, offensive smells are treated as nuisances for which a remedy will lie. See cases collected in Annotation, 18 A.L.R.2d 1033 (1950) (slaughterhouse). It is equally clear that a reasonable volume of noise (like a reasonable olfactory insult from industrial odors) must be endured as the price of living in a modern industrial society. See generally Restatement, Torts, § § 822-831. Freedom from noise can be a legally protected right.

[1] We come then to the facts of the case at bar. At the outset the parties concede that because of the wording of the Oregon Constitution, Art. I, § 18 (eminent domain), a plaintiff aggrieved by a public activity must show that there has been a taking of his property. There must be more than merely the suffering of some damage. See, e.g., Moeller et ux. v. Multnomah County, 218 Or. 413, 424, 430, 345 P.2d 813 (1959) (See Note, 40 Or.L.Rev. 241 (1961)); Tomasek v. Oregon State Highway Comm., supra note 1.

[2] A taking within the meaning of Oregon Constitution, Art. I, § 18, has been defined as "any destruction, restriction, or interruption of the common and necessary use and enjoyment of the property of a person for a public purpose * * *." Morrison v. Clackamas County, 141 Or. 564, 568, 18 P.2d 814, 816 (1933). See Note, 16 Or.L.Rev. 155 (1937). The definition from Morrison v. Clackamas County, supra, is broad enough to cover a continuing nuisance, and hence the plaintiffs' case, unless there is some policy reason for limiting its application.

[3] Since United States v. Causby, 328 U.S. 256, 66 S.Ct. 1062, 90 L.Ed. 1206 (1946), and particularly since Griggs v. Allegheny County, 369 U.S. 84, 82 S.Ct. 531, 7 L.Ed.2d 585 (1962), we know that easements can be taken by repeated low-level flights over private land. Such easements have been found in actions against the federal government (Causby) and in actions against municipal corporations (Griggs). When such easements are said to have been taken, compensation must be paid to the owners of the lands thus burdened. Thus much appears to be settled.

It is not so well settled, however, that the easements discussed in the Causby and Griggs cases are easements to impose upon lands near an airport a servitude of noise. Courts operating upon the theory that repeated trespasses form the basis of the easement have not found it necessary to decide whether a repeated nuisance, which may or may not have been an accompaniment of a

3. Where a slaughterhouse had maintained a stench for 20 years, held: it had acquired a prescriptive right to continue the nuisance. Dana v. Valentine, 5 Metc. 8, 46 Mass. 8 (1842). See other cases collected in Annotation, 152 A.L.R. 343 (1944), and notes, 13 Harv.L.Rev. 142 (1899); 21 Notre Dame Lawyer 358 (1946); 2 Wash. & Lee L.Rev. 159 (1940). The Oregon Court has recognized (dictum) that a prescriptive right to maintain a private nuisance could be created by continuous conduct for the statutory time, although the case under study involved a trespassory invasion (drainage). Laurance et al. v. Tucker, 160 Or. 474, 85 P.2d 374 (1939).

trespass, could equally give rise to a servitude upon neighboring land. It must be remembered that in both the Causby and Griggs cases the flights were virtually at tree-top level. Accordingly, both decisions could perhaps be supported on trespass theories exclusively. Following the Causby case, several federal district courts held that while repeated flights at low levels directly over private land may amount to a taking for which compensation must be paid, repeated flights nearby but not directly overhead must be endured as mere "damages" which, for various reasons, may not be compensable. See, e.g., Moore v. United States, 185 F.Supp. 399 (N.D.Tex.1960); Freeman v. United States, 167 F.Supp. 541 (W.D.Okl.1958); and see Cheskov v. Port of Seattle, 55 Wash.2d 416, 348 P.2d 673 (1960), where the court found no taking, but held that damages might be recoverable in proper case under the Washington constitution.[4]

After the case at bar had been argued and submitted, the United States Court of Appeals for the Tenth Circuit, which had previously held in Batten v. United States, 292 F.2d 144 (10th Cir. 1961), that a complaint sounding substantially in nuisance stated a cause of action under circumstances very like those now before us, held, on the merits in the same case, that the interference with the use and enjoyment of the land complained of was a consequential damage not amounting to a taking, and adopted the rule that there must be a trespass before there can be a taking. Batten v. United States, 306 F.2d 580 (10th Cir. 1962). As pointed out in a dissent by Murrah, Chief Judge, the interference proven was substantial enough to impose a servitude upon the lands of the plaintiffs, and under the Causby and Griggs cases equally could have constituted a taking. 306 F.2d at 585. In view of the importance of the question presented in the Batten case, and in view of the strong dissent by the chief judge, it would be premature to speculate now upon the final direction the federal courts will take. We believe the dissenting view in the Batten case presents the better-reasoned analysis of the legal principles involved, and that if the majority view in the Batten case can be defended it must be defended frankly upon the ground that considerations of public policy justify the result: i.e., that private rights must yield to public convenience in this class of cases. The rationale of the case is circular. The majority said in effect that there is no taking because the damages are consequential, and the damages are consequential because there is no taking.

As we noted in a recent case which involved a different aspect of the airport problem,[5] some of the decisions reveal internal ambivalence with reference to the theory upon which they proceed. In perhaps the leading case, United

4. Unlike ours, the constitutions of several states permit the recovery of compensation for property "taken or damaged" for a public purpose. The significance of these constitutional provisions was fully discussed in Moeller v. Multnomah County, supra. Compare Oregon Constitution, Art. I, § 18, and Washington Constitution, Art. I, § 16. See also Tomasek v. Oregon State Highway Comm., supra note 1; Metzger v. City of Gresham, 152 Or. 682, 54 P.2d 311 (1936); Morrison v. Clackamas County, supra. Compare Levene et ux. v. City of Salem, 191 Or. 182, 197, 229 P.2d 255 (1951), where we talked as if a trespass could be either a "mere nuisance" (presumably a noncompensable one) or a "taking."

5. Atkinson et al. v. Bernard, Inc., 223 Or. 624, 355 P.2d 229 (1960).

States v. Causby, supra, the court used language appropriate to the law of trespass more or less interchangeably with language appropriate to the law of nuisance.[6] It appears that the majority in the Batten case accepted the rule that only a trespass in the airspace directly overhead can give rise to an action for a taking, and that nuisance principles ought not to be applied in actions against the government. This may be a cogent policy argument, but it does violence to the law of servitudes.

The fact that the defendant in the case at bar is a governmental agency is of obvious importance, but, before we can decide whether to adopt one rule for governmental defendants and another for private parties, we need to know what the alternatives are. We need to know what the constitutional protection of private property means when balanced against those policy considerations which arise out of the governmental character of the defendant: In other words, as is frequently the case, we must balance apparently conflicting principles before we can tell whether or not this particular case is one for the jury.

While not every wrong committed by government will amount to a taking of private property, there are some wrongs which do constitute a taking. See, e.g., Cereghino et al. v. State by and through State Hwy. Comm., 74 Adv.Sh. 547, 370 P.2d 694 (1962), and Moeller et ux. v. Multnomah County, supra. Many of these wrongs involve trespassory activities. The inquiry must not beg the question, however, whether a nuisance can also amount to a taking. Whether a nuisance has, in fact, produced the results alleged by the plaintiff in this case is another matter; first we must decide whether a nusiance can ever constitute a taking. If there is a taking, then what is taken must be paid for. Armstrong v. United States, 364 U.S. 40, 48, 80 S.Ct. 1563, 4 L.Ed.2d 1554 (1960). And see Annotation, 84 A.L.R.2d 348, Eminent Domain–View–Interference (1962).

[4] The subject matter of inverse condemnation is always private property. Narrowed down to a meaningful definition for the purposes of this case, however, the only "property" right of the possessor of land which has any value is his ability to use and enjoy his land. This is true whatever estate the possessor holds, whether in fee, or for life, or for years, or merely an incorporeal interest such as an easement or profit. See Ackerman v. Port of Seattle, 55 Wash.2d 400, 348 P.2d 664, 77 A.L.R.2d 1344 (1960). If the government substantially deprives the owner of the use of his land, such deprivation is a taking for which the government must pay.[7] Cereghino et al. v. State Hwy. Comm., supra;

6. The case says that the landowner owns at least as much of the space above the ground as he can occupy or use in connection with the land, and that the landowner as an incident of ownership has a claim to it and invasions of it are in the same category as invasions of the surface. 328 U.S. at 264, 265, 66 S.Ct. 1062. In the same opinion, the court also says that "[f]lights over private land are not a taking, unless they are so low and so frequent as to be a direct and immediate interference with the enjoyment and use of the land. . . ." 328 U.S. at 266, 66 S.Ct. at 1068. The commingling of trespass and nuisance language has been noted elsewhere. See 51 Northw.U.L.Rev. 346 (1962).

7. Willamette Iron Works v. Oregon R. & Nav. Co., 26 Or. 224, 37 P. 1016, 29 L.R.A. 88 (1894); McQuaid v. Portland & V. Ry. Co., 18 Or. 237, 22 P. 899 (1889). See also Kurtz v. Southern Pacific, 80 Or. 213, 155 P. 367, 156 P. 794 (1916). Cf. Brand v. Multnomah County, 38 Or. 79, 60 P. 390, 62 P. 209, 50 L.R.A. 389 (1900).

Ackerman v. Port of Seattle, supra. If, on the other hand, the government merely commits some tort which does not deprive the owner of the use of his land, then there is no taking.[8]

[5] Therefore, unless there is some reason of public policy which bars compensation in cases of governmental nuisance as a matter of law, there is a question, in each case, as a matter of fact, whether or not the governmental activity complained of has resulted in so substantial an interference with use and enjoyment of one's land as to amount to a taking of private property for public use. This factual question, again barring some rule which says we may not ask it, is equally relevant whether the taking is trespassory or by a nuisance. A nuisance can be such an invasion of the rights of a possessor as to amount to a taking, in theory at least, any time a possessor is in fact ousted from the enjoyment of his land.

It now becomes relevant to consider whether a jury ought to be permitted to find that a given nuisance is so aggravated as to be a taking when the perpetrator of the nuisance happens to be the government. The Port argues that the plight of the plaintiffs in this case is indistinguishable from that of thousands of their fellow countrymen whose homes abut highways and railroads and who endure the noise without complaint. Granting the similarity, it must be noted, however, that the matter is one of degree.[9] We do not decide that the positions of the parties are the same. The Port points to our previous decisions in support of the proposition that nuisance (nontrespassory) invasions by government are not compensable. The cases cited by the Port did not, however, hold that a nuisance so aggravated as to amount to a complete ouster or deprivation of the beneficial use of property was not a taking. That question does not appear to have been passed upon by our court. But cf. Wilson v. City of Portland, 132 Or. 509, 514, 285 P. 1030 (1930), where there is *dictum* to the effect that nontrespassory incursions give rise to no liability. There are cases elsewhere which tend to support the Port's theory that nuisances, when committed by government, are "legal" and therefore can never be a taking in the constitutional sense, but must always be endured with fortitude. Indeed, some authorities hold that the king can do no wrong and that the government never perpetrates a nuisance. See cases

8. The general rule is thus stated by Nichols:

". . . [W]hen a municipal or a public service corporation, or other party to whom the power of eminent domain can be constitutionally delegated, inflicts injury upon private land under authority of and in compliance with an act of the legislature, and there has been no want of reasonable care or skill in the execution of the power, such party is not liable in an action at law for such injury, even though the same act if done without legislative sanction would be actionable, unless the injury is of such a character as to deprive the owner of the use and possession of his land, or compensation is required by special statutory or constitutional provision whenever property is damaged by the construction of a public improvement [citing cases]." 2 Nichols, Eminent Domain 293, § 6.38(1).

See also 4 Nichols, Eminent Domain 476, § 14.1(1), and cases collected in the annotation thereto.

9. ". . . The law is not indifferent to considerations of degree." Cardozo, J., concurring in Schechter Poultry Corp. v. United States, 295 U.S. 495, 554, 55 S.Ct. 837, 853, 79 L.Ed. 1570, 97 A.L.R. 947.

noted in 66 C.J.S. Nuisances § 17, p. 761. Again, "lawful" nuisances have been held to be of such public desirability (utility) that only those portions of the invasion that could be severed from the whole and characterized as trespass could be considered in an action for damages. See, e.g., Richards v. Washington Terminal Co., 233 U.S. 546, 34 S.Ct. 654, 58 L.Ed. 1088, L.R.A.1915A, 887 (1914), holding that railroad noises and smoke (but not soot) must be endured where the conduct that created the nuisance is in the public interest and has been encouraged by law. The reason for assigning mystical power to trespass *quare clausum fregit* is elusive. But Richards v. Washington Terminal Co. did not say that the public interest demands that all governmentally approved activities (except trespass) be endured without compensation. We have found no case which goes that far, and we doubt that the constitutional right to compensation can be so construed.

[6] The plaintiffs concede that single-instance torts, as torts, are not compensable. Inverse condemnation, however, provides the remedy where an injunction would not be in the public interest, and where the continued interference amounts to a taking for which the constitution demands a remedy. In summary, a taking occurs whenever government acts in such a way as substantially to deprive an owner of the useful possession of that which he owns, either by repeated trespasses or by repeated nontrespassory invasions called "nuisance." If reparations are to be denied, they should be denied for reasons of policy which are themselves strong enough to counterbalance the constitutional demand that reparations be paid. None has been pointed out to us in this case.

[7,8] If we accept, as we must upon established principles of the law of servitudes, the validity of the propositions that a noise can be a nuisance; that a nuisance can give rise to an easement; and that a noise coming straight down from above one's land can ripen into a taking if it is persistent enough and aggravated enough, then logically the same kind and degree of interference with the use and enjoyment of one's land can also be a taking even though the noise vector may come from some direction other than the perpendicular.

If a landowner has a right to be free from unreasonable interference caused by noise, as we hold that he has, then when does the noise burden become so unreasonable that the government must pay for the privilege of being permitted to continue to make the noise? Logically, the answer has to be given by the trier of fact (subject to the usual exercise of the proper function of the court in screening the evidence). See Restatement, Torts, § 826, Comment d. It may be contended that the jury is an imperfect instrument in these cases, but such an argument raises constitutional and legislative questions that are not now before us. See Holden v. Pioneer Broadcasting Co., 228 Or. 405, 365 P.2d 845.

While it is no doubt anticipatory to advert to the problem of instructing the jury in cases of this kind, it is relevant to point out that the nuisance theory provides the jury a useful method for balancing the gravity of the harm to the plaintiff against the social utility of the airport's conduct, in a way that would not be available if the trespass theory were used. In Restatement, Torts, §§ 826-831, we find principles for balancing gravity against utility which can be adapted to jury instruction so that the question of reasonableness need not be any more mysterious to the jury in this type of case than it is in an automobile accident case. The balancing of private rights and public necessity is not a novel problem.[10]

[9,10] Whether expressed in so many words or not, the principle found in the Causby, Griggs, and Ackerman cases is that when the government conducts an activity upon its own land which, after balancing the question of reasonableness, is sufficiently disturbing to the use and enjoyment of neighboring lands to amount to a taking thereof, then the public, and not the subservient landowner, should bear the cost of such public benefit. Under this principle, it was error to exclude the plaintiffs' proffered testimony concerning the jet flights near his land. The real question was not one of perpendicular extension of surface boundaries into the airspace, but a question of reasonableness based upon nuisance theories.[11] In effect, the inquiry should have been whether the government had undertaken a course of conduct on its own land which, in simple fairness to its neighbors, required it to obtain more land so that the substantial burdens of the activity would fall upon public land, rather than upon that of involuntary contributors who happen to lie in the path of progress.

[11] As noted above, this court has expressed a policy against allowing compensation in several situations where there was no actual physical injury to the real property. The cases used terms such as "consequential damages,"[12] or "damages which do not amount to a 'taking',"[13] or *"damnum absque injuria."*[14] Such expressions describe conclusions that the court reached when it had decided that the facts involved did not measure up to the standard necessary for a "taking." Such injuries were then held to be noncompensable as a matter of law, under the policy against allowing compensation for mere "damages." Such decisions, which were no doubt right in cases of single-instance wrongs, prove too much when applied to continuing and substantial interference with the use and enjoyment of property. Ordinarily, in a case of a continuing interference, whether it is substantial enough to constitute a taking will be for the jury to determine.

10. See Madison v. Copper Co. [Madison v. Ducktown Sulphur, Copper & Iron Co., 113 Tenn. 331, 83 S.W. 658], supra, where damages were allowed and the injunction was refused. And see the related case of State of Georgia v. Tennessee Copper Co., 206 U.S. 230, 27 S.Ct. 618, 51 L.Ed. 1038, 11 Ann.Cas. 488 (1907); 237 U.S. 474, 35 S.Ct. 631, 59 L.Ed. 1054 (1915); 240 U.S. 650, 36 S.Ct. 465, 60 L.Ed. 846 (1916). Similar considerations are discussed in Booth-Kelly Lumber Co. v. City of Eugene, 67 Or. 381, 136 P. 29 (1913) and York et ux. v. Stallings et al., 217 Or. 13, 341 P.2d 529(1959).

11. See Kellogg v. Mertens (La.App.) 30 So.2d 777 (1947), and cases discussed in Amphitheaters, Inc. v. Portland Meadows, 184 Or. 336, 198 P.2d 847, 5 A.L.R.2d 690 (1948), where the plaintiffs sought damages at law for a nuisance from excessive lights. And see York et ux. v. Stallings et al., supra note 10 (injunction denied); and Note, Airplane Noise: Problem in Tort Law and Federalism, 74 Harv.L.Rev. 1581 (1961). Cf. Antonik v. Chamberlain, 81 Ohio App. 465, 475, 477, 78 N.E.2d 752 (1947).

12. Brand v. Multnomah County, 38 Or. at 92, 60 P. 390, 62 P. 209, 50 L.R.A. 389.

13. Moeller et ux. v. Multnomah County, 218 Or. supra, at 427, 345 P.2d, at 820.

14. Barrett et al. v. Union Bridge Co. (on merits) 117 Or. 220, 243 P. 93, 45 A.L.R. 521 (on petition for rehearing) 117 Or. 566, 578, 245 P. 308, 45 A.L.R. 527 (1926), quoting with approval Less v. City of Butte, 28 Mont. 27, 31, 72 P. 140, 61 L.R.A. 601, 98 Am.St.Rep. 545 (1903).

Another assignment of error in the case at bar challenges the failure of the court to give a requested instruction with respect to low-level flights directly over plaintiffs' land.[15] The court instead instructed the jury that only such flights as were conducted over the land at altitudes of less than 500 feet could constitute a taking.[16]

[12] The challenged instruction requires us to decide when, if ever, an airport can be liable for taking property because it permits flights to and from it over private land, but within "navigable airspace." On this point, there is no doubt that a taking of private property can occur even though the flights are within navigable airspace as defined by law if the flights are below 500 feet. Matson v. United States, 171 F.Supp. 283, 145 Ct.Cl. 225 (1959), held that the plaintiff should recover for a taking, even though the court recognized that the taking was accomplished in what today would be navigable airspace.[17] Griggs v. Allegheny County, supra, is a square holding that taking of private property can be accomplished by planes taking off and landing within navigable airspace. 369 U.S. 84, 82 S.Ct. 531, 533, 7 L.Ed.2d 585, 588. There is, therefore, no merit in the defense argument that all flights within the navigable airspace are automatically free from liability.[18] The debate centers on the legal effect of the 500-foot rule.

The Port's argument that flights above 500 feet are immune from private litigation seems to be based on two grounds:

(1) As a result of the legislation by Congress in denominating navigable airspace and declaring a public right of transit through it, the landowner cannot

15. Requested:

"If you find from the evidence in this case that there have been flights of airplanes over plaintiffs' property originating from and going into the defendant airport during the period complained of in plaintiff's second amended complaint, and if you further find that such flights were at such a low altitude and at such a frequency over plaintiffs' property as to be a direct and an immediate interference with the use and enjoyment thereof, then I instruct you that said interference would constitute a partial taking of the plaintiffs' property under the Constitution of the United States and the State of Oregon."

16. Given:

". . . I instruct you that under the law, if you find that the aircraft which may have flown over the plaintiffs' property during the period complained of were flown at heights of five hundred feet or greater above the property, such flights are within the navigable airspace and cannot be made the basis of any recovery for the plaintiffs here and your verdict must be for the defendant."

17. In Matson v. United States, supra, the court said:

". . . We do not think, however, that the change in the definition of navigable airspace affects plaintiffs' causes of action. The Government's easement over plaintiffs' property may be perpetual. Although today navigable airspace with its public rights of transit . . . includes the glide, its use by the United States or other aeroplane operators at heights below the minimum altitudes of flight except where necessary for take-off or landing may require compensation. . . ." 171 F.Supp. at 285.

18. Since navigable airspace now includes both the cruising altitudes and the space needed for the glide, it is meaningless to say that flights in the navigable airspace cannot constitute a servitude on land. It is necessary to know how the flights affect the land. See Griggs v. Allegheny County, supra.

claim there has been a "trespass" through a column of air which he does not own.[19] Ownership of the navigable airspace is said to be in the public.[20]

(2) As a result of the same legislation, the landowner is in a position analogous to that of a person abutting a highway or a railroad right-of-way who must be content with the incidental inconveniences that are unavoidably attendant upon those operations.[21]

The instruction given below forces a choice between consistency, which is on the side of the plaintiffs, and public convenience, which is on the side of the Port. Logically, it makes no difference to a plaintiff disturbed in the use of his property whether the disturbing flights pass 501 feet or 499 feet above his land. If he is in fact ousted from the legitimate enjoyment of his land, it is to him an academic matter that the planes which have ousted him did not fly below 500 feet.[22] The rule adopted by the majority of the state and federal courts is, then, an arbitrary one. The barring of actions when the flights are above 500 feet is also difficult to reconcile with the theory that recovery should be based upon nuisance concepts rather than upon the trespass theory which we have rejected. Whether a plaintiff is entitled to recover should depend upon the fact of a taking, and not upon an arbitrary rule. The ultimate question is whether there was a sufficient interference with the landowner's use and enjoyment to be a taking.

It is sterile formality to say that the government takes an easement in private property when it repeatedly sends aircraft directly over the land at altitudes so low as to render the land unusable by its owner, but does not take an easement when it sends aircraft a few feet to the right or left of the

19. Title 49 U.S.C. (1952):

§ 176(a). "The United States of America is declared to possess and exercise complete and exclusive national sovereignty in the airspace above the United States . . ."

§ 403. "There is recognized and declared to exist in behalf of any citizen of the United States a public right of freedom of transit in air commerce through the navigable airspace of the United States."

§ 180. "As used in sections 171, 174-177, and 179-184 of this title, the term 'navigable airspace' means airspace above the minimum safe altitudes of flight prescribed by the Civil Aeronautics Authority, and such navigable airspace shall be subject to a public right of freedom of interstate and foreign air navigation in conformity with the requirements of said sections."

20. We need not here consider whether such ownership of the airspace is in the United States or in the individual states. See 57 Mich.L.Rev. 1214, 1223 (1959).

21. Brand v. Multnomah County, supra note 7; Richards v. Washington Terminal Co., 233 U.S. 546, 34 S.Ct. 654, 58 L.Ed. 1088, supra; and Matson v. United States, 171 F.Supp. 283, 145 Ct.Cl. 225, supra.

22. See 14 J. Air L. & Com. 112, 116, discussing a decision to the effect that "[t]he height at which an airplane operator may pass above the surface without trespassing is a question depending for solution on the facts in the particular case, and this question is unaffected by the regulations promulgated by the Department of Commerce, under the Air Commerce Act of 1926 . . . ." Cory v. Physical Culture Hotel, 14 F. Supp. 977, 982 (W.D.N.Y.1936). In any event, unless experts, equipped with the necessary instruments, have measured each flight, it is highly unlikely that trustworthy evidence would be produced to prove the exact altitude of flights over private land.

perpendicular boundaries (thereby rendering the same land equally unusable). The line on the ground which marks the landowner's right to deflect surface invaders has no particular relevance when the invasion is a noise nuisance. Neither is a 500-foot ceiling relevant, desirable though it may be as an administrative device. If the interest to be protected is worth protecting at all, it is necessary to employ a system of rules that will meet the problem. Whatever virtue the establishment of a 500-foot floor under the cruising flight of aircraft may have as a matter of public safety, there can be only one sound reason to make it a rule of the law of real property. That reason ought to be the knowledge, derived from factual data, that flights above 500 feet do not disturb the ordinary, reasonable landowner. This may be true. We do not know that it is. It may well be that only the most sensitive are offended by such flights. It may equally be true that some of the aircraft now in use are so disturbing to those on the ground that 500 feet of air will not provide protection to the landowner below. We are not justified in adopting the 500-foot rule as a rule of property law in cases of this character merely because to do so might make our work easier. The trier of fact in each case is best able to work out the solution. The difficulty was foreseen in the Causby case.[23] Congress may very properly declare certain airspace to be in the public domain for navigational purposes, but it does not necessarily follow that rights of navigation may be exercised unreasonably. The power to invade the rights of servient landowners no doubt reposes in the federal government, but there is a point beyond which such power may not be exercised without compensation. United States v. Causby, supra. The same limitation applies to lesser governmental agencies.[24] See Griggs v. Allegheny County, supra.

Unfortunately for trial judges trying to formulate instructions for juries, the cases have not dealt with the instructions to be given to the laymen who must work out the answer under Oregon law. In submitting to a jury a case such as we have before us, the trial court is confronted with the need to verbalize rules as abstract as any to be found in the law, but, as we have said before,[25] the ingenuity of trial judges in formulating meaningful instructions to juries is usually equal to the task.

23. "The airplane is part of the modern environment of life, and the inconveniences which it causes are normally not compensable under the Fifth Amendment. The airspace, apart from the immediate reaches above the land, is part of the public domain. We need not determine at this time what those precise limits are. Flights over private land are not a taking, unless they are so low and so frequent as to be a direct and immediate interference with the enjoyment and use of the land. We need not speculate on that phase of the present case. For the findings of the Court of Claims plainly established that there was a diminution in value of the property and that the frequent, low-level flights were the direct and immediate cause. We agree with the Court of Claims that a servitude has been imposed upon the land." United States v. Causby, supra 328 U.S. at 266, 267, 66 S.Ct. at 1068.

24. The question of who, under the current Federal definition of navigable airspace, ought to be liable for the taking is discussed in Comment, 57 Mich.L.Rev. 1214, 1225 (1959), and the possibility is suggested that suits could be brought against the United States. See also Harvey, Landowners' Rights in the Air Age: The Airport Dilemma, 56 Mich.L.Rev. 1313, 1326 (1958).

25. Williamson v. McKenna, 223 Or. 366, 401, 354 P.2d 56 (1960).

The idea that must be expressed to the jury is that before the plaintiff may recover for a taking of his property he must show by the necessary proof that the activities of the government are unreasonably interfering with his use of his property, and in so substantial a way as to deprive him of the practical enjoyment of his land. This loss must then be translated factually by the jury into a reduction in the market value of the land.

[13] We cannot say, as a matter of law, that jet or rocket or some other kind of noise within 500 feet, or within some other number of feet, of private land might not in a particular case cause a taking for public use. The question in each case must be decided by an appropriate tribunal. Our present constitution places this duty upon the jury. If the jury proves unequal to the task, that, as noted above, is a legislative problem. If the case should arise when it is claimed that insufficient evidence was placed before the jury to support a verdict, then will be time enough to pass upon the amount of evidence necessary to get to the jury. In the case at bar, much of the evidence was excluded. As we have noted, this exclusion was error.

Other assignments of error challenge various rulings which were made in a logical and consistent pattern which followed from the able trial court's view of the case as one controlled essentially by trespass concepts. On another trial, these rulings are not likely to be repeated, and need not detain us further now.

Reversed and remanded.

PERRY, Justice (dissenting).

I am unable to agree with the majority's views of the law of eminent domain. It should be noted that to reach a reversal of the judgment of the trial court, the majority rely upon the law of nuisance. The majority seem to admit that this has never been the law of this state, but argue that it should be. So far as I have been able to ascertain, no jurisdiction whose constitution reads as does ours has ever sustained such a proposition.

In substance, plaintiffs' assignments of error are: (1) the trial court refused to submit to the jury as evidence of a taking, evidence that airplanes did travel directly over the property owned by plaintiffs at a height of more than 500 feet, and (2) the trial court refused to submit to the jury evidence of airplane flights which do not travel over the plaintiffs' property but over property adjacent thereto. It is these adjacent flights which, if considered, must rest solely upon the law of nuisance.

Considering first the issue of flights above the 500-foot level, I am of the opinion that such flights may be considered in determining whether there has been a "taking" in the constitutional sense.

In the case of United States v. Causby, 328 U.S. 256, 66 S.Ct. 1062, 90 L.Ed. 1206, the rule of law was established that ownership in land could not be considered in this space age as extending upward "to the periphery of the universe" and that therefore Congress had the authority to declare that all navigable airspace above our land was a part of the public domain.

Congress had defined navigable airspace as that airspace above the minimum safe altitude of flight as prescribed by the Civil Aeronautics Authority. As applied to the matter before us, the minimum airspace established for safety is

500 feet. At first blush it would appear that all airspace above the 500-foot level of the plaintiffs' property, being within the public domain, plaintiffs would have no proprietary interest therein which could be taken, but I do not believe this conclusion can be sustained.

Subsequent to the determination of United States v. Causby, supra, the Civil Aeronautics Authority included in its determination of airspace the glide path and the take-off path to and from the 500-foot level to the airport. Griggs v. Allegheny County, 369 U.S. 84, 82 S.Ct. 531, 7 L.Ed.2d 585. The Supreme Court of the United States, in considering the effect of this additional regulation within the scope of the national airport plan, provided in 49 U.S.C.A. § 1101 et seq., stated that private ownership in land "presupposes" the use of some of the airspace above. The court therefore held there was a constitutional taking of an air easement over the plaintiff's property line directly in the glide and ascent path of the planes.

From this latter case it appears that the power of Congress to establish a navigable airspace as public domain may not authorize a trespass above the owner's property, if, as a consequence thereof, there is injury to the owner's reasonable use and enjoyment of his land.

It seems to me this is a proper rule to balance public and private interests arising from the abolishment of the common-law rule that ownership in land extended upward to the periphery of the universe, therefore, where the flight directly over the land, by reason of noise and vibration, can be said in fact to cause serious interference in the owner's use and enjoyment of the property, it is a trespass, which is a constitutional taking, and requires full compensation.

In the matter before us, however, after searching the record, I am unable to find any evidence that would support a judgment of a taking, based on interference with the plaintiff's use and enjoyment of the land by airplane flights above the 500-foot level. Therefore, in my opinion, the trial court did not err in refusing to submit this issue to the jury.

Turning now to the issue presented as to whether the flights over the lands of adjacent owners, which create a noise nuisance, can constitute a taking of the plaintiffs' property in a constitutional sense.

So far as material, our constitution, which provides for just compensation for property taken, reads as follows:

> "Private property shall not be taken for public use, * * * without just compensation." Art. I, § 18.

In the recent case of Cereghino v. State by and through State Hwy. Comm., 74 Adv. Sh. 547, 370 P.2d 694, a case of inverse condemnation, this court pointed out that the taking of property in the constitutional sense was the taking of all or a part of an individual's possessory right in the property, not just interference with its use and enjoyment. The court stated:

> "The Fifth Amendment of the Constitution of the United States and Article I, Section 18, of the Oregon Constitution are identical in language and meaning. The word 'property' in these provisions is not 'used in its vulgar and untechnical sense of the physical thing with respect to which

> the citizen exercises rights recognized by law', but 'to denote the group of rights inhering in the citizen's relation to the physical thing, as the right to possess, use and dispose of it'. United States v. General Motors Corp., 323 U.S. 373, 377-378, 65 S.Ct. 357, 359, 89 L.Ed. 311, 156 A.L.R. 390. When the sovereign exercises the power of eminent domain 'it deals with what lawyers term the individual's "interest" in the thing in question. That interest may comprise the group of rights for which the shorthand term is "a fee simple" or it may be an interest known as an "estate or tenancy for years," as in the present instance'. Ibid. See 1 Lewis, Eminent Domain (3d ed.) § § 63, 64. Or it may be such a right as is involved in this case."

That this same rule as to a constitutional taking in an inverse condemnation suit is adhered to by the United States is found in United States v. Causby, supra. In that case government planes (heavy bombers) were flown at an elevation of approximately 87 feet directly over the Causby property as they took off and returned to the airfield. The court stated:

> "* * * If, by reason of the frequency and altitude of the flights, respondents could not use this land for any purpose, their loss would be complete. It would be as complete as if the United States had entered upon the surface of the land and taken exclusive possession of it.
>
> "We agree that in those circumstances there would be a taking. *Though it would be only an easement of flight which was taken, that easement,* if permanent and not merely temporary, normally would be the equivalent of a *fee interest.* It would be a definite exercise of complete dominion and control *over the surface of the land.* The fact that the planes never touched the surface would be as irrelevant as the absence in this day of the feudal livery of seisin on the transfer of real estate. The owner's right to possess and exploit the land—that is to say, his beneficial ownership of it—would be destroyed. It would not be a case of incidental damages arising from a legalized nuisance such as was involved in Richards v. Washington Terminal Co., 233 U.S. 546, 34 S.Ct. 654, 58 L.Ed. 1088. In that case property owners whose lands adjoined a railroad line were denied recovery for damages resulting from the noise, vibrations, smoke and the like incidental to the operations of the trains. *In the supposed case, the line of flight is over the land. And the land is appropriated as directly and completely as if it were used for the runways themselves.*" (Emphasis mine.)

Again, that there may be no question of the rule of law, the court remanded the case for an accurate description of the easement taken. To the same effect is the recent case of Griggs v. Allegheny County, supra.

That the definition of a constitutional taking has consistently been grounded in the appropriation of an interest in the realty itself has been a rule of law of long standing under the Constitution of the United States is shown by the case of Portsmouth Harbor Land & Hotel Co. v. United States, 260 U.S. 327, 43 S.Ct. 135, 67 L.Ed. 287. In this case damages were sought in inverse condemnation because of the establishment of a fort in which there were gun emplacements and shells were fired over and across the plaintiff's land. Mr. Justice Holmes, speaking for the court, said: "This is a claim in respect of land which, *or an interest in which,* is alleged to have been taken by the United States Government. * * *" (Italics mine.)

This court has always recognized and maintained this distinction between the loss of a proprietary right and damage in inverse condemnation proceedings. This is borne out by the cases cited by the majority.

In Willamette Iron Works v. Oregon R. & Nav. Co., 26 Or. 224, 37 P. 1016, 29 L.R.A. 88, this court carefully pointed out that the owner of property adjacent to a street has a proprietary interest in the street. And thus having a proprietary interest, this interest cannot be taken without just compensation.

This same thought is carried out in the case of McQuaid v. Portland & V. Ry. Co., 18 Or. 237, 22 P. 899, and to show that the court had in mind the distinction between a constitutional taking for which compensation must be paid and the creation of a nuisance which does not require compensation, I quote:

> "* * * The latter will, doubtless, be obliged to submit to the ordinary inconveniences and consequences which the construction of a railroad track, and the moving of a locomotive and cars thereon, occasion—be compelled to endure the smoke, noise, and screeching which naturally result from the use of that character of vehicles; but they cannot be deprived of the right of ingress and egress, to and from their premises, without compensation. * * *"

In Brand v. Multnomah County, 38 Or. 79, 60 P. 390, 62 P. 209, 50 L.R.A. 389, also cited, the court simply held that a change of grade in a street did not create an additional servitude upon an abutting owner's interest in the street. This case has no application to the matter at hand.

In Kurtz v. Southern Pacific Co., 80 Or. 213, 155 P. 367, 156 P. 794, also cited, the basis of relief in the original opinion of the court is somewhat obscure, but no doubt is left in the opinion on rehearing. The relief of injunction was granted upon the fact that there had been no prior purchase or condemnation of the owner's proprietary interest in the land, "an easement of ingress and egress," the court stating:

> "The evidence discloses that the spur track of which complaint is made is a special injury affecting no other property owner than plaintiff, that it will materially and permanently affect his ingress and egress to and from his lots, and consequently his property rights are invaded in a manner which can only be lawfully done by compromise or condemnation."

Not a single Oregon case will support the theory that a mere nuisance can be considered a taking, as provided in our constitution, nor does any other jurisdiction where the language of the constitution is similar to ours hold that a mere nuisance can be considered a taking, nor does the majority cite any case so holding. The reason for this is fundamental. The law of trespass and nuisance is based upon different concepts of social justice.

A nuisance, although a tort, does not contemplate a physical invasion of the property of another, but the use of a person's own property in such a way as to interfere with another's free enjoyment of his property.

> "A nuisance, in the ordinary sense in which the word is used, is any thing that produces an annoyance—any thing that disturbs one or is offensive; but in legal phraseology it is applied to that class of wrongs that arise from the unreasonable, unwarrantable or unlawful use by a person of his own property, real or personal, or from his own improper, indecent or unlawful personal conduct, working an obstruction of, or injury to, a right of another or of the public, and producing such material annoyance, inconvenience, discomfort or hurt, that the law will presume a consequent damage. * * *." 1 Wood on Nuisances, 3d Ed., § 1, page 1.

While a nuisance may cause as much damage to a person's enjoyment of the use of his property as a trespass, this does not mean that because an individual has suffered a damage, this damage requires compensation by the public.

> "It goes without saying that the courts have never construed the 'just compensation' clause of a federal or state constitution as requiring payment for all injuries imposed upon persons or property by acts of government. Any such requirement would make government itself impossible. No legislature can enact an important statute which does not directly or indirectly impose a material loss on some property owners. The imposition of a tax, the establishment of a new banking system or currency reform, the enactment of a new protective tariff, will often inflict losses on many private citizens far in excess of the total loss imposed by the most drastic act of condemnation in the history of the world. Yet no compensation for these losses is required." 1 Orgal on Valuation Under Eminent Domain, 2d Ed., § 1, page 5.

Governmental acts may be detrimental to the personal interests of adjoining land owners, but this does not constitute a taking.

> "Sanitary Dist. [of Rockford] v. Johnson, 343 Ill. 11, 174 N.E. 862 (1931) (sewage reduction plant); [City of] Winchester v. Ring, 312 Ill. 544, 144 N.E. 333, 36 A.L.R. 520 (1924) (cemetery); Schuler v. Wilson, 322 Ill. 503, 153 N.E. 737, 48 A.L.R. 1027 (1926) (school); Frazer v. Chicago, 186 Ill. 480, 57 N.E. 1055, 51 L.R.A. 306 (1900) (smallpox hospital); Mayfield v. Board of Education, 118 Kan. 138, 233 Pac. 1024 (1925) (school); Barry v. Smith, 191 Mass. 78, 77 N.E. 1099, 5 L.R.A. (N.S.) 1028 (1906) (contagious disease hospital). In Conger v. Pierce County, 116 Wash. 27, 198 Pac. 377, 18 A.L.R. 393 (1921) the court said: 'Private property may be damaged, and its value lessened because it is located close to some public buildings, such as a jail, or hospital, or public hall, yet such damage is purely incidental and not recoverable. The noise consequent on the operation of railroad trains upon a private right of way may depreciate the value of adjoining private property, and be an

annoyance to those living in the immediate neighborhood, but such damage is purely consequential and is not recoverable.' " 1 Orgal on Valuation Under Eminent Domain, 2d Ed., § 1, page 6.

Practically all human activities engaged in carrying out a commercial enterprise may interfere with someone's enjoyment of his property. It is the right of an owner of land to use his land in any lawful manner, and it is only when the manner of use creates a grave interference with another's enjoyment of his property that the law will seek to redress this type of wrong. This is a natural requirement of organized society. There must be some give and take to promote the well-being of all. The underlying basis in nuisance law is the common-sense thought that in organized society there must be an adjustment between reasonable use and personal discomfort. No such consideration is involved in the law of trespass.

Trespass of property which, as has been pointed out, effects a taking in a constitutional sense, comprehends a physical invasion of the property either by the person or by causing a physical object to enter upon or over the property of another. Martin et ux. v. Reynolds Metals Co., 221 Or. 86, 342 P.2d 790.

> "One who intentionally and without a consensual or other privilege
>
> "(a) enters land in possession of another or any part thereof or causes a thing or third person so to do, or
>
> "(b) remains thereon, or
>
> "(c) permits to remain thereon a thing which the actor or his predecessor in legal interest brought thereon in the manner stated in §§ 160 and 161,
>
> "is liable as a trespasser to the other irrespective of whether harm is thereby caused to any of his legally protected interests." Restatement of the Law, Torts, Vol. 1, § 158.

Therefore, it is the taking of an owner's possessory interest in land as compared with interfering with an owner's use and enjoyment of his land that distinguishes a trespass which is a "taking" from a nuisance, which is not.

> "There is a distinction between a nuisance and a trespass, although many things are sometimes called nuisances which are mere trespasses, and it has been said that an action for a nuisance which violates a property right incident to the ownership of land is in the nature of one for trespass to realty. The difference is that a nuisance consists of a use of one's own property in such a manner as to cause injury to the property or other right or interest of another and generally results from the commission of an act beyond the limits of the property affected, while a trespass is a direct infringement of another's right of property. Thus, where there is no actual physical invasion of the plaintiff's property, the cause of action is for nuisance rather than trespass. * * *" 39 Am.Jur. 282, Nuisances, § 3.

Morgan v. High Penn Oil Co., 238 N.C. 185, 77 S.E.2d 682.

Since a nuisance interferes with the enjoyment of the right to possess land, different rules of law apply to the balancing of the interests of owners. An owner's use of his own land will not create liability unless his use causes substantial interference with another's enjoyment of his property. 4 Restatement of Torts, Interference with the Use of Land, Ch. 40, § 822, p. 226. Also, the utility of the use that creates the nuisance must be weighed against the "gravity of the harm." Id., Ch. 40, § 826, p. 241, and Ch. 40, § 828, p. 250.

Such considerations are foreign to the law of trespass. A trespass imports damage and permits recovery, though no actual damage is caused. This rule of law is so well established citation of authority is unnecessary. There can be no balancing of interests.

Where a permanent trespass is committed by government, the constitution will not permit a balancing of the value of the taking for the benefit of the public against the interests of an owner. The owner must be fully compensated for his loss.

As pointed out, different policy considerations are involved in the laws of trespass which can ripen into a taking, and the laws of nuisance. The people have established these policy differences through the constitution and the enactment of laws which provide for entirely different procedures and considerations. See ORS 281.210 et seq., and ORS 105.505 et seq. This court ought not to exceed its powers to establish a different policy.

The distinction between what the law is, and a belief of what the law ought to be, is pointed out in the case of Batten v. United States, 306 F.2d 580 (10th Cir. 1962). This case is directly in point with the issue before us, and the majority opinion therein sustains the position which I have taken here.

The majority here, as does Mr. Chief Judge Murrah in his dissent in Batten v. United States, supra, seeks to place consequential damage in the same category as a taking, without attempting to draw the distinction which has always existed in the law; that is, the taking of a possessory interest as opposed to damage.

A nuisance takes none of the title in the property. The full legal title rests in the owner. If the nuisance is abated in any manner, the damage suffered has ended and the land is again restored to its full value to the owner. On the other hand, if there is a taking, the property right of ownership or some interest therein has been transferred from the owner to the sovereign, and does not again revert to the original owner even though the use to which the property has been put by the sovereign ceases.

It may well be, as suggested by Chief Judge Murrah, that "fairness and justice, as between the State and the citizen, requires the burden imposed to be borne by the public and not by the individual alone." But the question of who should bear the burdens imposed by the creation and continuance of a great society created and maintained for the benefit of all, is, as pointed out herein, a political question to be resolved by a majority of the people through their elected representatives and not by judicial fiat.

As pointed out by the majority in Batten v. United States, supra, this course has been taken in many states by its citizens, and this is the course which should be taken in this state, if the entire burden is to be borne by the public.

In setting forth the principles of law which should prevent this court as a matter of law, as well as policy, from commingling the remedies afforded under the law of eminent domain and nuisance, I do not wish to convey the thought that the plaintiffs are without a remedy. The discussion that the plaintiffs may have a remedy requires consideration of the majority's statement to the effect that an easement of nuisance may be created as between private individuals. The rule has no application to public nuisances.

This court has established the rule that a damage action lies against a municipality, which has the same immunity from suit as does the state, for the creation of a nuisance for the benefit of the public. Wilson v. City of Portland, 153 Or. 679, 58 P.2d 257.

We have also stated that the "convenience of the public" will not authorize the public to acquire an easement of nuisance by prescription. Ulmen v. Town of Mt. Angel, 57 Or. 547, 112 P. 529, 36 L.R.A., N.S., 140.

A careful reading of the case of Richards v. Washington Terminal Co., 233 U.S. 546, 34 S.Ct. 654, 657, 58 L.Ed. 1088, cited by the majority, will show that this decision, which permitted a recovery of damages for a nuisance, was based upon the same principles announced by this court in Wilson v. City of Portland, supra.

It is true that the damage created by a nuisance may equal a taking of the whole, but this does not justify this court in stating that a nuisance may constitute a taking of a possessory interest in land, as contemplated by our constitution.

Since, as the plaintiffs state, this action was tried on the theory of inverse condemnation, the trial court committed no error in its rulings and the judgment should be affirmed. If the plaintiffs have suffered damage for a non-trespassory nuisance, they may seek redress in an action or suit, as provided by law.

For the reasons above set forth, I dissent.

McALLISTER, C.J., and ROSSMAN, J., concur in this dissent.

391 P. 2d 540
Glenn A. MARTIN and Claresta L. Martin,
his wife, et al., Respondents,
v.
The PORT OF SEATTLE, a municipal
corporation, Appellant.
Vern AARHUS et al., Respondents,
v.
The PORT OF SEATTLE, a municipal
corporation, Appellant.
No. 36996.
Supreme Court of Washington,
En Banc.
April 23, 1964.

Inverse condemnation action by property owners against the Port of Seattle, a municipal corporation, as owner of the Seattle-Tacoma International Airport. The property owners sought damages for an alleged taking or damaging of their property for public use caused by nearby low altitude flights of jet aircraft landing and taking off from the airport. The Superior Court, King County, Henry Clay Agnew, J., determined that the plaintiffs had stated a claim for relief. The defendant appealed. The Supreme Court, Finley, J., held that the plaintiffs, in pleading the interference with the use and enjoyment of their land, with a subsequent decline in market value, stated a claim upon which relief could be granted.

Affirmed.

1. Eminent Domain

"Inverse condemnation" is popular description of action brought against governmental entity having power of eminent domain to recover value of property which has been appropriated in fact, but with no formal exercise of the power.

2. Eminent Domain

The noise of jet aircraft in process of landing or taking off can amount to a "taking" or "damaging" of property for which the constitution requires that compensation be made. Const. art. 1, § 16 as amended, amend. 9.

3. Eminent Domain

The term "property" in constitutional amendment requiring that compensation be made for taking or damaging of property includes the unrestricted right to use, enjoy and dispose of the land. Const. art. 1, § 16 as amended, amend. 9.

4. Eminent Domain

When the noise and intense vibration produced by low-flying jet aircraft deprive owner of land of an essential element in his relationship to that land, the result should be the same whether the airport operator himself brings the action to "condemn" the right to so interfere with the land, or the landowner is forced to be the moving party.

5. Aviation

Aircraft are permitted to use air space which has been placed in the public domain subject only to federal regulation of their routes and operating procedure. Federal Aviation Act of 1958, § 101, 49 U.S.C.A. § 1301.

6. Eminent Domain

Recovery for landowner in respect to noise of jet aircraft in process of landing or taking off is supported upon reasoning akin to eminent domain, and taking of private property or rights for public benefit, and not upon any consideration of whether the taking should be classed as "wrongful" or tortious under any common-law theory. Const. art. 1, § 16 as amended, amend. 9.

7. Eminent Domain

The inability of landowner to enjoin use of navigable air space does not prevent him from recovering for decline in market value of his land which was brought about or inflicted for public benefit. Const. art. 1, § 16 as amended, amend. 9; Federal Aviation Act of 1958, § 101, 49 U.S.C.A. § 1301.

8. Aviation

The privilege to use the navigable air space does not automatically mean freedom from liability for damage or demonstratable pecuniary loss to property owners below; flights are not immune from private litigation, whether in process of take-off or landing. Const. art. 1, § 16 as amended, amend. 9; Federal Aviation Act of 1958, § 101, 49 U.S.C.A. § 1301.

9. Eminent Domain

No overflight or direct physical invasion of air space over land is necessary in order to maintain an action under the "taking or damaging" provisions of the state constitution. Const. art. 1, § 16 as amended, amend. 9.

10. Eminent Domain

The specific purpose of the word "damaging" in the constitutional requirement that compensation be made for taking or damaging of property is to avoid the distinctions attached to the word "taking" appropriate to a bygone era. Const. art. 1, § 16 as amended, amend. 9.

11. Eminent Domain

Terms "substantial" and "incidental" in inverse condemnation context are not pertinent in that when there is only an injury which is incidental there is no measurable or provable decline in market value.

12. Eminent Domain

"Inverse condemnation" is strongly analogous to eminent domain; it differs from eminent domain only in that the landowner institutes the action, rather than the entity possessing the condemnation power; in the inverse condemnation case the plaintiff landowner is usually claiming a partial taking or damaging rather than a total loss of the land itself.

13. Eminent Domain

In inverse condemnation the measure of recovery is injury to market value, and that alone.

14. Eminent Domain

Complaint by landowners alleging taking or damaging of their property for public use caused by nearby low altitude flights of jet aircraft landing and taking off from an airport owned by the defendant Port of Seattle, a municipal corporation, with a subsequent decline in market value, stated a claim upon which relief could be granted. Const. art. 1, § 16 as amended, amend. 9; U.S.C.A. Const. Amend. 14.

Bogle, Bogle & Gates, Robert W. Graham, Thomas L. Morrow, Richard L. Young, Seattle, for appellant.

Riddell, Williams, Voorhees, Ivie & Bullitt, R.H. Riddell, S.E. DeForest, Seattle, for Martin, et al.

Short, Cressman & Cable, Paul R. Cressman, Wm. L. Hintze, Seattle, for Aarhus, et al.

Lyman M. Tondel, Jr., Cleary, Gottlieb, Steen & Hamilton, New York City, John E. Stephen, Gen. Counsel, Air Transport Ass'n of America, Washington, D.C., amici curiae.

FINLEY, Judge.

[1] This is an "inverse condemnation"[1] action brought by 196 property owners against the Port of Seattle, a municipal corporation, as owner of the Seattle-Tacoma International Airport. The respondent property owners seek damages for an alleged taking or damaging of their property for public use caused by nearby low altitude flights of jet aircraft landing and taking off from the airport. The sole question on this appeal is whether the property owners have stated a claim for relief due to such jet aircraft flights. The question of actual individual monetary damage is by stipulation reserved for later separate trial.

The property in question is located directly south of the primary north-south runway of the Seattle-Tacoma Airport, in a rectangular area roughly one mile long and one-half mile wide, bounded by South 200th Street on the north, South 216th Street on the south, 16th Avenue South on the west, and 24th Avenue South on the east. The litigated area of approximately one-half square mile has been somewhat arbitrarily defined for the purposes of suit in such a manner that it is bisected by an imaginary flight line extended south along the

1. Inverse condemnation is the popular description of an action brought against a governmental entity having the power of eminent domain to recover the value of property which has been appropriated in fact, but with no formal exercise of the power. Thornburg v. Port of Portland (1962), 233 Or. 178, 376 P.2d 100.

direction of the runway. The northernmost edge of the litigated area is approximately 9/10ths of a mile from the end of the runway, and jet aircraft in the process of landing pass over this imaginary centerline of the area at altitudes of less than 500 feet.

The plaintiffs contend, in general, that the use of appellant's airport by jet aircraft[2] has unreasonably interfered with the use and enjoyment of their properties and caused substantial depreciation in the value of those properties. While the parties have been segregated for the purpose of suit in such a manner as stresses the presence or absence of an actual physical invasion of airspace,[3] the contentions of the plaintiffs make it clear that the gravamen of the complaint is the noise and vibration created by the aircraft rather than physical invasion,[4] making it apparent that any differentiation on this basis would be of little practical significance.

The plaintiffs make extensive claims of interference and damage flowing from the flights in close proximity to their land, some summary of which should be made here to indicate the extent of the growing societal problem of which the present action may be only a harbinger. The plaintiffs claim that, when jet aircraft pass over or in close proximity, conversation is halted, radio and television reception is disrupted, and the sound obliterated. The jets cause vibrations in the houses and of their contents, rendering it necessary to hammer the nails back into the siding of some of the homes at about six-month intervals, and to tighten light fixtures periodically. Sleep is disrupted, outdoor entertainment almost impossible, and the noise painful to many. The noise also causes fear, particularly in small children. It is asserted that the respondents cannot sell their homes, and that the property values are substantially reduced.

The trial court held that the plaintiffs had stated a claim for relief. The theory which forms the basis of this holding may be set out as follows. The property owners were conceptually divided into two groups, one group comprising those having land which was subjected to direct overflights by the jet aircraft, the second, those as to which no overflights were shown. Respecting the first group, the trial court held that the overflights amounted to a *taking* of an air easement without just compensation in violation of Art. I, § 16, Amendment 9, of the Washington Constitution and Amendment XIV of the United States Constitution. As to the second group, the trial court held that the regular low flights near by amounted to a *damaging* of the properties without payment of just compensation in violation of Art. I, § 16, Amendment 9, of the Washington

2. The record shows that the first regularly scheduled commercial jet flight was made on October 2, 1959, and the number of jet landings per month thereafter increased from 12 in January 1960 to 1,302 in August 1962.

3. The property owners are, for the purposes of suit, divided into three groups. The "A" group is comprised of owners subjected to direct overflights, the "B" group of owners for which it is disputed whether or not there are any overflights, and the "C" group of owners which suffer no overflights.

4. This distinction accepts the perhaps unwarranted assumption commonly found in the federal cases that sound and vibration waves cannot be considered a "physical invasion," thereby also avoiding the sterile arguments sometimes directed along those definitional lines.

Constitution. According to stipulation, judgment was entered only as to potential liability, leaving the matter of damages to proof on an individual plot-by-plot basis in subsequent proceedings.

We are substantially in agreement with the trial court. However, this court will not in this case stress any of the proposed distinctions between the "taking" and the "damaging" of a property right respecting the use and enjoyment of the land. As the Washington Constitution affords or provides a basis for compensation in either instance, subtle efforts at legal refinement to characterize and describe a particular interference can be expected to be more difficult and treacherous than convincing or utilitarian.

[2,3] There seems little doubt that the noise of jet aircraft in the process of landing or taking off can amount to a taking or damaging of property for which Amendment 9 of the Washington Constitution requires that compensation be made. The term "property," as used in that provision, was defined in Ackerman v. Port of Seattle (1960), 55 Wash.2d 400, 348 P.2d 664, 77 A.L.R. 2d 1344, to include the unrestricted right to use, enjoy, and dispose of the land. It was there held that the frequent flights over the land of the plaintiffs amounted to a taking for which compensation in terms of the decline in market value of the land was required. The defendant in Ackerman was the same entity here involved.

[4] An identical result follows in the instant case from the clear direction of the Constitution that just compensation be made for the taking or damaging of "property," as defined in Ackerman. The only remaining obstacle to the plaintiffs' recovery under this approach is the problem of proving measurable detriment to the market value of their land under the traditional rules of proof. Whether the "cause of action" for the recovery of compensation is viewed as resulting from the due process provisions of the Constitution, or as resulting from an adaptation of older ideas of eminent domain and the condemnation of private property for public use, is of little significance. When the noise and intense vibration produced by low-flying jet aircraft deprives the owner of land of an essential element in his relationship to that land, the result should be the same whether the airport operator himself brings the action to "condemn" the right to so interfere with the land, or the landowner is forced to be the moving party. It should be noted that the Federal Government has developed the practice of affirmatively moving to condemn so-called "air easements" in connection with the operation of their air bases. See United States v. 15,909 Acres, 176 F.Supp. 447 (S.D.Cal. 1958). It also appears that the right of a property owner to proceed against the federal government on a theory that the noise of jet aircraft have "taken" his right to use and enjoyment of land is well established, recognized, and accepted. Aaron v. United States, 311 F.2d 798 (Ct.Cl. 1963); Batten v. United States, 306 F.2d 580 (10th Cir. 1962); Jensen v. United States, 305 F.2d 444 (Ct.Cl. 1962); Davis v. United States, 295 F.2d 931 (Ct.Cl. 1961); Bacon v. United States, 295 F.2d 936 (Ct.Cl. 1961). Some state courts recognize that the noise of jet aircraft, and its interference with the use of land not included in a condemnation begun by the state, are additional elements of compensable damage includable in the payments required for the land or

airspace actually physically taken in the action. Bowling Green-Warren County Airport Board v. Long (Ky. 1962), 364 S.W.2d 167; Johnson v. Airport Authority of the City of Omaha (1962), 173 Neb. 801, 115 N.W.2d 426.

The appellants resist the conclusions that would seem to flow from the above reasoning with a series of arguments which may be roughly grouped within three broad contentions: (1) That the Congress of the United States has placed all navigable airspace within the public domain, with the result that no use of such airspace by the public can result in liability; (2) that there can be no "taking or damaging" in the constitutional sense in the absence of a direct overflight of the plaintiff's land; and (3) that recovery based upon an alleged interference with the exercise or enjoyment of property rights must be limited to those instances where a *substantial* interference is shown, as opposed to a mere "incidental" damaging. These contentions will be considered in the above sequence.

[5-7] The Congress has placed certain airspace in the public domain. Consequently, aircraft are permitted to use such airspace subject only to federal regulation of their routes and operating procedures. In the Federal Aviation Act of 1958, the "navigable airspace" of the United States was expressly extended to include any and all airspace "needed to insure safety in take-off and landing of aircraft."[5] It is the position of the appellant that such legislation creates such an unrestricted right of use as to prevent any action for trespass or for nuisance, or based on any other theory that would place a burden upon interstate commerce.[6] This approach, however, overlooks the fact that recovery for the landowner is supported upon reasoning akin to eminent domain, and the taking of private property or rights for the public benefit, and not upon any consideration of whether that taking should be classed as "wrongful" or tortious under any common-law theory. It does not follow from the inability of the landowner to enjoin the use of the navigable airspace, semantic difficulties aside, that he should be unable also to recover for a decline in the market value of his land which was brought about or inflicted for the public benefit.

In Griggs v. County of Allegheny (1962), 369 U.S. 84, 82 S.Ct. 531, 7 L.Ed.2d 585, the Supreme Court of the United States took specific notice of the 1958 Act:

> "Following the decision in the Causby case [United States v. Causby, 328 U.S. 256, 66 S.Ct. 1062, 90 L.Ed. 1206], Congress redefined 'navigable airspace' to mean 'airspace above the minimum altitudes of flight prescribed by regulations issued under this chapter, and shall include airspace needed to insure safety in take-off and landing of aircraft'. * * * By the present regulations the 'minimum safe altitudes' within the meaning of the statute are defined, so far as relevant here, as heights of 500 or

5. 72 Stat. 737, 49 U.S.C.A. § 1301(24) (Supp.1961).

6. It might also be noted here that the present lawsuit seeks just compensation not from the airlines or the federal government, but from the Port of Seattle, an entity subject to state law as well as federal regulation.

1,000 feet '[e]xcept where necessary for takeoff or landing'. But as we said in the Causby case, the use of land presupposes the use of some of the airspace above it."

[8] We are here in agreement with the Supreme Court, and find no merit in the argument that the privilege to use the navigable airspace automatically means freedom from liability for damage or demonstrable pecuniary loss to property owners below. Flights are not immune from private litigation, whether in the process of take-off or landing; Matson v. United States (1959), 171 F.Supp. 283, 145 Ct.Cl. 225, or above 500 feet, Thornburg v. Port of Portland (1962), 233 Or. 178, 376 P.2d 100.

[9] The appellants next contend that the terms "taking and damaging" of the Washington Constitution provide recovery in only those instances where a property right is taken by the passage of the aircraft directly over the land of the plaintiff. This requirement, that a landowner show a direct overflight as a condition precedent to recovery of the damages to his land, is presently stressed by some federal courts in construing the "taking" as contemplated by the Fourteenth Amendment to the Federal Constitution. Batten v. United States (10th Cir. 1962), 306 F.2d 580. We are unable to accept the premise that recovery for interference with the use of land should depend upon anything as irrelevant as whether the wing tip of the aircraft passes through some fraction of an inch of the airspace directly above the plaintiff's land. The plaintiffs are not seeking recovery for a technical trespass, but for a combination of circumstances engendered by the nearby flights which interfere with the use and enjoyment of their land.

Both United States v. Causby (1946), 328 U.S. 256, 66 S.Ct. 1062, 90 L.Ed. 1206, and Griggs v. Allegheny County (1962), 369 U.S. 84, 82 S.Ct. 531, 7 L.Ed.2d 585, allowed recovery for repeated low-level flights over private land. While a direct overflight or invasion in airspace is in fact involved in each case, it is not clear that the reasoning and approach of those cases is so limited. Realistically, it must be conceded that a major part of the damage in either case was engendered by noise and vibration, whether or not accompanied by a physical displacement of air above the property. Thus, in Causby, the noise which frightened the chickens to a point where that type of ranching became impossible would presumably be equally inimical to the use of the land whether it came from directly overhead or obliquely from flights through the adjoining airspace of a neighbor. Again in Griggs, the loss of sleep due to noise and vibration was stressed as an important factor in allowing recovery, in addition to the fears engendered by the physical passage of the aircraft above or in close proximity to the home. The reliance placed upon the high noise level by the Supreme Court in both decisions, without detectable preoccupation with its angle of incidence, strongly indicates that the holdings are not limited to those instances where the aircraft passes directly over the land.

A careful reading of the above considered cases leads this court to the conclusion that the limitations inherent in the common-law concepts of trespass and ouster of possession, while highly useful in some contexts, can rapidly become outmoded in dealing with current and evolving spaceage sonic and supersonic phenomena. It is more likely that the view of Chief Judge Murrah, dissenting in Batten, represents the position of the United States Supreme Court. Finding it unnecessary to adhere to a strict trespass rule, he suggests compensation whenever the interference with the use of land is of sufficient directness, peculiarity, and magnitude "that fairness and justice, as between the State and the citizen, requires the burden imposed to be borne by the public and not by the individual alone." We must agree that the problem of balancing the interests involved, public and private, seems much the same whether a physical trespass is or is not involved.

[10] In addition to the above, further reason exists in Washington for refusing to adopt the overly strict interpretation of "taking" pressed by the appellant. The language of the Ninth Amendment of the Washington Constitution provides for just compensation of not only a "taking," but also a "damaging." The specific purpose of the addition of language beyond that of the United States Constitution is to avoid the distinctions attached to the word "taking" appropriate to a bygone era. It is unnecessary to become embroiled in the technical differences between a taking and a damaging in order to accord the broader conceptual scope intended by the additional language. See Ackerman v. Port of Seattle, supra; 47 Minn.L.Rev. 889 (1963).

We hold that no overflight or direct physical invasion of the airspace over the land is necessary in order to maintain an action under the "taking or damaging" provisions of the state constitution.

[11-13] Lastly, the appellant directs his arguments to the showing of damage and interference with use and enjoyment which was made at the trial by the plaintiff-respondent landowners. It is argued that the interference with private property rights must be shown to be a "substantial" interference before it can amount to a "taking" or a "taking or damaging" within the purview of the constitutional language, and that any lesser showing must be considered a mere noncompensable "incidental" damaging. The terms "substantial injury" and "substantial interference" appear commonly in the decided cases, sometimes as if it were the *sine qua non* of recovery. The terms are not pertinent, however, in the "inverse condemnation" context, where the action is strongly analogous to the eminent domain proceeding. It differs from eminent domain only in that the landowner institutes the action, rather than the entity possessing the condemnation power. Also, the plaintiff landowner in the inverse condemnation setting is usually claiming a partial taking or damaging rather than a total loss of the land itself.

When this action is analyzed in this manner, the term "substantial" is of dubious relevancy or utility. It connotes a balancing of the interests of the public in general against those of the individual. Inherent is the idea that the individual must bear a certain amount of inconvenience and loss of peace and quiet as the cost of living in a modern, progressing society. In eminent domain, and in inverse condemnation, such a balancing does not have to be accomplished as a distinct process, simply because the individual seeks no recovery for his individual suffering, damage, loss of quiet, or other disturbance. These elements of damage are cognizable in a tort action, and such a balancing would thus be necessary. But in inverse condemnation the measure of recovery is injury to market value, and that alone.[7]

Therefore, the balance of interest inherently struck in this type of action comes about in the following manner. If the individual is unusually sensitive, and sustains a greater injury than might be suffered by the general public from such interference, the public interest in maintaining the flights leaves him to one remedy—to sell his property and move. This is no different than it would be had his land been condemned for forced sale to the state. But whichever way the state exacts such a "sale," it must pay the individual the amount he suffers in the diminishment of the value of his land, as reflected by the decrease in the amount he can receive in a sale to a willing buyer. Such lowering of market value reflects not the personal injury to the individual, but the lesser desirability of the land to the general public; i.e., to a ready, able, and willing buyer. When the land of an individual is diminished in value for the public benefit, then justice, and the constitution, require that the public pay.

In the above manner, the interests which would otherwise be protected by the requirement of a "substantial" injury are vindicated in two distinct ways. First, where there is only an injury of the extent such that it should be called or labeled "incidental," no measurable or provable decline in market value could be expected traceable to the flights. Recovery would not be forthcoming, but not because of some arbitrary rule set for convenience in administration of justice, but because of an inability to prove damages according to the common and well-understood rules of suit. Second, and even more significant to the balancing problem, the smaller the provable decline in market value, the slighter the burden cast upon the public in paying for it. Surely the protection of the public interest does not entail the refusal of *small* claims on the ground that the burden to the public is not great enough to pay for!

[14] Upon the reasoning hereinbefore set out, we therefore hold that the plaintiffs, in pleading the interference with the use and enjoyment of their land, with a subsequent decline in market value, have stated a claim upon which relief can be granted. The judgment should be affirmed in conformity with the conclusions reached herein. It is so ordered.

OTT, C.J., and HILL, ROSELLINI, WEAVER, DONWORTH, HUNTER, HAMILTON, and HALE, JJ., concur.

7. Ackerman v. Port of Seattle (1960), 55 Wash.2d 400, 348 P.2d 664, 77 A.L.R.2d 1344.

564 F.2d 1002
BRITISH AIRWAYS BOARD and
Compagnie Nationale Air France,
Plaintiffs-Appellees,
v.
The PORT AUTHORITY OF NEW YORK
AND NEW JERSEY, William J. Ronan,
Paul Stillman, James G. Hellmuth, Victor R. Yanitelli, Milton A. Gilbert, James C. Kellogg, III, Alan Sagner, Joseph F. Cullman, III, Jane Englehardt, Lewis L. Glucksman, Robert F. Wagner, Commissioners of the Port Authority of New York and New Jersey, and Howard Schulman, Commissioner Designate of the Port Authority of New York and New Jersey, Defendants-Appellants.

United States Court of Appeals,
Second Circuit.

Argued Sept. 19, 1977.

Decided Sept. 29, 1977.

Operators of supersonic jet airliner Concorde brought action seeking to enjoin Port Authority of New York and New Jersey from further banning operations of Concorde at John F. Kennedy International Airport. After the Court of Appeals, 558 F.2d 75, reversed summary judgment order, 431 F.Supp. 1216, entered in favor of operators of Concorde, the United States District Court for the Southern District of New York, 437 F.Supp. 804, Milton Pollack, J., again entered injunction against Port Authority, which appealed. The Court of Appeals, Irving R. Kaufman, Chief Judge, held that district court properly dissolved ban on supersonic transport flights at Kennedy International Airport, but district court's order would be modified insofar as it fixed airport's long-standing noise limitation as only possible standard against which Port Authority legally could measure permissible noise of supersonic aircraft at airport so that Port Authority would be authorized to adopt new, uniform and reasonable noise standard in the future if it determined that long-standing noise limitation was inadequate.

Affirmed as modified.

Mansfield, Circuit Judge, concurred in part and filed opinion.

1. Administrative Law and Procedure

Law will not tolerate denial of rights by unwarranted official inaction.

2. Aviation

Task of protecting local population from airport noise belongs to agency, usually of local government, that owns and operates airfield.

3. Aviation

Maintenance of fair and efficient system of air commerce mandates that each airport operator be circumscribed to the issuance of reasonable, nonarbitrary and nondiscriminatory rules defining permissible level of noise which can be created by aircraft using the airport.

4. Aviation

Court's task of monitoring airport proprietor's observance of strict statutory obligation to make its facility available for public use on fair and reasonable terms and without unjust discrimination was especially critical in the case of proprietor's refusal to allow British-French supersonic transport to land at important international port of call, for if each village and hamlet were suffered to summarily prohibit entry of foreign-made or owned aircraft without promulgating uniform rules, it could make a sham of our country's binding treaty commitments to subject air carriers of France and Britain only to evenly applied laws and regulations.

5. Aviation

District court's finding that studies by consultants of Port Authority of New York and New Jersey relating to appropriate noise regulation for supersonic aircraft were merely redundant of work already thoroughly performed by other agencies was not erroneous.

6. Aviation

While proprietor of airport was not under duty to slavishly accept Secretary of Transportation's conclusions with respect to noise limitations applied to supersonic aircraft, proprietor could not stall indefinitely in adopting noise regulations when all information at its disposal either confirmed supersonic aircraft's ability to meet existing noise rules or was impotent to dissuade other responsible officials that impact of aircraft's low-frequency energy emissions on airport neighbors would not be more than minimal at most.

7. Administrative Law and Procedure

While there are no absolute standards by which it may be determined that an inquiry is not being conducted by agency with reasonable dispatch, court will closely scrutinize nature and character of problems before agency to assess whether path it has chosen to pursue will resolve those issues in the reasonably foreseeable future.

8. Aviation

District court properly dissolved ban on flights of supersonic jet airliner Concorde at Kennedy International Airport, in view of evidence that Port Authority of New York and New Jersey, operator of airport, had failed to adopt fair noise regulation to be applied to supersonic aircraft within reasonable period of time and in view of evidence that Concorde could meet long-standing noise rule which had been applied to subsonic aircraft; however, district court injunction would be modified so as to allow Port Authority power to adopt new, uniform and reasonable noise standard in the future if it determined that long-standing noise rule was inadequate.

9. Aviation

Port Authority of New York and New Jersey had to afford all aircraft, including supersonic jet airliner Concorde, a fair and equal opportunity to meet requirements of any future noise rule.

Patrick J. Falvey, Gen. Counsel, The Port Authority of New York and New Jersey, New York City (Joseph Lesser, Isobel E. Muirhead, Arthur P. Berg, New York City, Vigdor Bernstein, Pomona, N. Y., Benjamin R. DeCosta, St. Albans, N. Y., Sholem Friedman, New York City, of counsel), for defendants-appellants.

Peter J. Nickles, Washington, D. C. (William C. Clarke, New York City, William H. Allen, Eugene D. Gulland, John Michael Clear and Covington & Burling, Washington, D. C., of counsel), for plaintiff-appellee British Airways Board.

John A. Wells, New York City (Stanley Godofsky, Stephen Froling, Timothy R. Cappel and Rogers & Wells, New York City, of counsel), for plaintiff-appellee Compagnie Nationale Air France.

William D. Denson, New York City, for amici curiae Town of Hempstead, Village of Lawrence, Village of Cedarhurst, Village of Atlantic Beach, and Robert F. Check, Mona Gottesman and Herbert Warshavsky.

Before KAUFMAN, Chief Judge, and MANSFIELD and VAN GRAAFEILAND, Circuit Judges.

IRVING R. KAUFMAN, Chief Judge:

Four days after oral argument of this case, the President of the United States decided to permit supersonic transport aircraft service to thirteen American cities under specified restrictions. The President's decision followed sixteen months of demonstration flights at Dulles International Airport in Virginia by the Anglo-French Concorde, during which the noise and vibration levels of the aircraft were carefully monitored. A similar test at New York's John F. Kennedy International Airport, requested by the Secretary of Transportation and which the President "continues to support . . . pending a decision on the final (federal) noise rule," has yet to commence because the airport's proprietor, the Port Authority of New York and New Jersey, refuses to promulgate an acceptable noise rule for supersonic aircraft. Our sole task is to determine the legality of the total ban, which has now endured for more than one and one-half years, imposed by the Port Authority on Concorde flights into Kennedy pending on alleged effort to develop a noise standard.

This case, of course, is no stranger to our court. More than three months ago, after a careful review, we held that the Port Authority possessed the power and bore the responsibility to establish fair, even-handed and nondiscriminatory regulations designed to abate the effect of airplane noise on surrounding communities. *British Airways v. Port Authority,* 558 F.2d 75 (2d Cir. 1977) ("Concorde I"). We urged in that opinion that the Port Authority conclude its study and fix reasonable noise standards "with dispatch", for it was apparent that procrastination would only exacerbate the economic injury already suffered by the airlines, hinder legitimate efforts to determine the technological and commercial feasibility of supersonic aviation and further strain our foreign relations. We also directed Judge Pollack to conduct an evidentiary hearing to determine whether the Port Authority's then 13 month delay in promulgating noise regulations applicable to supersonic aircraft was so excessive as to constitute unfair discrimination and an undue burden on commerce.

It was our intention, in deciding as we did, to give the Port Authority another opportunity to come to grips with the problems posed by this clash of opposing forces. We hoped it would resolve the strife being generated by this litigation by, at the least, deciding to promulgate a noise rule equally applicable to all planes landing at Kennedy, without the court's intervention on the details of the Rule.

To this day the Port Authority has demonstrated total resistance in responding to the airlines' desire to secure a fair test of their aircraft in New York. Moreover, it is plain from its public statements that the Authority has no intention to resolve this critical issue in the foreseeable future. We cannot countenance such abdication. Accordingly, we will affirm the order of the district court, enjoining further prohibition of Concorde operations at Kennedy Airport until the Port Authority promulgates a reasonable nonarbitrary and nondiscriminatory noise regulation that all aircraft are afforded an equal opportunity to meet. We have also found it necessary, however, to modify Judge Pollack's order as hereafter indicated.

I. Facts

The Port Authority's 112 PNdB Noise Rule. The onslaught of civil jet aviation after World War II sorely tested our nation's commitment to make technological progress environmentally acceptable. As the proprietor of two airports in America's most populous city, the Port Authority of New York and New Jersey was thrust at an early date into the forefront of efforts to accommodate the needs of commercial aviation with the understandable desire of airport neighbors to enjoy a reasonable degree of peace and tranquility. Thus, in 1951 the Authority adopted a regulation prohibiting use of any of its facilities without permission. This rule vividly demonstrated the Port Authority's determination to compel the manufacture of quieter aircraft, a desire which was soon underscored by its refusal to accord landing rights to certain jet airplanes whose din was deemed intolerable to surrounding communities.

Both the vital importance of the aviation industry to the national economy and basic considerations of fairness, however, required that even the appearance of whim and caprice be eliminated from critical decisions concerning airport access. The Port Authority accordingly retained a consulting firm in 1955, and charged it with developing a method of meaningful quantification of the relative reactions of individuals to the quite different character of noise produced by existing propeller driven aircraft and newer jet engines. By 1958 it was demonstrated that an ordinary person heard 112 PNdB (perceived noise in decibels) emitted by a jet as substantially equivalent to the sound produced by a DC–6B piston airplane. The Port Authority therefore adopted 112 PNdB, as registered at selected monitoring points, to be the maximum permissible noise limit for all aircraft wishing to use John F. Kennedy International Airport.

The Port Authority's noise standard, of course, was not intended to transform Jamaica Bay and environs into a sylvan glen. By requiring only that the next generation of civil aircraft be no louder than its noisiest predecessor, the Authority sought a standard which it believed would prevent further deterioration of the area surrounding JFK. The aircraft industry was assured that any plane able to meet the standard, either through quieter engines or noise abating operating procedures, would be welcome in New York. In fact, until the Port Authority imposed the ban on supersonic aircraft that is challenged in the instant suit, not a single jet airplane that met the long-standing 112 PNdB rule was denied access to Kennedy Airport.

SST Noise. Since New York is this country's most important international gateway, it is not surprising that the manufacturers of the Concorde, the world's first supersonic commercial passenger airplane, communicated their desire to use JFK to the Port Authority more than seven years ago. At that time John R. Wiley, the Authority's Director of Aviation, warned that SSTs would "be required to meet the same noise levels as will be demanded of subsonic aircraft." In fact, those who built the Concorde were well aware that its noise posed a serious objection to American acceptance of the plane. Accordingly, the French and British spent nearly $100 million on noise abatement alone.

Before requesting specific permission to use Kennedy Airport, the owners of Concorde compiled reams of data concerning the likely effects of its noise on airport neighbors. In a series of tests conducted in late 1974 at Casablanca, Morocco and Toulouse, France, the manufacturers of the aircraft proved—in conditions closely simulating those at JFK—that the Concorde could consistently meet a 109 PNdB standard. Indeed, it was reported that the "Boeing 707 under [its] flight path [had] a distinctly greater spectral content in the more annoying frequency range bands, compared with Concorde." Moreover, the incremental impact of adding several Concorde flights to an already busy airport was found to be minimal. And further testing in January, 1976 demonstrated that even fewer individuals than originally anticipated would be adversely affected by the introduction of Concorde at JFK.

Federal Action. In late summer 1975 British Airways and Air France, confident of their aircraft's ability to satisfy applicable regulations, applied to the Federal Aviation Administration for permission to use the SST in transatlantic service to the United States. A thorough Environmental Impact Statement was prepared, and formed the basis for Secretary of Transportation William T. Coleman's careful and comprehensive decision of February 4, 1976, to order provisional amendment of the airlines' operations specifications to permit each carrier to conduct up to two flights daily into Kennedy and one per day into Dulles International Airport. This grant was accompanied by stringent conditions. For example, the Concorde could not travel at supersonic speeds over land areas; it had to observe a 10 P.M. to 7 A.M. curfew; and the aircraft was directed to abide by strict noise abatement procedures as prescribed by the F.A.A. In addition, these amendments were not to be effective beyond sixteen months from the commencement of commercial service. Finally, Secretary Coleman explicitly provided that all flights would cease immediately "in the event of an emergency deemed harmful to the health, welfare or safety of the American people."

Before rendering his decision, which we have termed "the very paragon of a clear and considered administrative action," *Concorde I, supra* at 80, Secretary Coleman painstakingly discussed both the traditionally recognized component of Concorde noise (addressed by the Port Authority's 112 PNdB rule) and its purportedly unique capacity to emit substantial low frequency vibrations. Based on his review of voluminous data, Coleman concluded that the noise of a Concorde at its source was indeed louder than that produced by subsonic aircraft under similar conditions. But this revelation was only the beginning of analysis, for relevant regulations are carefully calculated to reflect the relative subjective impact of aircraft noise on individuals living in the vicinity of airports. In fact, to focus upon the absolute energy emission levels of Concorde's engines without considering the mitigating effect of noise abatement procedures—as the *amicus curiae* does in this case—is as empty an exercise as inquiring of a Kantian philosopher whether a tree falling in a deserted forest can be "heard."

Coleman thus turned for guidance to a federally prepared Noise Exposure Forecast (NEF), which described the cumulative effect of all aircraft operating at JFK within the course of 24 hours. This index, which included corrections for the discrete whine of certain jet aircraft and penalized flights scheduled during normal sleeping hours, revealed that the addition of eight Concorde flights a day would produce only a negligible impact on the communities surrounding JFK. More specifically, the descriptor indicated that the number of people residing within the NEF 30 contour—a term of art applying to those instances in which certain individuals "may complain"—would increase by only 0.4%, from 485,000 to 487,000; and within the NEF 40 zone—in which "repeated vigorous" complaints would be forthcoming—from 112,000 to 114,000, or by 2%. Overall noise in each contour would increase by about 0.3%. Although this meant that a greater number of people would be subjected to a somewhat noisier environment, the Secretary cogently noted that an identical effect would be created (without amending any operating certificates) simply by the addition of "a few extra flights by . . . B–707's or DC–8's."

Secretary Coleman also recognized that the sound produced by the Concorde's engines is of a relatively low pitch and thus qualitatively different from that emitted by subsonic aircraft. The plane's deep rumble, he said, would cause minor structural shaking; and the fact that its sound readily penetrates buildings would result in the rattling of dishes and other non-stationary objects within homes. Coleman concluded, however, after a comprehensive survey of the evidence, that "these vibrations do not present any danger of structural damage and little possibility of annoyance." In fact, under the strictly limited regime contemplated in his order, the Secretary was confident that the resulting irritation would be slight, and the Concorde induced vibrations "brief and barely perceptible."

In the end, Coleman recognized that a testing period of actual Concorde operations was an essential prelude both to the final decision on the aircraft's acceptability in the United States and to the determination whether public hostility in America's premier commercial center made the development of a second, quieter generation of SSTs economically unfeasible. Raw data alone cannot forecast community response to SSTs, for every individual reacts differently to noise. The sixteen-month demonstration ordered by Coleman was thus a crucible in which to assay subjective attitudes of airport neighbors and our willingness to fairly assess the issue of supersonic transportation. In the words of this court, "the very dimensions of the most significant environmental drawback of the Concorde are impossible to determine without an adequate test." *Concorde I, supra,* at 80.

The Port Authority's Response. While technicians strove to project scientifically the community response to Concorde noise, local leaders on the political scene lobbied to prevent SST landings at Kennedy. On January 5, 1976 New York State Commissioner of Transportation Raymond Schuler conveyed Governor Carey's unqualified opposition to Concorde to Secretary Coleman at a public hearing; he testified to the same effect six weeks later before the Port Authority's Operations Committee. The New York Legislature simultaneously passed a bill banning all SSTs from Kennedy Airport.[1] Although we do not know the impact of these actions on the Commissioners of the Port Authority, who are appointed by the Governors of New York and New Jersey, soon thereafter–on March 11, 1976–the Concorde was banned by the Authority from JFK for a period not to exceed six months, during which operations at Dulles, Charles de Gaulle and Heathrow Airports were to be monitored and analyzed.

In taking this action, the Port Authority did not apply its existing and well-established 112 PNdB rule to the Concorde. Rather, it suggested that the unique low frequency vibrations produced by the SST's engines "were not necessarily reflected" in the current noise standard. Although Secretary Coleman found the adverse environmental effects of the Concorde's low pitched sound to be negligible, the Port Authority concluded the issue warranted further

1. This legislation was not binding on the Port Authority, since a similar bill failed of enactment in the New Jersey legislature.

study. And while the Authority agreed with the Secretary that the subjective reaction of people exposed to SST noise needed further inquiry under actual operating conditions, it questioned whether such testing at JFK was in the "public interest."

The Authority also believed it was necessary to retain consultants who would further study the SST and quantify the vibration problem in a manner that would accurately predict community reaction to this unique component of the SST's noise profile. Accordingly, on May 24, 1976–the day that flights began in Washington, D.C. and more than three months after Coleman's exhaustive decision–the Port Authority engaged Dr. Karl Kryter of the Stanford Research Institute to examine Concorde noise.[2]

Dr. Kryter spent several months recording onto magnetic tape the noise of all types of aircraft, including the Concorde, at JFK, Dulles, Charles de Gaulle and Heathrow Airports. By February, 1977 he had developed a formula that, in his words "would allow one to a first order of approximation [to] say that if you had the 707 and the Concorde in a given mode of operation with a given level of noises commonly measured, what the relative difference in potential vibration would be." The critical importance of this research cannot be gain-said, for it demonstrates that eight months ago the Port Authority's principal consultant had devised a means of relating household vibration to the SST's absolute noise levels, a "vibration-rattle index." What Kryter had not been able to do was correlate this figure with the amount of irritation an individual would experience at a given level of noise and vibration.[3]

When Dr. Kryter reported these results to the Port Authority in early March, 1977, he was asked to outline a proposal for solving this elusive problem of "additivity." But the Authority has never actually engaged Kryter, or anyone else, to pursue such research. Moreover, he has testified that an additivity study would consume six months to a year, and cost between $500,000 and $1 million. The Port Authority refused to embark upon such an expedition, and has not authorized a single penny to be spent on its completion. Neither, of course, does it wish to assay subjective reaction to vibration through actual test flights, as Secretary Coleman suggested. Thus it is not at all clear to us how the Port Authority intends to solve this additivity dilemma, if indeed it ever expects or wants to do so.

Airlines Submit Revised Operating Procedures. While the Port Authority found that the problems of Concorde noise were either intractable or capable of logarithmic expansion, the airlines continued to refine existing data that

2. Six months later, on November 8, 1976, the Port Authority employed Dr. Aubrey McKennell, a British psychologist, to conduct an attitude survey of the people living near Heathrow Airport. Although McKennell observed in his final report, dated March, 1977, that "the majority of those who had heard Concorde said its noise was less disturbing than they had anticipated," he concluded that his study on the whole was "inconclusive."

3. Thus, the Port Authority's 112 PNdB standard is a subjective measure of annoyance that equates the irritation engendered by a jet engine and the noisiest piston-driven aircraft, a DC-6B. The problem Dr. Kryter was unable to solve was the relative annoyance caused, for example, by a B–707 that emitted 112 PNdB + 1 vibration unit and a Concorde SST that might emit 110 PNdB + 3 vibration units.

proved Concorde's ability to meet the longstanding 112 PNdB standard at JFK. Thus, by telex on March 7, 1977 the owners of Concorde detailed certain revised procedures entailing reduced operating weights, specific runway utilization assuring that 98% of departures would occur over water, and a "decelerated approach" making it graphically apparent that the Concorde's noise would not exceed 105 PNdB at any Port Authority meter. In addition, it was again established that the incremental disturbance of individuals within the NEF 30 and 40 contours would be negligible. On April 14 the F.A.A. confirmed the technical validity of the airlines newest submission. It was now clear not only that the Concorde met the established 112 PNdB rule, but also that its perceived noise "footprint"[4] was comparable to that of the B707–320B.

The Port Authority's Response. Although the Port Authority originally had banned the Concorde from JFK for a period not to exceed six months, the agency ultimately established March 10, 1977—a full year after its initial resolution—as the date it would render a definitive decision on this important issue. In the period of more than a year since Secretary Coleman's decision, a wealth of new data had been complied to aid the Authority in its task, including monthly progress reports on SST operations at Dulles. All consultants had completed their work and reported their conclusions, and the Port Authority had decided not to authorize any further funding for efforts to quantify Concorde noise. The Commissioners nevertheless answered the airlines' latest initiative by postponing consideration of Concorde landings from March 10 to "a later date." An accompanying press release claimed this course was chosen out of "fairness" to the airlines, implying that they had proved for the first time their aircraft's capability to meet the 112 PNdB rule. But in fact, from the first tests in 1974, there had never been a shred of evidence indicating the SST's inability to meet the rule, and the March 7 submission merely proved the Concorde even quieter than theretofore supposed. In this context it is not surprising that the airlines immediately notified the Port Authority that "our patience has run out," and sought relief in federal court.

Litigation, Round 1. On May 11, 1977 Judge Pollack dissolved the Port Authority's ban on Concorde, reasoning that Secretary Coleman's decision to accord the plane limited permission to land in this country preempted any contrary exercise of local authority. *British Airways v. Port Authority,* 431 F.Supp. 1216 (S.D.N.Y.1977). This court, with the concurrence of the government as *amicus,* reversed. We held that federal law contemplated a limited role for airport proprietors. We decided that their task was to promulgate reasonable rules to abate noise in the airport and its environs. We also remanded for an evidentiary hearing to ascertain whether the Port Authority had exercised its responsibility in a "fair, reasonable and nondiscriminatory manner" or whether, as urged by the airlines and the United States, the thirteen month delay—as it was then—in promulgating a uniform noise standard for the Concorde was unreasonable, discriminatory and hence illegal.

4. Much like isobars on a weather map, the noise "footprint" is created by drawing lines joining areas in the vicinity of an airport that experience the same level of noise from specific aircraft.

The Port Authority's Response. Five days before the mandated hearing, on July 7, 1977, the Port Authority's Commissioners voted to indefinitely extend the "temporary" ban imposed sixteen months earlier. The Authority merely reiterated what had been known for years—that the Concorde had "unique characteristics including that on landing [it] has a high level of low frequency energy." Despite the receipt of monthly progress reports from Dulles since the inception of service there, the Authority had now grasped another excuse for non-action: it would await a final federal compilation of Concorde data, due in late September. This is puzzling, of course, in light of the Port Authority's repeated disavowal of earlier federal studies favorable to the SST, and its assertion of complete independence in conducting its own examination of Concorde noise.[5] And even more perplexing, since the work of its consultants had ceased four months earlier, was the Authority's statement that a "vibration-rattle index is being further studied."

Judge Pollack's Decision. On August 17, the district judge again struck down the Port Authority's ban of SST flights after concluding that for over a year the agency had been "reploughing old ground and doing re-reviews of scientific and theoretical data previously available." In the view of the district court Dr. Kryter had established nothing beyond what was adequately considered and reported by Secretary Coleman, and the Port Authority had no intention of setting either 112 PNdB or any other noise standard for the Concorde. This total abdication constituted an unreasonable, discriminatory and unfair impingement on commerce. The Port Authority, accordingly, was enjoined from prohibiting further SST flights into JFK if they emitted no more noise than 112 PNdB.

Ensuing Action. Neither advocates nor opponents of the Concorde have declared a truce while awaiting our review of the district judge's order. Recently several members of Congress urged that the federal government restudy low frequency vibrations. But, on September 15, 1977 Secretary of Transportation Brock Adams, in separate letters to Elmer Staats, Comptroller of the Currency, and Port Authority Director of Aviation Morris Sloane, declared that it was "unnecessary to define and quantify a vibration-rattle index before initiating regulatory action on new noise standards." In fact, Secretary Adams reported, the vibrations emitted by the SST were no greater than those induced by long range subsonic aircraft, such as the B—747 and DC—10. And since these aircraft have been flying into JFK for several years without apparent rattle problems, the Secretary believed increased structural damage and annoyance to be "improbable." Indeed, the Dulles demonstration, Adams stated, had shown that vibration levels were even less than originally anticipated.[6] Dr. Kryter's report, in the opinion of the Department of Transportation, had not raised any new questions, and the existing data was sufficient to justify the

5. In fact, the media reported that President Carter's decision to permit Concorde landings in the United States has resulted in "no change" in the Port Authority's position.

6. Indeed, it has been found that the vibrations produced by the Concorde are no more annoying to those living under its flight path than the slamming of a door.

inception of public notice and comment procedures for certification of the Concorde without further delay.[7] This course was followed eight days later when President Carter decided to permit existing Concordes to fly into thirteen American cities, including New York, without requesting further vibration research.

II. Discussion

[1] The law simply will not tolerate the denial of rights by unwarranted official in-action. *Cf. NLRB v. Rutter-Rex Mfg. Co.*, 396 U.S. 258, 265–66, 90 S.Ct. 417, 24 L.Ed.2d 405 (1969); *Nader v. FCC*, 172 U.S. App.D.C. 1, 520 F.2d 182 (1975). If ever there was a case in which a major technological advance was in imminent danger of being studied into obsolescence, this is it. There comes a time when relegating the solution of an issue to the indefinite future can so sap petitioners of hope and resources that a failure to resolve the issue within a reasonable period is tantamount to refusing to address it at all. The same is true of studying the question in such a manner that the issue will disappear by sheer frustration or the assumption by another institution–in this case the courts–of the task of deciding a charged dispute whose resolution otherwise is the duty of the agency. The hour is at hand for the Port Authority's indefinite ban on Concorde flights to be recognized as an abdication of responsibility. The airlines should no longer be forced to suffer the consequences of such illegal delay.

[2] Our initial opinion in this case delineated the extremely limited role congress had reserved for airport proprietors in our system of aviation management. Common sense, of course, required that exclusive control of airspace allocation be concentrated at the national level, and communities were therefore preempted from attempting to regulate planes in flight. See *Allegheny Airlines v. Village of Cedarhurst,* 238 F.2d 812 (2d Cir. 1958); *American Airlines v. Town of Hempstead,* 398 F.2d 369 (2d Cir.), *cert. denied* 393 U.S. 1017, 89 S.Ct. 620, 21 L.Ed.2d 561 (1969). The task of protecting the local population from airport noise, however, has fallen to the agency, usually of local government, that owns and operates the airfield. *Air Transport Assn. v. Crotti,* 389 F.Supp. 58 (N.D.Cal.1975) (three-judge court); *National Aviation v. City of Hayward,* 418 F.Supp. 417 (N.D.Cal.1976). It seemed fair to assume that the proprietor's intimate knowledge of local conditions, as well as his ability to acquire property and air easements and assure compatible land use,

7. A Department of Transportation Information Brief, issued on September 1, 1977, and entitled "Noise Spectra of Concorde and Subsonic Aircraft During Approach" states:

> It seems probable that agreement and/or acceptance of any "vibration-rattle index" would be very unlikely, even after a lengthy and complex research program. Actually, such a program appears to be a useless undertaking. Recent analyses of the low frequency spectra of the Concorde and long-range subsonic aircraft indicate little difference in their potential for inducing structural vibration.

Moreover, despite protestations to the contrary by the appellants, our independent examination of recent reports issued by NASA and the Environmental Protection Agency similarly discloses no significant commitment to further study of SST vibrations.

cf. Griggs v. Allegheny County, 369 U.S. 84, 82 S.Ct. 531, 7 L.Ed. 585 (1962), would result in a rational weighing of the costs and benefits of proposed service. Congress has consistently reaffirmed its commitment to this two-tiered scheme,[8] and both the Supreme Court and executive branch have recognized the important role of the airport proprietor in developing noise abatement programs consonant with local conditions.[9]

[3, 4] The maintenance of a fair and efficient system of air commerce, of course, mandates that each airport operator be circumscribed to the issuance of reasonable, nonarbitrary and nondiscriminatory rules defining the permissible level of noise which can be created by aircraft using the airport. *Concorde I, supra* at 84. We must carefully scrutinize all exercises of local power under this rubric to insure that impermissible parochial considerations do not unconstitutionally burden interstate commerce or inhibit the accomplishment of legitimate national goals. See *Douglas v. Seacoast Products,* 431 U.S. 265, 97 S.Ct. 1740, 52 L.Ed.2d 304 (1977). See also 49 U.S.C. § 1651(a) ("provision of fast, safe, efficient and convenient transporation"); 49 U.S.C. § 1346 ("encourage . . . the development of civil aeronautics and air commerce"). And, of course, our task of monitoring the proprietor's observance of the strict statutory obligation to make his facility available for public use on fair and reasonable terms, and without unjust discrimination, 49 U.S.C. § 1718 (1),[10] is especially critical in the case of an important international port of call such as New York. For, if each village and hamlet were suffered to summarily prohibit the entry of foreign-made or owned aircraft without promulgating uniform rules, it could make a sham of our country's binding treaty commitments to subject the air carriers of France and Britain only to evenly applied "laws and regulations." See U.S.–France Air Services Agreement, Art. V, 62 Stat. 3445, T.I.A.S. No. 1679 (1947); Bermuda Agreement, Art. 5, 60 Stat. 1499, T.I.A.S. No. 1507 (1946), *renegotiated,* see Dep't of State Bulletin, Vol. LXXVII, No. 1990 (Aug. 15, 1977); see also Convention on International Civil Aviation (Chicago Convention), 61 Stat. 1180, T.I.A.S. No. 1591 (1946).

We thus urged in *Concorde I* that it was manifestly imperative under our cooperative scheme of aircraft regulation for the Port Authority expeditiously to establish reasonable, nonarbitrary and nondiscriminatory noise regulations at JFK. This it has not done. Rather, the Port Authority has steadfastly refused to accord landing rights to an airplane that is capable of meeting the rule that has consistently been applied to all other aircraft for nearly twenty years–112 PNdB.

8. See S.Rep. No. 1353, 90th Cong.2d Sess. 7 (1968) (accompanying 1968 amendments to Federal Aviation Act); H.R.Rep. No. 94-842, 92d Cong.2d Sess. 10 (1972), S.Rep. No. 92-1160, 92d Cong.2d Sess. 10-11 (1972), U.S. Code Cong. & Admin.News. 1972, p. 4655 (accompanying 1972 amendments to Noise Control Act).

9. See *City of Burbank v. Lockheed Air Terminal, Inc.,* 411 U.S. 624, 635 n. 14, 93 S.Ct. 1854, 36 L.Ed.2d 547 (1973); Department of Transportation, Aviation Noise Abatement Policy (Nov. 18, 1976).

10. See *City of Dallas v. Southwest Airlines Co.,* 494 F.2d 773 (5th Cir.), *cert. denied,* 419 U.S. 1079, 95 S.Ct. 668, 42 L.Ed.2d 674 (1974); *Aircraft Owners Pilots Ass'n. v. Port Authority,* 305 F.Supp. 93 (E.D.N.Y.1969).

[5, 6] The district judge, after a hearing, found that the studies by the Authority's consultants were merely redundant of work already thoroughly performed by other agencies. This finding by the judge is not erroneous. We are not, of course, to be understood as saying that the Port Authority must slavishly accept Secretary Coleman's conclusions; but neither can it stall indefinitely when all the information at its disposal either confirms the SST's ability to meet existing noise rules or is impotent to dissuade other responsible officials that the impact of Concorde's low frequency energy emissions on airport neighbors will not be more than minimal at most.

[7] While there are no absolute standards by which it may be determined that an inquiry is not being conducted with reasonable dispatch, a court will closely scrutinize the nature and character of the problems before the agency to assess whether the path it has chosen to pursue will resolve those issues in the reasonably foreseeable future. *Cf. Deering-Milliken, Inc. v. Johnston,* 295 F.2d 856 (4th Cir. 1961). Thus, the Port Authority claims that its consultants have found the low frequency vibrations of the Concorde a unique source of annoyance, and begs our indulgence as it petitions for federal aid to develop a "vibration-rattle index". But the federal government shows little interest in the vibration problem, and the President has determined to permit Concorde service in thirteen American cities despite the alleged rattle. We presume the President's decision was prompted by reports, after sixteen months of operations at Dulles, proving SST-induced vibrations—which Secretary Coleman had predicted to by "slight, brief and barely preceptible"—even less noticeable than originally anticipated and essentially equivalent to those emitted by long range subsonic aircraft. Accordingly, it is highly unlikely that the federal government will soon expend large amounts of money on a project—the development of a vibration-rattle index—that the Department of Transportation dubs a "useless undertaking."

Moreover, it is also clear that the Port Authority is not willing to finance such a project. Dr. Kryter as long ago as March of this year reported significant progress in quantifying a vibration-rattle index. In his opinion the elusive mystery of additivity could be unlocked in less than one year, although at considerable cost. The Port Authority has shown no inclination to fund such an endeavor, yet seeks our sanction to ban Concorde flights while we await development of a noise standard that may never eventuate. We would be remiss if we were to allow the Port Authority to dawdle further on the basis of studies that by its own admission are inconclusive in a manner that threatens irreparable economic injury[11] and constitutes treatment that is anything but even-handed. See *Office of Communication of the United Church of Christ v. FCC,* 138 U.S.App.D.C. 112, 425 F.2d 543 (1969) (Burger, J.).

The final reason assigned by the appellant for its delay in developing a vibration-rattle index and hence, a noise rule for SSTs is that the airlines' submission of revised operating procedures only six months ago forced Dr. Kryter

11. The airlines have submitted affidavits stating that they will lose $300,000 per week so long as the Port Authority's ban continues.

essentially to commence his research anew. But the airlines' specific runway utilization and other proposals merely confirmed what had been apparent for months—that the Concorde could meet and surpass the longstanding 112 PNdB standard at JFK. In fact, the revised procedures, whose technical validity was soon assured by the F.A.A., proved that the plane was even quieter than theretofore supposed and comparable in noise intensity to the subsonic B707–320B. It is hollow to assert the "tardiness" of this unrequested submission as a justification for the Port Authority's inability to devise a suitable noise rule, particularly in light of Dr. Kryter's testimony that the airlines' April 1 data in no way altered his conclusion concerning the vibration issue.

III. Relief

[8, 9] Accordingly, we affirm the order of the district court so far as it dissolves the ban on SST flights at Kennedy Airport and permits the Concorde to serve New York under conditions detailed in federal operations specifications. Our holding, however, does not deny the Port Authority the power to adopt a new, uniform and reasonable noise standard in the future,[12] assuming the longstanding 112 PNdB rule, which the Concorde concededly can meet, upon reasoned grounds is deemed inadequate. The district court's order is modified insofar as it fixes 112 PNdB as the only possible standard against which the Port Authority legally can measure the permissible noise of supersonic aircraft at JFK.

We underestimate neither the seriousness of the issues confronting the Port Authority nor the difficulties it has encountered in arriving at a suitable resolution. Its ultimate determination will have broad economic, political, social and environmental implications. But making sensitive decisions, and exercising sound judgment even in the face of some nagging uncertainty, is the daily fare of judges, administrators and other public officials. And we have asked no more of the Port Authority than that it meet its admittedly heavy responsibility by adopting a fair noise rule within a reasonable period of time.

MANSFIELD, Circuit Judge (concurring in part):

I agree that the district court's order, as modified, should be affirmed. However, I cannot agree with the majority's characterization of the Port Authority's failure to establish SST noise and vibration standards as "procrastination," "total resistance," "abdication of responsibility," or as "tantamount to refusing to address" the issue, much less that the Port Authority has been politically motivated or "anything but even-handed." In my view these characterizations are unwarranted and ignore the serious problems that have been encountered in obtaining the scientific and attitudinal data required for a decision of such long-range, far-reaching proportions for New York residents. The establishment of noise standards for SSTs at JFK Airport is a matter of vital importance, not

12. Of course, the Port Authority must afford all aircraft, including the Concorde, a fair and equal opportunity to meet the requirements of any future noise rule.

just to the plaintiff Airlines and to the maintenance of cordial international relations with England and France,[1] but to more than 500,000 people living near JFK. The commercial SST may not be synonymous with progress if the price is to be increasing noise pollution and vibration to deafening proportions for thousands. Because of this impact on human lives the issue has warranted most careful study even if some delay ensued.

If this case involved only a dispute over whether the Port Authority was entitled to ban temporarily commercial flights of a revolutionary new aircraft while it took the necessary steps to develop a suitable standard for regulating the levels of noise and vibration produced by the aircraft, I would uphold such a ban. The case, however, involves a "temporary" ban imposed over 18 months ago that was recently extended indefinitely. Moreover, the Port Authority now finds itself "caught on dead center" in its efforts to develop a noise regulation adapted to the peculiar characteristics of supersonic aircraft, which has led the district court to terminate the Port Authority's ban on Concorde flights. While I join in the affirmance of that order, I do so on different grounds than the majority.

I cannot agree with my distinguished colleagues that this record supports a finding that the Port Authority has acted in bad faith or has been derelict in its duty. I am willing to accept the Authority's contrary contention, which appears to be supported by evidence, that it has proceeded in good faith to make a conscientious effort to develop a noise and vibration standard that will be fair and reasonable to plaintiffs and to other prospective SST carriers seeking to use JFK as well as to the more than 500,000 people residing within the sound and vibration "footprint" of SST takeoffs from that airport but that it has been stumped by inability (1) to construct a "noise-vibration" measuring device or index that will be generally acceptable to acoustical scientists, and (2) to fix a maximum level on such an index that would properly balance the conflicting interests of the carriers and the airport's neighbors.

Nevertheless, I do not believe that any agency such as the Port Authority is entitled to exclude carriers indefinitely and unconditionally from the use of its facilities without making definitive findings, based on substantial evidence, that the proposed use would jeopardize the health, safety or welfare of the public. This the Port Authority cannot do at this stage. It finds itself in the difficult position of not having enough evidence at this stage to bar the Concorde completely and yet not having enough data to fix reasonable and non-discriminatory noise-vibration levels that will withstand scientific and legal scrutiny. The picture is complicated by the necessity of investing additional hundreds of thousands of dollars of public funds, over and above the more than $250,000 already spent by the Authority, on further research and attitudinal surveys needed to complete the job.

Under the circumstances, I concur in the view that continuation of the Port Authority's ban on the Concorde cannot be justified, not because of

1. Ironically it was Napoleon who said, "I have made noise enough in the world already." Reported in B. O'Meara, *Napoleon in Exile,* 1816 (AMS Press ed. 1969), as quoted in The Home Book of Quotations 625 (B. Stevenson ed. 1967).

any fault on its part but because there comes a time when the hourglass runs out and even a public agency must "fish or cut bait." That time has now passed. Moreover, the limited test use of JFK contemplated by the plaintiffs under the Secretary of Transportation's decision might serve the useful purpose of providing the very basis that the Authority needs for on-site monitoring and attitudinal surveys essential to the formulation of reasonable noise-vibration regulations for SST craft.

In my view, the problem of measuring the unique combination of noise and vibration generated by the Concorde and of establishing maximum levels of public tolerance is not nearly as simple as my colleagues would make it appear. If this were simply a case of securing SST compliance with the Port Authority's existing noise standard for subsonic jets—112 PNdB—there would be no justification for any Port Authority delay once the plaintiffs, in March 1977, finally developed new operating procedures for the Concorde at JFK that would minimize the plane's noise impact so that it could meet the existing subsonic test insofar as it creates noise of a conventional nature. But the problem is more difficult and far-reaching than that. The reasonableness of the Port Authority ban on Concorde flights must be considered in light of what the Port Authority knew about the noise and vibration impact of commercial supersonic air travel when it imposed the ban on March 11, 1976. As Secretary of Transportation William T. Coleman, Jr. observed in his February 4, 1976, decision allowing a 16-month test of the Concorde at Dulles, and, subject to Port Authority permission, at JFK, the Concorde possesses unique noise and vibration characteristics quite different from subsonic aircraft. Secretary Coleman's decision states:

> "Low frequency components of aircraft noise create community annoyance through induced vibrations of homes and buildings near airports. Because noise generated by the Concorde has a much greater low-frequency content than that of comparable subsonic jets, there has been substantial public concern about the effect of induced vibrations on historic and other buildings, structures, windows and interior furnishings such as pictures, lamps, and dishes. Low frequency sound travels much more readily through the atmosphere and through structures than does the sound produced by other jets. Thus, if the Concorde and a subsonic jet were to generate noise of equal intensity at the aircraft, the Concorde's noise would be of a greater intensity at greater distances from the aircraft, since its sound energy would not dissipate as rapidly. This effect was studied thoroughly by the FAA and is described fully in the final EIS."

He further noted that "[s]ince the noise of the Concorde has five times the low frequency content of the noise of most subsonic jets, the vibrational effect will be five times as great" and that "[t]he greatest possibility of annoyance stems from the fact that vibration induced in walls may for a few seconds rattle hanging pictures and dishes and other items which might be standing loose on shelves. Again, however, I emphasize that there is no evidence that structural damage will ensue."

The final Environmental Impact Statement prepared by the Federal Aviation Administration and released in September 1975, upon which Secretary Coleman based his decision, had reported:

> "From Figure 6B, the Concorde's perceived loudness or noisiness under the takeoff flight path is double that of a B–707, four times the noisiness of a B–747 and eight times as loud as a DC–10. The perceived loudness of the Concorde will be annoying. It will interfere with communications and may cause startle.
>
> "The Concorde's low frequency spectral content is five times that of present subsonic jet aircraft (Figure 19–22). This low frequency aspect will induce some perceptible vibrational impact. However, while perceptible, the vibrational impact will not exceed any existing standards for structural damage (See Section VI.C.2 and Figures 41–46). Since the low frequency content of Concorde's noise signature will produce some household rattle and interfere with communications, it will be annoying to residents in the immediate airport vicinity."

Comparing the Concorde's noise on takeoff with that of conventional subsonic jet aircraft, Secretary Coleman found:

> "On the Concorde's takeoff using noise abatement procedures, for example, 47.6 square miles of land are subjected to noise levels at or above 100 EPNdB; comparable figures for the B–707 and the B–747 are 7.49 square miles and 2.91 square miles, respectively. This level of noise, 100 EPNdB, is approximately equal to, or perhaps slightly less noisy than, heavy city traffic at a distance of 25 feet, although the period of exposure to the aircraft noise would be short, generally under a minute."

Secretary Coleman further projected that at JFK in 1978 approximately 485,000 people would reside in the NEF 30 contour and 114,000 people within the NEF 40 contour as compared with only 1,000 residents around Dulles Airport within the NEF 30 contour and none within the NEF 40 contour.[2]

2. The Federal Aviation Administration's final Environmental Impact Statement analyzes the noise impact of the Concorde in terms of four "noise descriptors," which are scientific methods of representing different aspects of a particular noise impact.

The Noise Exposure Forecast (NEF) is a "noise descriptor" that describes the cumulative noise impact of all the aircraft operating at a given airport during the course of a day. It includes corrections for irritating whines or discrete frequencies in aircraft noise, and for noises occurring during those periods of the day, such as late evening, when loud noises are more disturbing. Use of the NEF descriptor permits an assessment of the extent to which Concorde operations will increase the total noise impact on persons living near an airport.

Secretary Coleman stated that the following NEF values have been generally accepted as a valid means of assessing community reaction to aircraft noise exposure:

(1) Individuals residing in an area measured at between NEF 30 and NEF 40 "may complain";

(2) Individuals residing within an NEF contour greater than 40 can be expected to complain "vigorously and repeatedly";

(3) The threshold of "possible hearing loss" is reached at NEF 45.

The Secretary's Decision on Concorde Supersonic Transport 44-48 (Feb. 4, 1976).

He predicted that as a result of the limited Concorde test operations at JFK an "already severely affected area would be further degraded" whereas "on the basis of NEF data, the effect of the proposed Concorde operations at Dulles will be hardly perceptible." He concluded that this data gave him "no clear direction."

Secretary Coleman decided that the inadequacy of the data available to him in February of 1976, together with other policy considerations, justified a limited period of Concorde operations at Dulles and JFK, during which time new data would be collected so that subsequent decisions regarding Concorde operations in this country would be more fully informed. One month later, the Port Authority decided otherwise. Although it also deemed the information then available to be wanting, it chose to withhold approval of Concorde operations at JFK until it had conducted its own investigation of the noise and vibration impact of supersonic flights. In view of the conflicting evidence concerning the impact of the Concorde, as well as the Port Authority's legitimate doubts about the suitability of its 20-year old 112 PNdB standard for measuring supersonic aircraft noise and vibration, I do not view the agency's initial decision as unreasonable.

Moreover, the tests conducted at Dulles since Secretary Coleman's decision, while leading to a federal authorization of Concorde landings at various airports in the United States, subject to reasonable and non-discriminatory local regulations, have not indicated that the existing noise regulation at JFK would be adequate to provide reasonable protection against excessive noise pollution by SSTs in the future. Despite Secretary Coleman's prediction that the effect of the proposed Concorde operations at Dulles would be "hardly perceptible," the number of noise complaints at that airport has increased from a total of 77 during the three-year period prior to the introduction of the Concorde to a total of 1,762 complaints during the first 12 months of Concorde operations, of which 1,387 or 79% were complaints about the Concorde. See Statement of Henry S. Eschwege, Director, Community and Economic Development Division, United States General Accounting Office, before the Subcommittee on Environment, Energy and Natural Resources of the House Committee on Government Operations, September 7, 1977.

The lodging of some 1,387 complaints against Concorde noise during only one year of very limited test operations at Dulles, registered by those located in an area where only 1,000 people reside, would indicate that even though the Concorde may be able to meet existing Port Authority standards, it may also, because of its additional noise and vibration pollution, be so objectionable at JFK, where over 500,000 people reside within the same contours, as to necessitate more stringent, additional regulations. Even assuming, despite this disproportionately high number of protests from Dulles' neighbors that the Concorde would successfully "play in Peoria" or other less densely populated areas, this does not mean that it would go over, noisewise, in heavily-populated New York.

These circumstances, standing alone, might justify a substantial pause in the development of new noise-vibration standards at JFK. In addition, there are other justifications for much of the Port Authority's delay. First, of course, there has been the inherent difficulty in developing a method or index for measuring or quantifying the combination of "vibration plus noise" generated by the SST that will be generally acceptable to acoustical experts. Secondly—and most difficult of all—is the task of determining the level at which this "vibration plus noise" should be viewed as too excessive to be acceptable to the average "reasonable person" (assuming such a person is to be treated as the standard for this purpose). The Port Authority is not being called upon merely to fix a criterion for a few Concorde flights per day on a limited, experimental basis, but to establish a gauge that will be used for all future SSTs using JFK, of which there may be hundreds, if not thousands, of flights in the years to come. Last, but not least, the Port Authority faces the prospect that if the present trend toward increasing the liability of airport proprietors to their neighboring residents for excessive noise in takeoffs and landings should continue, see *Griggs v. Allegheny County,* 369 U.S. 84, 82 S.Ct. 531, 7 L.Ed.2d 585 (1962); *Greater Westchester Homeowners Assn. v. City of Los Angeles,* 13 Avi. 18, 116 Cal.Sup.Court 1976, the Authority faces possible exposure to many millions of dollars in damages in suits by residents in the vicinity of JFK, based on "taking" or "nuisance" theories, unless it adopts carefully-considered reasonable regulations tailored to the unique environmental problems created by the SST.

For these reasons I do not share the view that the Port Authority has in the past been at fault in banning Concorde flights at JFK while it sought to develop a new standard for regulating the noise and vibration produced by supersonic aircraft. However, the circumstances have now changed in a way that leads me to conclude that Concorde test flights into JFK for the period permitted under Secretary Coleman's decision should be permitted. The Port Authority's research effort has stopped at the point where its expert, Dr. Karl Kryter of the Stanford Research Institute, is able to assess only the comparative *potential* for vibration produced by supersonic and subsonic aircraft. Dr. Kryter virtually concedes that real-life attitudinal data is now essential to enable him to determine how much irritation caused to neighboring residents by Concorde noise and vibration will be reasonably tolerable. As both the majority here and Secretary Coleman have observed, reaction to noise and vibration is essentially a subjective phenomenon. The most sophisticated noise-vibration rattle index will not, by itself, enable the Port Authority to determine the point on the index beyond which an SST may not go because of the excessive irritation to airport neighbors. This judgment must be based, in part, on human experience, which cannot be measured intelligently without actual test flights.

The Port Authority contends that test flights should await further experimentation and study. This argument is untenable, however, in light of the Authority's own disinclination to fund further research, and the federal government's apparent satisfaction for its limited purposes with the information currently available.[3] The Port Authority's position has thus been reduced to the assertion that it can justify its ban indefinitely on the basis of its belief that the Concorde will exceed acceptable noise and vibration levels. Yet it is unwilling to define the standards that the airlines are expected to meet. This is an insufficient basis to justify the exclusion of an aircraft that concededly meets the Port Authority's only existing noise regulation. Although plaintiffs will now be permitted to go into JFK on the limited test basis authorized by Secretary Coleman, the Port Authority retains the power, if, as, and when it obtains the essential data, to prescribe reasonable noise and vibration standards that might have the effect of authorizing, limiting or barring the use of JFK by SSTs, depending on the Authority's findings.

NOTE: The Supreme Court declined review. (98 S.Ct. 291 [1977])

3. As Chief Judge Kaufman's opinion notes, Secretary of Transportation Brock Adams has recently taken the position, on the basis of a report by his Department's Office of Noise Abatement dated September 1, 1977, that it is unnecessary to define or quantify a "vibration-rattle" index before establishing new noise standards for aircraft in view of findings that structural vibrations and associated rattling of interior furnishings by Concorde landings were not essentially different from those caused by long-range subsonic aircraft. However, the underlying report made it clear that it was limited to landings, as distinguished from takeoffs, and even then to "Concorde SST approaches utilizing a decelerating procedure" in lieu of a "conventional stabilized approach procedure." With respect to the latter the report concluded:

> "Low-frequency aircraft noise may induce sympathic [sic] vibrations in structures located near aircraft flight paths. At a 'worst-case' location directly under the approach path one nautical mile from runway threshold, the low frequency noise levels generated by Concorde SSTs using a conventional stabilized approach procedure are higher than levels generated by long-range subsonic aircraft (differences in sound pressure level from 4 to 16 dB in one-third-octave bands centered at 125 Hertz and below.)"

Moreover, the foregoing represents solely the reaction of the Department of Transportation, obtained at the request of the United States General Accounting Office, to Dr. Karl Kryter's report regarding the prospective impact of Concorde noise around JFK, which predicted a severe reaction by residents to the rattle. The General Accounting Office reported to Congress on September 7, 1977, through Mr. Henry Eschwege, that the Kryter report was also under review by NASA and EPA, which would advise whether they favored the development of a vibration-rattle index.

It should further be noted that Secretary Brock Adams' decision on September 23, 1977, to permit Concorde SSTs to land at some 13 American cities is subject to the condition that airport proprietors, including the Port Authority, retain their right "to limit or ban aircraft operations at their airports through reasonable, non-discriminatory noise rules." Except for Dulles Airport, therefore, the federal government's interest in the matter remains a limited one, amounting to little more than a proposal as far as use of various city airports is concerned.

CHAPTER 4

Damages and Injuries on Ground

The next several cases examine the extent of liability of persons operating aircraft above land, and causing injury to persons and property on the land, by descent or ascent of the aircraft, or by dropping any object from the aircraft.

The Rochester Gas v. Dunlop, and the Wood v. United Airlines cases are landmark cases in the area of injuries caused by crashes or collisions of aircraft.

---

148 Misc. 849

ROCHESTER GAS & ELECTRIC CORPORATION v. DUNLOP.

(Cite as 266 N.Y.S. 469)

Monroe County Court.

Sept. 6, 1933.

1. Electricity

Electric company *held* not entitled to recover from pilot of aeroplane, crashing against tower carrying transmission line, for resulting damage thereto on ground of negligence under res ipsa loquitur theory.

2. Electricity

Whether pilot of aeroplane, crashing against tower carrying electric transmission line, was guilty of trespass, was law question for court.

3. Property

Maxim "cujus est solum ejus est usque ad coelum" does not mean that landowner owns space above land to indefinite height.

4. Trespass

Flying of aeroplane through air above surface of land is not trespass against owner of soil in every case.

5. Property

Landowner's exclusive right to space above surface to such height as he may build structure thereon cannot be abridged, except by sovereign police power.

6. Evidence

It is common knowledge that aeroplanes frequently fall from causes over which pilots have no control.

7. Property

Aerial navigation has no inherent superiority over landowners where their rights and claims are in actual conflict.

8. Negligence

Chance that properly equipped and well-handled aeroplane may crash on and injure private property must be borne by one who takes machine aloft, not owner of such property.

9. Electricity

Owner of electric transmission line carried on steel towers, one of which was damaged by aeroplane crashing against it, *held* entitled to recover damages from pilot for trespass.

Appeal from City Court of Rochester.

Action by the Rochester Gas & Electric Corporation against William Dunlop. Judgment for defendant, and plaintiff appeals.

Reversed, and new trial ordered.

Whitman, Dey & Nier, of Rochester (George D. Ogden, of Rochester, of counsel), for appellant.

Raines & Raines, of Rochester (Charles J. O'Brien, of Rochester, of counsel), for respondent.

LYNN, Judge.

In July, 1931, the plaintiff was the owner of an electric transmission line, crossing through the town of Brighton, at the intersection of the Barge Canal with the East Henrietta road, so-called. This line was carried on steel towers, fifty feet high. On the 14th day of the month, at about 10 o'clock at night, the defendant, who was flying an aeroplane in the vicinity, crashed against the tower, bending it over and damaging it to the amount, as claimed, of $545, to recover which this action was brought; plaintiff alleging in two separate counts negligence and trespass. The defendant counterclaimed, but no appeal has been taken from the dismissal of the counterclaim in the court below, so no question concerning it arises upon this appeal. At the close of the plaintiff's case, the court dismissed the cause of action based on negligence, and, after the proofs were in, submitted the question of trespass to the jury, having denied the plaintiff's motion for a direction of verdict for the amount of damages sustained. It was the plaintiff's contention that a trespass had been committed as a matter of law; and the question was properly raised by the motion, and the request to charge and exceptions to the charge. The jury found for the defendant.

The defendant's evidence was to the effect that he was flying about two thousand feet high, from Penn Yan to Rochester, intending to land at the Rochester Airport, when, as he was within three or four miles of the airport, his engine, from some unknown cause, stopped. In his attempt to make a landing, and not seeing the tower in the nighttime, he came against it. The plaintiff, of course, offered no evidence as to the cause of the collision.

[1] The plaintiff claimed, in the court below, the right to recover on the basis of negligence, on the theory of res ipsa loquitur, and raises that point upon appeal. For reasons shown hereafter, I am of the opinion that the court below correctly determined that question.

[2-5] The further question is whether the court below should have held that there was a trespass as a matter of law. On the subject of trespass, there seems not to have been any question for a jury. Assuming that there was a trespass, it may be that the jury had a right to determine the amount of damages, but whether or not there was a trespass should have been disposed of as a matter of law. There was no dispute of fact. The defendant, flying over the plaintiff's land, came in contact with plaintiff's tower and injured it. That was the defendant's own testimony, and it permitted no variety of inferences. What then, should the court have decided on the subject of trespass? This involves the broader question, What is, or is to be, the law regarding the ancient maxim, "Cujus est solum ejus est usque ad coelum?" Not to go beyond the necessities of this case, it may be confidently stated that, if that maxim ever meant that the owner of land owned the space above the land to an indefinite height, it is no longer the law. As said by the United States Circuit Court of Appeals, in Swetland v. Curtiss Airports Corporation, 55 F.(2d) 201, 203, 83 A.L.R. 319, 325: "In every case in which it [the maxim referred to] is to be found it was used in connection with occurrences common to the era, such as overhanging branches or eaves. These decisions are relied upon to define the rights of the new and rapidly growing business of aviation. This cannot be done consistently with the traditional policy of the courts to adapt the law to the economic and social needs of the times. * * * We cannot hold that in every case it is a trespass against the owner of the soil to fly an aeroplane through the airspace overlying the surface." See, also, Smith v. New England Aircraft Co., 270 Mass. 511, 170 N.E. 385, 69 A.L.R. 300.

It is plain, however, that, outside of the sovereign police power, no rule has been or will be made, which abridges the exclusive right of the owner of lands to the space above it, to such height as he may build a structure upon the land; therefore, for the purpose of this case, it may be assumed that, when the aeroplane came in contact with the top of this tower, the rights and responsibilities of the respective parties were exactly the same as they would have been had the aeroplane come in contact with the earth below. What are those rights and responsibilities? There apparently has been no decision exactly defining them. Able and resourceful counsel have failed to present any, and the court has found none. For the consideration of this question, we revert to the question of negligence involved in the other cause of action. Judge Vann, in discussing the doctrine of res ipsa loquitur, in the case of Robinson v. Consolidated Gas Company of New York, 194 N.Y. 37, uses this language on page 40, 86 N.E. 805, 807, 28 L.R.A. (N.S.) 586: "The res of that maxim, which is sometimes misused, is not simply an accident resulting in injury, but the accident and the surrounding circumstances, necessarily shown by proving how the accident occurred, or in other words the occurrence as it appears by proof of the accident. The doctrine does not permit a recovery without some proof of negligence, but it regulates the degree of proof required under certain circumstances. If proof of the occurrence shows that the accident was such as could not have happened without negligence according to the ordinary experience of mankind, the doctrine is applied even if the precise omission or act of negligence is not specified."

[6-9] The above and other cases are cited by the respondent's counsel, to prove that the doctrine of res ipsa loquitur did not properly govern in the case at bar, and for the reasons given by him in his brief in the following words: "It is common knowledge that airplanes fall in a great many instances from causes over which the pilot has absolutely no control. Time and again we read in the newspapers where a complete inspection of the plane is made before starting and that for some unknown reason the engine stops requiring a forced landing which often results in a crash." The correctness of that statement we believe cannot be questioned, at least in the present state of aircraft development. When, therefore, a man takes over another man's land a machine which he knows is liable to crash upon and do injury to that land and the structures upon it, can it be said that he is an accidental trespasser within the meaning of those decisions which have exempted the trespasser from liability? It seems to me that the plaintiff proved one or the other of its causes of action. It can be said from human experience that an aeroplane will not fall except through negligence, then the plaintiff proved a prima facie case under its first cause of action. If, on the other hand, common experience requires the opposite conclusion, namely, that, no matter how perfectly constructed or how carefully managed an aeroplane may be, it may still fall, then the man who takes it over another's land and kills his cow or knocks off his chimney has committed an inexcusable trespass. It must be kept in mind that, when damage occurs in such a case, one or the other party has to stand it, and no reason readily suggests itself why it should not be the one who has brought about the chance occurrence. As was said by Chief Judge Rugg, of the Supreme Judicial Court of Massachusetts, in the case of Smith v. New England Aircraft Co., supra (page 392 of 170 N.E., 270 Mass. 511, 528): "Aerial navigation, important as it may be, has no inherent superiority over the landowner where their rights and claims are in actual conflict." And again, on page 393 of 170 N.E., 270 Mass. 511, 530: "Air navigation, important as it is, cannot rightly levy toll upon the legal rights of others for its successful prosecution." To hold that the defendant here is absolved from liability, because he was himself free from negligence, is to hazard all the chimneys in the land, as well as live stock on the farms, and even the people in their homes. The other alternative seems by far the more reasonable, namely: Such chance as there may be that a properly equipped and well-handled aeroplane may still crash upon and injure private property shall be borne by him who takes the machine aloft. I am therefore of the opinion that the plaintiff's cause of action upon the ground of negligence was properly dismissed, and that the only question which should have been submitted to the jury was the amount of damages suffered by the plaintiff, for which amount the plaintiff should have been awarded judgment.

The judgment appealed from is reversed, and a new trial ordered, with $30 costs and disbursements to the appellant.

223 N.Y.S. 2d 692
Larmicia and Solomon WOOD v. UNITED AIR LINES, INC.,
Trans World Airlines, Inc.
Supreme Court, Special Term, Kings County, Part I.
Dec. 14, 1961.

Action by husband and wife for injuries to the wife as the result of an airplane crash in the vicinity of their apartment. The plaintiffs moved for summary judgment on the issue of liability in trespass. The Supreme Court, Kings County, John E. Cone, J., held that the airline was not liable in trespass to apartment dweller near scene of airplane crash which allegedly led to fire damage to building and apartment, where there was no showing of intent to crash or of any control over the airplane after the mid-air collision preceding the crash.

Motion denied.

1. Trespass

Generally, to constitute actionable trespass there must be intent to do very act which results in immediate damage.

2. Trespass

Airline was not liable in trespass to dweller in apartment near scene of airplane crash which allegedly led to fire damage of building and apartment where there was no showing of intent to crash or of any control over airplane after mid-air collision preceding crash.

3. Aviation

Flying is no longer an ultra-hazardous activity which requires imposition of absolute liability for any damage or injury caused in course thereof.

4. Judgment

Summary judgment in action for damages in trespass would, regardless of liability, have to be denied where some of facts upon which motion was predicated, including manner in which plaintiff's injuries were sustained, were exclusively within knowledge of plaintiff or clearly not within knowledge of defendant.

Morris Hirschhorn, New York City, for plaintiff.

Haight, Gardner, Poor & Havens, New York City, for defendant United Air Lines.

Bigham, Englar, Jones & Houston, New York City, for defendant Trans World Airlines.

JOHN E. CONE, Justice.

Plaintiffs move for summary judgment in their favor against defendant United Air Lines, on the issue of liability in trespass.

This is an action in which plaintiff Larmicia Wood (hereinafter referred to as plaintiff) seeks to recover for personal injuries which she claims to have sustained in her apartment when a jet aircraft belonging to the defendant United Air Lines (hereinafter referred to as defendant) crashed in the immediate vicinity of Sterling Place and Seventh Avenue, in the Borough of Brooklyn, as the result of a mid-air collision with an airplane owned by co-defendant Trans World Airlines. The crash allegedly caused damage to the building at premises No. 26 Seventh Avenue and to plaintiffs' apartment located in said building. The plaintiff, Solomon Wood, as husband of the injured plaintiff, sues for loss of services, etc. Both plaintiffs, in addition, seek recovery for personal property damage allegedly resulting from the crash.

The "amended" complaint, in addition to alleging negligence, charges that the crash and the resultant damage and injury to plaintiff constituted a wrongful invasion of person and property which was in the nature of a trespass. It is plaintiffs' claim, as set forth in the memorandum in support of the instant motion, that the crash occurred in the immediate vicinity of No. 26 Seventh Avenue, and that "the ensuing explosions, concussions and fires brought about by the great impact of the crash with the spillage of jet fuel, almost completely burned out several buildings in the vicinity, including the premises of plaintiff Larmicia Wood, who was a tenant occupying her apartment at the time of the accident."

The instant motion for summary judgment is predicated not upon the claim of negligence but upon the trespass theory of liability, plaintiffs contending that the "invasion" resulting from the crash constituted a trespass as a matter of law. The plaintiffs, in effect, invoke a doctrine of strict or absolute liability which would impose liability upon an airplane owner for injuries or damage, sustained as a result of the crash of the plane, to person and property located on the ground, irrespective of the absence of any negligence or of any intent to invade the rights of those on the ground.

To establish that there was a physical invasion of the premises here involved, plaintiffs submit a report of the New York City Fire Department which, it is claimed, shows that there was extensive damage to the building in which plaintiff's apartment was located and to the apartment itself. Also submitted in support of the motion, presumably to show the injuries here complained of were sustained in plaintiff's apartment, is a medical abstract of the Coney Island Hospital, to which plaintiff was removed following the crash, containing a history stating in effect that plaintiff was at home when the crash occurred.

Defendant argues in opposition to the motion that there can be no trespass as a matter of law under the facts here sought to be shown by plaintiffs on this motion. Defendant contends further that the plaintiffs' moving papers are insufficient in that there is no competent proof offered to support the claim that plaintiff's apartment, or any part of the building for that matter, was physically invaded by defendant's aircraft, or that the plaintiff sustained her injuries in the apartment and not elsewhere, or that the plaintiff or her husband had the necessary possessory interest in the damaged premises to maintain an action in trespass. Defendant contends that in any event there are triable issues as to the foregoing, particularly since the facts relative to certain aspects thereof are exclusively within the knowledge of the plaintiff or, at any rate, are clearly not within defendant's knowledge.

[1] For the reasons and consideration herein below set forth, I am of the opinion that the facts which plaintiffs have sought to show on this motion are insufficient to support a recovery in trespass as a matter of law. It may safely be stated as a general rule that to constitute an actionable trespass there must be an intent to do the very act which results in the immediate damage (Socony-Vacuum Oil Co. v. Bailey, 202 Misc. 364, 109 N.Y.S.2d 799). The determinative factor is stated as follows in Phillips v. Sun Oil Co., 307 N.Y. 328, 331, 121 N.E.2d 249, 250:

> "Trespass is an intentional harm at least to this extent: while the trespasser, to be liable, need not intend or expect the damaging consequence of his intrusion, *he must intend the act which amounts to or produces the unlawful invasion,* and the intrusion must at least be the immediate or inevitable consequence of what he willfully does, or which he does so negligently as to amount to willfullness (citing cases, among them Guille v. Swan, 19 Johns, 381)." [Emphasis supplied.]

[2] In the instant case it would seem to be apparent that there was no intent to crash. Neither is there any indication that the collision which led to the crash occurred during the course of attempting to make a landing. No evidentiary facts are adduced on the instant motion to show that the plane was in any wise under the pilot's control when, as alleged in the amended complaint, it "plunged down" onto the street; indeed, the plaintiffs do not profess to argue that any control or management of the plane was possible, following the mid-air collision.

Upon this motion, plaintiffs rely basically on the view expressed in 1822 in Guille v. Swan (cited in the Phillips case supra), that "the intent with which an act is done is by no means a test of the liability of a party to an action of trespass." But it cannot be gainsaid that the somewhat absolute and unqualified language of the foregoing judicial pronouncement, and its application generally, must be construed and understood in the light of the explicatory language contained in the Phillips case, hereinbefore quoted. Moreover, an analysis of the cases, cited by plaintiffs, in which the element of intent was ignored or in which it did not loom as an essential element of the trespass cause of action, discloses that the imposition of liability in those cases involving, as they did, aviation mishaps, was predicated upon the assumption that flying was an extra-hazardous activity (see also the Restatement of the Law of Torts, § 519, applying the doctrine of strict liability to cases involving ultra-hazardous activity, and section 520 which defines ultra-hazardous activity and includes aviation as an example thereof).

Thus, turning to the cases cited by plaintiffs we find that in the Guille case, the defendant, a balloonist, descended into plaintiff's garden, which was a short distance from the place of defendant's ascent. The court, in holding the balloonist liable for damage done to plaintiff's garden by a crowd which rushed to the balloonist's aid, wrote in part as follows (Guille v. Swan, 19 Johns. 381, at p. 382);

> "I will not say that ascending in a balloon is an unlawful act, for it is not so; but, it is certain, that the Aeronaut has no control over its motion horizontally; he is at the sport of the winds, and is to descend when and how he can; his reaching the earth is a matter of hazard."

The case of Rochester Gas & Electric Corp. v. Dunlop (Monroe County Court), 1933, 148 Misc. 849, 266 N.Y.S. 469, also cited by plaintiffs, was an action both in negligence and trespass for damage caused to a tower when the airplane piloted by the defendant in that case crashed against it. The defendant's evidence was to the effect that in attempting to make a landing at night, following an engine failure, he failed to see the tower so as to avoid the collision. The court, in reversing a judgment rendered in favor of defendant and ordering a new trial, considered the application of either the res ipsa loquitur doctrine or the theory of trespass to the facts in the case. Concluding that trespass was the applicable theory, the court in effect predicated its decision upon the assumption that "common experience requires * * * [the conclusion] * * * that no matter how perfectly constructed or how carefully managed an aeroplane may be, it may still fall * * *" (pp. 851-852, 266 N.Y.S. p. 473). The court then stated that "when damage occurs in such a case, one or the other party has to stand it, and no reason readily suggests itself why it should not be the one who has brought about the chance occurrence" (p. 852, 266 N.Y.S. p. 473).

The other two cases upon which plaintiffs place principal reliance are Hahn v. U.S. Airlines, 1954, 127 F.Supp. 950 (E.D.N.Y.) and Margosian v. U.S. Airlines, 1955, 127 F.Supp. 464 (E.D.N.Y.). Both cases dealt with the same mishap, involving the crash of an airplane in the Borough of Queens, causing property damage. In both cases the court, upon the issue of liability in trespass, granted summary judgment in favor of the respective plaintiffs and against the aircraft owner. But we find that the court in the Hahn case relied upon section 165(c) of the Restatement of the Law of Torts, with particular reference to illustration 8 thereof. The court pointed out that § 165, subd. "c" recognizes liability for such "intrusion" as was caused by the crash. Illustration 8, which the court quoted, as being applicable, offers the following example of strict liability: "A is skillfully navigating an airplane far above the surface of B's premises. Stress of weather renders the plane unmanageable, and it comes to land in B's field, damaging his crops. A is liable to B." There should be noted, in this connection, the rationale underlying the view that flying is an ultra-hazardous activity (rendering it subject to the application of the doctrine of strict liability), which finds expression in § 520 of the Restatement. Thus, in comment b to section 520, it is stated that "aviation *in its present state of development* is ultra-hazardous because the best constructed and maintained aeroplane is so incapable of complete control that flying creates a risk that the plane even though carefully constructed, maintained and operated, may crash to the injury of persons, structures and chattels on the land over which the flight is made" (emphasis supplied). And in comment "g" a distinction is made between airplanes and automobiles, upon the ground that "the use of automobiles has become so common to the great mass of inhabitants of the United States and the residuum of risk which cannot be eliminated by careful driving and maintenance is so small that the driving of ordinary types of automobiles is not regarded as ultra-hazardous. On the other hand, aviation has not as yet become either a common or essential means of transportation. This, coupled with the fact that as yet aeroplanes have not been so perfected as to make them subject to a certainty of control approximating that of which automobiles are capable, and with the serious character of harm which an aeroplane out of control is likely to do to persons, structures or chattels on the land over which it flies make it proper to regard aviation as an ultra-hazardous activity."

Returning, however, to a consideration of the cases cited by plaintiffs on the instant motion, we find that the court in the Margosian case, supra, while making reference to the Restatement, manifested some concern with finding an element of intent as a prerequisite for the imposition of liability in trespass. As appears there from the court's opinion, the pilot in that case was seeking to make a landing at Idlewild when the plane crashed. This fact, in itself, can serve to distinguish the Margosian case from the instant one where there has been no showing that the pilot was in the course of landing at the time of the collision, or that he had any measure of control over the descending plane, following the collision.

[3] In any event, I am of the opinion, in light of the technical progress achieved in the design, construction, operation and maintenance of aircraft generally, that flying should no longer be deemed to be an ultra-hazardous activity, requiring the imposition of absolute liability for any damage or injury caused in the course thereof. This view is in accord with the current trend of the law. (Boyd v. White, 128 Cal.App.2d 641, 276 P.2d 92 [D.Ct.App.1954]; Southern California Edison Co. v. Coleman, 150 Cal.App.2d Supp. 829, 310 P.2d 504 [Super.Ct.1957].) Cf. Rogow v. United States, D.C.S.D.N.Y.1959, 173 F.Supp. 547, 556, and cases there cited.

It is to be noted that the Restatement, which was adopted and promulgated in 1938, rested its view of flying, as being an ultra-hazardous activity, upon the state of development of aviation existing at that time. It is indisputable that aviation has since made tremendous strides, both technically and in its use as a common mode of transportation. The view which has continued to gain acceptance is (as observed by the court in the Boyd case, cited supra) well expressed in a summary of the law contained in a 1949 annotation in 4 A.L.R.2d 1306, which reads as follows:

> "The courts and the law formerly looked upon aviation with the viewpoint still expressed in the American Law Institute, Restatement, Torts, Vol. 3, § 520, holding that aviation is an ultra-hazardous activity, similar to the operation of automobiles in the early days of the horseless carriage, and requiring those who take part in it to observe the highest degree of care. The Uniform Aeronautic Act, adopted in time by twenty-three states, imposed absolute liability on the owner, as well as the operator or lessee, of every aircraft for any damage to person or property caused by its operation provided there was no contributory negligence on the part

of him who was thus harmed. With the passage of time, however, this view came to be modified, and the trend of decisions established it to be the general rule that, properly handled by a competent pilot exercising reasonable care, an airplane is not an inherently dangerous instrument, so that in the absence of statute the ordinary rules of negligence control, and the owner (or operator) of an airship is only liable for injury inflicted upon another when such damage is caused by a defect in the plane or its negligent operation. By 1945, coincident with the opening of the postwar civilian aviation period, the number of states retaining the portions of the Uniform Aeronautic Act dealing with an owner's liability had dropped to eighteen."

A similar view is to be found in the Rogow case, cited supra, in which Kaufman, J., wrote as follows (173 F.Supp 547, at page 556):

> "In the early days of aviation, perhaps, it could have been said that planes crashed frequently and mysteriously through no fault of pilot or maintenance personnel. Cf. Rochester Gas & Electric Corp. v. Dunlop, 1933, 148 Misc. 849, 266 N.Y.S. 469. But great technical progress in the last few years has brought the art of flying to the state where aircraft do not generally meet disaster in the absence of some negligence. The New York courts have recognized this fact by applying the res ipsa loquitur doctrine in airplane crash cases. (Cases cited.) The Federal courts applying New York law have also repeatedly upheld the doctrine. (Citing cases.)"

Although the airplane involved in the instant case was a jet and not a conventional aircraft, no compelling reason suggests itself for applying a different view where, as in the present case, the crash was not shown to have been brought about by a mysterious or unknown defect peculiar to the design, maintenance or operation of jets, but appears to have been the result of a mishap, the nature of which arose out of a hazard common to the operation of conventional as well as jet aircraft.

[4] Based upon the foregoing considerations, I am of the opinion that actionable trespass has not been shown on the instant motion papers and that summary judgment therefor is not warranted. I am of the view that, in any event, summary judgment must be denied because some of the facts upon which the motion is predicated, among which is included the manner in which the plaintiff's injuries were sustained, are exclusively within the knowledge of plaintiff or clearly not within the knowledge of defendant (DeFrance v. Oestrike, 8 A.D.2d 735, 187 N.Y.S.2d 186; Vignola v. Britts, 11 A.D.2d 801, 205 N.Y.S.2d 215).

Accordingly, the motion for summary judgment is denied. Settle order on notice.

In the area of aerial agriculture, and weather modification, there are several cases that can be summarized here, rather than present the entire case.

The task of pinpointing liability is impeded, by the difficulty of establishing the source of the harmful spray and, in proving the negligence of the defendant.

The following are brief descriptions of cases, where it was held that the aircraft operator was liable for injury to plant life or animal stock on the ground.

1. The case of Hammond Ranch Corporation v. Dodson, 136 SW 2d 484 (Ark. 1940), involved the unauthorized spraying, with herbicides or pesticides, of the plaintiff's property adjacent to the property intended to be sprayed, and resulting in the death of the plaintiff's cattle.
2. The case of Burke v. Thomas 313 P.2d 1082 (Okla. 1957), involved the destruction of shade trees as a result of the unauthorized spraying with pesticides or herbicides.
3. George v. Cox 261 SW 2d 201 (Tex. 1953), is a situation in which a farm crop was destroyed as a result of unauthorized spraying.
4. In Kentucky Aerospray Inc. v. Mays 251 SW 2d 460 (Ky. 1952), the unauthorized spraying resulted in killing fish in a pool of the plaintiff.
5. Gerrard Co. v. Tricher, 27 P.2d 678 (Ariz. 1953), involved the death of bees, caused by the application of spray near the hives, and by bees carrying the substance to the hive.

When a property owner contracts to have his land sprayed and the aerial spraying causes injury to plant or animal life of a neighboring property owner, the property owner has tried to avoid liability by claiming that the injury was caused by the aerial sprayer acting as an independent contractor. The question as to who is liable is resolved as an issue of fact regarding the amount of control exercised by the owner of land, over the work performed by the contractor. This question is discussed in Pitchfork Land and Cattle Company v. King, 346 SW 2d 598 (Texas 1965).

In the case of Kennedy v. Clayton 227 SW 2d 934 (Ark. 1950), the court held that in the application of 2-4-D by an independent contractor, the property owner is absolutely liable because of the inherently dangerous nature of the substance.

The basis for this decision is that the property owner, when using such a dangerous substance, has a duty to prevent injury to others, and he cannot avoid his duty by contracting with an independent contractor.

In the case of Slutsky v. City of New York, 97 N.Y.S.2d 328 (1950), the operator of a resort hotel claimed that his business would be injured by experiments conducted by New York City to artificially induce rain in the New York Watershed. The court denied an injunction, by stating that the public necessity for an adequate water supply outweighed the inability of the plaintiff to show irreparable injury to himself and, his lack of vested rights in the clouds or the moisture therein.

CHAPTER 5

Liability to Passengers and Others

The cases reported in this section emphasize the legal considerations involved when a pilot, passenger, or employee is injured as a result of an aircraft crash or collision.

The legal questions that arise are:

1. Whether the passenger has the burden of proving that the carrier was negligent; or whether the carrier has the burden of proving that it was not negligent.
2. The second consideration is to determine whether the lawsuit should be tried under the laws of the State in which the accident occurred; or whether the lawsuit should be tried under the Laws of Admiralty, or the Death on the High Seas Act; or whether it should be tried under the laws of the foreign country in which the plane is registered; or whether the case is covered by Workmen's Compensation Laws in the case of an employee.

   This question is important because in some cases State laws make it easier for a plaintiff to recover damages; or the laws of the foreign country make it difficult for a plaintiff to recover damages; or the Workmen's Compensation cases limit the amount of damages that a plaintiff may recover for injuries.
3. A third question that must be resolved is whether the Federal Government is an employer and whether it is liable for the acts of its employees under the Federal Tort Claims Act. The United States Government is not liable under the Federal Tort Claims Act if the facts in the case considered, come within one of the exceptions set forth in the Act.

Burden of Proof

The general question of who has the burden of proving negligence, or of disproving negligence is considered in the case of Capital Airlines v. Barger, which follows.

341 S.W. 2d 579
CAPITAL AIRLINES, INC.
v.
Frances S. BARGER, Admx.
Court of Appeals of Tennessee,
Eastern Section.
Aug. 1, 1960.
Rehearing Denied Sept. 8, 1960.
Certiorari Denied by Supreme Court
Dec. 9, 1960.

Action by passenger's widow-administratrix against airline for passenger's wrongful death when airline's passenger airplane crashed short of runway. The Circuit Court, Hamilton County, John T. Mahoney, J., entered judgment on verdict for widow-administratrix and overruled airline's motion for new trial and for directed verdict, and airline appealed in error. The Court of Appeals, Howard, J., held that question of negligence under doctrine of res ipsa loquitur was for jury, and that award of $110,000 damages was excessive and would be sustained only on condition of remittitur of $12,500.

Judgment affirmed on condition of remittitur; otherwise reversed, and case remanded for new trial.

1. Trial

Where dispute exists as to any material determinative evidence, or doubt exists as to conclusion to be drawn from all the evidence, motion for directed verdict must be overruled.

2. Carriers

In action by passenger's widow-administratrix against airline for passenger's wrongful death when airline's passenger airplane crashed short of runway, question of negligence under doctrine of res ipsa loquitur was for jury.

3. Carriers

Where, in action by passenger's widow-administratrix against airline for passenger's wrongful death when airline's passenger airplane crashed short of runway, evidence raised inference or presumption of negligence under doctrine of res ipsa loquitur, airlines had to rebut the inference or presumption by showing that crash was unavoidable and could not have been prevented by exercise of highest degree of care.

4. Negligence

In Tennessee, doctrine of res ipsa loquitur is a rule of evidence.

5. Evidence

In event of conflict, questions of evidence are governed by law of the forum.

6. Carriers

Rule of res ipsa loquitur could be charged in Tennessee wrongful death action arising from airplane crash in Michigan.

7. Trial

Where, in death action, entire charge was clear, comprehensive, and reasonably complete, and generally conformed with applicable law, giving of certain portions of charge and refusal to charge certain special requests was not reversible error. T.C.A. §§ 27-116, 27-117.

8. Death

Under Michigan law, measure of recovery in wrongful death action is to be based upon what decedent's family was accustomed to receive, or had reasonable expectation of receiving, during decedent's lifetime. Comp.Laws Mich.1948, § 691.582.

9. Death

Under Michigan law, testimony throwing any light upon what the pecuniary injury resulting from death would be is admissible in wrongful death action. Comp.Laws Mich.1948, § 691.582.

10. Death

Under Michigan law, evidence as to loving relationship between husband and his family or evidence of lack of such relationship would be admissible in action for husband's wrongful death. Comp.Laws Mich.1948, § 691.582.

11. Death

In action for husband's wrongful death, exclusion of testimony of husband's girl friend in regard to husband's relation to her at time when he was still married to plaintiff was, under Michigan law, error. Comp.Laws Mich.1948, § 691.582.

12. Death

Award, in wrongful death action, of $110,000 damages for wrongful death of 28-year-old husband, who had allegedly contributed about $4,800 to his family the previous year, was excessive and would be sustained only on condition of remittitur of $12,500, in view of exclusion of testimony pertinent to issue of damages. Comp.Laws Mich.1948, § 691.582.

On Petition to Rehear.

13. Death

Under Michigan Wrongful Death Act, award of $110,000 damages for wrongful death of husband was not excessive, as a matter of law, in view of evidence that, during prior year, husband had contributed two-thirds of his $7,247.15 salary to support of his family, was capable of earning in excess of $9,000 a year, and had had life expectancy of 42.15 years. Comp.Laws Mich. 1948, § 691.582.

14. Interest

Under statute providing that interest is to be computed on every judgment from day on which it is entered of record, interest is to be computed from date of judgment overruling motion for new trial. T.C.A. § 47.1610.

Folts, Bishop & Thomas, Chattanooga, for plaintiff in error.
Harry Berke and A.A. Wassick, Chattanooga, for defendant in error.

HOWARD, Judge.

Referring to the parties as they appeared below, this tort action grew out of an airplane accident which occurred when a four-motor Viscount passenger plane, owned and operated by the defendant, Capital Airlines, Inc., crashed in a field approximately 2,200 feet short of the south end of runway No. 5, at the Tri-City Airport near Saginaw, Michigan. The accident occurred on the night of April 6, 1958, at 11:19 P.M. under circumstances hereinafter appearing. At the time the plane was approaching said runway to make a routine landing at the Airport. Plaintiff's husband, Dan M. Barger, age 28, was a passenger on the ill-fated plane, and he and 43 other passengers and the crew of 3 all perished in the crash.

Plaintiff, who qualified as Administratrix of her husband's estate in Hamilton County, Tennessee, sued the defendant for damages for the death of her husband, as provided by the wrongful death statute of the State of Michigan, her declaration alleging that the plane crashed short of the runway because of the negligence of the defendant in the following respects: "Failing to land the plane in a careful manner; failing to have the plane under proper control; failing to keep a proper lookout ahead for the runway; failing to provide or use proper instruments to guide the plane to a landing; and in failing to exercise a high degree of care to transport plaintiff's husband to his destination."

By general plea the defendant denied liability, and being ordered to plead specially, the defendant averred: "That the plane was properly equipped, had recently undergone inspection and had been found in good mechanical condition; that the defendant complied with all the rules and regulations of the Civil Aeronautics Board with regard to all phases of operation, maintenance, repair and use of the aircraft and the competency, skill and physical condition of the pilots; that the pilot for this flight was well qualified and thoroughly experienced; that the plane was making a routine approach to landing and had straightened out on its final approach when the nose of the plane dropped abruptly and the plane dove into the ground; that the accident was the result of an act of God and occurred because of an unusual, unforeseeable meteorological phenomenon which caused the plane to become uncontrollable, humanly, mechanically, or otherwise."

By replication the plaintiff joined issue upon the special pleas, and, thereupon, the case proceeded to trial before a jury.

There were two trials in which the defendant made motions for peremptory instructions at the conclusion of all the evidence introduced upon each trial. These motions were overruled. The first trial resulted in a mistrial, because the jury was unable to agree, and by reason of the trial judge's refusal to sustain defendant's motion for peremptory instructions, the defendant preserved and has filed a Wayside Bill of Exceptions. The second trial resulted in a jury verdict for the plaintiff for $110,000, which the trial judge approved, and judgment was entered. Defendant filed motion for a new trial and for a directed verdict, which motion was overruled, and this appeal in error was prayed, granted and perfected.

The defendant concedes that the evidence introduced on both trials was substantially the same. This concession, therefore, obviates the procedural requirement of our reviewing here the record of the first trial, although we have carefully and painstakingly read the records of both trials, in order to get a more complete understanding of the case.

Defendant's assignments of error are directed to (1) the sufficiency of the evidence; (2) alleged errors in the charge; (3) the denying of certain requests; (4) the exclusion of certain evidence, and (5) the amount of the verdict.

[1] The rule is well settled that where there is any dispute as to any material determinative evidence, or any doubt as to the conclusion to be drawn from all the evidence, a motion for a directed verdict must be overruled. Lackey v. Metropolitan Life Ins. Co., 30 Tenn.App. 390, 206 S.W.2d 806; East Tenn. Natural Gas Co. v. Peltz, 38 Tenn.App. 100, 270 S.W.2d 591.

We shall now review briefly the evidence as reflected by the record:

On the night of the ill-fated crash, the proof showed that the weather was disagreeable, but not unusually hazardous for flying. There was a mixture of slight rain, sleet and snow, with gusts of wind ranging from 18 to 27 knots per hour. At 11 P.M., only a few minutes before the crash, the weather observer in the tower at the airport recorded a 900 foot ceiling overcast, with visibility of 3 miles. None of these conditions was described as dangerous for the safe landing of planes. In fact only a few minutes before the crash two other planes had landed safely on runway 5, and these pilots testified that they experienced no trouble, and had found the weather much better than reported to them by the weather observer.

As the ill-fated plane approached the airport for a landing, it appears that it made a wide swing and missed the runway; that after circling the airport in a slight bank, the plane returned and approached the runway much "slower and lower" than had planes previously at this point. On descending to a point about 2,200 feet short of the runway, the plane, traveling at an estimated height of from 250 to 500 feet, suddenly nosed down at an angle of from 45 to 60 degrees and crashed to the ground. By the force of the impact the motors were buried in the dirt about 3 feet, and the forward momentum of the plane caused it to flip over on its back. After coming to rest the tail of the plane was pointing toward the runway on which it had expected to land. On striking the ground the plane burst into flames, making it impossible for any of the passengers or crew to escape.

It further appears that the plane was fully loaded with passengers, and that at a stop only 20 minutes previously had been refueled; that the plane was bound to accumulate some ice under prevailing weather conditions, necessitating the use of the de-icer, and that as ice accumulated it was necessary to increase the power. There were admissions by defendant's witnesses that the Dowmic switch, a pre-stall warning device, was found to be in a malfunctioning condition after the crash, but that defendant's pilots did not rely upon this device. Also that the pilot of the ill-fated plane had made "below average grade" on some of the phases of his pre-flight tests.

An investigation following the accident by the Civil Aeronautics Board disclosed that the crash did not result from the failure of any structural parts of the plane, nor was there any proof whatsoever by pilots or weather observers of any unusual weather phenomenon in the area that caused or remotely contributed to the cause of the crash.

It was conceded that the defendant's pilot had the exclusive control and management of the plane; that defendant was a public carrier for hire; that plaintiff's intestate was a paying passenger, and that defendant owed him the highest degree of care.

On behalf of the defendant it is insisted here, as it was below, that the proof showed that it was impossible for a plane flying at the altitude of 250 to 500 feet to crash as did the plane in question; that under the prevailing conditions had there been a failure of motors, or had the pilot turned loose of the controls, or flown too low, the plane would not have nosed down abruptly, but would have mushed into a pancake landing and spread wreckage over a great area.

[2,3] Were the above facts sufficient to warrant the jury in finding an inference or presumption of negligence under the doctrine of res ipsa loquitur? We think that they were, as it devolved upon the defendant to rebut the inference or presumption by showing that the crash was unavoidable, and could not have been prevented by the exercise of the highest degree of care.

Regarding the application of the doctrine of res ipsa loquitur, the Middle Section of this Court, speaking through Felts, Judge, in Sullivan et ux. v. Crabtree, 36 Tenn.App. 469, 258 S.W.2d 782, 783, said:

> "The classic statement of the doctrine of res ipsa loquitur is this: '(W)here the thing (causing the harm) is shown to be under the management of defendant or his servants, and the accident is such as in the ordinary course of things does not happen if those who have the management use proper care, it affords reasonable evidence, in the absence of explanation by the defendants, that the accident arose from want of care'. Erle, C.J., Scott v. London and St. Katherine Docks Co. (1865), 3 H. & C. 596, 159 Eng. Reprint 665, 667.
>
> "This statement has been accepted in our cases. John Bouchard & Sons Co. v. Keaton, 9 Tenn.App. 467, 479; North Memphis Savings Bank v. Union Bridge & Const. Co., 138 Tenn. 161, 177, 196 S.W. 492; Lewis v. Casenburg, 157 Tenn. 187, 7 S.W.2d 808, 60 A.L.R. 254; Poor Sisters of St. Francis v. Long, 190 Tenn. 434, 230 S.W.2d 659.
>
> "The maxim res ipsa loquitur means that the facts of the occurrence evidence negligence; the circumstances unexplained justify an inference of negligence. In the principle of proof employed, a case of res ipsa loquitur does not differ from an ordinary case of circumstantial evidence. Res ipsa loquitur is not an arbitrary rule but rather 'a common sense appraisal of the probative value of circumstantial evidence'. Boykin v. Chase Bottling Works, 32 Tenn.App. 508, 520-523, 222 S.W.2d 889, 896.
>
> * * * * *
>
> " 'A res ipsa loquitur case is a circumstantial evidence case which permits a jury to infer negligence from the mere occurrence of the

accident itself'. Prosser, Res Ipsa Loquitur in California, 37 Cal.L.Rev. 183, 191. So after proof of the rem the adding of another fact or facts may supply the explanation and take the case out of the rule. For example, see Granert v. Bauer, 17 Tenn.App. 370, 373, 67 S.W.2d 748 (where driver ran out of road trying to miss a hole); Oliver v. Union Transfer Co., 17 Tenn.App. 694, 698, 71 S.W.2d 478 (where side of road caved in taking the bus with it).

* * * * *

"It is true there has been confusion in the cases as to the procedural effect of res ipsa loquitur, some cases giving it one and some another of these three different effects:

"(1) It warrants an inference of negligence which the jury may draw or not, as their judgment dictates. Poor Sisters of St. Francis v. Long, 190 Tenn. 434, 442-443, 230 S.W.2d 659; Boykin v. Chase Bottling Works, 32 Tenn.App. 508, 522-523, 222 S.W.2d 889.

"(2) It raises a presumption of negligence which requires the jury to find negligence if defendant does not produce evidence sufficient to rebut the presumption. Gill v. Brown, 130 Tenn. 174, 178, 169 S.W. 752; Kay v. Metropolitan Street R. Co., 163 N.Y. 447, 57 N.E. 751; Prosser on Torts, 304; cf. Foltis, Inc. v. City of New York, 287 N.Y. 108, 38 N.E.2d 455, 153 A.L.R. 1122; Annotation, 153 A.L.R. 1134.

"(3) It not only raises such a presumption but also shifts the ultimate burden of proof to defendant and requires him to prove by a preponderance of all the evidence that the injury was not caused by his negligence. Turnpike Co. v. Yates, 108 Tenn. 428, 434, 67 S.W. 69; Gorsuch v. Swan, 109 Tenn. 36, 69 S.W. 1113, 97 Am.St.Rep. 836; Prosser on Torts, 304, 305.

"For a review of the numerous cases and a clear and helpful discussion of the subject, see: Prosser, The Procedural Effect of Res Ipsa Loquitur (1936), 20 Minn.L.Rev. 241-271; Prosser, Res Ipsa Loquitur in California (1949), 37 Cal.L.Rev. 183-234; Prosser on Torts (1941), 291-310.

"The effect of a case of res ipsa loquitur, like that of any other case of circumstantial evidence, varies from case to case, depending on the particular facts of each case; and therefore such effect can no more be fitted into a fixed formula or reduced to a rigid rule than can the effect of other cases of circumstantial evidence. The only generalization that can be safely made is that, in the words of the definition of res ipsa loquitur, it affords 'reasonable evidence', in the absence of an explanation by defendant, that the accident arose from this negligence.

* * * * *

"In the ordinary case, however, res ipsa loquitur merely makes a case for the jury—merely permits the jury to choose the inference of defendant's negligence in preference to other permissible or reasonable inferences. North Memphis Savings Bank v. Union Bridge & Const. Co., 138

> Tenn. 161, 188, 196 S.W. 492; John Bouchard & Sons Co. v. Keaton, 9 Tenn.App. 467, 480-481; Boykin v. Chase Bottling Works, 32 Tenn.App. 508, 523, 222 S.W.2d 889; Poor Sisters of St. Francis v. Long, 190 Tenn. 434, 442-443, 230 S.W.2d 659; Prosser, Res Ipsa Loquitur in California, 37 Cal.L.Rev. 183, 217-225."

It is insisted, however, that in airplane crashes the doctrine of res ipsa loquitur has been rejected by the Courts of Tennessee, and defendant relies principally upon Boulineaux v. City of Knoxville, 20 Tenn.App. 404, 99 S.W.2d 557, and Towle v. Phillips, 180 Tenn. 121, 172 S.W.2d 806.

In the Boulineaux case, decided in 1935, the plaintiffs sued for injuries sustained by a crash of the plane which was carrying them as passengers for hire on a sight-seeing flight. The crash resulted from the stalling of the motor after the plane had proceeded approximately one-half mile from the point of take off. There was a judgment for the defendants, and on affirming the judgment this Court rejected the doctrine of res ipsa loquitur because "it is a common and not an unusual occurrence for airplanes to stall and fall while in operation, and without the intervention of any act upon the part of the operator." [20 Tenn. App. 404, 99 S.W.2d 561.]

In Towle v. Phillips, supra [180 Tenn. 121, 172 S.W.2d 808], decided in 1943, the Supreme Court refused to apply the doctrine of res ipsa loquitur because (1) the plane had dual controls, one of which was accessible to the passenger, and (2) the operation of aircraft had not attained the position "where the doctrine of cases dealing with stagecoaches or trolley cars or steam railways can be applied."

In this enlightened age, it is common knowledge that within the past two decades tremendous improvements have been effected in the design and construction of airplanes, and in their operation and maintenance. Today an airplane is considered as a reasonably safe means of rapid transportation. Daily there are thousands of transport planes flying according to fixed schedules throughout the world carrying thousands of passengers annually, and airplane lines are vigorously competing with railroads, bus lines and steam ships. When the Boulineaux and Towle cases were decided, the development of air transportation could be appropriately termed as being in its adolescent stages. But since World War II, the development of aviation has been amazingly rapid, and the modern trend of authority seems to hold the rule of res ipsa loquitur applicable to airplane cases. In the field of aviation, as in other fields of transportation, accomplishment and liability are inseparable, and it appears to us that the principles governing liability of other common carriers should now be equally applicable to transport airplanes operating as such.

In American Jurisprudence, it says:

> "The doctrine of res ipsa loquitur, which asserts that whenever a thing which produced an injury is shown to have been under the control and management of the defendant, and the occurrence is such as in the ordinary course of events does not happen, if due care has been exercised, the fact of injury itself will be deemed to afford sufficient evidence to

support a recovery in the absence of any explanation by the defendant tending to show that the injury was not due to his want of care, has generally been applied to airplane accidents. The doctrine has been applied most frequently in actions for the injury or death of passengers for hire, and it has been stated that to be peculiarly suitable in actions against common carriers, due to the higher degree of care required." Vol. 6, Sec. 77, p. 45.

For a review of the decisions of other States applying the rule of res ipsa loquitur to airplane cases, see 6 A.L.R.2d p. 528.

Accordingly, as the law is progressive and expansive, adapting itself to the new relations and interests which are constantly springing up in the progress of society, we are constrained to hold the doctrine of res ipsa loquitur applicable under the facts and circumstances presented in the instant case.

Defendant insists that the trial Court erred in charging the rule of res ipsa loquitur, because (1) the accident having occurred in the State of Michigan, the law of that State would govern; and (2) that the Courts of the State of Michigan have never adopted said doctrine.

[4-6] In this State, the doctrine of res ipsa loquitur has been recognized as a rule of evidence, Quinley v. Cocke, 183 Tenn. 428, 192 S.W.2d 992; Oliver v. Union Transfer Co., 17 Tenn.App. 694, 71 S.W.2d 478; and where there is a conflict, the questions of evidence are governed by the law of the forum. Shepard & Gluck v. Thomas, 147 Tenn. 338, 246 S.W. 836; 11 Am.Jur., Secs. 203, 204, pp. 521, 524; 31 C.J.S. Evidence § 5, p. 509.

In 31 C.J.S. § 5, supra, it says:

> "It is well established that the courts of one state or country are not bound by the rules of evidence adopted in another jurisdiction, but the admissibility of evidence, as well as the burden of proof, and weight and sufficiency of evidence, is always governed by the lex fori."

While it appears that the Courts of Michigan have rejected the term "res ipsa loquitur," Rebentisch v. Korda, 331 Mich. 656, 50 N.W.2d 192, 194, nevertheless, the Courts of that State have recognized and applied the principle in numerous cases under the circumstantial evidence rule. Barnowsky v. Helson, 89 Mich. 523, 50 N.W. 989, 15 L.R.A. 33; Sewell v. Detroit United Railway, 158 Mich. 407, 123 N.W. 2; Indiana Lumbermens Mut. Ins. Co. v. Matthew Stores, Inc., 349 Mich. 441, 84 N.W.2d 755, and cases cited therein.

[7] Defendant further complains (1) of other portions of the trial Judge's charge, and (2) his refusal to charge certain special requests. After carefully considering the portions complained of in the light of the general charge, we find no errors that would justify a reversal of the case. T.C.A. §§ 27-116, 27-117. Nor is there an affirmative showing that the requests which were refused affected the results of the trial. T.C.A. § 27-117. De Rossett v. Malone, 34 Tenn.App. 451, 239 S.W.2d 366. The entire charge, which covered several pages of the record, was clear, comprehensive and reasonably complete, and conformed generally with the law as stated in Sullivan et ux. v. Crabtree, supra, and cases cited therein.

Next the defendant complains because the trial Judge excluded from the jury portions of testimony offered by defendant's witness, Josephine Bosarge. The testimony excluded was put in the record and is before us. The substance of the excluded testimony is that plaintiff and her husband were separated at the time of his death; that they separated in Chattanooga in 1957, while decedent was employed as manager of a shoe store operated by the Butler Shoe Company, in Birmingham, Alabama; that, thereafter decedent saw Miss Bosarge regularly every weekend at her home in Biloxi, Mississippi; that when decedent would return to Chattanooga to visit his little daughter, Dianne, age 6, he would call this witness on the telephone every night; that after the decedent accepted a position as salesman with Dr. Scholl's and went to Chicago in March 1958, he called witness on the telephone on numerous occasions and corresponded regularly with her; that the witness and decedent had discussed marriage, and had planned to marry as soon as plaintiff and decedent were divorced.

Plaintiff had denied that she and her husband were separated at the time of his death, or that they were contemplating divorce at the time. To the contrary she testified that they were happily married, and that he had contributed most liberally toward the support of his family; that they had had only one estrangement in December, 1957, when they agreed to separate and she sued for divorce; that within 2 weeks after the divorce petition was filed, they became reconciled and the petition was later dismissed, and that they had been happy following reconciliation.

[8,9] The wrongful death Statute of the State of Michigan, Sec. 27-712, Comp. Laws 1948, § 691.582, provides that "the court or jury may give such damages, as, the court or jury, shall deem fair and just, with reference to the pecuniary injury resulting from such death." Under the Michigan decisions, the measure of recovery seems to be based upon what the family was accustomed to receive, or had *reasonable expectation of receiving during the decedent's lifetime.* Chicago & N.W. Ry. Co. v. Bayfield, 37 Mich. 205; Ingersoll v. Detroit & M. Ry. Co., 163 Mich. 268, 128 N.W. 227, 32 L.R.A.,N.S., 362; Meola v. Quincy Mining Co., 174 Mich. 305, 140 N.W. 460. Therefore, testimony throwing any light upon what the pecuniary injury resulting from such death would be, is admissible. Rajnowski v. Detroit, B.C. & A.R. Co., 74 Mich. 20, 41 N.W. 847. (Emphasis supplied.)

[10,11] Under the above decisions, it is apparent that the amount which a husband would be expected to contribute during his lifetime would in some measure be expected by his relationship with his family. If that relationship were amicable, intimate and close, then the contribution would be expected to be greater than if the relationship were distant, unfriendly and strained. Hence, evidence as to a loving relationship between a husband and his family would be admissible on the question of damages for his death, and by the same token evidence that no loving relationship existed between the husband and his family would likewise be admissible. See also 16 Am.Jur. 236, p. 157; Annotation 74 A.L.R. 31. Accordingly, for reasons stated, we think that the Court erred in excluding the testimony of this witness.

[12] Finally, the defendant urges that the amount awarded by the jury is excessive.

Decedent, who was 28 years of age at the time of his death, had a life expectancy of 42.15 years under the Tennessee Mortality Tables. He was born and reared in Chattanooga, and was a high school graduate. While in high school and after graduation, he worked for the Butler Shoe Company, which operates a chain of shoe stores in several Southern cities. In 1955, he was promoted to store manager, in which capacity he was thereafter sent to various cities, including Birmingham, Alabama, Biloxi, Mississippi, and Raleigh, North Carolina. His salary for the year 1957 amounted to $7,247.15, two-thirds of which, according to the plaintiff, he contributed to her and Dianne's support. About January 1, 1958, decedent accepted a position as salesman with the Dr. Scholl's Company, manufacturer of shoes, innersoles, etc., and was sent to school in Chicago by this Company where he was a student at the time of his death. Just what salary he would have earned in his new position is not indicated. Previous to the ill-fated crash, decedent had left Chicago and at the time was on his way to Flint, Michigan, where he intended to spend the weekend at the home of Mr. and Mrs. Mackay, an aunt and uncle of Josephine Bosarge.

Admittedly, the size of the judgment has given us much concern as we have been unable to find any Michigan cases, nor has counsel for plaintiff pointed to any cases from that jurisdiction, approving judgments of like amounts in death cases. Likewise, we have found none in Tennessee. As heretofore pointed out, portions of the testimony of defendant's witness Bosarge were improperly excluded, and while this excluded testimony did not go to the issue of liability, it was pertinent to the issue of damages and the jury should have been allowed to determine its value, in the light of plaintiff's testimony. Under these circumstances, we feel that the error could be corrected if a remittitur were granted. City of Maryville v. McConkey, 19 Tenn.App. 520, 90 S.W.2d 951; 5B C.J.S. Appeal and Error § 1869, p. 312. This would obviate the necessity of another trial and at the same time do substantial justice to both parties. For the reasons stated, we are, therefore, constrained to order a remittitur of $12,500, and if accepted, judgment will be entered here for $97,500, at plaintiff-in-error's costs. If rejected, the judgment below will be reversed and the case will be remanded for a new trial.

McAMIS, P.J., and HALE, J., concur.

On Petition to Rehear

HOWARD, Judge.

Defendant, Capital Airlines, Inc., has filed petition to rehear in which it is respectfully requested that we (1) respond to the 9th assignment of error, and (2) disallow interest on the judgment.

[13] By the 9th assignment of error it is urged "that the verdict of $110,000.00 was excessive as a matter of law because the best proof of the plaintiff under the Michigan Wrongful Death Act would have entitled her to a

maximum recovery of about $97,500.00."; that under the circumstances the trial Judge erred in refusing defendant a new trial.

As pointed out in our original opinion, the decedent's "salary for the year 1957 amounted to $7,247.15, two-thirds of which, according to the plaintiff, he contributed to her and Dianne's support." There was also proof, undisputed, that decedent was capable of earning in excess of $9,000 a year as a salesman.

Based upon what the decedent's family was accustomed to receiving, and taking into consideration what they had reasonable expectation of receiving during his life expectancy of 42.15 years, we cannot arbitrarily say as a matter of law that the amount awarded by the jury was excessive under the proof. Therefore, the 9th assignment of error is overruled.

[14] Regarding interest, T.C.A. § 47-1610 provides that "Interest shall be computed on every judgment from the day on which it was entered of record." In construing the above statute, our Courts have held that interest shall be computed from the date of judgment overruling motion for a new trial. Monday v. Millsaps, 197 Tenn. 295, 271 S.W.2d 857; Tenn. Elec. Power Co. v. Hanson, 18 Tenn.App. 542, 79 S.W.2d 818.

Accordingly, for reasons indicated, the petition to rehear is denied at petitioner's costs.

McAMIS, P.J., and HALE, J., concur.

Admiralty Laws and Death on High Seas Act

In 1920, Congress passed the Death on the High Seas Act (41 Stat. 537), and thereby created a remedy, or right of action, for death caused by wrongful act, neglect or default, on the high seas.

The First National Bank of Greenwich v. National Airlines, which follows in this section, demonstrates how the courts resolved the question of whether to apply the State law or the Death on the High Seas Act.

When the Death on the High Seas Act created the right of action to sue for death occurring on the high seas, several other aspects arose.

The first task was to determine whether to apply the law of the United States or the laws of the foreign country in which the aircraft was registered. This question is covered in three of the following cases, namely: Noel v. United Aircraft, Fernandez v. L.A.V., and Bergeron v. K.L.M.

The second task was to determine whether to afford the injured employee the relief of unlimited liability of employer, as provided by the Death on the High Seas Act; or whether to give the injured employee the limited liability of his employer as provided by the Workmen's Compensation laws. The courts' resolution of this aspect of the problem is set forth in the following cases: South Pacific Company v. Jensen, and King v. Pan American World Airways.

The laws and rules of Admiralty are old and settled. Some of these laws and rules have been made applicable to the law of aviation and others have not.

The cases of South Pacific Company v. Jensen, and Executive Jet Aviation Inc. v. City of Cleveland, both of which follow, examine this aspect of the relationship of Admiralty Law to Aviation Law.

Before reading the cases in this section, read and become familiar with, the provisions of extracts from Death on the High Seas Act, Extract C.

Refer to Extract C, D.H.S.A.
Section 1 and Section 2.

288 F. 2d 621
FIRST NATIONAL BANK IN GREENWICH as Administrator c.t.a. of the Estate of Frenelia Lillian Putnam, deceased, etc., Plaintiff-Appellant,
v.
NATIONAL AIRLINES, INCORPORATED, Defendant-Appellee.
Samuel KESSLER, as Administrator de bonis non of the Estate of Rodma Lewis Osman, deceased, Plaintiff-Appellant,
v.
NATIONAL AIRLINES, INCORPORATED, Defendant-Appellee.
Nos. 245, 246, Dockets 25915, 25916.
United States Court of Appeals
Second Circuit.
Argued Feb. 15, 1961.
Decided April 6, 1961.

Actions for wrongful death. The United States District Court for the Southern District of New York, Richard H. Levet, J., 171 F.Supp. 528, dismissed plaintiffs' diversity claims under the Alabama Wrongful Death Act, then proceeding in admiralty ruled that plaintiffs suffered no compensable damage, and they appealed. The Court of Appeals, Lumbard, Chief Judge, held, inter alia, that evidence failed to establish that a child of decedent sustained a pecuniary loss as the result of the death of her mother in an airplane accident on the high seas.

Affirmed.

See, also, D.C., 22 F.R.D. 46.

1. Death

Damages, under the Alabama Wrongful Death Act, are not designed to compensate decedent's relatives for pecuniary loss, but are fixed by defendant's degree of culpability and are designed to punish him and deter others from similar negligence. Code of Ala., Tit. 7, § 123.

2. Federal Civil Procedure

A pre-trial order providing that a state death action and an admiralty cause of action be consolidated for trial, and that separate verdicts and judgments be entered in respect of each claim, was not binding on trial judge, but rather was an order addressed to good sense of trial judge. Fed.Rules Civ.Proc. rule 16, 28 U.S.C.A.

3. Federal Civil Procedure

It was proper for trial court to try issue of jurisdiction before reaching questions of negligence and damages in consolidated causes of action for death under state law, and for damages under the Death on the High Seas Act. Fed. Rules Civ.Proc. rule 42(b), 28 U.S.C.A.

4. States

State's boundary extended only one league from shore.

5. Admiralty

Error, if any, of trial court in labeling as advisory, jury's response to question of whether an accident occurred over land area of a state or within one marine league of shore of the state, was not prejudicial where trial judge reached same conclusion, and jury had not been told that its function was merely to advise.

6. Evidence

Statement of witness who had searched for bodies from an airliner which crashed, that "they found some," off a certain island, was properly excluded as hearsay as it revealed on its face that witness was not present when bodies were found.

7. Federal Civil Procedure

Portion of deposition of witness that he was standing on shore at a certain time on day an airplane crashed and he heard an airplane going west toward the gulf was properly excluded as not being sufficiently relevant on location of crash, where there was nothing to show that airplane he heard was the one that crashed, and the airplane that crashed was in the air for at least ten minutes after time witness heard the airplane.

8. Death

Aunts and uncles who could not show they were dependent upon decedent were precluded from recovery for such death under the Death on the High Seas Act. Death on the High Seas Act, §§ 1-7, 46 U.S.C.A. §§ 761-767.

9. Death

A child of decedent in order to recover under the Death on the High Seas Act was required to establish a pecuniary loss. Death on the High Seas Act, §§ 1-7, 46 U.S.C.A. §§ 761-767.

10. Death

Evidence failed to establish that a child of decedent sustained a pecuniary loss as the result of the death of her mother in an airplane accident on the high seas. Death on the High Seas Act, §§ 1-7, 46 U.S.C.A. §§ 761-767.

Theodore E. Wolcott, New York City, for plaintiffs-appellants.

John G. Reilly, New York City (Robert F. Ewald, Bigham, Englar, Jones & Houston, New York City, on the brief), for defendant-appellee.

Before LUMBARD, Chief Judge, and CLARK and SMITH, Circuit Judges.

LUMBARD, Chief Judge.

On February 14, 1953, National Airlines Flight 470, en route from Tampa to New Orleans, met with winds of hurricane velocity and crashed in the Gulf of Mexico near the Alabama shore. None of the 46 on board survived the disaster and among those killed were Frenelia Lillian Putnam whose administrator, acting for the benefit of Mrs. Putnam's daughter, Muriel Putnam Smith, is the appellant in #25915, and Rodma Lewis Osman, whose administrator acting for the benefit of Mrs. Osman's aunts and uncles, is the appellant in #25916.

It was unclear where the accident occurred; whether within the territorial jurisdiction of Alabama, in which case the Alabama Wrongful Death Act, 7 Alabama Code § 123, was applicable and the district court had jurisdiction because of diversity of citizenship, or on the high seas beyond the jurisdiction of Alabama, in which case the Federal Death on the High Seas Act, 46 U.S.C.A. §§ 761-767, applied and jurisdiction lay in admiralty.[1] Claims under both statutes were joined and after a hearing in which the evidence was limited to the situs of the accident, Judge Levet, reaching the same result as had the jury which he termed "advisory," found that the accident occurred on the high seas more than one marine league from the Alabama shore. The court, therefore, dismissed the Alabama wrongful death action and proceeded in admiralty under the Death on the High Seas Act to try the issue of damages, National having admitted its liability for the accident. After trial, Judge Levet held that Mrs. Osman's aunts and uncles could not recover since they had not shown, as the statute requires, 46 U.S.C.A. § 761, that they were "dependent" relatives of Mrs. Osman; Mrs. Smith was denied recovery since she had failed to establish that the death of her mother, Mrs. Putnam, caused her a "pecuniary" loss as the Death on the High Seas Act requires, 46 U.S.C.A. § 762.[2]

[1] The plaintiffs now appeal from the order dismissing the Alabama claim, which was harmful to them since under the Alabama statute damages are not designed to compensate a decedent's relatives for "pecuniary" loss but are rather fixed by the defendant's degree of culpability and designed to punish him and deter others from similar negligence, Avery Freight Lines, Inc. v. Stewart, 1953, 258 Ala. 524, 63 So.2d 895, 897. They claim that the district court committed error in deciding the issue of situs before hearing evidence on negligence and damage, in treating the jury as advisory and in excluding certain evidence bearing upon the locale of the accident. We disagree and, since we also find that the trial court was correct in holding that the plaintiffs had failed to establish a right to recover under the Death on the High Seas Act, we affirm the judgment below.

1. The complaint under the Death on the High Seas Act was brought on the civil side of the district court. But after this court decided Noel v. Linea Aeropostal Venezolana, 2 Cir., 1957, 247 F.2d 677, 66 A.L.R.2d 997, holding that rights under the Death on the High Seas Act were cognizable only in admiralty, the appellants sought and Judge Bicks granted a transfer to the admiralty side of the court.

2. In a companion suit, Mrs. Smith recovered $38,930 on account of the pecuniary loss caused to her by the death of her father, Eben F. Putnam, who had been killed in the same crash.

I. *The dismissal of plaintiffs' claim under the Alabama Wrongful Death Act.*

The plaintiffs' first contention is that Judge Levet, by trying the issue of jurisdiction before reaching the questions of negligence and damage, violated Judge Bicks' pretrial order [referred to supra in footnote 1] that "the Alabama causes of action * * * and the cause of action alleged in admiralty be consolidated for trial and shall be tried together, the civil claims to be tried to a jury and the claim in admiralty simultaneously be tried to a court." The order continues to state "that separate and several verdicts and judgments shall be rendered and entered in respect of each claim in such form and manner as the Trial Court shall direct * * *"

[2] Though the procedure adopted by Judge Levet may not have been in accord with the letter of this order, we can see no reason why that order should be interpreted to prevent the judge trying the case from resolving the jurisdictional question before reaching the issues of liability and damages; in any event, Judge Bicks' order under the view of the "law of the case" concept taken in this circuit was not binding but rather addressed to the good sense of his colleagues. Higgins v. California Prune & Apricot Grower, Inc., 2 Cir., 1924, 3 F.2d 896, 898; Meyers v. Jay Street Connecting Railroad, 2 Cir., 288 F.2d 356, at Note 10. Cf. Federal Rules of Civil Procedure, Rule 16, 28 U.S.C.A.

[3] The procedure chosen by Judge Levet was permissible under Rule 42(b) of the Federal Rules of Civil Procedure and was eminently sensible. Since the elements of damages under the Alabama statute were different from those under the Death on the High Seas Act, it was wise to determine at the outset which statute was applicable in order to avoid the presentation of unnecessary evidence. The procedure adopted also prevented the waste of having a jury sit through a full trial only to find at the end that jurisdiction lay in admiralty and, therefore, their services were not needed.

[4,5] The plaintiffs next complain that the trial judge deprived them of their right to jury trial on the issue of where the accident occurred by labeling as "advisory" the jury's negative response to the question whether the accident had occurred "over the land area of Alabama or within a marine league of the shore of Alabama."[3] Since the trial judge reached the same conclusion as the jury and since the jury had not been told that their function was merely to advise, the plaintiffs' right to jury trial on the factual issue dispositive of the jurisdictional question was not impinged. There appears to be no right of jury trial on these jurisdictional issues, see 5 Moore para. 38.36, but in any event there was no prejudice to the plaintiffs since they had a jury trial.

[6] We find no merit in plaintiffs' contentions relating to the exclusion of evidence bearing upon the situs of the accident. The plaintiffs principally object to the exclusion of a portion of the deposition of George W. Roberson, a gulf seaman, wherein Roberson, who had said that he had joined some men who were

3. Judge Levet was correct in ruling that Alabama's boundary extends only one marine league from her shore. United States v. State of Louisiana, 1959, 363 U.S. 1, 82, 80 S.Ct. 961, 4 L.Ed.2d 1025.

searching for the bodies of the victims, stated that "we cruised this area two or three days. They found some off Petit Bois Island." The statement was properly excluded as hearsay since on its face it reveals that Roberson himself was not present when the bodies were found. Had he been present it is inconceivable that he would not have been questioned further on the precise location of the bodies.

[7] Excluded also was another portion of Roberson's deposition wherein he said that while standing on the shore at about 5:00 P.M. on the day of the accident he heard an airplane going west toward the gulf. Since there was nothing to show that this was Flight 417, since the plane Roberson heard was heading toward the gulf and since Flight 417 was in the air at least as late as 5:10, this testimony was properly excluded as not being sufficiently relevant.

We find no merit in the contention that Judge Levet conducted the trial on the jurisdictional issue in a prejudicial manner.

II. *Denial of Recovery under the Death on the High Seas Act.*

[8] In the Osman case, No. 25916, counsel for the plaintiffs admitted that he could not show that Mrs. Osman's aunts and uncles, and only relatives that survived her, were dependent upon her. Therefore, under § 761 of the Death on the High Seas Act, 46 U.S.C.A. § 761, which requires a showing of dependency on the part of all claimants except a wife, husband, parent or child of the decedent, the Osman plaintiffs were precluded from recovery.

[9,10] Mrs. Smith, as a child of Frenelia Putnam, did not have to show that she was dependent upon her mother but did have to establish a "pecuniary" loss. This she failed to do.

Mrs. Smith failed to come forward with specific evidence from which the trial court could estimate her pecuniary loss. Although she testified that she never had to go shopping because her mother delivered groceries from Dave's Market in Greenwich, nine miles from her house, she did not say how often her mother made these deliveries nor what, if any, expense or inconvenience she was put to with respect to such deliveries after her mother's death. There was no proof that Mrs. Putnam paid for the groceries that she brought to her daughter. Similarly Mrs. Smith did not say how often her mother took care of her two young children, or how often her mother brought toys to those children, or what the value of such toys was.

Without giving any details, Mrs. Smith testified that her mother advised and assisted her in the organization and management of her household. The district court held that such advice and assistance could not be measured by any "material standard" and therefore could not be compensated for in damages. Though Mrs. Smith was thirty-one years of age, married and set up in her own household, it is conceivable, though unlikely, that she could have shown that her mother's simple guidance in domestic affairs had a dollar and cents value. But the complete lack of proof of what her mother did and of any evidence from which the value of her help might be calculated, precludes her from recovery.

Whatever may be the rule for minor children, it is clear that those who have reached their majority must be very specific to show that their parents' guidance had a pecuniary value beyond the irreplaceable values of companionship and affection. Cf. Michigan Central R.R. Co. v. Vreeland, 1913, 227 U.S. 59, 73, 33 S.Ct. 192, 57 L.Ed. 417.

Affirmed.

Refer to Extract C, D.H.S.A. Section 1, and Section 4.

202 F. Supp. 556

Ruth M. NOEL et al., Libellants,

v.

UNITED AIRCRAFT CORP.,

Respondent.

No. 1781.

United States District Court

D. Delaware.

Jan. 9, 1962.

Action for death of an American citizen on Venezuelan airliner which crashed into high seas, brought against manufacturer of aircraft's propellers, a Delaware corporation. On the question of choice of law, the District Court, Layton, J., held that action for death of American citizen, in course of his intended trip which originated in United States, was maintainable exclusively under law of United States by way of Death on High Seas Act.

Disposition accordingly.

Death

Action for death of American citizen, on Venezuelan airliner which crashed into high seas in course of his intended trip which originated in United States, brought against manufacturer of airliner's propellers, a Delaware corporation, was maintainable exclusively under law of United States by way of Death on High Seas Act. Death on the High Seas Act, §§ 1-8, 46 U.S.C.A. §§ 761-768.

Murray M. Schwartz, Wilmington, Del., Stephen M. Feldman, Joseph G. Feldman, Philadelphia, Pa. (of Feldman & Feldman), Philadelphia, Pa., for libellants.

William Prickett, Wilmington, Del. (of Prickett, Prickett & Tybout), Wilmington, Del., for respondent.

LAYTON, District Judge.

In this action under the Death on the High Seas Act, 46 U.S.C.A. §§ 761-768, the estate of the decedent (Libellants) seeks to recover damages for decedent's death on a Venezuelan airliner which crashed into the sea on June 20, 1956, more than one marine league off the New Jersey coast. The suit is not against Linea Aeropostal Venezolana, the airline company, but rather against the manufacturer of the aircraft's propellers.

Some two years after this action was instigated and after a great deal of discovery had been had, Libellants moved to amend the complaint by adding a cause of action based upon an implied breach of warranty of fitness of the propellers.

Respondent has interposed a number of objections, disposition of which was temporarily delayed pending decision as to whether the law of Venezuela should govern the trial of this action. If so, the question of the amendment under United States law would become moot since Venezuela apparently does not recognize a cause of action for implied breach of warranty. It was the view of this Court that because the accident happened on a Venezuelan airliner over the high seas, the law of the flag of the airliner should govern the action.[1] See 191 F.Supp. 557. Accordingly, the parties were directed to furnish affidavits by experts on the law of Venezuela in an effort to ascertain whether the laws of that country provided a remedy under circumstances such as are here present. After a lengthy absence because of illness, the Court now approaches the disposition of that question.

The affidavits of Dr. Benson for the Respondent and of Dr. Nebreda for the Libellants have been filed and considered. Both experts agree that recovery under the Civil Aviation Code of Venezuela is precluded for the reason that the provisions of this Code apply only to air carriers or airlines and not to manufacturers of airplane parts. Both experts agree that where acts of third parties (manufacturers of airplane parts as opposed to the airline companies themselves) form the grounds for the suit, recovery may be had by way of the general negligence provisions of the Civil Code.[2] However, Dr. Nebreda's affidavit goes on to state that insofar as concerns the Venezuelan law of conflicts, the Bustamante Code governs and, more specifically, Section 168 of said Code, which reads:

> "Obligations arising from negligent acts or omissions not subject to criminal law, shall be governed by the law of the *place where the negligence has occurred.*" (Emphasis added.)

Dr. Nebreda therefore concludes as follows:

> "In conclusion, the law which will apply to the present action will be the law of the place where the negligent act or omission occurred. If this negligent act or omission occurred in the United States, Venezuelan law will not apply."

Dr. Nebreda's affidavit was filed more than a month before that of Dr. Benson, who presumably had an opportunity to see it. Yet, the Benson affidavit fails to mention the Bustamante Code or make any reference to the conflicts question. Nor has Dr. Benson made any attempt to file a supplementary affidavit for the purpose of negating the conclusions reached by Dr. Nebreda. Accordingly, Nebreda's affidavit is accepted as authoritative.

1. The moving reason for the result was the reluctance of this Court to infringe upon the sovereignty and laws of a foreign land, despite the fact that the numerous contracts and relationships in this case with the United States suggested the possibility of jurisdiction by way of Sec. 1 of the Death on the High Seas Act.

2. As translated, this article states:
"He who intentionally or negligently or imprudently has caused damage to another is obliged to repair it."

Two important considerations are immediately presented, (a) under what law should this case be tried and (b) the obvious lack of interest which Venezuela has in asserting jurisdiction over this problem.

As to the first point, counsel are in the sharpest disagreement. Respondent asserts that the language of Sec. 168 of the Bustamante Code simply throws the matter back to the scene of the crash which occurred on a Venezuelan airliner on the high seas and, thus, by the principle of renvoi we return full circle to the proposition that Venezuelan law governs. Libellants, on the other hand, contend that the disputed language of the Bustamante Code means that the case is to be governed by the general Admiralty law of the United States. Whatever the answer may be, it is far from clear. It most certainly was never the intention of this Court in its opinion (191 F.Supp. 557) to foist off upon the Libellants a doubtful remedy. As was there said:

> "If the law of Venezuela permits no recovery or if recovery, *is doubtful under its law,* then perhaps an action may be maintained under American law * * *."

The second consideration raised by the Nebreda affidavit is crystal clear, however, and that is that Venezuela has no particular interest in applying its own law to these facts but, rather, refers the parties to the law of the place where the "negligence has occurred," wherever that may be. This, then, removes from this case any fear of infringing upon the law of Venezuela, a fact of which this Court was unaware when it filed its opinion in 191 F.Supp. 557.

It is conceded that most of the important contacts and relationships in this case are with the United States rather than Venezuela.[3] The decedent was an American citizen. His intended trip originated in the United States. The propellers were not only manufactured in this country but sold to Linea Aeropostal Venezolana in this country. Respondent is a Delaware corporation. Applying the rationale of Lauritzen v. Larsen, 345 U.S. 571, 73 S.Ct. 921, 97 L.Ed. 1254 and Romero v. International Terminal Operating Co., 358 U.S. 354, 79 S.Ct. 468, 3 L.Ed.2d 368, it is the conclusion of this Court that this cause of action is maintainable exclusively under the law of the United States by way of section one of the Death on the High Seas Act.

Since Venezuelan law is here held inapplicable, the Court must now deal with Libellants' motion to amend its complaint by adding a cause of action based on breach of warranty of fitness. The point has already been extensively briefed and argued. However, in the event counsel should desire to file briefs supplementing those filed a number of months ago, these should be filed not later than January 29, 1962.

3. This Court noted in passing in 191 F.Supp. 557 that there were numerous contracts between the parties and happenings in this case and the United States but was perhaps unduly concerned at that stage with the fear of interfering with the sovereignty and laws of Venezuela.

Refer to Extract C, D.H.S.A. Section 1, and Section 4.

156 F. Supp. 94

Jenny FERNANDEZ and Herman Varela, as Administrators of the Estate of Elvia B. Varela, Deceased, Libellants,

v.

LINEA AEROPOSTAL VENEZOLANA, Respondent.

United States District Court
S.D. New York.
Oct. 21, 1957.

Libel in admiralty for death of a stewardess on an aircraft which crashed into the Atlantic Ocean more than one league from the United States shore. The United States District Court for the Southern District of New York, Dawson, J., held that the first cause of action was sufficient, that the second and fourth causes of action were insufficient and that motions to dismiss the third and fifth causes of action would be granted with leave to file an amended libel.

Judgment in accordance with the opinion.

1. Death

Congress in adopting the Death on the High Seas Act did not intend that no action would lie for wrongful death on the high seas unless death occurred on a plane or vessel which flew the flag of a nation which had by statute granted a cause of action for wrongful death. Death on the High Seas Act, §§ 1, 4, 46 U.S.C.A. §§ 761, 764.

2. Death

While the maintaining of a death action is sometimes loosely referred to as a substantive right, it is properly not a right but rather a power which removes a previous disability, and the right depends on whether a wrong has been committed and this depends upon where the act was committed.

3. Death

The Death on the High Seas Act does not create a cause of action or grant a right of recovery for death in every situation but only against those defendants which would have been liable if death had not ensued, and hence the liability for an accident causing death would be dependent upon law of the place where the accident happened. Death on the High Seas Act, §§ 1-7, 46 U.S.C.A. §§ 761-767.

4. Negligence

A right of action for negligence would depend upon the law of the place of the accident, but the power to maintain the action would not be dependent upon the locus thereof but rather upon the forum which exercised that power.

5. Master and Servant

Libel in admiralty for death of a stewardess on board a Venezuelan aircraft which crashed into the Atlantic Ocean more than one league from the United States shore was not dismissable on the ground that the only remedy available was that accorded by Venezuelan law. Death on the High Seas Act, §§ 1-7, 46 U.S.C.A. §§ 761-767.

6. Master and Servant

In libel in admiralty for death of a stewardess on a Venezuelan aircraft which crashed into the Atlantic Ocean more than one league from the United States shore, cause of action based on the Warsaw Convention was dismissable on the ground that such convention does not provide an independent action. Warsaw Convention, 49 Stat. 3000.

7. Evidence
Statutes

Foreign law is a matter of fact which must be pleaded and proved with definiteness.

8. Federal Civil Procedure

In libel in admiralty for death of a stewardess on a Venezuelan aircraft which crashed into the Atlantic Ocean more than one league from the United States shore, cause alleging that a cause of action had been afforded the libellants under the Laws of Venezuela was insufficient for failure to plead or prove the substance of the Venezuelan law. Death on the High Seas Act, §§ 1-7, 46 U.S.C.A. §§ 761-767; Admiralty Rules, rule 22, 28 U.S.C.A.; Fed.Rules Civ. Proc. rule 8, 28 U.S.C.A.

9. Death

An action for wrongful death does not exist at common law and is purely a creature of statute.

10. Death
Federal Civil Procedure

The Civil Aeronautics Act of 1938 did not create a new and independent action for wrongful death and the cause of action set forth in the libel for death of a stewardess in a plane accident was not transformed into a separate cause of action by the allegation that the carrier violated the Civil Aeronautics Act of 1938. Civil Aeronautics Act of 1938, § 1 et seq. as amended 49 U.S.C.A. § 401 et seq.

11. Insurance

In libel for death of stewardess in a plane accident cause alleging a policy in favor of the estate of the decedent and no part of which had been paid was insufficient where it was not alleged that the policy was issued by the respondent or that respondent was liable thereon.

Herbst & Herbst, New York City, for libellants, Jerome Golenbock, New York City, of counsel.

Brinsmade & Schafrann, New York City, for respondent, Hobart L. Brinsmade, New York City, of counsel.

DAWSON, District Judge.

Two motions have been presented to the Court. The first one brings up exceptions by the respondents to the five alleged causes of action contained in the libel, on the ground that the libel fails to state causes of action either in admiralty or at law. The second motion seeks to transfer the second, third, fourth and fifth causes of action from the admiralty to the civil docket.

The action was started by a libel in admiralty. It was brought by the administrators of the estate of Elvia B. Varela who is alleged to have been a stewardess on board an aircraft owned and operated by the respondents which crashed into the Atlantic Ocean more than one league from the shore line of the United States on June 20, 1956. It is alleged that the crash caused the death of the stewardess and that the occurrence was brought about by the negligent operation of respondent's aircraft.

Five causes of action are alleged. Respondents contend that none of the causes of action states a claim upon which relief can be granted.

The first cause of action alleges that a cause of action has been afforded to libellants by the Death on the High Seas Act, 46 U.S.C.A. § § 761-767.

Respondents deny that this act affords a cause of action under the circumstances set forth in the libel. The Court of Appeals for the Second Circuit has expressly reserved ruling on the question of whether this act grants a right of action for death in the airspace. See Noel v. Linea Aeropostal Venezolana, 2 Cir., 247 F.2d 677. However, the act has been deemed applicable to airplane crashes in a number of cases where the crash occurred over the ocean. Wilson v. Transocean Airlines, D.C.N.D.Cal.1954, 121 F.Supp. 85; Higa v. Transocean Airlines, D.C.Hawaii 1954, 124 F.Supp. 13; Choy v. Pan-American Airways Co., 1941 A.M.C. 483 (S.D.N.Y.1941). See also, 55 Colum.L.Rev. 907, n. 56; 41 Cornell L.Rev. 243 at p. 245 (1956).

[1] Respondents do not seek to dismiss the first cause of action on the general ground that the Death on the High Seas Act is not applicable to death resulting from an airplane crash. Rather they contend that the only part of the act applicable is § 4 of the act, 46 U.S.C.A. § 764,[1] which makes recovery contingent upon the right of action granted by the law of the foreign state.

1. "§ 764. Rights of action given by laws of foreign countries

"Whenever a right of action is granted by the law of any foreign State on account of death by wrongful act, neglect, or default occurring upon the high seas, such right may be maintained in an appropriate action in admiralty in the courts of the United States without abatement in respect to the amount for which recovery is authorized, any statute of the United States to the contrary notwithstanding. Mar. 30, 1920, c. 111, § 4, 41 Stat. 537."

Respondents contend that § 1 of the act, 46 U.S.C.A. § 761,[2] does not create a cause of action when death occurs on board a foreign flag ship or plane outside of the territorial waters of the United States, on the ground that under the circumstances only the law of the flag applies. They urge that the only remedy available to a representative of the person whose death occurred on board a foreign ship or plane outside of the territorial waters of the United States is that accorded by the foreign law, and that although an action may be brought in admiralty in this Court, pursuant to § 764 of Title 46, no independent cause of action (not growing out of the rights granted by the foreign law) may be maintained in this Court. This position would mean that no action would lie for wrongful death on the high seas unless death occurred on a plane or vessel which flew the flag of a nation which had by statute granted a cause of action for wrongful death. This would be a harsh rule and would hardly seem consonant with the intent of Congress in adopting the Death on the High Seas Act. If Congress had intended that only the law of the flag was applicable to actions for death on the high seas, then § 4 of the act would be sufficient to preserve such cause of action. But the act as passed preserved not merely rights under foreign law, but also, by § 1 of the act, gave an additional right to the personal representative of the deceased to maintain an action against the "vessel, person, or corporation which would have been liable if death had not ensued." As the court said in Wilson v. Transocean Airlines, supra, 121 F.Supp. at page 94: "By these words the statute gives a right of action where none existed before."

Whether Congress had the power to create such a cause of action, or intended to create such a cause of action, where death occurred on a foreign ship or plane on the high seas, has been the subject of much discussion.[3] It is urged that in Lauritzen v. Larsen, 1953, 345 U.S. 571, 73 S.Ct. 921, 97 L.Ed. 1254, a case dealing with the application of the Jones Act, 46 U.S.C.A. § 688 to foreign seamen on foreign ships, the Supreme Court held that in the absence of a clear showing of different Congressional intent, such maritime statutes would be considered to apply only to areas and transactions in which American law would be considered operative under prevalent doctrines of international law. However, the Jones Act was, in practical effect, a labor law regulating the rights of seamen; and in the absence of definite legislative intent to the contrary, it would be proper to assume that it was not intended to regulate the rights of foreign seamen on foreign ships. See O'Neill v. Cunard White Star Lines, 2 Cir., 1947, 160 F.2d 446, certiorari denied 332 U.S. 773, 68 S.Ct. 56, 92 L.Ed. 358.

2. "§ 761. Right of action; where and by whom brought

"Whenever the death of a person shall be caused by wrongful act, neglect, or default occurring on the high seas beyond a marine league from the shore of any State, or the District of Columbia, or the Territories or dependencies of the United States, the personal representative of the decedent may maintain a suit for damages in the district courts of the United States, in admiralty, for the exclusive benefit of the decedent's wife, husband, parent, child, or dependent relative against the vessel, person, or corporation which would have been liable if death had not ensued. Mar. 30, 1920, c. 111, § 1, 41 Stat. 537."

3. See Magruder & Grout, Wrongful Death Within the Admiralty Jurisdiction, 35 Yale L.J. 395 (1926); Robinson, Wrongful Death in Admiralty and the Conflict of Laws, 36 Colum. L.Rev. 406 (1936); Comment, 41 Cornell L.Q. 243 (1956).

[2-4] But when we are dealing with death acts, such as Lord Campbell's Act, 9 & 10 Vict., c. 93, or the Death on the High Seas Act, we are dealing with a different situation. The courts have held that in the absence of a statute an action could not be maintained for death caused by negligence. See The Harrisburgh, 1886, 119 U.S. 199, 7 S.Ct. 140, 30 L.Ed. 358. These cases did not develop from the principle that no right existed, or that no wrong had been done, but rather that whatever cause of action had existed had died with the death of the person injured and could no longer be asserted even by the next of kin or the estate of the deceased victim. To correct this situation death acts have been passed in nearly all jurisdictions. This still left a vacuum in the case of deaths which might result from accidents on the high seas. To allow actions to be maintained for deaths in this situation the Death on the High Seas Act was enacted. See Hughes, Death Actions in Admiralty, 36 Yale L.J. 115 (1921). While the maintaining of a death action is sometimes loosely referred to as a "substantive right," it is, properly speaking, not a "right" but rather a "power" which removes a previous "disability." See Fundamental Legal Conceptions as Applied in Judicial Reason, by Professor Hohfeld, 26 Yale L.J. 710 (1917). The "right" depends on whether a wrong has been committed and this, of course, depends upon where the act was committed. An act in one area may be a wrong, but in another area may not be a wrong. The Death on the High Seas Act recognizes this distinction for it does not create a cause of action or grant a right of recovery for death in every situation but only against those defendants "which would have been liable if death had not ensued." Thus the liability for an accident causing death would be dependent upon the law of the place where the accident happened—and if it happened on a foreign ship it might well be dependent upon the law which would be applicable to that ship. The right of action for negligence would depend upon the law of the place of the accident, but the "power" to maintain the action would not be dependent upon the locus of the accident but rather upon the forum which exercised that power. In this country the admiralty courts have assumed jurisdiction to the extent that the laws of the country extend that jurisdiction. Thus in The Buenos Aires, 2 Cir., 1924, 5 F.2d 425, the Court of Appeals for this Circuit held that under the Death on the High Seas Act a Spanish vessel was liable in an action *in rem* for the death of a seaman, even though there was no right of action *in rem* under the Spanish law.

In The Scotland, 105 U.S. 24, 29, 26 L.Ed. 1001, the Supreme Court said:

> "In administering justice between parties it is essential to know by what law or code or system of laws, their mutual rights are to be determined. When they arise in a particular country or State, they are generally to be determined by the laws of that State. Those laws pervade all transactions which take place where they prevail, and give them their color and legal effect. Hence if a collision should occur in British waters, at least between British ships, and the injured party should seek relief in our courts, we would administer justice according to the British law, so far as the rights and liabilities of the parties were concerned, provided it were shown what that law was. If not shown, we would apply our own law to

the case. In the French or Dutch tribunals they would do the same. But, if a collision occurs on the high seas, where the law of no particular State has exclusive force, but all are equal, any forum called upon to settle the rights of the parties would, *prima facie,* determine them by its own law as presumptively expressing the rules of justice; but if the contesting vessels belonged to the same foreign nation, the court would assume that they were subject to the law of their Nation carried under their common flag, and would determine the controversy accordingly. If they belonged to different Nations, having different laws, since it would be unjust to apply the laws of either to the exclusion of the other, the law of the forum, that is, the maritime law as received and practiced therein, would properly furnish the rule of decision. In all other cases, each Nation will also administer justice according to its own laws. And it will do this without respect of persons, to the stranger as well as to the citizen. If it be the legislative will that any particular privilege should be enjoyed by its own citizens alone, express provision will be made to that effect. Some laws, it is true, are necessarily special in their application to domestic ships, such as those relating to the forms of ownership, charter-party, and nationality; others follow the vessel wherever she goes, as the law of the flag, such as those which regulate the mutual relations of master and crew, and the power of the master to bind the ship or her owners. But the great mass of the laws are, or are intended to be, expressive of the rules of justice and right applicable alike to all."

The admiralty law of the United States, as expressed in the Death on the High Seas Act, now grants power to the admiralty courts to entertain an action for a wrong done on the high seas even though the person injured has died as a result of the wrong. This power granted to the courts is applicable even though the wrong occurred in an area not subject to the laws of the United States.

[5] The motion to dismiss the first cause of action is denied.

[6] The second cause of action alleges that a cause of action has been afforded to the libellants under the Convention for Unification of Certain Rules Relating to International Transportation by Air, 49 Stat. Part II, p. 3000 et seq. (1934), usually called the "Warsaw Convention." The Court of Appeals for this Circuit has held, in a case growing out of the same airplane accident, that the Warsaw Convention does not provide an independent cause of action. Noel v. Linea Aeropostal Venezolana, 2 Cir., 247 F.2d 677. The second cause of action is therefore dismissed.

The third cause of action alleges:

> "That a cause of action has been afforded the libellants herein under the statutes and laws of the foreign state of Venezuela."

Respondents object that this cause of action is insufficient in that this allegation is merely conclusory and insufficient to comply with Rule 22 of the Admiralty Rules, 28 U.S.C.A. which requires a libellant to allege the facts upon which he relies; and that the libel is insufficient since libellants have failed to plead the substance or text of the law of Venezuela upon which they rely.

A libel which had essentially the same allegation as to foreign law was dismissed by Judge Weinfeld with the statement:

> "The libellant may not rely upon such a conclusory allegation as to the effect of the foreign law but must set forth its substance. * * *" Iafrate v. Compagnie Generale Transatlantique, D.C.S.D.N.Y.1952, 106 F.Supp. 619, 622.

It is to be noted that Admiralty Rule 22 provides:

> "The libel shall also propound and allege in distinct articles the various allegations of fact upon which the libellant relies in support of the suit, so that the respondent or claimant may be able to answer distinctly and separately the several matters contained in each article * * *."

In this respect the Admiralty Rule is quite different from the Civil Rule which does not require the pleading of the *facts* but only the allegation of a *claim.* See Rule 8 of the Rules of Civil Procedure, 28 U.S.C.A.

[7] It has been established for a long time that foreign law is a matter of fact which must be pleaded and proved with definiteness. See Empresa Agricola Chicama Ltda v. Amtorg, D.C.S.D.N.Y.1944, 57 F.Supp. 649; Lehnertz v. Societe Anonyme, etc., D.C.S.D.N.Y.1948, 8 F.R.D. 319.

[8] The third cause of action is dismissed with leave, however, to the libellants to file an amended pleading within sixty days alleging the text or the substance of the foreign law on which they rely.

[9,10] The fourth cause of action alleges that the acts of the respondent violated the provisions of the Civil Aeronautics Act of 1938, 49 U.S.C.A. § 401 et seq., and the rules, regulations, orders and directives promulgated by the Civil Aeronautics Board and the Civil Aeronautics Authority, and that these violations were the proximate cause of the death of the decedent. The act, and the rules, regulations, orders and directives promulgated thereunder, might establish a standard of care which will be applicable in a proper action brought to recover damages for wrongful death, but neither the act nor the regulations create an action for wrongful death. An action for wrongful death does not exist at common law and is purely a creature of statute. The Harrisburgh, 1886, 119 U.S. 199, 7 S.Ct. 140, 30 L.Ed. 358. The wrongful death statutes differ widely in their provisions as to jurisdiction, venue, persons who may sue, damages recoverable, time for instituting the action, etc. The Civil Aeronautics Act of 1938 did not create a new and independent action for wrongful death and the cause of action set forth in the libel, to the extent that it exists at all, is not transformed into a separate cause of action by the allegation that the respondent violated the Civil Aeronautics Act of 1938. The fourth cause of action is dismissed.

[11] The fifth cause of action alleges that there was a policy of insurance in favor of the estate of the decedent in the sum of $10,000, no part of which has been paid. It is not alleged that the policy of insurance was issued by the respondent or that respondent is liable on this policy. There are no allegations in the fifth cause of action which set forth the basis of a claim against the respondent. The fifth cause of action is dismissed, subject to leave to submit an amended complaint within a period of sixty days.

In view of the disposition of the first part of the motion, it becomes unnecessary to consider so much of the motion as seeks to transfer the second, third, fourth and fifth causes of action from the admiralty to the civil docket.

The motion to dismiss the first cause of action is denied. The motions to dismiss the second and fourth causes of action are granted. The motions to dismiss the third and fifth causes of action are granted, with leave, however, to file an amended libel within a period of sixty days. So ordered.

Refer to Extract C, D.H.S.A.
Section 1, and Section 4.

188 F. Supp. 594

Phyllis A. BERGERON, as Administratrix of the Estates of Nancy M. Guy, Deceased, Kenneth Charles Guy, Deceased and Elaine Barbara Guy, Deceased, Libellant,

v.

KONINKLIJKE LUCHTVAART MAATSCHAPPIJ, N.V., also known as K.L.M./Royal Dutch Airlines, Respondent.

United States District Court
S.D. New York.
Nov. 14, 1960.

Action for deaths of United States citizens which occurred when Dutch airplane crashed into Atlantic Ocean. On motion of respondent to dismiss claim asserted under section of Death on the High Seas Act relating to American law and to dismiss claim based on Dutch Wrongful Death Statute, the District Court, Irving R. Kaufman, J., held that under circumstances, claims could only be maintained under section of Death on the High Seas Act relating to foreign law.

Motion granted.

1. Death

Where foreign law, under section in Death on the High Seas Act relating thereto, appeared to be applicable to give cause for recovery for deaths of United States citizens occurring when Dutch owned airplane crashed into Atlantic Ocean, no concurrent or additional cause was provided by section of act providing causes under American law. Death on the High Seas Act, §§ 1, 4, 46 U.S.C.A. §§ 761, 764.

2. Admiralty

Section of Death on the High Seas Act relating to actions under foreign law was exclusive in its sphere and precluded assertion of claims, on civil side of court, under Dutch death statute, for death of United States citizens occurring when Dutch airplane crashed into ocean. Death on the High Seas Act, § 4, 46 U.S.C.A. § 764.

Emile Z. Berman and A. Harold Frost, by Marvin V. Ausubel, New York City, for libellant.

Haight, Gardner, Poor & Havens, by Eugene C. Brugger, New York City, for respondent.

IRVING R. KAUFMAN, District Judge.

Libellant's decedents, who were all citizens and residents of the United States, met their death when an airplane owned and operated by the respondent, a Dutch airline, crashed into the Atlantic Ocean while en route from Shannon, Ireland, to New York. Libellant brought this action to recover for their alleged wrongful deaths, asserting three separate causes of action as to each decedent. Her first set of claims is based on Section 1 of the Death on the High Seas Act, 46 U.S.C.A. § 761, which, if applicable, affords a cause of action under American law. This section provides:

> "Whenever the death of a person shall be caused by wrongful act, neglect, or default occurring on the high seas beyond a marine league from the shore of any State, or the District of Columbia, or the Territories or dependencies of the United States, the personal representative of the decedent may maintain a suit for damages in the district courts of the United States, in admiralty, for the exclusive benefit of the decedent's wife, husband, parent, child or dependent relative against the vessel, person, or corporation which would have been liable if death had not ensued."

A second basis for relief, grounded in Dutch Law, is alleged pursuant to Section 4 of the Death on the High Seas Act, which provides:

> "Whenever a right of action is granted by the law of any foreign State on account of death by wrongful act, neglect, or default occurring upon the high seas, such right may be maintained in an appropriate action in admiralty in the courts of the United States without abatement in respect to the amount for which recovery is authorized any statute of the United States to the contrary notwithstanding."[1]

Finally, the libellant asserts claims *at law,* based upon the Dutch Wrongful Death Statute. Jurisdiction of these causes of action is premised on diversity of citizenship, and a jury trial is demanded.

Respondent has moved here to dismiss the claims based on Section 1 of the Death on the High Seas Act, and the common-law claims grounded in Dutch law, contending that an action under Section 4 of the Act is the exclusive remedy when the death sought to be redressed occurs on a foreign vessel on the high seas.

The question of the interaction between Section 1 and Section 4 has long been a perplexing one, and has evoked much scholarly comment. See, e.g., Robinson, Handbook of Admiralty Law 139 (1939); 67 Yale L.J. 1445 (1958); 71 Harv.L.Rev. 1152 (1958); 41 Cornell L.Q. 243 (1956). Relatively few cases, however, have dealt with the problem. The early cases took a position which would support respondent's contention that the two sections are mutually exclusive. Thus, in The Vestris, D.C.S.D.N.Y.1931, 53 F.2d 847, the court explicitly held that when the deaths involved took place on a foreign vessel, the claimants did not have the option of suing either under Section 1 or Section 4, but rather were required to bring their action under Section 4. A similar result was reached

1. It is clear that the primary purpose of the concluding clause is to render the Limitation of Shipowners' Liability Act, 46 U.S.C. §§ 183-189 inapplicable to actions brought under this section against foreign shipowners. See, e.g., The Vestris, D.C.S.D.N.Y.1931, 53 F.2d 847.

in The Vulcania. After the District Court sustained a libel brought under Section 1, even though a foreign vessel was involved, since foreign law had not been sufficiently pleaded, D.C.S.D.N.Y.1940, 32 F.Supp. 815, it later dismissed the Section 1 claim when it appeared that the foreign law had been sufficiently pleaded so as to provide the basis for a claim under Section 4. D.C.S.D.N.Y.1941, 41 F.Supp. 849. Thus, at least until 1952, it seemed clear that Section 1 was inapplicable when the death occurred on a foreign vessel, see Robinson, Handbook of Admiralty Law 139 (1939); no case had held otherwise.

In 1952, Judge Weinfeld, in Iafrate v. The Liberte, D.C.S.D.N.Y.1952, 106 F.Supp. 619, sustained a libel under Section 1 although the death occurred upon a French vessel. The problem of the relationship with Section 4 was not extensively discussed, although it is noteworthy that the court dismissed the claim based on French law on the ground that the French law had been insufficiently pleaded. Leave to serve an amended libel, containing proper allegations, was granted. Thus, the problem of a possible multiplicity of remedies was not squarely faced.

In Fernandez v. Linea Aeropostal Venezolana, D.C.S.D.N.Y.1957, 156 F.Supp. 94, the court purported to deal with this problem. The case involved an American citizen who met her death on a Venezuelan plane which crashed on the high seas. The respondent argued that only Venezuelan law, under Section 4, was applicable, and that there could be no cause of action based on American law under Section 1 for a death occurring on a foreign vessel or aircraft. The court rejected this contention, and sustained the libel under Section 1, in language indicating its belief that remedies under the two sections were cumulative. The court said:

> "But the act as passed preserved not merely rights under foreign law, but also, by § 1 of the act, gave an *additional* right to the personal representative of the deceased to maintain an action against the 'vessel, person, or corporation which would have been liable if death had not ensued'." (Emphasis supplied.) 156 F.Supp. at page 96.

But despite this broad language, which would indicate cumulative causes of action in all situations of American deaths on foreign vessels, the court clearly showed its primary concern over the situation in which the applicable foreign law did not grant a cause of action for wrongful death. Thus, to guard against this possibility, a cause of action under Section 1 was found. In this regard, it is again noteworthy that the court dismissed the cause of action asserted under Venezuelan law, with leave to amend, for failure to sufficiently plead the substance of that law. Therefore, it appeared uncertain whether or not a cause of action under Venezuelan law existed.

The last case to consider the problem was Noel v. Airponents, Inc., D.C.N.J. 1958, 169 F.Supp. 348, 351. The cause of action in that case arose from the same airplane disaster as gave rise to the Fernandez litigation. Here again the court sustained libellant's claim based on Section 1, although the death occurred on a foreign aircraft. But the court emphasized a number of factors which moved it to its conclusion. The libellant, an American citizen, asserted his claim against the agency which serviced the plane, an American corporation, rather than against the foreign carrier. Thus, both parties to the suit were American nationals. Further, the alleged tortious conduct occurred within the United States. In addition, it appeared that no cause of action under Venezuelan law existed, an opinion which was not disputed by the libellant. Thus, since virtually all of the relevant contacts pointed to the application of American law, the cause of action under Section 1 was sustained. The court did not hold that cumulative remedies under Section 1 and Section 4 were available; rather, the whole tenor of the opinion indicated that the court was seeking to find the *one* applicable body of law which could properly govern the entire claim.

In the present case, none of the factors influencing the court to apply American law in Noel are present. The respondent here is the foreign airlines. Furthermore, it appears that the Dutch law does provide a basis for recovery for wrongful death; it has been specifically pleaded by the libellant, and the respondent appears to concede its applicability. Thus, the question of whether, in a case in which foreign law under Section 4 appears to be applicable, there is an additional cause of action under Section 1, is squarely before the court.

[1] I am of the opinion that the "choice of law" approach adopted by Judge Smith in the Noel case is the most fruitful means for solving this admittedly perplexing problem. Cf. Lauritzen v. Larsen, 1952, 345 U.S. 571, 73 S.Ct. 921, 97 L.Ed. 1254. It is certainly anomalous for the representative of a decedent who died on a foreign vessel to have two bases for recovery, while the representative of a decedent dying on an American vessel is limited to a single cause of action under Section 1. It is most difficult to attribute such an intent to Congress. It seems clear that the primary purpose for the enactment of the Death on the High Seas Act was to assure that there would be *some* recovery for the wrongful death of American citizens dying in disasters on the high seas. See Fernandez v. Linea Aeropostal Venezolana, D.C.S.D.N.Y.1957, 156 F.Supp. 94, 96. Thus, the courts in Iafrate, Fernandez and Noel felt it necessary to apply American law when there appeared to be substantial doubt whether a cause of action under foreign law existed, in order to assure that *some* basis for recovery was present. But, when there is no such doubt, the presence of both Section 1 and Section 4 allows the Act to be applied with flexibility so as to arrive at the one proper choice of law to appropriately govern the litigation. And Section 4 itself, following the traditional and still-valid primacy accorded in admiralty to the "law of the flag," see Lauritzen v. Larsen, 1952, 345 U.S. 571, 584-585, 73 S.Ct. 921, 929, 97 L.Ed. 1254, appears to embody the additional policy that, in making this determination, when the death occurs on a foreign vessel, foreign law is to be applied. There is no reason to depart from this principle when, as in the instant case, the applicable foreign law provides a cause of action for wrongful death, and is sufficiently pleaded. When the foreign law provides no such action, or an examination of the relevant contact points indicate, as in Noel, a closer relation to American law, Section 1 will be available so as not to preclude

recovery. But there is no warrant in the statutory language or policy for the maintenance of concurrent causes of action under both American law (Section 1) and foreign law (Section 4). Thus, the libellant's first, fourth and seventh libels, seeking to assert claims under Section 1 of the Death on the High Seas Act, must be dismissed.

[2] Libellant also seeks to assert claims on the civil side, based on Dutch law. The controversy has long raged as to whether suits brought under the Death on the High Seas Act could be maintained at law as well as in admiralty. Both Section 1 and Section 4 contain language suggesting that actions can only be brought in admiralty. Section 1 provides "the personal representative of the decedent may maintain a suit for damages in the district courts of the United States, in admiralty * * *." Although earlier cases held that this language was merely permissive, and thus that an action could be brought under Section 1 at law, see, e.g., Choy v. Pan-American Airways Co., D.C.S.D.N.Y., 1941 A.M.C. 483, it now seems to be accepted that the language of the section is mandatory, and thus that jurisdiction is solely in admiralty. See Noel v. Linea Aeropostal Venezolana, 2 Cir., 247 F.2d 677, 66 A.L.R.2d 997, certiorari denied 1957, 355 U.S. 907, 78 S.Ct. 334, 2 L.Ed.2d 262; Higa v. Transocean Airlines, 9 Cir., 230 F.2d 780, certiorari dismissed, 1956, 352 U.S. 802, 77 S.Ct. 20, 1 L.Ed.2d 37; Wilson v. Transocean Airlines, D.C.N.D.Cal.1954, 121 F.Supp. 85. Since there was clearly no cause of action for wrongful death on American vessels prior to the passage of the Act, see The Harrisburg, 1886, 119 U.S. 199, 7 S.Ct. 140, 30 L.Ed. 358, there is plainly no basis for the maintenance of a civil action at law independent of the Act. See 41 Cornell L.Q. 241, 250 (1956).

However, libellant argues that Section 4 presents a different situation. This section, unlike Section 1, does not create an entirely new cause of action, but rather provides for the enforcement of rights of action granted by foreign law. But, the section provides, similar to Section 1, that "such right may be maintained in an appropriate action in admiralty in the courts of the United States." Judge Weinfeld, after a review of legislative history, has concluded that this language also is mandatory, and thus that actions under Section 4 can only be brought in admiralty. Iafrate v. The Liberte, D.C.S.D.N.Y.1952, 106 F.Supp. 619. Libellant seeks to avoid this holding by asserting the claims in her third, sixth and ninth causes of action, not under Section 4, but independently of the statute, with diversity of citizenship as a basis of jurisdiction. Foreign wrongful death statutes were enforced in American courts prior to the passage of the Act, albeit in admiralty rather than at law. See La Bourgogne, 1908, 210 U.S. 95, 28 S.Ct. 664, 52 L.Ed. 973. Thus, subsequent to its passage, some courts have sustained actions brought at law for the enforcement of rights granted by foreign wrongful death statutes, Powers v. Cunard S.S. Co., D.C.S.D.N.Y.1925, 32 F.2d 720; The Saturnia, D.C.S.D.N.Y.,1936 A.M.C. 469, presumably based on the "Savings-to-Suitors" clause, 28 U.S.C. § 1333(1). Cf. Egan v. Donaldson

Atlantic Line, D.C.S.D.N.Y.1941, 37 F.Supp. 909.[2] Considerations of uniformity and legislative intent would indicate that Section 4, like Section 1 should be exclusive in its sphere. See Iafrate v. The Liberte, supra. Moreover, it is once again difficult to believe that Congress would choose to discriminate between representatives of decedents dying on foreign vessels and those dying on American vessels, by allowing to the former, in addition to the traditional action in admiralty, an action at law with its concomitant right to jury trial, while limiting the latter to an admiralty action.[3] I am of the opinion that in an area such as this, courts should strive to reach a result which will foster uniformity and equality of treatment. Thus, the respondent's motion to dismiss the libellant's third, sixth and ninth causes of action is also granted. Settle order.

2. The decisions in both Powers and the Saturnia were rendered before an examination of legislative history by the courts indicated that actions under Section 1 and Section 4 could be brought only in admiralty. Thus, at the time these decisions were rendered, it was not anomalous to allow the representative of a decedent dying on a foreign vessel to bring a common-law action, since the same right to a jury was presumably available under the statute. But, in light of the subsequent holdings in such cases as Higa and Iafrate, it seems clear that the apparent rationale of Powers and The Saturnia should be re-examined. Moreover, neither of these cases dealt with the situation presented here, in which the libellant attempted to bring claims based on the same statutes both in admiralty and at law.

3. The administrative difficulties in allowing claims based on identical statutes to be brought in the same action both at law, with a jury, and in admiralty, without a jury, is also a factor which should be considered.

Refer to Extract C,
D.H.S.A. Section 1

244 U.S. 205

SOUTHERN PACIFIC COMPANY, Plff. in Err.,
v.
MARIE JENSEN.
(Cite as 37 S. Ct. 524)

COMMERCE–EMPLOYERS' LIABILITY–APPLICABILITY OF STATUTE TO OCEAN-GOING SHIPS–"Boat."

1. Congress did not establish a rule of liability with respect to injuries received by an employee on an ocean-going ship plying between ports of different states, owned and operated by a corporation which is also an interstate railway carrier, by enacting the provisions of the Employers' Liability Act of April 22, 1908 (35 Stat. at L. 65, chap. 149, Comp. Stat. 1916, §§ 8657–8665), giving a right of recovery against interstate carriers by railroad for the death or injury of employees while engaged in interstate commerce, caused by the negligence of the carriers' officers, agents, or employees, or by any defect or insufficiency, due to its negligence, in its "cars, engines, appliances, machinery, track, roadbed, works, boats, wharves, or other equipment." The word "boats" in the statute refers to vessels which may be properly regarded as in substance part of a railroad's extension or equipment, as understood and applied in common practice.

ADMIRALTY–EXCLUSIVENESS OF FEDERAL JURISDICTION–STATE LEGISLATION AFFECTING MARITIME LAW.

2. State legislation changing, modifying, or affecting the general maritime law which contravenes the essential purpose expressed by an act of Congress, or works material prejudice to the characteristic features of such general maritime law, or interferes with the proper harmony or uniformity of that law in its international and interstate relations, is invalid as being repugnant to U.S. Const. art. 3, § 2, extending the judicial power of the United States to all cases of admiralty and maritime jurisdiction, U.S. Const. art. 1, § 8, giving Congress power to make all laws necessary and proper to carry into execution the powers vested in the Federal government, and U.S. Judicial Code, §§ 24, 256, giving the Federal district courts exclusive original cognizance of all civil causes of admiralty and maritime jurisdiction, saving to suitors in all cases the right of a common-law remedy where the common law is competent to give it.

MASTER AND SERVANT–EXCLUSIVENESS OF FEDERAL JURISDICTION–STATE WORKMEN'S COMPENSATION LAWS.

3. The application to an injury sustained by a longshoreman while he was unloading in a New York port an ocean-going steamship owned by a nonresident corporation, and plying between ports of different states, of the provisions of the New York Workmen's Compensation Act (N.Y. Laws 1913, chap. 816; Laws 1914, chaps. 41, 316), which, in lieu of the common-law liability enforceable by suit in cases of negligence, imposes a liability upon employers, enforceable

without judicial action, to make compensation for disabling or fatal accidental injuries to employees, without regard to fault as a cause, graduating compensation for disabilities according to a prescribed scale based upon loss of earning power, and measuring death benefits according to the dependency of the surviving wife, husband, or infant children, renders the statute, to that extent, invalid as conflicting with U.S. Const. art. 3, § 2, extending the judicial power of the United States to all cases of admiralty and maritime jurisdiction, U.S. Const. art. 1, § 8, giving Congress power to make all laws necessary and proper to carry into execution the powers vested in the Federal government, and U.S. Judicial Code, §§ 24, 256, giving Federal district courts exclusive judicial cognizance of all civil causes of admiralty and maritime jurisdiction, saving to suitors in all cases the right to a common-law remedy where the common law is competent to give it, being also inconsistent with the policy of Congress to encourage investments in ships, manifested by U.S. Rev. Stat. §§ 4283-4285, Comp. Stat. 1916, §§ 8021-8023, Act of June 26, 1884 (23 Stat. at L. 57, chap. 121, Comp. Stat. 1916, § 8028), § 18, which declare a limitation upon the liability of their owners.

[No. 280.]

Argued February 28, 1916. Restored to docket for reargument November 13, 1916. Reargued January 31 and February 1, 1917. Decided May 21, 1917.

In error to the Supreme Court, Appellate Division, Third Department, of the State of New York, to review a judgment, affirmed by the Court of Appeals of that state, approving an award of the state Workmen's Compensation Commission to the dependents of a longshoreman killed on an ocean-going steamship. Reversed and remanded for further proceedings.

See same case below in court of appeals, 215 N.Y. 514, L.R.A.1916A, 403, 109 N.E. 600, Ann. Cas. 1916B, 276, 9 N.C.C.A. 286.

The facts are stated in the opinion.

Messrs. Norman B. Beecher and Ray Rood Allen for plaintiff in error.

Messrs. E. Clarence Aiken, Harold J. Hinman, and Mr. Egburt E. Woodbury, Attorney General of New York, for defendant in error.

Mr. Christopher M. Bradley as amicus curiae.

Mr. Justice McReynolds delivered the opinion of the court:

Upon a claim regularly presented, the Workmen's Compensation Commission of New York made the following findings of fact, rulings, and award, October 9, 1914:

1. "Christen Jensen, the deceased workman, was, on August 15, 1914, an employee of the Southern Pacific Company, a corporation of the state of Kentucky, where it has its principal office. It also has an office at Pier 49, North river, New York city. The Southern Pacific Company at said time was, and still is, a common carrier by railroad. It also owned and operated a steamship, El Oriente, plying between the ports of New York and Galveston, Texas.

2. "On August 15, 1914, said steamship was berthed for discharging and loading at Pier 49, North river, lying in navigable waters of the United States.

3. "On said date Christen Jensen was operating a small electric freight truck. His work consisted in driving the truck into the steamship El Oriente, where it was loaded with cargo, then driving the truck out of the vessel upon a gangway connecting the vessel with Pier 49, North river, and thence upon the pier, where the lumber was unloaded from the truck. The ship was about 10 feet distant from the pier. At about 10:15 A.M., after Jensen had been doing such work for about three hours that morning, he started out of the ship with his truck loaded with lumber, a part of the cargo of the steamship El Oriente, which was being transported from Galveston, Texas, to New York city. Jensen stood on the rear of the truck, the lumber coming about to his shoulder. In driving out of the port in the side of the vessel and upon the gangway, the truck became jammed against the guide pieces on the gangway. Jensen then reversed the direction of the truck and proceeded at third or full speed backward into the hatchway. He failed to lower his head and his head struck the ship at the top line, throwing his head forward and causing his chin to hit the lumber in front of him. His neck was broken and in this manner he met his death.

4. "The business of the Southern Pacific Company in this state consisted at the time of the accident and now consists solely in carrying passengers and merchandise between New York and other states. Jensen's work consisted solely in moving cargo destined to and from other states.

5. "Jensen left surviving him Marie Jensen, his widow, twenty-nine years of age, and Howard Jensen, his son, seven years of age, and Evelyn Jensen, his daughter, three years of age.

6. "Jensen's average weekly wage was $19.60 per week.

7. "The injury was an accidental injury and arose out of and in the course of Jensen's employment by the Southern Pacific Company, and his death was due to such injury. The injury did not result solely from the intoxication of the injured employee while on duty, and was not occasioned by the wilful intention of the injured employee to bring about the injury or death of himself or another.

"This claim comes within the meaning of chapter 67 of the Consolidated Laws as re-enacted and amended by chapter 41 of the Laws of 1914, and as amended by chapter 316 of the Laws of 1914.

"Award of compensation is hereby made to Marie Jensen, widow of the deceased, at the rate of $5.87 weekly during her widowhood, with two years' compensation in one sum in case of her marriage; to Harold Jensen, son of the deceased, at the rate of $1.96 per week, and to Evelyn Jensen, daughter of the deceased, at the rate of $1.96 per week until the said Harold Jensen and Evelyn Jensen respectively shall arrive at the age of eighteen years, and there is further allowed the sum of one hundred ($100) dollars for funeral expenses."

In due time the Southern Pacific Company objected to the award "upon the grounds that the act does not apply, because the workman was engaged in interstate commerce on board a vessel of a foreign corporation of the state of Kentucky, which was engaged solely in interstate commerce; that the injury was one with respect to which Congress may establish, and has established, a rule of liability, and under the language of § 114[1] [copied in the margin], the act has no application; on the ground that the act includes only those engaged in the operation of vessels other than those of other states and countries in foreign and interstate commerce, while the work upon which the deceased workman was engaged at the time of his death was part of the operation of a vessel of another state, engaged in interstate commerce, and hence does not come within the provisions of the act; further, that the act is unconstitutional, as it constitutes a regulation of and burden upon commerce among the several states, in violation of article 1, § 8, of the Constitution of the United States; in that it takes property without due process of law, in violation of the 14th Amendment of the Constitution; in that it denies the Southern Pacific Company the equal protection of the laws, in violation of the 14th Amendment of the Constitution, because the act does not afford an exclusive remedy, but leaves the employer and its vessels subject to suit in admiralty; also that the act is unconstitutional in that it violates article 3, § 2, of the Constitution, conferring admiralty jurisdiction upon the courts of the United States."

Without opinion, the appellate division approved the award and the court of appeals affirmed this action (215 N.Y. 514, L.R.A.1916A, 403, 109 N.E. 600, Ann. Cas. 1916B, 276), holding that the Workmen's Compensation Act applied to the employment in question and was not obnoxious to the Federal Constitution. It said: "The scheme of the statute is essentially and fundamentally one by the creation of a state fund to insure the payment of a prescribed compensation based on earnings for disability or death from accidental injuries sustained by employees engaged in certain enumerated hazardous employments. The state fund is created from premiums paid by employers based on the pay roll, the number of employees, and the hazards of the employment. The employer has the option of insuring with any stock corporation or mutual association authorized to transact such business, or of furnishing satisfactory proof to the Commission of his own financial ability to pay. If he does neither, he is liable to a penalty equal to the pro rata premium payable to the state fund during the period of his noncompliance, and is subject to a suit for damages by the injured employee, or his legal representative in case of death, in which he is deprived of the defenses of contributory negligence, assumed risk, and negligence of a fellow servant. By insuring in the state fund, or by himself or his insurance carrier paying the prescribed compensation, the employer is relieved from further liability for personal injuries or death sustained by employees.

1. Section 114. "The provisions of this chapter shall apply to employers and employees engaged in intrastate, and also in interstate or foreign commerce, for whom a rule of liability or method of compensation has been or may be established by the Congress of the United States, only to the extent that their mutual connection with intrastate work may and shall be clearly separable and distinguishable from interstate or foreign commerce, except that such employer and his employees working only in this state may, subject to the approval and in the manner provided by the Commission and so far as not forbidden by any act of Congress, accept and become bound by the provisions of this chapter in like manner and with the same effect in all respects as provided herein for other employers and their employees."

Compensation is to be made without regard to fault as a cause of the injury, except where it is occasioned by the wilful intention of the injured employee to bring about the injury or death of himself or another, or results solely from his intoxication while on duty. Compensation is not based on the rule of damages applied in negligence suits, but, in addition to providing for medical, surgical, or other attendance or treatment and funeral expenses, it is based solely on loss of earning power. Thus, the risk of accidental injuries occurring with or without fault on the part either of employee or employer is shared by both, and the burden of making compensation is distributed over all the enumerated hazardous employments in proportion to the risks involved." See also, Walker v. Clyde S.S. Co. 215 N.Y. 529, 109 N.E. 604, Ann. Cas. 1916B, 87.

In New York C.R. Co. v. White (decided March 6th), 243 U.S. 188, 61 L. ed. 667, 37 Sup. Ct. Rep. 247, we held the statute valid in certain respects; and, considering what was there said, only two of the grounds relied on for reversal now demand special consideration. First. Plaintiff in error, being an interstate common carrier by railroad, is responsible for injuries received by employees while engaged therein under the Federal Employers' Liability Act of April 22, 1908 (35 Stat. at L. chap. 149, p. 65, Comp. Stat. 1916, § 8657), and no state statute can impose any other or different liability. Second. As here applied, the Workmen's Compensation Act conflicts with the general maritime law, which constitutes an integral part of the Federal law under art. 3, § 2, of the Constitution, and to that extent is invalid.

The Southern Pacific Company, a Kentucky corporation, owns and operates a railroad as a common carrier; also the steamship El Oriente, plying between New York and Galveston, Texas. The claim is that therefore rights and liabilities of the parties here must be determined in accordance with the Federal Employers' Liability Act. But we think that act is not applicable in the circumstances.

The First Federal Employers' Liability Act (June 11, 1906, 34 Stat. at L. 232, chap. 3073) extended in terms to all common carriers engaged in interstate or foreign commerce, and, because it embraced subjects not within the constitutional authority of Congress, was declared invalid. Employers' Liability Cases (Howard v. Illinois C.R. Co.) 207 U.S. 463, 52 L. ed. 297, 28 Sup. Ct. Rep. 141, Jan. 6, 1908. The later act is carefully limited and provides that "every common carrier by railroad while engaging in commerce between any of the several states or territories, or between the District of Columbia and any of the states or territories, or between the District of Columbia or any of the states or territories and any foreign nation or nations, shall be liable in damages to any person suffering injury while he is employed by such carrier in such commerce, or, in case of the death of such employee, to his or her personal representatives, for the benefit of the surviving widow or husband and children of such employee; and, if none, then of such employee's parents; and, if none, then of the next of kin dependent upon such employee, for such injury or death resulting in whole or in part from the negligence of any of the officers, agents, or employees of such carrier, or by reason of any defect or insufficiency, due to its negligence, in its cars, engines, appliances, machinery, track, roadbed, works, boats, wharves, or other equipment."

Evidently the purpose was to prescribe a rule applicable where the parties are engaging in something having direct and substantial connection with railroad operations, and not with another kind of carriage recognized as separate and distinct from transportation on land and no mere adjunct thereto. It is unreasonable to suppose that Congress intended to change long-established rules applicable to maritime matters merely because the ocean-going ship concerned happened to be owned and operated by a company also a common carrier by railroad. The word "boats" in the statute refers to vessels which may be properly regarded as in substance but part of a railroad's extension or equipment as understood and applied in common practice.

The fundamental purpose of the Compensation Law, as declared by the court of appeals, is "the creation of a state fund to insure the payment of a prescribed compensation based on earnings for disability or death from accidental injuries sustained by employees engaged in certain enumerated hazardous employments," among them being "longshore work, including the loading or unloading of cargoes or parts of cargoes of grain, coal, ore, freight, general merchandise, lumber or other products or materials, or moving or handling the same, on any dock, platform or place, or in any warehouse or other place of storage." Its general provisions are specified in our opinion in New York C.R. Co. v. White, supra, and need not be repeated. Under the construction adopted by the state courts no ship may load or discharge her cargo at a dock therein without incurring a penalty, unless her owners comply with the act, which, in order to secure payment of compensation for accidents, generally without regard to fault, and based upon annual wages, provides (§ 50) that—"an employer shall secure compensation to his employees in one of the following ways:

"1. By insuring and keeping insured the payment of such compensation in the state fund, or 2. By insuring and keeping insured the payment of such compensation with any stock corporation or mutual association authorized to transact the business of workmen's compensation insurance in this state. If insurance be so effected in such a corporation of mutual association the employer shall forthwith file with the Commission, in form prescribed by it, a notice specifying the name of such insurance corporation or mutual association together with a copy of the contract or policy of insurance. 3. By furnishing satisfactory proof to the Commission of his financial ability to pay such compensation for himself, in which case the Commission may, in its discretion, require the deposit with the Commission of securities of the kind prescribed in section thirteen of the Insurance Law, in an amount to be determined by the Commission, to secure his liability to pay the compensation provided in this chapter."

"If an employer fail to comply with this section, he shall be liable to a penalty during which such failure continues of an amount equal to the pro rata premium which would have been payable for insurance in the state fund for such period of noncompliance to be recovered in an action brought by the Commission."

Article 3, § 2, of the Constitution, extends the judicial power of the United States "to all cases of admiralty and maritime jurisdiction"; and article 1,

§ 8, confers upon the Congress power "to make all laws which shall be necessary and proper for carrying into execution the foregoing powers and all other powers vested by this Constitution in the government of the United States or in any department or officer thereof." Considering our former opinions, it must now be accepted as settled doctrine that, in consequence of these provisions, Congress has paramount power to fix and determine the maritime law which shall prevail throughout the country. Butler v. Boston & S.S.S. Co. 130 U.S. 527, 32 L. ed. 1017, 9 Sup. Ct. Rep. 612; Re Garnett, 141 U.S. 1, 14, 35 L. ed. 631, 634, 11 Sup. Ct. Rep. 840. And further, that, in the absence of some controlling statute, the general maritime law, as accepted by the Federal courts, constitutes part of our national law, applicable to matters within the admiralty and maritime jurisdiction. The Lottawanna (Rodd v. Heartt) 21 Wall. 558, 22 L. ed. 654; Butler v. Boston & S.S.S. Co. 130 U.S. 527, 557, 32 L. ed. 1017, 1024, 9 Sup. Ct. Rep. 612; Workman v. New York, 179 U.S. 552, 45 L. ed. 314, 21 Sup. Ct. Rep. 212.

In The Lottawanna, Mr. Justice Bradley, speaking for the court, said: "That we have a maritime law of our own, operative throughout the United States, cannot be doubted. The general system of maritime law which was familiar to the lawyers and statesmen of the country when the Constitution was adopted was most certainly intended and referred to when it was declared in that instrument that the judicial power of the United States shall extend 'to all cases of admiralty and maritime jurisdiction'. . . . One thing, however, is unquestionable; the Constitution must have referred to a system of law coextensive with, and operating uniformly in, the whole country. It certainly could not have been the intention to place the rules and limits of maritime law under the disposal and regulation of the several states, as that would have defeated the uniformity and consistency at which the Constitution aimed on all subjects of a commercial character affecting the intercourse of the states with each other or with foreign states."

By § 9, Judiciary Act of 1789 (1 Stat. at L. 76, 77, chap. 20), the district courts of the United States were given "exclusive original cognizance of all civil causes of admiralty and maritime jurisdiction, . . . saving to suitors, in all cases, the right of a common-law remedy, where the common law is competent to give it." And this grant has been continued. Judicial Code, §§ 24 and 256 [36 Stat. at L. 1091, 1160, chap. 231, Comp. Stat. 1916, §§ 991 (1), 1233].

In view of these constitutional provisions and the Federal act it would be difficult, if not impossible, to define with exactness just how far the general maritime law may be changed, modified, or affected by state legislation. That this may be done to some extent cannot be denied. A lien upon a vessel for repairs in her own port may be given by state statute (The Lottawanna (Rodd v. Heartt) 21 Wall. 558, 579, 580, 22 L. ed. 654, 663, 664; The J.E. Rumbell, 148 U.S. 1, 37 L. ed. 345, 13 Sup. Ct. Rep. 498); pilotage fees fixed (Cooley v. Port Wardens, 12 How. 299, 13 L. ed. 996; Ex parte McNiel, 13 Wall. 236, 242, 20 L. ed. 624, 626); and the right given to recover in death cases (The Hamilton (Old Dominion S.S. Co. v. Gilmore) 207 U.S. 398, 52 L. ed. 264, 28 Sup. Ct. Rep. 133; La Bourgogne (Deslions v. La Compagnie Generale Transatlantique) 210 U.S. 95, 138, 52 L. ed. 973, 993, 28 Sup. Ct. Rep. 664). See The City of

Norwalk, 55 Fed. 98, 106. Equally well established is the rule that state statutes may not contravene an applicable act of Congress or affect the general maritime law beyond certain limits. They cannot authorize proceedings in rem according to the course in admiralty (The Moses Taylor, 4 Wall. 411, 18 L. ed. 397; American S.B. Co. v. Chase, 16 Wall. 522, 534, 21 L. ed. 369, 372; The Glide, 167 U.S. 606, 42 L. ed. 296, 17 Sup. Ct. Rep. 930); nor create liens for materials used in repairing a foreign ship (The Roanoke, 189 U.S. 185, 47 L. ed. 770, 23 Sup. Ct. Rep. 491). See Workman v. New York, 179 U.S. 552, 45 L. ed. 314, 21 Sup. Ct. Rep. 212. And plainly, we think, no such legislation is valid if it contravenes the essential purpose expressed by an act of Congress, or works material prejudice to the characteristic features of the general maritime law, or interferes with the proper harmony and uniformity of that law in its international and interstate relations. This limitation, at the least, is essential to the effective operation of the fundamental purposes for which such law was incorporated into our national laws by the Constitution itself. These purposes are forcefully indicated in the foregoing quotations from The Lottawanna.

A similar rule in respect to interstate commerce, deduced from the grant to Congress of power to regulate it, is now firmly established. "Where the subject is national in its character, and admits and requires uniformity of regulation, affecting alike all the states, such as transportation between the states, including the importation of goods from one state to another, Congress can alone act upon it and provide the needed regulations. The absence of any law of Congress on the subject is equivalent to its declaration that commerce in that matter shall be free." Bowman v. Chicago & N.W.R. Co. 125 U.S. 465, 507, 508, 31 L. ed. 700, 714, 715, 1 Inters. Com. Rep. 823, 8 Sup. Ct. Rep. 689, 1062; Vance v. W.A. Vandercook Co. 170 U.S. 438, 444, 42 L. ed. 1100, 1103, 18 Sup. Ct. Rep. 674; Clark Distilling Co. v. Western Maryland R. Co. 242 U.S. 311, 61 L. ed. 326, L.R.A. 1917B, 1218, 37 Sup. Ct. Rep. 180, decided January 8, 1917. And the same character of reasoning which supports this rule, we think, makes imperative the stated limitation upon the power of the states to interpose where maritime matters are involved.

The work of a stevedore, in which the deceased was engaging, is maritime in its nature; his employment was a maritime contract; the injuries which he received were likewise maritime; and the rights and liabilities of the parties in connection therewith were matters clearly within the admiralty jurisdiction. Atlantic Transport Co. v. Imbrovek, 234 U.S. 52, 59, 60, 58 L. ed. 1208, 1211, 1212, 51 L.R.A.(N.S.) 1157, 34 Sup. Ct. Rep. 733.

If New York can subject foreign ships coming into her ports to such obligations as those imposed by her Compensation Statute, other states may do likewise. The necessary consequence would be destruction of the very uniformity in respect to maritime matters which the Constitution was designed to establish; and freedom of navigation between the states and with foreign countries would be seriously hampered and impeded. A far more serious injury would result to commerce than could have been inflicted by the Washington statute authorizing a materialman's lien, condemned in The Roanoke. The legislature exceeded its authority in attempting to extend the statute under consideration to conditions like those here disclosed. So applied, it conflicts with the Constitution and to that extent is invalid.

Exclusive jurisdiction of all civil cases of admiralty and maritime jurisdiction is vested in the Federal district courts, "saving to suitors in all cases the right of a common-law remedy where the common law is competent to give it." The remedy which the Compensation Statute attempts to give is of a character wholly unknown to the common law, incapable of enforcement by the ordinary processes of any court, and is not saved to suitors from the grant of exclusive jurisdiction. The Hine v. Trevor, 4 Wall. 571, 572, 18 L. ed. 456; The Belfast, 7 Wall. 624, 644, 19 L. ed. 266, 272; American S.B. Co. v. Chase, 16 Wall. 522, 531, 533, 21 L. ed. 369, 371, 372; The Glide, 167 U.S. 606, 623, 42 L. ed. 296, 302, 17 Sup. Ct. Rep. 930. And finally, this remedy is not consistent with the policy of Congress to encourage investments in ships, manifested in the Acts of 1851 [9 Stat. at L. 635, chap. 43] and 1884 (Rev. Stat. 4283-4285, Comp. Stat. 1916, §§ 8021-8023; § 18, Act of June 26, 1884, 23 Stat. at L. 57, chap. 121, Comp. Stat. 1916, § 8028), which declare a limitation upon the liability of their owners. Richardson v. Harmon, 222 U.S. 96, 104, 56 L. ed. 110, 113, 32 Sup. Ct. Rep. 27.

The judgment of the court below must be reversed and the cause remanded for further proceedings not inconsistent with this opinion.

Reversed.

Mr. Justice Holmes, dissenting:

The Southern Pacific Company has been held liable under the statutes of New York for an accidental injury happening upon a gang-plank between a pier and the company's vessel, and causing the death of one of its employees. The company not having insured as permitted, the statute may be taken as if it simply imposed a limited but absolute liability in such a case. The short question is whether the power of the state to regulate the liability in that place and to enforce it in the state's own courts is taken away by the conferring of exclusive jurisdiction of all civil causes of admiralty and maritime jurisdiction upon the courts of the United States.

There is no doubt that the saving to suitors of the right of a common-law remedy leaves open the common-law jurisdiction of the state courts, and leaves some power of legislation, at least, to the states. For the latter I need do no more than refer to state pilotage statutes, and to liens created by state laws in aid of maritime contracts. Nearer to the point, it is decided that a statutory remedy for causing death may be enforced by the state courts, although the death was due to a collision upon the high seas. American S.B. Co. v. Chase, 16 Wall. 522, 21 L. ed. 369; Sherlock v. Alling, 93 U.S. 99, 104, 23 L. ed. 819, 820; Knapp, S. & Co. v. McCaffrey, 177 U.S. 638, 646, 44 L. ed. 921, 925, 20 Sup. Ct. Rep. 824; Minnesota Rate Cases (Simpson v. Shepard) 230 U.S. 352, 409, 57 L. ed. 1511, 1545, 48 L.R.A.(N.S.) 1151, 33 Sup. Ct. Rep. 729, Ann. Cas. 1916A, 18. The misgivings of Mr. Justice Bradley were adverted to in The Hamilton (Old Dominion S.S. Co. v. Gilmore) 207 U.S. 398, 52 L. ed. 264, 28 Sup. Ct. Rep. 133, and held at least insufficient to prevent the admiralty from recognizing such a state-created right in a proper case, if indeed they went to any such extent. La Bourgogne (Deslions v. La Compagnie Generale Transatlantique) 210 U.S. 95, 138, 52 L. ed. 973, 993, 28 Sup. Ct. Rep. 664.

The statute having been upheld in other respects (New York C.R. Co. v. White, 243 U.S. 188, 61 L. ed. 667, 37 Sup. Ct. Rep. 247), I should have thought these authorities conclusive. The liability created by the New York act ends in a money judgment, and the mode in which the amount is ascertained, or is to be paid, being one that the state constitutionally might adopt, cannot matter to the question before us if any liability can be imposed that was not known to the maritime law. And as such a liability can be imposed where it was unknown not only to the maritime but to the common law, I can see no difference between one otherwise constitutionally created for death caused by accident and one for death due to fault. Neither can the statutes limiting the liability of owners affect the case. Those statutes extend to nonmaritime torts, which, of course, are the creation of state law. Richardson v. Harmon, 222 U.S. 96, 104, 56 L. ed. 110, 113, 32 Sup. Ct. Rep. 27. They are paramount to but not inconsistent with the new cause of action. However, as my opinion stands on grounds that equally would support a judgment for a maritime tort not ending in death, with which admiralty courts have begun to deal, I will state the reasons that satisfy my mind.

No doubt there sometimes has been an air of benevolent gratuity in the admiralty's attitude about enforcing state laws. But of course there is no gratuity about it. Courts cannot give or withhold at pleasure. If the claim is enforced or recognized it is because the claim is a right, and if a claim depending upon a state statute is enforced, it is because the state had constitutional power to pass the law. Taking it as established that a state has constitutional power to pass laws giving rights and imposing liabilities for acts done upon the high seas when there were no such rights or liabilities before, what is there to hinder its doing so in the case of a maritime tort? Not the existence of an inconsistent law emanating from a superior source, that is, from the United States. There is no such law. The maritime law is not a corpus juris—it is a very limited body of customs and ordinances of the sea. The nearest to anything of the sort in question was the rule that a seaman was entitled to recover the expenses necessary for his cure when the master's negligence caused his hurt. The maritime law gave him no more. The Osceola, 189 U.S. 158, 175, 47 L. ed. 760, 764, 23 Sup. Ct. Rep. 483. One may affirm with the sanction of that case that it is an innovation to allow suits in the admiralty by seamen to recover damages for personal injuries caused by the negligence of the master, and to apply the common-law principles of tort.

Now, however, common-law principles have been applied to sustain a libel by a stevedore in personam against the master for personal injuries suffered while loading a ship. Atlantic Transport Co. v. Imbrovek, 234 U.S. 52, 58 L. ed. 1208, 51 L.R.A.(N.S.) 1157, 34 Sup. Ct. Rep. 733, and The Osceola recognizes that in some cases, at least, seamen may have similar relief. From what source do these new rights come? The earliest case relies upon "the analogies of the municipal law" (The Edith Godden, 23 Fed. 43, 46)—sufficient evidence of the obvious pattern, but inadequate for the specific origin. I recognize without hesitation that judges do and must legislate, but they can do so only interstitially; they are confined from molar to molecular motions. A common-law judge could not say, "I think the doctrine of consideration a bit of historical nonsense and shall not enforce it in my court." No more could a judge, exercising the limited jurisdiction of admiralty, say, "I think well of the common-law rules of master and servant, and propose to introduce them here en bloc." Certainly he could not in that way enlarge the exclusive jurisdiction of the district courts and cut down the power of the states. If admiralty adopts common-law rules without an act of Congress, it cannot extend the maritime law as understood by the Constitution. It must take the rights of the parties from a different authority, just as it does when it enforces a lien created by a state. The only authority available is the common law or statutes of a state. For from the often-repeated statement that there is no common law of the United States (Wheaton v. Peters, 8 Pet. 591, 658, 8 L. ed. 1055, 1079; Western U. Teleg. Co. v. Call Pub. Co. 181 U.S. 92, 101, 45 L. ed. 765, 770, 21 Sup. Ct. Rep. 561), and from the principles recognized in Atlantic Transport Co. v. Imbrovek having been unknown to the maritime law, the natural inference is that, in the silence of Congress, this court has believed the very limited law of the sea to be supplemented here as in England by the common law, and that here that means, by the common law of the state. Sherlock v. Alling, 93 U.S. 99, 104, 23 L. ed. 819, 820. Taylor v. Carryl, 20 How. 583, 598, 15 L. ed. 1028, 1033. So far as I know, the state courts have made this assumption without criticism or attempt at revision from the beginning to this day; e.g., Wilson v. MacKenzie, 7 Hill, 95, 42 Am. Dec. 51; Gabrielson v. Waydell, 135 N.Y. 1, 11, 17 L.R.A. 228, 31 Am. St. Rep. 793, 31 N.E. 969; Kalleck v. Deering, 161 Mass. 469, 37 N.E. 450, 42 Am. St. Rep. 421, 15 Am. Neg. Cas. 672. See Ogle v. Barnes, 8 T.R. 188, 101 Eng. Reprint, 1338; Nicholson v. Mounsey, 15 East, 384, 104 Eng. Reprint, 890, 13 Revised Rep. 501. Even where the admiralty has unquestioned jurisdiction the common law may have concurrent authority and the state courts concurrent power. Schoonmaker v. Gilmore, 102 U.S. 118, 26 L. ed. 95. The invalidity of state attempts to create a remedy for maritime contracts or torts, parallel to that in the admiralty, that was established in such cases as The Moses Taylor, 4 Wall. 411, 18 L. ed. 397, and The Hine v. Trevor, 4 Wall. 555, 18 L. ed. 451, is immaterial to the present point.

The common law is not a brooding omnipresence in the sky, but the articulate voice of some sovereign or quasi sovereign that can be identified; although some decisions with which I have disagreed seem to me to have forgotten the fact. It always is the law of some state, and if the district courts adopt the common law of torts, as they have shown a tendency to do, they thereby assume that a law not of maritime origin, and deriving its authority in that territory only from some particular state of this Union, also governs maritime torts in that territory—and if the common law, the statute law has at least equal force, as the discussion in The Osceola assumes. On the other hand, the refusal of the district courts to give remedies coextensive with the common law would prove no more than that they regarded their jurisdiction as limited by the ancient lines—not that they doubted that the common law might and would be enforced in the courts of the states as it always has been. This court has recognized that in some cases different principles of liability would be applied as the suit should happen to be brought in a common law or admiralty court. Compare The Max Morris, 137 U.S. 1, 34 L. ed. 586, 11 Sup. Ct. Rep. 29, with Belden v. Chase, 150 U.S. 674, 691, 37 L. ed. 1218, 1224, 14 Sup. Ct. Rep. 269. But hitherto it has not been doubted authoritatively, so far as I know, that even when the admiralty had a rule of its own to which it adhered, as in Workman v. New York, 179 U.S. 552, 45 L. ed. 314, 21 Sup. Ct. Rep. 212, the state law, common or statute, would prevail in the courts of the state. Happily such conflicts are few.

It might be asked why, if the grant of jurisdiction to the courts of the United States imports a power in Congress to legislate, the saving of a common-law remedy, i.e., in the state courts, did not import a like if subordinate power in the states. But leaving that question on one side, such cases as American S.B. Co. v. Chase, 16 Wall. 522, 21 L. ed. 369; The Hamilton (Old Dominion S.S. Co. v. Gilmore) 207 U.S. 398, 52 L. ed. 264, 28 Sup. Ct. Rep. 133, and Atlantic Transport Co. v. Imbrovek, supra, show that it is too late to say that the mere silence of Congress excludes the statute or common law of a state from supplementing the wholly inadequate maritime law of the time of the Constitution, in the regulation of personal rights, and I venture to say that it never has been supposed to do so, or had any such effect.

As to the specter of a lack of uniformity, I content myself with referring to The Hamilton (Old Dominion S.S. Co. v. Gilmore) 207 U.S. 398, 406, 52 L. ed. 264, 270, 28 Sup. Ct. Rep. 133. The difficulty really is not so great as in the case of interstate carriers by land, which, "in the absence of Federal statute providing a different rule, are answerable according to the law of the state for nonfeasance or misfeasance within its limits." Minnesota Rate Cases (Simpson v. Shepard) 230 U.S. 352, 408, 57 L. ed. 1511, 1545, 48 L.R.A.(N.S.) 1151, 33 Sup. Ct. Rep. 729, Ann. Cas. 1916A, 18, and cases cited. The conclusion that I reach accords with the considered cases of Lindstrom v. Mutual S.S. Co. 132 Minn. 328, L.R.A.1916D, 935, 156 N.W. 669; Kennerson v. Thames Towboat Co. 89 Conn. 367, L.R.A.1916A, 436, 94 Atl. 372; and North Pacific S.S. Co. v. Industrial Acci. Commission—Cal.—, 163 Pac. 199, as well as with the New York decision in this case. 215 N.Y. 514, L.R.A.1916A, 403, 109 N.E. 600, Ann. Cas. 1916B, 276, 9 N.C.C.A. 286.

Mr. Justice Pitney, dissenting:

While concurring substantially in the dissenting opinion of Mr. Justice Holmes, I deem it proper, in view of the momentous consequences of the decision, to present some additional considerations.

This dissent is confined to that part of the prevailing opinion which holds that the Workmen's Compensation Act of New York, as applied by the state court to a fatal injury sustained by a stevedore while engaged in work of a maritime nature upon navigable water within that state, conflicts with the Constitution of the United States and the act of Congress conferring admiralty and maritime jurisdiction in civil cases upon the district courts of the United States, and is to that extent invalid. Except for the statute, an action might have been brought in a court of admiralty. Atlantic Transport Co. v. Imbrovek, 234 U.S. 52, 62, 58 L. ed. 1208, 1212, 51 L.R.A.(N.S.) 1157, 34 Sup. Ct. Rep. 733. No question is raised respecting the jurisdiction of the state court over the subject-matter. But plaintiff in error contends, and the prevailing opinion holds, that it was a violation of a Federal right for the state court to apply the provisions of the local statute to a cause of action of maritime origin, because, by the Constitution of the United States, admiralty jurisdiction was conferred upon the Federal courts.

It should be stated, at the outset, that the case involves no question of penalties imposed by the New York act, but affects solely the responsibility of the employer to make compensation to the widow, in accordance with its provisions, which are outlined in New York C.R. Co. v. White, 243 U.S. 188, 192-195, 61 L. ed. 667, 37 Sup. Ct. Rep. 247.

The argument is that, even in the absence of any act of Congress prescribing the responsibility of a shipowner to his stevedore, the general maritime law, as accepted by the Federal courts when acting in the exercise of their admiralty jurisdiction, must be adopted as the rule of decision by state courts of common law when passing upon any case that might have been brought in the admiralty; and that, just as the absence of an act of Congress regulating interstate commerce in some cases is equivalent to a declaration by Congress that commerce in that respect shall be free, so nonaction by Congress amounts to an imperative limitation upon the power of the states to interpose where maritime matters are involved.

This view is so entirely unsupported by precedent, and will have such novel and far-reaching consequences, that it ought not to be accepted without the most thorough consideration.

Section 2 of article 3 of the Constitution reads as follows: "The judicial Power shall extend to all Cases, in Law and Equity, arising under this Constitution, the Laws of the United States, and Treaties made, or which shall be made, under their Authority; to all Cases affecting Ambassadors, other public Ministers and Consuls; to all Cases of admiralty and maritime Jurisdiction; to Controversies to which the United States shall be a party; to Controversies between two or more States; between a State and Citizens of another State; between Citizens of different States; between Citizens of the same State claiming Lands under Grants of different States, and between a State, or the Citizens thereof, and foreign States, Citizens or Subjects." Acting under the authority of article 1, § 8, which empowers Congress to make all laws necessary and proper for carrying into execution the powers vested in the government or in any department or officer thereof, the first Congress, in the original Judiciary Act (Act of September 24, 1789, chap. 20, § 9, 1 Stat. at L. 73, 77), conferred upon the Federal district courts "exclusive original cognizance of all civil causes of admiralty and maritime jurisdiction, . . . saving to suitors, in all cases, the right of a common-law remedy, where the common law is competent to give it." The saving clause has been preserved in all subsequent revisions. Rev. Stat. § 563 (8), Judicial Code, § 24 (3), 36 Stat. at L. 1087, 1091, chap. 231, Comp. Stat. 1916, §§ 968, 991 (3).

From the language quoted from the Constitution, read in the light of the general purpose of that instrument and the contemporaneous construction found in the Judiciary Act, with regard also to the mischiefs that called for the establishment of a national judiciary, and from what I believe to be the unbroken current of decisions in this court from that day until the present, I draw the following conclusions: (1) That the framers of the Constitution intended *to establish jurisdiction*—the power to hear and determine controversies of the various classes specified—and *not to prescribe particular codes or systems of law* for the decision of those controversies; (2) that the civil jurisdiction in admiralty was not intended to be exclusive of the courts of common law, at least not until Congress should deem it proper so to enact; (3) that by the law of England, and by the practice of the colonial governments, the courts of common law, of equity, and of admiralty, were controlled in their decisions by separate, and, in a sense, independent systems of substantive law, and the constitutional grant of judicial power in "all cases in law and equity," and in "all cases of admiralty and maritime jurisdiction," was no more intended (in the absence of legislation by Congress) to make the rules of maritime law binding upon the Federal courts of common law when exercising their concurrent jurisdiction, than to make the rules of the common law binding upon the courts of admiralty; (4) that, if not binding upon the Federal courts, it results, *a fortiori,* that the rules of maritime law were not intended to be made binding upon the courts of the states; (5) that it is not necessary, in order to give full effect to the grant of admiralty and maritime jurisdiction, to imply that the rules of decision prevailing in admiralty must be binding upon common-law courts exercising concurrent jurisdiction in civil causes of maritime origin, and to give such a construction to the Constitution is to render unconstitutional the saving clause in § 9 of the Judiciary Act, and also to trench upon the proper powers of the states by interfering with their control over their water-borne internal commerce; and (6) that, in the absence of legislation by Congress abrogating the saving clause, the states are at liberty to administer their own laws in their own courts when exercising a jurisdiction concurrent with that of admiralty, and at liberty to change those laws by statute.

That the language of § 2 of art. 3 of the Constitution speaks only of establishing jurisdiction, and does not prescribe the mode in which or the substantive law by which the exercise of that jurisdiction is to be governed, seems to me entirely plain; and upon this point I need only refer to the language itself, which I have quoted.

That this view is in harmony with the general purpose of the Constitution seems to me equally plain. At this late date it ought not to be necessary to repeat that the object of the framers of that instrument was to lay the foundations of a government, to set up its framework, and to establish merely the general principles by which it was to be animated; avoiding, as far as possible, any but the most fundamental regulations for controlling its operations, and these usually in the form of restrictions. Vanhorne v. Dorrance, 2 Dall. 304, 308, 1 L. ed. 391, 393, Fed. Cas. No. 16,857; Martin v. Hunter, 1 Wheat. 304, 326, 4 L. ed. 97, 102.

The object was to enumerate, rather than to define, the powers granted. Gibbons v. Ogden, 9 Wheat. 1, 189, 194, 6 L. ed. 23, 68, 69; Passenger Cases, 7 How. 283, 549, 12 L. ed. 702, 813; Lottery Case (Champion v. Ames) 188 U.S. 321, 346, 47 L. ed. 492, 497, 23 Sup. Ct. Rep. 321, 13 Am. Crim. Rep. 561. To delineate only the great outlines of the judicial power, leaving the details to Congress, while providing for the organization of the legislative department and the mode in which and the restrictions under which its authority should be exercised. Rhode Island v. Massachusetts, 12 Pet. 657, 721, 9 L. ed. 1233, 1259. The reason for adopting general outlines only was well expressed by Mr. Chief Justice Marshall in M'Culloch v. Maryland, 4 Wheat. 316, 407, 4 L. ed. 579, 601: "A constitution, to contain an accurate detail of all the subdivisions of which its great powers will admit, and of all the means by which they may be carried into execution, would partake of the prolixity of a legal code, and could scarcely be embraced by the human mind. It would probably never be understood by the public. Its nature, therefore, requires that only its great outlines should be marked, its important objects designated, and the minor ingredients which compose those objects be deduced from the nature of the objects themselves. That this idea was entertained by the framers of the American Constitution is not only to be inferred from the nature of the instrument, but from the language."

The adoption of any particular system of substantive law was not within the purpose of the Constitutional Convention; and the clause establishing the judicial power was ill-adapted to the purpose, had it existed. So far as they intended to prescribe permanent rules of substantive or even procedural law in connection with the establishment of the judicial system, the framers employed express terms for the purpose, as appears from other provisions of article 3, including the definition of treason, the character of proof required, the limitation of the punishment, and the requirement of a jury trial for this and other crimes.

In a somewhat exhaustive examination of various sources of information, including Elliot's Debates, Farrand's Records of the Federal Convention, and The Federalist, Nos. 80-83, I have been unable to find anything even remotely suggesting that the judicial clause was designed to establish the maritime code or any other system of laws for the determination of controversies in the courts by it established, much less any suggestion that the maritime code was to constitute the rule of decision in common-law courts, either Federal or state.

Certainly, there is nothing in the mere provision establishing jurisdiction in admiralty and maritime causes to have that effect, unless the jurisdiction so established was in its nature exclusive. But, in civil causes, the jurisdiction was not exclusive by the law of England and of the colonies, and it was not made an exclusive jurisdiction by the Constitution.

In discussing this point, the distinction between the instance court and the prize court of admiralty must be observed. It was held in England that the question of prize or no prize, and other questions arising out of it, were exclusively cognizable in the admiralty, because that court took jurisdiction owing to the fact of possession of a prize of war, and the controversy turned upon belligerent rights and was determinable by the law of nations, and not the particular municipal law of any country. Le Caux v. Eden (1781) 2 Dougl. K.B. 594, 602-613, 99 Eng. Reprint, 375, 379-385; Lindo v. Rodney, reported in a note to Le Caux v. Eden, 2 Dougl. K.B. 613, 99 Eng. Reprint, 385; Smart v. Wolff (1789) 3 T.R. 323, 340, et seq., 100 Eng. Reprint, 600; Camden v. Home (1791) 4 T.R. 382, 393, et seq., 100 Eng. Reprint, 1076, 6 Bro. P.C. 203, 2 Eng. Reprint, 1028, 2 H. Bl. 533, 126 Eng. Reprint, 687. But of civil actions in personam the instance court exercised a jurisdiction concurrent with that of the courts of common law. As Ld. Mansfield said in Lindo v. Rodney, 2 Dougl. K.B. 614: "A thing being done upon the high sea don't exclude the jurisdiction of the court of common law. For seizing, stopping, or taking a ship, upon the high sea, *not as prize,* an action will lie; but for taking *as prize,* no action will lie. The nature of the question excludes; not the locality." And again, referring to the effect of certain statutes (p. 615): "The taking a ship upon the high sea is triable at law to repair the plaintiff in damages; but a taking on the high sea as *prize* is not triable at law to repair the plaintiff in damages. The nature of the ground of the action—*prize or no prize*—not only authorizes the prize court, but excludes the common law. These statutes don't exclude the common law in any case, and they confine the admiralty by the locality of the thing done, which is the cause of action. It must be done upon the high sea."

So, with respect to actions ex contractu, Mr. Justice Blackstone says, 3 Bl. Com. 107: "It is no uncommon thing for a plaintiff to feign that a contract, really made at sea, was made at the royal exchange, or other inland place, in order to draw the cognizance of the suit from the courts of admiralty to those of Westminster Hall." The concurrent jurisdiction of the courts of common law was affirmed by Dr. Browne, the first edition of whose work was published in 1797-1799. 2 Browne, Civil & Admiralty Law, 1st Am. ed. 112, 115.

The declaration of Mr. Justice Nelson, speaking for this court in New Jersey Steam Nav. Co. v. Merchants' Bank, 6 How. 344, 390, 12 L. ed. 465, 485, that the lodging by the Constitution of the entire admiralty power in the Federal judiciary, and the 9th section of the Judiciary Act, with its saving of common-law remedies, left the concurrent power of the courts of common law and of admiralty where it stood at common law, was not a chance remark. It has been so ruled in many other cases, to which I shall refer hereafter. The principles and history of the common law were well known to the framers of the Constitution and the members of the first Congress; it was from that system that their terminology was derived; and the provisions of the Constitution and contemporaneous legislation must be interpreted accordingly.

The statement that there is no common law of the United States (Wheaton v. Peters, 8 Pet. 591, 658, 8 L. ed. 1055, 1079; Smith v. Alabama, 124 U.S. 465, 478, 31 L. ed. 508, 512, 1 Inters. Com. Rep. 804, 8 Sup. Ct. Rep. 564) is true only in the sense that the Constitution neither of its own force imposed, nor authorized Congress to impose, the common law or any other general body of laws upon the several states for the regulation of their internal affairs. As was pointed out in Smith v. Alabama (p. 478): "There is, however, one clear exception to the statement that there is no national common law. The interpretation of the Constitution of the United States is necessarily influenced by the fact that its provisions are framed in the language of the English common law, and are to be read in the light of its history."

As was well expressed by Shiras, District Judge, in Murray v. Chicago & N.W.R. Co. 62 Fed. 24, 31: "From them [citations of the decisions of this court] it appears beyond question, that the Constitution, the Judiciary Act of 1789, and all subsequent statutes upon the same subject, are based upon the general principles of the common law, and that, to a large extent, the legislative and judicial action of the government would be without support and without meaning if they cannot be interpreted in the light of the common law. When the Constitution was adopted, it was not the design of the framers thereof to create any new systems of general law, nor to supplant those already in existence. At that time there were in existence and in force in the colonies or states, and among the people thereof, the law of nations, the law admiralty and maritime, the common law, including commercial law, and the system of equity. Upon these foundations the Constitution was erected. The problem sought to be solved was not whether the Constitution should create or enact a law of nations, of admiralty, of equity, or the like, but rather how should the executive, legislative, and judicial powers and duties based upon these systems, and necessary for the proper development and enforcement thereof, be apportioned between the national and state governments."

And it is not to be supposed that the framers of the Constitution, familiar with the institutions and the principles of the common law, by which the admiralty jurisdiction was allowed on sufferance, and with a degree of jealousy born of the fact that the courts of admiralty were not courts of record, that they followed the practice of the civil law, allowed no trial by jury, and administered an exotic system of laws (3 Bl. Com. 69, 86, 87, 106-108)—it is not to be supposed, I say, that the framers of the Constitution, in granting judicial power over cases of admiralty and maritime jurisdiction, along with like power over all cases in law and equity arising under the laws of the United States, intended to exclude common-law courts, state or national, from any part of their concurrent jurisdiction in cases of maritime origin, or to deprive them of the judicial power, theretofore existing, to decide such cases according to the rules of the common law.

It is matter of familiar history that one of the chief weaknesses of the Confederation was in the absence of a judicial establishment possessed of general authority. Except that the Continental Congress, as an incident of the war power, was authorized to establish rules respecting captures and the disposition of prizes of war, and to appoint courts for the trial of piracies and felonies committed on the high sea, and for determining appeals in cases of capture, and except that the Congress itself, through commissioners, was to exercise jurisdiction in disputes between the states and in controversies respecting conflicting land grants of different states, there was no provision in the Articles of Confederation for establishing a judicial system under the authority of the general government.

The result was that not only private parties, in cases arising out of the laws of the Congress, but the United States themselves, were obliged to resort to the courts of the states for the enforcement of their rights. Many cases of this character are reported, some even antedating the Confederation. Respublica v. Sweers (1779) 1 Dall. 41, 1 L. ed. 29; Respublica v. Powell (1780) 1 Dall. 47, 1 L. ed. 31; Respublica v. De Longchamps (1784) 1 Dall. 111, 1 L. ed. 59. Even treason was punished in state courts and under state laws. See cases of Molder, Malin, Carlisle, and Roberts (1778) 1 Dall. 33-39, 1 L. ed. 25-27.

Before the Revolution, courts of admiralty jurisdiction were a part of the judicial systems of the several colonies. Waring v. Clarke, 5 How. 441, 454-456, 12 L. ed. 226, 232-234, Benedict, Admiralty, §§ 118-165. Upon the outbreak of the war questions of prize law became acute, and the colonial Congress, by resolutions of November 25, 1775, passed in the exercise of the war power (Penhallow v. Doane, 3 Dall. 54, 80, 1 L. ed. 507, 518), made appropriate recommendations for the treatment of prizes of war, but remitted the jurisdiction over such questions to the courts of the several colonies, reserving to itself only appellate authority. This system continued until the year 1780 (after the submission of the Articles of Confederation, but before their final ratification), when the Congress established a court for the hearing of appeals from the state courts of admiralty in cases of capture. The opinions of this court are reported in 2 Dall. 1-42, 1 L. ed. 263-281, and numerous cases decided without opinion, as well as some of those decided by committees of the Congress prior to the establishment of the court, are referred to in the late Bancroft Davis's "Federal Courts Before the Constitution," 131 U.S. xix-xlix, Appx. The weak point of this system was the want of power in the central government to enforce the judgment of the appellate tribunal when it chanced to reverse the decree of a state court. There were some curious cases of conflicting jurisdiction, illustrated by Doane v. Penhallow (1787) 1 Dall. 218, 221, 1 L. ed. 108, 109; Penhallow v. Doane (1795) 3 Dall. 54, 79, 86, 1 L. ed. 507, 517, 520; and United States v. Peters (1809) 5 Cranch, 115, 135, 137, 3 L. ed. 53, 59, 60.

It was under the influence of numerous experiences of the inefficiency of a general government unendowed with judicial authority that the Constitutional Convention assembled in the year 1787. The fundamental need, to which the Convention addressed itself in framing the judiciary article, was to set up a judicial power covering all subjects of national concern. There was no greater need to establish jurisdiction over admiralty and maritime causes than over controversies arising under the Constitution and laws of the Union. There was no purpose to establish a system of substantive law in any of the several classes of cases included within the grant of judicial power. The language employed makes it plain that, with the few express exceptions already noted (treason, etc.) the rules of decision were to be sought elsewhere. The entire absence of a purpose to establish a maritime code is manifest not only from the omission of any reference to the laws of Oleron, the laws of Wisbuy, or any other of the maritime codes recognized by the nations of Europe, but further from the fact that the colonies differed among themselves as to maritime law and admiralty practice, and that their system in general differed from that which was administered in England. The evident purpose, in this as in the other classes of controversy, was that the courts of admiralty should administer justice according to the previous course and practice of such courts in the colonies, just as the courts of common law and equity jurisdiction were to proceed according to the several systems of substantive law appropriate to courts of their respective kinds; subject, of course, to the power of Congress to change the rules of law respecting matters lying within its appropriate sphere of action.

Undoubtedly the framers of the Constitution were advised of the ancient controversy in England between the common-law courts and the courts of admiralty respecting the extent of the jurisdiction of the latter. They were aware of the dual function of the admiralty courts as courts of instance and as prize courts, and of the established rule that in civil causes the jurisdiction of the instance court was concurrent with that of the courts of common law. They must have known that, whatever question had existed as to the territorial limits of the jurisdiction of the admiralty, it never had been questioned that in suits for mariners' wages and suits upon policies of marine insurance, and in other actions ex contractu having a maritime character, and also in actions of tort arising upon the sea, the courts of common law exercised, and long had exercised, concurrent jurisdiction. Whatever early doubts may have existed had been based not upon any inherent incapacity of the common-law courts to deal with the subject-matters, but upon the ancient theory of the venue, and disappeared with the recognition of the fictitious venue.

The grant of judicial power in cases of admiralty and maritime jurisdiction never has been construed as excluding the jurisdiction of the courts of common law over civil causes that, before the Constitution, were subject to the concurrent jurisdiction of the courts of admiralty and the common-law courts. The first Congress did not so construe it, as the saving clause in the Judiciary Act conclusively shows. And, assuming that the states, in the absence of legislation by Congress, would be without power over the subject-matter, this saving clause, still maintained upon the statute book, is a sufficient grant of power. Jurisdiction in prize cases, as has been shown, springs out of the possession of a prize of war. Civil proceedings in rem, to be mentioned hereafter, are based upon the maritime lien, where possession in the claimant is neither necessary nor usual as is the case with common-law liens. With these exceptions, both resting upon grounds peculiar to the forum of the admiralty, concurrent jurisdiction of the courts of common law in civil cases of maritime origin always has been recognized by this court. New Jersey Steam Nav. Co. v. Merchants' Bank, 6 How. 344, 390, 12 L. ed. 465, 485; The Genesee Chief v. Fitzhugh, 12 How. 443, 458, 13 L. ed. 1058, 1065; The Belfast, 7 Wall. 624, 644, 645, 19 L. ed. 266, 272; New England Mut. M. Ins. Co. v. Dunham, 11 Wall. 1, 32, 20 L. ed. 90, 99; Leon v. Galceran, 11 Wall. 185, 187, 188, 20 L. ed. 74, 75; American S.B. Co. v. Chase, 16 Wall. 522, 533, 21 L. ed. 369, 372; Schoonmaker v. Gilmore, 102 U.S. 118, 26 L. ed. 95; Manchester v. Massachusetts, 139 U.S. 240, 262, 35 L. ed. 159, 166, 11 Sup. Ct. Rep. 559.

Nor is the reservation of a common-law remedy limited to such causes of action as were known to the common law at the time of the passage of the Judiciary Act. It includes statutory changes. American S.B. Co. v. Chase, 16 Wall. 522, 533, 534, 21 L. ed. 369, 372, 373; Knapp, S. & Co. v. McCaffrey, 177

U.S. 638, 644, 44 L. ed. 921, 924, 20 Sup. Ct. Rep. 824. Those remedies which were held not to be common-law remedies, within the saving clause, in The Moses Taylor, 4 Wall. 411, 427, 431, 18 L. ed. 397, 400, 402; The Hine v. Trevor, 4 Wall. 555, 571, 572, 18 L. ed. 451, 456; The Belfast, 7 Wall. 624, 644, 19 L. ed. 266, 272; American S.B. Co. v. Chase, 16 Wall. 522, 533, 21 L. ed. 369, 372, and The Glide, 167 U.S. 606, 623, 42 L. ed. 296, 302, 17 Sup. Ct. Rep. 930, provided for imposing a lien on the ship by proceedings in the nature of admiralty process in rem, and it was for this reason only that they were held to trench upon the exclusive admiralty jurisdiction of the courts of the United States. The distinction was noticed in Leon v. Galceran, 11 Wall. 185, 189, 20 L. ed. 74, 75, and again in Knapp, S. & Co. v. McCaffrey, 177 U.S. 638, 642, 44 L. ed. 921, 923, 20 Sup. Ct. Rep. 824. In the latter case it was pointed out (p. 644) that the reservation of a common-law remedy where the common law is competent to give it was not confined to common-law actions, but included remedies without action, such as a distress for rent or for the trespass of cattle; a bailee's remedy by detaining personal property until paid for work done upon it or for expenses incurred in keeping it; the lien of an innkeeper upon the goods of his guests, and that of a carrier upon things carried; the remedy of a nuisance by abatement, and others. The most recent definition of the rule laid down in The Hine v. Trevor and other cases of that class is in Rounds v. Cloverport Foundry & Mach. Co. 237 U.S. 303, 59 L. ed. 966, 35 Sup. Ct. Rep. 596.

I have endeavored to show, from a consideration of the phraseology of the constitutional grant of jurisdiction and the act of the first Congress, passed to give effect to it, from the history in the light of which the language of those instruments is to be interpreted, and from the uniform course of decision in this court, from the earliest time until the present, these propositions: first, that the grant of jurisdiction to the admiralty was not intended to be exclusive of the concurrent jurisdiction of the common-law courts theretofore recognized; and, secondly, that neither the Constitution nor the Judiciary Act was intended to prescribe a system of substantive law to govern the several courts in the exercise of their jurisdiction, much less to make the rules of decision, prevalent in any one court, obligatory upon others, exercising a distinct jurisdiction, or binding upon the courts of the states when acting within the bounds of their respective jurisdictions. In fact, while courts of admiralty undoubtedly were expected to administer justice according to the law of nations and the customs of the sea, they were left at liberty to lay hold of common-law principles where these were suitable to their purpose, and even of applicable state statutes, just as courts of common law were at liberty to adopt the rules of maritime law as guides in the proper performance of their duties. This eclectic method had been practised by the courts of each jurisdiction prior to the Constitution, and there is nothing in that instrument to constrain them to abandon it.

The decisions of this court show that the courts of admiralty in many matters are bound by local law. The doubt expressed by Mr. Justice Bradley in Butler v. Boston & S.S.S. Co. 130 U.S. 527, 558, 32 L. ed. 1017, 1024, 9 Sup. Ct. Rep. 612, as to whether a state law could have force to create a liability in a maritime case at all, was laid aside in The Corsair (Barton v. Brown) 145 U.S.

335, 36 L. ed. 727, 12 Sup. Ct. Rep. 949, and definitely set at rest in The Hamilton (Old Dominion S.S. Co. v. Gilmore) 207 U.S. 398, 404, 52 L. ed. 264, 269, 28 Sup. Ct. Rep. 133. The fact is that, long before Butler v. Boston & S.S.S. Co., it had been recognized that state laws might not merely create a liability in a maritime case, but impose a duty upon the admiralty courts of the United States to enforce such liability. Thus, while it was recognized that by the general maritime law a foreign ship, or a ship in a port of a state to which she did not belong, was subject to a suit in rem in the admiralty for repairs or necessaries, the case of a ship in a port of her home state was governed by the municipal law of the state, and no lien for repairs or necessaries would be implied unless recognized by that law. The General Smith (1819) 4 Wheat. 438, 443, 609, 611; The Lottawanna (Rodd v. Heartt) 21 Wall. 558, 571, 578, 22 L. ed. 654, 660, 663. Conversely, it was held in the case of Peyroux v. Howard (1833) 7 Pet. 324, 341, 8 L. ed. 700, 706, that a libel in rem in the admiralty might be maintained against a vessel for repairs done in her home port where a local statute gave a lien in such a case. To the same effect, The J.E. Rumbell, 148 U.S. 1, 12, 37 L. ed. 345, 347, 13 Sup. Ct. Rep. 498. As elsewhere pointed out herein, where a state statute conferred a lien operative strictly in rem, it was uniformly held not enforceable in the state courts, but only because it trenched upon the peculiar jurisdiction of the admiralty, and therefore was not a "common-law remedy" within the saving clause of the Judiciary Act of 1789. The Moses Taylor, 4 Wall. 411, 427, 431, 18 L. ed. 397, 400, 402; The Hine v. Trevor, 4 Wall. 555, 571, 572, 18 L. ed. 451, 456; The Belfast, 7 Wall. 624, 644, 19 L.ed. 266, 272; American S.B. Co. v. Chase, 16 Wall. 522, 533, 21 L. ed. 369, 372; The Glide, 167 U.S. 606, 623, 42 L. ed. 296, 302, 17 Sup. Ct. Rep. 930.

Under these decisions, and others to the same effect, the substance of the matter is that a state may, by statute, create a right to a lien upon a domestic vessel, in the nature of a maritime lien, which may be enforced in admiralty in the courts of the United States; but a state may not confer upon its own courts jurisdiction to enforce such a lien, because the Federal jurisdiction in admiralty is exclusive. The J.E. Rumbell, 148 U.S. 1, 12, 37 L. ed. 345, 347, 13 Sup. Ct. Rep. 498, and cases cited. But a lien imposed not upon the rem, but upon defendant's interest in the res, may be made enforceable in the state courts. Rounds v. Cloverport Foundry & Mach. Co. 237 U.S. 303, 307, 59 L. ed. 966, 968, 35 Sup. Ct. Rep. 596, and cases cited.

The Roanoke, 189 U.S. 185, 194, 198, 47 L. ed. 770, 772, 774, 23 Sup. Ct. Rep. 491, while approving The General Smith, Peyroux v. Howard, The Lottawanna, and The J.E. Rumbell, supra, gave a negative answer to the very different question whether a state could, without encroaching upon the Federal jurisdiction, create a lien against foreign vessels to be enforced in the courts of the United States.

In the present case there is no question of lien, and, I repeat, no question concerning the jurisdiction of the state court; the crucial inquiry is, to what law was it bound to conform in rendering its decision? Or, rather, the question is the narrower one: Do the Constitution and laws of the United States prevent a state court of common law from applying the state statutes in an action in personam arising upon navigable water within the state, there being no act of Congress applicable to the controversy? I confess that until this case and kindred cases submitted at the same time were brought here, I never had supposed that it was open to the least doubt that the reservation to suitors of the right of a common-law remedy had the effect of reserving at the same time the right to have their common-law actions determined according to the rules of the common law, or state statutes modifying those rules. This court repeatedly has so declared, at the same time recognizing fully that the point involves the question of state power. In United States v. Bevans, 3 Wheat. 336, 388, 4 L. ed. 404, 416, the court, by Mr. Chief Justice Marshall, said: "Can the cession of all cases of admiralty and maritime jurisdiction be construed into a cession of the waters on which those cases may arise? This is a question on which the court is incapable of feeling a doubt. The article which describes the judicial power of the United States is not intended for the cession of territory or of general jurisdiction. It is obviously designed for other purposes. . . . In describing the judicial power, the framers of our Constitution had not in view any cession of territory, or, which is essentially the same, of general jurisdiction. It is not questioned that whatever may be necessary to the full and unlimited exercise of admiralty and maritime jurisdiction is in the government of the Union. Congress may pass all laws which are necessary and proper for giving the most complete effect to this power. Still, the general jurisdiction over the place, subject to this grant of power, adheres to the territory, as a portion of the sovereignty not yet given away." In American S.B. Co. v. Chase, 16 Wall. 522, 533, 21 L. ed. 369, 372, the court, by Mr. Justice Clifford, said (p. 534): "State statutes, if applicable to the case, constitute the rules of decision in common-law actions, in the circuit courts as well as in the state courts."

In Atlee v. Northwestern Union Packet Co. 21 Wall. 389, 395, 396, 22 L. ed. 619, 621, the court, by Mr. Justice Miller, said: "The plaintiff has elected to bring his suit in an admiralty court, which has jurisdiction of the case, notwithstanding the concurrent right to sue at law. In this court the course of proceeding is in many respects different and the rules of decision are different. . . . An important difference as regards this case is the rule for estimating the damages. In the common-law court the defendant must pay all the damages or none. If there has been on the part of plaintiffs such carelessness or want of skill as the common law would esteem to be contributory negligence, they can recover nothing. By the rule of the admiralty court, where there has been such contributory negligence, or, in other words, when both have been in fault, the entire damages resulting from the collision must be equally divided between the parties. . . . Each court has its own set of rules for determining these questions, which may be in some respects the same, but in others vary materially." And see The Max Morris, 137 U.S. 1, 10, 34 L. ed. 586, 588; Belden v. Chase, 150 U.S. 674, 691, 37 L. ed. 1218, 1224, 14 Sup. Ct. Rep. 269; Benedict, Admiralty, § 201.

In the prevailing opinion, great stress is laid upon certain expressions quoted from The Lottawanna (Rodd v. Heartt) 21 Wall. 558, 574, 22 L. ed. 654, 661; but it seems to me they have been misunderstood, because read without regard to context and subject-matter. That was an admiralty appeal, and involved the question whether, by the general maritime law, as accepted in the United States, there was an implied lien for necessaries furnished to a vessel in her home port, where no such lien was recognized by the municipal law of the state. In the course of the discussion, the court, by Mr. Justice Bradley, said: "That we have a maritime law of our own, operative throughout the United States, cannot be doubted. The general system of maritime law which was familiar to the lawyers and statesmen of the country when the Constitution was adopted was most certainly intended and referred to when it was declared in that instrument that the judicial power of the United States shall extend 'to all cases of admiralty and maritime jurisdiction'. But by what criterion are we to ascertain the precise limits of the law thus adopted? *The Constitution does not define it.* It does not declare whether it was intended to embrace the entire maritime law as expounded in the treatises, or only the limited and restricted system which was received in England, or lastly, such modification of both of these as was accepted and recognized as law in this country. *Nor does the Constitution attempt to draw the boundary line between maritime law and local law; nor does it lay down any criterion for ascertaining that boundary.* It assumes that the meaning of the phrase 'admiralty and maritime jurisdiction' is well understood. It treats this matter as it does the cognate ones of common law and equity, when it speaks of 'cases in law and equity', or of 'suits at common law', *without defining those terms, assuming them to be known and understood.*"

In this language there is the clearest recognition that the Constitution, in establishing and distributing the judicial power, did not intend to define substantive law, or to make the rules of decision in one jurisdiction binding proprio vigore in tribunals exercising another jurisdiction. The courts of common law were to administer justice according to the common law, the courts of equity according to the principles of equity, and the courts of admiralty and maritime jurisdiction according to the maritime law. The expression on page 575 respecting the uniform operation of the maritime law was predicated only of the operation of that law as administered in the courts of admiralty, for it is not to be believed that there was any purpose to overrule Atlee v. Northwestern Union Packet Co. 21 Wall. 389, 395, 22 L. ed. 619, 621, decided at the same term and only about two months before The Lottawanna by a unanimous court, including Mr. Justice Bradley himself, in which it was held that where there was concurrent jurisdiction in the courts of common law and the courts of admiralty, each court was at liberty to adopt its own rules of decision. Moreover, the principal question at issue in The Lottawanna was whether the case of The General Smith, 4 Wheat. 438, 4 L. ed. 609, should be overruled, in which it had been held that, in the absence of state legislation imposing the lien, a ship was not subject to a libel in rem in the admiralty for repairs furnished in her home port. The general expressions referred to relate to that state of law—the absence of state legislation, as well as of legislation by Congress—and opon this the decision in The General Smith was upheld (p. 578). But in proceeding to discuss the subordinate question whether there was a lien under the state statute, it was held (p. 580):

"It seems to be settled in our jurisprudence that so long as Congress does not interpose to regulate the subject, the rights of materialmen furnishing necessaries to a vessel in her home port may be regulated in each state by state legislation." And again (p. 581): "Whatever may have been the origin of the practice, and whether or not it was based on the soundest principles, it became firmly settled, and it is now too late to question its validity. . . . It would undoubtedly be far more satisfactory to have a uniform law regulating such liens, but until such a law be adopted (supposing Congress to have the power) the authority of the states to legislate on the subject seems to be conceded by the uniform course of decisions."

Again, in Workman v. New York, 179 U.S. 552, 45 L. ed. 314, 21 Sup. Ct. Rep. 212, which, like The Lottawanna, was a proceeding in admiralty, the court, in quoting the declarations contained in that case respecting the general operation of the maritime law throughout the navigable waters of the United States, was dealing only with its application in the courts of admiralty. This is plain from what was said as a preface to the discussion (p. 557): "In examining the first question, that is, whether the local law of New York must prevail, though in conflict with the maritime law, it must be borne in mind that the issue is not—as was the case in Detroit v. Osborne (1890) 135 U.S. 492, 34 L. ed. 260, 10 Sup. Ct. Rep. 1012—whether the local law governs as to a controversy arising in the courts of common law or of equity of the United States, but does the local law, if in conflict with the maritime law, control a court of admiralty of the United States in the administration of maritime rights and duties, although judicial power with respect to such subjects has been expressly conferred by the Constitution (art. 3, § 2) upon the courts of the United States."

In the argument of the present case and companion cases, emphasis was laid upon the importance of uniformity in applying and enforcing the rules of admiralty and maritime law, because of their effect upon interstate and foreign commerce. This, in my judgment, is a matter to be determined by Congress. Concurrent jurisdiction and optional remedies in courts governed by different systems of law were familiar to the framers of the Constitution, as they were to English-speaking peoples generally. The judicial clause itself plainly contemplated a jurisdiction concurrent with that of the state courts in other controversies. In such a case, the option of choosing the jurisdiction is given primarily for the benefit of suitors, not of defendants. For extending it to defendants, removal proceedings are the appropriate means.

Certainly there is no greater need for uniformity of adjudication in cases such as the present than in cases arising on land and affecting the liability of interstate carriers to their employees. And, although the Constitution contains an express grant to Congress of the power to regulate interstate and foreign commerce, nevertheless, until Congress had acted, the responsibility of interstate carriers to their employees for injuries arising in interstate commerce was controlled by the laws of the states. This was because the subject was within the police power, and the divergent exercise of that power by the states did not regulate, but only incidentally affected, commerce among the states. Sherlock v. Alling, 93 U.S. 99, 103, 23 L. ed. 819, 820; Second Employers' Liability Cases

(Mondou v. New York, N.H. & H.R. Co.) 223 U.S. 1, 54, 56 L. ed. 327, 347, 38 L.R.A. (N.S.) 44, 32 Sup. Ct. Rep. 169, 1 N.C.C.A. 875. It required an act of Congress (Act of April 22, 1908, 35 Stat. at L. 65, chap. 149, Comp. Stat. 1916, § 8657) to impose a uniform measure of responsibility upon the carriers in such cases. So, it required an act of Congress (the so-called Carmack Amendment to the Hepburn Act of June 29, 1906, 34 Stat. at L. 584, 595, chap. 3591, Comp. Stat, §§ 8563, 8604a, 8604aa) to impose a uniform rule of liability upon rail carriers for losses of merchandise carried in interstate commerce. Adams Exp. Co. v. Croninger, 226 U.S. 491, 504, 57 L. ed. 314, 319, 44 L.R.A. (N.S.) 257, 33 Sup. Ct. Rep. 148. In a great number and variety of cases state laws and policies incidentally affecting interstate carriers in their commercial operations have been sustained by this court, in the absence of conflicting legislation by Congress. Among them are: Laws requiring locomotive engineers to be examined and licensed by the state authorities (Smith v. Alabama, 124 U.S. 465, 482, 31 L. ed. 508, 513, 1 Inters. Com. Rep. 804, 8 Sup. Ct. Rep. 564); requiring such engineers to be examined for defective eyesight (Nashville, C. & St. L.R. Co. v. Alabama, 128 U.S. 96, 100, 32 L. ed. 352, 354, 2 Inters. Com. Rep. 238, 9 Sup Ct. Rep. 28); requiring telegraph companies to receive despatches and transmit and delivery them diligently (Western U. Teleg. Co. v. James, 162 U.S. 650, 40 L. ed. 1105, 16 Sup. Ct. Rep. 934); forbidding the running of freight trains on Sunday (Hennington v. Georgia, 163 U.S. 299, 304, 308, etc. 41 L. ed. 166, 169, 170, 16 Sup. Ct. Rep. 1086); regulating the heating of passenger cars (New York, N.H. & H.R. Co. v. New York, 165 U.S. 628, 41 L. ed. 853, 17 Sup. Ct. Rep. 418); prohibiting a railroad company from obtaining by contract an exemption from the liability which would have existed had no contract been made (Chicago, M. & St. P.R. Co. v. Solan, 169 U.S. 133, 136, 137, 42 L. ed. 688, 691, 692, 18 Sup. Ct. Rep. 289); a like result arising from rules of law enforced in the state courts in the absence of statute (Pennsylvania R. Co. v. Hughes, 191 U.S. 477, 488, 491, 48 L. ed. 268, 272, 273, 24 Sup. Ct. Rep. 132); statutes prohibiting the transportation of diseased cattle in interstate commerce (Missouri, K. & T.R. Co. v. Haber, 169 U.S. 613, 630, 635, 42 L. ed. 878, 884, 885, 18 Sup. Ct. Rep. 488; Reid v. Colorado, 187 U.S. 137, 147, 151, 47 L. ed. 108, 114, 115, 23 Sup. Ct. Rep. 92, 12 Am. Crim. Rep. 506); statutes requiring the prompt settlement of claims for loss or damage to freight, applied incidentally to interstate commerce (Atlantic Coast Line R. Co. v. Mazursky, 216 U.S. 122, 54 L. ed. 411, 30 Sup. Ct. Rep. 378); even since the passage of the Carmack Amendment (Missouri, K. & T.R. Co. v. Harris, 234 U.S. 412, 417, 420, 58 L. ed. 1377, 1381, 1382, L.R.A.1915E, 942, 34 Sup. Ct. Rep. 790); statutes regulating the character of headlights used on locomotives employed in interstate commerce (Atlantic Coast Line R. Co. v. Georgia, 234 U.S. 280, 58 L. ed. 1312, 34 Sup. Ct. Rep. 829; Vandalia R. Co. v. Public Service Commission 242 U.S. 255, 61 L. ed. 276, 37 Sup. Ct. Rep. 93). All these cases affected the responsibility of interstate carriers. Until now, Congress has passed no act concerning their responsibility for personal injuries sustained by passengers or strangers, or for deaths resulting from such injuries, so that these matters still remain subject to the regulation of the several states. We have held recently that even the anti-pass provision of the Hepburn Act (34 Stat. at L. 584, 585, chap. 3591, § 1, Comp. Stat. 1916, § 8563) does not deprive a party who accepts gratuitous carriage in interstate commerce with the consent of the the carrier, in actual but unintentional violation of the prohibition of the act, of the benefit and protection of the law of the state imposing upon the carrier a duty to care for his safety (Southern P. Co. v. Schuyler, 227 U.S. 601, 612, 57 L. ed. 662, 669, 43 L.R.A. (N.S.) 901, 33 Sup. Ct. Rep. 277).

In the very realm of navigation, the authority of the states to establish regulations effective within their own borders, in the absence of exclusive legislation by Congress, has been recognized from the beginning of our government under the Constitution. As to pilotage regulations, it was recognized by the first Congress (Act of August 7, 1789, chap. 9, § 4, 1 Stat. at L. 53, 54, Rev. Stat. § 4235, Comp. Stat. 1916, § 7981), and this court, in many decisions, has sustained local regulations of that character (Cooley v. Port Wardens, 12 How. 299, 320, 13 L. ed. 996, 1005; Pacific Mail S.S. Co. v. Joliffe, 2 Wall. 450, 459, 17 L. ed. 805, 807; Ex parte McNiel, 13 Wall. 236, 241, 20 L. ed. 624, 626; Wilson v. McNamee, 102 U.S. 572, 26 L. ed. 234; Olsen v. Smith, 195 U.S. 332, 341; 49 L. ed. 224, 229, 25 Sup. Ct. Rep. 52; Anderson v. Pacific Coast S.S. Co. 225 U.S. 187, 195, 56 L. ed. 1047, 1051, 32 Sup. Ct. Rep. 625).

It is settled that a state, in the absence of conflicting legislation by Congress, may construct dams and bridges across navigable streams within its limits, notwithstanding an interference with accustomed navigation may result. Wilson v. Black Bird Creek Marsh Co. 2 Pet. 245, 252, 7 L. ed. 412, 414; Gilman v. Philadelphia, 3 Wall. 713, 18 L. ed. 96; Pound v. Turek, 95 U.S. 459, 24 L. ed. 525; Escanaba & L.M. Transp. Co. v. Chicago, 107 U.S. 678, 683, 27 L. ed. 442, 445, 2 Sup. Ct. Rep. 185; Cardwell v. American River Bridge Co. 113 U.S. 205, 208, 28 L. ed. 959, 960, 5 Sup. Ct. Rep. 423; Hamilton v. Vicksburg, S. & P.R. Co. 119 U.S. 280, 30 L. ed. 393, 7 Sup. Ct. Rep. 206; Willamette Iron Bridge Co. v. Hatch, 125 U.S. 1, 8, 31 L. ed. 629, 631, 8 Sup. Ct. Rep. 811; Lake Shore & M.S.R. Co. v. Ohio, 165 U.S. 365, 41 L. ed. 747, 17 Sup. Ct. Rep. 357; Manigault v. Springs, 199 U.S. 473, 478, 50 L. ed. 274, 277, 26 Sup. Ct. Rep. 127.

So, as to harbor improvements (Mobile County v. Kimball, 102 U.S. 691, 697, 26 L. ed. 238, 239); improvements and obstructions to navigation (Huse v. Glover, 119 U.S. 543, 548, 30 L. ed. 487, 490, 7 Sup. Ct. Rep. 313; Leovy v. United States, 177 U.S. 621, 625, 44 L. ed. 914, 916, 20 Sup. Ct. Rep. 797; Cummings v. Chicago, 188 U.S. 410, 427, 47 L. ed. 525, 530, 23 Sup. Ct. Rep. 472); inspection and quarantine laws (Gibbons v. Ogden, 9 Wheat. 1, 203, 6 L. ed. 23, 71); wharfage charges (Keokuk Northern Line Packet Co. v. Keokuk, 95 U.S. 80, 24 L. ed. 377; Cincinnati, P.B.S. & P. Packet Co. v. Catlettsburg, 105 U.S. 559, 563, 26 L. ed. 1169, 1171; Parkersburg & O. River Transp. Co. v. Parkersburg, 107 U.S. 691, 702, 27 L. ed. 584, 588, 2 Sup. Ct. Rep. 732; Ouachita & M. River Packet Co. v. Aiken, 121 U.S. 444, 447, 30 L. ed. 976, 977, 1 Inters. Com. Rep. 379, 7 Sup. Ct. Rep. 907); tolls for the use of an improved waterway (Sands v. Manistee River Improv. Co. 123 U.S. 288, 295, 31 L. ed. 149, 151, 8 Sup. Ct. Rep. 113).

So, of provisions fixing the tolls for transportation upon an interstate ferry (Port Richmond & B.P. Ferry Co. v. Hudson County, 234 U.S. 317, 331, 58 L. ed. 1330, 1336, 34 Sup. Ct. Rep. 821), or upon vessels plying between two ports located within the same state (Wilmington Transp. Co. v. Railroad Commission, 236 U.S. 151, 156, 59 L. ed. 508, 517, P.U.R.1915A, 845, 35 Sup. Ct. Rep. 276).

In each of these cases, except the last, which related to intrastate transport, the state regulation had an incidental effect upon the very conduct of navigation in interstate or foreign commerce. If in such cases the states possess the power of regulation in the absence of inconsistent action by Congress, much more clearly do they possess that power where Congress is silent, with respect to a liability which arises but casually, through the accidental injury or death of an employee engaged in a maritime occupation.

Indeed, with respect to injuries that result in death, it already is settled that although the general maritime law, like the common law, afforded no civil remedy for death by wrongful act (The Harrisburg, 119 U.S. 199, 30 L. ed. 358, 7 Sup. Ct. Rep. 140; The Alaska, 130 U.S. 201, 209, 32 L. ed. 923, 925, 9 Sup. Ct. Rep. 461), yet a right of action created by statute is enforceable in a state court although the tort was committed upon navigable water (American S.B. Co. v. Chase, 16 Wall. 522, 533, 21 L. ed. 369, 372; Sherlock v. Alling, 93 U.S. 99, 104, 23 L. ed. 819, 820), and the liability arising out of a state statute in such a case will be recognized and enforced in the admiralty (The Hamilton (Old Dominion S.S. Co. v. Gilmore) 207 U.S. 398, 52 L. ed. 264, 28 Sup. Ct. Rep. 133), although not by proceeding *in rem* unless the statute expressly creates a lien (The Corsair (Barton v. Brown) 145 U.S. 335, 347, 36 L. ed. 727, 731, 12 Sup. Ct. Rep. 949).

In Sherlock v. Alling, supra, which was an action in a state court and based upon a state statute to recover damages for a death by wrongful act occurring in interstate navigation, it was contended that the statute could not be applied to cases where the injury was caused by a marine tort, without interfering with the exclusive regulation of commerce vested in Congress. The court, after declaring that any regulation by Congress, or the liability for its infringement, would be exclusive of state authority, proceeded to say, by Mr. Justice Field (93 U.S. 104): "But with reference to a great variety of matters touching the rights and liabilities of persons engaged in commerce, either as owners or navigators of vessels, the laws of Congress are silent, and the laws of the state govern. The rules for the acquisition of property by persons engaged in navigation, and for its transfer and descent, are, with some exceptions, those prescribed by the state to which the vessels belong; and it may be said, generally, that the legislation of a state, not directed against commerce or any of its regulations, but relating to the rights, duties, and liabilities of citizens, and only indirectly and remotely affecting the operations of commerce, is of obligatory force upon citizens within its territorial jurisdiction, whether on land or water, or engaged in commerce, foreign or interstate, or in any other pursuit. In our judgment, the statute of Indiana falls under this class. Until Congress, therefore, makes some regulation touching the liability of parties for marine torts resulting in the death of the persons injured, we are of opinion that the statute of Indiana applies," etc.

I deem The Hamilton, supra, to be a controlling authority upon the question now presented. It was there held, not only that the constitutional grant of admiralty jurisdiction, followed and construed by the Judiciary Act of 1789, leaves open the common-law jurisdiction of the state courts over torts committed at sea, but also that it leaves the states at liberty to change the law respecting such torts by legislation, as by a statute creating a liability for death by wrongful act, which was the particular legislation there in question.

To what extent uniformity of decision should result from the grant of jurisdiction to the courts of the United States concurrent with that of the state courts is a subject that repeatedly has been under consideration in this court, but it never has been held that the jurisdictional grant required state courts to conform their decisions to those of the United States courts. The doctrine clearly deducible from the cases is that, in matters of commercial law and general jurisprudence, not subject to the authority of Congress, or where Congress has not exercised its authority, and in the absence of state legislation, the Federal courts will exercise an independent judgment and reach a conclusion upon considerations of right and justice generally applicable, the Federal jurisdiction having been established for the very purpose of avoiding the influence of local opinion; but that where the state has legislated, its will, thus declared, is binding, even upon the Federal courts, if it be not inconsistent with the expressed will of Congress respecting a matter that is within its constitutional power. The doctrine concedes as much independence to the courts of the states as it reserves for the courts of the Union. Burgess v. Seligman, 107 U.S. 20, 33, 34, 27 L. ed. 359, 365, 2 Sup. Ct. Rep. 10; East Alabama R. Co. v. Doe, 114 U.S. 340, 353, 29 L. ed. 136, 140, 5 Sup. Ct. Rep. 869; Gibson v. Lyon, 115 U.S. 439, 446, 29 L. ed. 440, 442, 6 Sup. Ct. Rep. 129; Anderson v. Santa Anna, 116 U.S. 356, 362, 29 L. ed. 633, 635, 6 Sup. Ct. Rep. 413; Baltimore & O.R. Co. v. Baugh, 149 U.S. 368, 372, 37 L. ed. 772, 775, 13 Sup. Ct. Rep. 914; Folsom v. Township 96, 159 U.S. 611, 625, 40 L. ed. 278, 283, 16 Sup. Ct. Rep. 174; Stanly County v. Coler, 190 U.S. 437, 444, 47 L. ed. 1126, 1131, 23 Sup. Ct. Rep. 811; Kuhn v. Fairmont Coal Co. 215 U.S. 349, 357, 360, 54 L. ed. 228, 233, 234, 30 Sup. Ct. Rep. 140.

In Baltimore & O.R. Co. v. Baugh, 149 U.S. 368, 372, 37 L. ed. 772, 775, 13 Sup. Ct. Rep. 914, the court had under review the judgment of a circuit court of the United States in an action by a locomotive fireman injured through negligence of the engineer. The cause of action arose in the state of Ohio, and the question presented was whether the engineer and the fireman were fellow servants. Under the decisions of the Ohio courts they were, but this court held that, as there was no state statute, the question should not be treated as a question of local law, to be settled by an examination merely of the decisions of the state court of last resort, but should be determined upon general principles; the courts of the United States being under an obligation to exercise an independent judgment. The court, by Mr. Justice Brewer, said (149 U.S. 378): "There is no question as to the power of the states to legislate and change the rules of the common law in this respect, as in others; but, in the absence of such legislation, the question is one determinable only by the general principles of that law.

Further than that, it is a question in which the nation as a whole is interested. It enters into the commerce of the country. Commerce between the states is a matter of national regulation, and to establish it as such was one of the principal causes which led to the adoption of our Constitution."

In other words, the general effect of the question upon interstate commerce rendered it one of the class that called for the application of general principles; nevertheless, state legislation would be controlling—in the absence of valid legislation by Congress, of course.

In Chicago, M. & St. P.R. Co. v. Solan, 169 U.S. 133, 136, 137, 42 L. ed. 688, 691, 692, 18 Sup. Ct. Rep. 289, the doctrine was concisely stated by Mr. Justice Gray, speaking for the court, as follows (169 U.S. 136): "The question of the right of a railroad corporation to contract for exemption from liability for its own negligence is, indeed, like other questions affecting its liability as a common carrier of goods or passengers, one of those questions not of merely local law, but of commercial law or general jurisprudence, upon which this court, in the absence of express statute regulating the subject, will exercise its own judgment, uncontrolled by the decisions of the courts of the state in which the cause of action arises. But the law to be applied is none the less the law of the state, and may be changed by its legislature, except so far as restrained by the Constitution of the state or by the Constitution or laws of the United States."

I freely concede the authority of Congress to modify the rules of maritime law so far as they are administered in the Federal courts, and to make them binding upon the courts of the states so far as they affect interstate or international relations, or regulate "commerce with foreign nations, and among the several states, and with the Indian tribes." What I contend is that the Constitution does not, proprio vigore, impose the maritime law upon the states except to the extent that the admiralty jurisdiction was exclusive of the courts of common law before the Constitution; that is to say, in the prize jurisdiction, and the peculiar maritime process in rem; and that as to civil actions in personam having a maritime origin, the courts of the states are left free, except as Congress, by legislation passed within its legitimate sphere of action, may control them; and that Congress, so far from enacting legislation of this character, has from the beginning left the state courts at liberty to apply their own systems of law in those cases where, prior to the Constitution, they had concurrent jurisdiction with the admiralty, for the saving clause in the Judiciary Act necessarily has this effect.

Surely it cannot be that the mere grant of judicial power in admiralty cases, with whatever general authority over the subject-matter can be raised *by implication,* can, in the absence of legislation, have a greater effect in limiting the legislative powers of the states than that which resulted from the *express* grant to Congress of an authority to regulate interstate commerce—the limited effect of which, in the absence of legislation by Congress, we already have seen. The prevailing opinion properly holds that, under the circumstances of the case at bar, although plaintiff in error was engaged in interstate commerce, and the deceased met his death while employed in such commerce, the provisions of the

Federal Employers' Liability Act (April 22, 1908, 35 Stat. at L. 65, chap. 149, Comp. Stat. 1916, § 8657) do not apply, because they cover only railroad operations and work connected therewith, wheras the deceased was employed upon an ocean-going ship. In effect it holds also that, in the absence of applicable legislation by Congress, the express grant of authority to regulate such commerce, as contained in the Constitution, does not exclude the operation of the state law. It seems to me a curious inconsistency to hold, at the same time, that the rules of the maritime law exclude the operation of a state statute without action by Congress although the Constitution contains no express grant of authority to establish rules of maritime law, and the authority must be implied from the mere constitutional grant of judicial power over the subject-matter; and most remarkable that this result is reached in the face of the fact that the judicial power in cases of admiralty jurisdiction has been put into effect by Congress subject to an express reservation of the previous concurrent jurisdiction of the courts of law over actions of this character. This, besides ignoring the reservation, gives a greater potency to an implied power than to a power expressly conferred.

The effect of the present decision cannot logically be confined to cases that arise in interstate or foreign commerce. It seems to be thought that the admiralty jurisdiction of the United States has limits coextensive with the authority of Congress to regulate commerce. But this is not true. The civil jurisdiction in admiralty in cases ex contractu is dependent upon the subject-matter; in cases ex delicto it is dependent upon locality. In cases of the latter class, if the cause of action arise upon navigable waters of the United States, even though it be upon a vessel engaged in commerce wholly intrastate, or upon one not engaged in commerce at all, or (probably) not upon any vessel, the maritime courts have jurisdiction. The Genesee Chief v. Fitzhugh, 12 How. 443, 452, 13 L. ed. 1058, 1062; The Commerce (Commercial Transp. Co. v. Fitzhugh) 1 Black, 574, 578, 579, 17 L. ed. 107, 109; The Belfast, 7 Wall. 624, 636, 638, 640, 19 L. ed. 266, 269-271; Ex parte Boyer, 109 U.S. 629, 632, 27 L. ed. 1056, 1057, 3 Sup. Ct. Rep. 434; Re Garnett, 141 U.S. 1, 15, 17, 35 L. ed. 631, 634, 635, 11 Sup. Ct. Rep. 840. It results that if the constitutional grant of judicial power to the United States in cases of admiralty and maritime jurisdiction is held by inference to make the rules of decision that prevail in the courts of admiralty binding proprio vigore upon state courts exercising a concurrent jurisdiction in cases of maritime origin, the effect will be to deprive the several states of their police power over navigable waters lying wholly within their respective limits, and of their authority to regulate their intrastate commerce so far as it is carried upon navigable waters.

The following additional consideration is entitled to great weight: The same Judiciary Act which, in its 9th section, conferred upon the district courts of the United States original cognizance of civil causes of admiralty and maritime jurisdiction, saving to suitors in all cases the right of a common-law remedy where the common law is competent to give it, in its 25th section allowed a writ of error from this court to review the final judgment or decree of a state court of last resort resulting from a decision overruling any special claim of right, privilege, or exemption based upon the construction of any clause of the Constitution or statutes of the United States. By later legislation the review was broadened (Act of February 5, 1867, chap. 28, § 2, 14 Stat. at L. 385, 386, § 709, Rev. Stat., § 237, Judicial Code, 36 Stat. at L. 1156, chap. 231, Comp. Stat. 1916, § 1214), and by recent legislation the writ of certiorari has been substituted for the writ of error in many cases (Act of September 6, 1916, chap. 448, 39 Stat. at L. 726, Comp. Stat. 1916, § 1207). But, at all times, the right to review in this court the decisions of the state courts upon questions of Federal law has existed, so that if, by the true construction of art. 3, § 2, of the Constitution, or of § 9 of the Judiciary Act of 1789, it had been the right of parties suing or sued in state courts upon causes of action of a maritime nature to insist that their cases should be determined according to the rules of decision found in the law maritime, this right or immunity might have been asserted as a Federal right, and its denial made the ground of a review of the resulting judgment, under a writ of error (or, now, a writ of certiorari) from this court to the state court of last resort. Yet, until the present case, and others submitted at the same time, the reported decisions of this court show not a trace of any such question raised. I can conceive of no stronger evidence to prove that from the foundation of the government until the present time it has been the opinion of the bar and of the judiciary, in the state courts as well as in the courts of the United States, that it was not the right of parties suing or sued in state courts of law or equity upon causes of action arising out of maritime affairs, to have them decided according to the principles that would have controlled the decision had the suits been brought in the admiralty courts.

There is no doubt that, throughout the entire life of the nation under Constitution, state courts not only have exercised concurrent jurisdiction with the courts of admiralty in actions ex contractu arising out of maritime transactions, and in actions ex delicto arising upon the navigable waters, but that, in exercising such jurisdiction, they have, without challenge until now, adopted as rules of decision their local laws and statutes, recognizing no obligation of a Federal nature to apply the law maritime. State courts of last resort, in several recent cases, have had occasion to consider the precise contention now made by plaintiff in error, and upon full consideration have rejected it. Lindstrom v. Mutual S.S. Co. 132 Minn. 328, L.R.A.1916D, 935, 156 N.W. 669; North Pacific S.S. Co. v. Industrial Acci. Commission—Cal.—163 Pac. 199; Kennerson v. Thames Towboat Co. 89 Conn. 367, 373, L.R.A.1916A, 436, 94 Atl. 372. See also Walker v. Clyde S.S. Co. 215 N.Y. 529, 531, 109 N.E. 604, Ann. Cas. 1916B, 87; Jensen v. Southern P. Co. 215 N.Y. 514, L.R.A.1916A, 403, 109 N.E. 600, Ann. Cas. 1916B, 276, 9 N.C.C.A. 286 (this case). I have found no case to the contrary except a decision by the United States district court for the northern district of Ohio in Schuede v. Zenith S.S. Co. 216 Fed. 566, now under consideration by this court. The reasoning is unsatisfactory, and it was repudiated in Keithley v. North Pacific S.S. Co. 232 Fed. 255, 259.

I may remark, in closing, that there is no conflict between the New York Workmen's Compensation Act and the acts of Congress for limiting the liability of shipowners (Rev. Stat. §§ 4283-4285, Comp. Stat. 1916, §§ 8021-8023;

Act of June 26, 1884, chap. 121, § 18, 23 Stat. at L. 53, 57, Comp. Stat. 1916, §§ 7707, 8028). So long as the aggregate liabilities of the owner, including that under the New York law, do not amount to as much as the interest of the owner in the vessel and freight pending, the act of Congress does not come into play. Where it does apply, it reduces all liabilities proportionally, under whatever law arising; the liability under the New York law along with the others. Butler v. Boston & S.S.S. Co. 130 U.S. 527, 552, 558, 32 L. ed. 1017, 1022, 1024, 9 Sup. Ct. Rep. 612; The Hamilton (Old Dominion S.S. Co. v. Gilmore) 207 U.S. 398, 406, 52 L. ed. 264, 270, 28 Sup. Ct. Rep. 133; Richardson v. Harmon, 222 U.S. 96, 104, 105, 56 L. ed. 110, 113, 114, 32 Sup. Ct. Rep. 27.

Mr. Justice **Brandeis** and Mr. Justice **Clarke** concur in the dissent, both upon the grounds stated by Mr. Justice **Holmes** and upon those stated by Mr. Justice **Pitney**.

Refer to Extract C, D.H.S.A. Section 1

270 F. 2d 355

Virginia J. KING, as Administratrix of the Estate of John Elvins King, Appellant,

v.

PAN AMERICAN WORLD AIRWAYS, a corporation, Appellee.

No. 16298.

United States Court of Appeals Ninth Circuit.

Aug. 27, 1959.

Rehearing Denied Dec. 8, 1959.

Administratrix brought action against airline company for wrongful death under the Death on the High Seas Act. The United States District Court for the Northern District of California, Southern Division, Louis E. Goodman, Chief Judge, 166 F.Supp. 136, entered judgment adverse to the administratrix, and administratrix appealed. The Court of Appeals, Jertberg, Circuit Judge, held that where duties of flight service supervisor of airline company required him to spend majority of his working time at San Francisco base and remaining working time in in-flight supervision and observation of pursers, stewards, and stewardesses employed on aircraft flying in and out of San Francisco, and, while in course of his employment aboard airliner, he was killed when airliner crashed on the high seas between the United States and Hawaii, sole remedy of his administratrix against company was under California Workmen's Compensation Act, which expressly provides compensation for death, outside the state, of an employee hired or regularly employed in the state, and that District Court did not have jurisdiction to entertain the action.

Judgment affirmed.

1. Workmen's Compensation

California Workmen's Compensation Act, which applies to all injuries whether occurring within California, or occurring outside territorial boundaries, if contract of employment was entered into in California or if employee was regularly employed in California, was not abrogated by Death on the High Seas Act. Death on the High Seas Act, § 1 et seq., 46 U.S.C.A. § 761 et seq.; West's Ann.Labor Code, §§ 3203, 3600, 3600.5, 3601, 3706, 5305.

2. Workmen's Compensation

Where duties of flight service supervisor of airline company required him to spend majority of his working time at San Francisco base and remaining working time in in-flight supervision and observation of pursers, stewards, and stewardesses employed on aircraft flying in and out of San Francisco, and, while in course of his employment aboard airliner, he was killed when airliner crashed on the high seas between the United States and Hawaii, sole remedy of his administratrix against company was under California Workmen's Compensation Act, which expressly provides compensation for death, outside the state, of an employee hired or regularly employed in the state, and federal District Court did not have jurisdiction to entertain action in admiralty for wrongful death under Death on the High Seas Act. Death on the High Seas Act, § 1 et seq., 46 U.S.C.A. § 761 et seq.; West's Ann.Labor Code, §§ 3203, 3600, 3600.5, 3601, 3706, 5305.

Smith, Parrish, Paduck & Clancy, Joseph Edward Smith, William Shannon Parrish, John B. Lewis, Oakland, Cal., Herbert Chamberlin, San Francisco, Cal., for appellant.

Steinhart, Goldberg, Feigenbaum & Ladar, Neil E. Falconer, John J. Goldberg, San Francisco, Cal., for appellee.

Before STEPHENS, HAMILIN and JERTBERG, Circuit Judges.

JERTBERG, Circuit Judge.

Appellant appeals from the final decree of the district court granting appellee's motion for a summary judgment in its favor. Jurisdiction of the district court was based on U.S.C. Title 28, Section 1333. Jurisdiction of this Court to review such decree is found in U.S.C. Title 28, Sections 1291 and 1294.

The parties agree that the sole and narrow question presented to this Court is whether the California Workmen's Compensation Act ousted the district court of jurisdiction to entertain a suit in admiralty against an employer for wrongful death under the Death on the High Seas Act by the administratrix of the estate of an airline employee who in the course of his employment was killed in the crash of an airliner on the high seas.

The stipulation of facts presented to the district court is as follows:

"(1) At all times relevant in this action, Respondent, Pan American World Airways, Inc., was and is a New York corporation, organized and existing under the laws of the State of New York with its airline operations divided into three separate divisions: The Pacific-Alaska Division (the Pacific area and Alaska) with headquarters at San Francisco, California; the Latin American Division (Central and South America) with headquarters at Miami, Florida; and the Atlantic Division (Europe and East) with headquarters at New York City, New York. Since 1944 the principal headquarters of the Pacific-Alaska Division has been located at the San Francisco International Airport, South San Francisco, California, and the principal headquarters of Pan American World Airways, Inc., for the transaction of business within the State of California has been located at the same place.

"(2) At all times relevant, the decedent, John Elvins King, and Libellant, Virginia J. King, were residents of the State of California;

"(3) The decedent John Elvins King, was first employed by Respondent, Pan American World Airways, Inc., on or about the 12th day of October, 1942, in San Francisco, California, and began his employment in San Francisco, California. The decedent, John Elvins King, was continuously employed by Respondent, Pan American World Airways, Inc., from the said 12th day of October,

1942, to and including the 8th day of November, 1957, and was continuously based at San Francisco since December 31, 1947.

"On May 1, 1957, said decedent was assigned the position of Flight Service Supervisor, stationed at the Pan American World Airways, Inc., base at the San Francisco International Airport, South San Francisco, California. That the duties of said employment provided that decedent John Elvins King would fly approximately 600 flying hours during a yearly employment of approximately 2080 hours.

"(4) At and prior to the time of the death of decedent, John Elvins King, on about November 8, 1957, Respondent, Pan American, had 'secured' the compensation rights of its employees under the California Workmen's Compensation Act by securing a policy of Workmen's Compensation Insurance issued by the Travelers Insurance Company, which said policy was in full force and effect at the time of the death of the decedent, John Elvins King.

"(5) The decedent, John Elvins King, left the San Francisco International Airport, South San Francisco, California, alive on November 8, 1957, on board Pan American Flight No. 7, the first stop of which was Territory of Hawaii, U.S.A. At the time of his death, decedent, John Elvins King, was performing services growing out of and incident to his employment, and was acting within the course of his employment, and his death was not caused by intoxication. On November 8, 1957, the airplane entered the water at a point between San Francisco, California, and the Territory of Hawaii (Hawaiian Islands), more than one marine league from any shoreline. Following said event John Elvins King was dead. The parties do not stipulate as to whether he died in the air or in the water.

"(6) Following the death of decedent, John Elvins King, Respondent, Pan American World Airways, Inc., and Travelers Insurance Company, its Workmen's Compensation Insurance carrier, on December 2, 1957, filed an application before the Industrial Accident Commission of the State of California, being Claim No. SF 183-024, in which Virginia J. King, Jean C. King-Freeman, Richard R. King and Melissa A. King, minors, by their Guardian Ad Litem and Trustee, Virginia J. King, were parties. Said application was filed to determine the liability of applicant, Pan American, for death benefit and burial expense under the California Workmen's Compensation Act. On February 20, 1958, a hearing was held before the Industrial Accident Commission upon said application. At said hearing, Virginia J. King appeared, through counsel, and contested the jurisdiction of the Industrial Accident Commission.

"At said time and place, said Virginia J. King advised that she was appearing specially, and that the application had been filed by Respondents without and against her consent. That Respondents agreed that defendants were not appearing voluntarily. That Libellant advised further that her appearance was not to be considered as a consent to jurisdiction of the Industrial Accident Commission either directly or indirectly, nor was she appearing for any reason other than the fact that she had been summoned to appear by the Industrial Accident Commission of the State of California after proceedings instituted by

Pan American World Airways, Inc. "As a result of said application and hearing, an order awarding a death benefit in favor of Virginia J. King, Richard R. King and Melissa A. King and against Travelers Insurance Company was made by the California Industrial Accident Commission on March 31, 1958.[1]

"A certified copy of said application (Exhibit 'A') and the order made by the Industrial Accident Commission with respect to said application (Exhibit 'B') in said proceeding are attached as Exhibits 'A' and 'B' hereof, and a certified copy of the opinion of the referee is attached hereto as Exhibit 'C' hereof.

"Entry of this stipulation shall not be deemed an admission by either party as to the relevancy or materiality of any of the facts stipulated to, and the parties reserve their rights in this regard."

Appellant's libel was based upon the Death on the High Seas Act (March 30, 1920, c. 111, Sections 1-7, 41 Stat. 537, 46 U.S.C.A. §§ 761-767). Relevant portions of that Act are as follows:

Section 1. "Whenever the death of a person shall be caused by wrongful act, neglect, or default occurring on the high seas beyond a marine league from the shore of any State, or the District of Columbia, or the Territories or dependencies of the United States, the personal representative of the decedent may maintain a suit for damages in the district courts of the United States, in admiralty, for the exclusive benefit of the decedent's wife, husband, parent, child, or dependent relative against the vessel, person, or corporation which would have been liable if death had not ensued."

Section 2. "The recovery in such suit shall be a fair and just compensation for the pecuniary loss sustained by the persons for whose benefit the suit is brought and shall be apportioned among them by the court in proportion to the loss they may severally have suffered by reason of the death of the person by whose representative the suit is brought."

Section 5. "If a person die as a result of such wrongful act, neglect, or default as is mentioned in section 761 of this title during the pendency in a court of admiralty of the United States of a suit to recover damages for personal injuries in respect of such act, neglect, or default, the personal representative of the decedent may be substituted as a party and the suit may proceed as a suit under this chapter for the recovery of the compensation provided in section 762 of this title."

Section 7. "The provisions of any State statute giving or regulating rights of action or remedies for death shall not be affected by this chapter. Nor shall this chapter apply to the Great Lakes or to any waters within the territorial limits of any State, or to any navigable waters in the Panama Canal Zone."

As a separate and special defense, the appellee alleged that the rights and obligations of the appellant were governed by the provisions of the California Workmen's Compensation Act, and that by virtue of the provisions thereof the rights and remedies afforded by said Workmen's Compensation Act provided the sole and exclusive right and remedy of appellant against the appellee for and on

1. At oral argument in this case appellant's counsel stated that payment of the award had been accepted by appellant.

account of the death of the deceased employee, and that by virtue thereof appellant is barred from maintaining the action.

The California Workmen's Compensation Act (cited as sections in the West's Ann.California Labor Code) in its pertinent parts provides:

Section 3600: "Liability for the compensation provided by this division, in lieu of any other liability whatsoever to any person except as provided in section 3706, shall, without regard to negligence, exist against an employer for any injury sustained by his employees arising out of and in the course of the employment and for the death of any employee if the injury proximately causes death, in those cases where the following conditions of compensation concur: * * *."

Section 3600.5: "(a) If an employee who has been hired or is regularly employed in this State receives personal injury by accident arising out of and in the course of such employment outside of this State, he, or his dependents in case of his death, shall be entitled to compensation according to the law of this State * * *."

Section 3601: "Where the conditions of compensation exist, the right to recover such compensation, pursuant to the provisions of this division is, except as provided in section 3706, the exclusive remedy against the employer for the injury or death."

Section 3706: "If an employer fails to secure the payment of compensation, any injured employee or his dependents may proceed against such employer by filing an application for compensation with the commission, and, in addition, may bring an action at law against such employer for damages, as if this division did not apply."

Section 5305: "The commission has jurisdiction over all controversies arising out of injuries suffered without the territorial limits of this State in those cases where the injured employee is a resident of this State at the time of the injury and the contract of hire was made in this State. Any such employee or his dependents shall be entitled to the compensation or death benefits provided by this division."

Section 3203: "The provisions of Division 4 and Division 5 shall not apply to employers or employments which, according to law, are so engaged in interstate commerce as not to be subject to the legislative power of the State, nor to employees injured while they are so engaged, except in so far as such divisions are permitted to apply under the * * * Constitution or laws of the United States."

The summary judgment was granted on the ground that the appellant's exclusive remedy was under the California Workmen's Compensation Act, and that appellant was therefore precluded from maintaining the admiralty remedy for wrongful death accorded by the Death on the High Seas Act. See King v. Pan American World Airways, D.C., 166 F.Supp. 136.

Appellant's main contentions are: (1) that the application of the California Workmen's Compensation Act to the instant case is invalid under the holding of the Supreme Court of the United States in Southern Pacific Co. v. Jensen, 1917, 244 U.S. 205, 37 S.Ct. 524, 61 L.Ed. 1086; (2) that the Death on the High Seas

Act abrogated the otherwise applicable Workmen's Compensation Act; and (3) that decisions of this Court compel us to hold that the Death on the High Seas Act abrogated the remedy afforded under the California Workmen's Compensation Act.

Before proceeding to discuss appellant's contentions we will note several general observations.

Neither party questions the power of Congress to enact the Death on the High Seas Act. If in the instant case the airplane had crashed on land, whether in the continental United States, in Hawaii, or in any foreign country, the remedy accorded under the Death on the High Seas Act would not have been applicable. If King had survived the crash in the instant case, no remedy would have been available to him under the Death on the High Seas Act.

It is not disputed that due to the interstate and foreign character of business of major airlines Congress has the power under the Constitution to enact a federal compensation act applicable to airline employees and their employers comparable to the specific federal laws enacted as to railroad workers, seamen, longshoremen, and others. Up to the present time Congress has chosen not to exercise such power.

Liability for the compensation provided by the California Workmen's Compensation Act exists against an employer without regard to negligence for any injury sustained by his employee arising out of and in the course of the employment and for the death of any employee if the injury proximately causes death. The right to recover such compensation is the exclusive remedy against the employer except under certain circumstances not here pertinent. The Act applies to all injuries whether occurring within the State of California, or occurring outside the territorial boundaries if the contract of employment was entered into in California or if the employee was regularly employed in California. In Alaska Packers Ass'n v. Industrial Accident Commission of California, etc., 294 U.S. 532, 55 S.Ct. 518, 79 L.Ed. 1044, the Supreme Court upheld an award made by the Industrial Accident Commission of California to an employee who was injured in the course of his employment in the Territory of Alaska, and whose contract of employment was entered into in California, and who had elected to be bound by the Alaska Workmen's Compensation Law, A.C.L.A.1949, § 43–3–1 et seq. Such extraterritorial jurisdiction has been sustained on the basis of a state's legitimate interest in protecting employees regularly employed within their state and their families from the consequences of industrial injuries. Cardillo v. Liberty Mutual Insurance Co., 330 U.S. 469, 67 S.Ct. 801, 91 L.Ed. 1028.

The applicable state workmen's compensation act has uniformly been held to govern industrial injuries sustained by employees of airlines in the course of their employment whether the crash occurred in this country or on foreign soil. Willingham v. Eastern Air Lines, 2 Cir., 199 F.2d 623; Severson v. Hanford Tri-State Air Line, Inc., 8 Cir., 105 F.2d 622, certiorari denied 309 U.S. 660, 60 S.Ct. 514, 84 L.Ed. 1008; Spelar v. American Overseas Air Lines, Inc., D.C., 80 F.Supp. 344; Urda v. Pan American Airways, 5 Cir., 211 F.2d 713. See also Duskin v. Pennsylvania-Central Air Lines, 6 Cir., 167 F.2d 727, certiorari denied

335 U.S. 829, 69 S.Ct. 56, 93 L.Ed. 382. In each of the above cited cases wherein a state wrongful death statute was involved it was held that the state workmen's compensation act excluded the operation of the otherwise applicable death act. None of the cases was based upon the Death on the High Seas Act. The rationale of these cases is that the applicable workmen's compensation law governs because it is the law in relation to which the parties contracted and the law affords a certain and speedy remedy to the injured employee, or his family in case of his death.

We will now discuss the appellant's contention: is the application of the California Workmen's Compensation Act to the instant case invalid under the doctrine announced by the Supreme Court in Southern Pacific Co. v. Jensen, supra? In the Jensen case the Supreme Court held that the New York State Workmen's Compensation Act could not be validly applied to the death of a stevedore killed while unloading a ship. The Court held that "the general maritime law" was part of our national law and that state legislation was invalid if it "works material prejudice to the characteristic features of the general maritime law." The Court further stated, "The work of a stevedore, in which the deceased was engaging, is maritime in its nature; his employment was a maritime contract; the injuries which he received were likewise maritime; and the rights and liabilities of the parties in connection therewith were matters clearly within the admiralty jurisdiction." 244 U.S. 217, 37 S.Ct. 529. The Jensen doctrine was reiterated by the Supreme Court in Knickerbocker Ice Co. v. Stewart, 1920, 253 U.S. 149, 40 S.Ct. 438, 441, 64 L.Ed. 834. In that case the decedent's death occurred while he was employed as a bargeman and doing business of a maritime nature, and the Court held that the Congressional Act in question was invalid because it attempted to sanction state compensation remedies "for injuries suffered by employes engaged in maritime work."

The Jensen doctrine was likewise applied by the Supreme Court in State of Washington v. W.C. Dawson & Co., 1924, 264 U.S. 219, 44 S.Ct. 302, 68 L.Ed. 646. The Court dealt jointly with two cases. By the Act of June 10, 1922 (42 Stat. 634) Congress amended Sections 24(3) and 256 of the Judicial Code relating to admiralty and maritime jurisdiction (28 U.S.C.A. §§ 41, subd. 3, 256), by adding to the saving clause of that Act, "and to claimants for compensation for injuries to or death of persons other than the master or members of the crew of a vessel their rights and remedies under the workmen's compensation law of any State, District, Territory, or possession of the United States, which rights and remedies when conferred by such law shall be exclusive." One of the cases presented the question "whether one engaged in the business of stevedoring, whose employees work only on board ships in the navigable waters of Puget Sound, can be compelled to contribute to the accident fund provided for by the Workmen's Compensation Act of Washington," [264 U.S. 219, 44 S.Ct. 303] and the other case presented the question as to whether the Industrial Accident Commission of the State of California had jurisdiction to award compensation for "the death of a workman killed while actually engaged in maritime work, under maritime contract, upon a vessel moored at her dock in San Francisco Bay and discharging her cargo."

It is clear from decisions of the Supreme Court after the Jensen case that the Jensen doctrine does not apply to all maritime torts. In Grant Smith-Porter Ship Co. v. Rohde, 1922, 257 U.S. 469, 42 S.Ct. 157, 66 L.Ed. 321, the Court held that in view of its exclusive features the Workmen's Compensation Act of the State of Oregon abrogated the right of the injured employee which would otherwise exist to recover damages in an admiralty court. The employee, a carpenter, was injured while working on a partially completed vessel lying at a dock in the Willamette River, at Portland, Oregon, which river is a part of the navigable waters of the United States. The Court held that jurisdiction in admiralty existed because the injury occurred on navigable waters. The Court stated, 257 U.S. at page 475, 42 S.Ct. at page 158:

"The contract for constructing 'The Ahala' was nonmaritime, and although the incompleted structure upon which the accident occurred was lying in navigable waters, neither Rohde's general employment, nor his activities at the time, had any direct relation to navigation or commerce. Thames Towboat Co. v. The Schooner 'Francis McDonald', 254 U.S. 242, 41 S.Ct. 65, 65 L.Ed. 245. The injury was suffered within a State whose positive enactment prescribed an exclusive remedy therefor. And as both parties had accepted and proceeded under the statute by making payments to the Industrial Accident Fund it cannot properly be said that they consciously contracted with each other in contemplation of the general system of maritime law. Union Fish Co. v. Erickson, 248 U.S. 308, 39 S.Ct. 112, 63 L.Ed. 261. Under such circumstances regulation of the rights, obligations and consequent liabilities of the parties, as between themselves, by a local rule would not necessarily work material prejudice to any characteristic feature of the general maritime law, or interfere with the proper harmony or uniformity of that law in its international or interstate relations. Southern Pacific Co. v. Jensen, 244 U.S. 205, 37 S.Ct. 524, 61 L.Ed. 1086; Western Fuel Co. v. Garcia, 257 U.S. 233, 42 S.Ct. 89, 66 L.Ed. 210."

In Alaska Packers' Ass'n v. Industrial Accident Commission, 1928, 276 U.S. 467, 48 S.Ct. 346, 72 L.Ed. 656, the injured workman was a resident of California and was employed by a California corporation to do work in Alaska. He agreed to go to Alaska as a seaman and after arriving in Alaska to work as directed. He made nets, fixed up boats, and served as a fisherman on one of them. He was injured while attempting to push a stranded fishing boat off the beach. The Supreme Court held that, assuming the injury to be within the admiralty jurisdiction, the injured employee was not engaged "in any work so directly connected with navigation and commerce that to permit the rights of the parties to be controlled by the local law would interfere with the essential uniformity of the general maritime law." Thereafter this Court upheld the application of the California Workmen's Compensation Act to two similarly employed cannery workers who met death in the wreck of a fishing schooner at sea. Alaska Packers Ass'n v. Marshall, 9 Cir., 95 F.2d 279. See also Millers' Indemnity Underwriters v. Braud, 1926, 270 U.S. 59, 46 S.Ct. 194, 70 L.Ed. 470.

The decedent was employed in a nonmaritime industry and performed no maritime work. As stated by the district court, "Indeed the only aspect of this case which gives it any maritime flavor whatsoever is the locale of the accident."

King v. Pan American World Airways, supra [166 F.Supp. 139]. Our study of the decisions of the Supreme Court above cited lead us to the conclusion that there is no constitutional barrier to the application of the California Workmen's Compensation Act to the facts of this case. In reaching that conclusion we have carefully reviewed the decisions of the Supreme Court in Standard Dredging Co. v. Murphy, 1943, 319 U.S. 306, 63 S.Ct. 1067. 87 L.Ed. 1416, and Pennsylvania Railway Co. v. O'Rourke, 1953, 344 U.S. 334, 73 S.Ct. 302, 97 L.Ed. 367, cited and relied upon by the appellant.

[1] Is the California Workmen's Compensation Act abrogated by the Death on the High Seas Act? The Death on the High Seas Act was enacted to fill a void in the maritime law which was found to exist by the Supreme Court in The Harrisburg, 119 U.S. 199, 7 S.Ct. 140, 30 L.Ed. 358. The Act provides an admiralty remedy for wrongful death where none existed before. The language of The Act does not purport to supersede a remedy afforded by a state workmen's compensation act for a death occurring on the high seas. Section 7 of the Act (supra) expressly provides that the provisions of any state statute giving or regulating rights of actions or remedies for death shall not be affected by the Act. The attitude of Congress at, prior and subsequent to the enactment of the Act toward state workmen's compensation acts was extremely friendly, as clearly reflected in the Congressional Acts declared unconstitutional in the Jensen, Knickerbocker and Dawson cases, supra. Decisions of the Supreme Court as cited supra hold that state workmen's compensation acts which provide an exclusive remedy to injured employees supersede the otherwise existing admiralty remedy for personal injuries in situations where the application of the state acts does not interfere with the uniformity of the maritime law. That the Death on the High Seas Act may have abrogated state wrongful death statutes for death occurring on the high seas is not persuasive that the Act likewise abrogates state workmen's compensation remedies. State wrongful death statutes require proof of fault. This same requirement is embodied in the Death on the High Seas Act. State wrongful death statutes in general do not purport or intend to apply outside the state's own boundaries. Uniformity perhaps in this field can only be achieved under the Death on the High Seas Act. Recovery under the Act may be uncertain and long delayed. The factors that might lead to the conclusion that the Death on the High Seas Act supplants or supersedes state wrongful death statutes do not apply and are not relevant to state workmen's compensation acts. Under such acts, compensation is payable without proof of fault but only on the basis of status as an employee. If death results in the course of employment, relief is prompt and certain.

In contending that the Death on the High Seas Act extends to wrongful death of employees, appellant has called to our attention the following cases: Pollard v. Seas Shipping Co. Inc., 2 Cir., 1945, 146 F.2d 875, 877; The Black Gull, 2 Cir., 1936, 82 F.2d 758, 759; Decker v. Moore-McCormack Lines, Inc., D.C.Mass.1950, 91 F.Supp. 560, 561; Batkiewicz v. Seas Shipping Co., D.C.N.Y.1943, 53 F.Supp. 802, 803; The Four Sisters, D.C.Mass.1947, 75 F.Supp. 399, 400. In the Pollard case, the plaintiff sued under the Jones Act (46 U.S.C.A. § 688), as administratrix of her husband's estate for damages for his death while in the course of his employment as a fireman on the "S.S. Algic" owned by the defendant. The jury returned a verdict for the plaintiff, and on appeal the defendant argued that drowning was not covered by the Jones Act. The Circuit Court affirmed the judgment. The Black Gull case involved an action to recover damages for the death of a harbor pilot killed by the negligence of a ship about to take him aboard. In sustaining the judgment against the defendant, the Court stated at page 761 of 82 F.2d: "We have assumed that a compulsory pilot is not an employee of the vessel in the sense that a member of her crew is such. Therefore any duty of protection owed to him * * * must rest on some other basis than employment." The Decker case involved the deaths of two seamen killed in a collision between two vessels. Actions to recover damages were brought not against the vessel operated by the decedents' employer, but against the owner of the other vessel. In the Batkiewicz case, the court permitted plaintiff to amend by adding a count under the Death on the High Seas Act to a count under the Jones Act. In the Four Sisters case, which also involved the death of a seaman, the question dealt with was whether or not an action under the Jones Act excluded a remedy under the Death on the High Seas Act. It is to be noted that all of the cases cited involved seamen. None involved a state workmen's compensation act with its exclusive remedy provision. None involved the substantive question of law presented by the instant case.

Appellant makes reference to the "twilight zone" cases under which appellant states that resort may be had at the election of the claimant to either a federal or state forum offering concurrent rights and remedies, and cites Davis v. Department of Labor, 317 U.S. 249, 63 S.Ct. 225, 87 L.Ed. 246, and Hahn v. Ross Island Sand & Gravel Co., 358 U.S. 272, 79 S.Ct. 266, 268, 3 L.Ed.2d 292. As stated by the Supreme Court in the Hahn case the Longshoremen's and Harbor Workers' Compensation Act, 33 U.S.C.A. § 901 et seq., does not apply if recovery for the disability or death through workmen's compensation may validly be provided by State law. The "twilight zone" was created in the Davis case, and as stated by Mr. Justice Stewart in his dissenting opinion in the Hahn case, "was a practical solution to a practical problem, a problem stemming from Southern Pacific Co. v. Jensen, 244 U.S. 205, 37 S.Ct. 524, 61 L.Ed. 1086, and one which 25 years of post-Jensen history had failed to solve. The problem was how to assure to injured waterfront employees the simple, prompt, and certain protection of workmen's compensation which Congress had clearly intended to give in enacting the federal statute. See 317 U.S. at page 254, 63 S.Ct. at page 228. The Davis decision in effect told the injured employee that in a doubtful case he would be assured of workmen's compensation whether he proceeded under a state workmen's compensation act or the federal statute." In the Davis case the occupation of the petitioner's decedent was in the "twilight zone." The Supreme Court of the State of Washington annulled an award to petitioner under the State Workmen's Compensation Law. The Supreme Court of the United States reversed and sustained the award. In the Hahn case, the Supreme Court stated:

"As to cases within this 'twilight zone', Davis, in effect, gave an injured waterfront employee an election to recover compensation under either the Longshoremen's Act or the Workmen's Compensation Law of the State in which the injury occurred. It seems plain enough that petitioner's injury occurred in the 'twilight zone', and that recovery for it 'through workmen's compensation proceedings', could have been, and in fact was, validly 'provided by State law'—the Oregon Workmen's Compensation Act. Ore.Rev.Stat. §§ 656.002–656.990. Therefore, the Longshoremen's Act did not bar petitioner's claim under state law. But since his employer had elected to reject them, the automatic compensation provisions of the Oregon Workmen's Compensation Act did not apply to the claim. Section 656.024 of that law provides, however, that when an employer has elected to reject the Act's automatic compensation provisions his injured employee may maintain in the courts a negligence action for damages. Of course, the employee could not do this if the case were not within the 'twilight zone', for then the Longshoremen's Act would provide the exclusive remedy. Since this case is within the 'twilight zone', it follows from what we held in Davis that nothing in the Longshoremen's Act or the United States Constitution prevents recovery."

In the instant case decedent's employment was not maritime. The California Workmen's Compensation Act was in full force and effect. There was no federal workmen's compensation act in effect. We find nothing in the "twilight zone" cases which ousts the California State Workmen's Compensation Act, or permits appellant to elect between it and the Death on the High Seas Act. To permit such an election would destroy the exclusive remedy provision which is an essential element to the California Workmen's Compensation Act.

In contending that the California Workmen's Compensation laws furnish no basis for the judgment of the district court, appellant relies on the case of Schellenger v. Zubik, D.C., 170 F.Supp. 92. The question presented in that case was whether or not a seaman who signs a state workmen's compensation agreement, receives payments thereunder, and executes a final receipt is barred from his right of recovery under the Jones Act and under the doctrine of unseaworthiness. We do not find this case apposite. We have heretofore pointed out the nonmaritime character of the decedent's employment and the exclusive provision of the California Workmen's Compensation Act which appellee relies upon in this case. We likewise are of the view that Occidental Indem. Co. v. Industrial Accident Commission, 24 Cal.2d 310, 149 P.2d 341, is not in point. In that case the California Supreme Court annulled an industrial accident award in the case of a seaman injured in the course of his employment. The Court held that seamen are governed by admiralty law over which federal law is paramount. The Betsy Ross case, 9 Cir., 145 F.2d 688, adds nothing since the same parties, the same injuries, and the same employment were involved in this case as were involved in the Occidental Indem. Company case. This Court agreed with the State Court that employment of the injured workman was maritime in character, which fact deprived the Industrial Accident Commission of the State of California of jurisdiction. Finally, under this head appellant contends that Section 3203, supra, of the California Workmen's Compensation Act makes such law self-subordinating to the Death on the High Seas Act. We feel that this point has been disposed of adversely to such contention by what has already been said in this opinion.

Appellant's final contention is that under the decisions of this Court in Higa v. Transocean Air Lines, 9 Cir., 230 F.2d 780, and Trihey v. Transocean Air Lines, Inc., 9 Cir., 255 F.2d 824, we are compelled to hold that the Death on the High Seas Act abrogated the remedy afforded under the California Workmen's Compensation Act. We do not agree. In the Higa case, Higa was a passenger on an airplane which crashed in the Pacific Ocean 300 to 400 miles from Wake Island, when flying toward Honolulu. The administrator of Higa's estate instituted an action alleging that Higa's death was caused by the plane crashing into the ocean. The action for damages was based on the Death on the High Seas Act and was brought as a common law civil suit rather than in admiralty. The district court dismissed the action because the action was not instituted on the admiralty side of the court. This Court affirmed the judgment of dismissal. The substantive question of law presented to us in this case was not involved in the Higa case. Although the Court by way of dictum expressed the view that a local wrongful death statute was not superseded by the Death on the High Seas Act, the wrongful death statute of the Territory of Hawaii was not mentioned in the opinion except in a footnote noting the existence of such an act. The Trihey case involved an action in admiralty for the wrongful death on the high seas of a passenger in an airplane which crashed. The district court found no negligence on the part of the defendants. This Court affirmed the judgment on the ground it could not say the findings of the district court were erroneous. Again the question of substantive law involved in the present case was not present in the Trihey case, nor even did it involve a local wrongful death statute. Appellant also relies on D'Aleman v. Pan American World Airways, 2 Cir., 259 F.2d 493. The decedent was a passenger on the defendant's airplane, flying from Puerto Rico to New York. Because of engine trouble and weather conditions the plane proceeded to Virginia where it made a normal landing. The passengers were advised while enroute that one engine was being "feathered" and that the flight would be on the three remaining engines, and because of weather conditions the plane would land in Virginia. Several days after landing the decedent died in New York. The plaintiff's first cause of action, based upon the Death on the High Seas Act, alleged that the deceased became so terrified by the "feathering" of the engine and the announcement of the unscheduled landing in Virginia that he went into a state of shock which resulted in his death. The second cause of action was based upon alleged failure of the defendant to provide adequate medical care to the deceased. None of the workmen's compensation laws were involved. The district court, under the first cause of action, sitting without a jury, found no negligence. A jury sitting under the second cause of action found likewise. The Circuit Court found that the first cause of action was properly heard in admiralty without a jury, and that the ruling of the district court in excluding evidence offered by the plaintiff under the second cause of action was proper. This case does not bear on the specific problem before us.

[2] We conclude that under the stipulated facts of this case and the applicable law appellant's sole remedy against the defendant is under the California Workmen's Compensation Act, and that the judgment of the district court must be and is hereby affirmed.

Refer to Extract A, U.S. Constitution Article III, Section 2

409 U.S. 249
EXECUTIVE JET AVIATION, INC.,
et al., Petitioners,
v.
CITY OF CLEVELAND, OHIO, et al.
(Cite as 93 S. Ct. 493)
No. 71–678.
Argued Nov. 15, 1972.
Decided Dec. 18, 1972.

Owners of airplane which crashed into navigable water on takeoff brought suit in admiralty for loss of the aircraft against city which owned and operated airport, airport manager, and air traffic controller. The United States District Court for the Northern District of Ohio dismissed the complaint, and appeal was taken. The Court of Appeals for the Sixth Circuit affirmed, 448 F.2d 151, and certiorari was granted. The Supreme Court, Mr. Justice Stewart, held that maritime locality alone is not a sufficient predicate for admiralty jurisdiction in aviation tort cases, and that in the absence of legislation to the contrary, claims arising from airplane accidents are not cognizable in admiralty unless the wrong bears a significant relationship to traditional maritime activities. The Court further held that there was no such significant relationship where land-based aircraft flying between points within the continental United States fell into the navigable waters of Lake Erie after striking a flock of seagulls over the runway on takeoff.

Affirmed.

1. Courts

Certiorari was granted to consider a seemingly important question affecting the jurisdiction of the federal courts: whether aviation torts occurring in or over navigable waters are within admiralty jurisdiction. 28 U.S.C.A. § 1333(1).

2. Admiralty

Maritime locality alone is not a sufficient predicate for admiralty jurisdiction in aviation tort cases; in the absence of legislation to the contrary, claims arising from airplane accidents are not cognizable in admiralty unless the wrong bears a significant relationship to traditional maritime activities. 28 U.S.C.A. § 1333(1); Longshoremen's and Harbor Workers' Compensation Act § 1 et seq. as amended 33 U.S.C.A. § 901 et seq.; Jones Act, 46 U.S.C.A. § 688; Admiralty Jurisdiction Extension Act, 46 U.S.C.A. § 740; Air Commerce Act of 1926, § 7, 49 U.S.C.A. § 177; Federal Aviation Act of 1958, § 1109(a), 49 U.S.C.A. § 1509(a).

3. Admiralty

Federal admiralty courts have jurisdiction of wrongful death actions arising out of airplane crashes on the high seas beyond a marine league from the shore of any state or the District of Columbia or the territories or dependencies of the United States. Death on the High Seas Act, § 1 et seq., 46 U.S.C.A. § 761 et seq.

4. Admiralty

With respect to determining admiralty jurisdiction of tort actions other than wrongful death actions, it was stated by the court an airplane crash on the high seas bears some relationship to maritime commerce, at least insofar as the aircraft is beyond state territorial waters and performing a function, transoceanic crossing, that previously would have been performed by waterborne vessels; but it was not determined whether such relationship is "significant" so as to warrant invoking admiralty jurisdiction. 28 U.S.C.A. § 1333(1); Death on the High Seas Act, § 1 et seq., 46 U.S.C.A. § 761 et seq.

5. Admiralty

Mere fact that alleged wrong "occurs" or "is located" on or over navigable waters is not of itself sufficient to turn a case of airplane negligence into a "maritime tort."

6. Admiralty

Neither the fact that an airplane goes down on navigable waters nor the fact that the negligence "occurs" while a plane is flying over such waters is enough to create such a relationship to traditional maritime activity as to justify the invocation of admiralty jurisdiction, despite alleged analogy between aircraft down at sea and sinking vessels. 28 U.S.C.A. § 1333(1).

7. Admiralty

Where land-based aircraft on flight which was intended to take it from Cleveland, Ohio, to Bangor, Maine, and then to White Plains, New York, struck a flock of seagulls over the runway after takeoff from a Cleveland airport and fell into and soon sank in navigable waters of Lake Erie, a short distance off shore, there was no significant relationship between such event and traditional maritime activity involving navigation and commerce on navigable waters, and thus owners of the aircraft could not invoke admiralty jurisdiction in their suit for loss of the aircraft against city which owned and operated airport, airport manager, and air traffic controller. 28 U.S.C.A. § 1333(1).

8. Admiralty

In suit by owner of aircraft, which fell into navigable waters of Lake Erie after striking seagulls on takeoff, against city which owned and operated airport,

airport manager and air traffic controller, pendency of a separate action against the United States in federal court under the Tort Claims Act had no relevance in determining whether the instant case should be heard in admiralty, with its federal substantive law. 28 U.S.C.A. §§ 1333(1), 1346(b), 2674.

9. Constitutional Law

If it is desirable that aviation tort cases should be governed by uniform substantive and procedural laws, proper course is for Congress to enact appropriate legislation under the commerce clause, rather than for the courts to invoke federal admiralty jurisdiction in a few fortuitous aircraft cases when accident occurs in or over navigable waters.

10. Admiralty

In the absence of legislation to the contrary, there is no federal admiralty jurisdiction over aviation tort claims arising from flights by land-based aircraft between points within the continental United States. 28 U.S.C.A. § 1333(1).

*Syllabus**

CERTIORARI TO THE UNITED STATES COURT
OF APPEALS FOR THE SIXTH CIRCUIT
No. 71–678.
Argued November 15, 1972.
Decided December 18, 1972.

Petitioners, invoking federal admiralty jurisdiction under 28 U.S.C. § 1333(1), brought suit for damages resulting from the crash-landing and sinking in the navigable waters of Lake Erie of their jet aircraft shortly after takeoff from a Cleveland airport. The District Court dismissed the complaint for lack of admiralty jurisdiction on the grounds that the alleged tort had neither a maritime locality nor a maritime nexus. The Court of Appeals affirmed on the first ground. *Held:* Neither the fact that an aircraft goes down on navigable waters nor that the negligence "occurs" while the aircraft is flying over such waters is sufficient to confer federal admiralty jurisdiction over aviation tort claims, and in the absence of legislation to the contrary such jurisdiction exists with respect to those claims only when there is a significant relationship to traditional maritime activity. Therefore, federal admiralty jurisdiction does not extend to aviation tort claims arising from flights like the one involved here between points within the continental United States. Pp. 497-507.

448 F.2d 151, affirmed.

---

*The syllabus constitutes no part of the opinion of the Court but has been prepared by the Reporter of Decisions for the convenience of the reader. See United States v. Detroit Timber & Lumber Co., 200 U.S. 321, 337, 26 S.Ct. 282, 287, 50 L.Ed. 499.

Phillip D. Bostwick, Washington, D.C., for petitioners.
Sol. Gen. Erwin N. Griswold, for respondents.

Mr. Justice STEWART delivered the opinion of the Court.

On July 28, 1968, a jet aircraft, owned and operated by the petitioners, struck a flock of seagulls as it was taking off from Burke Lakefront Airport in Cleveland, Ohio, adjacent to Lake Erie. As a result, the plane lost its power, crashed, and ultimately sank in the navigable waters of Lake Erie, a short distance from the airport. The question before us is whether the petitioners' suit for property damage to the aircraft, allegedly caused by the respondents' negligence, lies within federal admiralty jurisdiction.

When the crash occurred, the plane was manned by a pilot, a co-pilot, and a stewardess, and was departing Cleveland on a charter flight to Portland, Maine, where it was to pick up passengers and then continue to White Plains, New York. After being cleared for takeoff by the respondent Dicken, who was the federal air traffic controller at the airport, the plane took off, becoming airborne at about half the distance down the runway. The takeoff flushed the seagulls on the runway, and they rose into the airspace directly ahead of the ascending plane. Ingestion of the birds into the plane's jet engines caused an almost total loss of power. Descending back toward the runway in a semi-stalled condition, the plane veered slightly to the left, struck a portion of the airport perimeter fence and the top of a nearby pickup truck, and then settled in Lake Erie just off the end of the runway and less than one-fifth of a statute mile offshore. There were no injuries to the crew, but the aircraft soon sank and became a total loss.

Invoking federal admiralty jurisdiction under 28 U.S.C. § 1333(1),[1] the petitioners brought this suit for damages in the District Court for the Northern District of Ohio against Dicken and the other respondents[2] alleging that the crash had been caused by the respondents' negligent failure to keep the runway free of the birds or to give adequate warning of their presence.[3] The District Court, in an unreported opinion, held that the suit was not cognizable in admiralty and dismissed the complaint for lack of subject matter jurisdiction.

Relying primarily on the Sixth Circuit precedent of Chapman v. City of Grosse Pointe Farms, 385 F.2d 962 (1967), the District Court held that admiralty jurisdiction over torts may properly be invoked only when two criteria are met: (1) the locality where the alleged tortious wrong occurred must have been

1. That section provides:

"The district courts shall have original jurisdiction, exclusive of the courts of the States, of:

"(1) Any civil case of admiralty or maritime jurisdiction, saving to suitors in all cases all other remedies to which they are otherwise entitled."

2. Besides Dicken, the respondents are the City of Cleveland, as owner and operator of the airport, and Phillip A. Schwenz, the airport manager.

3. The petitioners also filed an action against Dicken's employer, the United States, under the Federal Tort Claims Act, 28 U.S.C. §§ 1346(b) and 2674, asserting the same claim. That action is pending in the District Court for the Northern District of Ohio.

on navigable waters; and (2) there must have been a relationship between the wrong and some maritime service, navigation, or commerce on navigable waters. The District Court found that the allegations of the petitioners' complaint satisfied neither of these criteria. With respect to the locality of the alleged wrong, the court stated that "the alleged negligence became operative upon the aircraft while it was over the land; and in this sense the 'impact' of the alleged negligence occurred when the gulls disabled the plane's engines [over the land]. . . . From this point on the plane was disabled and was caused to fall. Whether it came down upon land or upon water was largely fortuitous." Alternatively, the court concluded that the wrong bore no relationship to maritime service, navigation, or commerce:

> "Assuming . . . that air commerce bears some relationship to maritime commerce when the former is carried out over navigable waters, the relevant circumstances here were unconnected with the maritime facets of air commerce. The claimed 'wrong' in this case was the alleged failure to keep the runway free of birds and the failure to adequately warn the pilots of their presence upon the end of the runway. When the alleged negligence occurred, and when it became operative upon the aircraft, all the parties were engaged in functions common to all air commerce, whether over land or over sea.
>
> ". . . Thus, the conclusion here must be that the operative facts of the claim in this case are concerned with the land-connected aspects of air-commerce, namely, the maintenance and operation of an airport located on the land and the dangers encountered by an aircraft when using its runways for take-off."

[1] The Court of Appeals for the Sixth Circuit affirmed on the ground that "the alleged tort in this case occurred on land before the aircraft reached Lake Erie. . . . " 448 F.2d 151, 154 (1971). Hence, that court found it "not necessary to consider the question of maritime relationship or nexus discussed by this court in [*Chapman*]." *Ibid.* We granted certiorari to consider a seemingly important question affecting the jurisdiction of the federal courts. 405 U.S. 915, 92 S.Ct. 941, 30 L.Ed.2d 784 (1972).

I

Determination of the question whether a tort is "maritime" and thus within the admiralty jurisdiction of the federal courts has traditionally depended upon the locality of the wrong. If the wrong occurred on navigable waters, the action is within admiralty jurisdiction; if the wrong occurred on land, it is not. As early as 1813, Mr. Justice Story, on Circuit, stated this general principle:

> "In regard to torts I have always understood, that the jurisdiction of the admiralty is exclusively dependent upon the locality of the act. The admiralty has not, and never (I believe) deliberately claimed to have any jurisdiction over torts, except such as are maritime torts, that is, such as are

> committed on the high seas, or on waters within the ebb and flow of the tide." Thomas v. Lane, 23 Fed.Cas. pp. 957, 960, No. 13,902 (C.C.Me).

See also DeLovio v. Boit, 7 Fed.Cas. pp. 418, 444, No. 3,776 (C.C. Mass. 1815); Philadelphia, W. & B. R. Co. v. Philadelphia & Havre de Grace Steam Towboat Co., 23 How. 209, 215, 16 L.Ed. 433 (1860). Later, this locality test was expanded to include not only tidewaters, but all navigable waters, including lakes and rivers. The Genesee Chief v. Fitzhugh, 12 How. 443, 13 L.Ed. 1058 (1852).

In The Plymouth, 3 Wall. 20, 35, 36, 18 L.Ed. 125 (1866), the Court essayed a definition of when a tort is "located" on navigable waters:

> "[T]he wrong and injury complained of must have been committed wholly upon the high seas or navigable waters, or, at least, the substance and consummation of the same must have taken place upon these waters to be within the admiralty jurisdiction. . . .
>
> * * * * *
>
> ". . . The jurisdiction of the admiralty over maritime torts does not depend upon the wrong having been committed on board the vessel, but upon its having been committed on the high seas or other navigable waters.
>
> ". . . Every species of tort, however occurring, and whether on board a vessel or not, if upon the high seas or navigable waters, is of admiralty cognizance."

The Court has often reiterated this rule of locality.[4] As recently as last Term, in Victory Carries, Inc. v. Law, 404 U.S. 202, 205, 92 S.Ct. 418, 421, 30 L.Ed.2d 383, we repeated that "[t]he historic view of this Court has been that the maritime tort jurisdiction of the federal courts is determined by the locality of the accident and that maritime law governs only those torts occurring on the navigable waters of the United States."

This locality test, of course, was established and grew up in an era when it was difficult to conceive of a tortious occurrence on navigable waters other than in connection with a waterborne vessel. Indeed, for the traditional types of maritime torts, the traditional test has worked quite satisfactorily. As a leading admiralty text has put the matter:

> "It should be stressed that the important cases in admiralty are *not* the borderline cases on jurisdiction; these may exercise a perverse fascination in the occasion they afford for elaborate casuistry, but the main business of the [admiralty] court involves claims for cargo damage, collision, seamen's injuries and the like—all well and comfortably within the circle, and far from the penumbra." G. Gilmore & C. Black, The Law of Admiralty 24 n. 88 (1957).

4. In Victory Carriers, Inc. v. Law, 404 U.S. 202, 205 n. 2, 92 S.Ct. 418, 421, 30 L.Ed.2d 383 (1971), we cited over 40 cases to this effect.

But it is the perverse and casuistic borderline situations that have demonstrated some of the problems with the locality test of maritime tort jurisdiction. In Smith & Son v. Taylor, 276 U.S. 179, 48 S.Ct. 228, 72 L.Ed. 520 (1928), for instance, a longshoreman unloading a vessel was standing on the pier when he was struck by a cargo-laden sling from the ship and knocked into the water where he was later found dead. This Court held that there was no admiralty jurisdiction in that case, despite the fact that the longshoreman was knocked into the water, because the blow by the sling was what gave rise to the cause of action, and it took effect on the land. Hence, the Court concluded, "[t]he substance and consummation of the occurrence which gave rise to the cause of action took place on land." 276 U.S., at 182, 48 S.Ct., at 229. In the converse factual setting, however, where a longshoreman working on the deck of a vessel was struck by a hoist and knocked onto the pier, the Court upheld admiralty jurisdiction because the cause of action arose on the vessel. Minnie v. Port Huron Terminal Co., 295 U.S. 647, 55 S.Ct. 884, 79 L.Ed. 1631 (1935). See also The Admiral Peoples, 295 U.S. 649, 55 S.Ct. 885, 79 L.Ed. 1633 (1935).

Other serious difficulties with the locality test are illustrated by cases where the maritime locality of the tort is clear, but where the invocation of admiralty jurisdiction seems almost absurd. If a swimmer at a public beach is injured by another swimmer or by a submerged object on the bottom, or if a piece of machinery sustains water damage from being dropped into a harbor by a land-based crane, a literal application of the locality test invokes not only the jurisdiction of the federal courts, but the full panoply of the substantive admiralty law as well. In cases such as these, some courts have adhered to a mechanical application of the strict locality rule and have sustained admiralty jurisdiction despite the lack of any connection between the wrong and traditional forms of maritime commerce and navigation.[5] Other courts, however, have held in such situations that a maritime locality is not sufficient to bring the tort within federal admiralty jurisdiction, but that there must also be a maritime nexus—some relationship between the tort and traditional maritime activities, involving navigation or commerce on navigable waters. The Court of Appeals for the Sixth Circuit, for instance, in the *Chapman* case, where a swimmer at a public beach was injured, held that

> "[a]bsent such a relationship, admiralty jurisdiction would depend entirely upon the fact that a tort occurred on navigable waters; a fact which in and of itself, in light of the historical justification for federal admiralty

5. Davis v. City of Jacksonville Beach, Florida, 251 F.Supp. 327 (MD Fla. 1965) (injury to a swimmer by a surfboard); King v. Testerman, 214 F.Supp. 335, 336 (ED Tenn. 1963) (injuries to a water skier). See also Horton v. J. & J. Aircraft, Inc., 257 F.Supp. 120, 121 (SD Fla. 1966). Cf. Weinstein v. Eastern Airlines, Inc., 316 F.2d 758 (CA3 1963).

jurisdiction, are quite immaterial to any meaningful invocation of the jurisdiction of admiralty courts." 385 F.2d, at 966.[6]

As early as 1850, admiralty scholars began to suggest that a traditional maritime activity, as well as a maritime locality, is necessary to invoke admiralty jurisdiction over torts. In that year, Judge Benedict expressed his "celebrated doubt"[7] as to whether such jurisdiction did not depend, in addition to a maritime locality, upon some "relation of the parties to a ship or vessel, embracing only those tortious violation[s] of maritime right and duty which occur in vessels to which the Admiralty jurisdiction, in cases of contracts, applies." E. Benedict, The American Admiralty 173 (1850). More recently, commentators have actively criticized the rule of locality as the sole criterion for admiralty jurisdiction, and have recommended adoption of a maritime relationship requirement as well. See 7A J. Moore, Federal Practice, Admiralty ¶¶ .325 [3] and .325 [5] (2d ed. 1972); Black, Admiralty Jurisdiction: Critique and Suggestions, 50 Col.L.Rev. 259, 264 (1950). In 1969, the American Law Institute's Study of the Division of Jurisdiction Between State and Federal Courts (ALI Study) also made that recommendation, stating (at 233):

> "It is hard to think of any reason why access to federal court should be allowed without regard to amount in controversy or citizenship of the parties merely because of the fortuity that a tort occurred on navigable waters, rather than on other waters or on land. The federal courts should not be burdened with every case of an injured swimmer."

Despite the board language of cases like the Plymouth, 3 Wall. 20, 18 L.Ed. 125 (1866), the fact is that this Court has never explicitly held that a

6. In another injured-swimmer case, McGuire v. City of New York, 192 F.Supp. 866, 871-872 (SDNY 1961), the court stated:

"The proper scope of jurisdiction should include all matters relating to the business of the sea and the business conducted on navigable waters.

"The libel in this case does not relate to any tort which grows out of navigation. It alleges an ordinary tort, no different in substance because the injury occurred in shallow waters along the shore than if the injury had occurred on the sandy beach above the water line. Whether the City of New York should be held liable for the injury suffered by libellant is a question which can easily be determined in the courts of the locality. To endeavor to project such an action into the federal courts on the ground of admiralty jurisdiction is to misinterpret the nature of admiralty jurisdiction."

Other cases holding that admiralty jurisdiction was not properly invoked because the tort, while having a maritime locality, lacked a significant relationship to maritime navigation and commerce, include: Peytavin v. Government Employees Insurance Co., 453 F.2d 1121 (CA5 1972); Gowdy v. United States, 412 F.2d 525, 527-529 (CA6 1969); Smith v. Guerrant, 290 F.Supp. 111, 113-114 (SD Tex. 1968). See also J.W. Petersen Coal & Oil Co. v. United States, 323 F.Supp. 1198, 1201 (ND Ill. 1970); O'Connor & Co. v. City of Pascagoula, Miss., 304 F.Supp. 681, 683 (SD Miss. 1969); Hastings v. Mann, 226 F.Supp. 962, 964-965 (EDNC 1964), aff'd, 340 F.2d 910 (CA4 1965). A similar view is taken by the English courts. Queen v. Judge of the City of London Court. [1892]. 1 Q.B. 273.

7. Hough, Admiralty Jurisdiction—Of Late Years, 37 Harv.L.Rev. 529, 531 (1924).

maritime locality is the sole test of admiralty tort jurisdiction. The last time the Court considered the matter, the question was left open. Atlantic Transport Co. of West Virginia v. Imbrovek, 234 U.S. 52, 34, S.Ct. 733, 58 L.Ed. 1208 (1914). In that case, a stevedore brought suit for injuries sustained on board a vessel while loading and stowing copper. The petitioner admitted the maritime locality of the tort, but contended that no maritime relationship was present. The Court sustained federal admiralty jurisdiction, but found that it was not necessary to decide whether locality alone is sufficient:

> "Even if it be assumed that the requirement as to locality in tort cases, while indispensable, is not necessarily exclusive, still in the present case the wrong which was the subject of the suit was, we think, of a maritime nature and hence the District Court, from any point of view, had jurisdiction. . . .
>
> ". . . If more is required than the locality of the wrong in order to give the court jurisdiction, the relation of the wrong to maritime service, to navigation and to commerce on navigable waters, was quite sufficient." *Id.,* at 61, 62, 34 S.Ct., at 735.

Since the time of that decision the Court has not squarely dealt with the question left open there, although opinions in several cases have discussed the maritime or non-maritime nature of the tort and its relationship to maritime navigation. In Rodrigue v. Aetna Casualty & Surety Co., 395 U.S. 352, 89 S.Ct. 1835, 23 L.Ed.2d 360 (1969), for instance, we held that admiralty had no jurisdiction of wrongful-death actions under the Death on the High Seas Act, 41 Stat. 537, 46 U.S.C. § 761 et seq., arising out of accidents on artificial island drilling rigs in the Gulf of Mexico more than a marine league offshore. We relied in that case on the fact that the accidents bore no relation to any navigational function:

> "The accidents in question here involved no collision with a vessel, and the structures were not navigational aids. They were islands, albeit artificial ones, . . . and the accidents had no more connection with the ordinary stuff of admiralty than do accidents on piers." *Id.,* at 360, 89 S.Ct., at 1839.

See also The Raithmoor, 241 U.S. 166, 176-177, 36 S.Ct. 514, 516-517, 60 L.Ed. 937 (1916); Chelentis v. Luckenbach S.S. Co., 247 U.S. 372, 382, 38 S.Ct. 501, 503, 62 L.Ed. 1171 (1918); Great Lakes Dredge & Dock Co. v. Kierejewski, 261 U.S. 479, 481, 43 S.Ct. 418, 67 L.Ed. 756 (1923); Robins Dry Dock & Repair Co. v. Dahl, 266 U.S. 449, 457, 45 S.Ct. 157, 158, 69 L.Ed. 372 (1925); London Guarantee & Accident Co. v. Industrial Accident Comm'n, 279 U.S. 109, 123, 49 S.Ct. 296, 299, 73 L.Ed. 632 (1929).

Apart from the difficulties involved in trying to apply the locality rule as the sole test of admiralty tort jurisdiction, another indictment of that test is to be found in the number of times the federal courts and the Congress, in the interests of justice, have had to create exceptions to it in the converse situation—*i.e.,* when the tort has no maritime locality, but does bear a relationship to maritime service, commerce, or navigation. See 7A J. Moore, Federal Practice,

Admiralty ¶ .325 [4] (2d ed. 1972). For example, in O'Donnell v. Great Lakes Dredge & Dock Co., 318 U.S. 36, 63 S.Ct. 488, 87 L.Ed. 596 (1943), the Court sustained the application of the Jones Act, 41 Stat. 1007, 46 U.S.C. § 688, to injuries to a seaman on land, because of the seaman's connection with maritime commerce. We relied in that case on an analogy to maintenance and cure:

> "[T]he maritime law, as recognized in the federal courts, has not in general allowed recovery for personal injuries occurring on land. But there is an important exception to this generalization in the case of maintenance and cure. From its dawn, the maritime law has recognized the seaman's right to maintenance and cure for injuries suffered in the course of his service to his vessel, whether occurring on sea or on land." *Id.,* at 41-42, 63 S.Ct., at 491.

Similarly, the doctrine of unseaworthiness has been extended to permit a seaman or a longshoreman to recover from a ship owner for injuries sustained wholly on land, so long as those injuries were caused by defects in the ship or its gear. Gutierrez v. Waterman S.S. Corp., 373 U.S. 206, 214-215, 83 S.Ct. 1185, 1190-1191, 10 L.Ed.2d 297 (1963). See also Strika v. Netherlands Ministry of Traffic, 185 F.2d 555 (CA2 1950).

Congress, too, has extended admiralty jurisdiction predicated on the relation of the wrong to maritime activities, regardless of the locality of the tort. In the Extension of Admiralty Jurisdiction Act, 62 Stat. 496, 46 U.S.C. § 740, enacted in 1948, Congress provided:

> "The admiralty and maritime jurisdiction of the United States shall extend to and include all cases of damage or injury, to person or property, caused by a vessel on navigable water, notwithstanding that such damage or injury be done or consummated on land."

This Act was passed specifically to overrule cases, such as *The Plymouth, supra,* holding that admiralty does not provide a remedy for damage done to land structures by ships on navigable waters. Victory Carriers, Inc. v. Law, 404 U.S., at 209 n. 8, 92 S.Ct., at 423; Gutierrez v. Waterman S.S. Corp., 373 U.S., at 209-210, 83 S.Ct., at 1187-1188.[8]

In sum, there has existed over the years a judicial, legislative, and scholarly recognition that, in determining whether there is admiralty jurisdiction over a particular tort or class of torts, reliance on the relationship of the wrong to traditional maritime activity is often more sensible and more consonant with the

8. The Court has held, however, that there is no admiralty jurisdiction under the Extension of Admiralty Jurisdiction Act over suits brought by longshoremen injured while working on a pier, when such injuries were caused, not by ships, but by pier-based equipment. Victory Carriers, Inc. v. Law, *supra*; Nacirema Operating Co. v. Johnson, 396 U.S. 212, 223, 90 S.Ct. 347, 353, 24 L.Ed.2d 371 (1969). The Longshoremen's and Harbor Workers' Compensation Act, 33 U.S.C. § 901 et seq., was amended in 1972 to cover employees working on those areas of the shore customarily used in loading, unloading, repairing, or building a vessel. Pub. L.No. 92-576, § 2, 86 Stat. 1251.

purposes of maritime law than is a purely mechanical application of the locality test.

II

[2] One area in which locality as the exclusive test of admiralty tort jurisdiction has given rise to serious problems in application is that of aviation. For the reasons discussed above and those to be discussed, we have concluded that maritime locality alone is not a sufficient predicate for admiralty jurisdiction in aviation tort cases.

In one of the earliest aircraft cases brought in admiralty, The Crawford Bros., No. 2, 215 F. 269, 271 (WD Wash. 1914), in which a libel *in rem* for repairs was brought against an airplane that had crashed into Puget Sound, the federal court declined to assume jurisdiction, reasoning that an airplane could not be characterized as a maritime vessel. *The Crawford Bros.* was followed by a number of cases dealing with seaplanes, in which the courts restricted admiralty jurisdiction to occurrences involving planes that were afloat on navigable waters.[9] Continuing doubt as to the applicability of admiralty law to aircraft was illustrated by cases in the 1930s and 1940s holding that aircraft owners could not invoke the benefits of the maritime doctrine of limitation of liability,[10] and that crimes committed on board aircraft flying over international waters were not punishable under criminal statutes proscribing acts committed on the high seas.[11] Moreover, Congress exempted all aircraft from conformity with United States navigation and shipping laws.[12]

[3] The first major extension of admiralty jurisdiction to land-based aircraft came in wrongful-death actions arising out of aircraft crashes at sea and brought under the Death on the High Seas Act, 46 U.S.C. § 761 et seq. The federal courts took jurisdiction of such cases because the literal provisions of that statute appeared to be clearly applicable. The Death on the High Seas Act, enacted in 1920, provides:

> "Whenever the death of a person shall be caused by wrongful act, neglect, or default occurring on the high seas beyond a marine league from

9. Matter of Reinhardt v. Newport Flying Service Corp., 232 N.Y. 115, 117-118, 133 N.E. 371, 372 (1921); United States v. Northwest Air Service, Inc., 80 F.2d 804, 805 (CA9 1935). See also Lambros Seaplane Base v. The Batory, 215 F.2d 228, 231 (CA2 1954).

10. Dollins v. Pan-American Grace Airways, Inc., 27 F.Supp. 487, 488-489 (SDNY 1939); Noakes v. Imperial Airways, Ltd., 29 F.Supp. 412, 413 (SDNY 1939).

11. United States v. Peoples, 50 F.Supp. 462 (ND Cal. 1943); United States v. Cordova, 89 F.Supp. 298 (EDNY 1950).

In 1952, however, Congress amended the criminal jurisdiction of admiralty to include crimes committed aboard aircraft while in flight over the high seas or any other waters within the admiralty jurisdiction of the United States except waters within the territorial jurisdiction of any State. 18 U.S.C. § 7(5).

12. The Federal Aviation Act of 1958, 72 Stat. 799, as amended, 49 U.S.C. § 1509(a), the successor to the Air Commerce Act of 1926, 44 Stat. 572, formerly 49 U.S.C. § 177 (1952 ed.).

the shore of any State, or the District of Columbia, or the Territories or dependencies of the United States, the personal representative of the decedent may maintain a suit for damages in the district courts of the United States, in admiralty. . . . "

The first aviation case brought pursuant to the Death on the High Seas Act was apparently Choy v. Pan American Airways Co., 1941 A.M.C. 483 (SDNY), where death was caused by the crash of a seaplane into the Pacific Ocean during a transoceanic flight. The District Court upheld admiralty jurisdiction on the ground that the language of the Act was broad and made no reference to surface vessels. According to the court:

> "The statute certainly includes the phrase 'on the high seas' but there is no reason why this should make the law operable only on a horizontal plane. The very next phrase 'beyond a marine league from the shore of any State' may be said to include a vertical sense and another dimension." *Id.,* at 484.

Since *Choy,* many actions for wrongful death arising out of aircraft crashes into the high seas beyond one marine league from shore have been brought under the Death on the High Seas Act, and federal jurisdiction has consistently been sustained in those cases.[13] Indeed, it may be considered as settled today that this specific federal statute gives the federal admiralty courts jurisdiction of such wrongful-death actions.

[4] In recent years, however, some federal courts have been persuaded in aviation cases to extend their admiralty jurisdiction beyond the statutory coverage of the Death on the High Seas Act. Several cases have held that actions for *personal injuries* arising out of aircraft crashes into the high seas more than one league off shore or arising out of aircraft accidents in the airspace over the high seas were cognizable in admiralty because of their maritime locality, although they were not within the scope of the Death on the High Seas Act or any other federal legislation.[14] These cases, as well as most of those brought under the Death on the High Seas Act, involved torts both with a maritime locality, in that

13. See, e.g., Wyman v. Pan American Airways, Inc., 181 Misc. 963, 966, 43 N.Y.S. 2d 420, 423, aff'd, 267 App.Div. 947, 48 N.Y.S.2d 459, aff'd, 293 N.Y. 878, 59 N.E.2d 785 (1944); Higa v. Transocean Airlines, 230 F.2d 780 (CA9 1955); Noel v. Linea Aeropostal Venezolana, 247 F.2d 677, 680 (CA2 1957); Trihey v. Transocean Air Lines, 255 F.2d 824, 827 (CA9 1958); Lacey v. L.W. Wiggins Airways, Inc., 95 F.Supp. 916 (Mass. 1951); Wilson v. Transocean Airlines, 121 F.Supp. 85 (ND Cal. 1954); Stiles v. National Airlines, Inc., 161 F.Supp. 125 (ED La. 1958), aff'd, 268 F.2d 400 (CA5 1959); Noel v. Airponents, Inc., 169 F.Supp. 348 (NJ 1958); Lavello v. Danko, 175 F.Supp. 92 (SDNY 1959); Blumenthal v. United States, 189 F.Supp. 439, 445 (ED Pa. 1960), aff'd, 306 F.2d 16 (CA3 1962); Pardonnet v. Flying Tiger Line, Inc., 233 F.Supp. 683 (ND Ill. 1964); Kropp v. Douglas Aircraft Co., 329 F.Supp. 447, 453-455 (ED NY 1971). Cf. D'Aleman v. Pan American World Airways, 259 F.2d 493 (CA2 1958).

14. Bergeron v. Aero Associates, Inc., 213 F.Supp. 936 (ED La. 1963); Notarian v. Trans World Airlines, Inc., 244 F.Supp. 874 (WD Pa. 1965); Horton v. J. & J. Aircraft, Inc., 257 F.Supp. 120 (SD Fla. 1966).

the alleged negligence became operative while the aircraft was on or over navigable waters, and also with some relationship to maritime commerce, at least insofar as the aircraft was beyond state territorial waters and performing a function–transoceanic crossing–that previously would have been performed by waterborne vessels.[15]

But a further extension of admiralty jurisdiction was created when courts began to sustain that jurisdiction in situations such as the one now before us–when the claim arose out of an aircraft accident that occurred on or over navigable waters *within* state territorial limits, and when the aircraft was not on a transoceanic flight. Apparently, the first such case grew out of a 1960 crash of a commercial jet, bound from Boston to Philadelphia, that collided with a flock of birds over the airport runway and crashed into Boston Harbor within one minute after takeoff. Weinstein v. Eastern Airlines, Inc., 316 F.2d 758 (CA3 1963). In deciding that a wrongful-death action arising from this crash was within admiralty jurisdiction, the Court of Appeals for the Third Circuit applied the strict locality rule and found that the tort had a maritime locality. The court further justified the invocation of admiralty jurisdiction in that case by an analogy to the Death on the High Seas Act:

> "If, as it has been held, a tort claim arising out of the crash of an airplane beyond the one marine league line is within the jurisdiction of admiralty, then *a fortiori* a crash of an aircraft just short of that line but still within the navigable waters is within that jurisdiction as well." *Id.,* at 765.

There have been a few subsequent cases to like effect.[16] To the contrary, of course, is the decision of the Court of Appeals for the Sixth Circuit in the present case.

III

These latter cases graphically demonstrate the problems involved in applying a locality-alone test of admiralty tort jurisdiction to the crashes of aircraft. Airplanes, unlike waterborne vessels, are not limited by physical boundaries and can and do operate over both land and navigable bodies of water. As Professor Moore and his colleague Professor Pelaez have stated, "In both death and injury cases . . . it is evident that while distinctions based on locality often are in fact quite relevant where water vessels are concerned, they entirely lose their significance where aircraft, which are not geographically restrained, are concerned." 7A J. Moore, Federal Practice, Admiralty ¶ .330 [5], pp. 3772-3773 (2d ed.

15. Whether this type of relationship to maritime commerce is a sufficient maritime nexus to justify admiralty jurisdiction over airplane accidents is discussed *infra,* at 505-506. We do not decide that question in this case.

16. Hornsby v. Fish Meal Co., 431 F.2d 865 (CA5 1970); Harris v. United Air Lines, Inc., 275 F.Supp. 431, 432 (SD Iowa 1967). Cf. Scott v. Eastern Air Lines, Inc., 309 F.2d 14, 21-22 (CA3 1968) (en banc).

1972). In flights within the continental United States, which are principally over land, the fact that an aircraft happens to fall in navigable waters, rather than on land, is wholly fortuitous. The ALI Study, in criticizing the *Weinstein* decision, observed:

> "If a plane takes off from Boston's Logan Airport bound for Philadelphia, and crashes on takeoff, it makes little sense that the next of kin of the passengers killed should be left to their usual remedies, ordinarily in state court, if the plane crashes on land, but that they have access to a federal court, and the distinctive substantive law of admiralty applies, if the wrecked plane ends up in the waters of Boston Harbor." ALI Study 231.[17]

Moreover, not only is the locality test in such cases wholly adventitious, but it is sometimes almost impossible to apply with any degree of certainty. Under the locality test, the tort "occurs" where the alleged negligence took effect, *The Plymouth, supra*; Smith & Son v. Taylor, 276 U.S. 179, 48 S.Ct. 228, 72 L.Ed. 520 (1928); and in the case of aircraft that locus is often most difficult to determine.

The case before us provides a good example of these difficulties. The petitioners contend that since their aircraft crashed into the navigable waters of Lake Erie and was totally destroyed when it sank in those waters, the locality of the tort, or the place where the alleged negligence took effect, was there. The fact that the major damage to their plane would not have occurred if it had not landed in the lake indicates, they say, that the substance and consummation of the wrong took place in navigable waters. The respondents, on the other hand, argue that the alleged negligence took effect when the plane collided with the birds—over land. Relying on cases such as Smith & Son v. Taylor, *supra,* where admiralty jurisdiction was denied in the case of a longshoreman struck by a ship's sling while standing on a pier, and knocked into the water, the respondents contend that a tort "occurs" at the point of first impact of the alleged negligence. Here, they say, the cause of action arose as soon as the plane struck the birds; from then on, the plane was destined to fall, and whether it came down on land or water should not affect "the locality of the act." See Thomas v. Lane, 23 Fed.Cas., at 960.

In the view we take of the question before us, we need not decide who has the better of this dispute. It is enough to note that either position gives rise to the problems inherent in applying the strict locality test of admiralty tort jurisdiction in aviation accident cases. The petitioners' argument, if accepted, would make jurisdiction depend on where the plane ended up—a circumstance that could be wholly fortuitous and completely unrelated to the tort itself. The anomaly is well illustrated by the hypothetical case of two aircraft colliding at a

17. See also Comment, Admiralty Jurisdiction: Airplanes and Wrongful Death in Territorial Waters, 64 Col.L.Rev. 1084, 1091-1092 (1964).

high altitude, with one crashing on land and the other in a navigable river. If, on the other hand, the respondents' position were adopted, jurisdiction would depend on whether the plane happened to be flying over land or water when the original impact of the alleged negligence occurred. This circumstance, too, could be totally fortuitous. If the plane in the present case struck the birds over Cleveland's Lakefront Airport, admiralty jurisdiction would not lie; but if the plane had just crossed the shoreline when it struck the birds, admiralty jurisdiction would attach, even if the plane were then able to make it back to the airport and crashland there. These are hardly the types of distinctions with which admiralty law was designed to deal.

[5] All these and other difficulties that can arise in attempting to apply the locality test of admiralty jurisdiction to aeronautical torts are, of course, attributable to the inherent nature of aircraft. Unlike waterborne vessels, they are not restrained by one-dimensional geographic and physical boundaries. For this elementary reason, we conclude that the mere fact that the alleged wrong "occurs" or "is located" on or over navigable waters—whatever that means in an aviation context—is not of itself sufficient to turn an airplane negligence case into a "maritime tort." It is far more consistent with the history and purpose of admiralty to require also that the wrong bear a significant relationship to traditional maritime activity. We hold that unless such a relationship exists, claims arising from airplane accidents are not cognizable in admiralty in the absence of legislation to the contrary.

IV

[6] This conclusion, however, does not end our inquiry, for there remains the question of what constitutes, in the context of aviation, a significant relationship to traditional maritime activity. The petitioners argue that any aircraft falling into navigable waters has a sufficient relationship to maritime activity to satisfy the test. The relevant analogy, they say, is not between flying aircraft and sailing ships, but between a downed plane and a sinking ship. Quoting from the *Weinstein* opinion, they contend: "When an aircraft crashes into navigable waters, the dangers to persons and property are much the same as those arising out of the sinking of a ship or a collision between two vessels." 316 F.2d, at 763. The dissenting opinion in the Court of Appeals in the present case made the same argument:

> "I believe that there are many comparisons between the problems of aircraft over navigable waters and those of the ships which the aircraft are rapidly replacing. . . .
>
> ". . . Problems posed for aircraft landing on, crashing on, or sinking into navigable waters differ markedly from landings upon land. . . . In such instances, wind and wave and water, the normal problems of the mariner, become the approach or survival problems of the pilot and his passengers. . . . What I would hold is that tort cases arising out of aircraft crashes into navigable waters are cognizable in admiralty jurisdiction even if the negligent conduct is alleged to have happened wholly on land." 448 F.2d at 163.

We cannot accept that definition of traditional maritime activity. It is true that in a literal sense there may be some similarities between the problems posed for a plane downed on water and those faced by a sinking ship. But the differences between the two modes of transportation are far greater, in terms of their basic qualities and traditions and consequently in terms of the conceptual expertise of the law to be applied.[18] The law of admiralty has evolved over many centuries, designed and molded to handle problems of vessels relegated to ply the waterways of the world, beyond whose shores they cannot go. That law deals with navigational rules—rules that govern the manner and direction those vessels may rightly move upon the waters. When a collision occurs or a ship founders at sea, the law of admiralty looks to those rules to determine fault, liability, and all other questions that may arise from such a catastrophe. Through long experience, the law of the sea knows how to determine whether a particular ship is seaworthy, and it knows the nature of maintenance and cure. It is concerned with maritime liens, the general average, captures and prizes, limitation of liability, cargo damage, and claims for salvage.

Rules and concepts such as these are wholly alien to air commerce, whose vehicles operate in a totally different element, unhindered by geographical boundaries and exempt from the navigational rules of the maritime road. The matters with which admiralty is basically concerned have no conceivable bearing on the operation of aircraft, whether over land or water. Indeed, in contexts other than tort, Congress and the courts have recognized that, because of these differences, aircraft are not subject to maritime law.[19] Although dangers of wind and wave faced by a plane that has crashed on navigable waters may be superficially similar to those encountered by a sinking ship, the plane's unexpected descent will almost invariably have been attributable to a cause unrelated to the sea—be it pilot error, defective design or manufacture of airframe or engine, error of a traffic controller at an airport, or some other cause; and the determination of liability will thus be based on factual and conceptual inquiries unfamiliar to the law of admiralty. It is clear, therefore, that neither the fact that a plane goes down on navigable waters nor the fact that the negligence "occurs" while a plane is flying over such waters is enough to create such a relationship to traditional maritime activity as to justify the invocation of admiralty jurisdiction.

We need not decide today whether an aviation tort can ever, under any circumstances bear a sufficient relationship to traditional maritime activity to come within admiralty jurisdiction in the absence of legislation.[20] It could be

18. Moreover, if the mere happenstance that an aircraft falls into navigable waters creates a maritime relationship because of the maritime dangers to a sinking plane, then the maritime relationship test would be the same as the petitioners' view of the maritime-locality test, with the same inherent fortuity.

19. See *supra*, at 501.

20. Of course, under the Death on the High Seas Act, a wrongful-death action arising out of an airplane crash on the high seas beyond a marine league from the shore of a State may clearly be brought in a federal admiralty court.

argued, for instance, that if a plane flying from New York to London crashed in the mid-Atlantic, there would be admiralty jurisdiction over resulting tort claims even absent a specific statute.[21] An aircraft in that situation might be thought to bear a significant relationship to traditional maritime activity because it would be performing a function traditionally performed by waterborne vessels.[22] Moreover, other factors might come into play in the area of international air commerce—choice-of-forum problems, choice of law problems,[23] international-law problems, problems involving multi-nation conventions and treaties, and so on.

[7] But none of these considerations is of concern in the case before us. The flight of the petitioners' land-based aircraft was to be from Cleveland to Portland, Maine, and thence to White Plains, New York—a flight that would have been almost entirely over land and within the continental United States. After it struck the flock of seagulls over the runway, the plane descended and settled in Lake Erie within the territorial waters of Ohio. We can find no significant relationship between such an event befalling a land-based plane flying from one point in the continental United States to another, and traditional maritime activity involving navigation and commerce on navigable waters.

[8] Just last Term, in Victory Carriers, Inc. v. Law, 404 U.S., at 212, 92 S.Ct., at 425, we observed that in determining whether to expand admiralty jurisdiction "we should proceed with caution. . . ." Quoting from Healy v. Ratta, 292 U.S. 263, 270, 54 S.Ct. 700, 703, 78 L.Ed. 1248 (1934), we stated:

> " 'The power reserved to the states, under the Constitution, to provide for the determination of controversies in their courts may be restricted only by the action of Congress in conformity to the judiciary sections of the Constitution. . . . Due regard for the rightful independence

21. But see 7A J. Moore, Federal Practice, Admiralty ¶ .330 [5], p. 3772 (2d ed. 1972):
"What possible rational basis is there, for instance, in holding that the personal representative of a passenger killed in the crash of an airplane traveling from Shannon, Ireland to Logan Field in Boston has a cause of action within the admiralty jurisdiction if the plane goes down three miles from shore; may have a cause of action within the admiralty jurisdiction if the plane goes down within an area circumscribed by the shore and the three-mile limit; and will not have a cause of action within the admiralty jurisdiction if the plane managed to remain airborne until reaching the Massachusetts coast? And this notwithstanding that in all instances the plane may have developed engine trouble or been the victim of pilot error at an identical site far out over the Atlantic."

22. Apart from transoceanic flights, the Government's brief suggests that another example where admiralty jurisdiction might properly be invoked in an airplane accident case on the ground that the plane was performing a function traditionally performed by waterborne vessels, is shown in Hornsby v. Fish Meal Co., 431 F.2d 865 (CA5 1970), which involved the mid-air collision of two light aircraft used in spotting schools of fish and the crash of those aircraft into the Gulf of Mexico within one marine league of the Louisiana shore.

23. In such a situation, it has been stated:
"Were the maritime law not applicable, it is argued that the recovery would depend upon a confusing consideration of what substantive law to apply, *i.e.,* the law of the forum, the law of the place where each decedent [or injured party] purchased his ticket, the law of the place where the plane took off, or, perhaps, the law of the point of destination." 7A J. Moore, Federal Practice, Admiralty ¶ .330 [5], p. 3774 (2d ed. 1972).

> of state governments, which should actuate federal courts, requires that they scrupulously confine their own jurisdiction to the precise limits which [a federal] statute has defined.' "

In the situation before us, which is only fortuitously and incidentally connected to navigable waters and which bears no relationship to traditional maritime activity, the Ohio courts could plainly exercise jurisdiction over the suit,[24] and could plainly apply familiar concepts of Ohio tort law without any effect on maritime endeavors.[25]

[9] It may be, as the petitioners argue, that aviation tort cases should be governed by uniform substantive and procedural laws and that such actions should be heard in the federal courts so as to avoid divergent results and duplicitous litigation in multi-party cases. But for this Court to uphold federal admiralty jurisdiction in a few wholly fortuitous aircraft cases would be a most quixotic way of approaching that goal. If federal uniformity is the desired goal with respect to claims arising from aviation accidents, Congress is free under the Commerce Clause to enact legislation applicable to all such accidents, whether occurring on land or water, and adapted to the specific characteristics of air commerce.

[10] For the reasons stated in this opinion we hold that, in the absence of legislation to the contrary, there is no federal admiralty jurisdiction over aviation tort claims arising from flights by land-based aircraft between points within the continental United States.[26]

The judgment is affirmed.

Affirmed.

24. There is no diversity of citizenship between petitioners and the City of Cleveland.

25. The United States, respondent Dicken's employer, can be sued, of course, only in federal district court under the Federal Tort Claims Act, 28 U.S.C. §§ 1346(b) and 2674. Such an action has been filed by the petitioners here, but even in that suit the federal court will apply the substantive tort law of Ohio. Thus, Ohio law will not be ousted in this case, and the pendency of the action under the Tort Claims Act has no relevance in determining whether the instant case should be heard in admiralty, with its federal substantive law.

The possibility that the petitioners would have to litigate the same claim in two forums is the same possibility that would exist if their plane had stopped on the shore of the lake, instead of going into the water, and is the same possibility that exists every time a plane goes down on land, negligence of the federal air traffic controller is alleged, and there is no diversity of citizenship. This problem cannot be solved merely by upholding admiralty jurisdiction in cases where the plane happens to fall on navigable waters.

26. Some such flights, *e.g.,* New York City to Miami, Florida, no doubt involve passage over "the high seas beyond a marine league from the shore of any State." To the extent that the terms of the Death on the High Seas Act become applicable to such flights, that Act, of course, is "legislation to the contrary."

United States and the Federal Tort Claims Act

The cases in Section II discussed application of the Federal Tort Claims Act (1946) to airports and the liability of airports to their neighbors.

Two cases reported in this section examine the application of the Federal Tort Claims Act on the liability of the United States Government in military activities, as in U.S. v. Reynolds; and application of the Act where there is a conflict between the different laws of two different states, as in the case of Richards v. U.S.

Before reading the cases in this section, read, and become familiar with, the provisions of extracts from Federal Tort Claims Act, Extract D.

---

345 U.S. 1
UNITED STATES v. REYNOLDS et al.
(Cite as 73 S. Ct. 528)
No. 21.
Argued Oct. 21, 1952.
Decided March 9, 1953.

Three separate actions under Federal Tort Claims Act by widows of civilians killed in crash of an Air Force plane. The United States District Court for the Eastern District of Pennsylvania, 10 F.R.D. 468, rendered judgments for plaintiffs, and the United States appealed. The Court of Appeals, 192 F.2d 987, affirmed, and the Supreme Court granted certiorari. The Supreme Court, Mr. Chief Justice Vinson, held that when formal claim of privilege of Air Force report of accident was filed by Secretary of Air Force, under circumstances indicating reasonable possibility that military secrets were involved, there was sufficient showing of privilege to cut off further demand for production.

Reversed and remanded.

Mr. Justice Black, Mr. Justice Frankfurter, and Mr. Justice Jackson, dissented.

1. Courts

Certiorari would be granted by Supreme Court as to suits brought under Federal Tort Claims Act for death of three civilians in crash of Air Force plane, when important question of Government's privilege to resist discovery was involved. 28 U.S.C.A. §§ 1346, 2674; Fed.Rules Civ.Proc. rule 34, 28 U.S.C.A.; 5 U.S.C.A. § 22.

2. Federal Civil Procedure

Federal Rule of Civil Procedure, relating to discovery and compelling production only of matters not privileged, uses the term "privileged" as that term is understood in the law of evidence, and includes the Government's privilege against revealing military secrets. Fed.Rules Civ.Proc. rules 1 et seq., 34, 37, 28 U.S.C.A.; 5 U.S.C.A. § 22.

3. Federal Civil Procedure

The Government has a privilege against revealing military secrets, and it cannot ordinarily be required to produce documents containing such secrets.

4. Federal Civil Procedure

The privilege against revealing military secrets belongs to the Government and must be asserted by it, and it can neither be claimed nor waived by a private party, but there must be formal claim of privilege, lodged by head of department having control over the matter, after actual personal consideration by that officer. Fed.Rules Civ.Proc. rules 1 et seq., 34, 37, 28 U.S.C.A.; 5 U.S.C.A. § 22.

5. Federal Civil Procedure

Where, on motion for production of document, Government asserts privilege against revealing military secrets, court must determine whether circumstances are appropriate for claim of privilege, without forcing disclosure of very thing the privilege is designed to protect, and consequently plea should be accepted if court is satisfied from all evidence and circumstances that there is reasonable danger that compulsion of the evidence will expose military matters which, in the interest of national security, should not be divulged. Fed.Rules Civ.Proc. rules 1 et seq., 34, 37, 28 U.S.C.A.; 5 U.S.C.A. § 22.

6. Evidence

In determining propriety of trial court's denial of Government's plea of privilege against production of Air Force reports of accident in which three civilians were killed, the Supreme Court would take judicial notice that time was one of vigorous preparation for national defense, that air power was potent weapon in scheme of defense, and that newly developed electronic devices, such as those being tested at time of accident, had greatly enhanced effective use of air power, and that such devices must be kept secret if their military advantages were to be properly exploited. Fed.Rules Civ.Proc. rules 1 et seq., 34, 37, 28 U.S.C.A.; 5 U.S.C.A. § 22.

7. Federal Civil Procedure

In view of fact that Rules of Civil Procedure are applicable to suits against United States under Tort Claims Act, and fact that under Federal Rules, production of only unprivileged documents is required, when formal claim of privilege was filed by Secretary of Air Force in actions by widows of civilians killed in crash of Air Force plane which had gone aloft to test secret electronic equipment, there was a sufficient showing of privilege to cut off further demand for production of documents. Fed.Rules Civ.Proc. rules 1 et seq., 34, 37, 28 U.S.C.A.; 5 U.S.C.A. § 22.

8. Federal Civil Procedure

Where plea of privilege against revealing military secrets is entered by Government in suit under Federal Tort Claims Act, showing of necessity for production of document will determine how far court should probe in satisfying itself that occasion for invoking privilege is appropriate, but even the most compelling necessity cannot overcome claim of privilege if court is ultimately satisfied that military secrets are at stake, and where necessity is dubious, a formal claim of privilege, made under circumstances indicating reasonable possibility that military secrets are involved, is entitled to prevail. Fed.Rules Civ.Proc. rules 1 et seq., 34, 37, 28 U.S.C.A.; 5 U.S.C.A. § 22.

9. Federal Civil Procedure

The principle applicable in criminal cases that Government, when prosecuting an accused, has duty to see that justice is done, and it cannot unconscionably invoke governmental privileges to deprive accused of anything material to his defense, has no application in civil forum where Government is not the moving party, but is a defendant only on terms to which it has consented. Fed.Rules Civ.Proc. rules 1 et seq., 34, 37, 28 U.S.C.A.; 5 U.S.C.A. § 22.

2

Mr. Samuel D. Slade, Washington, D.C., for petitioner.
Mr. Charles J. Biddle, Philadelphia, Pa., for respondents.

Mr. Chief Justice VINSON delivered the opinion of the Court.

[1] These suits under the Tort Claims Act[1] arise from the death of three civilians in the crash of a B-29 aircraft at

3

Waycross, Georgia, on October 6, 1948. Because an important question of the Government's privilege to resist discovery[2] is involved, we granted certiorari. 343 U.S. 918, 72 S.Ct. 678, 96 L.Ed. 1332.

The aircraft had taken flight for the purpose of testing secret electronic equipment, with four civilian observers aboard. While aloft, fire broke out in one of the bomber's engines. Six of the nine crew members, and three of the four civilian observers were killed in the crash.

The widows of the three deceased civilian observers brought consolidated suits against the United States. In the pretrial stages the plaintiffs moved, under Rule 34 of the Federal Rules of Civil Procedure,[3] for production of the Air

1. 28 U.S.C. §§ 1346, 2674, 28 U.S.C.A. §§ 1346, 2674.

2. Federal Rules of Civil Procedure, Rule 34, 28 U.S.C.A.

3. "Rule 34. *Discovery and Production of Documents and Things for Inspection, Copying, or Photographing.* Upon motion of any party showing good cause therefor and upon notice to all other parties, and subject to the provisions of Rule 30(b), the court in which an action is pending may (1) order any party to produce and permit the inspection and copying for photographing, by or on behalf of the moving party, of any designated documents, papers, books, accounts, letters, photographs, objects, or tangible things, not privileged, which constitute or contain evidence relating to any of the matters within the scope of the examination permitted by Rule 26(b) and which are in his possession, custody, or control; or (2) order any party to permit entry upon designated land or other property in his possession or control for the purpose of inspecting, measuring, surveying, or photographing the property or any designated object or operation thereon within the scope of the examination permitted by Rule 26(b). The order shall specify the time, place, and manner of making the inspection and taking the copies and photographs and may prescribe such terms and conditions as are just."

Force's official accident investigation report and the statements of the three surviving crew members, taken in connection with the official investigation. The Government moved to quash the motion, claiming that these matters were privileged against disclosure pursuant

4

to Air Force regulations promulgated under R.S. § 161.[4] The District Judge sustained plaintiffs' motion, holding that good cause for production had been shown.[5] The claim of privilege under R.S. § 161 was rejected on the premise that the Tort Claims Act, in making the Government liable "in the same manner" as a private individual[6] had waived any privilege based upon executive control over governmental documents.

Shortly after this decision, the District Court received a letter from the Secretary of the Air Force, stating that "it has been determined that it would not be in the public interest to furnish this report * * *." The court allowed a rehearing on its earlier order, and at the rehearing the Secretary of the Air Force filed a formal "Claim of Privilege." This document repeated the prior claim based generally on R.S. § 161, and then stated that the Government further objected to production of the documents "for the reason that the aircraft in question, together with the personnel on board, were engaged in a highly secret mission of the Air Force." An affidavit of the Judge Advocate General, United States Air Force, was also filed

5

with the court, which asserted that the demanded material could not be furnished "without seriously hampering national security, flying safety and the development of highly technical and secret military equipment." The same affidavit offered to produce the three surviving crew members, without cost, for examination by the plaintiffs. The witnesses would be allowed to refresh their memories from any statement made by them to the Air Force, and authorized to testify as to all matters except those of a "classified nature."

4. 5 U.S.C. § 22, 5 U.S.C.A. § 22:

"The head of each department is authorized to prescribe regulations, not inconsistent with law, for the government of his department, the conduct of its officers and clerks, the distribution and performance of its business, and the custody, use, and preservation of the records, papers, and property appertaining to it."

Air Force Regulation No. 62–7(5) (b) provides:

"Reports of boards of officers, special accident reports, or extracts therefrom will not be furnished or made available to persons outside the authorized chain of command without the specific approval of the Secretary of the Air Force."

5. 10 F.R.D. 468.

6. 28 U.S.C. § 2674, 28 U.S.C.A. § 2674:

"The United States shall be liable, respecting the provisions of this title relating to tort claims, in the same manner and to the same extent as a private individual under like circumstances, but shall not be liable for interest prior to judgment or for punitive damages."

The District Court ordered the Government to produce the documents in order that the court might determine whether they contained privileged matter. The Government declined, so the court entered an order, under Rule 37(b)(2)(i),[7] that the facts on the issue of negligence would be taken as established in plaintiffs' favor. After a hearing to determine damages, final judgment was entered for the plaintiffs. The Court of Appeals affirmed,[8] both as to the showing of good cause for production of the documents, and as to the ultimate disposition of the case as a consequence of the Government's refusal to produce the documents.

6

We have had broad propositions pressed upon us for decision. On behalf of the Government it has been urged that the executive department heads have power to withhold any documents in their custody from judicial view if they deem it to be in the public interest.[9] Respondents have asserted that the executive's power to withhold documents was waived by the Tort Claims Act. Both positions have constitutional overtones which we find it unnecessary to pass upon, there being a narrower ground for decision. Touhy v. Ragen, 1951, 340 U.S. 462, 71 S.Ct. 416, 95 L.Ed. 417; Rescue Army v. Municipal Court of Los Angeles, 1947, 331 U.S. 549, 574-585, 67 S.Ct. 1409, 1422-1427, 91 L.Ed. 1666.

[2,3] The Tort Claims Act expressly makes the Federal Rules of Civil Procedure applicable to suits against the United States.[10] The judgment in this case imposed liability upon the Government by operation of Rule 37, for refusal to produce documents under Rule 34. Since Rule 34 compels production only of matters "not privileged," the essential question is whether there was a valid claim of privilege under the Rule. We hold that there was, and that, therefore, the judgment below subjected the United States to liability on terms to which Congress did not consent by the Tort Claims Act.

7. "Rule 37. *Refusal to Make Discovery: Consequences*

* * * * *

"(b) Failure to Comply With Order.

* * * * *

"(2) *Other Consequences.* If any party or an officer or managing agent of a party refuses to obey . . . an order made under Rule 34 to produce any document . . ., the court may make such orders in regard to the refusal as are just, and among others the following:

"(i) An order that the matters regarding which the questions were asked, or the character or description of the thing or land, or the contents of the paper, or the physical or mental condition of the party, or any other designated facts shall be taken to be established for the purposes of the action in accordance with the claim of the party obtaining the order;. . . ."

8. 192 F.2d 987.

9. While claim of executive power to suppress documents is based mor immediately upon R.S. § 161 (see supra, note 4), the roots go much deeper. It is said that R.S. § 161 is only a legislative recognition of an inherent executive power which is protected in the constitutional system of separation of power.

10. 28 U.S.C. (1946 ed.) § 932; United States v. Yellow Cab Co., 1951, 340 U.S. 543, 553, 71 S.Ct. 399, 406, 95 L.Ed. 523.

We think it should be clear that the term "not privileged" as used in Rule 34, refers to "privileges" as that term is understood in the law of evidence. When the Secretary of the Air Force lodged his formal "Claim of Privilege," he attempted therein to invoke the privilege against revealing military secrets, a privilege which is well

7

established in the law of evidence.[11] The existence of the privilege is conceded by the court below,[12] and, indeed, by the most outspoken critics of governmental claims to privilege.[13]

[4,5] Judicial experience with the privilege which protects military and state secrets has been limited in this country.[14] English experience has been more extensive, but still relatively slight compared with other evidentiary privileges.[15] Nevertheless, the principles which control the application of the privilege emerge quite clearly from the available precedents. The privilege belongs to the Government and must be asserted by it; it can neither be claimed[16] nor waived[17] by a private party. It is not to be lightly invoked.[18] There must be a formal claim

8

of privilege, lodged by the head of the department which has control over the matter,[19] after actual personal consideration by that officer.[20] The court itself must determine whether the circumstances are appropriate for

11. Totten v. United States, 1875, 92 U.S. 105, 107, 23 L.Ed. 605; Firth Sterling Steel Co. v. Bethlehem Steel Co., D.C.E.D.Pa.1912, 199 F. 353; Pollen v. Ford Instrument Co., D.C.E.D.N.Y.1939, 26 F.Supp. 583; Cresmer v. United States, D.C.E.D.N.Y.1949, 9 F.R.D. 203; see Bank Line v. United States, D.C.S.D.N.Y.1946, 68 F.Supp. 587, Id., 2 Cir., 1947, 163 F.2d 133. 8 Wigmore on Evidence (3d ed.) § 2212(a), p. 161, and § 2378(g) (5), at pp. 785 et seq.; 1 Greenleaf on Evidence (16th ed.) §§ 250-251; Sanford, Evidentiary Privileges Against the Production of Data Within the Control of Executive Departments, 3 Vanderbilt L.Rev. 73, 74-75 (1950).

12. 192 F.2d 987, 996.

13. See Wigmore, op. cit. supra, note 11.

14. See cases cited supra, note 11.

15. Most of the English precedents are reviewed in the recent case of Duncan v. Cammell, Laird & Co., [1942] A.C. 624.

16. Firth Sterling Steel Co. v. Bethlehem Steel Co., D.C.E.D.Pa.1912, 199 F. 353.

17. In re Grove, 3 Cir., 1910, 180 F. 62.

18. Marshall, C.J., in the Aaron Burr trial, I Robertson's Reports 186: "That there may be matter; the production of which the court would not require, is certain. . . . What ought to be done, under such circumstances, presents a delicate question, the discussion of which, it is hoped, will never be rendered necessary in this country."

19. Firth case, supra, note 16.

20. "The essential matter is that the decision to object should be taken by the minister who is the political head of the department, and that he should have seen and considered the contents of the documents and himself have formed the view that on grounds of public interest they ought not be produced. . . ." Duncan v. Cammell, Laird & Co., [1942] A.C. 624, 638.

the claim of privilege,[21] and yet do so without forcing a disclosure of the very thing the privilege is designed to protect.[22] The latter requirement is the only one which presents real difficulty. As to it, we find it helpful to draw upon judicial experience in dealing with an analogous privilege, the privilege against self-incrimination.

The privilege against self-incrimination presented the courts with a similar sort of problem. Too much judicial inquiry into the claim of privilege would force disclosure of the thing the privilege was meant to protect, while a complete abandonment of judicial control would lead to intolerable abuses. Indeed, in the earlier stages

9

of judicial experience with the problem, both extremes were advocated, some saying that the bare assertion by the witness must be taken as conclusive, and others saying that the witness should be required to reveal the matter behind his claim of privilege to the judge for verification.[23] Neither extreme prevailed, and a sound formula of compromise was developed. This formula received authoritative expression in this country as early as the Burr trial.[24] There are differences in phraseology, but in substance it is agreed that the court must be satisfied from all the evidence and circumstances, and "from the implications of the question, in the setting in which it is asked, that a responsive answer to the question or an explanation of why it cannot be answered might be dangerous because injurious exposure could result." Hoffman v. United States, 1951, 341 U.S. 479, 486-487, 71 S.Ct. 814, 818, 95 L.Ed. 1118.[25] If the court is so satisfied, the claim of the privilege will be accepted without requiring further disclosure.

21. Id., at page 642:

"Although an objection validly taken to production, on the ground that this would be injurious to the public interest, is conclusive, it is important to remember that *the decision ruling out such documents is the decision of the judge*. . . . It is the judge who is in control of the trial, not the executive. . . ." (Emphasis supplied.)

22. Id., at pages 638-642; cf. the language of this Court in Hoffman v. United States, 1951, 341 U.S. 479, 486, 71 S.Ct. 814, 818, 95 L.Ed. 1118, speaking of the analogous hazard of probing too far in derogation of the claim of privilege against self-incrimination:

"However, if the witness, upon interposing his claim, were required to prove the hazard in the sense in which a claim is usually required to be established in court, *he would be compelled to surrender the very protection which the privilege is designed to guarantee.*" (Emphasis supplied.)

23. Compare the expressions of Rolfe, B. and Willes, C.J., in Regina v. Garbett, 2 C. & K. 474, 492 [1847]; see 8 Wigmore on Evidence (3d ed.) § 2271.

24. I Robertson's Reports 244:

"When a question is propounded, it belongs to the Court to consider and decide whether any direct answer to it can implicate the witness; if this be decided in the negative, then he may answer it without violating the privilege which is secured to him by law. If a direct answer to it may criminate himself, then he must be the sole judge what his answer would be. The Court cannot participate with him in this judgment, because they cannot decide on the effect of his answer without knowing what it would be, and a disclosure of that fact to the judges would strip him of the privilege which the law allows and which he claims."

25. Brown v. United States, 1928, 276 U.S. 134, 48 S.Ct. 288, 72 L.Ed. 500; Mason v. United States, 1917, 244 U.S. 362, 37 S.Ct. 621, 61 L.Ed. 1198.

Regardless of how it is articulated, some like formula of compromise must be applied here. Judicial control over the evidence in a case cannot be abdicated to the

10

caprice of executive officers. Yet we will not go so far as to say that the court may automatically require a complete disclosure to the judge before the claim of privilege will be accepted in any case. It may be possible to satisfy the court, from all the circumstances of the case, that there is a reasonable danger that compulsion of the evidence will expose military matters which, in the interest of national security, should not be divulged. When this is the case, the occasion for the privilege is appropriate, and the court should not jeopardize the security which the privilege is meant to protect by insisting upon an examination of the evidence, even by the judge alone, in chambers.

[6] In the instant case we cannot escape judicial notice that this is a time of vigorous preparation for national defense. Experience in the past war has made it common knowledge that air power is one of the most potent weapons in our scheme of defense, and that newly developing electronic devices have greatly enhanced the effective use of air power. It is equally apparent that these electronic devices must be kept secret if their full military advantage is to be exploited in the national interests. On the record before the trial court it appeared that this accident occurred to a military plane which had gone aloft to test secret electronic equipment. Certainly there was a reasonable danger that the accident investigation report would contain references to the secret electronic equipment which was the primary concern of the mission.

[7] Of course, even with this information before him, the trial judge was in no position to decide that the report was privileged until there had been a formal claim of privilege. Thus it was entirely proper to rule initially that petitioner had shown probable cause for discovery of the documents. Thereafter, when the formal claim of privilege was filed by the Secretary of the Air Force, under

11

circumstances indicating a reasonable possibility that military secrets were involved, there was certainly a sufficient showing of privilege to cut off further demand for the document on the showing of necessity for its compulsion that had then been made.

[8] In each case, the showing of necessity which is made will determine how far the court should probe in satisfying itself that the occasion for invoking the privilege is appropriate. Where there is a strong showing of necessity, the claim of privilege should not be lightly accepted, but even the most compelling necessity cannot overcome the claim of privilege if the court is ultimately satisfied that military secrets are at stake.[26] *A fortiori,* where necessity is dubious, a

26. See Totten v. United States, 1875, 92 U.S. 105, 23 L.Ed. 605, where the very subject matter of the action, a contract to perform espionage, was a matter of state secret. The action was dismissed on the pleadings without ever reaching the question of evidence, since it was so obvious that the action should never prevail over the privilege.

formal claim of privilege, made under the circumstances of this case, will have to prevail. Here, necessity was greatly minimized by an available alternative, which might have given respondents the evidence to make out their case without forcing a showdown on the claim of privilege. By their failure to pursue that alternative, respondents have posed the privilege question for decision with the formal claim of privilege set against a dubious showing of necessity.

There is nothing to suggest that the electronic equipment, in this case, had any causal connection with the accident. Therefore, it should be possible for respondents to adduce the essential facts as to causation without resort to material touching upon military secrets. Respondents were given a reasonable opportunity to do just that, when petitioner formally offered to make the surviving crew members available for examination. We think that offer should have been accepted.

12

[9] Respondents have cited us to those cases in the criminal field, where it has been held that the Government can invoke its evidentiary privileges only at the price of letting the defendant go free.[27] The rationale of the criminal cases is that, since the Government which prosecutes an accused also has the duty to see that justice is done, it is unconscionable to allow it to undertake prosecution and then invoke its governmental privileges to deprive the accused of anything which might be material to his defense. Such rationale has no application in a civil forum where the Government is not the moving party, but is a defendant only on terms to which it has consented.

The decision of the Court of Appeals is reversed and the case will be remanded to the District Court for further proceedings consistent with the views expressed in this opinion.

Reversed and remanded.

Mr. Justice BLACK, Mr. Justice FRANKFURTER, and Mr. Justice JACKSON dissent substantially for the reasons set forth in the opinion of Judge Maris below. 192 F.2d 987.

---

27. United States v. Andolschek, 2 Cir., 1944, 142 F. 2d 503; United States v. Beckman, 22 Cir., 1946, 155 F. 2d 580.

Refer to Extract D, F.T.C.A. Section 1346(b), and Section 2674

369 U.S. 1

Suzanne Thomas RICHARDS, etc., et al.,
Petitioners,
v.
UNITED STATES of America et al.
(Cite as 82 S. Ct. 585)
No. 59.
Argued Nov. 15, 1961.
Decided Feb. 26, 1962.

Actions under the Federal Tort Claims Act and under the Oklahoma Wrongful Death Act, for death of passengers who lost their lives when an aircraft operated by an airline subject to federal regulation crashed in Missouri. The government asserted a right of indemnity against the airline. The United States District Court for the Northern District of Oklahoma entered judgment dismissing the action and appeals were taken. The Court of Appeals, 285 F.2d 521, affirmed, and certiorari was granted. The Supreme Court, Mr. Chief Justice Warren, held that complaints failed to state claims upon which relief could be granted under the Federal Tort Claims Act or under Oklahoma Wrongful Death Act, where act of negligence allegedly occurred in Oklahoma, and death in Missouri, and plaintiffs received maximum amount recoverable under Missouri Death Act.

Affirmed.

1. Courts

Certiorari would be granted to resolve a conflict between circuits as to law a federal district court should apply in an action brought under the Federal Tort Claims Act where an act of negligence occurs in one state and results in an injury and death in another state, and to enunciate a rule that could be applied uniformly in Federal Tort Claims Act cases. 28 U.S.C.A. §§ 1346(b), 2674.

2. United States

The Federal Tort Claims Act was designed primarily to remove sovereign immunity of the United States from suits in tort, and with certain specific exceptions to render the Government liable in tort as a private individual would be under like circumstances. 28 U.S.C.A. §§ 1346(b), 2674.

3. United States

The Federal Tort Claims Act was not patterned to operate with complete independence from principles of law developed in common law and refined by statute, but was designed to build upon legal relationships formulated and characterized by the states. 28 U.S.C.A. §§ 1346(b), 2674.

4. Statutes

It is assumed that legislative purpose is expressed by ordinary meaning of words used.

5. United States

The Federal Tort Claims Act requires federal courts, in multistate tort actions, to look in the first instance to law of the place where the acts of negligence took place, and does not, through use of the words "act or omission," refer to the place where the negligence had its operative effect. 28 U.S.C.A. § § 1346(b), 2674.

6. Statutes

A section of a statute should not be read in isolation from context of the whole act, and in interpreting legislation, Supreme Court must not be guided by a single sentence or member of a sentence, but should look to provisions of the whole law and to its object and policy.

7. United States

A federal district court should apply the whole law, including choice-of-law rules of the state where the negligent act or omission occurred, in an action brought under the Federal Tort Claims Act, where negligence occurs in one state and results in injury and death in another state, and the court should not apply merely internal law of place where operative effect of the negligence took place. 28 U.S.C.A. § § 1346(b), 2674.

8. States

If more than one state has sufficiently substantial contact with an activity, the forum state, by analysis of the interests possessed by the states involved, could constitutionally apply to decision of the case the law of one or another state having such an interest in the multistate activity.

9. Negligence

An Oklahoma state court was free to apply either its own law, the place where the negligence occurred, or the law of Missouri, the place where the injury occurred, to an action brought in its court and involving such factual situation.

10. Death
United States

Under Oklahoma law, an action for wrongful death is based on statute of the place where the injury occurred that caused the death, and therefore, Missouri wrongful death statute controlled maximum recovery in a wrongful death action brought under the Federal Tort Claims Act, and under Oklahoma Wrongful Death Act, where act of negligence occurred in Oklahoma, and injury that caused the death occurred in Missouri. V.A.M.S. § 537.090; 28 U.S.C.A. § § 1346(b), 2674.

11. Courts

Supreme Court ordinarily accepts determinations of Courts of Appeal on questions of state law, and would do so where petitioners seeking certiorari did not contend there was an erroneous interpretation of state law.

12. United States

Complaints for wrongful death of plaintiffs' decedents, under the Federal Tort Claims Act, and under the Oklahoma Wrongful Death Act failed to state claims upon which relief could be granted, where act of negligence allegedly occurred in Oklahoma, and death in Missouri, and plaintiffs received maximum amount recoverable under the Missouri Death Act. V.A.M.S. § 537.090; 28 U.S.C.A. §§ 1346(b), 2674.

13. Death

Payment of maximum amounts recoverable under Missouri statute for wrongful deaths which occurred in Missouri precluded recovery under the Federal Tort Claims Act and under Oklahoma Wrongful Death Act, even though acts of negligence which caused the fatal accident allegedly occurred in Oklahoma. V.A.M.S. § 537.090; 12 O.S.1951 §§ 1051-1054; 28 U.S.C.A. §§ 1346(b), 2674.

2

Truman B. Rucker, Tulsa, Okl., for petitioners.

Richard J. Medalie, Washington, D.C., for respondent, the United States.

W.B. Patterson, Dallas, Tex., for respondent, American Airlines, Inc.

Mr. Chief Justice WARREN delivered the opinion of the Court.

The question to be decided in this case is what law a Federal District Court should apply in an action brought under the Federal Tort Claims Act[1] where an act of negligence occurs in one State and results in an injury and death in another State. The basic provision of the Tort Claims Act states that the Government shall be liable for tortious conduct committed by its employees acting within the scope of their employment "under circumstances where the United States, if a private person, would be liable to the claimant in accordance with the

3

law of the place where the act or omission occurred."[2] The parties urge that the alternatives in selecting the law to determine liability under this statute are: (1) the internal law of the place where the negligence occurred, or (2) the whole law (including choice-of-law rules) of the place where the negligence occurred, or (3) the internal law of the place where the operative effect of the negligence took place.

Although the particular facts of this case are relatively unimportant in deciding the question before us, a brief recitation of them is necessary to set the context for our decision. The petitioners are the personal representatives of passengers killed when an airplane, owned by the respondent American Airlines, crashed in Missouri while en route from Tulsa, Oklahoma, to New York City. Suit was brought by the petitioners against the United States in the Federal

1. The provisions of the Tort Claims Act are now found in 28 U.S.C. §§ 1291, 1346, 1402, 1504, 2110, 2401, 2402, 2411, 2412, and 2671-2680, 28 U.S.C.A. §§ 1291, 1346, 1402, 1504, 2110, 2401, 2402, 2411, 2412, 2671-2680.

2. 28 U.S.C. § 1346(b), 28 U.S.C.A. § 1346(b).

District Court for the Northern District of Oklahoma, on the theory that the Government, through the Civil Aviation Agency, had "negligently failed to enforce the terms of the Civil Aeronautics Act and the regulations thereunder which prohibited the practices then being used by American Airlines, Inc., in the overhaul depot of Tulsa, Oklahoma."[3] The petitioners in each case either had already received a $15,000 settlement from the Airlines, the maximum amount recoverable under the Missouri Wrongful Death Act,[4] amount had been tendered that amount. They sought additional amounts from the United States under the Oklahoma

4

Wrongful Death Act[5] which contains no limitation on the amount a single person may recover from a tortfeasor. The Government filed a third-party complaint against American Airlines, seeking reimbursement for any amount that the petitioners might recover against the United States.

After a pretrial hearing, the District Court ruled that the complaints failed to state claims upon which relief could be granted under the Oklahoma Act since that statute could not be applied extraterritorially "where an act or omission occurring in Oklahoma results in injury and death in the State of Missouri."[6] Alternatively, the court noted that if Oklahoma law was applicable under the Federal Tort Claims Act, "then the general law of Oklahoma, including its conflicts of law rule, is applicable thereunder," thus precluding further recovery since the Oklahoma conflicts rule would refer the court to the law of Missouri, the place where the negligence had its operative effect.[7] In dismissing the petitioners' complaints against the United States, the court found it unnecessary to pass upon the third-party complaint asserted by the Government against American. On appeal, the Court of Appeals for the Tenth Circuit affirmed the judgment by a divided vote,[8] the majority agreeing with the lower court that the complaints failed to state a cause of action upon which relief could be based under either the Oklahoma or the Missouri Wrongful Death Act. In dissent, the chief judge, believing that Congress intended the internal law of the place where the act or omission occurred to control the rights and liabilities of the parties, stated that he thought it was error to apply the Oklahoma

3. Under 72 Stat. 778, 49 U.S.C. § 1425, 49 U.S.C.A. § 1425, the Administrator of the Federal Aviation Agency is charged with the responsibility of enforcing rules and regulations controlling inspection, maintenance, overhaul and repair of all equipment used in air transportation.

4. Mo.Rev.Stat.1949, § 537.090, V.A.M.S. Subsequent to the origination of these actions the Missouri Code was amended to provide for maximum damages of $25,000. Mo.Rev. Stat.1959, § 537.090.

5. Okl.Stat., 1951, Tit. 12, §§ 1051-1054.

6. The opinion of the District Court is not reported.

7. Gochenour v. St. Louis-San Francisco R. Co., 205 Okl. 594, 239 P.2d 769.

8. 285 F.2d 521.

5

conflict-of-laws rule, and would have remanded the case for a determination of liability under the Oklahoma Act.

[1] That the question confronting us is an important one and of a recurring nature is made apparent by the conflicting views expressed in its solution by the lower federal courts. In the five circuits in which it has arisen, resolution of the question has been reached by adoption of one or another of the alternatives urged upon us by the parties to this suit. The petitioners' contention, that the reference in Section 1346(b) to the "place where the act or omission occurred" directs application of only the internal law of that State—here, Oklahoma—is supported by the Seventh Circuit's decision in Voytas v. United States, 256 F.2d 786, and by the District of Columbia Circuit in Eastern Air Lines v. Union Trust Co., 95 U.S.App. D.C. 189, 221 F.2d 62, as well as by the dissenting judge of the Tenth Circuit in the instant case. The Government's interpretation of the Act, that in order also to give effect to Section 2674,[9] providing that the United States shall be liable in the same manner as a private individual, a court must refer to the whole law of the State where the act or omission occurred, was adhered to by the Second Circuit in Landon v. United States, 197 F.2d 128, as well as by the Tenth Circuit in the case at bar. American Airlines, although willing to abide by the interpretation advanced by the Government, suggests, as an alternative, that the internal law of the place where the negligence had its operative effect—here, Missouri—should control. This construction of the Act is supported by the Ninth Circuit's decision in United States v. Marshall, 230 F.2d 183, and by the dissenting opinion in the Union Trust case, supra. It was to resolve the threefold conflict and to enunciate a rule that can be applied uniformly in Tort Claims Act cases that we granted certiorari. 366 U.S. 916, 81 S.Ct. 1093, 6 L.Ed.2d 240.

I.

6

The principal provision of the Federal Tort Claims Act, originally enacted as Title IV of the Legislative Reorganization Act of 1946,[10] is Section 1346(b), reading in pertinent part:

> "* * * the district courts * * * shall have exclusive jurisdiction of civil actions on claims against the United States, for money damages * * * for injury or loss of property, or personal injury or death caused by the negligent or wrongful act or omission of any employee of the Government while acting within the scope of his office or employment, under circumstances where the United States, if a private person, would be liable to the claimant in accordance with the law of the place where the act or omission occurred."

9. 28 U.S.C. § 2674, 28 U.S.C.A. § 2674.
10. 60 Stat. 842 (1946).

Section 2674, also relevant to our decision, provides:

> "The United States shall be liable, respecting * * * tort claims, in the same manner and to the same extent as a private individual under like circumstances, but shall not be liable for interest prior to judgment or for punitive damages."

[2,3] The Tort Claims Act was designed primarily to remove the sovereign immunity of the United States from suits in tort and, with certain specific exceptions, to render the Government liable in tort as a private individual would be under like circumstances.[11] It is evident that the Act was not patterned to operate with complete independence

7

from the principles of law developed in the common law and refined by statute and judicial decision in the various States. Rather, it was designed to build upon the legal relationships formulated and characterized by the States, and, to that extent, the statutory scheme is exemplary of the generally interstitial character of federal law. If Congress had meant to alter or supplant the legal relationships developed by the States, it could specifically have done so to further the limited objectives of the Tort Claims Act. That is, notwithstanding the generally interstitial character of the law, Congress, in waiving the immunity of the Government for tortious conduct of its employees, could have imposed restrictions and conditions on the extent and substance of its liability.[12] We must determine whether, and to what extent, Congress exercised this power in selecting a rule for the choice of laws to be applied in suits brought under the Act. And, because the issue of the applicable law is controlled by a formal expression of the will of Congress, we need not pause to consider the question whether the conflict-of-laws rule applied in suits where federal jurisdiction rests upon diversity of citizenship shall be extended to a case such as this, in which jurisdiction is based upon a federal statute.[13] In addition, and even though Congress has left to judicial implication the task of giving content to its will in selecting the controlling law, because of the formal expression found in the Act itself, we are presented with a situation wholly distinguishable from those cases in which our initial inquiry has been whether the appropriate rule should be the simple adoption of state

11. See Feres v. United States, 340 U.S. 135, 71 S.Ct. 153, 95 L.Ed. 152, for a detailed analysis of the purposes of the Federal Tort Claims Act in the context of its legislative history.

12. Soriano v. United States, 352 U.S. 270, 77 S.Ct. 269, 1 L.Ed.2d 306; United States v. Sherwood, 312 U.S. 584, 61 S.Ct. 767, 85 L.Ed. 1058.

13. Klaxon Co. v. Stentor Electric Mfg. Co., 313 U.S. 487, 61 S.Ct. 1020, 85 L.Ed. 1477. See Vanston Bondholders Protective Committee v. Green, 329 U.S. 156, 67 S.Ct. 237, 91 L.Ed. 162: McKenzie v. Irving Trust Co., 323 U.S. 365, 65 S.Ct. 405, 89 L.Ed. 305; D'Oench, Duhme & Co. v. Federal Deposit Ins. Corp., 315 U.S. 447, 62 S.Ct. 676, 86 L.Ed. 956.

8

law.[14] Here, we must decide, first, to which State the words "where the act or omission occurred" direct us, and, second, whether application of the internal law or the whole law of that State would be most consistent with the legislative purpose in enacting the Tort Claims Act.

II.

The legislative history of the Act, although generally extensive,[15] is not, except in a negative way, helpful in solving the problem of the law to be applied in a multistate tort action such as is presented by the facts of this case. It has been repeatedly observed that Congress did not consider choice-of-law problems during the long period that the legislation was being prepared for enactment.[16] The concern of Congress, as illustrated by the legislative history,[17] was the problem of a person injured by an employee operating a government vehicle or otherwise acting within the scope of his employment, situations

9

rarely involving a conflict-of-laws question.[18] In these instances, where the negligence and the injury normally occur simultaneously and in a single jurisdiction, the law to be applied is clear, and no solution to the meaning of the words "the law of the place where the act or omission occurred" is required. Here, however, we are faced with events touching more than one "place"—a problem which Congress apparently did not explicitly consider—and, thus, we are compelled to give content to those critical words.

14. See, e.g., Holmberg v. Armbrecht, 327 U.S. 392, 66 S.Ct. 582, 90 L.Ed. 743; Clearfield Trust Co. v. United States, 318 U.S. 363, 63 S.Ct. 573, 87 L.Ed. 838; D'Oench, Duhme & Co. v. Federal Deposit Ins. Corp., 315 U.S. 447, 62 S.Ct. 676, 86 L.Ed. 956; Royal Indemnity Co. v. United States, 313 U.S. 289, 61 S.Ct. 995, 85 L.Ed. 1; Board of Com'rs of Jackson County v. United States, 308 U.S. 343, 60 S.Ct. 285, 84 L.Ed. 313. See also discussion in Hart and Wechsler, The Federal Courts and the Federal System, 679 et seq.

15. Hearings before House Committee on the Judiciary on H.R. 5373 and H.R. 6463, 77th Cong., 2d Sess.; S.Rep. No. 1196, 77th Cong., 2d Sess.; H.R.Rep. No. 2245, 77th Cong., 2d Sess.; No. 1287, 79th Cong., 1st Sess.

16. See e.g., 68 Harv.L.Rev. 1455 (1955); 45 Iowa L.Rev. 125 (1959); 6 N.Y.L.F. 484, 488-490 (1960).

17. See H.R.Rep. No. 2428, 76th Cong., 3d Sess. 3; Hearings on H.R. 5373 and H.R. 6463, note 15, supra, 39, 66; Hearings before a Subcommittee of the House Committee on the Judiciary on H.R. 7236, 76th Cong., 3d Sess. 7, 16; Hearings before a Subcommittee of the Senate Committee on the Judiciary on S. 2690, 76th Cong., 3d Sess. 9; 69 Cong.Rec. 2192, 2193, 3118; 86 Cong.Rec. 12024.

18. See, e.g., Knecht v. United States, 3 Cir., 242 F.2d 929; Irish v. United States, 9 Cir., 225 F.2d 3; United States v. Praylon, 4 Cir., 208 F.2d 291; Somerset Seafood Co. v. United States, 4 Cir., 193 F.2d 631; D'Anna v. United States, 4 Cir., 181 F.2d 335; Olson v. United States, 8 Cir., 175 F.2d 510; Modla v. United States, D.C., 151 F.Supp. 198; Irvin v. United States, D.C., 148 F.Supp. 25.

[4,5] In the Tort Claims Act Congress has expressly stated that the Government's liability is to be determined by the application of a particular law, the law of the place where the act or omission occurred,[19] and we must, of course, start with the assumption that the legislative purpose is expressed by the ordinary meaning of the words used. We believe that it would be difficult to conceive of any more precise language Congress could have used to command application of the law of the place where the negligence occurred than the words it did employ in the Tort Claims Act. Thus we first reject the alternative urged by American Airlines. The legislative materials cited to us by American[20] not only lack probative force

10

in a judicial sense, but they are completely unpersuasive to support the argument that Congress intended the words "act or omission" to refer to the place where the negligence had its operative effect. The ease of application inherent in the rule urged by American lends a certain attractiveness, but we are bound to operate within the framework of the words chosen by Congress and not to question the wisdom of the latter in the process of construction. We conclude that Congress has, in the Tort Claims Act, enacted a rule which requires federal courts, in multistate tort actions, to look in the first instance to the law of the place where the acts of negligence took place.

III.

However, our task is not completed. Having rejected the third alternative stated initially as inconsistent with the express terminology of the Act, we must now determine the reach of the words "law of the place." Do they embrace the whole law of the place where the negligence occurred, or only the internal law of that place? This problem, unlike the initial question discussed under II, supra, has not been dealt with by any formal expression of Congress and we must therefore establish the rule to be applied uniformly by lower federal courts, with due regard to the variant interests and policies expressed by the Tort Claims Act legislation.

19. 28 U.S.C. § 1346(b), 28 U.S.C.A. § 1346(b).

20. Hearings before House Committee on the Judiciary on H.R. 5373 and H.R. 6463, 77th Cong., 2d Sess. 9, 30. American suggests that support for its argument is found in the testimony of Mr. Francis Shea, then Assistant Attorney General of the United States, before the House Committee on the Judiciary, who stated, when asked where a claimant might bring suit under the Act, that the venue provision allowed suit to be brought either where the claimant resides or where the injury took place. Because the venue provision of the Act also contains the words "wherein the act or omission complained of occurred" (28 U.S.C. § 1402(b)), 28 U.S.C.A. § 1402(b), American contends that the reference to the place where the injury occurred should control the meaning of the "act or omission" language in Section 1346(b). In addition to the fact that this testimony bears no relation to the choice-of-laws problems, and that considerations underlying the problem of venue are substantially different from those determining applicable law, we are not persuaded to allow an isolated piece of legislative history to detract from the Act the words Congress expressly employed.

11

[6,7] We believe it fundamental that a section of a statute should not be read in isolation from the context of the whole Act,[21] and that in fulfilling our responsibility in interpreting legislation, "we must not be guided by a single sentence or member of a sentence, but [should] look to the provisions of the whole law, and to its object and policy."[22] We should not assume that Congress intended to set the courts completely adrift from state law with regard to questions for which it has not provided a specific and definite answer in an act such as the one before us which, as we have indicated, is so intimately related to state law. Thus, we conclude that a reading of the statute as a whole, with due regard to its purpose, requires application of the whole law of the State where the act or omission occurred.

We are led to our conclusion by other persuasive factors notwithstanding the fact that the very conflict among the lower federal courts that we must here resolve illustrates the also reasonable alternative view expressed by the petitioners. First, our interpretation enables the federal courts to treat the United States as a "private individual under like circumstances," and thus is consistent with the Act considered as a whole.[23] The general conflict-of-laws rule, followed by a vast majority of the States,[24] is to apply the law of the place of injury to the

12

substantive rights of the parties. Therefore, where the forum State is the same as the one in which the act or omission occurred, our interpretation will enable the federal courts to treat the United States as an individual would be treated under like circumstances.[25] Moreover, this interpretation of the Act provides a degree of flexibility to the law to be applied in federal courts that would not be possible under the view advanced either by the petitioners or by American.

21. National Labor Relations Board v. Lion Oil Co., 352 U.S. 282, 288, 77 S.Ct. 330, 333, 1 L.Ed.2d 331; Cherokee Intermarriage Cases, 203 U.S. 76, 89, 27 S.Ct. 29, 34, 51 L.Ed. 96; Panama Refining Co. v. Ryan, 293 U.S. 388, 439, 55 S.Ct. 241, 256, 79 L.Ed. 446 (Cardozo, J., dissenting).

22. Mastro Plastics Corp. v. National Labor Relations Board, 350 U.S. 270, 285, 76 S.Ct. 349, 359, 100 L.Ed. 309, quoting from United States v. Boisdore's Heirs, 8 How. 113, 122, 12 L.Ed. 1009.

23. 28 U.S.C. § 2674, 28 U.S.C.A. § 2674, quoted in the text, supra, as well as 28 U.S.C. § 1346(b), 28 U.S.C.A. § 1346(b), provides that the United States should be treated as an individual defendant would be under like circumstances.

24. Restatement, Conflict of Laws, §§ 377, 378 and 391. This rule has been repeated so frequently that a citation of cases here would serve no purpose. For a collection of cases, see Goodrich, Conflict of Laws, 263-264; Stumberg, Conflict of Laws, 182-187; 25 C.J.S. Death § 28, nn. 27-30.

25. For example, had the petitioners in the instant case brought suit against American as well as the United States, the petitioners' interpretation of the Act would have the District Court determine the American's liability by the law of Missouri and the United States' by the law of Oklahoma. Under our construction of the Act, however, both defendants' liability would be determined by the law of Missouri. However, because of the venue provision in the statute, allowing suit to be brought where all the plaintiffs reside as well as where the act or omission occurred (28 U.S.C. § 1402(b), 28 U.S.C.A. § 1402(b); see Knecht v. United States, 3 Cir., 242 F.2d 929; Olson v. United States, 8 Cir., 175 F.2d 510), a situation may arise where a District Court could not determine the Government's and a private individual's liability in exactly the same manner.

Recently there has been a tendency on the part of some States to depart from the general conflicts rule in order to take into account the interests of the State having significant contact with the parties to the litigation.[26] We can see no compelling reason to saddle the Act with an interpretation that would

13

prevent the federal courts from implementing this policy in choice-of-law rules where the State in which the negligence occurred has adopted it. Should the States continue this rejection of the older rule in those situations where its application might appear inappropriate or inequitable,[27] the flexibility inherent in our interpretation will also be more in step with that judicial approach, as well as with the character of the legislation and with the purpose of the Act considered as a whole.

In the absence of persuasive evidence to the contrary, we do not believe that Congress intended to adopt the inflexible rule urged upon us by the petitioners. Despite the power of Congress to enact for litigation of this type a federal conflict-of-laws rule independent of the States' development of such rules, we should not, particularly in the type of interstitial legislation involved here, assume that it has done so. Nor are we persuaded to require such an independent federal rule by the petitioners' argument that there are other instances, specifically set forth in the Act,[28]

26. Grant v. McAuliffe, 41 Cal.2d 859, 264 P.2d 944. 42 A.L.R.2d 1162; Schmidt v. Driscoll Hotel, Inc., 249 Minn. 376, 82 N.W.2d 365; Haumschild v. Continental Casualty Co., 7 Wis.2d 130, 95 N.W.2d 814. See Currie, Survival of Actions: Adjudication versus Automation in the Conflict of Laws, 10 Stan.L.Rev. 205 (1958). Cf. Vrooman v. Beech Aircraft Corp., 10 Cir., 183 F.2d 479; Levy v. Daniels' U-Drive Auto Renting Co., 108 Conn. 333, 143 A. 163, 61 A.L.R. 846; Caldwell v. Gore, 175 La. 501, 143 So. 387; Burkett v. Globe Indemnity Co., 182 Miss. 423, 181 So. 316.

27. In addition to the cases cited in note 26, supra, see the opinion by Mr. Justice Black in Vanston Bondholders Protective Committee v. Green, 329 U.S. 156, 161-162, 67 S.Ct. 237, 239, 91 L.Ed. 162, where it is stated in context to a different but analogous problem:

"In determining which contact is the most significant in a particular transaction, courts can seldom find a complete solution in the mechanical formulae of the conflicts of law. Determination requires the exercise of an informed judgment in the balancing of all the interests of the states with the most significant contacts in order best to accommodate the equities among the parties to the policies of those states."

28. The Act permits claimants to sue only in the federal courts, and not in the state courts which are available in actions against a private individual, § 1346(b); the Act prescribes its own period of limitations which may be shorter or longer than that of the State, § 2401(b); the claimant cannot obtain a trial by jury under the Act, although he could against a private individual, § 2402; the claimant cannot obtain interest prior to judgment in suits under the Act regardless of the state rule governing private individuals, § 2674; the claimant cannot obtain punitive damages under the Act, even though state law may provide for it as against a private defendant, § 2674; the claimant cannot recover any damages against the United States on any claim arising out of assault, battery, flase imprisonment, false arrest, malicious prosecution, abuse of process, libel, slander, misrepresentation, deceit, or interference with contract rights, whereas he could recover such damages against a private individual, § 2680(h); the claimant cannot obtain any recovery against the United States on a claim arising in a foreign country, although he could against a private individual, § 2680(k); and the Act exempts the Government from liability for claims based on various types of activities, although a private individual would be liable in the same circumstances, § 2680.

14

where the liability of the United States is not coextensive with that of a private person under state law. It seems sufficient to note that Congress has been specific in those instances where it intended the federal courts to depart completely from state law and, also, that this list of exceptions contains no direct or indirect modification of the principles controlling application of choice-of-law rules. Certainly there is nothing in the legislative history that even remotely supports the argument that Congress did not intend state conflict rules to apply to multistate tort actions brought against the Government.[29]

15

Under our interpretation of the Act we find it unnecessary to judge the effect of the Oklahoma courts' pronouncements that the Oklahoma Wrongful Death Act cannot be given extraterritorial effect.[30]

IV.

[8-11] Our view of a State's power to adopt an appropriate conflict-of-laws doctrine in a situation touching more than one place has been indicated by our discussion in Part III of this opinion.[31] Where more than one State has sufficiently substantial contact with the activity in question, the forum State, by analysis of the interests possessed by the States involved, could constitutionally apply to the decision of the case the law of one or another state having such an interest in the multistate activity.[32] Thus, an Oklahoma state court would be free to apply either its own law, the law of the place where the negligence occurred, or the law of Missouri, the law of the place where the injury occurred,

29. In fact, despite the ambiguity that exists in the history due to the fact that Congress did not specifically consider the choice-of-laws problem, the legislative material indicates that Congress thought in terms of state law being applicable. The term "law of the place where the act or omission occurred" was particularized as (1) the law of the situs of the wrongful act of omission. Hearings before House Committee on the Judiciary on H.R. 5373 and H.R. 6463. 77th Cong., 2d Sess. 35; (2) local law, id., at 26, 27, 30, 59 and 61; S.Rep. No. 1196, 77th Cong., 2d Sess. 6: H.R.Rep. No. 2245, 77th Cong., 2d Sess. 9; H.R.Rep. No. 1287, 79th Cong., 1st Sess. 4; S.Rep. No. 1400, 79th Cong., 2d Sess. 32; (3) local tort law. Hearings before House Committee on the Judiciary on H.R. 5373 and H.R. 6463, 77th Cong., 2d Sess. 30; (4) the law of the situs of the alleged tort. Hearings before a Subcommittee of the Senate Committee on the Judiciary on S. 2690, 76th Cong., 3d Sess. 44; and (5) the locale of the injury or damage. Hearings before the House Committee on the Judiciary on H.R. 5373 and H.R. 6463, 77th Cong., 2d Sess. 9.

30. Gochenour v. St. Louis-San Francisco R. Co., 205 Okl. 594, 239 P.2d 769. See Fenton v. Sinclair Refining Co., 206 Okl. 19, 240 P.2d 748.

31. Supra, 369 U.S., pp. 12-13, 82 S.Ct., pp. 593-594 and cases cited. See also Carroll v. Lanza, 349 U.S. 408, 75 S.Ct. 804, 99 L.Ed. 1183; Watson v. Employers Liability Corp., 348 U.S. 66, 75 S.Ct. 166, 99 L.Ed. 74; Pacific Employers Ins. Co. v. Industrial Accident Comm., 306 U.S. 493, 59 S.Ct. 629, 83 L.Ed. 940. Cf. Hartford Accident & Indemnity Co. v. Delta & Pine Land Co., 292 U.S. 143, 54 S.Ct. 634, 78 L.Ed. 1178; Home Insurance Co. v. Dick, 281 U.S. 397, 50 S.Ct. 338, 74 L.Ed. 926.

32. See, e.g., the cases cited in note 26, supra.

to an action brought in its courts and involving this factual situation.[33] Both the Federal District

16

Court sitting in Oklahoma, and the Court of Appeals for the Tenth Circuit, have interpreted the pertinent Oklahoma decisions,[34] which we have held are controlling, to declare that an action for wrongful death is based on the statute of the place where the injury occurred that caused the death.[35] Therefore, Missouri's statute controls the case at bar. It is conceded that each petitioner has received $15,000, the maximum amount recoverable under the Missouri Act, and the petitioners thus have received full compensation for their claims. Accordingly, the courts below were correct in holding that, in accordance with Oklahoma law, petitioners had failed to state claims upon which relief could be granted. The judgment is affirmed.

Affirmed.

---

33. Alabama G.S.R. Co. v. Carroll, 97 Ala. 126, 11 So. 803, 18 L.R.A. 433; Otey v. Midland Valley R. Co., 108 Kan. 755, 197 P. 203; Connecticut Valley Lumber Co. v. Maine Central R. Co., 78 N.H. 553, 103 A. 263; El Paso & N.W.R. Co. v. McComus, 36 Tex.Civ.App. 170, 81 S.W. 760 (holding that the law of the place of injury controls) and Schmidt v. Driscoll Hotel, Inc., 249 Minn. 376, 82 N.W.2d 365 (holding that the law of the place of negligence controls). See also Hunter v. Derby Foods, 2 Cir., 110 F.2d 970, 133 A.L.R. 255; 35 Col.L.Rev. 202.

34. Gochenour v. St. Louis-San Francisco R. Co., 205 Okl. 594, 239 P.2d 769; Miller v. Tennis. 140 Okl. 185, 282 P. 345. See Fenton v. Sinclair Refining Co., 206 Okl. 19, 240 P.2d 748.

35. We are aware that in the Oklahoma cases cited in note 34, supra, both the injury and negligence occurred in the same sister State, and that the two courts below relied largely on dictum in those cases to conclude that Oklahoma would follow the general rule that the law of the place of injury would control even had the negligence that caused the injury taken place in Oklahoma. The petitioners here do not contend that this was an erroneous interpretation of state law. We ordinarily accept the determinations of Courts of Appeals on questions of state law and do so here under the circumstances presented. General Box Co. v. United States, 351 U.S. 159, 165, 76 S.Ct. 728, 732, 100 L.Ed. 1055; Estate of Spiegel v. Commissioner, 335 U.S. 701, 707-708, 69 S.Ct. 301, 303-304, 93 L.Ed. 330; Huddleston v. Dwyer, 322 U.S. 232, 237, 64 S.Ct. 1015, 1018, 88 L.Ed. 1246.

The next several cases are summarized below, rather than reporting the entire case. It is felt that summarizing these particular cases would better illustrate special applications of provisions of the Federal Tort Claims Act (FTCA):

1. FTCA Section 2680 (k) states that FTCA shall not apply to a claim arising in a foreign country. In U.S. v. Spelar, 338 U.S. 217 (1949), the court ruled that a military base in Newfoundland, leased to U.S. for a long term, was considered a foreign country for purposes of 2680 (k), and therefore U.S. was not liable.
2. FTCA Section 1346 (b) recites that negligence must be by an employee of the U.S. in order to apply FTCA against the U.S. In Pattno v. U.S., 311 F.2d 604 (1962), the court ruled that Air National Guard personnel not on active federal service are not employees of the U.S. within the meaning of 1346 (b). Pearl v. U.S., 230 F.2d 243 (1956), held that members of the Civil Air Patrol are not employees of the U.S. within the meaning of 1346 (b). The case of U.S. v. Maryland, 322 F.2d 1009 (1963), involved a mid-air collision of an Air National Guard aircraft and a commercial airliner. It was determined that the cause of the collision was the negligence of a mechanic who failed to hook up a meter in the National Guard aircraft. The mechanic was in the National Guard, and was also hired by the Federal Government to maintain the Federally owned plane. The court held that the mechanic was an employee within the meaning of 1346 (b), and therefore the U.S. was liable.
3. In the case of Eastern Airlines v. Union Trust Co., 221 F.2d 62 (1954), the executors of deceased bring the action for death arising out of a mid-air collision between a commercial airliner and a privately owned surplus fighter aircraft. The Airport was owned by the U.S. Government. It was determined that the negligence of the tower operator controlling aircraft movement was the proximate cause of the accident and of the death. The court held that the U.S. was liable because the tower operator was a Federal employee within the meaning of 1346 (b).

   In order to escape liability the defendant U.S. Government advanced two arguments:

   a. The airport was a discretionary function and therefore U.S. Government was not liable under FTCA Section 2680 (a).
   b. A private individual could not perform this function and therefore U.S. Government was not liable within the meaning of FTCA Section 2674.

      The court rejected both of the government's arguments and ruled that the government was liable because the airport function was not discretionary; and that anyone can operate an airport, hire tower operators, and get them certified by the Federal Government.

4. Three additional cases in which the courts held that the discretionary function provision of Section 2680 (a) did not preclude a suit under FTCA are as follows:
   a. U.S. v. Lawter 219 F.2d 559 (1955) which held that where a death resulted from an unsuccessful rescue from water by an helicopter, the government was liable.
   b. Bullock v. U.S., 133 F.Supp. 885 (Utah 1955), in which the court ruled that the fallout damage to a flock of sheep as a result of nuclear tests conducted by the Atomic Energy Commission, did not prevent a suit under FTCA.
   c. Dahstrom v. U.S., 228 F.2d 819 (1956), held that where an injury resulted from the bolting of a team of horses frightened by a low-flying Federal aircraft conducting a survey, the government was liable.

CHAPTER 6

Tariffs—Limitation of Liability

A tariff is a list or schedule of charges, for services, and for transportation of goods and people; and the conditions therefor.

The study of tariffs in aviation cuts across many fields of study including the Warsaw Convention, and the Interstate Commerce Commission.

In the industry, tariffs for air carriage must be filed with the Civil Aeronautics Board. Properly filed, tariffs become a part of the contract of the carriage between the carriers and the shipper, and therefore, are binding on both parties. Tariff rates and schedules have been held to be binding on all parties whether or not the shipper has knowledge of the tariff rates and schedules.

Before reading the cases in this section, read, and become familiar with, the provisions of Extracts from the Federal Aviation Act, Extract B; and with Extracts from Interstate Commerce Act, Part II, Extract E.

The United States Supreme Court has applied its Interstate Commerce Act tariff rulings, to cases under the FAA and under the CAB. Following are several cases decided by the United States Supreme Court under the Interstate Commerce Commission, as applicable to cases that might be brought under the Civil Aeronautics Board:

1. In Boston & M.R. Company v. Hooker, 233 U.S. 97 (1914), the passenger had no actual notice of the tariff provision that limited his recovery to $100.00, for damage to his baggage, unless he declared the actual higher value and paid an excess charge for same. The Supreme Court held that the passenger was limited to a recovery of $100.00 for loss of his baggage.
2. In Western Union Telegraph Company v. Esteve Brothers & Company, 256 U.S. 566 (1921), the Supreme Court held that the Telegraph Company's liability was limited to the amount of the tolls collected. In this case the Telegraph Company made an error in the transmission of an unrepeated cablegram. The tariff provided for different rates for repeated and unrepeated cablegrams.
3. In the case of Texas & Pacific R.R. Company v. Mugg & Dryden, 202 U.S. 242, the shipper was quoted a lower rate than that filed with the Interstate Commerce Commission. The Supreme Court held that the shipper must pay the full rate recited in the tariff.

4. In Chicago & Atlantic R.R. Company v. Kirby, 255 U.S. 155 (1912), a carrier agreed to expedite a shipment of horses over its own lines in order to make connections with a fast freight train of a second carrier. The first carrier was not able to make the connection, and the shipper sued for recovery of damages for breach of an agreement. The Supreme Court held that the shipper could not recover damages for breach of an agreement, because the agreement constituted an unreasonable preference, forbidden by the Interstate Commerce Act. The shipper was charged only regular through rates with no provision for such service.
5. In Jones v. Northwest Airlines 157 P.2d 728 (1945), the court applied the rulings under the ICC, to aviation cases and tariffs filed under CAB. The tariff in question permitted the carrier to cancel a flight at any time it deemed necessary and further stated that the carrier was not responsible for failure of the aircraft to depart or arrive on the scheduled time. The Court held that, even though the passenger claimed he had a special contract with carrier which recognized the limited time he had for the trip, the alleged contract was void because it was inconsistent with the terms of the tariff schedules. The court stated that the ticket was sold subject to tariff regulations, which regulations were in conflict with the alleged contract.

The general reasoning of many courts in cases similar to the above, is based, not on the fiction of constructive notice or of lack of contracts, but rather on the requirement for equality and uniformity of rates, and the application thereof.

The Mack v. Eastern Airlines case is presented here as historical comment on the method used to regulate tariffs and rates by the Civil Aeronautics Board before enactment of the Airline Deregulation Act of 1978.

It should be noted here that the Airline Deregulation Act of 1978 has brought about, and will bring about, many changes in airline regulation. Some of the changes will take the form of court decisions in the absence of specific statutory regulation. Other changes will take the form of transfer of regulation to other existing statutes and agencies, such as U.S. anti-trust laws.

Generally speaking, the Airline Deregulation Act of 1978 reduced economic regulation of the airline industry by the Civil Aeronautics Board. A brief description of some of the changes are as follows:

1. Relaxed entry requirements into the air industry and into new markets; and relaxed route authority.
2. Relaxation, and termination of Civil Aeronautics Board authority over air carrier fares, and terms and conditions of the contract of carriage.
3. Termination of the Civil Aeronautics Board in 1985.

87 F. Supp. 113

MACK v. EASTERN AIR LINES, Inc.

Civ. No. 7941.

United States District Court

D. Massachusetts.

June 2, 1949.

Action by Chester W. Mack against Eastern Air Lines, Inc., for damages because of defendant's failure to transport plaintiff beyond New York on plane flight from Boston to Washington, D.C.

The United States District Court, District of Massachusetts, Wyzanski, J., granted the defendant's motion for summary judgment.

1. Carriers

The rules of airline carrier providing that carrier should not be liable for failure to operate any scheduled flight with or without notice to passenger and fixing the rights of the passenger were within the authority conferred by the Civil Aeronautics Act of 1938 and became a part of the contract between the carrier and the passenger. Civil Aeronautics Act of 1938, § 1 et seq., 49 U.S.C.A. § 401 et seq.

2. Carriers

The section of the Civil Aeronautics Act of 1938 providing that remedies existing at common law or by some other statute were not abrogated by such act merely preserved existing remedies and did not preserve existing obligations or rights or contractual arrangements. Civil Aeronautics Act of 1938, § 1106, 49 U.S.C.A. § 676.

3. Carriers

Contractual arrangements and obligations of air carriers are governed by the Civil Aeronautics Act and not by common law or some other statute. Civil Aeronautics Act of 1938, § 1106, 49 U.S.C.A. § 676.

4. Carriers

The rules of airline carrier that carrier should not be liable for its failure to operate any flight with or without notice to passenger and fixing rights of passenger were incorporated in contract between passenger and carrier and passenger was bound by the conditions specified therein.

5. Carriers

Under rules of airline carrier, the carrier had the right to change schedule of flight without previous notice to passenger and to remove at New York passenger who had purchased transportation from Boston to Washington, D.C., in view of weather or other conditions beyond carrier's control.

6. Carriers

Airline carrier's failure to inform passenger in Boston of the weather and carrier's removal of passenger from plane in New York and excellent condition of weather in Washington an hour after the passenger left plane in New York were irrelevant as respects carrier's liability to passenger who had purchased transportation from Boston to Washington, D.C.

Chester W. Mack, Boston, Mass., Lambert H. Bigelow, Boston, Mass., for plaintiff.

Warren F. Farr, Ropes, Gray, Best, Coolidge & Rugg, Boston, Mass., for defendant.

WYZANSKI, District Judge.

This is an action by a passenger on defendant's air line bound from Boston to Washington, D.C. for damages because of defendant's failure to transport him beyond New York. Defendant has moved for summary judgment under the provisions of Federal Rules of Civil Procedure, rule 56(b), 28 U.S.C.A.

By the pleadings, admissions of plaintiff on file and affidavits attached to defendant's motion it appears that there is no dispute as to the following facts. Plaintiff purchased a ticket from Boston to Washington, D.C. for passage on Flight No. 633 on August 27, 1947. That flight was scheduled to leave Boston at 4:00 p.m. for Jacksonville and Miami, Florida, with scheduled stops at LaGuardia Field, New York at 5:05 p.m. and at Washington, D.C. at 6:37 p.m. Plaintiff was a passenger on that flight. The flight did not leave Boston until 5:34 p.m. and arrived at LaGuardia Field, New York at 6:35 p.m.

At 6:00 p.m. while Flight No. 633 was in the air en route to New York, the Washington Air Route Traffic Control Center, a facility of the Civil Aeronautics Administration, issued an order stopping air traffic into Washington, D.C. until further notice due to emergency conditions. Upon the arrival of Flight No. 633 at LaGuardia Field defendant's Flight Superintendent ordered the flight to omit its scheduled stop at Washington, D.C. because of this indefinite suspension of traffic into the Washington airport. All passengers bound for Washington, D.C., including plaintiff, were requested to deplane and did so. Flight No. 633 departed from LaGuardia Field for Jacksonville at 7:13 p.m. Plaintiff refused a refund of the one-way fare from New York to Washington, D.C. and demanded that defendant pay him $30.80, being the amount of the full fare from Boston to Washington, D.C. plus hotel and telephone expenses.

Thereafter he brought this suit in which he set forth three causes of action: Count 1, in tort, alleging that defendant negligently failed to apprise him that the flight to Washington might not be completed and that defendant negligently failed to carry him beyond New York; Count 2, in tort, alleging that defendant negligently refused to complete the air passage to Washington, D.C.; and Count 3, in contract, alleging breach of contract to carry plaintiff to Washington, D.C.

At the argument on the motion for summary judgment filed by defendant, plaintiff said he was prepared to show first, that the defendant did not act reasonably in that it failed to inform plaintiff in Boston of the weather conditions and likelihood of no stop in Washington, D.C.; second, that defendant acted unreasonably in New York in requiring Washington passengers to deplane at LaGuardia Field. Plaintiff also stated that he was prepared to show that within an hour after the plane left LaGuardia Field weather conditions in Washington, D.C. were excellent and it would have been practicable for the defendant to have carried him from LaGuardia Field to Washington, D.C. virtually as scheduled.

It takes no extended discussion to show that defendant is entitled to the summary judgment for which it asks and that plaintiff's contentions are entirely devoid of merit.

Section 403 of the Civil Aeronautics Act of 1938, 49 U.S.C.A. § 483, provides for the filing, posting and publishing of tariffs by air carriers and requires that contracts of carriage shall correspond to such tariffs. Pursuant to that provision of law defendant before August 27, 1947 filed, posted and published Local and Joint Passenger Rules Tariff No. PR-2. Paragraph 2(A) of these Rules Tariff provided that the Rules contained therein "shall constitute the terms and conditions upon which each participating carrier furnishes, or agrees to furnish, transportation at such fares and charges, to the same extent as if such Rules were included as terms and conditions in the contract of carriage and expressly agreed to by passengers." Rule 11(A) and (B) of the Rules Tariff provided:

"(A) Liability of participating carriers.

Except to the extent provided in paragraphs (B) and (C) of this Rule, no participating carrier shall be liable for failing to operate any flight according to schedule or for changing the schedule of any flight, with or without notice to the passenger.

"(B) Options of passengers and carriers—General.

Except as provided in paragraph (C) of this Rule, whenever any participating carrier fails to operate any flight according to schedule, or changes the schedule of any flight, or cancels the reservation of any passenger pursuant to Rule 13(A), said carrier will, at the request of the passenger—

(1) Transport the passenger on the next flight on which space is available;

(2) Endorse the unused portion of his ticket for purposes of rerouting;

(3) Refund an amount determined in accordance with Rule 15(a) upon surrender of the unused portion of his ticket * * *

(4) If the carrier so elects, reroute the passenger, or secure for him accommodations by other means of transportation." Paragraph (C) of the Rule deals with the options of passengers and carriers when the passenger misses a connecting flight on which space has been reserved, and is inapplicable to the present case. Rule 14 of the Rules Tariff provided in its pertinent parts as follows:

"(A) General. Each participating carrier reserves the right to refuse to transport, or to remove at any point, any passenger—

(1) Whenever such action is necessary to comply with any governmental regulation, or whenever it deems such action necessary or advisable by reason of weather or other conditions beyond its control;

* * * * *

"(E) Liability. No participating carrier shall be liable for its refusal to transport any passenger in accordance with the preceding paragraphs of this Rule, or for its removal of any passenger in accordance with paragraph (A) or (B) of this Rule, but such carrier will, at the request of the passenger and upon surrender of the unused portion of his ticket, refund an amount determined in accordance with Rule 15(a)." Rule 15 of the Rules Tariff provided:

"(A) Involuntary. The amount of the refund which any participating carrier will make, pursuant to Rule 11(B) (3), 11(C) (3), or 14(E) will be—

* * * * *

(2) If a portion of the ticket has been used, either—

(a) An amount equal to the one way fare and charges applicable to the transportation covered by the unused portion of the ticket, less the same rate of discount that was applied in computing the original cost of the ticket; or

(b) If the flight on which the passenger was being transported was terminated at a point not on the routing designated by the passenger's ticket" [various other amounts].

[1-3] There can be no question that these Rules were within the authority conferred by the Civil Aeronautics Act of 1938 and became a part of the contract between the carrier and the passenger. Boston & Maine Railroad v. Hooker, 233 U.S. 97, 34 S.Ct. 526, 58 L.Ed. 868, L.R.A.1915B, 450, Ann.Cas. 1915D, 593; Western Union, Telegraph Co. v. Esteve Brothers & Co., 256 U.S. 566, 571, 573, 41 S.Ct. 584, 65 L.Ed. 1094. There is nothing in Section 1106 of the Civil Aeronautics Act of 1938, 49 U.S.C.A. § 676, which is to the contrary. That section merely provides that *remedies* now existing at common law or by some other statute are not abrogated by the Civil Aeronautics Act of 1938, 49 U.S.C.A. § 401 et seq. What it preserves are pre-existing remedies, not pre-existing obligations or rights or contractual arrangements. Contractual arrangements and obligations are governed by the Civil Aeronautics Act and not by common law or some other statute. If Schwartzman v. United Air Lines Transport Corp., D.C.Neb., 6 F.R.D. 517, is to the contrary, I decline to follow it.

[4] Inasmuch as the Rules 11, 14 and 15 of the Rules Tariff were incorporated in the contract between plaintiff and defendant, there can be no question that plaintiff is bound by the conditions specified therein. Jones v. Northwest Airlines, Inc., 22 Wash.2d 863, 157 P.2d 728; Boston & Maine Railroad v. Hooker, supra; Western Union Telegraph Co. v. Esteve Brothers & Co., supra.

[5] Under Rule 11(A) defendant had the right to change the schedule of Flight No. 633 without previous notice to plaintiff. Also under Rule 14 defendant had the right to remove plaintiff at LaGuardia Field because it determined such action advisable because of weather or other conditions beyond its control.

[6] It is entirely irrelevant as a matter of law that defendant did not inform plaintiff in Boston of the weather, that defendant removed plaintiff from the plane in New York and that the weather in Washington was in fact excellent an hour after plaintiff left the plane in New York. Since all these facts are irrelevant as a matter of law, there is no genuine issue as to any material fact and defendant as the moving party is entitled to a judgment as a matter of law. F.R.C.P. Rule 56(c), as amended.

Judgment for defendant with costs.

CHAPTER 7

Workmen's Compensation Limitation of Liability

Workmen's compensation acts are within the province of the states and therefore are covered by state laws and statutes. Workmen's compensation acts provide benefits and care to employees who suffer injury or death in connection with their employment. The cost of these benefits is borne by the employer.

The primary task in workmen's compensation cases is to determine whether the injury or death of an employee occurred during the course of his employment. These are fact situations that are peculiar in themselves and cannot be readily applied to other cases.

The following are summaries of cases in which it was held that the injury or death of the employee occurred during the course of his employment and therefore the employee was covered by the workmen's compensation act of his state:

1. In Markoholz v. General Electric Co., 243 N.Y.S.2d 853 (1963), an employee was on a one-week personal visit to Italy, after attending a business conference in France. The court held that his death occurred while he was in the course of business and therefore covered by workmen's compensation act.
2. In Dunham Co. v. Industrial Commission, 156 N.E.2d 560 (Ill. 1959), an engineer was traveling as a passenger from Chicago to Seattle in a commercial airliner which was destroyed in mid-air by an act of sabotage. The court held that his death occurred during the course of his employment and therefore he was covered by the workmen's compensation act of his state.
3. In Galloway v. Department of Motor Vehicles, 57 S.E.2d 799 (1950), a state highway patrolman, trying to locate a suspect in a wooded area, was flying in a private aircraft, which crashed in the wooded area. The court held, in this case, that the patrolman was covered by Workmen's Compensation Act of his state because the injury occurred during the course of his employment.
4. In Indiana Steel Products Company v. Leonard, 131 N.E.2d 162 (Ind. 1956), a salesman piloting a rented aircraft to make a call on a customer, crashed the aircraft; and the court held he was covered by Workmen's Compensation Act.

The Markoholz v. General Electric court case is presented below to illustrate a factual situation in which the court found that the employee was covered by the State's Workmen's Compensation Act, and the reasoning of court in arriving at its decision.

---

13 N.Y.2d 163

Claim of William MARKOHOLZ, as Guardian of William Martino and Others, Infant Children of Michael Martino, Deceased, Appellant, v. GENERAL ELECTRIC COMPANY, Employer, et al., Respondents. Workmen's Compensation Board, Respondent.

(Cite as 243 N.Y.S. 2d 853)

Court of Appeals of New York.

Oct. 10, 1963.

Workmen's compensation proceeding in which the employer appealed from an award of the Workmen's Compensation Board for the claimant. The Appellate Division of the Supreme Court in the Third Judicial Department, 18 A.D.2d 857, 236 N.Y.S.2d 341, entered an order reversing the award and dismissing the claim and the claimant appealed. The Court of Appeals, Desmond, C.J., held that employee who was killed in airplane crash while flying, with his wife, from Milan to Paris after a six day vacation following close of conference at Paris to which his employer had sent him was deemed to have been in his employment for purpose of compensability under Workmen's Compensation Act, where he was to have taken a plane from Paris to home after only a three hour stop in Paris.

Order reversed and award reinstated.

Van Voorhis, J., dissented.

1. Workmen's Compensation

Courts are bound by Workmen's Compensation Board's fact findings which, including ultimate fact of "arising out of and in the course of," must stand unless erroneous in law. Workmen's Compensation Law, § 23.

2. Workmen's Compensation

Employee who was killed in airplane crash while flying, with his wife, from Milan to Paris after a six day vacation following close of conference at Paris to which his employer had sent him was deemed to have been in his employment for purposes of compensability under Workmen's Compensation Act, where he was to have taken a plane from Paris to home after three hour stop in Paris. Workmen's Compensation Law, § 23.

164

Abraham Markhoff, New York City, for appellant.

George B. Smith, Schenectady, for General Electric Co. and another, respondents.

No appearance for Workmen's Compensation Bd., respondent.

DESMOND, Chief Judge.

Michael Martino, on behalf of whose three children this workmen's compensation death claim was filed, was in 1959 an employee of respondent General Electric Company at Schenectady, N.Y. He and his wife were killed in an airplane crash on a flight from Milan to Paris six days after the close of an international conference held in Paris and which Martino, before going to Italy, had attended at the request of and at the expense of his employer and with the permission of the United States Atomic Energy Commission. The claim was contested by the employer and carrier on the asserted ground that the accidental death did not arise out of or during

165

his employment since at the time of the fatal plane crash Martino was in fact returning to Paris from a vacation trip. The Referee rejected the claim but the Workmen's Compensation Board allowed it, holding that under the circumstances Martino's visit to a country other than France was a reasonable activity within the area of the work which had taken him to Paris and that his death was a risk of his employment. The Appellate Division reversed, the majority being of the view that during Martino's week's vacation (June 21 to June 27) he was on a purely personal venture.

One Justice dissented, suggesting that the case should be remitted to the board for further proof as to whether when he left Milan Martino had begun his homeward journey to New York and Schenectady with a brief stop only at Paris and had thus resumed his employment. Claimant appeals here as of right.

We order a reversal and reinstatement of the claim, being of the opinion that the record contains factual justification for the board's holding of "arising out of and in the course of his employment" and that the Appellate Division should not have held on the law that this finding was without support.

The principal facts were stipulated and are tersely summarized in the Appellate Division memorandum as follows: "Decedent had spent the period from June 15 to 20, 1959, attending a conference in Paris, France, at which he represented the employer. The employer agreed to pay his transportation from New York to Paris, his hotel and personal expenses while at the conference, and his return fare from Paris to New York. Decedent also had permission to take his wife with him to Europe and to take a week's vacation fromJune 21 to June 27, 1959, after the Paris conference had concluded. However, decedent was to pay all of his wife's transportation and other expenses, and was to pay all expenses for both himself and his wife during the vacation week. Following the Paris conference decedent and his wife went to Milan, Italy, where they spent the week's vacation, and while they were returning by commercial plane from Milan to Paris where they were to take another plane for New York, the plane crashed on June 26, and both were killed." To that summary we add other material which appears in the

166

record and which shows the following itinerary arranged for and followed by Martino and his wife:

'Lv. Paris	June 20	5.50pm	UT715
Arr Nice		7.55pm	
Lv. Milan	June 26	5.05pm	TWA891
Arr Paris		7.00pm	
Lv. Paris		10.00pm	TW801
Arr New York	27	7.25am."	

That means that the Martinos, after having left France for Italy when the conference ended on June 20, stayed in Nice and in Italy until the afternoon of June 26 on which date they left Milan at 5:05 P.M. on a TWA flight for Paris which was due in the latter city at 7:00 P.M. but crashed en route, and that they were booked to fly out of Paris at 10 o'clock that same evening on another TWA flight due to arrive in New York the next morning.

[1,2] The courts are bound by the Workmen's Compensation Board's fact findings which, including the ultimate fact of "arising out of and in the course of," must stand unless erroneous in law and whether or not conflicting inferences are available (Workmen's Compensation Law, Consol.Laws c. 67, § 23; Matter of Glielmi v. Netherland Dairy Co., 254 N.Y. 60, 64, 171 N.E. 906, 907). Applying that concept to this case, the award must stand if there is support for the board's finding, made here as it was made in Matter of Scott v. U.S.O. Camp Shows, 274 App.Div. 862, 82 N.Y.S.2d 118, affd. 298 N.Y. 896, 84 N.E.2d 808, that the employee had returned to the employment when the accident happened. The Scott case is a controlling and convincing authority for reversal of the order now on appeal. Susan Scott was a professional dancer employed to do U.S.O. shows for United States soldiers in Europe. It was a term of her contract that after three months in the American occupation zone in Germany she was to have a week's vacation with pay. When that vacation time began at the close of a performance she with other members of the cast went on an automobile trip to Paris for sightseeing and shopping. A week later while returning by automobile to Germany to resume her performances she was injured in an automobile accident. The Workmen's Compensation Board, the Appellate Division and this court held that the authorized and paid vacation was an incident of

167

her employment, especially since the accident occurred when she was on her way back to the place where she would resume work. It is true that in the present case Martino's journey from Milan back to the United States was to be broken by a stopover in Paris but that interruption was for three hours only and he was to continue on a plane of the same airline which had transported him from Milan. If he could have booked a direct flight from Milan to New York there would probably be no dispute of the claim. But the actual stopover in Paris was not to carry out some separate private purpose of Martino's but came about because of the way his tour was worked out by a travel agency. The employer itself recognized this when in its first report of injury in response to the question "What was employee doing when accident occurred?" it answered "Returning from trip which involved attendance at International Conference on Information Processing, Paris, France (June 15-20) & vacation (June 22-26)." This confirms the fact that he was on a return journey to his work in Schenectady via Paris whither his employer's business had taken him.

The rule of coverage applied in our decisions in Matter of Scott v. U.S.O. Camp Shows, 298 N.Y. 896, 84 N.E.2d 808, supra and Matter of Lyons v. U.S.O. Camp Shows, 298 N.Y. 897, 84 N.E.2d 808, are not to be limited to traveling actors. Martino, too, was, like claimants Scott and Lyons, on his way to resume his employment when the disaster occurred and it follows that he, too, must be deemed to have been in the employment for purposes of compensability.

Matter of Davis v. Newsweek Magazine, 305 N.Y. 20, 24-26, 110 N.E.2d 406, 407-409 rejected the compensation claim but only because the travels of Davis "though * * * twofold in purpose, were predominantly in furtherance of the personally motivated vacation trip, except for which he would not have gone." It is clear from the Davis record that he and his wife were on a vacation trip with no obligation to write any articles for his employer but a vague thought that he should do so if he cared to. Relevant here is Matter of Lewis v. Knappen Tippetts Abbett Engineering Company, 304 N.Y. 461, 108 N.E.2d 609, where the employee, hired to work in Israel and having completed his work there, went off on a sightseeing trip without any particular permission from his employer during the course of which he was shot and killed by an Arab soldier. This court pointed out in Lewis that he

168

and the claimants in Matter of Scott v. U.S.O. Camp Shows, 298 N.Y. 896, 84 N.E.2d 808, supra and Matter of Lyons v. U.S.O. Camp Shows, 298 N.Y. 897, 84 N.E.2d 808, supra, were all on personal vacation trips but returning to work when injured or killed. In Lewis, as here, the argument was that the journey during which Lewis was shot "was a voluntary one unrelated to the employment and undertaken by decedent for his own pleasure" (304 N.Y. 461, 466, 108 N.E.2d 609, 611). We, rejecting this, said that "the courts have been most reluctant to come to such a conclusion (if indeed, they have ever so come in any reported case) in situations where the employment is far from home, the employee has no fixed hours, excursions to nearby places of interest are available and expected, and where the employment itself exposes claimant, generally, to the rise." We noted in the Lewis opinion (304 N.Y. p. 467, 108 N.E.2d pp. 611-612) that claimant when killed by a random bullet was "waiting passage to Greece" where he had another business engagement for his employer.

We see no necessity for remitting the case for further proof with respect to the question whether Martino had begun his homeward journey when he left Milan. There is enough in this record to justify an inference that he had. The Workmen's Compensation Board validly drew that inference.

The order should be reversed and the award reinstated, with costs to appellant in this court.

DYE, FULD, BURKE, FOSTER and SCILEPPI, JJ., concur with DESMOND, C.J.; VAN VOORHIS, J., dissents and votes to affirm upon the memorandum opinion of the Appellate Division.

Order reversed, with costs against respondent and carrier, and the award of the Workmen's Compensation Board reinstated.

The following are summaries of cases in which the courts held that the employee's injury or death did not occur within his duties of employment.

1. In Ruffi v. American Fly Away Service Inc. 104 N.W.2d 37 (Ohio 1950), a pilot ferrying an aircraft, departed from flight altitude, buzzed a fishing boat and, as a consequence, crashed the aircraft. The court held that he was not acting within the scope of his employment and therefore not covered by Workmen's Compensation Law of his state.
2. In Lange v. Memphis, St. Paul Metropolitan Airports Commission 99 N.W.2d 915 (Minn. 1959), an airport supervisor was instructed by his employer that flying aircraft was not a part of his duties and that flying was not permitted during working hours. The Supervisor, while flying in violation of these instructions, crashed the aircraft. The court held he was not covered by Workmen's Compensation Act of his state.
3. In Williams v. Central Flying Service Inc., 368 S.W.2d 87 (Ark. 1963), a part-time employee of a fixed-base operator, crashed in an aircraft, while flying as a passenger. The court held that the employee was not acting within the scope of his employment and therefore not covered by the State's Workmen's Compensation Act.
4. In Gaumer v. The Industrial Commission of Arizona, 382 Pac.2d 673 (1963), a full-time employee of a fixed-base operator, while piloting an aircraft during working hours crashed the plane. The aircraft was owned by the third party, and the employee was preparing the aircraft for a later ferry flight, as an independent contractor. The court held that the employee was not acting within the scope of his employment and therefore not covered by Workmen's Compensation.
5. In Whitely v. King Radio Corporation 375 Pac.2d 593 (Kansas 1962), an engineer was taking flying lessons at the expense of his employer. The flying, however, had no relationship to the duties of his employment. The court held he was not covered by Workmen's Compensation.

The Ruffi v. American court case is presented below to illustrate a factual situation in which the court found that the employee was not covered by the State's Workmen's Compensation Act, and the reasoning of the court in arriving at its decision.

104 N.E. 2d 37
RUFFI v. AMERICAN FLY AWAY SERVICE, Inc.
Court of Appeals of Ohio,
Montgomery County.
Dec. 15, 1950.

Proceeding under the Workmen's Compensation Act by Cecelia W. Ruffi against the American Fly Away Service, Inc. The Court of Common Pleas denied the plaintiff the right to participate in the Workmen's Compensation Fund and the plaintiff appealed on questions of law. The Court of Appeals, Miller, P.J., held that the plaintiff's decedent was not an independent contractor.

Judgment affirmed.

1. Workmen's Compensation

Workmen's Compensation Act does not apply where the injured person is an independent contractor and the relation of employer and employee does not exist.

2. Workmen's Compensation

Whether one is an independent contractor or an employee depends upon the facts of each case.

3. Workmen's Compensation

Where employer, who hired pilot to fly new or used aircraft to various locations throughout the United States, had not reserved the right to control the manner or means of doing the work, and pilot was to be responsible to the employer only for the result, an independent contractor relationship not within workmen's compensation law existed.

4. Workmen's Compensation

An injury to be compensable under the compensation law must have been received while employee was engaged in the promotion of employer's business and in the furtherance of his affairs.

5. Workmen's Compensation

Where pilot who had been employed to pilot airplanes on as direct a route as possible and at an altitude commensurate with terrain and weather conditions, was killed when he deliberately departed from his course and dove his plane down to a lake to "buzz" a fishing boat, not only on one occasion, but a second time, pilot was not acting within the scope of his employment at the time he met his death.

6. Workmen's Compensation

Where plaintiff's motion to make Industrial Commission of Ohio a party defendant in workmen's compensation action, was not made until after the verdict had been rendered in favor of defendant, motion was not timely made and was properly overruled.

Vradelis, McCray and McCray, Dayton, for plaintiff-appellant.
Pickrel, Schaeffer & Ebeling, Dayton, for defendant-appellee.

MILLER, Presiding Judge.

This is a law appeal from the judgment of the Court of Common Pleas denying the plaintiff-appellant the right to participate in the Workmen's Compensation Fund. At the close of all of the evidence the defendant moved for an instructed verdict for the defendant for the following reasons:

1. The plaintiff's decedent was not an employee as defined in the Workmen's Compensation Act.

2. The plaintiff's decedent was not killed in the course of his employment, if he was an employee.

The court sustained the motion on each of the grounds set forth and a judgment was rendered on the verdict. The appellant urges that the record presented issues of fact which should have been submitted to the jury for its determination.

The record discloses that the defendant, the American Fly Away Service, Inc., was engaged in the business of ferrying small airplanes from the place of manufacture to various places of distribution and sale located throughout the United States on the date on which the plaintiff's decedent was killed; that the defendant's business had been in operation for several years; that it was quite extensive, at times having as many as fifty pilots engaged in this service. The decedent was one of the pilots and at the time of his death was making delivery of an airplane for the defendant.

The record discloses that on June 5, 1946, the plaintiff's decedent and the defendant entered into a written agreement containing the following provisions pertinent to the issues here presented: The parties to the contract will be referred to as "pilot" and defendant."

Item 1. The pilot agreed to fly new or used aircraft to various locations throughout the United States.

2. Pilot to be paid compensation in advance.

3. * * *

4. All expenses incurred by the pilot as the result of delays to be borne by the pilot unless it exceeded two days through no fault of his own, in which event the expenses beyond the two days would be paid by the defendant.

5. Pilot shall pay all of his traveling expenses and shall have exclusive right to determine the mode of his transportation, routes, etc.

6. The pilot was to be the sole judge of the route to fly and under what weather conditions he would fly, but it was specifically agreed that the pilot would abide by the rules and regulations prescribed by competent authorities; that all methods and means of delivery shall be determined by the pilot who was to be responsible to the defendant for the results.

7. The pilot was to furnish all necessary equipment such as navigation maps, charts, etc.

8. The pilot agreed to operate each and every aircraft in accordance with the manufacturer's recommendation.

9. The pilot agreed to furnish all gas and oil necessary to be used and to be responsible for having the aircraft properly tied down or hangared at night and to bear all necessary expenses for this.

10. If grounded for any reason the pilot agreed to remain with the aircraft at his own expense until a representative of the defendant arrived. In case that he stopped over night the pilot agreed to wire his location and his expected future itinerary to the defendant at his own expense.

11. The pilot was not compelled to accept any aircraft offered to him, having the right to refuse the same without stating the cause.

12. The pilot agreed to incur no expense on the defendant without advance authorization.

13. * * *

14. * * *

15. The pilot reserved the right to work when he pleased and to engage in other occupations of his choice, such as flight instruction, etc.

16. * * *

17. The pilot agreed that when he accepted an aircraft for delivery he would do so as soon as possible and that he would not at any time or under any circumstances use the aircraft for any purpose whatsoever not absolutely necessary for the delivery of said aircraft.

18. The pilot agreed to be responsible for his own acts, being an independent contractor, and would not be protected under the policy of insurance carried by the defendant.

19. The pilot agreed to reimburse the defendant for damage to any aircraft in amounts not covered by the defendant's policies of insurance.

20. * * *

21. The pilot agreed not to carry passengers at any time except when requested to do so by the defendant and when so requested he was to be paid additional compensation.

22. * * *

23. * * *

The record discloses further that on July 23, 1946, the date of the fatal accident, the plaintiff's decedent piloted an airplane from Middletown, Ohio, to Washington, D.C., under the said contract. At approximately 3:30 p.m. the same day he was assigned another airplane to fly from Washington, D.C., to Chicago, Illinois. While flying near Deep Creek Lake, Maryland, he swerved approximately half a mile off of his course in order to fly low or buzz a fishing boat on the lake. His plane was the lead plane followed by two others. He signalled them to buzz the fishing boat with him, which they did. However, the decedent decided to return and buzz the boat again, which he did, but this time he went too low and struck a cable, which caused him to lose control of his airplane, resulting in his death.

The evidence discloses that upon the delivery of an airplane the decedent was directed to pick up a release and receipt which released the defendant from liability and he was also directed by defendant to pick up payment for the delivery charge, which was to be returned to the defendant.

[1,2] The evidence offered was sufficient to make the defendant amenable to the act provided the deceased was an employee acting within the scope of his employment. The compensation law does not apply where the injured person is an independent contractor and the relation of employer and employee does not exist. Industrial Commission v. McAdow, 126 Ohio St. 198, 184 N.E. 759. Whether one is an independent contractor or an employee depends upon the facts of each case.

In Gillum v. Industrial Commission, 141 Ohio St. 373, 48 N.E.2d 234, syllabus 2 in part provides: "* * * The principal test applied to determine the character of the arrangement is that if the employer reserves the right to control the manner or means of doing the work, the relation created is that of master and servant, while if the manner or means of doing the work or job is left to one who is responsible to the employer only for the result, an independent contractor relationship is thereby created."

[3] It is our conclusion that there was no evidence presented to show that the defendant herein reserved the right to control the manner or means of doing the work herein; that all the evidence clearly showed that the pilot was to be responsible to the employer only for the result and that therefore an independent contractor relationship existed.

[4,5] We shall next consider the question whether or not the plaintiff's decedent, if he were an employee, was acting within the scope of his employment at the time he met his untimely death. The appellant urges that the hazard of monotony while flying an airplane is a hazard that has a causal relationship or connection with the accident. We concede that monotony may be such a hazard, and injuries resulting therefrom would be compensable, but here we have a different situation. The plaintiff's decedent deliberately departed from his course and dove his plane down to the lake, not only on one occasion, but a second time, which resulted in his death. We think that this was clearly a departure from the scope of employment. In order to be compensable the injury must have been received while the employee was engaged in the promotion of the employer's business and in the furtherance of his affairs. Industrial Commission of Ohio v. Bateman, 126 Ohio St. 279, 185 N.E. 50. Georgejakakis v. Wheeling Steel Corporation, 151 Ohio St. 458, 86 N.E.2d 594. The appellant cites the cause of Laudato v. Hunkin-Conkey Construction Company, 135 Ohio St. 127, 19 N.E.2d 898, but we think this case is distinguishable on the facts from the case at bar. In the cited case the employee's duties required him to ascend to an upper floor and then to descend to the ground floor in the performance of his duties of unloading certain debris for his employer. While performing such duties he was injured. In the case at bar the plaintiff's decedent was not under contract or required to descend from a high altitude to a low altitude in order to see how close he could come to a fishing boat on the surface of the lake. He was under contract to fly a plane on as direct a route as possible and at an altitude commensurate with terrain and weather conditions, and there is nothing in the record to indicate that these conditions caused him to descend in the manner in which he did. We think the court ruled properly in sustaining the defendant's motion.

[6] The second error assigned is that the court erred in overruling the plaintiff's motion to make the Industrial Commission of Ohio a party defendant. This motion, the record discloses, was not made until after the verdict had been rendered in favor of the defendant. It was therefore not seasonably made and the trial court did not err in its ruling.

The judgment will be affirmed.

HORNBECK and WISEMAN, JJ., concur.

CHAPTER 8

Warsaw Convention Limitation of Liability

The Warsaw Convention of 1929 (The Convention for the Unification of Certain Rules Relating to International Transportation by Air), is a treaty to which the United States became a party on June 15, 1934, when the United States Senate gave its "advice and consent."

The purpose of the Warsaw Convention was to limit the liability of the Air Carriers in the fledgling aviation industry of the 1920's. It is felt, in some quarters, that the airline industry does not now need the protection that it was afforded in its young years.

There is legal opinion that the limited liability provision (Article 22), and the venue provision (Article 28), of the Warsaw Convention deny equal rights of American Citizens under the U.S. Constitution. In November 7, 1968, Judge Nicholas J. Bua of the Circuit Court of Cook County, Illinois handed down a lengthy Memorandum Opinion on this question (Burdell v. Canadian Pacific Airlines, No. 66L–10799, Cook County Circuit Court, Nov. 7, 1968). This case did not go to a higher court for appeal, because it was settled for $215,000.00 in favor of the plaintiff. The air carrier requested the court to withdraw that part of the ruling which related to constitutionality. The court granted the motion, but stated that, as concerns this case, the venue and damage limitation provisions of the Warsaw Convention were unconstitutional. This opinion, therefore, remains an important precedent on the constitutionality of Warsaw Articles 22, and 28. (Also refer to Illinois Bar Journal, February 1970, John J. Kennelly.)

The following case of Grey v. American Airlines presents a discussion of several articles of the Warsaw Convention. This case will illustrate how the Convention is applied to a factual situation.

Refer to Extract F, Warsaw Convention, Articles 22 and 25

227 F. 2d 282

Doris Sylvia GREY, infant, and Howard Martin Grey, infant, children of Harry M. Goldberg, deceased, and Sophie Goldberg, deceased, by Esther Weiner, their guardian ad litem, Plaintiffs-Appellants,

v.

AMERICAN AIRLINES, Inc., Defendant-Appellee.

No. 73, Docket 23601.

United States Court of Appeals Second Circuit.

Argued Oct. 7, 1955.

Decided Nov. 7, 1955.

Action against airline for death of passengers. The United States District Court for the Southern District of New York, Edward A. Conger, J., set aside verdict for plaintiffs and directed judgment for plaintiffs in amount of $16,600 only, and plaintiffs appealed. The Court of Appeals, Medina, J., held that where plaintiffs relied on Warsaw Convention provision excepting cases of wilful misconduct from provision limiting recovery, evidence was insufficient to take to jury question whether airline had been guilty of wilful misconduct.

Affirmed.

1. Carriers

That airplane passenger tickets did not make reference to intermediate agreed stopping places did not render Warsaw Convention limitation of liability defenses inapplicable to action for death of passengers in crash at one of the intermediate points. Warsaw Convention of Oct. 29, 1934, art. 8, 49 Stats. 3000 et seq., 3016.

2. Federal Civil Procedure

In action against airline for death of passengers, wherein airline, at outset and in motions for directed verdicts at close of plaintiffs' case, urged that there could be no recovery in excess of Warsaw Convention limitation, and raised contention again at close of all evidence, that motion at close of all evidence made no specific reference to one of the deceased passengers did not deprive trial court of power to set aside verdict and direct judgment for plaintiffs for limited recovery for all deaths. Fed.Rules Civ.Proc. rule 50(b), 28 U.S.C.A.; Warsaw Convention of Oct. 29, 1934, art. 17, 49 Stat. 3018.

3. Carriers

In an action against an airline for death of passengers, airline, under Warsaw Convention, had burden of proving that it took all necessary measures to avoid damage or that it was impossible to take them. Warsaw Convention of Oct. 29, 1934, arts. 17, 20(1), 22(1), 25, 49 Stats. 3018, 3019, 3020.

4. Carriers

In action, under Warsaw Convention, against airline for death of passengers, plaintiffs, in attempt to avoid Convention provision limiting recovery except in cases of wilful misconduct, had burden of proving misconduct by a fair preponderance of credible evidence. Warsaw Convention of Oct. 29, 1934, arts. 17, 20(1), 22(1), 25, 49 Stats. 3018, 3019, 3020.

5. Carriers

"Wilful misconduct," within Warsaw Convention provision limiting recovery for airline passengers' death except in case of wilful misconduct, requires proof of a conscious intent to do or omit doing an act from which harm results to another, or an intentional omission of a manifest duty, and there must be a realization of the probability of injury from conduct, and a disregard of probable consequences of such conduct. Warsaw Convention of Oct. 29, 1934, arts. 17, 20(1), 22(1), 25, 49 Stats. 3018, 3019, 3020.

6. Carriers

In action against airline for death of passengers, all questions of credibility were for jury, and where conflicting inferences were rationally admissible, it was function of jury to take those which they considered most consistent with general pattern of proofs.

7. Courts

On appeal from orders setting aside verdict for plaintiffs in action against airline for death of passengers and directing verdict for defendants, plaintiffs were entitled to have evidence viewed in light most favorable to themselves.

8. Federal Civil Procedure

In action against airline for death of passengers, wherein plaintiffs alleged, for purposes of circumventing Warsaw Convention limitations, wilful misconduct on part of airline, trial judge had right to reject finding of wilful misconduct only if, on no possible view of evidence, could reasonable men have reached that conclusion.

9. Carriers

In action against airlines for death of passengers, wherein plaintiffs relied on Warsaw Convention provision excepting cases of wilful misconduct from provision limiting recovery, evidence was insufficient to take to jury question whether airline had been guilty of wilful misconduct. Warsaw Convention of Oct. 29, 1934, arts. 20(1), 25, 49 Stats. 3019, 3020.

10. Carriers

Jury in action against airline for death of passengers was entitled to disregard testimony of one witness, or any part of it, and to accept testimony of another in its entirety.

Manes, Sturim, Donovan & Laufer, New York City (Arthur M. Laufer and Samuel S. Sturim, New York City, on the brief), for plaintiffs-appellants.

Haight, Gardner, Poor & Havens, New York City (William J. Junkerman and James B. McQuillan, New York City, of counsel), for defendant-appellee.

Before HAND, MEDINA and LUMBARD, Circuit Judges.

MEDINA, Circuit Judge.

The parents of the infant plaintiffs and twenty-six other persons met their deaths during the early hours of the morning of November 29, 1949, when defendant's Douglas DC-6 airplane, on an international flight from New York to Mexico City, crashed at Love Field, Dallas, Texas.

[1] While plaintiffs contended that the Warsaw Convention was not applicable, because the passenger tickets issued to decedents did not make reference to the intermediate "agreed stopping places"[1] of Washington, D.C., and Dallas, Texas, motions to strike the usual Warsaw Convention limitation of liability defenses, based upon this technical and wholly unsubstantial alleged omission, were denied before trial by Judge Noonan. We agree with Judge Noonan's reasoning and see no occasion to elaborate upon his carefully prepared opinion. Grey v. American Airlines, D.C.S.D.N.Y.1950, 95 F.Supp. 756.

At the trial the principal issue was whether or not plaintiffs had adduced evidence sufficient to support a finding that the disaster was due to "wilful misconduct" on the part of defendant's employees, or any of them. The jury found that it was; but the trial judge, after taking under advisement defendant's motion to set aside the verdicts and direct judgment in favor of plaintiffs for $16,600, or the limited amount of $8300 on account of the death of each decedent, reviewed the evidence in some detail and, in the order now appealed from, granted the motion.

[2] *In limine* plaintiffs contend that the trial judge lacked power to entertain the motion, at least with reference to so much of plaintiffs' claim as arises out of the death of the mother, Sophie Goldberg, under Fed.Rules Civ. Proc. rule 50(b), 28 U.S.C.A. because no motion for a directed verdict was made by defendant "at the close of all the evidence" to the effect that the jury should find in plaintiffs' favor for the sum of $8300 "arising out of the death of Sophie Goldberg." We had supposed the winds of time had long since carried into oblivion such flimsy excuses for avoiding a consideration of the merits of a case. From the outset defendant urged that there could be no recovery in excess of $8300 for the death of either decedent; motions for directed verdicts with respect to the claims arising out of each of the two deaths were made at the close of plaintiffs' case; the contention was again made *in extenso* at the close of all the evidence. It was mere inadvertence that no reference was again made specifically to Sophie Goldberg. Accordingly, the trial judge had ample authority under Rule 50(b) to set aside or disregard the verdicts and dispose of the case with finality, subject to appellate review.

1. Presidential Proclamation of October 29, 1934, 49 Stat. Pt. 2 at p. 3000 et seq.

The plane left La Guardia Airport at 10:30 P.M.; took off from Washington, D.C., for Dallas at 12:54 A.M., and, when in the vicinity of Nashville, Tennessee, the outboard engine on the port wing, known as the #1 engine, commenced to backfire, as a result of which it was feathered and shut off. Without further incident Dallas was sighted and the plane was cleared to land on runway 36. We are concerned with what occurred between the time the plane crossed the boundary of the airport at an altitude of 200 feet, until it crashed on top of the hangar of the Dallas Aviation School on the edge of the airport opposite the direction tower. The crew, consisting of the Captain, the First Officer and the Flight Engineer, survived; and their testimony gives us a certain amount of data, together with some flat contradictions and a mass of conflicting possible inferences. Before giving a brief resume of the evidence, it will be well to set forth the applicable law.

[3] The scheme of the Warsaw Convention is pretty plain on its face. Chapter III is the one which concerns us here. Article 17 imposes an absolute liability upon the carrier for all personal injuries, regardless of fault, "if the accident which caused the damage so sustained took place on board the aircraft." But this liability is excused by Article 20(1), if "the carrier proves" that it has "taken all necessary measures to avoid the damage or that it was impossible" for it to take them. As to this it is plain that the burden of proof is upon the carrier. And, in passing, it may be noted that in most if not all serious accidents, whether or not members of the crew survive, the difficulties in avoiding this presumptive liability would seem to be almost if not quite insurmountable.

Against this background we come to Article 25, which provides that the carrier shall not be entitled to avail itself "of the provisions of this convention which exclude or limit" its liability, if the damage is caused by its "wilful misconduct." The exclusion refers to Article 20(1), and the limitation to Article 22(1), which provides that "the liability of the carrier for each passenger shall be limited" to $8300. Upon whom is the burden of proving wilful misconduct?

The trial court here instructed the jury that the burden of proving wilful misconduct rested upon plaintiffs, and plaintiffs acquiesced in this, virtually conceding that it was not incumbent upon defendant to sustain the onus of proving a negative. As will shortly appear, the real cause of the crash still remains in doubt, and we feel that the interest of justice requires that we decide this question, even though the parties have apparently taken the answer for granted.

[4] We hold that the trial judge ruled correctly when he charged the jury that plaintiffs could recover no more than $8300 on account of the death of each decedent, unless plaintiffs proved by a fair preponderance of the credible evidence that there was wilful misconduct on the part of defendant's employees, or any of them, which was a "substantial contributing factor" to the accident. The specific language of Article 20(1), above quoted, and the absence of corresponding words in Article 25 would seem to make admissible no other interpretation of the Convention. But perhaps of greater significance is the general purpose of protecting international air carriers from the burden of excessive claims connected with the loss of aircraft under circumstances which make it

impossible, or virtually so, to determine the mechanical or human shortcomings which caused the disaster, because of the death of all on board and the destruction of the plane. We find implicit in the terms of the Convention an intention to relieve the carriers of this burden of proof, whilst at the same time giving the injured parties the opportunity to prove wilful misconduct, if they can.

[5] There is no dispute as to what constitutes wilful misconduct. The instructions required proof of "a conscious intent to do or omit doing an act from which harm results to another, or an intentional omission of a manifest duty. There must be a realization of the probability of injury from the conduct, and a disregard of the probable consequences of such conduct." This was in accordance with precedent. American Airlines v. Ulen, 1949, 87 U.S.App.D.C. 307, 186 F.2d 529; Pekelis v. Transcontinental & Western Air, Inc., 2 Cir., 1951, 187 F.2d 122, 23 A.L.R.2d 1349; Goepp v. American Overseas Airlines, 1952, 281 App.Div. 105, 117 N.Y.S.2d 276, affirmed 305 N.Y. 830, 114 N.E.2d 37, certiorari denied 346 U.S. 874, 74 S.Ct. 124, 98 L.Ed. 382.

[6-8] Moreover, as this is a jury case, plaintiffs are entitled to have the evidence viewed in the light most favorable to plaintiffs. All questions of credibility were for the jury. It was within their province to pick and choose, to accept a part or the whole of the testimony of any particular witness, and to reject the rest. Where conflicting inferences were rationally admissible, it was a function of the jury to take those which they considered most consistent with the general pattern of the proofs. And this congeries is summed up in the general verdicts. The trial judge had a right to reject the finding of wilful misconduct only if, on no possible view of the evidence, could reasonable men reach that conclusion. Binder v. Commercial Travelers, 2 Cir., 1948, 165 F.2d 896; 3 Moore, Federal Practice § 50.01 (1938).

We now return to the evidence of the events which crowded into the brief interval of time between the crossing of the boundary of the airport at a height of 200 feet and the crash.

The Flight Engineer suddenly reported that the fuel flow gauge on engine #4, the outboard starboard engine, read zero. The Captain at once ordered the fuel booster pump applied, and the Captain testified that he felt that engine "surge," which caused the left wing to dip 20° and the plane to swerve to the left and out of line with the runway. Reduction of power on the #3 and #4 engines and increase of power on #2 apparently brought the plane level and she was about 30 or 40 feet above the ground. The Captain says he ordered the landing gear retracted and the flaps raised, with full take-off power on the three operating engines. The First Officer says he did not hear any order but knew from the actions of the Captain that he was attempting to pull up and make another try for the field. That the plane gained altitude is apparent from the fact of where she hit on top of the hangar of the Dallas Aviation School.

But in the interval, without any order from the Captain, the First Officer feathered the #4 engine, and the Captain claims that this was what caused the crash. The First Officer says the instruments indicated that #4 was "windmilling," that the unfeathered propeller without power behind it would operate as a drag, and that he left the flaps as they were because to level them off would, in his opinion, have resulted in an immediate loss of altitude. There was testimony that there was still power in #4 and that the levelling of the flaps would have helped the plane to rise, although this seems improbable in view of her position so close to the ground. In any event, the plane stalled and fell.

If defendant had the burden of proving that there was no wilful misconduct on the part of any member of the crew, we think a jury would have been warranted in finding on this record that the burden had not been sustained. There are too many gaps and imponderables, to say nothing of the conflicts and inconsistencies, some of which we have not thought it necessary to collate.

[9] But we cannot discover anything in the case to warrant a finding that there was wilful misconduct. It is said that the Captain was in command and that he was the only one authorized by Civil Air Regulations 61.301, 61.310, to act in an emergency. But we find nothing in the Regulations to justify this conclusion. The plane was *in extremis;* whatever the First Officer did or failed to do was done to save the plane and the lives of all on board including his own.

[10] True it is that the jury were entitled to disregard the testimony of the First Officer, or any part of it, and to accept the testimony of the Captain in its entirety. But even so the record is still devoid of any evidence of wilful misconduct.

Much is also said on plaintiffs' behalf of defective instruments and previous backfiring by the engine which was feathered when near Nashville, but it is abundantly plain to us that each and every member of the crew thought the plane was airworthy when they left Washington, D.C. for Dallas; and the evidence referred to is of trivial consequence.

Other alleged errors seem to us not to warrant discussion.

Affirmed.

The following several summarized cases utilize and refer to several articles of the Warsaw Convention. In order to understand the meaning of the decisions refer to the relevant Warsaw Convention Articles in Extract F.

In Ross v. Pan American Airlines 85 N.E.2d 881 (N.Y. 1949), a carrier airline chartered an aircraft to the U.S. Government to carry a U.S.O. entertainment troupe overseas. The tickets for the flight were delivered to the liaison officer in charge of the U.S.O. troupe. The plaintiff, a member of the entertainment troupe was injured in a crash, during the flight. The defendant air carrier, in this case, asserted that the limited liability provisions of Warsaw Article 22 applied, and therefore, the carrier's liability was limited to $8,300.00.

> In an effort to remove the limited liability provisions of the Warsaw Convention from protecting the carrier and the U.S. Government, the plaintiff asserted two claims.
>
> The Plaintiff asserted that Warsaw Convention Article 2 applied because the flight was being made "directly" by the U.S. and if so, then the limited liability of the Warsaw Convention would not apply to the U.S. Government. The court held that the flight was chartered by the U.S. Government and therefore the limited liability of Warsaw Convention Article 22 applied.
>
> Secondly, the Plaintiff asserted that there was not sufficient delivery of tickets to passengers as required by Warsaw Convention Article 3, and therefore the limited liability of the Warsaw Convention did not apply. The court also rejected this assertion and stated that delivery to the liaison officer constituted sufficient delivery of tickets to the members of the U.S.O. troupe. Therefore the limited liability of Article 22 applied.

In Mertens v. Flying Tiger Lines, 341 F.2d 851 (Feb. 16, 1965), an aircraft, with crew, was chartered to the U.S. Government, and the tickets were not delivered to passengers until after the aircraft was airborne. The plaintiff passenger, in this case, asserted that there was not sufficient delivery of tickets under Warsaw Convention Article 3, and therefore the limited liability provisions of the Warsaw Convention did not apply to the air carrier. The court held that there was not sufficient delivery and therefore the limited liability provisions of Warsaw Convention Article 22 was not applicable.

In Kraus v. K.L.M., 92 N.Y.S.2d 315 (Oct. 17, 1949), an air freight "airwaybill" did not give a list of agreed stopping places as required by Warsaw Convention Article 8. However, the air freight "airwaybill" did make reference to a timetable list of scheduled stopping places. The plaintiff shipper asserted that since the "airwaybill" did not set forth the stopping places, then Warsaw Convention Article 9 would apply and the carrier would not be able to use the limited liability provisions of the Convention. The court held that the reference to the timetable was sufficient compliance with Warsaw Convention Article 8, and therefore the limited liability provided by Article 20 would be applied in favor of the carrier defendant.

CHAPTER 9

Liability of Manufacturers and Repairers

The liability of manufacturers and repairers to the buyers or passengers of their products is a dynamic aspect of aviation law. The two landmark cases, set forth here in their entirety as they are presented in the West Legal Reporter System, are MacPherson v. Buick, and Goldberg v. Kollsman.

The first question that must be resolved in manufacturer liability cases, is whether there is privity of contract between the buyer and the manufacturer; and whether that privity of contract is necessary to hold the manufacturer liable to the buyer for injury inflicted on the buyer from the manufacturer's products.

The courts have held that privity of contract is not necessary to hold the manufacturer liable.

The second question that must be resolved is whether the manufacturer is liable to the buyer on the legal theory that there is a tort, or on the theory that there is a breach of contract liability. This is an important question to be resolved.

If the manufacturer is liable on the basis of torts, then the plaintiff buyer has the burden of proving that the defendant manufacturer is negligent, because the manufacturer is presumed innocent until proved negligent. In addition, the defendant manufacturer has the following defenses by which he can wholly or partially escape liability:

1. The defendant can allege contributory negligence by the plaintiff buyer.
2. The defendant can allege that the plaintiff buyer assumed an unjustifiable risk.
3. The defendant can allege that the plaintiff violated a statute or ordinance.

If the manufacturer is liable on the contractual basis, whether it is actually written or implied, then the same manufacturer can be sued by the buyer on the basis that the manufacturer breached a warranty of contract. The warranty can be written or implied. Of course in this contractual situation the plaintiff is in a stronger position than in that of tort liability. If the plaintiff buyer can sue the defendant manufacturer on the basis that the manufacturer breached a warranty of contract, then the advantage to the plaintiff is threefold:

1. The plaintiff buyer does not have the burden of proving that defendant manufacturer is negligent.
2. The defendant manufacturer is presumed negligent and therefore has the burden of proving that he was not negligent.
3. The defendant does not have the three defenses set forth above in the theory of tort liability.

The case of MacPherson v. Buick covers the general analysis of the liability theories.

The case of Goldberg v. Kollsman applies the theory to the aircraft.

---

217 N.Y. 382
MacPHERSON v. BUICK MOTOR CO.
(Cite as 111 N.E. 1050)
(Court of Appeals of New York.
March 14, 1916.)

1. Negligence—Liability of Manufacturers—Character of Goods

The principle that the manufacturer or seller of goods is liable for injuries to persons due to defects therein, is not limited to things which, in their normal operation, are implements of destruction, but if the nature of the thing is such that it is reasonably certain to place persons in peril when negligently made, the liability attaches, irrespective of contract for failure properly to inspect and discover defects, coupled with knowledge of probable danger therefrom.

2. Negligence—Liability of Manufacturers—Probable Danger

The mere fact that danger may possibly result from the character of the goods sold is insufficient to make the manufacturer liable for injuries, and it must appear that injury would probably result.

3. Negligence—Liability of Manufacturers—Questions for Jury

Whether the character of an article manufactured is such that injury would probably result from its use may be a question for the court or for the jury.

4. Negligence—Liability of Manufacturer—Knowledge of Danger

In order to make the manufacturer liable for defects in goods sold, he must have knowledge that in the usual course of events the danger will be shared by others than the buyer, although mere knowledge alone is insufficient to create his liability.

5. Negligence—Liability of Manufacturer—Duty to Inspect

The duty of a manufacturer to inspect his goods so as to guard against injuries to persons therefrom is independent of contract, and the obligation arises at law.

6. Negligence—Liability of Manufacturers—Duty to Inspect—Dangerous Articles

An automobile is such a dangerous article that a manufacturer thereof is under duty carefully to inspect in order to prevent injuries to persons arising from defects therein.

7. Negligence–Liability of Manufacturers–Knowledge of Use

Where an automobile manufacturer knew that the car which he sold would be used by persons other than the buyer, and the ultimate buyer of the car was injured when a wheel, made of defective wood and defectively constructed, collapsed, the manufacturer was liable for the injuries.

8. Negligence–Liability of Manufacturers–Imminence of Danger

The liability of a manufacturer for injuries caused by a defectively constructed automobile, if danger was to be reasonably expected therefrom, attached regardless of whether the danger was inherent or only imminent, so that it was not error to instruct that the automobile was not an inherently dangerous machine.

9. Negligence–Liability of Manufacturers–Duty to Inspect

A manufacturer of automobiles is not absolved from the duty of inspection because he bought the wheels from a reputable manufacturer, but he is responsible for the finished product.

10. Negligence–Liability of Manufacturers–
Character of Danger–Duty of Inspection

The duty of a manufacturer to inspect goods produced by him varies with the nature of the thing to be inspected, and is higher where the article itself is dangerous and greater degree of caution is required.

Willard Bartlett, C.J., dissenting.

Appeal from Supreme Court, Appellate Division, Third Department.

Action by Donald C. MacPherson against the Buick Motor Company. From a judgment of the Appellate Division (160 App. Div. 55, 145 N.Y. Supp. 462), affirming a judgment of the Supreme Court for plaintiff, defendant appeals. Affirmed.

William Van Dyke, of Detroit, Mich., for appellant. Edgar T. Brackett, of Saratoga Springs, for respondent.

CARDOZO, J. The defendant is a manufacturer of automobiles. It sold an automobile to a retail dealer. The retail dealer resold to the plaintiff. While the plaintiff was in the car it suddenly collapsed. He was thrown out and injured. One of the wheels was made of defective wood, and its spokes crumbled into fragments. The wheel was not made by the defendant; it was bought from another manufacturer. There is evidence, however, that its defects could have been discovered by reasonable inspection, and that inspection was omitted. There is no claim that the defendant knew of the defect and willfully concealed it. The case, in other words, is not brought within the rule of Kuelling v. Lean Mfg. Co., 183 N.Y. 78, 75 N.E. 1098, 2 L.R.A. (N.S.) 303, 111 Am. St. Rep. 691, 5 Ann. Cas. 124. The charge is one, not of fraud, but of negligence. The question to be determined is whether the defendant owed a duty of care and vigilance to any one but the immediate purchaser.

The foundations of this branch of the law, at least in this state, were laid in Thomas v. Winchester, 6 N.Y. 397, 57 Am. Dec. 455. A poison was falsely labeled. The sale was made to a druggist, who in turn sold to a customer. The customer recovered damages from the seller who affixed the label. "The defendant's negligence," it was said, "put human life in imminent danger." A poison, falsely labeled, is likely to injure any one who gets it. Because the danger is to be foreseen, there is a duty to avoid the injury. Cases were cited by way of illustration in which manufacturers were not subject to any duty irrespective of contract. The distinction was said to be that their conduct, though negligent, was not likely to result in injury to any one except the purchaser. We are not required to say whether the chance of injury was always as remote as the distinction assumes. Some of the illustrations might be rejected to-day. The principle of the distinction is, for present purposes, the important thing. Thomas v. Winchester became quickly a landmark of the law. In the application of its principle there may, at times, have been uncertainty or even error. There has never in this state been doubt or disavowal of the principle itself. The chief cases are well known, yet to recall some of them will be helpful. Loop v. Litchfield, 42 N.Y. 351, 1 Am. Rep. 513, is the earliest. It was the case of a defect in a small balance wheel used on a circular saw. The manufacturer pointed out the defect to the buyer, who wished a cheap article and was ready to assume the risk. The risk can hardly have been an imminent one, for the wheel lasted five years before it broke. In the meanwhile the buyer had made a lease of the machinery. It was held that the manufacturer was not answerable to the lessee. Loop v. Litchfield was followed in Losee v. Clute, 51 N.Y. 494, 10 Am. Rep. 638, the case of the explosion of a steam boiler. That decision has been criticized (Thompson on Negligence, 233; Shearman & Redfield on Negligence [6th Ed.] § 117); but it must be confined to its special facts. It was put upon the ground that the risk of injury was too remote. The buyer in that case had not only accepted the boiler, but had tested it. The manufacturer knew that his own test was not the final one. The finality of the test has a bearing on the measure of diligence owing to persons other than the purchaser. Beven, Negligence (3d Ed.) pp. 50, 51, 54; Wharton, Negligence (2d Ed.) § 134.

These early cases suggest a narrow construction of the rule. Later cases, however, evince a more liberal spirit. First in importance is Devlin v. Smith, 89 N.Y. 470, 42 Am. Rep. 311. The defendant, a contractor, built a scaffold for a painter. The painter's servants were injured. The contractor was held liable. He knew that the scaffold, if improperly constructed, was a most dangerous trap. He knew that it was to be used by the workmen. He was building it for that very purpose. Building it for their use, he owed them a duty, irrespective of his contract with their master, to build it with care.

From Devlin v. Smith we pass over intermediate cases and turn to the latest case in this court in which Thomas v. Winchester was followed. That case is Statler v. Ray Mfg. Co., 195 N.Y. 478, 480, 88 N.E. 1063. The defendant manufactured a large coffee urn. It was installed in a restaurant. When heated, the urn exploded and injured the plaintiff. We held that the manufacturer was liable. We said that the urn "was of such a character inherently that, when applied to the purposes for which it was designed, it was liable to become a source of great danger to many people if not carefully and properly constructed."

It may be that Devlin v. Smith and Statler v. Ray Mfg. Co. have extended the rule of Thomas v. Winchester. If so, this court is committed to the extension. The defendant argues that things imminently dangerous to life are poisons, explosives, deadly weapons—things whose normal function it is to injure or destroy. But whatever the rule in Thomas v. Winchester may once have been, it has no longer that restricted meaning. A scaffold (Devlin v. Smith, supra) is not inherently a destructive instrument. It becomes destructive only if imperfectly constructed. A large coffee urn (Statler v. Ray Mfg. Co., supra) may have within itself, if negligently made, the potency of danger, yet no one thinks of it as an implement whose normal function is destruction. What is true of the coffee urn is equally true of bottles of aerated water. Torgesen v. Schultz, 192 N.Y. 156, 84 N.E. 956, 18 L.R.A. (N.S.) 726, 127 Am. St. Rep. 894. We have mentioned only cases in this court. But the rule has received a like extension in our courts of intermediate appeal. In Burke v. Ireland, 26 App. Div. 487, 50 N.Y. Supp. 369, in an opinion by Cullen, J., it was applied to a builder who constructed a defective building; in Kahner v. Otis Elevator Co., 96 App. Div. 169, 89 N.Y. Supp. 185, to the manufacturer of an elevator; in Davies v. Pelham Hod Elevating Co., 65 Hun, 573, 20 N.Y. Supp. 523, affirmed in this court without opinion, 146 N.Y. 363, 41 N.E. 88, to a contractor who furnished a defective rope with knowledge of the purpose for which the rope was to be used. We are not required at this time either to approve or to disapprove the application of the rule that was made in these cases. It is enough that they help to characterize the trend of judicial thought.

Devlin v. Smith was decided in 1882. A year later a very similar case came before the Court of Appeal in England (Heaven v. Pender, 11 Q.B.D. 503). We find in the opinion of Brett, M.R., afterwards Lord Esher, the same conception of a duty, irrespective of contract, imposed upon the manufacturer by the law itself:

> "Whenever one person supplies goods or machinery, or the like, for the purpose of their being used by another person under such circumstances that every one of ordinary sense would, if he thought, recognize at once that unless he used ordinary care and skill with regard to the condition of the thing supplied, or the mode of supplying it, there will be danger of injury to the person or property of him for whose use the thing is supplied, and who is to use it, a duty arises to use ordinary care and skill as to the condition or manner of supplying such thing."

He then points out that for a neglect of such ordinary care or skill whereby injury happens, the appropriate remedy is an action for negligence. The right to enforce this liability is not to be confined to the immediate buyer. The right, he says, extends to the persons or class of persons for whose use the thing is supplied. It is enough that the goods "would in all probability be used at once * * * before a reasonable opportunity for discovering any defect which might exist," and that the thing supplied is of such a nature "that a neglect of ordinary care or skill as to its condition or the manner of supplying it would probably cause danger to the person or property of the person for whose use it was supplied, and who was about to use it." On the other hand, he would exclude a case "in which the goods are supplied under circumstances in which it would be a chance by whom they would be used or whether they would be used or not, or whether they would be used before there would probably be means of observing any defect," or where the goods are of such a nature that "a want of care or skill as to their condition or the manner of supplying them would not probably produce danger of injury to person or property." What was said by Lord Esher in that case did not command the full assent of his associates. His opinion has been criticized "as requiring every man to take affirmative precautions to protect his neighbors as well as to refrain from injuring them." Bohlen, Affirmative Obligations in the Law of Torts, 44 Am. Law Reg. (N.S.) 341. It may not be an accurate exposition of the law of England. Perhaps it may need some qualification even in our own state. Like most attempts at comprehensive definition, it may involve errors of inclusion and of exclusion. But its tests and standards, at least in their underlying principles, with whatever qualification may be called for as they are applied to varying conditions, are the tests and standards of our law.

[1-4] We hold, then, that the principle of Thomas v. Winchester is not limited to poisons, explosives, and things of like nature, to things which in their normal operation are implements of destruction. If the nature of a thing is such that it is reasonably certain to place life and limb in peril when negligently made, it is then a thing of danger. Its nature gives warning of the consequences to be expected. If to the element of danger there is added knowledge that the thing will be used by persons other than the purchaser, and used without new tests, then, irrespective of contract, the manufacturer of this thing of danger is under a duty to make it carefully. That is as far as we are required to go for the decision of this case. There must be knowledge of a danger, not merely possible, but probable. It is possible to use almost anything in a way that will make it dangerous if defective. That is not enough to charge the manufacturer with a duty independent of his contract. Whether a given thing is dangerous may be sometimes a question for the court and sometimes a question for the jury. There must also be knowledge that in the usual course of events the danger will be shared by others than the buyer. Such knowledge may often be inferred from the nature of the transaction. But it is possible that even knowledge of the danger and of the use will not always be enough. The proximity or remoteness of the relation is a factor to be considered. We are dealing now with the liability of the manufacturer of the finished product, who puts it on the market to be used without inspection by his customers. If he is negligent, where danger is to be foreseen, a liability will follow.

[5] We are not required, at this time, to say that it is legitimate to go back of the manufacturer of the finished product and hold the manufacturers of the component parts. To make their negligence a cause of imminent danger, an independent cause must often intervene; the manufacturer of the finished product must also fail in his duty of inspection. It may be that in those circumstances

the negligence of the earlier members of the series is too remote to constitute, as to the ultimate user, an actionable wrong. Beven on Negligence (3d Ed.) 50, 51, 54; Wharton on Negligence (2d Ed.) § 134; Leeds v. N.Y. Tel. Co., 178 N.Y. 118, 70 N.E. 219; Sweet v. Perkins, 196 N.Y. 482, 90 N.E. 50; Hayes v. Hyde Park, 153 Mass. 514, 516, 27 N.E. 522, 12 L.R.A. 249. We leave that question open. We shall have to deal with it when it arises. The difficulty which it suggests is not present in this case. There is here no break in the chain of cause and effect. In such circumstances, the presence of a known danger, attendant upon a known use, makes vigilance a duty. We have put aside the notion that the duty to safeguard life and limb, when the consequences of negligence may be foreseen, grows out of contract and nothing else. We have put the source of the obligation where it ought to be. We have put its source in the law.

[6,7] From this survey of the decisions, there thus emerges a definition of the duty of a manufacturer which enables us to measure this defendant's liability. Beyond all question, the nature of an automobile gives warning of probable danger if its construction is defective. This automobile was designed to go 50 miles an hour. Unless its wheels were sound and strong, injury was almost certain. It was as much a thing of danger as a defective engine for a railroad. The defendant knew the danger. It knew also that the car would be used by persons other than the buyer. This was apparent from its size; there were seats for three persons. It was apparent also from the fact that the buyer was a dealer in cars, who bought to resell. The maker of this car supplied it for the use of purchasers from the dealer just as plainly as the contractor in Devlin v. Smith supplied the scaffold for use by the servants of the owner. The dealer was indeed the one person of whom it might be said with some approach to certainty that by him the car would not be used. Yet the defendant would have us say that he was the one person whom it was under a legal duty to protect. The law does not lead us to so inconsequent a conclusion. Precedents drawn from the days of travel by stagecoach do not fit the conditions of travel to-day. The principle that the danger must be imminent does not change, but the things subject to the principle do change. They are whatever the needs of life in a developing civilization require them to be.

In reaching this conclusion, we do not ignore the decisions to the contrary in other jurisdictions. It was held in Cadillac Co. v. Johnson, 221 Fed. 801, 137 C.C.A. 279, L.R.A. 1915E, 287, that an automobile is not within the rule of Thomas v. Winchester. There was, however, a vigorous dissent. Opposed to that decision is one of the Court of Appeals of Kentucky. Olds Motor Works v. Shaffer, 145 Ky. 616, 140 S.W. 1047, 37 L.R.A. (N.S.) 560, Ann. Cas. 1913B, 689. The earlier cases are summarized by Judge Sanborn in Huset v. J.I. Case Threshing Machine Co., 120 Fed. 865, 57 C.C.A. 237, 61 L.R.A. 303. Some of them, at first sight inconsistent with our conclusion, may be reconciled upon the ground that the negligence was too remote, and that another cause had intervened. But even when they cannot be reconciled; the difference is rather in the application of the principle than in the principle itself. Judge Sanborn says, for example, that the contractor who builds a bridge, or the manufacturer who builds a car, cannot ordinarily foresee injury to other persons than the owner as the probable result. 120 Fed. 865, at page 867, 57 C.C.A. 237, at page 239, 61 L.R.A. 303. We take a different view. We think that injury to others is to be foreseen not merely as a possible, but as an almost inevitable, result. See the trenchant criticism in Bohlen, supra, at page 351. Indeed, Judge Sanborn concedes that his view is not to be reconciled with our decision in Devlin v. Smith, supra. The doctrine of that decision has now become the settled law of this state, and we have no desire to depart from it.

In England the limits of the rule are still unsettled. Winterbottom v. Wright, 10 M. & W. 109, is often cited. The defendant undertook to provide a mail coach to carry the mail bags. The coach broke down from latent defects in its construction. The defendant, however, was not the manufacturer. The court held that he was not liable for injuries to a passenger. The case was decided on a demurrer to the declaration. Lord Esher points out in Heaven v. Pender, supra, at page 513, that the form of the declaration was subject to criticism. It did not fairly suggest the existence of a duty aside from the special contract which was the plaintiff's main reliance. See the criticism of Winterbottom v. Wright, in Bohlen, supra, at pages 281, 283. At all events, in Heaven v. Pender, supra, the defendant, a dock owner, who put up a staging outside a ship, was held liable to the servants of the shipowner. In Elliot v. Hall, 15 Q.B.D. 315, the defendant sent out a defective truck laden with goods which he had sold. The buyer's servants unloaded it, and were injured because of the defects. It was held that the defendant was under a duty "not to be guilty of negligence with regard to the state and condition of the truck." There seems to have been a return to the doctrine of Winterbottom v. Wright in Earl v. Lubbock [1905] 1 K.B. 253. In that case, however, as in the earlier one, the defendant was not the manufacturer. He had merely made a contract to keep the van in repair. A later case (White v. Steadman [1913] 3 K.B. 340, 348) emphasizes that element. A livery stable keeper who sent out a vicious horse was held liable, not merely to his customer, but also to another occupant of the carriage, and Thomas v. Winchester was cited and followed, White v. Steadman, supra, at pages 348, 349. It was again cited and followed in Dominion Natural Gas Co. v. Collins [1909] A.C. 640, 646. From these cases a consistent principle is with difficulty extracted. The English courts, however, agree with ours in holding that one who invites another to make use of an appliance is bound to the exercise of reasonable care. Caledonian Ry. Co. v. Mulholland [1898] A.C. 216, 227; Inderman v. Dames, L.R. [1 C.P.] 274. That at bottom is the underlying principle of Devlin v. Smith. The contractor who builds the scaffold invites the owner's workmen to use it. The manufacturer who sells the automobile to the retail dealer invites the dealer's customers to use it. The invitation is addressed in the one case to determinate persons and in the other to an indeterminate class, but in each case it is equally plain, and in each its consequences must be the same.

There is nothing anomalous in a rule which imposes upon A., who has contracted with B., a duty to C. and D. and others according as he knows or does not know that the subject-matter of the contract is intended for their use. We may find an analogy in the law which measures the liability of landlords. If A. leases to B. a tumble-down house, he is not liable, in the absence of fraud, to

B.'s guests who enter it and are injured. This is because B. is then under the duty to repair it, the lessor has the right to suppose that he will fulfill that duty, and, if he omits to do so, his guests must look to him. Bohlen, supra, at page 276. But if A. leases a building to be used by the lessee at once as a place of public entertainment, the rule is different. There injury to persons other than the lessee is to be foreseen, and foresight of the consequences involves the creation of a duty. Junkermann v. Tilyou R. Co., 213 N.Y. 404, 108 N.E. 190, L.R.A. 1915F, 700, and cases there cited.

[8] In this view of the defendant's liability there is nothing inconsistent with the theory of liability on which the case was tried. It is true that the court told the jury that "an automobile is not an inherently dangerous vehicle." The meaning, however, is made plain by the context. The meaning is that danger is not to be expected when the vehicle is well constructed. The court left it to the jury to say whether the defendant ought to have foreseen that the car, if negligently constructed, would become "imminently dangerous." Subtle distinctions are drawn by the defendant between things inherently dangerous and things imminently dangerous, but the case does not turn upon these verbal niceties. If danger was to be expected as reasonably certain, there was a duty of vigilance, and this whether you call the danger inherent or imminent. In varying forms that thought was put before the jury. We do not say that the court would not have been justified in ruling as a matter of law that the car was a dangerous thing. If there was any error, it was none of which the defendant can complain.

[9,10] We think the defendant was not absolved from a duty of inspection because it bought the wheels from a reputable manufacturer. It was not merely a dealer in automobiles. It was a manufacturer of automobiles. It was responsible for the finished product. It was not at liberty to put the finished product on the market without subjecting the component parts to ordinary and simple tests. Richmond & Danville R.R. Co. v. Elliott, 149 U.S. 266, 272, 13 Sup.Ct. 837, 37 L. Ed. 728. Under the charge of the trial judge nothing more was required of it. The obligation to inspect must vary with the nature of the thing to be inspected. The more probable the danger the greater the need of caution.

There is little analogy between this case and Carlson v. Phoenix Bridge Co., 132 N.Y. 273, 30 N.E. 750, where the defendant bought a tool for a servant's use. The making of tools was not the business in which the master was engaged. Reliance on the skill of the manufacturer was proper and almost inevitable. But that is not the defendant's situation. Both by its relation to the work and by the nature of its business, it is charged with a stricter duty.

Other rulings complained of have been considered, but no error has been found in them.

The judgment should be affirmed, with costs.

WILLARD BARTLETT, C.J. (dissenting). The plaintiff was injured in consequence of the collapse of a wheel of an automobile manufactured by the defendant corporation which sold it to a firm of automobile dealers in Schenectady, who in turn sold the car to the plaintiff. The wheel was purchased by the Buick Motor Company, ready made, from the Imperial Wheel Company of Flint, Mich., a reputable manufacturer of automobile wheels which had furnished the defendant with 80,000 wheels, none of which had proved to be made of defective wood prior to the accident in the present case. The defendant relied upon the wheel manufacturer to make all necessary tests as to the strength of the material therein, and made no such test itself. The present suit is an action for negligence, brought by the subvendee of the motor car against the manufacturer as the original vendor. The evidence warranted a finding by the jury that the wheel which collapsed was defective when it left the hands of the defendant. The automobile was being prudently operated at the time of the accident, and was moving at a speed of only eight miles an hour. There was no allegation or proof of any actual knowledge of the defect on the part of the defendant, or any suggestion that any element of fraud or deceit or misrepresentation entered into the sale.

The theory upon which the case was submitted to the jury by the learned judge who presided at the trial was that, although an automobile is not an inherently dangerous vehicle, it may become such if equipped with a weak wheel; and that if the motor car in question, when it was put upon the market was in itself inherently dangerous by reason of its being equipped with a weak wheel, the defendant was chargeable with a knowledge of the defect so far as it might be discovered by a reasonable inspection and the application of reasonable tests. This liability, it was further held, was not limited to the original vendee, but extended to a subvendee like the plaintiff, who was not a party to the original contract of sale.

I think that these rulings, which have been approved by the Appellate Division, extend the liability of the vendor of a manufactured article further than any case which has yet received the sanction of this court. It has heretofore been held in this state that the liability of the vendor of a manufactured article for negligence arising out of the existence of defects therein does not extend to strangers injured in consequence of such defects, but is confined to the immediate vendee. The exceptions to this general rule which have thus far been recognized in New York are cases in which the article sold was of such a character that danger to life or limb was involved in the ordinary use thereof; in other words, where the article sold was inherently dangerous. As has already been pointed out, the learned trial judge instructed the jury that an automobile is not an inherently dangerous vehicle.

The late Chief Justice Cooley of Michigan, one of the most learned and accurate of American law writers, states the general rule thus:

> "The general rule is that a contractor, manufacturer, vendor or furnisher of an article is not liable to third parties who have no contractual relations with him, for negligence in the construction, manufacture, or sale of such article." 2 Cooley on Torts (3d Ed.), 1486.

The leading English authority in support of this rule, to which all the later cases on the same subject refer, is Winterbottom v. Wright, 10 Meeson & Welsby, 109, which was an action by the driver of a stagecoach against a contractor who had agreed with the postmaster general to provide and keep the vehicle in repair for the purpose of conveying the royal mail over a prescribed route. The coach broke down and upset, injuring the driver, who sought to recover against the contractor on account of its defective construction. The Court of Exchequer denied him any right of recovery on the ground that there was no privity of contract between the parties, the agreement having been made with the postmaster general alone.

> "If the plaintiff can sue," said Lord Abinger, the Chief Baron, "every passenger or even any person passing along the road who was injured by the upsetting of the coach might bring a similar action. Unless we confine the operation of such contracts as this to the parties who enter into them the most absurd and outrageous consequences, to which I can see no limit, would ensue."

The doctrine of that decision was recognized as the law of this state by the leading New York case of Thomas v. Winchester, 6 N.Y. 397, 408, 57 Am. Dec. 455, which, however, involved an exception to the general rule. There the defendant, who was a dealer in medicines, sold to a druggist a quantity of belladonna, which is a deadly poison, negligently labeled as extract of dandelion. The druggist in good faith used the poison in filling a prescription calling for the harmless dandelion extract, and the plaintiff for whom the prescription was put up was poisoned by the belladonna. This court held that the original vendor was liable for the injuries suffered by the patient. Chief Judge Ruggles, who delivered the opinion of the court, distinguished between an act of negligence imminently dangerous to the lives of others and one that is not so, saying:

> "If A. build a wagon and sell it to B., who sells it to C., and C. hires it to D., who in consequence of the gross negligence of A. in building the wagon is overturned and injured, D. cannot recover damages against A., the builder. A.'s obligation to build the wagon faithfully arises solely out of his contract with B. The public have nothing to do with it. * * * So, for the same reason, if a horse be defectively shod by a smith, and a person hiring the horse from the owner is thrown and injured in consequence of the smith's negligence in shoeing, the smith is not liable for the injury."

In Torgesen v. Schultz, 192 N.Y. 156, 159, 84 N.E. 956, 18 L.R.A. (N.S.) 726, 127 Am. St. Rep. 894, the defendant was the vendor of bottles of aerated water which were charged under high pressure and likely to explode unless used with precaution when exposed to sudden changes of temperature. The plaintiff, who was a servant of the purchaser, was injured by the explosion of one of these bottles. There was evidence tending to show that it had not been properly tested in order to insure users against such accidents. We held that the defendant corporation was liable notwithstanding the absence of any contract relation between it and the plaintiff—

> "under the doctrine of Thomas v. Winchester, supra, and similar cases based upon the duty of the vendor of an article dangerous in its nature, or likely to become so in the course of the ordinary usage to be contemplated by the vendor, either to exercise due care to warn users of the danger or to

take reasonable care to prevent the article sold from proving dangerous when subjected only to customary usage."

The character of the exception to the general rule limiting liability for negligence to the original parties to the contract of sale, was still more clearly stated by Judge Hiscock, writing for the court in Statler v. Ray Manufacturing Co., 195 N.Y. 478, 482, 88 N.E. 1063, where he said that:

> "In the case of an article of an inherently dangerous nature, a manufacturer may become liable for a negligent construction which, when added to the inherent character of the appliance, makes it imminently dangerous, and causes or contributes to a resulting injury not necessarily incident to the use of such an article if properly constructed, but naturally following from a defective construction."

In that case the injuries were inflicted by the explosion of a battery of steam-driven coffee urns, constituting an appliance liable to become dangerous in the course of ordinary usage.

The case of Devlin v. Smith, 89 N.Y. 470, 42 Am. Rep. 311, is cited as an authority in conflict with the view that the liability of the manufacturer and vendor extends to third parties only when the article manufactured and sold is inherently dangerous. In that case the builder of a scaffold 90 feet high, which was erected for the purpose of enabling painters to stand upon it, was held to be liable to the administratrix of a painter who fell therefrom and was killed, being at the time in the employ of the person for whom the scaffold was built. It is said that the scaffold, if properly constructed, was not inherently dangerous, and hence that this decision affirms the existence of liability in the case of an article not dangerous in itself, but made so only in consequence of negligent construction. Whatever logical force there may be in this view it seems to be clear from the language of Judge Rapallo, who wrote the opinion of the court that the scaffold was deemed to be an inherently dangerous structure, and that the case was decided as it was because the court entertained that view. Otherwise he would hardly have said, as he did, that the circumstances seemed to bring the case fairly within the principle of Thomas v. Winchester.

I do not see how we can uphold the judgment in the present case without overruling what has been so often said by this court and other courts of like authority in reference to the absence of any liability for negligence on the part of the original vendor of an ordinary carriage to any one except his immediate vendee. The absence of such liability was the very point actually decided in the English case of Winterbottom v. Wright, supra, and the illustration quoted from the opinion of Chief Judge Ruggles in Thomas v. Winchester, supra, assumes that the law on the subject was so plain that the statement would be accepted almost as a matter of course. In the case at bar the defective wheel on an automobile, moving only eight miles an hour, was not any more dangerous to the occupants of the car than a similarly defective wheel would be to the occupants of a carriage drawn by a horse at the same speed, and yet, unless the courts have been all wrong on this question up to the present time, there would be no liability to strangers to the original sale in the case of the horse-drawn carriage.

The rule upon which, in my judgment, the determination of this case depends, and the recognized exceptions thereto, were discussed by Circuit Judge Sanborn, of the United States Circuit Court of Appeals in the Eighth Circuit, in Huset v. J.I. Case Threshing Machine Co., 120 Fed. 865, 57 C.C.A. 237, 61 L.R.A. 303, in an opinion which reviews all the leading American and English decisions on the subject up to the time when it was rendered (1903). I have already discussed the leading New York cases, but as to the rest I feel that I can add nothing to the learning of that opinion or the cogency of its reasoning. I have examined the cases to which Judge Sanborn refers, but if I were to discuss them at length, I should be forced merely to paraphrase his language, as a study of the authorities he cites has led me to the same conclusion; and the repetition of what has already been so well said would contribute nothing to the advantage of the bench, the bar, or the individual litigants whose case is before us.

A few cases decided since his opinion was written, however, may be noticed. In Earl v. Lubbock [1905] L.R. 1 K.B. Div. 253, the Court of Appeal in 1904 considered and approved the propositions of law laid down by the Court of Exchequer in Winterbottom v. Wright, supra, declaring that the decision in that case, since the year 1842, had stood the test of repeated discussion. The Master of the Rolls approved the principles laid down by Lord Abinger as based upon sound reasoning; and all the members of the court agreed that his decision was a controlling authority which must be followed. That the federal courts still adhere to the general rule, as I have stated it, appears by the decision of the Circuit Court of Appeal in the Second Circuit, in March, 1915, in the case of Cadillac Motor Car Co. v. Johnson, 221 Fed. 801, 137 C.C.A. 279, L.R.A. 1915E, 287. That case, like this, was an action by a subvendee against a manufacturer of automobiles for negligence in failing to discover that one of its wheels was defective, the court holding that such an action could not be maintained. It is true there was a dissenting opinion in that case, but it was based chiefly upon the proposition that rules applicable to stagecoaches are archaic when applied to automobiles, and that if the law did not afford a remedy to strangers to the contract, the law should be changed. If this be true, the change should be effected by the Legislature and not by the courts. A perusal of the opinion in that case and in the Huset Case will disclose how uniformly the courts throughout this country have adhered to the rule and how consistently they have refused to broaden the scope of the exceptions. I think we should adhere to it in the case at bar, and therefore I vote for a reversal of this judgment.

HISCOCK, CHASE, and CUDDEBACK, JJ., concur with CARDOZO, J., and HOGAN, J., concurs in result. WILLARD BARTLETT, C.J., reads dissenting opinion. POUND, J., not voting.

Judgment affirmed.

12 N.Y. 2d 432

Anneliese GOLDBERG, as Administratrix of the Estate of Edith Feis, Deceased, Appellant, v. KOLLSMAN INSTRUMENT CORPORATION et al., Respondents, and American Airlines, Inc., Defendant.

(Cite as 240 N.Y.S. 2d 592)

Court of Appeals of New York.

May 9, 1963.

Action for wrongful death of airplane passenger brought against air carrier, manufacturer of airplane, and manufacturer of altimeter on the airplane. From an order of the Supreme Court, Special Term, New York County, Aron Steuer, J., 23 Misc.2d 215, 199 N.Y.S.2d 134, dismissing the causes of action as to the manufacturers of the airplane and the altimeter, the plaintiff appealed. The Supreme Court, Appellate Division, First Judicial Department, 12 A.D.2d 906, 214 N.Y.S.2d 640, and 12 A.D.2d 906, 214 N.Y.S.2d 641, affirmed and permission to appeal was granted. The Court of Appeals, Desmond, C.J., held that airplane manufacturer's implied warranty of fitness of airplane for contemplated use ran in favor of airline passenger riding on such plane despite lack of privity of contract, but implied warranty did not apply as to manufacturer of altimeter on the airplane.

Judgment modified so as to provide for dismissal of cause of action as to altimeter manufacturer only and affirmed as modified.

Burke, Van Voorhis and Scileppi, JJ., dissented.

1. Sales

A breach of warranty is not only a violation of sales contract out of which warranty arises but is a tortious wrong suable by a noncontracting party whose use of warranted article is within reasonable contemplation of vendor or manufacturer.

2. Sales

Where an article is of such character that when used for purpose for which it is made it is likely to be a source of danger to several or many people if not properly designed and fashioned, manufacturer, as well as vendor, is liable for breach of law-implied warranties to persons whose use is contemplated.

3. Sales

Airplane manufacturer's implied warranty of fitness of airplane for contemplated use ran in favor of airline passenger riding on such plane, which had been purchased by an air carrier, despite lack of privity of contract, but implied warranty did not apply as to manufacturer of altimeter on airplane.

433

William L. Shumate, Edward M. O'Brien and Stuart M. Speiser, New York City, for appellant.

Benjamin E. Haller, New York City, for Lockheed Aircraft Corp., respondent.

434

Arthur Richenthal, Irving M. Moss and David Abrams, New York City, for Kollsman Instrument Corp., respondent.

DESMOND, Chief Judge.

We granted leave to appeal in order to take another step toward a complete solution of the problem partially cleared up in Greenberg v. Lorenz, 9 N.Y.2d 195, 213 N.Y.S.2d 39, 173 N.E.2d 773 and Randy Knitwear, Inc. v. American Cyanamid Co., 11 N.Y.2d 5, 226 N.Y.S.2d 363, 181 N.E.2d 399 (both decided after the making of the Special Term and Appellate Division orders here appealed from). The question now to be answered is: does a manufacturer's implied warranty

435

of fitness of his product for its contemplated use run in favor of all its intended users, despite lack of privity of contract?

The suit is by an administratrix for damages for the death of her daughter-intestate as the result of injuries suffered in the crash near La Guardia Airport, New York City, of an airplane in which the daughter was a fare-paying passenger on a flight from Chicago to New York. American Airlines, Inc., owner and operator of the plane, is sued here for negligence (with present respondents Lockheed and Kollsman) but that cause of action is not the subject of this appeal. The two causes of action, from the dismissal of which for insufficiency plaintiff appeals to us, run against Kollsman Instrument Corporation, manufacturer or supplier of the plane's altimeter, and Lockheed Aircraft Corporation, maker of the plane itself. Kollsman and Lockheed are charged with breaching their respective implied warranties of merchantability and fitness. Those breaches, it is alleged, caused the fatal crash.

There is nothing in the complaint that says where the plane or its altimeter were manufactured or sold nor does the pleading inform us as to decedent's place of residence, although it is alleged that plaintiff's appointment as administratrix was by a New York court. Plaintiff argues that California law should apply on the "grouping of contracts" theory and it is clear (indeed in effect conceded by respondents) that California law allows recovery for a proven breach of implied warranties as to dangerous instrumentalities (see Peterson v. Lamb Rubber Co., 54 Cal.2d 339, 347, 5 Cal.Rptr. 863, 353 P.2d 575; Greenman v. Yuba Power Prods., Inc., 59 Cal.2d 67, 27 Cal.Rptr. 697, 377 P.2d 897). Special Term, however, said in its opinion in the present case that the governing law is that of New York State where the accident took place, citing Poplar v. Bourjois, Inc., 298 N.Y. 62, 80 N.E.2d 334 and that under New York law no claim for breach of implied warranty may be enforced by one not in privity with the warrantor. The Appellate Division, affirming, wrote no opinion. The Special Term opinion, as we have said above, was filed before our Greenberg and Randy Knitwear decisions (supra) and Greenberg and Randy Knitwear declared that in New York privity of contract is not always a requisite for breach of warranty recoveries. The Randy Knitwear opinion (11 N.Y.2d p. 16, 226 N.Y.S.2d p. 370, 181 N.E.2d p. 404) at least suggested that all requirements of privity have been dispensed with in our State. That is the immediate,

436

or at least the logical and necessary result of our decisions and, accordingly, it really makes no difference whether New York or California law be applied, since in this respect both States use the same rules.

[1] The enormous literature on this subject and the historical development of the law of warranties to its present state need not be reviewed beyond the references in our Greenberg and Randy Knitwear opinions (supra). A breach of warranty, it is now clear, is not only a violation of the sales contract out of which the warranty arises but is a tortious wrong suable by a noncontracting party whose use of the warranted article is within the reasonable contemplation of the vendor or manufacturer. As to foodstuffs we definitively ruled in Greenberg v. Lorenz, 9 N.Y.2d 195, supra, 213 N.Y.S.2d 39, 173 N.E.2d 773, that the persons thus protected and eligible to sue include the purchaser's family. We went no further in that case because the facts required no farther reach of the rule.

[2] The concept that as to "things of danger" the manufacturer must answer to intended users for faulty design or manufacture is an old one in this State. The most famous decision is MacPherson v. Buick Motor Co., 217 N.Y. 382, 111 N.E. 1050, L.R.A.1961F, 696, holding the manufacturer liable in negligence to one who purchased a faulty Buick automobile from a dealer (see the recent and similar case of Markel v. Spencer, 5 A.D.2d 400, 171 N.Y.S.2d 770, affd. 5 N.Y.2d 958, 184 N.Y.S.2d 835, 157 N.E.2d 713). But the MacPherson opinion cites much older cases such as Devlin v. Smith, 89 N.Y. 470 [1882], where one who negligently built a scaffold for a contractor was adjudged liable to the contractor's injured employee. MacPherson and its successors dispelled the idea that a manufacturer was immune from liability in tort for violation of his duty to make his manufactures fit and safe. In MacPherson's day enforcement required a suit in negligence. Today, we know from Greenberg v. Lorenz; Randy Knitwear Inc. v. American Cyanamid Co. (supra) and many another decision in this and other States (see, for instance, Henningsen v. Bloomfield Motors, Inc., 32 N.J. 358, 161 A.2d 69, 75 A.L.R.2d 1, and Thomas v. Leary, 15 A.D.2d 438, 225 N.Y.S.2d 137) that, at least where an article is of such a character that when used for the purpose for which it is made it is likely to be a source of danger to several or many people if not properly designed and fashioned, the manufacturer as well as the vendor is liable, for breach of law-implied warranties, to the persons

437

whose use is contemplated. The MacPherson holding was an "extension" of existing court-made liability law. In a sense, Greenberg v. Lorenz and Randy Knitwear, Inc. v. American Cyanamid Co. (supra) were extensions in favor of noncontracting consumers. But it is no extension at all to include airplanes and the passengers for whose use they are built—and, indeed, decisions are at hand which have upheld complaints, sounding in breach of warranty, against manufacturers of aircraft where passengers lost their lives when the planes crashed (see, e.g., Conlon v. Republic Aviation Corp., D.C., 204 F.Supp. 865; Middleton v. United Aircraft Corp., D.C., 204 F.Supp. 856; Ewing v. Lockheed Aircraft Corp., D.C., 202 F.Supp. 216; Hinton v. Republic Aviation Corp., D.C., 180 F.Supp. 31).

[3] As we all know, a number of courts outside New York State have for the best of reasons dispensed with the privity requirement (see Jaeger, Privity of Warranty: Has the Tocsin Sounded?, 1 Duquesne U.L.Rev. 1). Very recently the Supreme Court of California (Greenman v. Yuba Power Prods., Inc., 59 Cal.2d 67, 27 Cal.Rptr. 697, 377 P.2d 897 [1963], supra) in a unanimous opinion imposed "strict tort liability" (surely a more accurate phrase) regardless of privity on a manufacturer in a case where a power tool threw a piece of wood at a user who was not the purchaser. The California court said that the purpose of such a holding is to see to it that the costs of injuries resulting from defective products are borne by the manufacturers who put the products on the market rather than by injured persons who are powerless to protect themselves and that implicit in putting such articles on the market are representations that they will safely do the job for which they were built. However, for the present at least we do not think it necessary so to extend this rule as to hold liable the manufacturer (defendant Kollsman) of a component part. Adequate protection is provided for the passengers by casting in liability the airplane manufacturer which put into the market the completed aircraft.

The judgment appealed from should be modified, without costs, so as to provide for the dismissal of the third (Kollsman) cause of action only and, as so modified, affirmed.

BURKE, Judge (dissenting). We dissent.

If this were a case in which a manufacturer made express representations concerning the quality of its product calculated

438

to promote its sale or use by persons in the plaintiff's position, our decision in Randy Knitwear, Inc. v. American Cyanamid Co., 11 N.Y.2d 5, 226 N.Y.S.2d 363, 181 N.E.2d 399, would allow a recovery. If it were a case where a defendant sold a food or other household product to a member of a family, the warranty incident thereto would extend to all for whose consumption or use the product was obviously purchased. (Greenberg v. Lorenz, 9 N.Y.2d 195, 213 N.Y.S.2d 39, 173 N.E.2d 773; Greenman v. Yuba Power Prods., Inc., 59 Cal.2d 67, 27 Cal.Rptr. 697, 377 P.2d 897.) The conclusion reached by the majority might be correct even if the defective product were sold to an employer for the use of his employees. (Thomas v. Leary, 15 A.D.2d 438, 225 N.Y.S.2d 137; Peterson v. Lamb Rubber Co., 54 Cal.2d 339, 5 Cal.Rptr. 863, 353 P.2d 575.) This, however, is none of those cases. The conditions present, in those cases are entirely different. There the manufacturer knew that the article he made was not to be inspected thereafter. Here Federal regulations provide for rigorous inspection and certification from the Federal Aviation Agency. There the risk of loss was a trap for the unwary. Here all are aware of the hazards attending air travel and accident and special insurance is readily available at moderate rates. Plaintiff[1] is a purchaser of a service from an airline seeking to assert a warranty cause of action against

1. Edith Feis, for whose death this action is brought, will be referred to herein as plaintiff.

Lockheed, the assembler of an airplane, and Kollsman, the manufacturer of an allegedly defective component part thereof. In such a situation we see no satisfactory basis on which to uphold against Lockheed a cause of action not grounded in negligence, while disallowing it against the manufacturer of an alleged defective part.

First, we do not find a cause of action stated under the implied warranty provisions of section 96 of the Personal Property Law, Consol. Laws, c. 41. Plaintiff purchased no goods; she entered into a contract of carriage with American Airlines. By a long line of cases in this court, the most recent being Kilberg v. Northeast Airlines, Inc., 9 N.Y.2d 34, 211 N.Y.S.2d 133, 172 N.E.2d 526, it is settled that the measure of American Airlines' duty towards plaintiff was an undertaking of reasonably safe carriage. This duty is, of course, discharged by the use of due care. Crucial is the fact that this duty would be unaffected if American assembled its own planes, even if they contained a latent defect. Why, then, should plaintiff's rights

439

be any greater simply because American chose to contract this work out instead of doing it itself? Absent some equity of direct reliance on the advertised representations of one of the manufacturers, which might invoke the reasoning of Randy Knitwear, Inc. v. American Cyanamid Co., 11 N.Y.2d 5, 226 N.Y.S.2d 363, 181 N.E.2d 399, supra, it is no concern of plaintiff how the person with whom she dealt, American, subdivided its responsibility of furnishing the machines and services in discharge of its undertaking of safe carriage.

Of course, plaintiff's right to due care cannot be diminished by American's delegating certain tasks to others. What would be actionable negligence if done by American is not less so because done by another; such a person may be sued by plaintiff, and so may American if the negligence was discoverable by it. By the same token, however, plaintiff's primary right to care from American (and, indeed, all whose actions foreseeably affect her) should not be enlarged to insurance protection simply because American chose to have a certain task performed by another. We note that the argument made in some cases based on the avoidance of a multiplicity of actions is inapplicable here. In such cases, the plaintiff himself is the recipient of a warranty incident to the sale of goods and if the defect is in the manufacture it is at least reasonable to suggest a procedure by which liability may be imposed by the person entitled to the recovery directly against the one who, through a chain of warranties, is ultimately liable. Here, however, plaintiff (or her family, etc.) was not sold the chattel which caused her injury and hence there is no warranty.

It is true we have extended the benefit of an implied warranty beyond the immediate purchaser to those who could be fairly called indirect vendees of the product. (Greenberg v. Lorenz, 9 N.Y.2d 195, 213 N.Y.S.2d 39, 173 N.E.2d 773, supra.) Without stressing the weakness of the analogy that plaintiff here is the indirect vendee of the airplane and its parts, or the effect of the interposition between plaintiff and defendants of a federally regulated service industry of dominant economic and legal significance, it must be recognized that the true grounds of decision in a case of this sort lie outside the purpose and policy of the Sales Act and must be evaluated accordingly. Most scholars who have considered this question acknowledge that the warranty rationale is at best a useful

440

fiction. (See, e.g., Prosser, The Assault upon the Citadel [Strict Liability to the Consumer], 69 Yale L.J. 1099; James, Products Liability, 34 Tex.L.Rev. 192.) If a strict products or enterprise liability is to be imposed here, this court cannot escape the responsibility of justifying it. We cannot accept the implication of the majority that the difference between warranty and strict products liability is merely one of phrasing.

Inherent in the question of strict products or enterprise liability is the question of the proper enterprise on which to fasten it. Here the majority have imposed this burden on the assembler of the finished product, Lockheed. The principle of selection stated is that the injured passenger needs no more protection. We suggest that this approach to the identification of an appropriate defendant does not answer the question: Which enterprise should be selected if the selection is to be in accord with the rationale upon which the doctrine of strict products liability rests?

The purpose of such liability is not to regulate conduct with a view to eliminating accidents,[2] but rather to remove the economic consequences of accidents from the victim who is unprepared to bear them and place the risk on the enterprise in the course of whose business they arise. The risk, it is said, becomes part of the cost of doing business and can be effectively distributed among the public through insurance or by a direct reflection in the price of the goods or service. As applied to this case we think the enterprise to which accidents such as the present are incident is the carriage of passengers by air—American Airlines. The fact that this accident was due to a defective altimeter should be of no legal significance to plaintiff absent some fault (negligence) on the part of Kollsman or Lockheed. Here, the dominant enterprise and the one with which plaintiff did business and relied upon was the airline.

If the carrier which immediately profited from plaintiff's custom is the proper party on which to fasten whatever enterprise

441

liability the social conscience demands, enterprises which supply the devices with which the carrier conducts its business should not be subject to an action based on this theory. This seems most persuasive where the business that deals directly with the public is not merely a conduit for the distribution of the manufacturer's consumer goods but assumes the responsibility of selecting and using those goods itself as a

2. In view of the ease with which lack of care can be brought to light through devices such as *res ipsa loquitur,* any marginal increase in the stimulus to care would be clearly outweighed by the harshness of the means used to achieve it—the removal of due care as a defense. Prosser, The Assault upon the Citadel (Strict Liability to the Consumer), 69 Yale L.J. 1099, 1119. Apparently the majority agree since Kollsman, the actual manufacturer of the chattel that allegedly caused the accident, is not held liable.

capital asset in the conduct of a service enterprise such as common carriage. In such a case the relationship between the assembler of these goods and the air traveller is minimal as compared to that obtaining between the traveller and the carrier. In a theory of liability based, not on the regulation of conduct, but on economic considerations of distributing the risk of accidents that occur through no one's neglect, the enterprise most strategically placed to perform this function—the carrier rather than the enterprise that supplies an assembled chattel thereto, is the logical subject of the liability, if liability there is to be.

Whatever conclusions may flow from the fact that the accident was caused by a defective altimeter should be merged in whatever responsibility the law may place on the airline with which plaintiff did business. To extend warranty law to allow plaintiff to select a defendant from a multiplicity of enterprises in a case such as this would not comport with the rationale of enterprise liability and would only have the effect of destroying whatever rights that exist among the potential defendants by virtue of agreement among themselves. If, on the other hand, plaintiff's maximum rights lie against the carrier, the rules of warranty can perform their real function of adjusting the rights of the parties to the agreements through which the airline acquired the chattel that caused the accident. If, as we maintain in this case, the true theory relied on by plaintiff is enterprise liability, then the rights of those from whom compensation is sought, no less than of those who seek it, "ought not to be made to depend upon the intricacies of the law of sales." (Ketterer v. Armour & Co., 2 Cir., 200 F. 322, 323.)

We are therefore of the opinion that any claim in respect of an airplane accident that is grounded in strict enterprise liability should be fixed on the airline or none at all. Only in this way do we meet and resolve, one way or another, the anomaly presented by the reasoning of the majority, which, through reliance

442

on warranty incident to sales, grants a recovery to a passenger injured through a nonnegligent failure of equipment but denies it to one injured through a nonnegligent failure of maintenance or operation.

Although no such claim is raised by the pleadings, as we stated earlier, it is clear that our cases limit the airline's duty to that of due care. (McPadden v. New York Cent. R.R. Co., 44 N.Y. 478; Stierle v. Union Ry. Co., 156 N.Y. 70, 50 N.E. 419; Williams v. Long Island R.R. Co., 294 N.Y. 318, 62 N.E.2d 212; Kilberg v. Northeast Airlines, Inc., 9 N.Y.2d 34, 211 N.Y.S.2d 133, 172 N.E.2d 526, supra.) It is this rule avowedly formed to deal with the problem of accidents, that must be re-evaluated by those who would support the theory of strict enterprise liability. A stricter rule is not without precedent in this court (Alden v. New York Cent. R.R. Co., 26 N.Y. 102, holding that the carrier "must be held accountable, in every event, to furnish a road-worthy coach; and that, if the event proved it not to have been so, he must suffer the consequences" [26 N.Y. p. 104]; see, also, cases collected in McLean v. Triboro Coach Corp., 302 N.Y. 49, 96 N.E.2d 83). However, as long as our law holds a carrier chargeable only with negligence, what part of reason is it to hold to a greater duty an enterprise which supplied an assembled aircraft which was certified for commercial service by the Federal Aviation Agency?

Our reluctance to hold an air carrier to strict liability for the inevitable toll of injury incident to its enterprise is only the counsel of prudence. Aside from the responsibility imposed on us to be slow to cast aside well-established law in deference to a theory of social planning that is still much in dispute (Prosser, Torts [2d ed.] § 84; Patterson, The Apportionment of Business Risks through Legal Devices, 24 Colum.L.Rev. 335, 358; Pound, Introduction to the Philosophy of Law 100-104 [1954]), there remains the inquiry whether the facts fit the theory. It is easy, in a completely free economy, to envision the unimpeded distribution of risk by an enterprise on which it is imposed; but how well will such a scheme work in an industry which is closely regulated by Federal agencies? In consideration of international competition and other factors weighed by those responsible for rate regulation, how likely is it that rate scales will rise in reflection of increased liability? (See Pound, supra, pp. 102-103.) In turn, how likely is it that the additional risk

443

will be effectively distributed as a cost of doing business? Such questions can be intelligently resolved only by analysis of facts and figures compiled after hearings in which all interested groups have an opportunity to present economic arguments. These matters, which are the factual cornerstones supporting the theory adopted by the majority, aside from our view that they apply it to the wrong enterprise, are classically within the special competence of the Legislature to ascertain. For a court to assume them in order to support a theory that displaces much of the law of negligence from its ancestral environment involves an omniscience not shared by us. For a court to apply them, not to the enterprise with which plaintiff dealt and relied upon, or to the enterprise which manufactured the alleged defective part, but to the assembler of the aircraft used by the carrier, involves a principle of selection which is purely arbitrary.

DYE, FULD and FOSTER, JJ., concur with DESMOND, C.J.

BURKE, J., dissents in an opinion in which VAN VOORHIS and SCILEPPI, JJ., concur.

Judgment modified in accordance with the opinion herein and, as so modified, affirmed, without costs.

CHAPTER 10

Learning Guides for the Student and Teacher

Contents of the Guides

There are seven Learning Guides. Explanatory instructions are given at the bottom of each Guide.

The seven Guides are as follows:

Homework Guide Outline	Guide 1
Test Form	Guide 2
Instructions for Appeal Moot Court	Guide 3
Form of Brief for Appeal (Appellant)	Guide 4
Form of Brief for Appeal (Appellee)	Guide 5
Form Used by Associate Judges to Grade Advocates	Guide 6
Form Used by Chief Judge (Instructor) to Grade Students as Advocates and as Associate Judges	Guide 7

How to Use the Guides

Purpose of the Homework Guide 1 is to enable the students to analyze the cases in the book and to present their analysis in class. The instructor evaluates the students' analyses and then dictates to the class the particular analysis that he, the instructor, wants the students to learn.

The students analyze every case in the book or as many as the instructor desires.

Purpose of Test Form Guide 2 is for the student to read two hypothetical cases given as a test. Each of the cases has a set of facts that is identical to one of the cases given for homework. The student must be able to identify the homework case that is similar to the test case and then write the homework case in the form of the Test Guide.

Purpose of Guides 3 through 7 is to enable the students to prepare their Moot Court case.

The cases used for the Moot Court are taken from the book and are those cases that have a dissenting opinion as well as a majority opinion to enable both the Appellants and Appellees to develop their arguments in the case.

The cases that the instructor can use for Moot Court are marked "Moot Court" in the "Index to Cases."

All the students of the class are divided into groups; four students in each group. Each group of four students is assigned an actual court case for presentation. However, all students are required to read all the cases in order to be able to evaluate the presentation by the other student Advocates.

Two students of each group of four act as Counsel for the Appellants in the case, and the other two students act as opposing Counsel for the Appellees. The four students at this stage are called Advocates and are graded as such in accordance with the following Guides 3 through 7 inclusive.

While the four students of one group are acting as Advocates and are arguing their case before the Chief Judge, the other students in the class are acting as Associate Judges and are making evaluations of the presentation of the Advocates.

The form used by the students as Associate Judges to evaluate the students as Advocates is self explanatory and is shown as Guide 6.

The Chief Judge grades the students in their capacity as Advocates based on their presentation. The Chief Judge also grades the students in their capacity as Associate Judges based on the relevancy of their evaluations of the student Advocates.

The four student Advocates are required to present their arguments before the class. The instructor acts as Chief Judge and questions the Advocates during their presentation. The spectator students are the Associate Judges at this point.

Those students who are not presenting a case and are therefore Associate Judges, are required to listen to the presentation of the four student Advocates, and make evaluations, give grades, and give reasons for the evaluations and grades.

When the spectators or Associate Judges present their own case then they become Advocates and the other students of the class act as Associate Judges.

Therefore, every student is both an Advocate and an Associate Judge and is graded in both capacities.

GUIDE 1
HOMEWORK GUIDE OUTLINE

	Names	Who Prevailed
1. Plaintiff:	____________________	__________
2. Defendant:	____________________	__________
3. Appellant:	____________________	__________
4. Appellee:	____________________	__________

5. Court or Courts (Names): A. B.

6. Description of Case (Distinguishing Features):

7. Question of Law or Fact:

8. A. Allegations of Plaintiff.

   B. Defenses of Defendant.

9. Court Decision: & Court Reason:
   - A. Who Prevailed
   - B. General Principle Decided
   - C. Reasons
   - D. Statutes, Laws Used

10. Dissenting Opinion:

11. Court's Dicta:

12. Then State Your Opinion—Whether You Agree or Disagree: And Your Reasons Why: Cite Cases.

EXPLANATION: Students read the cases for homework and brief them in accordance with the information required by this Guide (on their own notebook paper). The instructor then asks the students questions on the cases, in class, and they can read their answers from their notes, not from their textbooks. After the question period has been completed, the instructor then gives the students the information in the case that he wants them to know on the Guide. This information is in abbreviated form and is written in the form of the Guide.

GUIDE 2
TEST FORM

1. Plaintiff:

2. Defendant:

3. Case Relied On:

4. Question of Law or Fact:

5. A. Allegations of Plaintiff.

   B. Defenses of Defendant.

6. Court Decision and Reasoning:
   A. Who Prevailed
   B. General Principle Decided
   C. Reasons
   D. Statutes, Laws, Constitution, Used & Considered in Decision.

7. Dissenting Opinion:

8. Court Dicta:

9. Your Opinion—Whether You Agree or Disagree: And Your Reasons Why: Cite Cases.

Suggestion: For Each Case—Write in the Above Numbers and Headings (May Be Abbreviated) on Your Paper, Before Writing in the Required Information.

EXPLANATION: For the test, the instructor gives the students 2 hypothetical cases with facts that can be identified only with two of the cases that they have had for homework. The real names of the parties in the homework cases are disguised in the test cases. Then the students answer the questions on the Test Form in accordance with the information answers they were given by the instructor on Guide 1.

GUIDE 3
INSTRUCTIONS FOR APPEAL MOOT COURT

1. Brief should be typewritten (8 1/2 x 11), double space, 6 pages, 1/2 inch margins.
2. Copy of Appellant Brief should be submitted to the court, and to the Counsel for Appellee, on ____________________.
3. Copy of Appellee brief should be submitted to the Counsel for Appellant, and to the court, 1 week later, on ____________________ .
4. Hearing Date of arguments shall be 2 weeks after filing of Appellant brief, namely on ____________________.
5. Counsel for parties should be ready for oral argument before the court, and for Questions by the court, on hearing date.
6. Counsel for Appellant shall present the declaration of their Arguments; 5 minutes for each counsellor.
7. Counsel for Appellee shall present their oral Answer to Appellant's Arguments, 5 minutes for each counsellor.
8. Appellant's Counsel, shall present their oral reply 3 minutes for each counsellor.
9. Appellee's Counsel shall present their oral rejoinder, 3 minutes for each counsellor.

EXPLANATION: These are instructions for the brief and for the time schedule. The cases used for the Moot Court are marked in the book (they have a majority and dissenting opinions so both sides can develop their arguments). All students read all the Moot Court cases even though they act as "Advocates" for only 1 case. This is done because they have to know all the cases in order to act as "Associate Judge" for those students who are the "Advocates" for their one "Moot Court case." If the students are to be "Associate Judges" in a "Moot Court case" they will brief the case in accordance with Guide 1, hand in the original, and keep a carbon copy of the brief.

GUIDE 4
FORM OF BRIEF FOR APPEAL (APPELLANT)
AVI 261 Appeal Court Practice

In The

Appeal Moot Court of the Miami-Dade Community College-South

________________Term, 19_______ No.______

________________________________, Appellant

VS.

________________________________, Appellee

Brief For the Appellant

BRIEF SHALL BE IN FOUR PARTS; NUMBERED 1 THROUGH 4 ON YOUR PAPER, AND MUST CONTAIN THE INFORMATION LISTED BELOW IN EACH RESPECTIVE PART.

1. A statement of the case, and points of law involved, in a clear and concise manner.
2. A statement of the Facts of the case.
3. Argument in Support of the position of the Appellant.
4. An Appendix which shall contain a copy of the material portions of the order, judgment or decree appealed from, together with any opinion of the Court filed in the case. The appendix should also contain a copy of such parts of the original record, material to the points presented, as the Appellant desires the Court to read.

"CONCLUSION"

"For the reasons stated, it is respectfully submitted that the order of the Court below should be reversed."

____

____

Counsel for the Appellant

Date ____________________

EXPLANATION: This is the form for the Appellant Brief. It is 6 pages in length, typed, double spaced, and graded for neatness and accuracy.

GUIDE 5
FORM OF BRIEF FOR APPEAL (APPELLEE)
AVI 261 Appeal Court Practice
In The
Appeal Moot Court of the Miami-Dade Community College-South

________________ Term, 19_______ No._______

________________________________, Appellant

VS.

________________________________, Appellee

Brief For the Appellee

BRIEF SHALL BE IN FOUR PARTS; NUMBERED 1 THROUGH 4 ON YOUR PAPER, AND MUST CONTAIN THE INFORMATION LISTED BELOW IN EACH RESPECTIVE PART.

1. Statement of the case and points of law involved, in a clear and concise manner.
2. A statement of the facts of the case which are necessary to correct or amplify the statement in Appellant's brief in so far as it is deemed erroneous or inadequate.
3. Argument on each point presented by Appellant and such additional points as Appellee desires to present.
4. An appendix which shall contain a copy of the material portions of the order, judgment or decree appealed from, together with any opinion of the Court filed in the case. Appendix should also contain a copy of such parts of the record as appellee desires the Court to read.

"CONCLUSION"

"For the reasons stated it is respectfully submitted that the order of the Court below should be affirmed."

____

____

Counsel for the Appellee

Date____________________

EXPLANATION: This is the form for the Appellee Brief. It is 6 pages in length, typed, double spaced, and graded for neatness and accuracy.

GUIDE 6
ASSOCIATE JUDGE GRADING SHEET

Associate Judge's Name ______________________

Case No.: ______________ Case Name: ______________

Attorneys for Appellant 1. ______________ 2. ______________

Attorneys for Appellees 3. ______________ 4. ______________

1. He presents case well (clear, concise, complete, understandable).
2. He answered questions to point.
3. He answered questions in self-assured manner.
4. He knew the facts of his case well.
5. He knew the law of the case.

Answer "Yes" or "No" After Because

Circle Grade

Appellant Attorney No. 1. ______________ Grade A B C D F

Because 1.____ 2.____ 3.____ 4.____ 5.____

Comment

Appellant Attorney No. 2. ______________ Grade A B C D F

Because 1.____ 2.____ 3.____ 4.____ 5.____

Comment

Appellee Attorney No. 3. ______________ Grade A B C D F

Because 1.____ 2.____ 3.____ 4.____ 5.____

Comment

Appellee Attorney No. 4. ______________ Grade A B C D F

Because 1.____ 2.____ 3.____ 4.____ 5.____

Comment

EXPLANATION: The "Advocates" are not graded on these evaluations. The instructor grades the "Associate Judges" on how well they analyze the "Advocates." The student "Associate Judges" are each given 2 copies of this Guide 6, (with carbon). After the "Associate Judges" have made their evaluations of each group of Advocates, the instructor collects the original copy and the student keeps the carbon. The instructor then asks the "Associate Judges" questions at the end of the "Advocates" presentation of their case.

GUIDE 7
STUDENT GRADES

Name of Student: *Jack Learner*

As Advocate: (Knowledge of Case, Analysis, Ability to Answer Questions)

Court Case No.: *1* Style *U.S. v. Causby*

Appellant *Jack Learner* Grade *30 points*

or

Appellee ______ Grade ______

As Writer of Briefs: (Clarity, Phraseology, Neatness, Typing, Spelling)

Grade *30 points*

As Associate Judge: (Knowledge of Case, Analysis of Advocate, Phraseology, Spelling)

Case No. *2* , *N.W. v. Minnesota* Grade *10 points*

Case No. *3* , *Griggs v. Allegheny* Grade *10 points*

Case No. *4* , *Thornburg v. Portland* Grade *10 points*

Case No. *5* , *Southern Pacific v. Jensen* Grade *10 points*

Case No. ______ , ______ Grade ______

Case No. ______ , ______ Grade ______

Case No. ______ , ______ Grade ______

Case No. ______ , ______ Grade ______

Moot Court Grade *100 points (is "A")*

EXPLANATION: This Guide 7 is used by the instructor to grade students in the "Moot Court Cases." The top portion is used to grade a student as "Advocate." The instructor as "Chief Judge" asks the "Advocates" questions while they are presenting their case. Added to this grade is the grade the student made while acting as "Associate Judge," (the lower portion). This "Moot Court" grade is then incorporated with the student's grade to arrive at the total grade for the term.

A sample is written above: A student is an "Appellant Advocate" for 1 case, and is "Associate Judge" for 4 cases. (Total of 5 cases, 20 students, 4 students to each case).

CHAPTER 11

Legal Definitions

Ad valorem—In proportion to the value.

Allegation—The statement of a plaintiff, in a pleading, setting out what he expects to prove.

Appellant—One who appeals to a higher court from the decision of a lower court.

Appellee—One against whom an appeal is taken.

Applicant—A person who applies for a specific action to be taken by a board. (But not against another party.)

Certiorari—An auxiliary writ to enable an appellate (higher court) to review the record of an inferior court, or administrative body. It is immediate, and to determine whether authority below was abused or exceeded.

Chattels—An article of personal property (not a fee in land).

Congeries—Collection of parts, particles into one mass, or aggregation.

Contributory negligence—Set up as a defense, means negligence of plaintiff which contributed to the injury as a proximate cause.

Defendant—A defending party; a person being sued or being accused.

Defenses—Statements of a defendant, setting out what he intends to prove.

Duty of care—Slight, reasonable, or great care required of a reasonable person if he were acting for himself under the circumstances.

Effect of releases—(1) Express release (specific terms); (2) Implied release (arises from acts); (3) Operation by law (law presumes release because of act, i.e., release of joint obligor).

e.g. (exempli gratia)—For example.

Fact and scope of employment—Term is defined by statute and depends on circumstances and facts even though master servant, or some other form of contractual relationship exists or does not exist.

Forum—A body that hears the argument and makes a decision on it. (tribunal)

id. (idem)—The same.

i.e. (id est)—That is.

In extremis—At the point of death.

Infra—Below.

Injunction—A prohibitive writ issued by a court of equity directed to a defendant to do or refrain from doing a particular act.

Inter alia—Among other things.

Intervenors—A person who voluntarily interposes in an action or other proceeding with leave of the court or board.

Judge's province—To determine the application of law to facts of the case.

Jurisdiction—Means the court with the power or authority to decide a case.

Jury province—To determine questions of fact, credibility of witnesses.

League—3 miles.

Liability—The state of being bound in law or justice to perform an obligation.

Lien—A charge imposed on specific property by which the property is made security for payment of any debt or duty.

Mandamus—A writ from an appellate (or higher) court and directed to a private, municipal, corporation, officers, administrative body or inferior court, commanding performance of a person to do or to refrain from doing a particular act.

Negligence—Failure to exercise that care which a prudent, reasonable person would exercise (Tort).

Nexus—Connection.

Obiter dictum—Incidental passing remark. Judicial opinion on a point other than the precise issue involved in the case.

Petitioner—A person who requests a specific action be taken by a board or court (against another party).

Plaintiff—A person who brings a suit into a court of law (one who complains against another party).

Privity—A direct relationship between two parties to a contract.

Procedural law—The method (form of action, manner) by which one party attempts to enforce a particular right or obligation to which he is entitled.

Proximate cause—That which stands next in causation to effect, not necessarily in time or space, but in causal relation.

Proximity—The state or quality of being near (in time, space, etc.).

Remand—To send a case back to a lower court, with directions concerning additional proceedings.

Res ipsa loquitur—The thing (fact) speaks for itself. (A rebuttable presumption that defendant was negligent.)

Respondent—One who answers in certain lawsuits or proceedings.

Subrogation–Putting a third person, who has paid a debt, in the place of the creditor to whom he paid it, so that he may exercise against the debtor all the rights which the creditor, if unpaid, might have done.

Subrogee–A person who is subrogated; one who succeeds to the rights of another, by subrogation.

Substantive law–Are the general principles that determine the rights and obligations of individuals or groups.

Sui generis–Of its own kind, peculiar to itself.

Supra–Above.

Tariff–Is a list or schedule of charges for services and for transportation of goods and people; and the conditions therefor.

Tort–Any wrongful act (not involving contract) to which a civil action can be brought.

Venue–Means the particular county, city, or district in which a court with jurisdiction may hear the case (geographical).

Willful Misconduct–A conscious intent to do or omit doing an act from which harm results to another, or an intentional omission of a manifest duty.

Writ–An instrument in writing in form of letter directed to an inferior court or a defendant.

CHAPTER 12

Extracts of Statutes for Cases

EXTRACT A

Extracts from

The Constitution of the United States

ARTICLE I.

SECTION 1. All legislative powers herein granted shall be vested in a Congress of the United States, which shall consist of a Senate and House of Representatives.

SECTION 8. The Congress shall have power to lay and collect taxes, duties, imposts and excises, to pay the debts and provide for the common defence and general welfare of the United States; but all duties, imposts and excises shall be uniform throughout the United States:

To borrow money on the credit of the United States:

To regulate commerce with foreign nations, and among the several states, and with the Indian tribes:

To establish an uniform rule of naturalization, and uniform laws on the subject of bankruptcies throughout the United States:

To coin money, regulate the value thereof, and of foreign coin, and fix the standard of weights and measures:

To provide for the punishment of counterfeiting the securities and current coin of the United States:

To establish post-offices and post-roads:

To promote the progress of science and useful arts, by securing for limited times to authors and inventors the exclusive right to their respective writings and discoveries:

To constitute tribunals inferior to the supreme court:

To define and punish piracies and felonies committed on the high seas, and offences against the law of nations:

To declare war, grant letters of marque and reprisal, and make rules concerning captures on land and water:

To raise and support armies, but no appropriation of money to that use shall be for a longer term than two years:

To provide and maintain a navy:

To make rules for the government and regulation of the land and naval forces:

To provide for calling forth the militia to execute the laws of the union, suppress insurrections and repel invasions:

To provide for organizing, arming and disciplining the militia, and for governing such part of them as may be employed in the service of the United States, reserving to the states respectively, the appointment of the officers, and the authority of training the militia according to the discipline prescribed by Congress:

To exercise exclusive legislation in all cases whatsoever, over such district (not exceeding ten miles square) as may, by cession of particular states, and the acceptance of Congress, become the seat of the government of the United States, and to exercise like authority over all places purchased by the consent of the legislature of the state in which the same shall be, for the erection of forts, magazines, arsenals, dock-yards, and other needful buildings: And,

To make all laws which shall be necessary and proper for carrying into execution the foregoing powers, and all other powers vested by this Constitution in the government of the United States, or in any department or officer thereof.

SECTION 9. The privilege of the writ of habeas corpus shall not be suspended, unless when in cases of rebellion or invasion the public safety may require it.

No bill of attainder or ex post facto law shall be passed.

No capitation, or other direct tax shall be laid unless in proportion to the census or enumeration herein before directed to be taken.

No tax or duty shall be laid on articles exported from any state.

No preference shall be given by any regulation of commerce or revenue to the ports of one state over those of another: nor shall vessels bound to, or from one state, be obliged to enter, clear, or pay duties in another.

No money shall be drawn from the treasury but in consequence of appropriations made by law; and a regular statement and account of the receipts and expenditures of all public money shall be published from time to time.

ARTICLE II.

SECTION 1. The executive power shall be vested in a President of the United States of America. He shall hold his office during the term of four years, and, together with the Vice President, chosen for the same term, be elected as follows:

Each state shall appoint, in such manner as the legislature thereof may direct, a number of electors, equal to the whole number of senators and representatives to which the state may be entitled in the Congress; but no senator or representative, or person holding an office of trust or profit under the United States, shall be appointed an elector.

Before he enter on the execution of his office, he shall take the following oath or affirmation:

"I do solemnly swear (or affirm) that I will faithfully execute the office of President of the United States, and will to the best of my ability, preserve, protect and defend the Constitution of the United States."

SECTION 2. The President shall be commander in chief of the army and navy of the United States, and of the militia of the several states, when called into the actual service of the United States; he may require the opinion, in writing, of the principal officer in each of the executive departments, upon any subject relating to the duties of their respective offices, and he shall have power to grant reprieves and pardons for offences against the United States, except in cases of impeachment.

He shall have power, by and with the advice and consent of the Senate, to make treaties, provided two-thirds of the senators present concur; and he shall nominate, and by and with the advice and consent of the Senate, shall appoint ambassadors, other public ministers and consuls, judges of the supreme court, and all other officers of the United States, whose appointments are not herein otherwise provided for, and which shall be established by law. But the Congress may by law vest the appointment of such inferior officers, as they think proper in the President alone, in the courts of law, or in the heads of departments.

SECTION 4. The President, Vice President, and all civil officers of the United States shall be removed from office on impeachment for, and conviction of, treason, bribery, or other high crimes and misdemeanors.

ARTICLE III.

SECTION 1. The judicial power of the United States, shall be vested in one supreme court, and in such inferior courts as the Congress may, from time to time, ordain and establish. The judges, both of the supreme and inferior courts, shall hold their offices during good behavior, and shall, at stated times, receive for their services a compensation, which shall not be diminished during their continuance in office.

SECTION 2. The judicial power shall extend to all cases, in law and equity, arising under this Constitution, the laws of the United States, and treaties made, or which shall be made under their authority; to all cases affecting ambassadors, other public ministers and consuls; to all cases of admiralty and maritime jurisdiction; to controversies to which the United States shall be a party: to controversies between two or more states, *between a state and citizens of another state,* between citizens of different states, between citizens of the same state, claiming lands under grants of different states, and between a state, or the citizens thereof, and foreign states, *citizens or subjects.*

In all cases affecting ambassadors, other public ministers and consuls, and those in which a state shall be party, the supreme court shall have original jurisdiction. In all the other cases before-mentioned, the supreme court shall have appellate jurisdiction, both as to law and fact, with such exceptions, and under such regulations as the Congress shall make.

The trial of all crimes, except in cases of impeachment, shall be by jury; and such trial shall be held in the state where the said crimes shall have been committed; but when not committed within any state, the trial shall be at such place or places as the Congress may by law have directed.

These two italicized passages are limited by Amendment XI.

SECTION 3. Treason against the United States shall consist only in levying war against them, or in adhering to their enemies, giving them aid and comfort. No person shall be convicted of treason unless on the testimony of two witnesses to the same overt act, or on confession in open court.

The Congress shall have power to declare the punishment of treason, but no attainder of treason shall work corruption of blood, or forfeiture, except during the life of the person attainted.

ARTICLE IV.

SECTION 1. Full faith and credit shall be given in each state to the public acts, records and judicial proceedings of every other state. And the Congress may by general laws prescribe the manner in which such acts, records and proceedings shall be proved, and the effect thereof.

SECTION 2. The citizens of each state shall be entitled to all privileges and immunities of citizens in the several states.

A person charged in any state with treason, felony, or other crime, who shall flee from justice, and be found in another state, shall, on demand of the executive authority of the state from which he fled, be delivered up, to be removed to the state having jurisdiction of the crime.

SECTION 3. New states may be admitted by the Congress into this union; but no new state shall be formed or erected within the jurisdiction of any other state, nor any state be formed by the junction of two or more states, or parts of states, without the consent of the legislatures of the states concerned as well as of the Congress.

The Congress shall have power to dispose of and make all needful rules and regulations respecting the territory or other property belonging to the United States; and nothing in this Constitution shall be so construed as to prejudice any claims of the United States, or of any particular state.

SECTION 4. The United States shall guarantee to every state in this union a republican form of government, and shall protect each of them against invasion; and on application of the legislature, or of the executive (when the legislature cannot be convened), against domestic violence.

ARTICLE VI.

All debts contracted and engagements entered into, before the adoption of this Constitution, shall be as valid against the United States under this Constitution, as under the confederation.

This Constitution, and the laws of the United States which shall be made in pursuance thereof; and all treaties made, or which shall be made, under the authority of the United States, shall be the supreme law of the land; and the judges in every state shall be bound thereby, any thing in the constitution or laws of any state to the contrary notwithstanding.

The senators and representatives before-mentioned, and the members of the several state legislatures, and all executive and judicial officers, both of the United States and of the several states, shall be bound by oath or affirmation, to support this Constitution; but no religious test shall ever be required as a qualification to any office or public trust under the United States.

AMENDMENTS TO THE CONSTITUTION

(The first ten Amendments, usually called the Bill of Rights, went into effect December 15, 1791.)

AMENDMENT I.

Congress shall make no law respecting an establishment of religion, or prohibiting the free exercise thereof; or abridging the freedom of speech or of the press; or the right of the people peaceably to assemble, and to petition the government for a redress of grievances.

AMENDMENT II.

A well-regulated militia being necessary to the security of a free state, the right of the people to keep and bear arms shall not be infringed.

AMENDMENT III.

No soldier shall, in time of peace, be quartered in any house without the consent of the owner, nor in time of war but in a manner to be prescribed by law.

AMENDMENT IV.

The right of the people to be secure in their persons, houses, papers, and effects, against unreasonable searches and seizures, shall not be violated, and no warrants shall issue but upon probable cause, supported by oath or affirmation, and particularly describing the place to be searched, and the persons or things to be seized.

AMENDMENT V.

No person shall be held to answer for a capital or other infamous crime unless on a presentment or indictment of a grand jury, except in cases arising in the land or naval forces, or in the militia, when in actual service, in time of war or public danger; nor shall any person be subject for the same offence to be twice put in jeopardy of life or limb; nor shall be compelled in any criminal case to be a witness against himself, nor be deprived of life, liberty, or property, without due process of law; nor shall private property be taken for public use without just compensation.

AMENDMENT VI.

In all criminal prosecutions, the accused shall enjoy the right to a speedy and public trial, by an impartial jury of the state and district wherein the crime shall have been committed, which district shall have been previously ascertained by law, and to be informed of the nature and cause of the accusation; to be confronted with the witnesses against him; to have compulsory process for obtaining witnesses in his favor, and to have the assistance of counsel for his defence.

AMENDMENT VII.

In suits at common law, where the value in controversy shall exceed twenty dollars, the right of trial by jury shall be preserved, and no fact tried by a jury shall be otherwise re-examined in any court of the United States than according to the rules of the common law.

AMENDMENT VIII.

Excessive bail shall not be required, nor excessive fines imposed, nor cruel and unusual punishments inflicted.

AMENDMENT IX.

The enumeration in the Constitution of certain rights shall not be construed to deny or disparage others retained by the people.

AMENDMENT X.

The powers not delegated to the United States by the Constitution, nor prohibited by it to the states, are reserved to the states respectively, or to the people.

AMENDMENT XI.
(adopted 1798)

The judicial power of the United States shall not be construed to extend to any suit in law or equity, commenced or prosecuted against one of the United States, by citizens of another state, or by citizens or subjects of any foreign state.

AMENDMENT XIV.
(adopted 1868)

SECTION 1. All persons born or naturalized in the United States, and subject to the jurisdiction thereof, are citizens of the United States and of the state wherein they reside. No state shall make or enforce any law which shall abridge the privileges or immunities of citizens of the United States; nor shall any state deprive any person of life, liberty, or property without due process of law; nor deny to any person within its jurisdiction the equal protection of the law.

EXTRACT B

Extracts from

Federal Aviation Act of 1958

(49 U.S. Code, Sections 1304, et seq.)
49 U.S. Code 1304 (F.A.A. Sec. 104)
49 U.S. Code 1321 (F.A.A. Sec. 201)
49 U.S. Code 1373 (F.A.A. Sec. 403)
49 U.S. Code 1374 (F.A.A. Sec. 404)
49 U.S. Code 1508 (F.A.A. Sec. 1108)

§ 1304. Public right of transit.

There is recognized and declared to exist in behalf of any citizen of the United States a public right of freedom of transit through the navigable airspace of the United States. (Pub. L. 85-726, title I, § 104, Aug. 23, 1958, 72 Stat. 740.)

SUBCHAPTER II–CIVIL AERONAUTICS BOARD; GENERAL POWERS

§ 1321. Agency of the United States.

(a) Continuation; membership; removal of members; political affiliation; chairman; compensation.

(1) The Civil Aeronautics Board, created and established under the name "Civil Aeronautics Authority" by section 201 of the Civil Aeronautics Act of 1938 and redesignated as the "Civil Aeronautics Board" by Reorganization Plan No. IV of 1940, is continued as an agency of the United States, and shall continue to be composed of five members appointed by the President, by and with the advice and consent of the Senate, for terms of six years, beginning upon the expiration of the terms for which their predecessors were appointed, except that any person appointed to fill a vacancy occurring prior to the expiration of the term for which his predecessor was appointed shall be appointed only for the remainder of such term; but upon the expiration of his term of office a member shall continue to serve until his successor is appointed and shall have qualified.

(2) The members of the Board may be removed by the President for inefficiency, neglect of duty, or malfeasance in office. No more than three of the members shall be appointed from the same political party. The President shall

designate annually one of the members of the Board to serve as chairman and one of the members to serve as vice chairman, who shall act as chairman in the absence or incapacity of the chairman. Each member of the Board shall receive a salary at the rate of $20,000 per annum, except that the member serving as chairman shall receive a salary at the rate of $20,500 per annum.

§ 1373. Tariffs of air carriers.

(a) Filing, posting, and publication; rejection of tariffs.

Every air carrier and every foreign air carrier shall file with the Board, and print, and keep open to public inspection, tariffs showing all rates, fares, and charges for air transportation between points served by it, and between points served by it and points served by any other air carrier or foreign air carrier when through service and through rates shall have been established, and showing to the extent required by regulations of the Board, all classifications, rules, regulations, practices, and services in connection with such air transportation. Tariffs shall be filed, posted, and published in such form and manner, and shall contain such information, as the Board shall by regulation prescribe; and the Board is empowered to reject any tariff so filed which is not consistent with this section and such regulations. Any tariff so rejected shall be void. The rates, fares, and charges shown in any tariff shall be stated in terms of lawful money of the United States, but such tariffs may also state rates, fares, and charges in terms of currencies other than lawful money of the United States, and may, in the case of foreign air transportation, contain such information as may be required under the laws of any country in or to which an air carrier or foreign air carrier is authorized to operate.

(b) Observance of tariffs; granting of rebates.

No air carrier or foreign air carrier shall charge or demand or collect or receive a regulation, or practice affecting such rate, fare, or charge, or the value of the service greater or less or different compensation for air transportation, or for any service in connection therewith, than the rates, fares, and charges specified in its currently effective tariffs; and no air carrier or foreign air carrier shall, in any manner or by any device, directly or indirectly, or through any agent or broker, or otherwise, refund or remit any portion of the rates, fares, or charges so specified, or extend to any person any privileges or facilities, with respect to matters required by the Board to be specified in such tariffs, except those specified therein. Nothing in this chapter shall prohibit such air carriers or foreign air carriers, under such terms and conditions as the Board may prescribe, from issuing or interchanging tickets or passes for free or reduced-rate transportation to their directors, officers, and employees and their immediate families; witnesses and attorneys attending any legal investigation in which any such air carrier is interested; persons injured in aircraft accidents and physicians and nurses attending such persons; and any person or property with the object of providing relief in cases of general epidemic, pestilence, or other calamitous visitation; and, in the case of overseas or foreign air transportation, to such other persons and under such other circumstances as the Board may be regulations prescribe. Any air carrier or foreign air carrier, under such terms and conditions as the Board may prescribe, may grant reduced-rate transportation to ministers of religion on a space-available basis.

(c) Notice of change in tariff.

No change shall be made in any rate, fare, or charge, or any classification, rule, regulation, or practice affecting such rate, fare, or charge, or value of service thereunder, specified in any effective tariff of any air carrier or foreign air carrier, except after thirty days' notice of the proposed change filed, posted, and published in accordance with subsection (a) of this section. Such notice shall plainly state the change proposed to be made and the time such change will take effect. The Board may in the public interest, by regulation or otherwise, allow such change upon notice less than that herein specified, or modify the requirements of this section with respect to filing and posting of tariffs, either in particular instances or by general order applicable to special or peculiar circumstances or conditions.

(d) Filing of divisions of rates and charges.

Every air carrier of foreign air carrier shall keep currently on file with the Board, if the Board so requires, the established divisions of all joint rates, fares, and charges for air transportation in which such air carrier or foreign air carrier participates. (Pub. L. 85-726, title IV, § 403, Aug. 23, 1958, 72 Stat. 758.)

§ 1374. Rates for carriage of persons and property; duty to provide service, rates, and divisions; discrimination.

(a) It shall be the duty of every air carrier to provide and furnish interstate and overseas air transportation, as authorized by its certificate, upon reasonable request therefor and to provide reasonable through service in such air transportation in connection with other air carriers; to provide safe and adequate service, equipment, and facilities in connection with such transportation; to establish, observe, and enforce just and reasonable individual and joint rates, fares, and charges, and just and reasonable classifications, rules, regulations, and practices relating to such air transportation; and, in case of such joint rates, fares, and charges, to establish just, reasonable, and equitable divisions thereof as between air carriers participating therein which shall not unduly prefer or prejudice any of such participating air carriers.

(b) No air carrier or foreign air carrier shall make, give, or cause any undue or unreasonable preference or advantage to any particular person, port, locality, or description of traffic in air transportation in any respect whatsoever or subject any particular person, port, locality, or description of traffic in air transportation to any unjust discrimination or any undue or unreasonable prejudice or disadvantage in any respect whatsoever. (Pub. L. 85-726, title IV, § 404, Aug. 23, 1958, 72 Stat. 760.)

§ 1508. Declaration of national sovereignty in air space; operation of foreign aircraft.

(a) The United States of America is declared to possess and exercise complete and exclusive national sovereignty in the airspace of the United States, including the airspace above all inland waters and the airspace above those portions of the adjacent marginal high seas, bays, and lakes, over which by international law or treaty or convention the United States exercises national jurisdiction. Aircraft of the armed forces of any foreign nation shall not be navigated in the United States, including the Canal Zone, except in accordance with an authorization granted by the Secretary of State.

(b) Foreign aircraft, which are not a part of the armed forces of a foreign nation, may be navigated in the United States by airmen holding certificates or licenses issued or rendered valid by the United States or by the nation in which the aircraft is registered if such foreign nation grants a similar privilege with respect to aircraft of the United States and only if such navigation is authorized by permit, order, or regulation issued by the Board hereunder, and in accordance with the terms, conditions, and limitations thereof. The Board shall issue such permits, orders, or regulations to such extent only as it shall find such action to be in the interest of the public: *Provided, however,* That in exercising its powers hereunder, the Board shall do so consistently with any treaty, convention, or agreement which may be in force between the United States and any foreign country or countries. Foreign civil aircraft permitted to navigate in the United States under this subsection may be authorized by the Board to engage in air commerce within the United States except that they shall not take on at any point within the United States, persons, property, or mail carried for compensation or hire and destined for another point within the United States. Nothing contained in this subsection shall be deemed to limit, modify, or amend section 1372 of this title, but any foreign air carrier holding a permit under said section shall not be required to obtain additional authorization under this subsection with respect to any operation authorized by said permit. (Pub. L. 85-726, title XI, § 1108, Aug. 23, 1958, 72 Stat. 798.)

EXTRACT C

Extracts from

Death on High Seas Act

(46 U.S. Code, Sec. 761-768)
(Note: D.H.S.A. Sections 1 through 8, is same as U.S.C.A. Sec. 761 through 768.)

Chapter 21.–DEATH ON THE HIGH SEAS BY WRONGFUL ACT

Sec.
761. Right of action; where and by whom brought.
762. Amount and apportionment of recovery.
763. Limitations.
764. Rights of action given by laws of foreign countries.
765. Death of plaintiff pending action.
766. Contributory negligence.
767. Exceptions from operation of chapter.
768. Pending suits.

§ 761. Right of action; where and by whom brought.

Whenever the death of a person shall be caused by wrongful act, neglect, or default occurring on the high seas beyond a marine league from the shore of any State, or the District of Columbia, or the Territories or dependencies of the United States, the personal representative of the decedent may maintain a suit for damages in the district courts of the United States, in admiralty, for the exclusive benefit of the decedent's wife, husband, parent, child, or dependent relative against the vessel, person, or corporation which would have been liable if death had not ensued. (Mar. 30, 1920, ch. 111, § 1, 41 Stat. 537.)

§ 762. Amount and apportionment of recovery.

The recovery in such suit shall be a fair and just compensation for the pecuniary loss sustained by the persons for whose benefit the suit is brought and shall be apportioned among them by the court in proportion to the loss they may severally have suffered by reason of the death of the person by whose representative the suit is brought. (Mar. 30, 1920, ch. 111, § 2, 41 Stat. 537.)

CROSS REFERENCES

Death of plaintiff pending action, see section 765 of this title.

§ 763. Limitations.

Suit shall be begun within 2 years from the date of such wrongful act, neglect, or default, unless during that period there has not been reasonable opportunity for securing jurisdiction of the vessel, person, or corporation sought to be charged; but after the expiration of such period of two years the right of action hereby given shall not be deemed to have lapsed until ninety days after a reasonable opportunity to secure jurisdiction has offered. (Mar. 30, 1920, ch. 111, § 3, 41 Stat. 537.)

§ 764. Rights of action given by laws of foreign countries.

Whenever a right of action is granted by the law of any foreign State on account of death by wrongful act, neglect, or default occurring upon the high seas, such right may be maintained in an appropriate action in admiralty in the courts of the United States without abatement in respect to the amount for which recovery is authorized, any statute of the United States to the contrary notwithstanding. (Mar. 30, 1920, ch. 111, § 4, 41 Stat. 537.)

§ 765. Death of plaintiff pending action.

If a person die as the result of such wrongful act, neglect, or default as is mentioned in section 761 of this title during the pendency in a court of admiralty of the United States of a suit to recover damages for personal injuries in respect of such act, neglect, or default, the personal representative of the decedent may be substituted as a party and the suit may proceed as a suit under this chapter for the recovery of the compensation provided in section 762 of this title. (Mar. 30, 1920, ch. 111, § 5, 41 Stat. 537.)

§ 766. Contributory negligence.

In suits under this chapter the fact that the decedent has been guilty of contributory negligence shall not bar recovery, but the court shall take into consideration the degree of negligence attributable to the decedent and reduce the recovery accordingly. (Mar. 30, 1920, ch. 111, § 6, 41 Stat. 537.)

§ 767. Exceptions from operation of chapter.

The provisions of any State statue giving or regulating rights of action or remedies for death shall not be affected by this chapter. Nor shall this chapter apply to the Great Lakes or to any waters within the territorial limits of any State, or to any navigable waters in the Panama Canal Zone. (Mar. 30, 1920, ch. 111, § 7, 41 Stat. 538.)

§ 768. Pending suits.

CODIFICATION

Section, act Mar. 30, 1920, ch. 111, § 8, 41 Stat. 538, provided that this chapter should not affect suits pending on March 30, 1920.

EXTRACT D

Extracts from

Federal Tort Claims Act (1946)

(28 U.S. Code, Sec. 1346, et seq.)
[Including provisions of Tucker Act, (1887) Sec. 1346(a)(2)]

§ 1346. United States as defendant.

(a) The district courts shall have original jurisdiction, concurrent with the Court of Claims, of:

(1) Any civil action against the United States for the recovery of any internal-revenue tax alleged to have been erroneonusly or illegally assessed or collected, or any penalty claimed to have been collected without authority or any sum alleged to have been excessive or in any manner wrongfully collected under the internal-revenue laws;

(2) Any other civil action or claim against the United States, not exceeding $10,000 in amount, founded either upon the Constitution, or any Act of Congress, or any regulation of an executive department, or upon any express or implied contract with the United States, or for liquidated or unliquidated damages in cases not sounding in tort.

(b) Subject to the provisions of chapter 171 of this title, the district courts, together with the United States District Court for the District of the Canal Zone and the District Court of the Virgin Islands, shall have exclusive jurisdiction of civil actions on claims against the United States, for money damages, accruing on and after January 1, 1945, for injury or loss of property, or personal injury or death caused by the negligent or wrongful act or omission of any employee of the Government while acting within the scope of his office or employment, under circumstances where the United States, if a private person, would be liable to the claimant in accordance with the law of the place where the act or omission occurred.

(c) The jurisdiction conferred by this section includes jurisdiction of any set-off, counterclaim, or other claim or demand whatever on the part of the United States against any plaintiff commencing an action under this section.

(d) The district courts shall not have jurisdiction under this section of:

(1) Any civil action or claim for a pension;

(2) Any civil action or claim to recover fees, salary, or compensation for official services of officers or employees of the United States.

§ 1402. United States as defendant.

(a) Any civil action against the United States under subsection (a) of section 1346 of this title may be prosecuted only:

(1) Except as provided in paragraph (2), in the judicial district where the plaintiff resides;

(2) In the case of a civil action by a corporation under paragraph (1) of subsection (a) of section 1346, in the judicial district in which is located the principal place of business or principal office or agency of the corporation; or if it has no principal place of business or principal office or agency in any judicial district (A) in the judicial district in which is located the office to which was made the return of the tax in respect of which the claim is made, or (B) if no return was made, in the judicial district in which lies the District of Columbia. Notwithstanding the foregoing provisions of this paragraph a district court, for the convenience of the parties and witnesses, in the interest of justice, may transfer any such action to any other district or division.

(b) Any civil action on a tort claim against the United States under subsection (b) of section 1346 of this title may be prosecuted only in the judicial district where the plaintiff resides or wherein the act or omission complained of occurred. (June 25, 1948, ch. 646, 62 Stat. 937; Sept. 2, 1958, Pub. L. 85–920, 72 Stat. 1770.)

§ 1504. Tort claims.

The Court of Claims shall have jurisdiction to review by appeal final judgments in the district courts in civil actions based on tort claims brought under section 1346 (b) of this title if the notice of appeal filed in the district court has affixed thereto the written consent on behalf of all the appellees that the appeal be taken to the Court of Claims. (June 25, 1948, ch. 646, 62 Stat. 942.)

§ 2402. Jury trial in actions against United States.

Any action against the United States under section 1346 shall be tried by the court without a jury, except that any action against the United States under section 1346 (a) (1) shall, at the request of either party to such action, be tried by the court with a jury. (June 25, 1948, ch. 646, 62 Stat. 971; July 30, 1954, ch. 648, § 2 (a), 68 Stat. 589.)

§ 2674. Liability of United States.

The United States shall be liable, respecting the provisions of this title relating to tort claims, in the same manner and to the same extent as a private individual under like circumstances, but shall not be liable for interest prior to judgment or for punitive damages.

If, however, in any case wherein death was caused, the law of the place where the act or omission complained of occurred provides, or has been construed to provide, for damages only punitive in nature, the United States shall be liable for actual or compensatory damages, measured by the pecuniary injuries resulting from such death to the persons respectively, for whose benefit the action was brought, in lieu thereof. (June 25, 1948, ch. 646, 62 Stat. 983.)

§ 2679. Exclusiveness of remedy.

The authority of any federal agency to sue and be sued in its own name shall not be construed to authorize suits against such federal agency on claims which are cognizable under section 1346 (b) of this title, and the remedies provided by this title in such cases shall be exclusive. (June 25, 1948, ch. 646, 62 Stat. 984.)

§ 2680. Exceptions.

The provisions of this chapter and section 1346 (b) of this title shall not apply to—

(a) Any claim based upon an act or omission of an employee of the Government, exercising due care, in the execution of a statute or regulation, whether or not such statute or regulation be valid, or based upon the exercise or performance or the failure to exercise or perform a discretionary function or duty on the part of a federal agency or an employee of the Government, whether or not the discretion involved be abused.

(b) Any claim arising out of the loss, miscarriage, or negligent transmission of letters or postal matter.

(c) Any claim arising in respect of the assessment or collection of any tax or customs duty, or the detention of any goods or merchandise by any officer of customs or excise or any other law-enforcement officer.

(d) Any claim for which a remedy is provided by sections 741-752, 781-790 of Title 46, relating to claims or suits in admiralty against the United States.

(e) Any claim arising out of an act or omission of any employee of the Government in administering the provisions of sections 1-31 of Title 50, Appendix.

(f) Any claim for damages caused by the imposition or establishment of a quarantine by the United States.

(g) Repealed. Sept. 26, 1950, ch. 1049, § 13 (5), 64 Stat. 1043.

(h) Any claim arising out of assault, battery, false imprisonment, false arrest, malicious prosecution, abuse of process, libel, slander, misrepresentation, deceit, or interference with contract rights.

(i) Any claim for damages caused by the fiscal operations of the Treasury or by the regulation of the monetary system.

(j) Any claim arising out of the combatant activities of the military or naval forces, or the Coast Guard, during time of war.

(k) Any claim arising in a foreign country.

(l) Any claim arising from the activities of the Tennessee Valley Authority.

(m) Any claim arising from the activities of the Panama Canal Company. (June 25, 1948, ch. 646, 63 Stat. 984; July 16, 1949, ch. 340, 63 Stat. 444; Sept. 26, 1950, ch. 1049, §§ 2 (a) (2), 13 (5), 64 Stat. 1038.)

EXTRACT E

Extracts from

Interstate Commerce Act, Part II

(49 U.S. Code, Sec. 303-304)

§ 303. Definitions and exceptions.

(b) Vehicles excepted from operation of law.

Nothing in this chapter, except the provisions of section 304 of this title relative to qualifications and maximum hours of service of employees and safety of operation or standards of equipment shall be construed to include

(7a) the transportation of persons or property by motor vehicle when incidental to transportation by aircraft;

§ 304. Powers and duties of Commission.

(a) Powers and duties generally.

It shall be the duty of the Commission—

(1) To regulate common carriers by motor vehicle as provided in this chapter, and to that end the Commission may establish reasonable requirements with respect to continuous and adequate service, transportation of baggage and express, uniform systems of accounts, records, and reports, preservation of records, qualifications and maximum hours of service of employees, and safety of operation and equipment.

(2) To regulate contract carriers by motor vehicle as provided in this chapter, and to that end the Commission may establish reasonable requirements with respect to uniform systems of accounts, records, and reports, preservation of records, qualifications and maximum hours of service of employees, and safety of operation and equipment.

(3) To establish for private carriers of property by motor vehicle, if need therefor is found, reasonable requirements to promote safety of operation, and to that end prescribe qualifications and maximum hours of service of employees, and standards of equipment. In the event such requirements are established, the term "motor carrier" shall be construed to include private carriers of property by motor vehicle in the administration of subsection (c) of this section and sections 305, 320, 321, 322 (a), (b), (d), (f), and (g), and 324 of this title.

(5) For the purpose of carrying out the provisions pertaining to safety, the Commission may avail itself of the assistance of any of the several research agencies of the Federal Government having special knowledge of any such matter, to conduct such scientific and technical researches, investigations, and tests as may be necessary to promote the safety of operation and equipment of motor vehicles as provided in this chapter; the Commission may transfer to such agency or agencies such funds as may be necessary and available to make this provision effective.

(6) To administer, execute, and enforce all provisions of this chapter, to make all necessary orders in connection therewith, and to prescribe rules, regulations, and procedure for such administration.

EXTRACT F

Extracts from

Warsaw Convention (1929)

(49 U.S. Statutes, Page 3014)

CHAPTER I. SCOPE–DEFINITIONS

Article 1

(1) This convention shall apply to all international transportation of persons, baggage, or goods performed by aircraft for hire. It shall apply equally to gratuitous transportation by aircraft performed by an air transportation enterprise.

(2) For the purposes of this convention the expression "international transportation" shall mean any transportation in which, according to the contract made by the parties, the place of departure and the place of destination, whether or not there be a break in the transportation or a transshipment, are situated either within the territories of two High Contracting Parties, or within the territory of a single High Contracting Party, if there is an agreed stopping place within a territory subject to the sovereignty, suzerainty, mandate or authority of another power, even though that power is not a party to this convention. Transportation without such an agreed stopping place between territories subject to the sovereignty, suzerainty, mandate, or authority of the same High Contracting Party shall not be deemed to be international for the purposes of this convention.

(3) Transportation to be performed by several successive air carriers shall be deemed, for the purposes of this convention, to be one undivided transportation, if it has been regarded by the parties as a single operation, whether it has been agreed upon under the form of a single contract or of a series of contracts, and it shall not lose its international character merely because one contract or a series of contracts is to be performed entirely within a territory subject to the sovereignty, suzerainty, mandate, or authority of the same High Contracting Party.

Article 2

(1) This convention shall apply to transportation performed by the state or by legal entities constituted under public law provided it falls within the conditions laid down in article 1.

(2) This convention shall not apply to transportation performed under the terms of any international postal convention.

CHAPTER II. TRANSPORTATION DOCUMENTS

SECTION I—PASSENGER TICKET

Article 3

(1) For the transportation of passengers the carrier must deliver a passenger ticket which shall contain the following particulars:

(a) The place and date of issue;

(b) The place of departure and of destination;

(c) The agreed stopping places, provided that the carrier may reserve the right to alter the stopping places in case of necessity, and that if he exercises that right, the alteration shall not have the effect of depriving the transportation of its international character;

(d) The name and address of the carrier or carriers;

(e) A statement that the transportation is subject to the rules relating to liability established by this convention.

(2) The absence, irregularity, or loss of the passenger ticket shall not affect the existence or the validity of the contract of transportation, which shall none the less be subject to the rules of this convention. Nevertheless, if the carrier accepts a passenger without a passenger ticket having been delivered he shall not be entitled to avail himself of those provisions of this convention which exclude or limit his liability.

SECTION II.—BAGGAGE CHECK

Article 4

(1) For the transportation of baggage, other than small personal objects of which the passenger takes charge himself, the carrier must deliver a baggage check.

(2) The baggage check shall be made out in duplicate, one part for the passenger and the other part for the carrier.

(3) The baggage check shall contain the following particulars:

(a) The place and date of issue;

(b) The place of departure and of destination;

(c) The name and address of the carrier or carriers;

(d) The number of the passenger ticket;

(e) A statement that delivery of the baggage will be made to the bearer of the baggage check;

(f) The number and weight of the packages;

(g) The amount of the value declared in accordance with article 22 (2);

(h) A statement that the transportation is subject to the rules relating to liability established by this convention.

(4) The absence, irregularity, or loss of the baggage check shall not affect the existence or the validity of the contract of transportation which shall none

the less be subject to the rules of this convention. Nevertheless, if the carrier accepts baggage without a baggage check having been delivered, or if the baggage check does not contain the particulars set out at (d), (f), and (h) above, the carrier shall not be entitled to avail himself of those provisions of the convention which exclude or limit his liability.

Article 8

The air waybill shall contain the following particulars:

(a) The place and date of its execution;

(b) The place of departure and of destination;

(c) The agreed stopping places, provided that the carrier may reserve the right to alter the stopping places in case of necessity, and that if he exercises that right the alteration shall not have the effect of depriving the transportation of its international character;

(d) The name and address of the consignor;

(e) The name and address of the first carrier;

(f) The name and address of the consignee, if the case so requires;

(g) The nature of the goods;

(h) The number of packages, the method of packing, and the particular marks or numbers upon them;

(i) The weight, the quantity, the volume, or dimensions of the goods;

(j) The apparent condition of the goods and of the packing;

(k) The freight, if it has been agreed upon, the date and place of payment, and the person who is to pay it;

(l) If the goods are sent for payment on delivery, the price of the goods, , and, if the case so requires, the amount of the expenses incurred;

(m) The amount of the value declared in accordance with article 22 (2);

(n) The number of parts of the air waybill;

(o) The documents handed to the carrier to accompany the air waybill;

(p) The time fixed for the completion of the transportation and a brief note of the route to be followed, if these matters have been agreed upon;

(q) A statement that the transportation is subject to the rules relating to liability established by this convention.

Article 9

If the carrier accepts goods without an air waybill having been made out, or if the air waybill does not contain all the particulars set out in article 8 (a) to (i), inclusive, and (q), the carrier shall not be entitled to avail himself of the provisions of this convention which exclude or limit his liability.

Article 17

The carrier shall be liable for damage sustained in the event of the death or wounding of a passenger or any other bodily injury suffered by a passenger, if the accident which caused the damage so sustained took place on board the aircraft or in the course of any of the operations of embarking or disembarking.

Article 20

(1) The carrier shall not be liable if he proves that he and his agents have taken all necessary measures to avoid the damage or that it was impossible for him or them to take such measures.

(2) In the transportation of goods and baggage the carrier shall not be liable if he proves that the damage was occasioned by an error in piloting, in the handling of the aircraft, or in navigation and that, in all other respects, he and his agents have taken all necessary measures to avoid the damage.

Article 22

(1) In the transportation of passengers the liability of the carrier for each passenger shall be limited to the sum of 125,000 francs. Where, in accordance with the law of the court to which the case is submitted, damages may be awarded in the form of periodical payments, the equivalent capital value of the said payments shall not exceed 125,000 francs. Nevertheless, by special contract, the carrier and the passenger may agree to a higher limit of liability.

(2) In the transportation of checked baggage and of goods, the liability of the carrier shall be limited to a sum of 250 francs per kilogram, unless the consignor has made, at the time when the package was handed over to the carrier, a special declaration of the value at delivery and has paid a supplementary sum if the case so requires. In that case the carrier will be liable to pay a sum not exceeding the declared sum, unless he proves that that sum is greater than the actual value to the consignor at delivery.

(3) As regards objects of which the passenger takes charge himself the liability of the carrier shall be limited to 5,000 francs per passenger.

(4) The sums mentioned above shall be deemed to refer to the French franc consisting of 65 1/2 milligrams of gold at the standard of fineness of nine hundred thousandths. These sums may be converted into any national currency in round figures.

Article 25

(1) The carrier shall not be entitled to avail himself of the provisions of this convention which exclude or limit his liability, if the damage is caused by his wilful misconduct or by such default on his part as, in accordance with the law of the court to which the case is submitted, is considered to be equivalent to wilful misconduct.

(2) Similarly the carrier shall not be entitled to avail himself of the said provisions, if the damage is caused under the same circumstances by any agent of the carrier acting within the scope of his employment.

Article 28

(1) Any action for damages must be brought, at the option of the plaintiff, in the territory of one of the High Contracting Parties, either before the court of the domicile of the carrier or of his principal place of business, or where he has a place of business through which the contract has been made, or before the court at the place of destination.

Article 29

(1) The right to damages shall be extinguished if an action is not brought within 2 years, reckoned from the date of arrival at the destination, or from the date on which the aircraft ought to have arrived, or from the date on which the transportation stopped.

(2) The method of calculating the period of limitation shall be determined by the law of the court to which the case is submitted.

Article 34

This convention shall not apply to international transportation by air performed by way of experimental trial by air navigation enterprises with the view to the establishment of regular lines of air navigation, nor shall it apply to transportation performed in extraordinary circumstances outside the normal scope of an air carrier's business.

SECTION TWO

Legal Checklist for Aviation Activities

Index for Section Two

CHAPTER 13

Introduction to Section Two

This section is designed to provide only general information relative to the subject matter covered. It is designed to acquaint the reader with some of the practices and pitfalls in aviation activities. It is hoped that the checklist of activities provided herein will act as a "red flag" and will alert the reader to obtain the services of a competent attorney when necessary.

The function of this section is to serve a dual purpose. First, as a text for undergraduate college students to supplement Section One. Secondly, as a checklist for those persons or organizations who participate in aviation activities.

The reader can obtain much helpful information from the "AIRCRAFT OWNERS AND PILOTS ASSOCIATION" an organization with main offices in Bethesda, Maryland, and Washington, D.C.

This is not a "do it yourself" kind of manual. It is to serve as a checklist to identify those complicated and technical areas that require caution and the legal advice of a competent attorney. Words of caution are sprinkled throughout this section to remind the reader of the wisdom and importance of early and preventive legal counsel, and mechanical repair, and maintenance.

CHAPTER 14

Aviation Activities by Persons or Organizations

A. Owner's Responsibility

The owner of an aircraft is legally bound to use reasonable care to prevent injury or damage to persons or property.

A pilot who does not own the aircraft, and who causes injury to persons, or damage to property is liable for the losses. The liability of the pilot can be carried over to the owner, who authorizes the pilot to use his aircraft.

The laws of many states vary with the facts of the case. A lawyer would be required to recognize the differences in liability. Adequate insurance coverage is another important consideration.

In general, it is always wise to "follow the book." This is so whether it be as a pilot or as an owner who lends his aircraft to a friend.

If you "follow the book" you are less likely to have an accident. If you have an accident and have "followed the book" or "followed the regulations," you are less likely to be considered the tort feasor, or the wrongdoer, because you can say and show that you have acted as a prudent and reasonable person would have acted. With this kind of defense, a person is less likely to be liable for the damages accrued by the accident.

B. Buyer of Aircraft

Before agreeing to buy an aircraft, the prospective buyer should obtain a title search of the aircraft from the F.A.A. records office in Oklahoma City. This can be obtained through the assistance of an attorney. This search will disclose the following information:

1. The present registered owner. (He should sign the Bill of Sale.)
2. The mortgage holder or lien holder, if any. (They must be paid and execute releases at time of sale.)
3. The previous registered owners. (They can provide a history of condition of aircraft.)

Additional documents that should be inspected before executing a buy-sell agreement are as follows:

1. Bill of sale.
2. Airworthiness certificate.

3. Maintenance records including engine and aircraft log books.
4. Maintenance manual.
5. Aircraft flight manual.
6. Written documentation that all directives and manufacturers' bulletins have been complied with.
7. Equipment list.
8. Weight and balance data.

The following is a checklist for buying a new or used aircraft; some of the items will apply to new aircraft, some will apply to used aircraft, and some will apply to both:

1. Determine your requirements for the aircraft you want to buy; such as range, capacity, make, style, etc.
2. Study used aircraft advertisements to get an idea of price ranges for various aircraft.
3. Deal with reputable dealers and get statements of representations about aircraft in writing.
4. Obtain a title search before you commit yourself to buy the aircraft. F.A.A. has title registration office in Oklahoma City, Oklahoma.
5. Check log books to see whether all F.A.A. air worthiness directives have been complied with.
6. Determine from records whether aircraft has been in accident and properly repaired. Selling price should be lower for aircraft that has been in an accident.
7. Determine availability and cost of hull insurance and liability insurance.
8. Determine if parts are unavailable for the particular make, type, or style of aircraft.
9. Determine the condition of the aircraft by having it inspected by a competent mechanic.
10. See preceding item for additional documents that should be inspected before buying an aircraft.

A further checklist as to the items of the aircraft to be inspected by the mechanic and/or the buyer are:

1. Number of hours aircraft has flown and number of hours since last inspection.
2. Determine whether there is metal corrosion inside wings and tail section.
3. Determine the gallons of gas consumed per hour by the aircraft; and the amount of oil consumed.
4. Determine the condition of instruments and/or radio by flight checking them; and whether they are F.A.A. accepted.
5. Ascertain the condition of the engine by checking such items as:
   Total time on engine.
   Overhaul time.

Appearance–rust, clean, sign of oil leaks.
Condition of hose, connection, clamps.
Compression of cylinders.

6. Ascertain the condition of propeller by examining such items as:
   Condition of finish and blade surface.
   Tightness or looseness of prop.
   Compliance with all prop bulletins.
7. Ascertain the condition of wings by examining such items as:
   Condition of leading edge, breaks or cuts.
   Inspection plates.
   Loose fabric on fabric covered wings.
   Loose rivets on metal wings.
   Loose bolts or structural members.
8. Ascertain the condition of cowling by examining such items as:
   Missing fasteners.
   Loose rivets.
   Good or bad fit.
   Existence of cracks.
9. Ascertain the working condition of the cabin doors and the appearance of the interior of the aircraft.

C. Written Agreement

A contract for the purchase of the aircraft should be drawn by the attorneys for both the buyer and the seller. It should contain at least the following:

1. Names of buyer and seller.
2. Description of aircraft.
3. Price of aircraft and financing terms.
4. Affidavit by seller that aircraft is in airworthy condition, and meets F.A.A. standards, and will pass current F.A.A. inspection.
5. List of defects or deficiencies of the aircraft that are acceptable to the buyer.
6. Representation that the aircraft and engine and accessories have been checked by a reputable repair station.
7. Seller will transfer F.A.A. registration to buyer.
8. Delivery to buyer with title clear of encumbrances or liens.
9. Possession to buyer at closing.
10. Controversy from transaction to be settled by arbitration according to rules of American Arbitration Association.

D. Recording Conveyances and Security Interests

The Federal Aviation Act established a system of registration and recordation of title to aircraft, mortgages, liens for labor and materials and other interests connected with a particular aircraft. The purpose of the recording provisions is to protect the person who, in good faith, is the first to record his interest with the F.A.A. office in Oklahoma City.

Included among the items that should be recorded are:

1. Title to aircraft.
2. Chattel mortgages.
3. Conditional sales contracts.
4. Liens for labor and material furnished to improve or repair the aircraft.
5. Other security agreements or security interests that may affect the title of the aircraft.

E. Title Search by Lender and Buyer

A prospective buyer should obtain a title search of aircraft records from the F.A.A. records office in Oklahoma City. The purpose of this search (as described in "Buyer of Aircraft" above) is to obtain information as to name of the present registered owner; and identity of mortgage holders and lien holders and other holders of security interests in the aircraft. The prospective buyer wants to get a bill of sale and title from the real or registered owner; and the new owner also wants to make certain that he knows all the debts and liens that he must pay if he buys the aircraft; or the new owner may require that the present owner pay off the existing debts before the sale. These are some of the matters to which the buyer's attorney should attend.

A prospective individual lender or lending institution who is financing the purchase of the aircraft will also obtain a title search before lending any money. The purpose of the search for the lender is to obtain the identity of the seller, and identity of any mortgage holders or lien holders or other holders of security interests in the aircraft. The prospective lender wants to have a first lien or first mortgage against the newly purchased aircraft and therefore has to see that all existing mortgages and liens are paid off before lending new money to the buyer for purchase of the aircraft.

F. Title Transfer

In order to take title to the aircraft, the new buyer must submit to the F.A.A. records office in Oklahoma City, the following:

1. A bill of sale signed by the seller.
2. An application for registration of the aircraft signed by the new owner.
3. If the mortgage and liens on the aircraft have been satisfied, then the buyer must send in releases signed by the creditors who held these security interests.

These recordings should be accomplished as quickly as possible after the closing of the sale since the filing date of documents determines the priority of these documents in the event that there is a conflict of interests. This is another important function of a buyer's attorney.

G. Lending, Borrowing or Renting Aircraft—from Others or to Others

The owner of an aircraft who rents or lends his aircraft to another may be subject to liability from:

1. The person who has possession or is piloting the owner's aircraft.
2. Third persons who are injured by the aircraft whether they be passengers in the owned aircraft, passengers in another aircraft or persons on the ground.

Liability is not imposed on the owner by the simple fact of ownership. Common law rules of liability are complex and have been altered by statutory law. When injury to persons, or damage to property, results from the operation of an aircraft, there are many factors that must be considered. A few factors that may impose liability on the owner are:

1. The owner may have been negligent in permitting an unqualified pilot to operate the aircraft.
2. The pilot may have been an employee or an agent of the owner.
3. The cause of the accident may have been a mechanical defect in the aircraft or in one or more of its parts.
4. A state law may impose liability on the owner.
5. There may be a civil penalty imposed by the Federal Aviation Administration for violation of its regulations.

The person who borrows or rents an aircraft may be liable for injury to persons, or damage to property. The liability of the pilot-borrower may extend to the following:

1. Injury to passengers in the borrowed aircraft he is piloting.
2. Injury to passengers in other aircraft.
3. Injury to persons on the ground.
4. Damage to other person's property whether in the air or on the ground.
5. Damage to the borrowed aircraft which the borrower is piloting.

A note of caution here for the borrower or renter of an aircraft: The owner of an aircraft may have owner's insurance for damage to his aircraft. The owner may be paid for damages that the pilot-borrower inflicts on the aircraft. However after the insurance company has paid the owner, then the insurance company may sue the pilot-borrower or the pilot-renter for the amount of the damages. In order for a renter-pilot or borrower-pilot to protect himself against such a claim, he must make certain that the owner or fixed base operator has insurance that protects the renter-pilot or borrower-pilot; or the renter-pilot or borrower-pilot must obtain his own insurance protection.

H. Aircraft Maintenance by Pilot

The holder of a pilot certificate is authorized to perform "preventive maintenance" on an aircraft owned or operated by him that is not used for air carrier service. This authorization is contained in Federal Aviation Regulation Part 43.

Caution is necessary here to distinguish between "preventive" and "major" work. If a pilot performs repair work for which he is not competent or that is not defined as "preventive" the following may be the consequences:

1. Safety of aircraft can be in jeopardy.
2. Federal Aviation Regulations may be violated.
3. Insurance coverage may be affected.
4. Accident liability may be affected.

Assistance in determining the classification of "Preventive Maintenance" can be obtained from the maintenance inspector of the local F.A.A. office, or from a competent A&P mechanic. The following types of work are defined as "preventive maintenance" in F.A.R., Part 43, Appendix A:

1. Removal, installation, and repair of landing gear tires.
2. Replacing elastic shock absorber cords on landing gear.
3. Servicing landing gear shock struts by adding oil, air, or both.
4. Servicing landing gear wheel bearings, such as cleaning and greasing.
5. Replacing defective safety wiring or cotter keys.
6. Lubrication not requiring disassembly other than removal of non-structural items such as cover plates, cowlings, and fairings.
7. Making simple fabric patches not requiring rib stitching or the removal of structural parts or control surfaces.
8. Replenishing hydraulic fluid in the hydraulic reservoir.
9. Refinishing decorative coating of fuselage, wings, tail group surfaces (excluding balanced control surfaces), fairings, cowling, landing gear, cabin, or cockpit interior when removal or disassembly of any primary structure or operating system is not required.
10. Applying preservative or protective material to components where no disassembly of any primary structure or operating system is involved and where such coating is not prohibited or is not contrary to good practices.
11. Repairing upholstery and decorative furnishings of the cabin or cockpit interior when the repairing does not require disassembly of any primary structure or operating system or interfere with an operating system or affect primary structure of the aircraft.
12. Making small simple repairs to fairings, non-structural cover plates, cowlings, and small patches and reinforcements not changing the contour so as to interfere with proper airflow.
13. Replacing side windows where that work does not interfere with the structure or any operating system such as controls, electrical equipment, etc.
14. Replacing safety belts.
15. Replacing seats or seat parts with replacement parts approved for the aircraft, not involving disassembly of any primary structure or operating system.

16. Trouble shooting and repairing broken circuits in landing light wiring circuits.
17. Replacing bulbs, reflectors, and lenses of position and landing lights.
18. Replacing wheels and skis where no weight and balance computation is involved.
19. Replacing any cowling not requiring removal of the propeller or disconnection of flight controls.
20. Replacing or cleaning spark plugs and setting of spark plug gap clearance.
21. Replacing any hose connection except hydraulic connections.
22. Replacing prefabricated fuel lines.
23. Cleaning fuel and oil strainers.
24. Replacing batteries and checking fluid level and specific gravity.
25. Removing and installing glider wings and tail surfaces that are specifically designed for quick removal and installation and when such removal and installation can be accomplished by the pilot.

I. Fixed Base Operators

A fixed base operator's activities may be varied and diverse. Because of the nature of his operations, factors relating to a fixed base operator may be found in other parts of this section.

A fixed base operator is required by law to exercise *due diligence* and *reasonable care* when performing his work or providing a service to an aircraft.

An F.B.O. acting as a repair shop is required to inspect an aircraft, detect and correct, or warn the aircraft owner of dangerous conditions that may exist in the aircraft. Failure to properly perform these tasks can be considered negligence on the part of the fixed base operator. This negligence, in turn, can and may subject the repair facility to liability for injuries or damages resulting from the defects which should have been detected or repaired. The courts use a standard of care that a "reasonable person" would exercise. The fixed base operator may be able to show that he exercised reasonable care if he used the procedures, practices and equipment that are utilized and accepted in the industry.

Again it is wise to "follow the book" and to follow accepted industry practices. "Short cuts" are a dangerous practice in any field of endeavor; in the aviation industry "short cuts" can be especially costly, dangerous and fatal.

The repairman also has a duty to exercise reasonable care to protect an aircraft against loss, damage or destruction, when it is left for repair. He has a duty to return the aircraft to the owner in as good a condition, at least, as he received it. Again the question of liability of the repairman will be determined by whether he acted in a "negligent manner" or whether he exercised "due care" and acted as a "reasonable person" would have acted.

A flight school owes a high duty of care to its student pilots. It also has the duty of giving the student adequate training and testing, with competent instructors and appropriate equipment. If the flight school does not meet the standards in one or more of these areas it may be liable, for injury or damages, not only to its students but also to third persons whose property or persons are damaged or injured by the student pilot.

A fixed base operator has a legal duty to exercise "reasonable care" for the protection and preservation of the aircraft in his possession. An individual borrowing his friend's plane also has a legal duty to exercise "reasonable care." The degree of "care" that a person must exercise is determined by such factors as whether there is a contract, whether he is being paid for possessing or holding the aircraft, or whether he is holding the aircraft as a favor to the owner. In all cases "reasonable care" must be used by the possessor of the aircraft. Negligence or lack of due care on the part of the possessor can impose a liability for loss or damage to the plane while in his possession.

Hangarkeepers liability generally stems from a bailor-bailee relationship when the subject matter of the bailment, the aircraft, is damaged or destroyed while in the custody of the bailee for storage, repair or safekeeping.

J. Airport Owners or Operators

The diversity and number of activities at an airport depend upon the size and nature of the airport. A local airport would provide fewer activities than a large international airport. Among the activities which would create liability for an airport owner or operator are the following:

1. Aircraft operation.
2. Aircraft storage.
3. Fuel and oil service.
4. Maintenance and repair service.
5. Ramp and runway service.
6. Rescue and fire fighting service.
7. Rental airline passenger ticket services and baggage checking areas.
8. Operation of automobile parking lots.
9. Hotel operation.
10. Elevators and escalators.
11. Hallways and stairways.
12. Restaurants and food catering.
13. Rental car lots.
14. Rental retail stores.

Persons to whom a duty is owed and therefore to whom an airport may have liability may include:

1. General aircraft owners.
2. Airline companies and employees.
3. Passengers.
4. Retail and other airport lessees and employees.
5. Visitors.
6. Hotel guests.
7. Restaurant patrons.
8. Retail lessees' patrons.

Generally the airport is obligated to maintain airport premises in safe condition for all persons using it and to provide suitable warnings for hazardous conditions which the operator knows or should know, and which a visitor cannot reasonably be expected to know.

K. Flying Clubs

A flying club can be organized by the following methods:

1. Oral agreement.
2. Written agreement.
3. Informal agreement.
4. Formal agreement.
5. Incorporation (articles of incorporation and bylaws constitute the written agreement).

A flying club can own an aircraft by the following methods:

1. Partnership ownership by the members. (The disadvantage in this is the possibility that each member may be held personally liable for the accidents or negligence of another member.)
2. Non-profit corporate ownership. (Each member is personally liable only for his own negligence; although the corporation entity may be liable for a member's negligence.)
3. Rental arrangements for leasing aircraft for use by members.

In any one of the arrangements, adequate liability insurance for each member or group of members is a necessity.

When a group buys an aircraft the same steps and requirements should be observed as set forth in "Buyer of Aircraft"; "Written Agreement"; "Recording Conveyances"; "Title Search"; and "Title Transfer."

Adequate insurance is a necessity. Insurance coverage should be obtained; and competent insurance advice should be secured.

Included in the kinds of coverage that should be obtained are:

1. Liability Insurance.
2. Bodily injury.
3. Property damage.
4. Passenger Insurance.
5. Hull Insurance.

L. Liability of Airlines, Manufacturers, and Others

The consideration of, and the factors affecting the liability of various members of the aviation community to other members are very complex and do not lend themselves to adequate treatment here. Section One of this book under Chapters 4, 5, 6, 7, 8, and 9 covers this subject quite extensively, and provides cases that demonstrate the complexity of the subject matter.

The best advice in the way of preventive law that can be offered in this complex area is to always act with prudence, and with due care; exercise the care of a "reasonable person"; do not act negligently; and secure adequate insurance when available. If you are involved in an accident after taking the above precautions then secure competent legal counsel.

An airline operator, a taxi operator or a charter operator are considered "common carriers" and as such are required to exercise the highest degree of care towards their passengers. They "warrant" or "guarantee" safe passage of their passengers.

A passenger who is a gratuitous passenger in a friend's aircraft or in an airline aircraft often does not have as much right for recovery of damages as a paying passenger. Caution should always be exercised in this area. The following factors should be considered in this area:

1. Some states have "guest statutes." In these states, a person accepting a ride in a "friend's" aircraft, and not paying for same, does not have a right of action against the pilot for the negligent acts of the pilot.
2. In some states such a passenger is not covered by insurance.
3. If a passenger or plaintiff is also negligent he is considered "contributorily negligent."

   In some states the plaintiff's recovery against a defendant carrier, manufacturer, repair facility, government, or others, is prorated in direct proportion to the percentage of negligence that can be attributed to the passenger or plaintiff, and the percentage of negligence attributable to the carrier or other defendant.

   In some states, a passenger or defendant who is contributorily negligent cannot recover any compensation from the carrier or other defendant.

   Contributory negligence occurs when a passenger or plaintiff fails to exercise reasonable care for his own safety and thereby contributes to his own injury.
4. Employees of airlines or passengers who ride on passes often are required to waive or give up their rights to sue the carrier in cases of injuries.
5. When a passenger buys an airline ticket it constitutes a contract for safe passage. The airline liability for luggage is limited. If the luggage is worth more than the limit, then the passenger must pay for special handling.
6. An employee of an airline, or of a fixed base operator, or of an airport, while acting or "working" outside the scope of his primary employment is not covered by the benefits of his primary employer. See Section One, Chapter 7 for examples.
7. A manufacturer is liable to the buyer of a product and also to third parties who are likely to use the product or come in contact with it, when the product has a defect. A manufacturer is also liable for damages for failure to instruct the buyer on the proper usage of the product.

8. United States law, and individual state laws are adopted principally from the common law of England. Under the common law the state could not be sued.

   The United States and the individual states have passed laws granting, to its citizens, the right to sue the government for certain wrongs.

   The Federal Tort Claims Act gave United States citizens the right to sue the United States government when the lawsuit is founded on:

   a. The constitution.
   b. An act of congress.
   c. A regulation of an executive department.
   d. Contract with the United States.
   e. Torts (negligent acts) committed by employees of the United States while in the performance of their duties as employees.

   Generally, the Federal Government or State Governments cannot be sued for acts that are discretionary in nature (can be performed only by a government). Acts by the government that are commercial in nature may impose liability on the government, if those acts are performed in a negligent manner.

9. Military aircraft negligently operated or maintained, causing property damage, or injury or death, impose a liability on the government as provided in the Federal Tort Claims Act.

CHAPTER 15

Fundamental Definitions and Concepts of Aviation Law

(a) *COMMON LAW* is that body of law and juristic theory which was originated, developed and formulated and is administered in England, and has been adopted by most of the states of the United States. It comprises the body of those principles and rules of action which derive their authority from usages and customs of long standing, or from judgments and decrees of courts.

It is to be distinguished from *Statutory Law*—which are the laws created by the enactment of legislatures.

(b) *AVIATION LAW* has some Common Law influence; and Aviation Law has adopted some Common Law principles. However, there were no "flying machines" during the time that the "Common Law" was established in England. Therefore cases involving "Aircraft" are generally Statute Law or laws enacted by legislatures.

(c) *BAILMENT* is a delivery of personal property by one person (Bailor) to another (Bailee), for the purpose of performing a special object in relation to the property, and property is returned when the purpose is accomplished.

Example: A repairman is a bailee, and aircraft owner is a bailor. A hangarman is a bailee, and aircraft owner is a bailor.

(d) *BAILOR* is the person who bails or delivers personal property to a second party (or bailee) for the purpose of performing a special object in relation to the property. (After purpose is accomplished, the second party returns property to bailor.)

(e) *BAILEE* is the party to whom personal property is delivered for the purpose of performing a special object in relation to the property. (After purpose is accomplished bailee returns property to bailor.)

(f) *ADMINISTRATIVE LAW* is that branch of public law which deals with the various agencies of the sovereign power; their regulations and the enforcement of their regulations; for example: The Federal Aviation Administration, Civil Aeronautics Board, The National Transportation Safety

Board. The rules and regulations of these aviation agencies are part of the body of Administrative Law.

(g) *CASE LAW* is "judge made law" resulting from a decision in a particular situation with a particular set of facts.

(h) *NEGLIGENCE* is ordinarily the failure to use such reasonable care and caution as would be expected of a prudent man. Negligence is the breach of a duty, and consists of doing or omission to do something which results in damage or injury to another person.

Negligence is the most active phase of Aviation Law and is covered under Chapter 14 of this Section Two; and is also covered by court cases under Chapters 3, 4, 5, 6, 7, 8, and 9, of Section One.

A pilot is held to a standard of conduct that a "reasonable person" would exercise. A pilot is expected to be competent and is expected to use good judgment in the operation of his aircraft. A pilot in command is responsible for the negligent operation of his aircraft by another person in his aircraft.

(i) *WILLFUL NEGLIGENCE* is a more aggravated form of negligence. It means a willful determination not to perform a known duty, or a reckless disregard of the safety or the rights of others.

(j) *CONTRIBUTORY NEGLIGENCE* is the negligence of the plaintiff that contributes to his own injury and may bar the plaintiff from a recovery. In some states the plaintiff would get a recovery prorated on the basis of his percentage of negligence as compared with the defendant's degree of negligence.

(k) *ACT OF GOD:* may be used as a defense to action on contract or in tort. Defendant must show:

1. Act or event complained of was the result of an act of God.
2. Defendant was not responsible and his negligence did not contribute to it in any way.

(l) *ASSUMPTION OF RISK:* In negligence cases it is a recognized principle that one who knowingly and voluntarily assumes the risk of injury from a known danger or defect, cannot recover. While often associated with contributory negligence it is distinguishable. Usually this defense is invoked in cases involving a contractual relationship between plaintiff and defendant (lessor and lessee, employer and employee, or other relationship), but it can be used in other cases as well.

Defendant must show:

1. An unreasonable risk by the plaintiff in the situation or thing causing the injury to the plaintiff.
2. Knowledge of the risk by the injured plaintiff at the time.

(m) *FEDERAL LAW* are the laws enacted by Federal Legislature—the U.S. Congress. These laws apply to the areas that are within the province of the Federal Government.

For example: Interstate commerce; air safety for all aircraft; and law suits between citizens of different states.

(n) *STATE LAW* are the laws passed by the legislatures of the individual states. These laws may, and do, vary from state to state. These laws apply to the areas that are within the province of the State Government. For example: Laws of negligence and liability for accidents involving an aircraft; crimes of theft or fire involving an aircraft; and civil law suits resulting from agreements involving aircraft.

(o) *AGREEMENTS* are contracts expressed or implied, written or oral between two or more people. Contracts arise when a pilot or mechanic or businessman buys an aircraft; or sells an aircraft; buys insurance; leases an aircraft or rents an aircraft or borrows an aircraft from a friend; or lends his aircraft to a friend; rents tie-down space; joins a flying club; has his aircraft repaired; or repairs aircraft; or is a passenger in an aircraft.

(p) *HANGARKEEPERS:* liability generally stems from a bailor-bailee relationship when the subject matter of the bailment, the aircraft, is damaged or destroyed while in the custody of the bailee for storage, repair, or safekeeping.

CHAPTER 16

Compensation for Loss

COMPENSATION for loss can be in one or more of three areas:

1. Death of a person.
2. Injury to a person.
3. Damage to property.

The determination of compensation for loss of life or injury or property damage is very complex. It is not a science and is determined largely by juries of ordinary citizens after conflicting facts and figures have been presented to them in court by opposing attorneys.

Among the elements that are considered to determine the compensation for loss of life and injury to persons are the following:

1. Loss of earnings.
2. Medical expenses.
3. Loss of future support of family members.
4. Pain and suffering of injured person.
5. Loss of love and affection by family.

Among the elements that are considered for damages to property are the following:

1. Damage to aircraft.
2. Damage to property on the ground.
3. Loss of aircraft or property on ground.
4. Loss of use of aircraft or property.

The award of compensation, or judgment for the injured party, is a claim against the defendant or the person who is adjudged to have been negligent. This can be levied against the estate of the defendant even if the defendant died in the accident.

It is important that a pilot have adequate liability insurance. An employee pilot should also see that his employer has adequate liability insurance.

CHAPTER 17

Insurance

An insurance policy represents a contract between the insured and the insurer. It is often a complex document with many ambiguous clauses, phrases, and paragraphs. Caution should be exercised both in completing the application form and in accepting a policy, the terms and provisions of which, you do not understand. Ask the insurer or its agent as many questions for clarification as is necessary to make certain that the type of insurance coverage and the extent of coverage is what you need or want.

Be accurate in the information that you provide on the application form. A "misrepresentation" or "inaccuracy" may render the policy void, because it may be considered a fraud on the insurance company. You may be paying premiums for insurance coverage that you will not receive when you need it, if the error in the application is sufficiently significant to void the policy.

Whether the terms of an insurance policy are "good" or "bad" is ultimately decided when you make a claim—and then it is too late to change the terms. So it is wise to seek impartial competent advice *before* buying insurance coverage rather than after an accident.

A. Among the Various Kinds of Insurance Coverage that Are Available Are:

1. Aircraft Hull.
   - All risks (covers aircraft while parked, taxiing, and in flight).
   - All risks while not in motion (covers aircraft while parked).
   - All risks while not in flight (covers aircraft while taxiing and parked).
2. Aircraft Liability (Protection Against "Third Party" Claims).
   - Owners and Pilots Insurance.
   - Bodily injury excluding passengers loss of life.
   - Loss of life.
   - Loss of income.
   - Property damage.
   - Passenger bodily injury.
   - Medical payments for passenger and crew.
   - Corporation Aircraft non-ownership liability.
   - Individual Aircraft non-ownership liability.

- Airport Liability.
    - Premises.
    - Contractual.
    - Construction.
    - Products.
    - Hangarkeepers.
- Aviation Products Liability.
    - Manufacturers.
    - Modifiers.
    - Repairers.
    - Suppliers.
- Workmen's Compensation.
    - Personal and Business Aircraft (covering flying crew members).
    - Other aviation risks (covering all employees).

B. Investigation After Accidents

An agent of the insurance company usually visits the insured after an accident. The purpose is usually to obtain information favorable to the insurer. Any statement by the insured to the insurer may later be used against the insured. It is therefore wise for the insured to defer making any statement to anyone until he has recovered from the physical and emotional strain of the accident.

C. Workmen's Compensation

The specific provisions of a Workmen's Compensation Law is based on the state law; and each state has its own workmen's compensation law.

In order to establish a right to workmen's compensation there must be a relationship of employer and employee. The rationale of workmen's compensation is that the employee is automatically covered by insurance for injuries received during employment. The employee does not have to prove that the employer was negligent; and the employer cannot use contributory negligence of the employee to reduce or preclude the employee's claim. Therefore the employee receives only limited damages or compensation for specified injuries or for death, in return for the automatic insurance coverage. The important condition however, is that the employee, at the time of the accident, must have been acting within the scope of his employment.

There have been many decisions that have outlined the essentials of such a relationship in aviation activities.

Section One, Chapter 7, sets out several examples in which the courts decided that the employee was acting within scope of employment and therefore was covered by workmen's compensation; or the employee was not acting within scope of employment and therefore was not covered by workmen's compensation.

D. Rating Insurance

The factors upon which an aircraft insurance policy is rated are as follows:

1. Type of aircraft to be insured.
   Age.
   Construction.
   Configuration.
2. The abilities of the pilot.
   Certificate.
   Ratings.
   Flying hours.
3. Geographic conditions.
   Terrain.
   Prevailing weather conditions.
   Geography of the airports used and areas of concentrated flying.
4. Purpose for which aircraft is to be used.
   Airline.
   Private business and pleasure.
   Industrial aid (corporations).
   Commercial use (charter, taxi, etc.).
   Special uses (require waivers from F.A.A.).

E. Aircraft Hull Insurance

The term "aircraft hull" refers to physical damage to the aircraft itself. The coverages are as follows:

All risk basis, ground and flight.
All risk basis, while not in motion.
All risk basis except while in flight.

The insurer's limits of liability under an Aircraft Hull Policy are determined by statements made in the application and in the declaration of the policy such as:

Value of aircraft.
Deductibles.
Cash value or replacement cost.

Loss can be made payable to a lien holder or a creditor with a mortgage on the aircraft.

F. Breach of Warranty Invalidates Insurance

Policies often contain provisions and requirements that must not be breached. The following are some instances of breach of warranties where insurance companies have been relieved of liability on the policy:

1. Where pilot flies contrary to federal regulations, and an accident happens.

2. Where pilot or copilot did not have valid certificate or proper ratings.
3. Where pilot is not authorized by policy.
4. Use of personal craft for instructional purposes.
5. Operation of aircraft by student pilot.
6. Where payment for flight is received.
7. Where aircraft is used outside geographical limits described in policy.

G. Aircraft Liability Insurance

Liability insurance provides the policy holder with protection against "third party" claims resulting from bodily injury or property damage as a result of his ownership, maintenance or use of the aircraft. The coverages provided are as follows:

Bodily injury excluding passenger liability.
Passenger bodily injury liability.
  Medical payments for injured passengers.
  Voluntary settlement to injured passengers.
Property damage liability.
Use of other aircraft policy.
Aircraft non-ownership liability policy.

H. Insurance for Liability of Owners and Operators of Airport

Liability insurance for owners and operators of airports provides the policy holder with protection against "third party" claims resulting from bodily injury or property damage as a result of ownership or operation of airport. The principle areas of airport liability and their classification may be summarized as follows:

1. AIRCRAFT OPERATIONS resulting in liability to bailees, tenants, and invitees (including liability of ramp service operators):
   Aircraft accidents.
   Fueling.
   Hangarkeepers.
   Loading stand.
   Maintenance and service.
   Rescue.
2. PREMISES OPERATIONS resulting in liability to tenants and invitees:
   Automobile parking lots.
   Elevators and escalators.
   Police and security.
   Slip and fall.
   Special events.
   Tenants and contractors.
   Vehicles.

I. Insurance for Liability of Manufacturer or Repairmen

Claims against a manufacturer or repairer can be generally classified as:

1. Those in which the direct purchaser seeks damages.
2. Those in which remote purchaser seeks damages.
3. Those in which third persons such as passengers seek damages.

A summary of the causes and sources of said liability is as follows:

1. Failure to exercise reasonable care in design of the product.
2. Negligence in selection of material.
3. Negligence in construction and fabrication.
4. Defects in the testing and quality control of the final product.

CHAPTER 18

Flight Preparation and Operation of Aircraft

This is the phase of aviation activity by a pilot which should be conducted in a systematic and thorough manner. This is so for two reasons:

1. It may prevent an accident.
2. If an accident does occur then the pilot who was thorough can point to his actions as being those of a "reasonable" and "prudent" person; he was not negligent and therefore was not the person who caused the accident.

A. Flight Plan

A flight plan should be filed at all times even when not required because it permits the pilot to make a conscious and thorough review and evaluation of conditions that will exist during the flight, including weather reports and forecasts; and it assists search and rescue operations if it is ever necessary. The items that should be included in a flight plan are:

1. Name of pilot.
2. Address of pilot and home base of aircraft.
3. Number of persons in aircraft.
4. Color of aircraft.
5. Type of aircraft.
6. Aircraft identification.
7. Radio call signal and radio frequencies to be used.
8. Cruising altitude and air speed.
9. Point and proposed time of departure.
10. Proposed route.
11. Destination—airport, city, state.
12. Changes of altitude en route.
13. Estimated time en route.
14. Fuel on board (in hours).
15. Alternate airport for emergency.

B. Preflight Inspection of Aircraft

The following checklist is general in nature and may be adapted to individual circumstances and aircraft:

1. Magnetos off and landing gear locked.
2. Check all openings in aircraft for foreign objects or birds nests.
3. Check wings.
   Tips, leading and trailing edge and surfaces.
   Struts, airlerons, flaps, hinges, control cable.
   Remove obstructions if any.
4. Check fuselage.
   Damage to skin.
   Inspection plates.
   Static ports for obstruction.
5. Check empennage.
   Damage to skin.
   Brace wires.
   Control surface hinges and cables.
   Remove obstructions if any.
6. Check undercarriage.
   Tires (wear and inflation).
   Struts.
   Nuts and bolts.
   Brake lines for damage or leaks.
   Remove obstructions if any.
7. Check fuel system.
   Visual check for quantity and quality.
   Gas caps and breather hole.
   Drain lines and tanks of sediment and water.
8. Check propeller.
   Blades.
   Hub (nuts and bolts).
   Spinner.
9. Check engine.
   Mounts, battery, wiring.
   Exhaust manifold.
   Oil level with dip stick.
   Secure cowl.
10. Check lights by turning on master switch.
11. Remove chocks and untie ropes.

The starting, pre-takeoff, takeoff, in-flight, and landing procedures are too varied and detailed to set forth here. However, the standard procedures should always be followed in detail with no "short cuts." The thoroughness with which a pilot follows these procedures may determine whether or not there is an accident and, if an accident, whether or not the pilot is considered the negligent party.

In all aircraft operations from pre-flight, through in-flight, to landing, the pilot should use good judgment. And one of the methods of evaluating whether the pilot has used good judgment, is to determine whether he has "followed the book'' for the proper procedures in all phases of the flight. This practice should be followed even though it may seem repetitive. This can be called ''Preventive Practices'' to keep from having accidents.

C. Aircraft Accident Reporting

A pilot must immediately notify the F.A.A. or National Transportation Safety Board (N.T.S.B.) of any accident, or in-flight hazards that result in damage to aircraft or property and injury to persons, by the most expeditious means possible.

CHAPTER 19

Government Agencies

A. Civil Aeronautics Board

In general the Civil Aeronautics Board performs two major functions:

1. Regulation of the economic aspects of domestic and international United States air carrier operation; and of foreign air carriers to and from the United States.
2. Participation in establishment and development of international air transportation.

In 1978 U.S. Congress passed the Airline Deregulation Act of 1978. One of the provisions of this Act is that the Civil Aeronautics Board may be terminated in 1985. If this is accomplished then the functions of the Civil Aeronautics Board will be transferred to and divided among other existing government agencies, such as Department of Justice, National Transportation Safety Board, Department of Transportation, and the Federal Aviation Administration.

The Civil Aeronautics Board and its functions do not have a direct effect on general aviation and therefore we will not describe its functions and operations in any more detail.

B. National Transportation Safety Board

The National Transportation Safety Board consists of five members, each appointed for a five-year term by the President, with the advice and consent of the U.S. Senate.

In general the duties of the NTSB include determining the cause or probable cause of transportation accidents and reporting the facts, conditions and circumstances surrounding the accident. The NTSB is also responsible for reviewing, on appeal, the suspension, amendment, modification, revocation or denial of a certificate or license issued by the F.A.A.

The NTSB has this limited relationship to general aviation pilots, mechanics, fixed base operators, hangarman, etc. Therefore we will not describe its functions and operations in any more detail at this point. We shall refer to its functions in connection with the operations of the Federal Aviation Administration, when it is applicable.

C. Federal Aviation Administration (F.A.A.)

The Federal Aviation Administration is headed by an Administrator. The Administrator is appointed by the President with the advice and consent of the U.S. Senate.

In general the responsibilities of the Federal Aviation Administrator are as follows:

1. The regulation of Air commerce to promote its development and safety and to promote the national defense.
2. The control of the use of the navigable airspace of the United States in the interest of safety and efficiency.
3. The development and operation of a system of air traffic control and navigation for both military and civil aircraft.
4. The consolidation of research and development of air navigation facilities as well as the installation and operation of such a system.

Kinds of Enforcement Actions

(a) When an F.A.A. designated physician has REFUSED TO ISSUE MEDICAL CERTIFICATE, the pilot can petition the Federal Air Surgeon for reconsideration.

If the Air Surgeon denies the medical certificate, the pilot can then appeal to the National Transportation Safety Board for a petition to review the Administrator's action.

If the NTSB denies the medical certificate, the pilot can then appeal to the U.S. Circuit Court of Appeals.

In all of the above hearings the pilot has the burden of proving the sufficiency of his medical qualifications.

If the F.A.A. administrator believes that the pilot's physical condition is such that he constitutes a danger to air traffic, then the Administrator may exercise EMERGENCY REVOCATION OF PILOT'S MEDICAL CERTIFICATE in the interest of public safety. Under these conditions:

1. The Administrator must initiate a hearing before The National Transportation Safety Board which must review The Administrator's actions and either reverse or affirm the emergency revocation.
2. The hearing must also be initiated and concluded within sixty days, so as not to work a hardship on the pilot.
3. The Administrator has the burden of proving that the pilot's medical qualifications do not meet the requirements.

(b) When the F.A.A. Administrator issues an order REVOCATION OR SUSPENSION OF PILOT'S CERTIFICATE, the F.A.A. legal department will issue a notice of the proposed action, and the pilot must respond to said notice.

The pilot can proceed in one or more of the following ways:

1. He may admit the charges.
2. He may answer the charges and deny them, in which case he has fifteen days from receipt of notice to make his reply.
3. He may request an informal conference.
4. He may not respond, in which case the Administrator will issue the order.
5. In the situation cited in paragraphs 2, 3, and 4 above, the pilot can appeal to the National Transportation Safety Board for a review of the Administrator's actions.

The Administrator may issue an EMERGENCY ORDER OF REVOCATION OR SUSPENSION OF PILOT'S CERTIFICATE. This is done in the interest of public safety when the Administrator believes that the pilot's continued flying constitutes a danger to air traffic.

In this case the pilot is grounded immediately. The pilot however is entitled to a speedy hearing before the National Transportation Safety Board, to either affirm or reverse the action of the Administrator. This hearing must be initiated and concluded within sixty days from date that pilot receives notice.

(c) In the REISSUANCE OF CERTIFICATE AFTER SUSPENSION OR REVOCATION, generally, at the end of a period of suspension the pilot will resume his privileges as they previously existed. Where a revocation has been effected, the pilot must qualify all over again to regain his privileges.

(d) A CIVIL MONEY PENALTY may be charged, if it is determined by the F.A.A. legal department that the pilot's violation is a comparatively non-serious violation, such as failure to secure inspections, or lack of proper documents, etc.

A civil money penalty is imposed for such minor violations instead of imposing a certificate revocation of suspension.

A notice of the civil money penalty is sent to the pilot, which sets forth the amount of money constituting the fine, and the facts of alleged violation for which the fine is imposed.

An informal conference is established to provide an opportunity for all parties to be heard and to try to settle the matter before formal proceedings commence.

The pilot should be careful not to admit to the commission of the alleged violation and a statement of no admission of guilt should accompany any compromise settlement with the F.A.A. An admission of guilt at this point can be used against the pilot in the event that a subsequent civil suit is brought against the pilot by a third party, for damages to the third party resulting from commission of the alleged violation.

If no settlement is made with the F.A.A. then the fine or penalty is referred to the U.S. Attorneys for collection in the U.S. District Court.

The procedures and practices are technical and it is recommended that a pilot, at the outset, use the services of a competent attorney when confronted with a violation.

(e) F.A.A. inspectors are required to make CRIMINAL REPORTS of suspected violations of certain criminal laws related to aircraft and air commerce. These reports are submitted to the appropriate agency such as Federal Bureau of Investigation, Immigration and Naturalization Service, Federal Bureau of Narcotics, and Customs Bureau.

Here again, it is wise not to become involved in these areas of violations of law. However if a pilot inadvertantly finds himself involved then he should obtain the services of a competent attorney.

(f) NOTICE TO AIRMEN (NOTAM) is an F.A.A. notice to airmen containing information concerning any component of, or hazard in, the airspace system; and it identifies the facility, service or danger to aircraft in flight being reported upon. The NOTAM is transmitted by code on weather teletype circuit. The complete NOTAM code is available at any location having a weather teletype circuit.

(g) A SEIZURE OF AIRCRAFT may be ordered by the F.A.A. Administrator where the aircraft is involved in violation of a Federal Aviation Regulation that is subject to a civil penalty; or where aircraft is involved in a more serious violation; and where the Administrator has reason to believe that the owner or pilot will not or cannot pay the penalty and/or comply with the Federal Aviation Regulation.

After the aircraft is seized and impounded, the owner and all registered parties of interest in the aircraft are notified of the time, place, and date of seizure; where plane is impounded; the alleged or determined violations; and the amount of the civil penalty as determined by a U.S. District Court. The cost to the owner will include the penalty, storage, maintenance and costs of seizure.

A seized aircraft will be ordered released by the Administrator whenever the owner:

1. Posts a bond sufficient to cover the penalty, cost, storage, and maintenance.
2. The owner pays the total amount determined.
3. The aircraft is subject to a lien enforced by a U.S. District court.
4. The U.S. Attorney informs the F.A.A. that he will not proceed with the allegations contained in the F.A.A. order of seizure.

Procedures for Enforcement Actions

The procedures, rules and regulations, and the substantive rights and obligations are very complex. If a pilot becomes involved with these proceedings it is wise and prudent to obtain the services of a competent attorney familiar with enforcement procedures.

The following is a very brief synopsis of the procedures. They are presented here only to indicate the general nature of the task, and indicate some "road signs" and are not designed to provide the pilot with a "do it yourself" guide:

1. An F.A.A. Flight Standards Inspector makes an investigation of the accident or violation; and then writes or calls the pilot; notifying the pilot of the information he has obtained; and asking for a reply to determine informally if a violation has occurred.
2. The pilot then gives his statement and provides the information he has regarding the incident under investigation. Extreme caution is needed here because any statement by the pilot, oral or written will become a part of the record and may be used in a civil or criminal charge that may later grow out of the incident or accident. Therefore caution should be used in whatever is said, the advice of a competent lawyer should be obtained, and the excitement and shock of the incident or accident should be permitted to subside before a statement is made orally or in writing.
3. If the F.A.A. inspector determines that the violation does not affect safety he then issues a safety compliance notice that sets forth the remedial action to correct the violation. Although there is no penalty a violation will be recorded in the pilot's record.
4. If the inspector determines that the violation does affect safety he then refers the matter to F.A.A. Regional Attorney. The Attorney then determines if he can prove up the violation from the facts and data in the file. If he feels he cannot—he closes the case. If he feels that he can prove up the case, he brings the appropriate action of either certificate suspension or revocation or civil money penalty.
5. The F.A.A. legal department sends a notice to the pilot.
6. The pilot responds to the notice. The caution expressed in paragraph two above applies here as well.
7. Informal conference with the F.A.A. attorney is then arranged where the pilot can effectively present his side of the facts. The pilot, at all times, should be polite, responsive, cooperative and exhibit an attitude that recognizes the importance of safety practices in aviation.
8. The pilot can appeal a decision of the F.A.A. Administrator to the National Transportation Safety Board.
9. The pilot can appeal the decision of the National Transportation Safety Board to the U.S. Circuit Court of Appeals.